12/23 $2

D1130329

376 pages
start at page 7

GEORGE
GISSING

GEORGE GISSING

A Life

PAUL DELANY

Weidenfeld & Nicolson
LONDON

First published in Great Britain in 2008
by Weidenfeld & Nicolson

1 3 5 7 9 10 8 6 4 2

A CIP catalogue record for this book
is available from the British Library.

ISBN-13 978 0 297 85212 4

Typeset by Input Data Services Ltd, Frome

Printed and bound by Butler and Tanner,
Frome and London

Weidenfeld & Nicolson

The Orion Publishing Group Ltd
Orion House
5 Upper Saint Martin's Lane
London, WC2H 9EA

An Hachette Livre UK Company

The Orion Publishing Group's policy is to use papers that
are natural, renewable and recyclable products and made
from wood grown in sustainable forests. The logging and
manufacturing processes are expected to conform to the
environmental regulations of the country of origin.

www.orionbooks.co.uk

Contents

	List of Illustrations	vii
	Introduction	ix
1	Unclassed	1
2	*Workers in the Dawn*	26
3	Under Harrison's Wing	50
4	Love With a Lady	74
5	Low Life	89
6	*Thyrza*	111
7	The Death of Nell	134
8	*The Emancipated*	156
9	Second Wife	175
10	Father and Son	193
11	Brixton	210
12	Unhappy Family	231
13	Breaking Away	252
14	The Shores of the Mediterranean	273
15	Gabrielle	292
16	The Private Life of Monsieur Gissing	313
17	Looking Homeward	335
18	Death in Exile	350
	Afterword	377
	Notes	382
	Bibliography	414
	Acknowledgements	419
	Index	421

List of Illustrations

1. Thomas Waller Gissing (*Arthur C. Young*)
2. Margaret Gissing (*Pierre Coustillas*)
3. Ellen Gissing (*Pierre Coustillas*)
4. and 5. Bellevue Prison, Hyde Road, Manchester (*Manchester Public Library*)
6. Gissing in 1884 (*Naudin*)
7. Marianne Helen ('Nell') Harrison (*Xavier Pétremand*)
8. Domenichino, *The Hunt of Diana* (*Galleria Borghese Rome/Bridgeman Art Library*)
9. Mrs Sarah Gaussen (*Pierre Coustillas*)
10. Rosalind Williams (*Barbara Caine, Destined to be Wives*)
11. Clara Collet (*Pierre Coustillas*)
12. The Marylebone Workhouse (*Peter Higginbotham/ Victoriaengland.co.uk*)
13. 'The Home Quartett: Mrs Vernon Lushington and Children', by Arthur Hughes, 1883 (*Private collection/Bridgeman Art Library*)
14. Edith Underwood (*Xavier Pétremand*)
15. Gissing in September 1893, by Alfred Ellis (*Xavier Pétremand*)
16. Queen Victoria's Diamond Jubilee, 1897 (*Towneley Hall Art Gallery and Museums, Burnley/Bridgeman Art Library*)
17. Gissing in Rome, 1898 (*Royal Gettmann, George Gissing and H.G. Wells*)
18. Gabrielle Edith Fleury (*Pierre Coustillas*)
19. Anna Fleury (*Pierre Coustillas*)
20. Gissing at Trient, Switzerland, in 1899 (*Xavier Petrémand*)
21. *Our Friend the Charlatan*, 1901, illustration by Launcelot Speed
22. Gissing, May 1901 (*Elliott & Fry*)
23. The sanatorium at Nayland, Suffolk (*Jonathan Frank*)
24. Maison Elgue, Ispoure, St Jean Pied de Port, where Gissing died (*Pierre Coustillas*)

Introduction

In April 1946 George Orwell was asked by a publisher to write a biography of George Gissing. Three years before, in *Tribune*, he had said that Gissing was 'perhaps the best novelist England has produced'. He would have liked to write the biography, but had to refuse because he was about to leave for the Island of Jura, where he would be unable to do any research into Gissing's life. Instead of a book like this one, Orwell wrote a novel, *Nineteen Eighty-Four*.[1]

No one will regret the choice that Orwell made; but his feeling for Gissing can help to draw the map of English literature from 1880 to 1950. Orwell was born in the year that Gissing died, 1903. Both of them lived forty-six years and died of lung disease. It is likely enough that Orwell borrowed the first name of his pseudonym from Gissing, as if to show that he planned to carry on Gissing's work, in a direct line from *The Nether World* to *Down and Out in Paris and London*. Orwell, though, chose to live among the poor to begin a lifelong commitment to leftist politics. Gissing became poor only by bad luck and bad judgement, and came to believe that political solutions were unlikely to abolish human misery.

Gissing said that the great subject of his novels was the situation of educated people with 'not enough money'. Orwell agreed that the struggle for subsistence was the essence of modern life and that too many English novelists, whatever their other talents, had failed to take that struggle seriously. Think of the legacies, fortunate marriages and cushy jobs that rain down on heroes and heroines at the end of most Victorian novels. Novelists who were not serious about 'the material question' (as Gurdjieff called it) might not be truly serious about anything else. Dickens, Orwell said in his brief 1943 essay on Gissing, was 'as unable to pass a joke as some people are to pass a pub'.[2] The proper job of a novelist was to expose the terrible workings of the social machine that every individual was up against. In Gissing's novels, those with the hardest battle against the machine were the class who were one step up from the bottom of the ladder. His subject,

Orwell said, was 'the cruel, grinding, "respectable" poverty of underfed clerks, downtrodden governesses and bankrupt tradesmen'. Poverty was worse when you had both to keep up appearances, and to deny yourself the rough and ready pleasures of the working class.

Orwell praised Gissing for recognising the *relentlessness* of the struggle to provide for oneself. Economic individualism had been a great engine of progress since the eighteenth century, making Britain into the world's pre-eminent nation. Yet the other side of the coin – the only side that Gissing saw – was the indifference of capitalism to individual failure. For Gissing, capitalism was a system that kicked you into the gutter and said: 'Enjoy yourself there.' Soon after his death, social security arrived, promising that no one would now be left in the gutter. Yet Gissing predicted the horrors of global war and totalitarianism that were about to arrive too. The consumer society may have blunted the tooth of poverty, yet for many people *Nineteen Eighty-Four* still conveys best what the twentieth century was about. A sense of doom is often more compelling than a sense of humour.

Where did Gissing's sense of doom come from? One of the tensions in biography is between seeing the person you write about as a unique case, and as a socially determined type. Millions of late Victorians had to contend with economic insecurity and the injuries of class; only Gissing created his particular anguished response. In 1895 he explained to Clara Collet the kind of novelist he had to be:

> One thing you say is particularly true – that I am never quite at ease save in dealing with forms of life where there enters pecuniary struggle. I think it will always be so. I find it a great effort to understand the daily life of people free from money cares. Never for one hour since I was out of boyhood have I been free from that harassing thought, and of course it affects my imagination.

In fact, Gissing had quite a comfortable childhood, and once he arrived at Owens College, Manchester, he won so many scholarships that he always had money in his pocket. His pecuniary struggle began only when he fell in love with a young prostitute, Nell Harrison, and stole money to keep up with her demands. Nell had a completely different attitude to money than Gissing. She got it in any way she could, and spent it at once on drink and fast company. The struggle over money was something that Gissing imposed on himself. He worked grimly at tutoring and writing, and consistently earned at least twice the average wage for the time. He felt harassed because his income was never secure, and because he tried to provide for everyone in his family as well as for himself.

Few people feel that they have as much money as they would like, but they experience the lack differently, according to their class and temperament. Gissing was born into the provincial lower middle class, and in spirit he never left it. He scorned its piety and its puritanism, and in the later part of his writing career he earned enough to live on a more comfortable scale. But he could never free himself from lower-middle-class instincts of frugality, order, self-discipline and constant work. He was consistent with his origins in taking his aspirations from the class above him, and in his fundamental distrust of the class below. Yet he could not stand at arm's length from his own character, and see what had made him the kind of person he was.

Gissing's obsessiveness and emotional rigidity limited the use he could make of his remarkable intelligence. He was one of the cleverest and most learned of English writers, and one of the most blinkered. He drew a marvellous portrait of an obsessive character in Mr Widdowson of *The Odd Women*, yet he lived always in the iron cage of his own obsessions. He insisted that there was no solution either to the problem of subsistence, or to the suffering inflicted by the Victorian sexual system. The economic marketplace worked to keep you poor and anxious; the sexual one to keep you frustrated and misunderstood. Even worse, economic and sexual need worked hand in glove. If you were poor, no desirable woman would have you; without a woman, you would be too lonely to do good work. Gissing's world-view was shaped by a deep cynicism about people's motives. They could not like you for yourself, only for the comforts you might be able to offer them. There were hardly any true individuals in his novels, just victims of circumstances.

A man at least had the chance of making money, and thereby bringing some pleasure into his life. Women could find pleasures only by attaching themselves to a man who was able to provide them. At Owens College, Gissing met upper-class young ladies who entranced him and who, he knew, would never consider him an eligible suitor. He also met Nell Harrison, who would go with any man who gave her money and drink. Gissing clung to the idea that all women had an ideal nature. If they lost their virtue, the blame lay with their male seducers. Yet almost any woman had the power to provide sexual comfort to lonely and deprived men. It seemed to Gissing that they used their power mostly to withhold, rarely to be generous.

One way to tell the story of Gissing's life is in three parts, each one about a failed relationship with a woman. The prologue could be his failed relationship with his mother. Each part would reveal a different aspect of the Victorian gender system, and how Gissing was defeated by it. Oppressive as the system may have been – and especially for the lower middle class – it worked in some fashion for most of the population. Gissing, though, was sexually defeated wherever he turned. We can blame his innate gloominess or his male chauvinism, and say that no woman could make him happy, or he them. Yet we can also see that he failed because he had too much insight into what was wrong with Victorian sexual arrangements.

There were many privileged males of the time – the Pre-Raphaelites, say, or Engels or the author of *My Secret Life* – who found pleasure, inspiration and sometimes love with uneducated women. Gissing's troubles came, first, because he was not privileged enough. In his first two marriages, he hoped to make his brides into presentable companions who could support his work and his social ambitions. Instead, his wives pulled him down. He would have liked to be a generous host, but found it impossible to invite any guest to his home. As H. G. Wells rose out of the lower middle class, his second wife added buoyancy to his ascent. Gissing tied himself to an anvil, and after Nell died he did it again.

Edmund Wilson suggested that 'the greatest novelists are men caught between the social classes, like Dostoevsky and Dickens'.[3] If so, novelists still may be caught in different ways. By his mid-twenties Gissing had a dress suit for dinner invitations, spoke with an impeccable accent, and had a Latin quotation for every occasion. By his mid-thirties he was earning a regular middle-class income. Yet he considered himself, in his own phrase, one of 'the unclassed'. This did not mean that he tried to ignore class distinctions, or that he viewed the class system with the critical eye of an outsider. It was more that his lack of a secure position made him feel excluded and devalued. No one from the lower middle class, he observed, would boast about the class they belonged to. Gissing felt his origins as a stigma, without being able to find any secure alternative position, other than the pipe dream of Henry Ryecroft in his Devon cottage.

After the degradation of prison, Gissing's only path to social rehabilitation was through success in the literary marketplace. The story of his life is the story of his books, yet he experienced their production as an immensely alienating task. His writing was a labour imposed from without, rather than an expression of his creative self. It is partly for this reason that I am not offering here a critical biography, in the sense of a full assessment of all of Gissing's books. Rather, I have tried to read the twenty-two novels, and the various other works, with a biographer's eye. Gissing was a neurotic writer, in the sense that much in his novels needs to be understood as a symptom of inner conflicts. Everything in his later life was determined by the twin disasters of his imprisonment and his marriage to Nell Harrison. But nothing was to be said about them. Prison he concealed altogether. He spoke about prostitution in his early novels, but cut out the most revealing passages about it in *The Unclassed* when he revised for a second edition. He argued that Dickens was completely justified in concealing both his childhood stint in the blacking factory, and his attachment to Ellen Ternan.

Gissing said that Godwin Peak, the hero of *Born in Exile*, was 'myself – one phase of myself'. Peak tried to ingratiate himself with Mr Warricombe, and marry his daughter, by posing as an orthodox Christian. Earlier, he had published an atheistical pamphlet under an assumed name; when this became known, his life was ruined. Gissing had a crucial patron in real life, Frederic Harrison, who was a follower of Auguste Comte. For a while, Gissing was an enthusiastic Comtean too; but he lost his faith and wrote an essay rebutting it, 'The Hope of Pessimism'. He chose not to publish the essay, rather than offend Harrison by announcing his defection from the movement. We might argue that Gissing deserves credit for respecting Harrison's beliefs; alternatively, we might condemn him for choosing his bread and butter over his intellectual integrity. But we can surely say that Gissing viewed honesty as a luxury, something you could afford only if you were financially and socially secure. The self you present to the world is a strategic one, because to be authentic is to be vulnerable.

We could simplify Gissing's dilemma by saying that Victorian society rested on hypocrisy, so that everyone was required to lie about their desires. But the major figures in Gissing's novels are almost always bad liars. This was true of Gissing's life, also. It was not just a case of having made a mistake in youth, and then trying to cover it over for the rest of his life. The mistake created daily misery that he could never shake off. If Gissing had been a consistent cynical determinist he would have deserved the label that critics tried to stick on him, that of an 'English Zola'. He would also have been a much less interesting figure than the Gissing who could never heal his self-inflicted wounds, and who gives us better than anyone the flavour of London in the 1880s and 1890s: a compound of wet streets, fog, coal smoke, narrow horizons, and an imagination equal to it all.

Unclassed

In the small hours of 26 May 1894, George Gissing left his Brixton home and walked five miles across London, in the cold and rain, to Liverpool Street Station. He was going to Southwold, Suffolk, to see if it would be a good place for a summer holiday. When he arrived he soon realised that the bleak and shingly beach would not suit his wife and small son. On his way back he had to change at Halesworth, and decided to spend a few hours in the town where his father had been born. Gissing wandered around, and found the record of his father's baptism in the church. When he went back to the station he spotted the bright orange cover of the latest *English Illustrated Magazine*, with his story 'The Honeymoon' inside. 'How proud he would have been,' Gissing thought, 'the dear, kind Father! How little could he dream, when a lad running about lanes and fields, that, more than half a century hence, his son's literary work would be sold, to that son himself, at Halesworth!'[1]

Biographies begin with their subject's ancestry, the roots that give rise to the tree. Gissing's story is about breaking with one's roots, in order to climb the ladder of class. Thomas Waller Gissing was born the eldest son of a Halesworth shoemaker, Robert Foulsham Gissing, in 1829. His mother, Jane, was the daughter of a farmer and public-house keeper at Theberton, not far away. Thomas was a bright little boy, who in the usual run of events would have become another shoemaker, like his father and grandfather before him. His stroke of luck was that one of his aunts, Emily Waller, had become the paid companion of a rich lady, Sophia Whittington, who offered to pay Thomas's fees at Harvey's Academy for Boys in Halesworth. Before the Education Acts of the 1870s, this was the only way that a boy like Thomas could escape from the shoemaker's bench.

Thomas Gissing was a clever lad, but there was no chance of his going on from his Academy to Oxford or Cambridge. That would be too big a leap for a single generation. After his schooling he was apprenticed to a pharmaceutical chemist. In 1856, when he was twenty-seven, he bought his own business in Wakefield, Yorkshire. He produced his own drugs as well as selling them across the counter. Perhaps Miss Whittington helped him again by putting up the capital. Wakefield was a thriving manufacturing town, and Thomas soon became one of its leading tradesmen. Within a year of his arrival in Wakefield he married Margaret Bedford, a woman of twenty-five from Worcestershire. The Bedfords owned land around Worcester and were somewhat better off than the Suffolk Gissings, but little of their good fortune came Margaret's way. She was the youngest of three sisters, whose mother and father both died within a year of Margaret's birth, probably from the terrible cholera epidemic of 1832–3. William Bedford was a solicitor's clerk who was only thirty-two when he died, and his little girls were not well provided for. Gissing may have drawn on his mother's story for the orphaned Madden sisters in *The Odd Women*: there is £800 to support all of them, and they are farmed out to 'a lady of small means' who brings them up. Margaret Bedford's eldest sister died at fifteen; her middle sister, Elizabeth, worked as a shop assistant in Worcester. Margaret had little education, and probably never read her son's books. On his side, he felt duty towards her rather than love.

The Bedfords, like the Gissings, were decent undistinguished English provincial folk. How the meeting between Thomas and Margaret came about is a mystery. The only clue comes in *Born in Exile*, where Godwin Peak's mother is said to have been a nursemaid to a local doctor's family before she married Peak's father. We know that Thomas Gissing was a romantic youth who published three slender volumes of poetry before he left Suffolk.[2] The third of them had a title poem that became a fateful part of the Gissing family mythology. 'Margaret' is a passionate plea for a young woman who loses her virtue, and is then made an outcast by a hypocritical society.[3] Soon after writing it, Thomas met his own Margaret and married her. She answered his fantasy in name but not in anything else. In a picture some years later she still looks like a pretty and cheerful young woman, though her hair and dress are severe. Later, everything about her would be severe. Margaret had no father to give her away, and no home to be married from. Thomas took her to be married in Grasmere church, where Wordsworth lay in the churchyard.

After the romantic wedding, married life began over the chemist's shop on Westgate. Turning left out of the shop brought you to Wakefield Cathedral; turning right to Wakefield Prison, now the place where Britain locks up its monsters, cannibals and child-murderers. The Victorians had no qualms about deterrence, and the children of Wakefield knew that to prison they would go, if they were not good. Thomas and Margaret Gissing came home to the shop in February 1857, and on 22 November their son George Robert was born. Perhaps his father named him after Lord Byron; few writers can have led a less Byronic life. After his marriage, Thomas mixed potions rather than writing poetry, and Margaret soon bore him five children. The first three were boys, George, William and Algernon, followed by Margaret and Ellen. In calling his first daughter Margaret, Thomas held on to his dreams about the eternal feminine.

Thomas Gissing was an exceptional man who had no real prospect of breaking out of his provincial and predictable existence. He worked hard at his trade and did well in it. To succeed one had to do one's share of civic duties; Thomas did more than his share, and found pleasure in the doing. His great hobby was botanising, and he managed to publish two little books about his expeditions.[4] George loved going out with his father to comb the countryside for rare plants. When he visited Thomas Hardy in Dorchester, some twenty years later, it gave him pleasure to see that Hardy's knowledge of wild plants was much inferior to his own.

As the oldest son, George modelled himself on his father and gave him absolute respect and love. Any child could see that Victorian husbands and wives were different beings with different lives. Difference meant conflict, and conflict meant choosing sides. George was completely on the side of his father, while his four siblings took the side of their mother. This put George out of harmony with his brothers and sisters all his life, even as he did his best to be loyal to them. The fundamental division of the Gissing family appears in a passage that Gissing cut from his first novel, *Workers in the Dawn*. An old printer, Mr Tollady, is reminiscing about his father:

> Perhaps his favourite study of all was Botany, a taste for which, as you know, I have inherited from him. How many a long walk have I had with him in the summer mornings, before breakfast, when I carried for him the tin-case in which he placed the plants he wished to take home. I used to beg my mother to let me stay at home from church on Sunday to help him in pressing these. My poor mother deemed it very shocking that the Sundays should be spent in this manner, and it was seldom I could obtain her leave to absent myself from Church. I have often thought these enforced hours of make-believe attention to litanies and sermons did me very much harm. At all events they created in my mind such an intense hatred of Churches and everything connected therewith that it remains undiminished to this day.[5]

Gissing had reason to cut the passage, because people in Wakefield would realise how closely it followed his own experience. For Mrs Gissing, criticism of religion was wickedness, and faith was not subject to question. For

Thomas, faith was just nonsense. He liked to ridicule the idea that the world was created by 'a man standing up and ordering it to exist'.[6] *The Origin of Species* was published on George's second birthday, and the battle over evolution would be a major theme in his novel *Born in Exile*. He and his father would worship in the Temple of Nature, not in a temple made by man. It was not just that George disliked the services that his mother forced on him; he also wanted to be doing something he loved instead, and in his father's company. His whole life would be shaped by rebellion against the evangelical Anglicanism of his mother.

George had much less of his father's company than he would have liked. Thomas Gissing worked obsessively, a trait that he would pass on to his eldest son. He was said to have done a full day's work before his assistants even came into the shop in the morning. As he prospered, and his family grew, he expanded into the Georgian house at the back of the shop. In 1865 Thomas bought the whole complex at auction, including a second shop next to his. The price was £2,940, a serious sum for the time; some local Tories ran up the price against him because he was a prominent Liberal.[7] It was not hard to make money in Wakefield if you knew your business, and Thomas surely did.

For a rising tradesman like Thomas Gissing, business and politics could scarcely be separated. Within a year of his arrival at Wakefield he was elected to the executive committee of the Mechanics Institution, the central cultural and political body of the town. These Institutions provided cheap access to books, periodicals, courses and lectures, at a time when the state provided neither free libraries nor free education. The Institutions were also the strong right hand of the Liberal Party, especially its more radical and anti-clerical elements. Thomas Gissing was a Victorian progressive to his fingertips, inspired by the political energies released by the first Reform Bill of 1832. The Liberal Party was his alternative to religious zeal, and the instrument of civic good works. He became treasurer of the local party, a town councillor from 1867, a committee member for the new Art School, the Hospital, and much else. If he had not died young, Thomas surely would have been elected mayor of Wakefield or an MP, and have become wealthy along the way. A lower-middle-class hero was what he wanted to be, and what he made himself into.

George Gissing had to find a way to imitate his father without being a mere copy of him. He would always be his father's child rather than his mother's, but he had a darker temperament than either of them. He held to his father's political allegiance, yet steadily lost hope that political action could make for a better world. The mid-Victorian optimism of Thomas

Gissing helped to build Wakefield. His son became an observer only, one who refused to join any group or run for any office. George started out feeling that 'something must be done' about the sufferings of the poor, but ended up believing that you couldn't be a Radical if you really knew what the lower classes were like.

George was sent to school from the age of four. The Back Lane School was just around the corner from his house, next to the new railway station (which came when George was ten) and almost under the shadow of the great wall of the prison. The Infants' section was in the charge of Miss Milner, a maiden sister of the prison doctor. 'I owe her much,' Gissing said later, 'as all do to their first teachers.'[8] All five of the Gissing children went to Miss Milner, and when she died, in 1887, she left £50 to each of George's sisters. From the Infant School he progressed to the Collegiate School for boys, in the same building, where the Reverend Joseph Harrison introduced him to the Greek and Latin classics. George stayed there till he was thirteen, beginning his education as a gentleman. The Gissing boys and girls did not play with the children of other shopkeepers. A pharmaceutical chemist needed academic learning, a butcher or draper did not. Thomas Gissing was friendly with doctors and lawyers, and might have become their equal in time. George's closest friend at the school was Henry Hick, a future doctor and son of the chemist who had sold Thomas Gissing his pharmaceutical business.

What sort of boy was George Gissing? When asked what was the best preparation for becoming a writer, Ernest Hemingway replied: 'An unhappy childhood.' There is no sign that George was unhappy until misfortune struck him from outside, when he was thirteen and his father died. He was so good at his schoolwork that when he was eight Miss Milner told his parents that he had to be moved up in school because she had taught him everything she knew. He loved holidays by the sea in Cumbria or Northumberland, where the children fished and hiked and searched for plants:

> whatever holiday or excursion was planned, his favourite expression was, 'Let us go in a body'; he always had a particular dislike of anyone being left out. In his earlier days it was impossible for him to be attracted to people outside his own family, unless he could admire their intellectual gifts.[9]

Memories of those early days in a large family lay behind Gissing's anguished complaints of loneliness in his adult life. First, the family was broken by his father's death; his marriage to Nell Harrison was never accepted by his mother or sisters; his novels shocked the conventional views of everyone else in the family; finally, Gissing's attempts to create a united family of his own met with complete failure. No one of his brothers and sisters, his mother, his legal wife, or his two children would be with him when he died. His path led inexorably away from his first home, to solitude and exile.

By choosing the life of an artist Gissing became, in his own terms, one of the 'unclassed'. A creative vocation called for doing more than just following the school curriculum and coming top in every exam. Gissing's first ambitions were in the visual arts: he drew, painted, and took instruction at the art school that his father had helped to establish. Some caricatures have survived from when he was twelve, making fun of himself and his brothers. He had plenty of whimsical ideas, but no great skill with the pencil. Although Gissing never became a painter, he knew a lot about painting, sculpture and architecture. The artist's life figured prominently in several of his novels, such as *The Emancipated, Denzil Quarrier*, and *Will Warburton*.

If things had gone smoothly for the Gissing family, George's creative side might have remained a minor interest while he pursued a solid professional career. He had started to write poetry by the age of eleven; it was smooth, correct and completely imitative of poets like Byron or Wordsworth. At that age he was able to put Virgil's First Eclogue into English verse. Originality was the last thing a Victorian schoolmaster would have been looking for, and a talent for imitation could count for brilliance. What first cut across Gissing's primrose path to academic success was his father's early death. Thomas Gissing probably had TB, but he did not allow illness to interfere with his frantic round of work and politics. Three days after Christmas of 1870 he died, with little warning, at the age of forty-one.[10]

In *Workers in the Dawn*, Tollady cannot cry at his father's burial in the snowy churchyard: 'it was not till I went to bed that, all of a sudden, the reality of my loss forced itself upon me, and I wept bitterly far into the night. Whether other children suffer so much at the loss of their parents, I know not. I only know that I cannot conceive agony more intense than I went through that night.' As it happens, there was a report in the local paper that George stood by his father's grave with eyes that were red with weeping.[11] No doubt he was torn between giving way to grief and being a little stoic, ready to step into his father's shoes. But the person with real power was his mother, who had to decide how to carry on and raise her children. At least she was far from poor. In 1867 Thomas Gissing had received a bequest of £1,000 from his aunt Emily Waller, who had inherited £8,000 from her friend Miss Whittington. Emily also left the Gissing boys

£500 each at age twenty-one, though they were not told this. Unlike Dr Madden of *The Odd Women*, Thomas had also managed to insure his life for £1,300. The pharmaceutical business was sold for another £1,300, and the house and shops brought just enough to pay off the mortgage on them. Margaret Gissing faced the future with about £3,300, and another £1,500 for the boys later on. She was thirty-eight years old, but she never remarried or took up any employment. Instead she would live quietly on the income from her inherited capital.

At a 4 per cent return, Mrs Gissing's income would be about £132 a year, twice or three times the average income in Wakefield. She invested mainly in house property, in and around the town. Having sold the house that went with Thomas's business, she moved to a smaller rented house in Stamp Office Yard, near the cattle market. Her other decisive move was to send the three boys away to boarding school. The two little girls, who were seven and four, would stay with her. It might seem callous to uproot the boys – the youngest, Algernon, was only ten – so soon after their father's death. Mrs Gissing's chief motive was that boys should have a firm patri-archal hand to guide them. The best alternative to their father was a good schoolmaster, and she already knew one: James Wood, the headmaster of the Lindow Grove School at Alderley Edge, Cheshire. She may also have felt that no local school could bring out the best in her boys, and that having sons at boarding school was a claim to middle-class status. If Thomas Gissing had lived, he might have felt differently. The boys could have stayed at the school next door, and enjoyed the comforts of home. But Mrs Gissing knew James Wood as a family friend, and had confidence that he would take good care of her boys. He was thirty-six years old in 1870, and had trained as a teacher at the Quaker Flounders Institute, a few miles from Wakefield.[12] Lindow Grove was just getting under way; it was already clear that George was a safe bet to win scholarships and raise the school's reputation. Probably Wood offered Mrs Gissing a discount on the school's usual fees.

Although James Wood had an extraordinary pupil in George Gissing, he was not an extraordinary teacher, and we cannot give him any great credit for Gissing's later career. A back-handed tribute to him said: 'As with many strong men, thought and action were often almost concurrent with him and he rarely repented of his resolutions.'[13] Wood prepared his boys well for their exams, and was liked by them, but there is no sign of intellectual creativity in his career. Nor would such a person be likely to employ teachers more creative than himself. One teacher said of his school: 'Best of all, boys were taught to be gentlemen, to have a hatred of all meanness, and insincerity, and a love of all things lovely, true, and of good report.'[14] This might be a good recipe for success in the mainstream of Victorian life, but not for becoming a novelist. Gissing would find his preparation for that in other places than Lindow Grove.

James Wood's school faced competition from hundreds of other private boarding schools, including many that were wealthier and more famous. He needed to attract students by pointing to good results in national examinations. Lindow Grove was nominally a Quaker school, but the boys could go to Anglican services if they preferred. Wood had married into the Quaker faith without really believing in it. He was an enthusiastic imperialist of the 'my country right or wrong' type, and he employed a grizzled veteran of the Crimean War, Sergeant St Ruth, to drill the boys once a week. This made the school more attractive to the sons of the gentry. In *The Private Papers of Henry Ryecroft*, Gissing would describe how much he hated the drill and being addressed by a number rather than a name. Lindow Grove inspired him with a lifelong hatred of nationalism and militarism.

But he had no objection to the discipline of acquiring knowledge. At Lindow Grove Gissing worked immensely hard at his books, whether he liked the subject or not. The school's pressure for academic glory was minor in comparison with the pressure he imposed on himself. He did what was required in sports, and went for long walks by way of amusement. The rest of his time went on cramming for exams. Gissing was ambitious, of course, but there was also a pattern that would only harden for the rest of his life. None of the memoirs of his time at Lindow Grove mention any emotional turmoil over his father's death. Instead, all his unhappiness was displaced into compulsive work, as if that was the way to sterilise grief and loss. For a boy at boarding school, that may have been a good survival strategy. Later, though, Gissing's way of dealing with problems in his marriages was to retreat into his study for endless hours of work. This helped to finish a novel in record time, but was not a good formula for domestic happiness.

The first target for Gissing's academic ambitions was the Oxford Junior Local Examination. This would normally be taken at age sixteen, followed by the Oxford Senior a year later. Gissing took the Oxford Junior at fourteen after two years at Lindow Grove, in the early summer of 1872. Mr Wood knew what he could do and saw no reason to hold him back. The boy who came top in the Manchester region would get a full scholarship to the new local university, Owens College. Gissing carried off the prize, and was ranked twelfth in the whole country. He entered Owens in October 1872, starting at the equivalent of sixth-form level (though his prowess in

Greek and Latin was already far beyond any sixth-former of today).

Owens College was a symbol of the rise of Victorian Manchester. It had opened its doors in 1851 on a bequest of £96,000 from the textile merchant John Owens, who wanted nonconformists like himself to be able to go to university. Unlike Oxford and Cambridge, no student would have to profess Anglicanism in order to be admitted, nor would there be any religious observances at the college.[15] Owens students needed only to be fourteen years old, and male. In *Born in Exile*, Gissing called 'Whitelaw College' 'an institute which had conferred humane distinction on the money-making Midland town'.[16] Like other red-brick universities founded around this time, Owens was particularly friendly to scientific studies. One of Gissing's classmates was J. J. Thomson, who would receive the Nobel Prize in 1906 for his discovery of the electron. Twenty-three former students of Owens and its successor, the university of Manchester, have received Nobels in science or economics.

To become a scientist would be to follow directly in his father's footsteps, and Gissing had no interest in doing that. His heart lay in English and French literature, and in the classics. For his first two years at Owens he continued to live at Lindow Grove, where he had his school friends and his two brothers. He could go into Manchester by train each day, and return to his peaceful country village at night. Mr Wood was happy to have him stay there because he could use Gissing as a part-time teacher at the school, at a small salary or perhaps just in exchange for his board and lodging. Wood was also something of a father-figure for Gissing. For his first Easter holiday from Owens, in April 1873, Gissing went to stay at Wood's house in Colwyn Bay, North Wales. On his last day he walked twenty-five miles to see the Menai Bridge. The next day, Wood had to go back to Lindow Grove for the beginning of term, and he suggested that Gissing should follow him on foot. Gissing left that afternoon and arrived at Alderley Edge for lunch two days later, having walked sixty-seven miles in forty-six hours. When he went back to Wood's house in July he walked by himself to the summit of Snowdon and most of the way back. Gissing called this sort of walk 'glorious'; most people would have collapsed long before the end.

Gissing's close friends were still his fellow students at Lindow Grove. Arthur Bowes was a year younger than him. They went to Shakespeare productions together, and Gissing told Bowes that he was the only boy at Lindow Grove he really cared for. There is no hint that this friendship had any homoerotic side to it. An older friend was William Summers, who came from a wealthy Manchester family and had gone directly to Oxford from Lindow Grove. He invited Gissing to stay with his family in

Manchester in July 1873. This was Gissing's first inside look at an upper-class household. He told a friend that he 'enjoyed himself rarely' at the Summerses, though in *Born in Exile* Godwin Peak goes to visit a similar family, the Warricombes, and makes 'no very favourable impression on his hostess'.[17] Gissing was still only fifteen and bound to feel awkward in a large and luxurious house. In addition, if *Born in Exile* is taken from life, he became infatuated with William Summers's younger sister, who was engaged to a wealthy cotton manufacturer called Abel Buckley. Godwin Peak becomes engaged to Sidwell Warricombe himself, until a lie about his past catches up with him.

Within six months of Gissing's arrival at Owens College his teachers realised that every academic prize lay within his grasp. His first essay for his favourite professor, Adolphus Ward, ran to sixty-eight pages.[18] Gissing won the poetry prize for *Ravenna*, in twenty-two Spenserian stanzas (the same metre as his father's poem 'Margaret'). At the prize-giving in July – a scene described in the first chapter of *Born in Exile* – he took a first prize in Classics. The reward was an eight-volume set of Gibbon's *Decline and Fall of the Roman Empire*, which became one of Gissing's key works. It combined classical lore with large helpings of gloom and doom. As he went up again and again for more prizes he was no longer a shy newcomer to the college, but someone who had acquired a halo of future success. The way was opening up to a subsequent Oxford or Cambridge degree, and to a brilliant professional career.

Gissing spent two more years on the same track at Owens, without fundamentally changing his way of life. He continued to live and to teach part-time at Lindow Grove. Owens College moved in the autumn of 1873 to a fine new campus on Oxford Road, on the southern outskirts of Manchester. The main buildings were designed by John Waterhouse, the leading architect of the style known as 'Manchester Gothic'. This was a casemented and tessellated blend of English and Italian medieval styles. The college was rising, and Gissing with it. He aimed to spend at least four years there, taking a cab-load of prizes home each July. After his First at Oxbridge he would teach Classics or English at some university. The new Victorian system of competitive examinations was defining Gissing's identity by the obstacle course that led from the lower middle class to the comfort and security of academic life. But in the autumn of 1875, when Gissing was not yet eighteen, he became a boy with no future.

Around October, Gissing left Lindow Grove and moved into lodgings at 43 Grafton Street, a terraced block just at the southern edge of the Owens College campus. One reason for doing so was that he could now afford it.

His entrance scholarship expired that summer, but at the end of June he sat for the first BA of the university of London. If you passed, you could become a London graduate without ever having set foot in the university. Anyone in England, male or female, could take the exams. They were rigorous, but narrowly factual, along the lines of 'describe the main events of Shakespeare's life up to 1603'. Gissing took the English and Latin exams, and on 1 September 1875 he learnt that he had been ranked first in England in both subjects, which no one had succeeded in doing before. His reward was £40 a year for two years for the Latin, and £30 for the English. In October he won the Owens College Shakespeare scholarship, another £40 a year for two years. Instead of being a dormitory monitor and general dogsbody at Lindow Grove, he could now afford to be a young man around Manchester, spending time with his friends and editing the college magazine. What Gissing did not realise was how unprepared he was to make good use of his freedom.

'I shall continue to go to Owens for perhaps two more years,' he told his grandfather, 'They seem to wish me to continue my studies quietly.'[19] All he knew of life was preparing for the next exam, as we see in his solemn advice to his eight-year-old sister Ellen: 'The time goes so quickly that we cannot afford to waste a single minute, and I only wish I could have two or three years back again, to make better use of them. Nothing makes one more comfortable than to think that no time has been wasted; and I am sure you have not wasted much yet.'[20] Even so, Gissing left his books behind from time to time, and Morley Roberts first spotted him acting the young dog:

> in a little hotel not very far from the College where some of us young fellows used to go between the intervals of lectures to play a game of billiards. I remember quite well seeing him sit on a little table swinging his legs. . . . He was curiously bright, with a very mobile face. He had abundant masses of brown hair combed backwards over his head, grey-blue eyes, a very sympathetic mouth, an extraordinarily well-shaped chin – although perhaps both mouth and chin were a little weak – and a great capacity for talking and laughing.[21]

Roberts was more of an adventurer and less of a scholar than Gissing, but they struck up a friendship that lasted for the rest of Gissing's life.

Within a few months of moving into Manchester Gissing started to waste time in a spectacular way, and to destroy his brilliant academic career. Why? He blamed much of his trouble on the shock of the utter loneliness he felt in his lodgings: 'It was a cruel and most undesirable thing that I, at the age of sixteen, should have been turned loose in a big city, compelled to live alone in lodgings, with nobody interested in me but those at the college. I see now that one of my sisters should certainly have been sent with me to [Manchester].'[22] It is hard to see how Gissing's thirteen-year-old sister Margaret would have kept him on the straight and narrow; he had some sentimental notion that a pure girl would protect him from a fallen one. He got into trouble because he was living alone, for the first time in his life; because he now cut a fine figure at the college and had money in his pocket; and because of his complete inexperience with women.

Between 1870 and 1875 Gissing had spent almost all his time in exclusively male environments. His contact with women was limited to his mother and sisters, and an occasional meeting with a young woman of his own class. Such women were attainable only through marriage, and a student would not consider marriage possible until he had finished his studies and gained an income. Gissing was idealistic by temperament, and doubly so when it came to young ladies. When Godwin Peak encounters two of them at the prize-giving in *Born in Exile*, he thinks he is being visited by divine beings:

> On the seat behind him were two girls whose intermittent talk held him with irresistible charm throughout the whole ceremony. He had not imagined that girls could display such intelligence, and the sweet clearness of their intonation, the purity of their accent, the grace of their habitual phrases, were things altogether beyond his experience.[23]

At Owens, Gissing could only dream of one day possessing such a domestic angel. Meanwhile, he was reading Latin poets like Ovid and Martial who took a brutally cynical view both of women's feelings and their bodies. How to reconcile such radically different visions? Perhaps Gissing found a clue in a poem published six years before. Dante Gabriel Rossetti's 'Jenny' was inspired by a fallen woman, like Thomas Gissing's 'Margaret'.[24] The poet speaks through a young college student, who has fallen in love with 'lazy laughing languid Jenny / Fond of a kiss and fond of a guinea'. He goes home with Jenny, but she falls asleep before they can make love, and he lies awake thinking about her life. In the morning he leaves her some guineas and leaves before she wakes up. Jenny is dishonoured, yet innocent; all the fault lies with the 'flagrant man-swine' who have made her what she is. The poet can adore Jenny as much as he does his fiancée and cousin Nell, who is genteel, pure and good. 'Jenny' conveys the Victorian belief that even a prostitute starts out with the ideal qualities that all women possess. That is why she is called *fallen*, because she was dragged down into the mire where the 'man-swine' have always lived.

Whether directly inspired by Rossetti's 'Jenny' or not, Gissing acted out its story. Owens College was first housed in a Georgian mansion on Quay Street in the centre of Manchester.[25] Behind the college, along the left bank of the river Irwell, were some of the foulest slums in Europe, reeking courtyards full of Irish immigrants and people who had moved in from the countryside. If the story 'The Sins of the Fathers' is true to life, Gissing found Marianne Helen ('Nell') Harrison in one of those courts that both shocked and tempted passers-by:

A broad archway, the gloom of its chill, murky shadow only deepened by the flicker of the shattered gas-lamp that hangs from the centre, its silence only broken by the agonized weeping of a poor girl who strives to still the throbbing of her temples by pressing them against the clammy stones; whilst, little as one would imagine it, but a few paces separate her from the crowd and glare of the wide streets – such a scene is but too common after nightfall in the heart of a great English manufacturing town. As such it did not at first produce a very startling effect upon Leonard Vincent, who, as he was hurrying home by short cuts from a social gathering of fellow-students, was stopped at the mouth of the archway by the sounds of distress that fell upon his ear; but his interest was more vividly awakened as he caught a glimpse of the upturned face faintly illumined by the light which just then a gust of wind blew into a flame. The dark, flashing eyes, the long, black hair all unkempt and streaming over the girl's shoulders, the face, lovely in its outlines, now weird with its look of agony and ghastly pale, made a picture such as he had never looked on, and held him for a moment as immovable as though he had been gazing upon the head of Medusa.[26]

Nell was seventeen years old in January 1876, when she met Gissing. She lived around the corner from the old Owens College in a brothel on Water Street, conveniently located for the students. She was a Shropshire lass, born in Shrewsbury, and 'The Sins of the Fathers' gives a probable sketch of her early life.[27] 'Laura Lindon' lives happily on a small farm until her father dies and her mother marries their rich landlord. He treats Laura so cruelly that she runs away with a friend to the north of England. They try to support themselves by sewing, but Laura's friend gives up the struggle and turns to prostitution, while Laura clings to her virtue. In the story, the stepfather's main offence is that he has a snobbish dislike of Laura's friends,

who are ordinary farm girls. This hardly seems reason enough to leave
home, and it is more likely that Nell ran off to Manchester because her
stepfather was sexually abusing her, or trying to. She was already an alcoholic in her teens, finding in drink a refuge from the pain of a prostitute's
life. There is no record of Nell having any contact with her mother after
she met Gissing. Either the mother was dead, or she had sided with her
second husband against her daughter.

Gissing knew that he should step forward to comfort a maiden in distress,
but he was ill equipped to understand the sexual trauma that was the most
likely cause of Nell's fall. His idea of saving her was to turn her into a lady –
to destroy the identity she had, rather than to give her the kind of acceptance
that might have restored her faith in herself. By February Gissing had
commissioned a photograph of Nell with flowing hair in Pre-Raphaelite
style, and was showing it to his friends. Morley Roberts commented that
he 'had about as little *savoir-faire* as anybody I had ever met up to that time,
or anybody I could ever expect to meet'.[28] Many Owens students made an
occasional visit to a brothel, with no harm to their future careers. Gissing
brought doom on himself by deciding to save Nell from her way of life,
and eventually to marry her.

Gissing visited Nell in her room on Water Street, but so did others. One
of them was Gissing's friend John George Black. When he went there
looking for Gissing one day, Nell was alone, and she got him into her bed –
against his will, he claimed. 'I had no desire for her – never felt so peculiar
in my life; my head swam, and I hardly knew what I was doing.'[29] When
Gissing wrote him that he had fallen in love with Nell, Black apologised
for betraying his friend, and explained that while Gissing loved Nell, he
loved Gissing:

> Gradually we have come together, and gradually an affection has sprung
> up in me for you such as I never felt for any other; and that this affair should
> cause any difference between us gives me at the thought infinite sorrow. . . .
> Hitherto I have had no friend; I have been a solitary creature consuming
> my own reflections.[30]

For Black, this was an affair in which Nell was a means to be intimate with
Gissing, the real object of his affection. They all had something else to
share, thanks to Nell:

> The irritation continued growing worse, and on examination, I found the
> prepuce swollen, and on turning it down, I found the whole of the inside
> salmon-coloured, as you called it, only little spots as though the skin had

been eaten away so as to show the flesh, and it almost looked as though it were bleeding. I applied a little of the subtilissimus, but the end continues to be irritated. The prepuce is a little hard as well; & there was a drop or two of yellow matter near the red spots.[31]

These symptoms most resemble the onset of either a herpes attack, or syphilis. But diagnostic tests for particular infections did not exist before the twentieth century. Someone who lived as Nell did would play host to a swarm of bacteria, viruses and parasites. No drugs existed that would kill them off. Later, Nell almost certainly had tertiary syphilis. At the end of the nineteenth century, one estimate was that 15 per cent of the adult population of Paris had syphilis; for prostitutes the rate must have been much higher.[32] Since Nell continued to prostitute herself during the six years or so that she lived with Gissing, it is likely that she infected him at some point. Some of his illnesses in later life are consistent with a diagnosis of syphilis. At the very least, he must have lived in fear of this shameful and incurable disease. Yet the infection he and Black picked up from her made no difference to his romantic infatuation with Nell, and the self-destructive behaviour that followed.

What kind of person was Nell? She had a pretty face, to judge by the one surviving photograph, but very little education. Her accent would have been Shropshire with some Manchester laid over it; Gissing tried, without success, to make her speak Standard English. In October 1894 he wrote a short story, 'The Fate of Humphrey Snell', which may contain a portrait of Nell. Humphrey is a young man who wanders the countryside, collecting herbs for a living. One night in Wells, Somerset, he comes across a weeping girl, an unemployed servant who has nowhere to sleep:

> She seemed to be about eighteen, and betrayed a weakness of character even in excess of the failing common to her kind; her manner was childish, and could not have excited suspicion in the most experienced observer. Humphrey ... felt a profound pity as he listened to her; and therewith blended that other vague emotion stirred by the first sound from her lips – an emotion which reminded him of early manhood, when he was wont to shrink from girls, and yet to worship afar off. ... [she was] foolishly pretty, with round eyes and baby lips, and neither nose nor chin to speak of; on the whole, good-natured in expression, and even through the traces of tears displaying a coquettish self-consciousness.[33]

Gissing's portrayal of 'Annie Frost' is coloured by his later cynicism about feminine wiles, and self-contempt for being betrayed by his own idealism. But he also sees how egotistical loneliness can set a trap for a man:

Humphrey, when he ventured to give an account of himself, perceived with a tremor of exquisite surprise that the girl willingly lent ear; at each meeting she grew more confidential, and seemed to regard him with a trust, an appealing simplicity, which thrilled him to the heart. Never in his life before had he revealed himself as to this girl. He imagined she understood him, that her mute attention meant sympathy. Yet of a sudden she asked: 'Don't you think you could earn more if you was to try?'

Although Gissing had his male friends at Owens, most of them were also rivals to be overcome. His education had separated him from his immediate family, and there was no home in Manchester where he was known and welcomed. In *Born in Exile*, Godwin Peak laments that 'It looked indeed as if there were no one in the world who cared what became of him.'[34] Gissing's isolation might be blamed on his own aloofness, compulsive work habits, and self-pity. Yet he longed for the tender reassurance that only a woman could provide. Like D. H. Lawrence, he felt that he could not face the world without a woman at his back to support him. Unlike Lawrence, though, Gissing had no mother-complex, except in reverse. He conformed to Simenon's definition of a novelist: 'a man who never received mother-love'.[35] All the more reason, then, to completely lose his head when Nell first took him in her arms. His joy at being physically and emotionally accepted completely overwhelmed both the stigma of prostitution, and his own common sense.

As Gissing's affair with Nell unfolded, the sting was in the tail. Gissing had £110 a year in scholarships. Yet his relationship with Nell was such a drain on his income that within six months of meeting her he had become a habitual thief. Undeterred by his dose of VD, he took Nell for a seaside holiday at Southport, the closest resort to Manchester. They stayed there for at least two weeks, while Gissing's teachers wondered why he had disappeared from their classes. When he came back, his friends begged him to stop seeing Nell; instead, he told them that he and Nell hoped to get married. Was it the discovery of sex that drove Gissing to stay on such a disastrous course? He probably had been a virgin when he met Nell, but plenty of his classmates consorted with prostitutes without wanting to marry them. Sex with Nell cannot have been very pleasant when both had florid cases of VD. His infatuation was not based on what was actually happening, but on how things would be when he had removed Nell from her sordid existence and remade her closer to his heart's desire. Gissing still believed in women's angelic nature; if they fell short, male lust or a callous society deserved all the blame.

Gissing and Nell came back to Manchester from Southport around the middle of April 1876, and the final catastrophe unfolded. Morley Roberts believed that Gissing was truly in love with Nell, 'and out of that affection there grew up, very naturally, a horror in his sensitive mind for the life this poor child was leading. He haunted the streets which she haunted, and sometimes saw her with other men.'[36] Gissing was desperate to have Nell to himself, if necessary by outbidding her other clients. He even bought Nell a sewing machine in the hope that she could support herself with it. Nell took all the money Gissing gave her, and asked for more. Some of it went on her health: there was a Dr Wahltuch to treat her VD, and she may already have been suffering from epilepsy. But much of Gissing's scholarship money was spent by Nell down at the pub.

That spring, students at Owens started to notice that books and articles of clothing were disappearing, followed by money that they had left in their coats in the downstairs cloakroom. J. G. Greenwood, the College Principal, brought in the police. On Wednesday 31 May a plain-clothes detective put some marked money in the pocket of a coat, then hid in a little room beside the cloakroom. He saw Gissing come and take the money, and arrested him on the spot. Soon the whole college would have known why he had done it. Letters that John George Black had written to Gissing about Nell were found by the police when they searched Gissing's room. The letters were turned over to Greenwood, and made a cast-iron case against the college's star student.

The next day Gissing came before the magistrate, charged with the theft of 5/2d (something like £50 in today's money).[37] He was kept in prison on remand, which meant easier conditions and the right to keep one's own clothes.[38] Six days after his arrest, Gissing appeared in Sessional Court and was sentenced to one month at hard labour. He had no grounds for a defence. As soon as sentence was pronounced he was taken to Bellevue Prison on Hyde Road, on the east side of Manchester. Bellevue, which had opened in 1849, was one of the grim human warehouses of the Victorian prison system.[39] The ramshackle jails of the eighteenth century had been replaced by the orderly nineteenth-century penitentiary, thanks largely to Quaker reformers determined to prevent the transmission of evil from one prisoner to another, through pastimes like gambling, singing and drinking. In the new prisons every prisoner would be kept in silent, solitary confinement. Each cell was to be a place of meditation and repentance. Windows would be set high up: not to see out of, but to remind inmates that they should receive God's light into their souls.

All too often, the new prisons did not drive inmates to repentance, but to madness. During his month in Bellevue, Gissing probably did not exchange one friendly word with other inmates or with guards. If a guard had anything to say to a prisoner, he would use his cell number, not his name. The prison was built in the classic 'Panopticon' style with five spokes around a central hub, from which the wardens could look down all the ranges of cells. There were 851 cells, of which nearly 30 per cent were for women (British prisons today are 95 per cent male). Gissing was one of nearly twelve thousand prisoners who served time in Bellevue during 1876. Victorian Britain believed in sending great numbers to prison, and treating them very harshly: penitence and punishment were expected to reinforce each other. Most of the inmates were there for drunkenness, prostitution or assault. Every night the Manchester police combed through the slums by the river Irwell and delivered petty offenders to the courts. A typical sentence would be a choice between a week in jail and a five-shilling fine. When Gissing stood in the intake line at Bellevue the woman behind him was a 'common prostitute', Bridget Monahan. She was fifty-five years old, four feet ten inches tall, and had sixty-seven previous convictions. Here was a portent of what Nell might become, if Gissing had eyes to see it.

Gissing's sentence was more than just being left alone for a month to contemplate his crime and the destruction of his hopes. He had committed a social, an academic and a sexual crime, all in one. On arrival he was bathed, had his head shaved, and was put in a prison uniform with its 'chicken track' pattern. Hard labour, at Bellevue, meant walking on a treadmill. Prisoners had to climb the equivalent of more than ten thousand vertical feet a day. Their diet (for the first month of their sentence) was about twenty ounces of bread, nine ounces of potatoes, an ounce of meat, two ounces of gruel, and three ounces of soup (made from one ox-head for a hundred servings). This gave about 2,500 calories, a third or a quarter of what a manual worker normally ate. Anyone on this regime was being deliberately starved; Oscar Wilde lost twenty-two pounds in the first few weeks of his imprisonment. For the first month, hard-labour prisoners typically had to sleep on bare boards, with a block of wood for a pillow.

A sentence of hard labour meant that the state was physically torturing the prisoner; to this was added the mental torture that a prisoner like Gissing would inflict on himself. He kept his prison sentence a secret for the rest of his life, and said very little about prison in his novels. In *The Unclassed* Ida Starr is wrongly convicted of theft, and surrenders her mind for six months to 'unvaried brooding upon one vast misery'.[40] Harry Mutimer, in *Demos*, gets three months' hard labour for stealing from his employer.

When he comes out, 'Punishment had had its usual effect; 'Arry was obstinately taciturn, conscious of his degradation, inwardly at war with all his kind.'[41] For Gissing, silence seemed the only possible response to his experience. Having first been sentenced to a month of silence by the law, he passed the same sentence on himself for another twenty-six years. We can guess at his motives from what he wrote about Dickens's secret, his childhood service in the blacking factory: 'as the boy had suffered from a sense of undeserved humiliation, so did the man feel hurt in his deepest sensibilities whenever he reflected on that evil time. His silence regarding it was a very natural reserve.'[42]

After his ordeal at Bellevue, Gissing had to bear the burden of his conviction for the rest of his life. An anonymous white-collar criminal tells what that meant:

> To the man in a good position, it is moral death, accompanied with ruin and disgrace to his family and relatives. The actual punishment to men in my position is not the confinement, the coarse but wholesome food, the discomforts, and work: it is the terrible fall in social position, the stigma that clings to a man not only all his life, but, after his life is ended, to his children.[43]

Gissing was released from prison on 5 July and met by Matthew Hick, the man from whom Thomas Gissing had purchased his Wakefield business. Owens College had expelled Gissing the day after he entered prison, and had cancelled his scholarship. His money from the university of London stopped also, since he was no longer a student. Most likely Matthew Hick took Gissing back to hide out in his mother's house; with his pallor and his prison haircut he would want to stay off the streets. As he licked his wounds, the powers-that-be at Owens were feeling some remorse at his fate. Everyone's first concern would be to separate him from Nell, the temptress who had ruined him. The safest course was to put him beyond her reach by sending him to America. A fund was quietly established at Owens to help him. The Governors of the College pledged £5 each, and Gissing probably received at least £50 to speed him on his way.[44]

Gissing remained in England for two months after his release. He passed the time by writing poetry, though it showed no sign of the terrible days he had passed in prison. There would be no 'Ballad of Bellevue Jail' from Gissing. He wrote a long poem about Narcissus falling in love with his own image, and a series of sonnets about Shakespeare's heroines.[45] 'To Sleep' ended with a fantasy of suicide as an escape from troubles; Gissing would talk of suicide from time to time in his adult life, and several of his protagonists kill themselves. There are two poems, 'A Farewell' and 'The Two Gardens', that seem to be addressed to Nell, or rather an idea of her:

> To-morrow's eve will see me far
> Upon the Ocean's swell,
> And all alone with moon and star;
> Farewell, my love, farewell!

The poem ends with a hope of the lovers' reunion across the sea. Gissing and Nell kept on writing to each other; he stuck to her like a limpet, in spite of everything. His idealisation of Nell seems to have been an emotional necessity for him. If she was just an ordinary girl of the streets, then Gissing had been a great fool. He preferred to think of himself as a great lover who had paid the price for his love.

Gissing's first idea of America was that he would do well there, and be able to bring Nell over and marry her. He left Liverpool for Boston early in September 1876. Boston was still the intellectual capital of the US, and Gissing had some introductions to help him get established there. The new steamships had reduced the voyage to about nine days, and the fare to £5. In the final pages of *Workers in the Dawn*, Arthur Golding is thrilled by the crossing:

> When he lay in his berth at night, listening to the lash and thunder of the waves against the sides of the vessel; to the cracking and straining of the masts and cordage, to the shrill whistle upon deck, now and then making itself heard above the duller noises, his heart was filled with a wild wish that the winds might sweep yet more fiercely upon the heaving water, that the ocean might swell up to mountainous waves, such deep delight did he experience in the midst of the grand new scene.[46]

Gissing arrived in the America of the Gilded Age, and soon decided that it did not suit him. From the Boston docks he walked up Bunker Hill and found a boarding house at 71 Bartlett Street, near the new monument to the battle of 1775. He had to pay ten dollars a week (about £2), which was much more expensive than England, though he found the food excellent. It would take Gissing almost four months to find a job, so he must have had a good sum in his pocket when he arrived in the New World. His only idea about supporting himself was to become a writer or journalist of some sort; he had written odds and ends for the Owens College magazine and assumed he could do something similar in Boston. He had an introduction to the great abolitionist William Lloyd Garrison, and Gissing hoped –

vainly, as it turned out – that Garrison could get him a job on the *Atlantic Monthly*. As Gissing arrived, the US was still caught up in a patriotic frenzy of celebrating the centennial of the Declaration of Independence. Garrison, with his root-and-branch hostility to the American way, gave Gissing an alternative view. Before the Civil War, Garrison had publicly burnt a copy of the constitution, saying that it supported slavery. Gissing found some intellectual society through Garrison, but could not get any of his sketches of English life published. In his spare time he worked at a translation of Heine. Gissing's lack of success at journalism was not surprising, since he never had the quickness of response and the instinct for popular taste of writers like Kipling or R. L. Stevenson. Still, he had come out of prison with a firm resolve to write for a living. It would be twelve years before he could support himself on his literary earnings alone, years of immense labour for small reward.

If Gissing's writings were not in demand, he had a more marketable skill as a teacher of Classics, foreign languages and English literature. At the beginning of January, just as his money was running out, he was hired as a replacement teacher at Waltham High School. His salary was fifteen dollars a week and he could earn more by giving private lessons. He paid eight dollars a week for room and board with the chairman of the school board, a Unitarian minister. The job was an easy one for him, and at first every-thing went swimmingly. 'A High-School teacher is an important person here,' he wrote home, and he was pleased by the respectful behaviour of the students.[47] It was something new for Gissing that the school had no fees, and was co-educational. He disliked the democratic manners of Ameri-cans in their social life, but made an exception for the friendliness of his students.

Once Gissing had his foot on any academic ladder, his intellectual gifts guaranteed that he would climb up it at speed. Within ten years he could easily have been a professor of Classics at an Ivy League university, leading a blameless and prosperous life. The small-town society of Waltham wel-comed this young and presentable Englishman, and Boston was only ten miles away. But Gissing's youth, and his compulsion to tempt fate, brought on another expulsion. He was only a year or two older than his students, and still emotionally vulnerable. Martha McCullough Barnes was a graduating senior in English and Classics, a bright student and a 'singularly attractive girl'. Perhaps she came to Gissing for some of those private lessons. Soon he was in love, but something went wrong. Either Martha Barnes rejected him, or the school authorities sniffed out the flirtation and sent Gissing packing. The *Waltham Free Press* reported his departure:

We regret to learn that Mr Gissing, the accomplished assistant teacher of
our High School left town suddenly and unexpectedly on Thursday of last
week in a distracted state of mind in consequence of a disappointment he
had suffered. His departure is a great loss for he was a man of rare scholarship
and his high toned character and the interesting general manner of con-
ducting the lessons of his classes won the affection and respect of his pupils.[48]

Many times in the future Gissing would give way to impulse, and lose
all sense of proportion about how to handle some awkward situation.
Perhaps Martha told her parents about a declaration of love from Gissing,
and he could not face the humiliation of people knowing that he had been
rebuffed by one of his students. With a little more prudence, he might have
kept his job and become a proper suitor for Martha after her graduation in
June. Instead he was once again cast adrift, with less than fifty dollars to his
name. Adventure beckoned in the far west, as far as California if possible.
Gissing did not have enough money to get there, so he went as far as he
could, to Chicago. In *New Grub Street*, Whelpdale goes west on an 'emigrant
train', the cheapest way to travel but also the most uncomfortable. These
trains were packed with people just off the boat, who slept on wooden
benches and had no food except for what they brought with them. In winter
they were bitterly cold. It is not surprising that after riding on an emigrant
train Gissing had no further desire to be an emigrant.

Gissing arrived in Chicago on the weekend of 3–4 March 1877. He may
have stopped briefly at Niagara Falls on the way, since there is a vivid
description of the falls in winter at the end of *Workers in the Dawn*. The last
of his money went for a week's board and lodging at a house on Wabash
Avenue, not far from the station. On Monday he managed to see the editor
of the *Chicago Tribune*, and was told he could submit a story for the Saturday
supplement. Gissing was under the gun; he walked up and down the freezing lakefront, trying to think out a story. Then he had to write it in the
noisy common room of his boarding house, because his bedroom was too
cold. In two days he finished the story and took it to the editor, who
accepted it for Saturday's paper. Within a week of his arrival in Chicago
Gissing was a published author and had eighteen dollars in hand, enough
to live on for another month.

The story Gissing wrote was 'The Sins of the Fathers'. If you have to
write a story in two days or be out on the street, there is not much scope
for fresh invention. Gissing took his experiences with Nell and with Martha
Barnes, and patched them together into a melodramatic tale. Leonard
Vincent is a student who comes across a girl, Laura, sobbing in an archway.
He helps her to live by getting her sewing; he wants to marry her, but his

rich father sends him off to America as a trial of his love. The father then tricks Leonard into believing that his beloved is dead, and he falls in love with Minnie Warren, a student at the school where he teaches: 'She is not tall, but her figure is perfect in symmetry; Minnie is grace itself, from the little slipper with the blue bow which now and then peeps from beneath the muslin, to the simple but jaunty coil of rich brown hair that sits on the back of her head.'[49] Leonard marries Minnie, but Laura then turns up as a travelling actress. She leads him to a frozen river and madly pulls him out on to the ice, where they both drown. Leonard is flattered to have Laura's love, but realises too late that it is deadly to him. The deeper message, though, is that Leonard is not responsible for what he does because stronger wills — those of Laura and his father — have dragged him along from beginning to end.

The point about 'The Sins of the Fathers' was not how good it was, but how Gissing was able to write it under the ultimate pressure. 'How can such an one write?' he would ask in later life. 'He never starved.' Morley Roberts was impressed by Gissing's resourcefulness in Chicago:

> I can imagine the state that he must have been in, and how desperate he must have become, to get out of his difficulties in the way that he actually employed. The endeavour to obtain work in a hustling country like the United States is ever a desperate proceeding for a nervous and sensitive man, and what it must have been to Henry Maitland to do what he did with the editor of the *Chicago Tribune* can only be imagined by those who knew him. In many ways he was the most modest and the shyest man who ever lived.[50]

Once Gissing had his first success with the *Tribune* it was much easier for him to continue, and he had another story published three weeks after his first one. 'R.I.P.' was a rather limp imitation of Edgar Allan Poe. Over a period of five months, eleven stories by Gissing appeared in various Chicago papers. Most of them were quite long, so he may have earned something between $150 and $200 in all. This was hardly enough to live on, and Gissing had to belabour his imagination to come up with enough plots. Some of them were taken from the English life he knew, featuring odd coincidences and fatal acts of dishonesty, themes that would reappear in his mature work. Others continued in the vein of fantasy, with peculiar deaths scattered across the landscape.

It was impressive that Gissing could produce a steady flow of commercial work, even if it was no more than competent. Yet he made no literary use at all of the American scene. Morley Roberts would journey through the

American and Canadian West some years later and write *The Western Avernus* about his adventures. R. L. Stevenson took the emigrant train two years after Gissing, and wrote about it in *An Amateur Emigrant*. Gissing, soon after he had settled in Chicago, decided that all he wanted was to go back to England. America was not a dynamic new world of opportunity. Rather it was a country that just ground you down. The stories Gissing wrote in Chicago bore no trace of how he was living when he wrote them. He had left England only bodily. He was still writing to Nell and planning to be reunited with her, as if he had learnt nothing from being sent to prison.

From Chicago Gissing took the train back to New York, to take ship for England. Apart from his difficulties in finding steady employment, his disillusionment with the US seems to have come from his social failure, like that of Arthur Golding in *Workers in the Dawn:*

> For a year he had not known what it was to hear the voice of a friend. Naturally retiring in his disposition, he seldom, if ever, addressed a stranger. Such of the Americans as he had had the opportunity of seeing more closely he could not persuade himself to like. He had nothing in common with them; their taste seemed to him hopelessly vulgar.[51]

At nineteen, Gissing was already too set in his ways to adapt to a different culture. The openness of American social life offended his lower-middle-class snobbishness and reserve. The American solution to his disaster at Owens College had failed. He had made no fortune, and faced a bleak future in England as an ex-convict. Nonetheless, he was desperate to return; but when he arrived in New York, in early July 1877, he lacked the $25 or so he needed for a steerage berth back to Liverpool. He tried to write another story for the New York papers, without success. Then, in mid-July, he saw his first Chicago story, 'The Sins of the Fathers', reprinted in a newspaper from Troy, in upstate New York. Perhaps that newspaper would also take the one he was currently writing?

Gissing took a steamboat up the Hudson to Troy, only to be told by the newspaper editor that he could offer no work. Without enough money to return to New York, Gissing took a room and lived on peanuts he bought in the street – loathsome food, he found, as a regular diet.[52] Then he heard that a travelling photographer needed an assistant. For the rest of July and August Gissing travelled across Massachusetts and up to Portland Maine, touting for work with little success. Still, the photographer kept him going until he could scrape up his fare back to England. He borrowed the money from an English friend at his Boston boarding-house, Robert Petremant.

The loan was secured by a trunk containing Gissing's books, manuscripts and spare clothes; it would take him four years to get it all back. With no fortune to show for his journey to the west, Gissing took ship in Boston at the end of September. He had eaten the bread of exile, and wanted only to return, on any terms he could get.

Workers in the Dawn

In the Year of Jubilee's Lionel Tarrant comes back to England from America in steerage, 'a trial such as he had never known, amid squalid discomforts which enraged even more than they disgusted him'. All he has gained from his year in America is 'to have studied with tolerable thoroughness the most hateful form of society yet developed'.[1] Gissing, similarly, had no affection for the US, and he never went back. From Liverpool he went to Wakefield for a few days with his family, then set off for London with whatever money his mother could spare. When he arrived at King's Cross it was too late to look for a room, so he spent the night at a coffee house near the station. He found lodgings at 62 Swinton Street, but moved on after a few days to 22 Colville Place, where he would stay for the next eleven months.

In his later writings Gissing would endlessly condemn the heartlessness of London, a giant battlefield where, every day, thousands die in silence. Yet London was the only place in the world for him to go, and it would do more to inspire his fiction than anywhere else. He could not go back to live in Manchester or Wakefield, where there would still be many to point the finger at him on the street. In London he could create a new identity from scratch, just another young man from the provinces in search of a job. And for anyone who wanted to become a writer London was the place to be.

London was also the place where Gissing could be reunited with Nell. He had written to her faithfully from America, and it never seems to have occurred to him that the best way to cleanse his record was to have nothing further to do with her. Instead, he still cherished hopes of making her into a ladylike companion. She may have been in the city already: William Gissing believed that Dr Louis Borchardt of Manchester had 'found some place for her' in London.[2] Borchardt was a German political refugee involved in charitable work and children's medicine. His 'place' might refer either to a job in domestic service, or to an institution for the reform of prostitutes. There were several in London, such as the Marylebone Female

Protection Society which sought 'to reclaim young Women from all parts of the country who have, by one false step, fallen from the path of virtue. They are cared for in their trouble, if expecting to become mothers; and, after suitable training, are placed in service, where needful help is given them in supporting their infants, lest, through want, they should fall again into sin.'[3] If Borchardt sent Nell to London to be made into a new woman, his effort failed. Whatever he or Gissing might do, she would always be drawn back to life on the street.

Whether Nell was living in a house of refuge or as a domestic servant, it would have been very difficult for Gissing to see her, and almost impossible for them to sleep together. An unmarried couple were not allowed to be alone, if employers or landladies had any say in it. Even if Nell was nearby, rather than back in Manchester, Gissing's early months in London were cursed by poverty and loneliness, two malignant presences in almost every book he would write. Innumerable young men and women had to suffer as he did. London had more money and more people – nearly four million in 1877 – than anywhere else in the world. But its good things were not there for all. The first place to look for comfort in such an overwhelming place was to one's family. Gissing had two married aunts in London, his father's sisters. Ann Stannard lived in Paddington with her husband William, a decorator; Maria Rahardt was married to a grocer of German origin and lived in Hackney. Gissing thought of going to stay with the Stannards, where his paternal grandfather also lived, but there would be too much watching over his comings and goings. His aunt Maria had been asking why he had left Wakefield; his London relatives did not know that he had gone to America, still less why he had gone. Gissing went to see the Stannards and Rahardts from time to time, but he was determined to live independently, no matter how miserable his lodgings might be. He walked the streets in search of employment, and survived on small sums of money sent him from Wakefield.

Gissing had taken the cheapest possible lodgings, an attic room just off Tottenham Court Road. It was close to the British Museum library, where he could hope to get his foot on the first rung of the Grub Street ladder. He soon found a pupil to coach for the London matriculation exam (the one in which he had come first in England himself). St Vincent Mercier was the well-to-do son of a former captain in the Navy, now treasurer of St John's Hospital for Diseases of the Skin. At that time dermatology also included the treatment of venereal disease, and the recently founded hospital was conveniently located in Leicester Square, at the heart of the London sex trade. St Vincent Mercier got himself appointed secretary to the hospital, and in April of 1878 he was able to give Gissing some part-time work as an admitting clerk. That would have given him a thorough knowledge of venereal disease (though it was not the kind of knowledge one could use in a Victorian novel). Gissing gives his hero, Reardon, a similar job in chapter 17 of *New Grub Street*.

In that novel, Reardon also has a garret like Gissing's, and pays 3/6d a week for it. His food costs a shilling a day, his clothes five pounds a year. Gissing could have lived on about twelve to fifteen shillings a week at Colville Place, out of which he still managed to buy second-hand books. His story 'The Last Half-Crown' describes the life he led there:

> No vehicles pass through Colville Place, for it is paved all across, and so makes a capital play-ground for the poor children who swarm in the neighbourhood. Harold Sansom would scarcely have chosen such modest lodgings of his own free will; once he had known the comforts of a very different home, but a miserable chain of circumstances had changed all that, and for some months he had been glad to rent a little garret at half-a-crown a week, furnished with a bed, a broken-seated chair, and an apology for a table. The sloping roof scarcely permitted him to stand upright, but that mattered little, for, when not wandering about in hopeless search for employment, he either lay upon his bed, seeking forgetfulness in the pages of one or two dear old books which still remained to him, or else sat at the crazy table, making desperate efforts to write something which might bring him bread.[4]

Gissing would become the poet laureate of the miseries of London lodging-houses, and of the struggle to come up with the weekly rent. There was only one sure escape from that struggle, the one taken by Sansom when he loses his last half-crown:

> Walk about London, reader, any part of it, and at any time of the day, and you are sure to notice more than one such figure, the bent shoulders, the drooping head, the worn, careless attire, above all that fixed, hopeless look indicating too clearly a mind warped and spirit crushed in the brutalizing struggle with his fellow men, a struggle compared with which to have fought with beasts at Ephesus were nought. The coarser natures wear long, resist to the end. Those of more delicate mould are soon driven to strange extremities, and become familiar with dread ideas from which a healthy mind shrinks in horror.[5]

Gissing returns often to the idea that London has its own cure for the miseries it inflicts. Those who cannot bear to wander the streets any longer can walk to the Embankment and throw themselves in the Thames. This is what Harold Sansom does, and Gissing often thought of doing.

While living in his garret, Gissing encountered one of his favourite books, Henri Murger's *Scènes de la Vie de Bohème*. Parisian garrets, he learned, had wine, song, poetry, friends, and beautiful girls of easy virtue. On Colville Place Gissing had no pleasures except the imaginary ones he found in books. The narrator of *The Private Papers of Henry Ryecroft* speaks of going without food in order to buy a book he covets. One day he finds a first edition of Gibbon's *Decline and Fall* in six volumes at a shilling each. He walks home to Islington to get the money, then has to make two trips to carry the heavy books home. Twenty miles of walking across London, and more than a week's rent, to acquire a favourite book![6] Gissing never had enough money to take the bus or Tube regularly; if *Ryecroft* is to be believed, on some days he covered fifty miles of London streets, at a pace of five miles an hour. He was tormented by the smells of food he could not afford, and sometimes had to beg to survive. 'I could shed tears,' Ryecroft says, 'over that spectacle of rare vitality condemned to sordid strife. The pity of it! And – if our conscience mean anything at all – the bitter wrong!'[7]

One might say that in exchange for his sufferings Gissing was acquiring what he needed as a novelist: a matchless knowledge of life in the great city, from top to bottom. Much of his suffering was self-inflicted; he would not waste time (as he saw it) on casual acquaintances, and would rather spend money on a book than on a good meal or a pint of beer in a pub. There were millions of people in London as poor as he was, but almost all of them were bent on finding whatever small pleasures they could. 'Only by contrast with this thick-witted multitude,' Ryecroft says, 'can I pride myself upon my youth of endurance and of combat. I had a goal before me, and *not* the goal of the average man. Even when pinched with hunger, I did not abandon my purposes, which were of the mind.' A Freudian might speak of repression and sublimation when looking at Gissing's youth; it might be more to the point to say that Gissing was a poor man who was determined to rise. His regime of self-denial had no religious basis, since he had firmly rejected Christianity. Nor was he economically ambitious, like a diligent clerk trying to climb the ladder of promotion. Everything that he endured was for the higher aim of becoming a writer. That was his path to a life of the mind when, through his crime, he had shut himself out of the other learned professions.

Gissing knew that he must make his way in Grub Street, and that he faced years of great labour for small reward. Coaching students for exams was intellectual work of a sort, and his chief means of putting bread on the table for the next ten years. Then there was hack-work of the kind done by

Mr Yule in *New Grub Street*; Gissing had hopes of working on a series of translations from Latin, but nothing came of it. Finally, the true path to literary success was to write fiction. In January 1878 Gissing sold one of his Chicago stories, 'The Artist's Child', to *Tinsley's Magazine*; but after that his luck with short stories dried up for several years. No matter; the way forward was to write a novel, and by January he was steadily at work on his first effort. From the beginning he was able to produce quantity in fiction; quality would come more slowly. On a day when he had no other tasks he would sit in his garret and cover twelve sheets of foolscap (each about twice the size of today's standard sheets). On other days he had his tutoring or clerking to do, or he studied in the British Museum library, where he had acquired a reader's ticket in November 1877.[8] By the end of June 1878 Gissing had finished his novel and sent it off to a publisher. We know nothing about the book except that it finished with a murder trial. When it was turned down, Gissing gave up on it and, at some point, threw out the manuscript. Before he had even received his rejection letter he had started another novel, which he expected to be 'infinitely better'.[9]

Gissing was twenty when he wrote his first novel. In spite of his imprisonment and exile, his experience of life was limited by his anti-social temperament, which conflicted with the novelist's need to soak up the details of how people rub along together. Dickens did not get started as a novelist until his mid-twenties; Thackeray, George Eliot and Trollope later than that. Apart from the short stories he had written in America, Gissing did not feel the need to serve an apprenticeship as a novelist. Writing a novel was for him rather like writing an exam: you made a plan in your head and then poured it out on to the page at a fast and steady rate. This had worked well for him in his academic career, and it was a method he persisted in. His surviving manuscripts show that his work had few discarded passages or substantial revisions – unlike Dickens, who did an immense amount of revision at each stage of composition. Gissing's project was to be productive at all costs, to live under a daily discipline and have something to show for it. To write at such a rate required a model to follow, and Gissing's first novels were pale copies of Dickens, so far as we can tell from the scraps of plot he mentions – trials, crimes, fortunate inheritances. Twenty years on, Gissing would write a splendid critical appreciation of Dickens's work. Dickens had served his five months as a child in the blacking factory, and everything in his later life grew from that seed, as a constant widening of his imagination and his social sympathy. For Gissing, his imprisonment had an almost opposite effect: every genial possibility in his life had to be subordinated to self-discipline. His literary imagination was constrained by the kind of life he allowed himself, and his novels could never be playful or lyrical as Dickens's were. The qualities they had all derived from the stern realities of Gissing's existence.

By the autumn of 1878 Gissing had survived a year in London, even if, like Ryecroft, he had been forced to move from his garret room to one in the basement that was sixpence a week cheaper. He had written a novel and started another, though neither would be published. He had three pupils who together brought him 18/6d a week, plus occasional work at the hospital. In August Algernon had sent him some money, and it was probably on the strength of this that Gissing moved in with Nell on 13 September 1878. They took a single room at 31 Gower Place, up at the top of Bloomsbury near Euston Station. The cost was only 6/6d a week, little more than at Colville Place. But how could Gissing expect to feed and clothe Nell when he could barely do that for himself?

Nell was twenty years old when she came to live with Gissing, and her only skill was needlework to make purses and knick-knacks. One of the problems that emerged when she and Gissing took their room was that there was so little housekeeping to occupy her. While he sat writing his novels or studying, Nell had nothing to do but watch, and she was not the kind of person to be satisfied with that. She wanted company and she wanted something to drink; when neither were on offer at home, she went out to find them. Gissing had no money to spare, and probably there was only one way for her to get what she needed. Euston provided a stream of single men arriving from the North. Gissing and Nell quarrelled with their landlord and left Gower Place after three months; perhaps she had tried to do business at home while Gissing was with his pupils or at the British Museum.

In *The Unclassed*, Gissing took the unbearable truth about his life with Nell and turned it into a drama of four people. There are two intellectual young men, Julian Casti and Osmond Waymark, and two young prostitutes, Harriet Smales and Ida Starr. Casti is too sensitive to cope, and dies young; Waymark survives and prospers. Harriet dies too, after having a fit and falling down stairs, whereas Ida reforms, inherits money, and educates herself. Waymark falls in love with Ida while she is still a prostitute, but his conscience will not allow him to sleep with her:

> What right had he to endeavour to gain her love, having nothing but mere beggarly devotion to offer her in return? ... In fact, it amounted to this: any hint of love on his part was a request that she would yield him gratis what others paid for; he would become a pensioner on her bounty. Needless to say, a wholly intolerable situation.[10]

Waymark will only love Ida platonically until she has become a lady and
accepted his proposal of marriage. There was no such convenient solution
for Gissing. The money that Nell brought home was needed to keep the
household running. It is hard to imagine that he would refuse to have
intercourse with Nell, when they had only the one room and one bed; but
his conscience was surely troubled by the situation. Not just his conscience,
either, since by now Nell was almost certainly syphilitic.

Living with Nell brought sexual relief, and sexual trouble. Her other
health problems brought more trouble yet. She had scrofula, a chronic
inflammation of the lymph glands in the neck caused by a combination of
TB, poverty and malnutrition. Like many prostitutes, she was an alcoholic;
she also had epilepsy, at that time a mysterious and stigmatising disease. In
The Unclassed, Harriet Smales has a seizure:

> A change suddenly came over Harriet's face; her eyelids drooped, and her
> mouth began to work compulsively. Then her arms fell to her sides, and in
> a moment she was stiffening on a chair; her head fell back, and, with a low
> moaning and a struggling, she slipped sideways, and at length fell heavily
> to the ground.[11]

Gissing describes what he has seen, Jacksonian epilepsy followed by a *grand
mal* seizure. The Victorians had no scientific knowledge of the causes of
epilepsy; Nell would simply be seen as a sickly and even a sinister creature.
Her disorder may have come from a head injury, or a tapeworm infestation
of her brain (the poor often ate 'measly pork' with tapeworm cysts in it).
The most likely cause, though, was Nell's alcoholism. Alcoholic epilepsy
was easy to miss because it was a disease of withdrawal – the seizures would
come on several hours after the victim had *stopped* drinking. Sub-
consciously, Nell may have realised that she was less likely to have a seizure
when she was drunk than when she was sober. But her drinking brought
problems that were loaded on to Gissing's already full plate: money wasted
in pubs, sexual promiscuity, quarrels with landlords. In *The Unclassed*,
Gissing shows sympathy for Emily Enderby's drinking: 'The poor creature,
as we know, took refuge in drink; it would procure her the pleasurable
excitement which otherwise she could never have known, and be followed
by the unconsciousness which was perhaps a yet greater boon.'[12] Refuge or
not, Nell's attempts to drown her sorrows made more sorrows come, both
for her and for her sober guardian.

On the financial front, at least, the autumn of 1878 brought Gissing some
luck. In July he had told Algernon that he had 'given up all hope of anything
but starvation and wretchedness', and he started to make enquiries about

getting some kind of teaching position on the Continent.[13] But in August he heard from his grandfather Robert Gissing that he was due to receive a legacy of about £500 on his twenty-first birthday, 22 November. The money emerged, quite unexpectedly, from a convoluted family intrigue. After inheriting £8,000 from Miss Whittington, Emily Waller made a late marriage to one Trevor Williams (the money had made her desirable, another Gissing theme). When Emily died in 1867 she left £1,000 to her favourite nephew, Thomas Gissing, and £500 in trust to each of his three sons.

It took three years for the Gissings to get any money from Trevor Williams, and that was in the year that Thomas died. Mrs Gissing got £1,300 in hand, but had to sue Williams for the balance of £1,200. That money was held in Chancery until the boys were twenty-one. George would be entitled to his share of the Chancery money at twenty-one, plus £100 from the money held by his mother. Most likely, he let her keep that for herself and the girls. He could look forward to £424 as his twenty-first birthday present, perhaps £100,000 in today's money – more, if one considers that £400 was enough to buy a decent London house. Both Gissing and his brother William, who was working in a bank, agreed that the prudent thing was to preserve the capital and spend only the interest of about £20 a year. It was not enough to live on, but it would pay the rent for Gissing and Nell's rooms at Gower Place, with £5 left over. Alternatively, he could look for some small business to invest in. The actual payment of his legacy would be delayed for several months, but William's birthday letter to him spoke for the expectations of all three brothers: 'Your prospects have materially brightened, since I wrote to you on this day last year. Plans are formed, and we have something definite to look forward to. It remains to realize all our hopes.'[14]

Meanwhile, the brothers had to scramble for a start in life. George and Nell moved at the end of 1878 from Gower Place to 70 Huntley Street nearby. The new home was another garret, and even that they owed to George's uncle Stannard, who had lent him £10 against his forthcoming legacy. When George paid him back four months later, Stannard charged him a pound in interest – a rate of 30 per cent a year! Algernon was hoping to launch himself by doing well in the London matriculation exam in December, for which he would come to town and stay with George and Nell. William's hopes were never to be realised. In June 1878 he was terrified to find himself spitting blood. He went back to his bank after some time off, and moved out of Manchester to Wilmslow, near Alderley Edge, where all three brothers had gone to school. By December William had to give up his job at the bank. Now he would try to make a living at what he really wanted to do, which was play the organ and teach music. He made up circulars for the middle-class houses in the neighbourhood, and found a few children to whom he gave lessons over the next two years. He was painfully earnest and hard-working; but he could not play any instrument really well, and had no formal training in music. With his legacy he hoped to take a degree.

George's hopes rested on his second novel, which he was writing through the second half of 1878. It also has disappeared, and that may be no great loss. From the few details we have, it seems to have been anecdotal and melodramatic. Gissing needed to distil some philosophy from what he saw on the street, so that he could write a novel containing thought as well as incident. Experience was flooding in on him fast enough; what he needed was enough intellectual maturity to be able to cope with it. He missed the books he had left in Boston, and was scraping together replacements from the second-hand shops. That he had no full-time job freed him to be an omnivorous reader for more of the day, in at least four languages other than English: Greek, Latin, French and German. Later he would add Italian and Spanish. Few English novelists can have had as much learning.

Gissing was in that exhilarating stage of life when he was both developing new ideas and, equally important, expelling old ones. His radicalism had begun literally at his father's knee, when Thomas Gissing read Darwin and the radical press of his time, and passed those ideas on to George. William Gissing, however, took his ideas from his mother and remained completely pious and conventional. He made an argument against George that is still popular: 'They reject with derision the idea of a God, because they cannot touch him or see him. They, nevertheless, accept with acclamation the Darwinian theory, equally wanting in proof. Such pitiful inconsistency.'[15] George did accept Darwinism, of course, and backed it up with enthusiasm for David Strauss's *Leben Jesu* (1835), which presented Jesus as man rather than God. He waxed indignant about the powers and privileges of the Church of England.

Beneath the intellectual substance of Gissing's radicalism lay his contempt for conventional beliefs and his sense of superiority over the general run of mankind. That disposition began with pride in his cleverness and academic success, followed by the humiliation of his conviction for theft. Gissing was taught the rude lesson that his brilliance did not exempt him from the rules set for all. Yet in *The Unclassed*, when Ida Starr is arrested for theft, Waymark tries to exempt her too: 'To Waymark the word "guilt", applied to such circumstances, connoted no moral reprobation; had he used it, in speech or thought, it would merely have borne the technical sense. In his habitual conviction of the relativity of all names and things, he could not possibly bring himself to regard this act as a crime.'[16] Waymark does not indignantly protest his beloved's innocence; he attacks the very idea of labelling her as guilty. Perhaps Gissing was drawing on Raskolnikov for his portrait of Waymark; he read *Crime and Punishment* sometime before the end of 1887, and considered it a magnificent novel.[17] If Gissing's prison sentence was meant to make him respect authority, it failed (though it did teach him not to break the rules again).

A large part of Gissing's intellectual development up to the autumn of 1878 – when he turned twenty-one – was negative. Strauss and Darwin undermined the foundations of Christianity, so that all Gissing's musings on human destiny started from a godless world. In politics and economics he started with a negative reaction: horror at the condition of London's poor. But he had not yet developed any systematic political programme, beyond the radical liberalism of his father. In the chapter 'Mind-Growth' of *Workers in the Dawn*, Helen Norman largely recapitulates Gissing's own development. She goes to study at the university of Tübingen in 1868, which she chooses because Strauss taught there.[18] She begins with *Leben Jesu* and *The Origin of Species*, then is told by one of her teachers to go on to Schopenhauer, whose message is: 'That the origin of all evil is to be found in the desire for life, and that he is the perfect man who succeeds in altogether uprooting this desire from his mind, losing the sense of his own identity, fixing his thoughts eternally in an absolutely passionless calm.' But once she has read Schopenhauer herself, Helen finds a very different message:

> It appears to me that his pessimism is the least valuable part of Schopen-
> hauer's teaching. The really excellent part of him is his wonderfully strong
> sympathy with the sufferings of mankind. Again and again he tells us that
> we should lose the consciousness of self in care for others, in fact identify
> ourselves with all our fellows, see only one great *self* in the whole world.
> For this doctrine alone I thank him heartily.[19]

From great thinkers, people take different messages, according to need. Schopenhauer's doctrine of stoic impersonality, noble as it might be, had little use for someone wanting to write novels. His call for universal sympathy was another matter; Gissing could see the sufferings of mankind all around him, and that provided both the morality and the material for his novels.

To sympathise with the masses was not enough; Gissing also needed a theory that would help him to understand them. Like Helen Norman, he fell under the spell of Auguste Comte – in part, surely, because of an almost eerie resemblance to his own history. Comte, who died in the year of Gissing's birth, came from the provincial lower middle class and was launched on a brilliant academic career by his skill at taking examinations. Then his erratic and rebellious disposition caused him to drop out of the Ecole Polytechnique. He married a former prostitute, whom he had first met as a client, and led a hand-to-mouth existence in Paris. At one point he tried to commit suicide by jumping in the Seine. In the 1830s he developed his great system of 'Positive Philosophy', which was popularised in England by such figures as George Henry Lewes, John Stuart Mill, Harriet Martineau and Frederic Harrison.

Comte, like his English counterpart Herbert Spencer, constructed a mighty 'theory of everything' to replace the dogmas shattered by the French Revolution and the decline of religious authority. He wanted to make a second revolution in France, but without forming a political party or rallying at any barricades. His first aim was to build a comprehensive understanding of social processes, for which he coined the term *sociology*. If the theory was correct, political power would follow after. Comte proposed a grand narrative of progress in rationality: mankind began by being superstitious, then became metaphysical, and now was becoming scientific. Science had already achieved deep understanding of the natural world; the next step was to apply scientific method to the social world. Once we understood social laws, we could control the future and eliminate injustice and disorder.

Comte's system appealed to Gissing because it argued that the most pressing task was to understand the practical workings of society in order to improve it. In *Workers in the Dawn*, Helen Norman finds that it is a natural step to go from Schopenhauer to Comte:

> First and foremost, Comte discards metaphysics, thereby earning my heartiest approbation. ... How delighted I am with his masterly following of the history of mankind through every stage of its development. There is something entrancing to me in these firmly-fixed laws, these *positive* investigations. Comte is for me the supplement to Darwin; the theories of both point to the same result, and *must* be true! ... How grand to feel that one is actually helping on the progress of humanity, as every one is doing who seeks earnestly to learn and to propagate the truth.[20]

As Gissing pondered his Comte in the British Museum, he could look across the room to where Karl Marx was building his rival system. Gissing knew of Marx's work, but the doctrine of class struggle had little appeal for him. Marxism was apocalyptic, looking forward to a final battle between capitalism and socialism; Comte foresaw a harmonious future where all would be united in the 'religion of humanity'. Gissing liked Comte's elitist utopianism. Old strongholds of privilege would be swept away and the world would be ruled by unselfish intellectuals, chosen by merit rather than birth.

Gissing did recognise a problem with Comte's theory: only one person in a thousand was capable of understanding it. Rather than change the theory, the solution was to change the populace:

> The establishment of a complete system of education, supplemented by a thorough net-work of free libraries, is the first thing to be aimed at. To that end we have a destructive task to perform; we must destroy the State-church, and do our utmost to weaken its hold upon the popular mind. By hacking away here, and ploughing there, surely the field will at length be got into something like a state fit for the sower.[21]

Gissing was now preaching Comteanism to the eighteen-year-old Algernon, having given up on William. He was becoming the kind of crank who would later be satirised in his own novels. Half of his life was dreaming of vast social reforms, or giving long lectures to his uncle Stannard's radical club. The other half was rubbing his few pennies together and telling his brothers that they should try eating nothing but lentils. A large part of Gissing's dislike of the Church of England was how rich it was; no bishop was eating lentils. If you were a Comtean, there was no political party to belong to; you just spent hours in the library trying to master all knowledge, and dreaming of a gloriously rational future. Further, Comte had been dead for twenty years and no dynamic leader had emerged to implement his ideas in the real world. Comteanism had a wide intellectual impact, but (unlike Marxism) it never developed a practical wing. Perhaps impractical people were specially attracted to it, Gissing among them.

In January 1879 Gissing at last found some company for his lonely musings. He was rubbing shoulders with other young readers at the British Museum; that he remained solitary showed that he would not make friends with anyone except on his own strict terms. With his legacy on the way he could hope for a more comfortable social life, and so he replied to a newspaper advertisement that went something like this:

> WANTED, human companionship. A young man of four-and-twenty wishes to find a congenial associate of about his own age. He is a student of

ancient and modern literatures, a free-thinker in religion, a lover of art in
all its forms, a hater of conventionalism.[22]

The man who had placed the advertisement was Eduard Bertz, twenty-four
years old, a socialist exile from Germany who was living in the same hand-
to-mouth way as Gissing. He survived on occasional bits of teaching and
journalism. That he was a foreigner distanced him from Gissing's prickly
concerns about social status. He had the solid knowledge of French,
German and Russian literature that, in Gissing's view, educated Englishmen almost always lacked.

In *The Unclassed* Waymark is living alone when Julian Casti (the Bertz
surrogate) comes to visit him for the first time: 'The contrast in mere
appearance between the two was very pronounced; both seemed in some
degree to be aware of it. Waymark seemed more rugged than in ordinary
companionship; the slightly effeminate beauty of Casti, and his diffident,
shyly graceful manners, were more noticeable than usual.'[23] This passage
suggests a homoerotic friendship, but there is no indication of that in
Gissing's relations with Bertz. Although Bertz never married, he was a
fussy and hypochondriac recluse, rather than any kind of homosexual. He
promoted Whitman's poetry in Germany, but then denounced him as a
pervert when he realised what Whitman's love-life was like. If there was
any sexual element in the friendship between Bertz and Gissing, it lay in
their masculine alliance against coarse and wayward femininity, of the kind
displayed by Harriet Smales in *The Unclassed*, and by Nell in real life. Their
idea of fun was to shut the door on women and spend long evenings in
front of the fire, puffing on their pipes and discussing the classics. Bertz
was also a shrewd and sympathetic critic of Gissing's novels, all the more
welcome because Gissing's other close friend, Morley Roberts, was much
less reliable. Gissing encouraged Bertz's writing, in return, though he never
had any great literary success. Another of their shared enthusiasms was for
German philosophers; thanks to Bertz, Gissing was one of the first British
intellectuals to appreciate Nietzsche.[24] Part of the closeness between Gissing
and Bertz was their belief that no one else in London thought as they did.
To both of them, friendship was synonymous with excluding outsiders.

At the beginning of April 1879 Gissing finally received his legacy, and
could look at his prospects with a fresh eye. In June he told Algernon that
he had £300 invested, so he must have paid off some debts and kept cash in
hand. He and Nell moved to better quarters at the end of June, two rooms
at 38 Edward Street, off Hampstead Road.[25] The rooms were closer to
Regent's Park, but at nine shillings a week were actually cheaper than

Huntley Street. Gissing was not lashing out on his small fortune. He could have bought a six-room house in Islington for £300 and rented out part of it, but he feared the complications of owning property, and never in his life would he succeed in buying cheap or selling dear. One minor luxury was to send Nell for a rest-cure in the country. William came into London to meet her (thinking that she and George were married), and it was arranged that she would go to a spare room in William's lodgings at Wilmslow.

Nell came to Wilmslow on 17 May, and stayed for four weeks. On the evening of her arrival she could not eat; soon after she had a seizure, and went on having them through the night. William had probably seen Nell's seizures before, but his landlady was frightened by having to deal with them. The seizures may have been triggered by alcohol withdrawal; Nell continued to have them during her stay at Wilmslow, though her health improved otherwise. Fresh air and good food were given credit for making her better. William did his best for Nell, but when she became ill again in October he did not volunteer to help. Gissing could not turn her into a country girl, any more than a lady or an intellectual. Nell continued to feel better for a while after she returned to London, which helped Gissing to make progress with his third attempt at a novel. The second one, written in the latter part of 1878, had run into the sand. It contained a lot of callow radicalism; William could not find anything good to say about the book, and that probably contributed to Gissing's abandoning it. He was establishing a pattern: rather than revising a novel, he preferred to set it aside and start a new one. If his first enthusiasm carried him through to the end, well and good, but often enough he turned against his own work. Rather than trying to repair it, he would literally reach for a clean sheet and begin another.

Gissing wrote steadily through the summer of 1879 and finished his massive novel – about 300,000 words – in early November. He called it 'Far, Far Away' after the children's song about a distant, happy land. He was two years older and much richer in experience than when he had written his first novel, soon after returning from America. Although this novel's hero, Arthur Golding, was a projection of Gissing's own concerns, he had chosen a less melodramatic and more documentary plot than before. 'The *idea* of the book,' Gissing told Algernon, 'is very greatly directed to social problems, principally the condition and prospects of the poorest classes.'[26] He had found the major theme of most of the novels he would write over the next nine years.

As Gissing was completing the book, he gave another hostage to fortune by marrying Nell, in the Anglican church of St James on Hampstead Road. He had been connected with her for four years, and her contributions to their partnership had been a dose of VD, imprisonment, exile in America, poverty, sickness, and endless trouble with landlords. Most of the time she just made him miserable; perhaps she tried to make up for these misfortunes by giving him love, in whatever way she could show it. If she did, Gissing never recorded it; nor did he ever write that he loved her. The closest he came was the idealistic sonnets that he wrote when he was on his way to America; but all his life he could hardly ever write of love except as a distant ideal, removed from the flesh and blood of a beloved's presence. Given the trouble he had already had with Nell, perhaps he married her for convenience, to avoid trouble with landlords, doctors and the like. Gissing was at his most militant stage of opposition to the Anglican Church, so Nell must have talked him into getting married in one. Afterwards, he refused in principle to attend any marriage, including his brother Algernon's. Marriage could do nothing to improve the cat-and-dog life he led with Nell; later, it made it impossible for him to seek the love of a woman of his own class, even after he and Nell had separated. In that sense, his half-hour in St James's was an eight-year sentence to loneliness and misery.

Gissing and Nell moved yet again at the end of November; her doctors had said that she might improve if she lived further north, where the air was supposedly better. They took two rooms and a garret at 5 Hanover Street (now Noel Road) in Islington. The street backed on to the Grand Union Canal, and Gissing enjoyed looking out from his study on to its quiet waters. Islington was then a seedy district of mainly artisan houses; Nell complained of loneliness, and Gissing tried unsuccessfully to find a companion for her. With no friends at home, it was a short walk for Nell to the bright lights and sawdust of the Angel and other pubs. She and Gissing stayed at Hanover Street for more than a year, and the house by the canal in Islington is part of the standard picture of Gissing's life in London. The canal really did make London fog thicker, and Gissing spent much of his first winter there in the murk.

Although Gissing's two previous novels have been lost, it seems fair to assume that *Workers in the Dawn* – the title that replaced 'Far, Far Away' – was the first of his novels that deserved to be published. He sent it off to Chatto & Windus around 12 November 1879, perhaps because they published Wilkie Collins, the closest living successor to Dickens. By Christmas he still had not heard from them, and he faced a cheerless holiday. William and Algernon would be at Wakefield for Christmas, but marriage had not changed Gissing's family situation. His mother did not want Nell at Wakefield, and Gissing would not go there on his own. He made an excuse that he could not afford to travel home, and made the best of it with

Nell in Islington. Immediately after Christmas, Chatto & Windus told him that there was no room for his novel on their list. He sent it to Smith, Elder, who reported that *Workers* had 'a great deal of graphic power', but not enough dramatic interest.[27] Next was Sampson, Low, who gave another reason to reject it:

> *Workers in the Dawn* is undoubtedly very ably written, that is our reader's opinion; but we are sorry to say he does not recommend it to us, on account of its rationalistic tendency, and certain details of a profligate character. We do not believe in fiction being the proper vehicle for conveying doctrinal opinions, for one reason that most readers will not read them. We should have been glad to have taken the work but for these reasons.[28]

This anticipated a good chunk of the reviews that Gissing would receive in the course of his career. He told Algernon that the complaints were foolish: 'It is not *I* who propagate a doctrine, but the characters whose lives I tell.'[29] This was too subtle a point for the average Victorian publisher. If Gissing populated his novels with rebellious and atheistical characters, subscribers to Mudie's library – the bulk of the novel-reading public – were bound to complain that the chef had put too much salt in their soup. They were not going to be satisfied with the reply that this particular soup was meant to be salty. William Gissing was certainly a dim bulb when it came to literary criticism but, just for that reason, his advice about marketing the novel was very much to the point:

> I should think you are well able to write a novel, historical or otherwise, which would bring you a good return, without touching upon any of the great questions of the day. I consider that the greatest advantage is to be derived from reticence – not eternal. We are constantly changing. If therefore we change certain opinions we have not to regret the publishing of our previous notions.[30]

This might seem a feeble way of looking at the issue, except that William grasped the fundamental point: if you wanted to be a successful writer, your task was to please your readers, not to please yourself. But to Algernon's criticism of *Workers*, Gissing simply said: 'I couldn't write otherwise, and I had a reason for every line.'[31] In the long run, indeed, Gissing was taking the right path to become a novelist to be reckoned with. In the moment, he had to absorb the lesson of the proverb: 'the way of transgressors is hard.'

Gissing was still convinced that *Workers in the Dawn* would find a publisher, and impress its readers. He sent the manuscript to the fourth publisher on his list, Kegan Paul, and started another novel that was planned to be just as long. In his spare moments he ran off some short stories and sent them to various magazines; all he got was more rejection slips. He also wrote a novella, 'All For Love', which has survived.[32] It was an attempt to write a straightforward piece of commercial fiction, about a middle-class couple with a guilty secret. 'All For Love' was poor stuff and no one would publish it, but it was revealing of Gissing's obsession with the theme of the double. Philip Vanstone is a degenerate thief, Laurence Bloomfield a worthy doctor. They are linked to the same woman, and exchange identities when Bloomfield murders Vanstone and their bodies end up in the same canal. Gissing looked out on the Regent Canal as he wrote the story, and perhaps was tempted to make the canal the solution to his own guilty and chaotic life.

After Kegan Paul turned down *Workers*, Gissing tried a much less prominent publisher, Remington & Co. Within a few days he was overjoyed to hear that his novel was going to appear, on the basis of 'shared profits'. He was too naive to realise that this arrangement was designed for him to make a loss and Remington to make a profit. The usual split was that after production costs had been covered, publisher and author would each get half of the profits. Gissing was impressed by Remington's offer of two-thirds of the profits; but Remington knew, of course, that there wouldn't be any profits to divide. Gissing would pay £125 to Remington to cover all the 'costs' of production. In fact, Remington could hide a comfortable profit for themselves in the supposed costs. They would publish *Workers* in three volumes at a price of one guinea, and spend £25 on advertising out of Gissing's payment. He probably calculated that the sale of twenty-five copies or so would pay off the advertising, and then he would get fourteen shillings a copy – two-thirds of the proceeds. It would only take sales of two hundred copies to get his investment back, and then the money would roll in with every new copy sold. In fact, a three-decker novel by an unknown author would only sell to libraries if it sold at all, and they would pay much less than list, say twelve shillings. Remington printed 277 copies, so they had charged Gissing about nine shillings a copy for publishing the book; their actual production costs might be four shillings or less. The book was nicely printed and bound, but that was because Gissing had paid for it.

Gissing signed his agreement with Remington on 26 February 1880, and the book would be published three months later, around 26 May. He complained that it took so long, though by modern standards Victorian publishers did everything with amazing speed. As soon as he had the contract, Gissing tidied up the manuscript for the press and made substantial revisions. All of these were cuts, amounting to about 8 per cent of the original length. When the first proofs were pulled, someone at Remington must have realised that *Workers in the Dawn* was at least 50 per cent longer than the usual three-decker: about 275,000 words instead of the usual 160,000 or so. Remington then asked Gissing to cut the book by half as it was going through the press, in order to reduce production costs. Gissing flatly refused to do this. The cuts that he had made already probably improved the book.[33] He cut some peripheral episodes, and reduced the amount of direct address to the reader by the author. Gissing over-indulged in direct address in his earlier novels (though such passages are helpful to a biographer). He cut some of his affectionate descriptions of Samuel Tollady, whom he had modelled on his own father. Passages about Arthur Golding's dalliance with prostitutes were also cut. *Workers in the Dawn* was never reprinted in Gissing's lifetime, but at some point in the 1890s he hoped for a new edition and started cutting the text again. He came to feel that all his novels in the three-decker format would benefit from being trimmed. But *The Unclassed* and *Thyrza* were the only ones that he managed to publish in England in a shorter edition.

Gissing was enjoying the thrill of reading proofs of his first book when terrible news about his brother William arrived. In June 1878 William had suffered a bronchial haemorrhage, and his health had been shaky ever since. At the end of March 1880 Algernon came to stay with him at Wilmslow, and one day they walked twenty miles across country. Three weeks later William fell ill and wrote to his mother; she arrived from Wakefield on the evening of 16 April. At eleven that night she was at his bedside when another haemorrhage killed him in a few minutes. William had lived a frustrated and limited life of twenty years. He was a gentle puritan who never understood his elder brother's passionate criticisms of religion and the social order.

Algernon and Mrs Gissing were at Wilmslow for William's burial in the churchyard there, but Gissing did not make the journey. He took a steely view of his brother's death: 'Poor Will is safely released from all cares and anxieties, but *we* still have to struggle to keep the wolf from the door, and we know very well that Will would receive no pleasure, could he see us, from the prospect of listless mourning.'[34] The proper response to tragedy, he believed, was to be found in Comte:

> For, though I myself look forward to no future world where the negligences
> of this may be made up for, I do not on that account say, 'let us eat and drink
> for to-morrow we die.' The immortality of man consists in this reflection –

that not a word we utter, not a thought we think, not a battle we win, not a temptation we yield to, but has, and *must* have, influence upon those living in contact with us, and from them, like the circles spreading in a pool, extends to the whole future human race. Therefore is it of vast importance to me whether I set an example of an ignorant and foolish man, or of one bent upon using his faculties to the utmost.[35]

Yet if everyone made it their aim to live for others, no one would have a reason to live for themselves. Gissing found in Comte a kind of mirror-image of what he had observed in the London slums. Life as it exists is a war of all against all; in life as it should be, everyone will sacrifice personal interest to the common good.

William died five months short of his twenty-first birthday, when he would have inherited more than £400. If he left no will, the intestacy rules would have given half the money to his mother, half to his four siblings. Gissing's share would have been about £55. A probable clue to the settlement was that in September 1880 – the month of William's majority – Mrs Gissing, Algernon, Margaret and Ellen moved to a larger and more comfortable house at 2 Stoneleigh Terrace, Agbrigg. It was on the other side of the river Calder from Wakefield, on the edge of open country. Gissing's windfall, if he received one, was probably swallowed up by Nell's constant medical expenses. His main hopes rested on reaping profits from *Workers in the Dawn*. Before any reviews had appeared, he heard of hostile rumours circulating in Wakefield about the book. It is not clear how these started, since hardly anyone in the town can have read it through. Algernon was put in an awkward position, because he was articled to one of the most pious and conservative solicitors in Wakefield. He told George that he didn't approve of the book's tone, and probably told his employer that as well. George was eager to receive a detailed response to *Workers* from his brother; he waited for months, but Algernon never delivered – no doubt because he had nothing good *to* deliver.

Gissing sent Algernon an open letter defending his book against any mutterings in Wakefield. *Workers*, he said, was not a novel in the usual sense; it was a critique of religious orthodoxy and of the government's failure to relieve 'terrible social evils':

In doing all this, I have been obliged to touch upon matters which will only be sufferable to those who read the book in as serious a spirit as mine when I wrote it. It is *not* a book for women and children, but for thinking and struggling *men*. If readers can put faith in the desperate sincerity of the author, they will not be disgusted with the book; otherwise, it is far better they should not read it. .... I fear it is the fate of many men to incur odium by their opinions, but the odium is only cast by those who cannot realize the sincerity of minds differently constituted from their own.[36]

Gissing was naive to think that mere sincerity would shield him from criticism. A stronger argument was that he had actually lived among the London poor, and knew much more about social evils than his genteel critics. But it would have been risky to boast in Wakefield about his personal experience of the lower depths. The *Athenaeum* review of *Workers*, the first to appear, attacked Gissing from the other side, complaining that he was not really educated and suffered from 'social inexperience'. But the reviewer also said that Gissing had 'done his subject the justice of sparing no graphic detail of the miseries of the vicious and the poor', and that he had 'considerable readiness and fluency of style, much power of vituperation, and an honest partisanship'.[37] The keynote of the review was respect, but grudging respect, something that Gissing would have to get used to in the years to come.

When *Workers in the Dawn* was accepted by Remington, in February 1880, Gissing had immediately started another novel. Set in the industrial towns around Manchester, it was to be about 'the dissipation of illusions, the destruction of ideals, in short the failure of a number of people to gain ends they have set up for their lives, or, if they *do* gain them, their failure to find the enjoyment they expectedt'.[38] The title was 'A Son of the Age'. The novel's central character would be 'particularly a product of our time, and a very evil product. The book will not, however, contain anything against orthodox religion, nor will it be concerned with those social abysses whence are taken so many of the characters of my first work.'[39] Feeling that he was himself doomed to failure, Gissing took a morbid interest in those destined for success. By the end of July the novel was half done; but then Gissing's world was turned upside down by a letter from Frederic Harrison, and he abandoned 'A Son of the Age' in favour of new opportunities.[40]

In June, Gissing had sent one of his precious author's copies to the leader of the English Comteans, Frederic Harrison. This was surely the most fortunate gift that Gissing ever made (to match the most unfortunate, the stolen money he gave to Nell, four years before). Frederic Harrison was forty-nine, and had been a Comtean since he was at Oxford, where he was converted by his tutor Richard Congreve. At the time Gissing sent him *Workers in the Dawn* Harrison was a prominent and wealthy lawyer, living in Bayswater with his wife and four children. He was the president of the

English Positivist committee. Gissing told Harrison that he was appealing to him because no one so far had understood his social and artistic aims:

> So truly is the book a product of passionate sympathy with many and diverse orders of men, that I cannot bring myself to relinquish so soon all faith in the vitality of the thing.
>
> To Comte I owe in the largest measure the enthusiasm to which I have here given expression, and it was by your writings, sir, that I first was led to Comte.[41]

Harrison replied before he had even finished the book. He was both deeply impressed by Gissing's work, and deeply distrustful of it. A Comtean novel should have a positive message, and Harrison had not found one yet:

> I am no critic, and very rarely read a modern romance, and I especially hate the so-called realism of Zola. But your painting of dark life seems to me as good as his, and to have a better social purpose – at least I hope so. . . . Your book therefore goes against all my sympathies in art, so that my admiration for its imaginative power is wrung from me. Whether prostitutes, thieves, and debauchees talk as you make them talk in the night houses of the Haymarket, I do not know, nor wish to know. It is possible that they are introduced to good purpose. I will try to see it.[42]

Harrison's qualms were roused by the chapter 'A Priestess of Venus' in volume III. Gissing did not write about sex directly, as Zola did; rather, he attacked the coarseness and bad behaviour associated with the buying and selling of women's bodies. Nor, in that chapter, did he present a sentimental, 'soiled dove' view of prostitutes: it is they who take the lead in violating marriage and the home. Part of Gissing's trouble with women was that he could not settle on either a sentimental or a cynical view of them. Harrison wanted a conventional and moralistic treatment of London's sexual underworld. He kept hoping to find it in *Workers*, and would be deeply shocked when Gissing went further into the world of prostitution in his next published novel, *The Unclassed*. But none of this took away from Harrison's enthusiasm for Gissing's achievement as a sociological novelist:

> There are scenes I am sure, which can hold their ground with the first things in modern fiction. The circulating libraries will be very shy of it. I do not think girls ought to read it at all. But men of insight will very soon discover its power. I will myself take care that one or two such read it, and I will urge my own opinion on the editor of more than one literary review. . . . You will be neglected for a few months, abused for two or three, and in six have a distinct (but not altogether tranquil) reputation.[43]

In his reply, Gissing reassured Harrison that he had not read any of Zola's books, so he could not be spreading the infection of 'realism' in England. He was not a realist, but an idealist who had fallen by chance into the lower depths:

> Rather than to any literary influence, I think I must trace the story to my own strongly excitable temperament, operated upon by hideous experiences of low life. For some years I have unavoidably come in contact with the very poor, uneducated and ignoble people; I have seen with what utter apathy these natures regard the most horrible manifestations of mental and moral depravity; and then, reflecting upon those more cultured grades, which I have also known, I was shocked by the gap between the two classes – not in the mere commonplace matter of material comfort, but in the power of comprehending each other's rule of life.[44]

Later, Gissing remarked that he had developed the literary method of *Workers in the Dawn* by studying George Eliot's novels.[45] Eliot too had been a disciple of Comte, and *Middlemarch* was the very type of a progressive sociological novel (though more positive in spirit than anything Gissing could manage). Both novelists proposed a correlation between society's movement to a higher phase of consciousness, and a similar movement in the personal life of the novel's protagonists. Where Gissing differed from Eliot was in the brutal collision between his respectable upbringing and the poverty-stricken masses of London. It was not just a difference in terms of class, where some people had fewer material goods than others, but even more in culture, where there was a clash of values. Gissing did not hesitate to say that the poor had no morals. Yet he was something more than just a comfortably placed scold, a type all too common in Victorian times. He struggled with two troublesome issues. One was the question of blame: were the poor depraved by nature, or because of the conditions under which they lived? Second, what about his own fall into sexual vice, and the punishment that followed it? It was not just that he observed depravity around him, as he walked the streets. Married to Nell, he dragged depravity out of the pub at closing time, and then shared a bed with it. He was part of the nether world that he deplored.

Gissing's 'excitable temperament' pointed to another contradiction in his writing. He knew that he was a passionate man, and bore the scars to prove it. Yet he also believed in the Comtean ideal of scientific detachment from the human world:

> Unfortunately, the subject I have most desire to master is nothing less than the laws of the universe, – in other words the science of all sciences. I want

to know what are the laws which govern the evolution of species on the earth, physically considered, and then to know the laws by which the mind of man is governed; for it is evident that the science of Psychology will soon become as definite as that of Physiology.[46]

Gissing wanted to achieve a godlike perspective on the universe, and to make sense of his own experience of struggle and confusion. But in *Workers in the Dawn*, sociological knowledge provides no salvation for the hero, Arthur Golding. His ideal beloved, Helen Norman, dies far away from him, of TB; his drunken wife, Carrie Mitchell, dies of syphilis. Gissing told Frederic Harrison that he had never known any actual woman like Helen; he did know one like Carrie, and nothing in Comte was of any use in coping with her.[47] The only solution for Arthur Golding is to throw himself over Niagara Falls. The coarseness of everyday life appals him; but neither can he find peace through intellectual detachment. The main achievement of *Workers in the Dawn* is Gissing's depiction of that which defeats both him and his hero: the culture of London's slums.

Gissing refused in *Workers* to provide a standard Victorian plot where love overcomes all obstacles, and is rewarded at the end with marriage, legacies, and a country cottage.[48] The protagonists of *Workers* are all dead at the end of the novel; the destructive element prevails over all efforts to resist it. Those who survive are either little people, or people taken in the mass. The arresting invocation with which Gissing begins his novel introduces his readers not to individual characters, but to a mob:

> Walk with me, reader, into Whitecross Street. It is Saturday night, the market-night of the poor; also one evening in the week which the weary toilers of our great city can devote to ease and recreation in the sweet assurance of a morrow unenslaved. . . .
>
> As we suddenly turn northwards out of the dim and quiet regions of Barbican, we are at first confused by the glare of lights and the hubbub of cries. Pressing through an ever-moving crowd, we find ourselves in a long and narrow street, forming, from end to end, one busy market. Besides the ordinary shops, amongst which the conspicuous fronts of the butchers' and the grocers' predominate, the street is lined along either pavement with rows of stalls and booths, each illuminated with flaring naphtha-lamps, the flames of which shoot up fiercely at each stronger gust of wind, filling the air around with a sickly odour, and throwing a weird light upon the multitudinous faces.[49]

Linguistically we get nothing but collective terms: crowd, multitude, throng, group, pile, customers, purchasers. It is not until page 11 that anyone is given a proper name; before that they are known only by the category they belong to. That was the essence of London for Gissing; it was a city in which most individuals counted for little. Its middle-class inhabitants might keep their singular dignity within their protected social world, but at Gissing's level he saw the insignificance of individual striving. Everyone around him seemed to be what he was himself, 'a victim of circumstances'.[50]

Gissing saw London thus, yet he also was aware of himself as having an alienated vision; he was someone who saw differently than most, and even saw badly:

> It must be confessed that the majority do not seem unhappy; they jest with each other amid their squalor; they have an evident pleasure in buying and selling; they would be surprised if they knew you pitied them. And the very fact that they are unconscious of their degradation afflicts one with all the keener pity.[51]

With the arrogance of youth, Gissing substitutes his own consciousness for that of the workers he observes. It never occurs to him that the degradation and misery might be within himself, rather than in those he judges. Gissing denied himself the three pleasures that workers enjoyed: sociability, drink, and sex. It was deeply engrained in him that these were the domains of waste and sin. Gissing the apprentice Comtean went into London's teeming streets in search of the 'laws of the universe'; Gissing the man was a soul adrift – not one who was 'born in exile', but who brought exile upon himself.

Under Harrison's Wing

If it were not for Frederic Harrison, *Workers in the Dawn* would have done little to help Gissing's career. Harrison constructed Gissing's early literary reputation almost single-handed. He wrote to five editors of reviews, and other influential literary figures of his acquaintance. He promoted Gissing as part of his campaign for Positivism; but Harrison was also a generous man who sensed how much hardship Gissing had endured, and who wanted to smooth his way in future. That meant inviting Gissing to his home and launching him on literary society. Two very long and quite favourable reviews of *Workers in the Dawn* appeared in September 1880, in the *Manchester Examiner* and *The Spectator*. George Saintsbury, in a briefer note, praised Gissing's sincerity and imagination. He made the shrewd point that although Gissing blamed society for human suffering, 'Yet, oddly enough, the bad ends to which nearly all, rich and poor, come are occasioned almost in every single instance by some personal error or folly which it is difficult to connect with the social system at all.'[1]

Harrison introduced Gissing to John Morley, the most prominent Liberal man of letters, editor of both the *Fortnightly Review* and the *Pall Mall Gazette*. Within a month Morley published three articles by Gissing on Social Democracy. He had learnt quite a lot about the German Social Democrats from Eduard Bertz, and did more research on his own account. He gave a respectful mention of Marx's *Capital* and the *Communist Manifesto* (though this does not prove that he actually read them). Gissing liked the idea of a society managed by intellectuals rather than by the market, and he despised the 'pig-sticking' of the German socialists by Bismarck. But even before he had written his major proletarian novels, he made it clear that he did not have much faith in the proletariat:

> Before the Socialist state is possible, the masses must be taught what they really need, why they need it, and how they must act to obtain it; in other words, it is not enough to agitate them with vague ideals: they must be, in

every sense of the word, educated to progress. . . . Human beings who live from day to day under much worse conditions than our cattle reared for slaughter are scarcely in a promising condition for the reception of intellectual and moral truths.[2]

Morley paid eight guineas for these articles, a substantial price. He also commissioned Gissing to report on various working-class events. For this work he had to go in costume, and he told Algernon that 'I am wearing my workman's clothing so much, I shall soon forget whether that or the more respectable suit is my proper attire.'[3] These outings did not lead to any published articles, though they convinced Gissing to start a new novel with 'a strongly and distinctly Socialistic flavour'.[4] This was a brave enterprise, given that Gissing had just heard from Remington that, so far, *Workers in the Dawn* had sold twenty-nine copies. Gissing had been trying to make a living from writing for four years. He had started four novels, abandoned three of them, and lost £125 on the one he had published. His contact with Morley might easily have led to a career in journalism, if Gissing had been more like the literary opportunist Jasper Milvain of *New Grub Street*. Instead, he decided that he did not have enough time or energy for journalism. His new novel was more important.

One journalism commission, though, Gissing could not refuse. Turgenev, then living in Paris, was looking for a London correspondent to write a quarterly survey of English affairs for *Vyestnik Evropy* ('The Messenger of Europe'), published in St Petersburg. This journal was the leading organ of the liberal Westernisers in Russia, traditionally opposed to the Slavophiles. Turgenev asked Edward Beesly, a professor of History at the university of London, to find someone; Beesly nominated Gissing. There was a kind of freemasonry of Positivist sympathisers, with Harrison at its centre. Beesly, Morley and Vernon Lushington were all recruited to put food on Gissing's table. Gissing's first deadline for *Vyestnik Evropy* would be in January 1881, and Turgenev asked him to write about political events rather than literature. Gissing had to supply long accounts of Parliamentary debates over Irish Home Rule (he supported it) and similar issues of the day. It was not inspiring work, but the pay was good at £8 per article, and Turgenev promised to raise it to £10 before long. Steady work like this paid the rent, and allowed Gissing to think of himself as carrying on the work of Enlightenment on a Continental scale, from his little study overlooking the Grand Union Canal.

Gissing should have been well pleased with the opportunities that had come his way through the publication of *Workers* and the support he was getting from the Positivists. He was increasing his income from teaching and writing, and probably received another £50 or £100 at this time from William's inheritance. The problem was that Nell's medical expenses quickly soaked up any extra money. Her health was breaking down so comprehensively that it is impossible to say, at this distance of time, what precisely was happening to her. There was childhood TB, scrofula, syphilis and alcoholism; from these came seizures, rashes, mysterious swellings and infections. In late October Gissing got her into the German hospital at Dalston, thanks to his uncle Paul Rahardt, the Peckham grocer. Then Rahardt spoiled his good turn by slandering Gissing as a wife-abuser and friend to the scoundrel Eduard Bertz. Rahardt's motives were unclear, except that he felt slighted by his Gissing relatives, and angry that Gissing had refused to invest in his shop. There may have been some fire to go with the smoke: Gissing had reached the end of his tether with Nell, and had no scruples about using force to restrain her.

At home in Islington, Gissing faced sickness and squalor; elsewhere he spent part of his day in some of the most cultured and comfortable homes in London. At the end of 1880, Harrison employed Gissing on a regular contract to teach his sons, Bernard and Austin, who were nine and seven years old. In January Gissing also took on the three daughters of Vernon Lushington, a judge, poet and Positivist. A painting by Arthur Hughes shows Mrs Lushington playing the piano accompanied by her daughters on violins, a utopian domestic scene in William Morris style. The Lushingtons were at the centre of the intellectual upper middle class. They were close friends with the Stephen family (Lesley Stephen had been a Positivist fellow-traveller for a while). Virginia Stephen was not yet born, but in time she would make Kitty, the eldest Lushington daughter, her model for *Mrs Dalloway*. Gissing was paid five shillings an hour at the Lushingtons, compared with little more than a shilling for some of his pupils when he started out. His income from teaching was now £2.10 a week. By all accounts, Gissing was a skilled and patient teacher, who knew how to bring out the best in his pupils. Yet it was not what he really wanted to do, and it often left him too tired to make progress on his novels. Further, if he gained a reputable teaching job, how could he hide Nell away from his colleagues? As a private tutor he lived two lives, four miles apart, going between the well-ordered homes of Bayswater and his Islington rooms, where drunk and dirty Nell awaited him. The travel was too much, even for Gissing, and he realised he must leave Islington and move to the west.

As he mingled with the Positivists, Gissing became a more militant Positivist himself, going to their meetings and even dating his letters by the Positivist calendar, where the months were named after great thinkers of the past. He was invited to Positivist houses for dinner, and felt that he was acquiring what he called the Science of Social Life. Local government caught his interest, and he thought of reviving Wakefield by starting a newspaper there, edited by himself and Algernon:

> I look forward to a day when something of the civic spirit of old Greece shall animate one and all of our towns. . . . I dislike the immense predominance of London. Germany, with its great number of university-towns and publishing-towns, is far nearer the ideal. Who ever sees a book worth having come from anywhere but London, – I mean of course of English books? . . . London is increasing in size beyond all reason, her evils growing simultaneously.[5]

Positivism had caused Gissing to take on a crushing load of obligations. While he tried to acquire universal knowledge, he had to teach the Harrison boys every morning and other pupils in the afternoons. He tried to work at his novel in the early mornings, and from five to nine in the evenings. Every night from 11.00 to 1.30 he read classical authors in Greek or Latin. It is not surprising that Nell tried to entertain herself elsewhere.

Gissing complained that his clothes were constantly splashed with mud from the streets, and he was wearing out a pair of boots every three weeks. At the end of February 1881 he and Nell moved to 55 Wornington Road in Westbourne Park, only a fifteen-minute walk from the Harrisons. The rent was lower, too – seven shillings, as against 8/6d. But Nell was now far away from any friends she might have made in Islington, and she still had only scraps of her husband's company, at meals or at other odd moments. It was costing them £3 a week to live, and Gissing's income from tutoring fell a bit short of this; his legacy money was going on everyday needs. 'I can never hope,' he told Algernon, 'to get much more than my bread and cheese; but that at least I feel to be my due, as I work all my waking hours without ceasing. I should think few people have less recreation of any kind.'[6] If Gissing had been single, 1881 might have been the year that launched him into literary society. Instead, it was a grim year with little to show for his struggles.

Bertz gave Gissing some congenial company by taking rooms in a nearby street, but the burden of Nell's ill-health kept on increasing. Soon after moving to Wornington Road, Gissing came home late at night and was told that Nell was having a fit in the chemist's nearby: 'I ran off, and found her in a fearful state, one moment insensible, the next delirious. A doctor had to be sent for at once, and, with the help of two of the shopmen, we

carried her home. I was up half the night, until she at length got to sleep.'[7]
The doctor agreed to come regularly and provide medicine for 10/6d a
week, but that was nearly a quarter of Gissing's income from tutoring.
Nell's seizures may also have included public incontinence, horribly embarrassing for someone of Gissing's disposition.

In May Gissing confessed to Algernon that the strain of coping with Nell
was starting to overwhelm him:

> I am getting most frightfully nervous, indeed so completely nervous that I
> dread the slightest variation from my hum-drum life. The door-bell ringing,
> even, or the postman's sudden knock puts me into palpitation and head-
> swimming, and I don't know what. This is very greatly the consequence, I
> know, of home circumstances, and I fear they will continue to work upon
> me. I only hope I shan't be rendered incapable of literary work.[8]

He had hoped to finish his socialist novel in time to get it published before
Christmas, but conditions were too hostile for him to create worthwhile
writing in 1881. Nonetheless, once Harrison took him under his wing,
Gissing would never be truly poor again. Charles Booth estimated, around
this time, that only 15 per cent of the London working class earned forty
shillings a week or more.[9] Gissing had about sixty shillings, and on a fairly
steady basis, since Harrison paid him quarterly, as did *Vyestnik Evropy*.
Since 1879 he had also received about £500 in legacies, of which only a
quarter had gone to Remington. What kept him complaining about money
was the constant drain of Nell's medical expenses. We can guess, also, that
Gissing spent substantial sums on books (though he could fairly claim that
he needed them for his work). Ultimately, his sense of poverty came from
his relative position and what he considered due to a man of his education
and talents. When he taught in upper-middle-class homes, he became
sharply aware that a truly civilised existence was far beyond his reach.

Living with Nell also cut Gissing off from having any secure social
position; he was condemned to a divided, in-between kind of life. Nell was
violently jealous of Eduard Bertz, so that Gissing could not receive him at
home. He lost even that companionship when Bertz gave up on England in
July 1881 and joined a utopian colony at Rugby, Tennessee, founded by
Thomas Hughes (the author of *Tom Brown's Schooldays*). Gissing's sister
Margaret, now seventeen, came to London to stay with friends in May.
Gissing saw her two or three times, but kept her away from Wornington
Road because his mother would have objected to Margaret having any
contact with Nell. He was doggedly faithful to his family, no matter how
much they disapproved of his writings and his way of life. Gissing kept

Algernon as his closest confidant, even though he was immovably conservative on politics, religion and Positivism. Algernon always defended the status quo, Gissing defended its enemies:

I always regret hearing you speak in the vein of the average British Philistine. As a Positivist, it is none of my principle to go about recommending political assassination. . . . But in Russia very, very much has been endured, more than we know, and of peaceful reform there seems extremely little chance. . . . Men are not born with a love of assassination, and when they take to it so resolutely as in Russia, reason compels us to admit that there *must* be some serious cause for it. Those are grievously to blame who resolutely obstruct political and social development. Their blood be on their own heads![10]

The blood here was that of Tsar Alexander II, recently killed by the Narodniks. In his article for *Vyestnik Evropy*, Gissing had praised British-style freedom of the press, and the Russian censors had let this pass. They did not mind hearing about Home Rule for Ireland, but Home Rule for Poland was not on the Tsar's agenda (it was a Polish suicide bomber who killed him). Gissing argued that if people did terrible things it proved that terrible things had first been done to them. When it came to his marriage, though, he never seemed to excuse Nell on the grounds that she led a terrible life before she met him. In his novels, similarly, prostitutes like Carrie Mitchell or Harriet Smales are shown as predisposed to evil and incorrigible. Gissing was not the first or the last person to be a Liberal in the world and a Tory at home.

From the summer of 1881 to the summer of 1882 Gissing went through a chaotic period in which he achieved little in his writing. In retrospect, we can see that his troubles with Nell had become unbearable and he was separating from her by fits and starts. At the beginning of July 1881 Gissing took her down to stay in lodgings at Hastings, hoping that she would remain there for several months. As soon as she was gone, though, he started to suffer from morbid loneliness. He decided to move back to Gower Place, where he had lived before at the end of 1878. 'I long for the neighbourhood of life and bustle and noise,' he told Algernon. 'Here in this wretched workman's suburb it grows intolerable.'[11] Over the next three years, Gissing would move six times. Apart from his year and a half in Chelsea, all his lodgings would be in the areas to the south and east of Regent's Park. He usually ended up within a five-minute walk of the stations serving the north of England, in an arc from Marylebone to King's

Cross. These great stations were the cathedrals of Victorian London, and Gissing liked the excitement they created.

No sooner had Gissing moved to 15 Gower Place than Nell returned from Hastings: she too had been lonely, and could only bear a month by the sea. The marriage was now entering its last act. Gissing was desperate to finish his socialist novel, which he had been working on for more than a year. 'I struggle with absolute anguish,' he told Algernon, 'for a couple of hours of freedom every day, and can only obtain the semblance of whole-hearted application. To say that I am like a man toiling up a hill with a frightful burden upon his back is absolutely no figure of speech with me; often, very often, I am on the point of stumbling and going no further!'[12] He was suffering from a writer's block brought on by his troubles with Nell. In addition, his grandiose plan prescribed by Comte, to master all knowledge, was a way of avoiding the immediate task of producing a successor to *Workers in the Dawn*. He had a bad case of second-novel jitters.

A first novel might be written straight from the heart, but after that Gissing believed in research. In 1880 he began to keep the 'Scrapbook' that would be a mainstay of his career for the next twenty years or so.[13] It was not precisely a scrapbook, but a personal filing system in which Gissing took notes or pasted clippings on foolscap sheets, then taped the sheets together into folders. As a novelist, he felt that he had a duty to the facts, and that a store of facts would be an asset to his work. Some other novelist might just introduce a typical 'ballet girl'. Gissing took the trouble to find out that she would be paid 21/- to 18/- a week if she danced in the front row, 15/- if she was in the second. A girl in a match factory would get 11/-.[14] Gissing was surprised that before 1855 Dickens did not prepare for his novels with research notes of this sort. Respect for the particularities of the real world was part of the novelist's vocation, Gissing felt. On a practical level, he had to write fast in order to survive, and having a dossier of facts was insurance against his constant fear of drying up. That meant living within range of a good public library where he could ferret through news-papers and magazines, looking for useful anecdotes. Memory or ima-gination might fail, documentation could be relied on.

When Nell returned in August, Gissing went off to visit his mother and sisters in Agbrigg. He stayed there for ten days, trying to get some writing done. When he returned, Algernon also came down to London to study for his Bachelor of Law degree; he could support himself with the legacy he was about to receive on his twenty-first birthday. Gissing gave Ellen, now fourteen, a lecture on life in the 'huge wilderness' of London (which she had never visited):

Struggling for a living in London is very much like holding yourself up, after a shipwreck, first by one floating spar and then another. You are too much taken up with the effort of saving yourself to raise your head and look if anyone else is struggling in the waves, and if you *do* come into contact with anyone else, ten to one it is only to fight and struggle for a piece of floating wood. For people who are not anxious about to-morrow's dinner life in London is very fine; otherwise it is a cruel sort of business.[15]

The image may have come from Carlyle's *Latter-day Pamphlets*. Carlyle had died that February – two months after George Eliot – and the two deaths made Gissing think of his time as an age of decline. His bleak view of London conflicted with Positivism's progressive creed; Gissing stopped dating his letters by the Positivist calendar, and was moving towards a darker view of English society.

For all Gissing's groans about London, the main trouble in his life had started in Manchester. In the autumn or early winter of 1881 Nell became an in-patient at the National Hospital for Diseases of the Heart and Paralysis, at 32 Soho Square ('Paralysis' at that time included epilepsy). Gissing was extremely sceptical about this hospital, and the fifteen shillings a week it charged its patients. He accused one of its physicians, Dr Ridsdale, of 'astounding villainy'.[16] On 13 January 1882 Nell insisted on leaving the hospital and coming home to Gower Place. She went out shopping the next day, against Gissing's wishes, and had a series of seizures. Finally he got Nell to nearby University Hospital in a cab, where 'we were inspected by half a dozen very young students (she still in fits) with the usual worse than nullity of result'.[17]

Gissing was affected, inevitably, by Victorian prejudices about epilepsy. The disease was feared because it was not understood, and because treatments for it did not work. All Nell knew was that she was desperate to go out – probably in search of drink, since Gissing found a bottle of gin hidden in one of her boxes. It did not matter to her where her seizures might happen. But Gissing hated the shame of trying to deal with Nell's seizures in a public place. A Victorian textbook says that an epileptic seizure is 'striking and horrible', and that 'a marked neurotic taint is to be found in the lineage of epileptics'.[18] Some doctors believed that seizures were caused by masturbation, or were a form of sexual hysteria; they prescribed sodium bromide, to suppress erotic urges. Gissing wanted above all to keep Nell's illness out of sight. One night when she tried to go out he locked the door and put the key in his pocket: 'I write in a strange mood; a sort of light-headedness, I fancy, from dreadfully wrought nerves. Whether I am behaving in a brutal fashion I know not. . . . I greatly fear she will end in a lunatic asylum.'[19] A hint in another letter suggests that Gissing sometimes lost control altogether and beat Nell with a stair-rod (these were wood or metal, about three feet long, used to hold down stair-carpets). He was no better than most of his male contemporaries in believing that women and children should be beaten into submission when all else failed (his story 'The Riding-Whip' proposed that beatings were good for scoundrelly males too). At the same time, as he told Algernon, he wondered whether 'she is to be blamed for all this, seeing that, without a doubt, her mind is affected'.[20] Their six years together had now brought out the worst in each. Blame, fury and sex had reached a toxic concentration. Nell wanted to go on, but Gissing felt that things had to come to a stop. In January 1882 he arranged for her to stay in Battersea with two ladies, the Misses Waskett, who took care of invalids for fifteen shillings a week. His only contact with her would be on Sunday afternoon visits.

Gissing's life settled down once he was no longer dividing it between Nell and his pupils, who included two sons of a knight and a nephew of the Duke of Sutherland. 'The queerest part of the business,' he noted, 'is that I find them no whit better or wiser than other people. Perhaps I was not without suspicion of this fact even before.'[21] Soon after Nell went to Battersea, Gissing left Gower Place, probably because all the eruptions had made it embarrassing to stay. He moved west to 29 Dorchester Place, Blandford Square, which also was closer to his pupils' homes. In the last throes of his relationship with Nell, Gissing had managed to write another short book: 'a violent attack upon the present state of society, and dire threatenings of evil to come, if we do not mend our ways. I call it "Watching the Storm Clouds", – a good name, I think.'[22] This was probably a political tract rather than fiction; as Gissing predicted, no publisher would take it, and the manuscript has disappeared. The socialist novel he had started in 1880 was abandoned, sometime during the crisis with Nell, and a new one was under way, called 'Mrs Grundy's Enemies'. This was now Gissing's sixth novel, with one published.

Nell stayed for about three months with the Misses Waskett in Battersea, then moved down to the Sussex coast at Seaford. In the middle of May 1882 she came back to London, and Gissing found a room for her in Kennington. Soon she decided that she preferred being back at the Hospital for Heart and Paralysis in Soho. Gissing felt that the hospital did Nell little good, and only wanted her for the money she paid; but he was willing to get rid of her at the price of £1 a week. 'I shall not myself go to the Hospital ever. . . . I only can't understand why she determined ever to leave the place, for I am convinced that the atmosphere of vulgar gossip is essentially congenial to her.'[23] Nell had needs that went far beyond what could be cured by the gift of a pound a week. Gissing, unable or unwilling to meet those needs, felt that his obligations stopped with giving material support to a woman who was too sick and disturbed to support herself.

For most of 1882 the separation from Nell allowed Gissing to make progress with his writing, while also carrying a heavy load of teaching. Algernon had come to live in London for the autumn of 1881 and the first part of 1882. He failed his Bachelor of Laws exams in January, but took them again in April and passed. After that he went wandering off to the north of England on holiday; he applied for work in some solicitors' offices, but his success in the exams was the last he would enjoy in the field of law.

With Algernon and Bertz both gone, Gissing found company in his old college friend John George Black, who was now married and living in London. It was six years since they had shared Nell's favours in Manchester; they went for long walks around Richmond Park and rowed on the Thames. Gissing moved again on 6 September 1882 to 17 Oakley Crescent in Chelsea. He had become dissatisfied with his landlady at Blandford Square, and wanted to be closer to the Blacks. His idea of a good time in London was to seek out quiet corners where you could pretend you were in the country; what he loathed was the sight of Londoners having *their* idea of a good time:

> Never is so clearly to be seen the vulgarity of the people as at these holiday-times. Their notion of a holiday is to rush in crowds to some sweltering place, such as the Crystal Palace, and there eat and drink and quarrel themselves into stupidity. Miserable children are lugged about yelling at the top of their voices, and are beaten because they yell. ... Places like Hampstead Heath and the various parks and commons are packed with screeching drunkards, one general mass of dust and heat and rage and exhaustion. Yet this is the best kind of holiday the people are capable of.[24]

Gissing was still enough of a Comtean to believe that the masses would behave in a more seemly way if they were given more free time and cultural opportunities. All the necessary work of the world could be done in three or four hours a day, and then people would learn how to use leisure well:

> There is so much labour just because there is so much money-grubbing. Every man has to fight for a living with his neighbour, and the grocer who keeps his shop open till half an hour after midnight has an advantage over him who closes at twelve. Work in itself is *not an end; only a means*; but we now-a-days make it an end, and three fourths of the world cannot understand anything else.[25]

With Nell out of the way, Gissing could forge ahead with his polemical novel, 'Mrs Grundy's Enemies'. He began the novel around the beginning of May and finished it by the beginning of September – three volumes in about four months. There was only one crisis with Nell. She left the hospital in Soho Square and went off to live with friends – according to Gissing, 'vile people, who write me abusive letters for my "neglect and cruelty".'[26] One Saturday night she turned up at the Misses Waskett with two drunken friends, and a policeman was called to get rid of them. In October, though, Gissing relented and brought Nell back to live with him at Oakley Crescent. She had just had an operation on her eyes, and needed nursing while she recovered. Gissing did his best, but could only manage for a month, since he got almost no sleep. 'These broken nights are fearful,' he told Algernon, 'I wonder much what they would result in if continued.'[27] He meant, presumably, that he would have killed himself. Later, Gissing told a friend that this was a time when he 'touched the lowest depths of despair'.[28] On 7 November Nell went into the Westminster Hospital for another operation, on her arm, perhaps for a syphilitic ulcer. She stayed there until 15 December, then returned to Chelsea for the last act of the marriage. On Christmas Day, Gissing often seemed to take a perverse pleasure in wallowing in gloom; he ate his dinner alone at a café on Oxford Street. He would not go out with Nell, for fear of her having a seizure. Who knows what kind of dinner *she* had?

On Boxing Day Gissing received a letter from George Bentley, the publisher, offering fifty guineas for the copyright of 'Mrs Grundy's Enemies'. The novel had been sent first to Smith, Elder, in September, and drew a typical rejection note: 'It exhibits a great deal of dramatic power and is certainly not wanting in vigour, but in our judgment it is too painful to please the ordinary novel reader and treats of scenes that can never attract the subscribers to Mr Mudie's library.'[29] After this snub, it was sweet indeed to have an acceptance from Bentley's, a long-established firm and the official publisher to the Queen. Gissing had spent six years as an ink-stained wretch. Now, it seemed, he had his foot on the ladder of success. It no longer mattered that his articles for *Vyestnik Evropy* were coming to an end, and the regular income they brought. But having been cheated and disappointed by Remington, Gissing was now going to receive another lesson on the way of a publisher with an author.

With the good news from Bentley in hand, Gissing dug in his heels on the domestic front. Two days after Christmas Nell left – or was pushed out of – Oakley Crescent, taking with her half the furniture. She went to live with friends in Brixton, and this time the separation was final. Gissing would send her a pound a week, which he paid faithfully. To make ends meet, he moved into a smaller room at Oakley Crescent, costing only seven shillings a week. Recently he had added two pupils, from whom he received a guinea and a half a week for fifteen hours of teaching. Prospects looked reasonably bright, and as soon as Nell was gone Gissing started another novel. He hoped to see 'Mrs Grundy's Enemies' published in the spring of 1883, followed by the new novel before the end of the year. He would then be fairly launched, and less dependent on Frederic Harrison, who had done so much for him over the past two and a half years. Gissing was moving away from Positivism and Harrison, it would become evident, was moving away from him.

In September 1882 Gissing had just finished 'Mrs Grundy', and decided to spend a month on writing a philosophical essay. He had the ambition of becoming a Victorian sage in the style of two men he greatly admired, Carlyle and Ruskin. Carlyle had died earlier in the year, in his house just around the corner from where Gissing was now living.[30] Gissing responded to the contempt, in both Carlyle and Ruskin, for Victorian materialism and its Gospel of Progress. He was realising that Progress was really the new religion of the Positivists. To create his own philosophy, he needed to begin with a refutation of Comte. This would mean a break with Harrison, and Gissing's solution to this dilemma anticipated the duplicity of Godwin Peak in *Born in Exile*. He would write the essay, but not publish it. Meanwhile, he would continue to teach Harrison's children and enjoy his bounty, while saying nothing about any loss of faith in the Positivist creed. Having just finished a novel attacking censorship, Gissing quietly decided to censor himself, in the cause of keeping his bread buttered on the right side. Perhaps that is unfair: Gissing was truly grateful to Harrison, and was reluctant to hurt his feelings by coming out as an opponent of Positivism. Moreover, Gissing's strongest motive in writing his essay, 'The Hope of Pessimism', was to set his own thoughts in order about where he stood in the world. Publication, or the lack of it, was a secondary concern.

'The Hope of Pessimism' began with the observation that the era of belief in God was coming to an end. How would this affect the mass emotions of modern society? The Positivists claimed that the religion of God would be replaced by the religion of Humanity, and the world would be a better place in consequence. Such a happy outcome depended on two assumptions. One was that 'a realistic interpretation of the universe' would make people cheerful. The other was that once people knew that there was nothing above them, they would value each other more highly:

When we have ceased, – it is urged – to peer into the clouds after impossible explanations of our being; when we have convinced ourselves of the purely natural sanctions of morality; when we have learned to regard the earth as our true and only home, and one capable of being made delightful to all creatures; then, and not till then, will our hearts overflow with the single love of Humanity, and 'to live for others' be recognized as at once the noblest moral theory and the highest practical blessedness.[31]

Against this sunny vision, Gissing suggested that a world without God would not be cheerful, but nihilistic. Instead of loving their neighbour, people would plunge fiercely into what Herbert Spencer called 'the battle of life':

Let [the religion of earthly optimism] constitute a man's creed, and, consciously or unconsciously, he will inevitably make it his first object to secure possession of his birthright. The social results which directly issue from such a conviction in the individual are only too plain before our eyes. Hence this scheme of commercial competition tempered by the police-code, to which we are pleased to give the name of a social order. ... Does not science – the very newest – assure us that only the fittest shall survive? If we tread upon a feeble competitor and have the misfortune to crush the life out of him, we are merely illustrating the law of natural selection.[32]

Once gloomy Christianity has given way to Comtean progress, the result will be a great flowering of egotism. Since we cannot crawl back to a false creed, the only alternative Gissing sees is Schopenhauerian pessimism, a tragic sense of 'the weariness of being'. We can neither hope for happiness in heaven, nor expect it here on earth. Instead of plunging into the 'battle of life', we should 'cultivate our perception of man's weakness, learn thoroughly the pathos inherent in a struggle between the finite and the infinite. We are shipmates, tossed on the ocean of eternity, and one fate awaits us all. Let this excite our tenderness.' Gissing had given up on the idea that we can master our fate through scientific knowledge. The world will always be too much for any individual, and all are doomed to a sticky end. The progressive optimism of Comte is therefore just another of humanity's mirages – a successor to the Christian illusion, not a triumph over it.

Gissing leaves one grain of hope: that we can find consolation in the realm of art. Schopenhauer had led the way, and was followed by Nietzsche in *The Birth of Tragedy* (1872). Only through art, Gissing suggests, can we overcome egotism and remove ourselves from the Battle of Life:

In the mood of artistic contemplation the will is destroyed, self is eliminated, the world of phenomena resolves itself into pictures of absolute significance, and the heart rejoices itself before images of pure beauty. Here, indeed, good does prevail over evil, and there is excellence in the sum of things. Herein is one explanation of the optimism of the Hellenic religion: it was the faith of a people of artists.[33]

Comte's *Positive Philosophy* had little to say about art, and it was not clear what a Comtean art would look like, beyond being scientific and progressive. What gave Gissing's art its particular flavour was that even before he had written his major novels of social criticism – *Demos, Thyrza, The Nether World* – he had renounced the Comtean belief that such criticism could lead to a perfected social order. At the same time, his fiction did not aspire to Schopenhauerian aesthetic harmony and detachment. Nor, finally, did he follow Ruskin and the aesthetes in trying to create a world elsewhere, in medievalism, fantasy or dream. Gissing knew that his early novels were binding his imagination to an uncongenial ground, the dirty streets of actual London; but he did not see any way of escaping that bondage.

When Gissing had completed 'The Hope of Pessimism' he did not even try to get it published. He could afford to write for his desk drawer because 'Mrs Grundy's Enemies' was in the press, and another novel was soon under way. This was 'The Burden of Life', eventually to appear as *The Unclassed*. But then, at the beginning of February 1883, George Bentley took a look at the proofs of 'Mrs Grundy'. He may not have read the book at all before that; now, he told Gissing that he needed to soften the description and dialogue. Harrison advised him to make whatever changes Bentley asked for, but Gissing was in a defiant mood. 'I shall fight these prejudices to the end,' he told Algernon, 'cost what it may.' Not only that, he would add a polemical preface to the novel: 'This book is addressed to those to whom Art is dear for its own sake. Also to those who, possessing their own Ideal of social and personal morality, find themselves able to allow the relativity of all Ideals whatsoever.'[34] This was a bit of Comtean jargon, that Positivism would 'render relative the ideas which were at first absolute', as humanity progressed from theology to science.[35]

Bentley now sent the manuscript of the novel to his friend Evelyn Abbott for his opinion. Abbott was a bachelor don at Balliol College, Oxford, paralysed from the waist down, and not obviously qualified to pass judgement on Gissing's work. In the meantime, Bentley's continued to set type and send proofs to Gissing. This made no sense, because if any significant changes were made the whole book would have to be reset. But George

Bentley was sick at his home in Wales and unable to make decisions, except to tell Gissing that it would be better to publish 'Mrs Grundy' much later in 1883. He sent Gissing a cheque for £50 in mid-April, but then fell silent for several months.[36]

Gissing could only peg away at his new novel, and hope for the best on 'Mrs Grundy'. When he got his money from Bentley, he thought again of the Wakefield newspaper project. Algernon had opened a law office in the town, using his inheritance, but he sat there day after day with no clients. Gissing perhaps realised that Algernon was not likely to be more successful as a newspaper editor than as a lawyer. Or, in the long run, as anything else, though it would take time for this to become clear. Now that Nell was being paid to stay away, Gissing could live more tranquilly than for a long time. By the end of May 1883 he had finished two volumes of *The Unclassed*, and planned to write sonnets once the third volume was done. The sonnets he did write were watered-down Wordsworth, and did not add anything to his reputation; few were published.

Margaret Gissing, now nineteen, complained to her brother that men were more egotistical than women, and drew a thoughtful reply:

> Your censure upon men at large I also believe to be thoroughly warranted; to myself, for instance, it applies very completely. The fact is, however, that the thinking much of oneself is just that quality which, in its best form, results in work of value. No one would produce, for instance, a work of art, who had not considerable self-esteem. But observe; it is only when this self-esteem is co-incident with *self-knowledge* that the trait ceases to be offensive to others.[37]

This was both shrewd, and self-serving. Women were more generous, Gissing conceded, but men were more productive – some men, at least. Egotism was justified by its results; on the other hand, a male who was both an egotist and a fool was contemptible. Gissing surely believed that most women were both nicer than men, and inferior to them. Later he would argue strongly that female inferiority could be cured by education. In any case, he would have to admit that his own dealings with women had been a complete failure; no masculine superiority there.

As he tried to justify his harsh treatment of Nell, Gissing was moving away from the 'Religion of Humanity' – Comtean altruism – and towards the Religion of Art:

> Philosophy has done all it can for me, and now scarcely interests me any more. My attitude henceforth is that of the artist pure and simple. The world is for me a collection of phenomena, which are to be studied and reproduced

artistically. In the midst of the most serious complications of life, I find myself suddenly possessed with a great calm, withdrawn, as it were, from the immediate interests of the moment, and able to regard everything as a picture. I watch and observe myself just as much as others. . . . This, I rather think, is at last the final stage of my development, coming after so many and various phases. Brutal and egotistic it would be called by most people. What has that to do with me, if it is a fact?[38]

Gissing accused himself of detachment rather than egotism, a stance that verged on callousness when he observed the sufferings of other people and thought only of how he might represent them in his fiction. We might see this as Gissing adopting the principles of Flaubert, where the artist is an ideal spectator. But Gissing had arrived there by a different path. Detachment was a strategy of self-preservation, forced on him by the insoluble problems of living for five years with Nell. He had grown a protective shell against her demands; he then transposed his withdrawal into a different key, as the observant indifference of the artist. Yet when it came to the point, Gissing could not write his novels with the cold eye of a Flaubert.

Gissing's new stance was first put to the test by the return of Eduard Bertz from Tennessee, after two years away. The experimental community at Rugby had collapsed into bankruptcy, taking a good chunk of Bertz's capital with it. When he came back to London he became a follower of the Salvation Army and the Blue Ribbon Army (a Christian temperance movement, founded by a repentant rum-smuggler). Gissing was appalled:

Whether this means weakening of the brain, I can't say: I stand and I marvel, but protest has been in vain. It is shocking to think how many people take this turn. Happily I don't fear for myself: my position has long been a very clear one.[39]

Gissing's position was not altogether consistent. He scorned Christian revelation, and explained to Margaret that we can only know the world through our fallible senses. His own gave him no evidence that God existed. Yet he was also as ferociously moralistic as any Presbyterian elder. He lavished praise on Algernon's letter to a Wakefield newspaper, which deplored the 'blasphemy, obsceneness and impurity' of a woman he had encountered on her night out. Whatever the foundations of morality might be, Gissing was sure that women were more to blame than men when they behaved badly, because their proper role was to be an 'angel of goodness'.[40]

The question of woman's nature soon arose close to home, in an episode that does not show Gissing in a pretty light. On 24 September, a police sergeant came to Oakley Crescent to tell Gissing that Nell had made a charge of 'criminal assault' – that is, rape – against three men:

> He told me she was described in the neighbourhood, as an habitual drunkard,
> well known in all public-houses, and generally regarded as in all respects a
> bad character. The assault took place at 1.30 a.m., in a place where business
> could not possibly have taken her. At the station she wished to back out of
> the charge, but of course was not allowed to. The officer told me he very
> much doubted her innocence. In any case, her bad character will go against
> her.[41]

Most likely the men had either refused to pay after having intercourse with
Nell, or had simply raped her. The Victorian judgement, which Gissing
also took for granted, was that a prostitute was to blame for her clients'
misdeeds. 'Don't think this upsets me,' Gissing told Algernon, 'I am really
very calm about it. I don't think it will even affect my work.'[42] Instead of
defending Nell, Gissing saw the incident as a golden chance of getting a
divorce, by proving that Nell led an immoral life. Charges against the three
men were dropped, and the police sergeant volunteered – in exchange for
a guinea a week – to spy on Nell and prove that she was a prostitute.

Frederic Harrison advised Gissing to push ahead with a divorce, and
offered to lend him money for his legal costs. For a few weeks Gissing
consulted lawyers and tried to confirm evidence against Nell. In theory, he
was in a position to divorce her on the grounds of adultery. But only a few
hundred divorces were granted each year in England, and the cost would
be a large chunk of his annual income. Whatever happened, he planned to
go on paying Nell £1 a week for her maintenance, and he could not afford
to keep paying his spy a guinea a week. After a couple of months, Gissing
simply gave up on the divorce. In October he had gone up to Aberdeen on
a mysterious trip that, he said, would be 'the foundation for better things'.[43]
Perhaps he was interviewed for a job; if so, nothing came of his first and
last trip to Scotland.

Nell's rape completed Gissing's emotional separation from her; so far as
we know, he would never see her again until she was lying dead. A woman
defiled was a woman to be discarded. Meanwhile, Gissing was writing
sentimental poems about pubescent innocence:

> O maiden, simple, pale and sweet,
> > You know not of the soul that's growing;
> You could not else so calmly meet,
> > O maiden sweet,
> The passion in my own eyes glowing.[44]

One wonders if Gissing's poem was inspired by his students, fifteen-year-old Kitty Lushington and her younger sister Margaret. The 'growing soul' is sexuality, which lives behind a veil inside the girl; at the right time it will break through the veil and show itself. Apart from its curious metaphor, the poem assumed that well-brought-up girls would be completely unconscious of sex until puberty. 'Most women, before their marriages, are passionless,' Gissing would say later. He comforted himself by musing about sexual innocence, as he tried to free himself from the all-too-sexual Nell.

In October, Bentley's announced that 'Mrs Grundy's Enemies' would appear in November or December, 'a novel dealing with a grade of society not often treated since Dickens's "Oliver Twist"'. But two months after the announcement, there was no sign of the novel. Someone at Bentley's still had cold feet. Perhaps because of a guilty conscience, Bentley accepted two contributions from Gissing to *Temple Bar*, which he edited. 'Song', the poem about the modest maiden, brought Gissing a guinea; a short story, 'Phoebe', brought more. This was a sad tale about a poor girl who finds some money in her room; she confides in a girl she meets on the street, who then steals the money. The story was typical in its combination of sympathy for the struggling poor with cynicism about the ways in which they preyed on each other. On 14 December Gissing wrote to Bentley saying that he had completed *The Unclassed* and would have to offer it to another publisher. Bentley asked to see the novel anyway, but soon told Gissing that it was immoral through and through:

> You will see what the reader says and about the heroine who is a prostitute being represented as good and noble and pure.
>
> Though we know in this unfortunate class there are many with kindly instincts yet the nature of the life tends to deaden and in time destroy the good originally present. It does not appear to me wholesome, to hold up the idea that a life of vice can be lived without loss of purity and womanly nature. I confess that I am of the opinion that the realistic treatment of such a subject works for evil as well as good, and possibly more for the former. I do not doubt your motive, which I believe is the noble one of bringing before the public a class, not enough considered with a view to an amendment of their condition and removal of their temptations.[45]

Bentley was complaining that the worst thing in *The Unclassed* was Gissing's representation of Ida Starr: a prostitute who raises herself to become a cultured and virtuous woman, worthy of the hero's love. If prostitutes are to be present at all, they should be shown on a one-way street to degradation. Bentley was a determinist who believed that prostitutes were

entirely trapped by their environment. Gissing's argument was that children were already endowed with a fixed moral nature. Bad Harriet Smales
belongs to the underworld of promiscuity and drunkenness; good Ida Starr
can cleanse herself and leave that world behind.

Gissing did not argue with Bentley's rejection of *The Unclassed*, but
asked yet again when 'Mrs Grundy's Enemies' would appear. Bentley
gave no answer; he now seemed likely to sit on it indefinitely. Algernon
suggested that Gissing might sue Bentley for failure to publish; Gissing
replied that he had already asked Harrison about doing so, and had been
told that 'you cannot force a man to publish a book which would be an
offence against morality'. Gissing also believed that he had no case because
Bentley had agreed to purchase the copyright, not to publish the book![46] It
was becoming evident that Bentley had no intention of publishing 'Mrs
Grundy', but Gissing remained hypnotised by the prestige of the firm and
the fact that Bentley had actually paid cash down for the novel. Six years
later, Bentley would indeed publish a Gissing novel, *The Emancipated*.
Meanwhile, Gissing formed the peculiar idea that he should give Bentley
another novel for no further money. In January 1884 he started another
'quite inoffensive' novel with Bentley in mind, calling it 'A Graven Image'.
He toiled away at it for four hours every night, after his day's teaching, but
it joined the ghostly company of his unfinished works.

Gissing stored up more trouble for himself through his dealings with
Algernon in the winter of 1883–4. Algernon sat in his law office waiting
for clients who never came, and writing letters to Wakefield newspapers
about unseemly behaviour that he had seen around town. At his brother's
suggestion, Algernon sent copies to Ruskin, who replied with cautious
politeness. Gissing encouraged Algernon to try writing articles and stories;
none of these met with success, but Gissing had planted the idea that
Algernon might become a professional writer if the law practice did not
thrive. Algernon had some talent; what he lacked was self-confidence,
imagination, and dogged devotion to work. Those were his brother's qualities; yet George was far from making a living from writing, after seven
years of trying. As he failed in his law practice, Algernon was starting to
flounder from one scheme to another, on his way to becoming a leech on
his brother and his other relatives.

Gissing, at least, was about to reach a great milestone as a writer: to both
be paid for a novel, and see it published. *The Unclassed* was rejected unread
by Chatto & Windus, then sent to Chapman & Hall. On 13 February
1884, Gissing met with Frederic Chapman, the head of the firm, and his
publisher's reader. They told Gissing they would pay £50 for the first

edition of the novel, and a royalty for subsequent printings. If Gissing would spend a week making some revisions, they would meet again and confirm the agreement. Gissing said that he had never worked so hard as in that week, so he must have done a major rewriting of the novel.[47] Chapman then told him that he would have a contract, and that 'his reader has scarcely ever spoken so strongly of a MS'.[48] But when the contract arrived, it was for £30, not £50. Gissing, grinding his teeth, felt he had to accept. Chapman & Hall had already started to set type, and Gissing's first concern had to be that they publish the book as soon as possible. He could hope to make more money from *The Unclassed* if it sold out the first printing of four hundred copies; but the hope was a faint one and, like many of Gissing's hopes, it remained unfulfilled.

The Unclassed led to an important friendship with Chapman's reader. Gissing had not recognised him at their first meetings, but then discovered that he was the poet and novelist George Meredith. For the rest of his life, Gissing was firm in his belief that Meredith was by far the greatest living English novelist. 'It is amazing that such a man is so neglected,' Gissing wrote later. 'For the last thirty years he has been producing work unspeakably above the best of any living writer, and yet no one reads him outside a small circle of highly cultured people. And perhaps that is better than being popular – a hateful word.'[49] Their friendship remained a cautious one, in that both were highly secretive about their social origins and their youthful follies. Meredith's great shame was that his father was a gentlemen's tailor who had gone bankrupt and fled to South Africa. Meredith had made his way in the literary world without a university education, and had married the upper-middle-class Mary Ellen Nicholls. She was a daughter of the novelist T. L. Peacock and the widow of a naval officer who had drowned. Her marriage to Meredith was unhappy, and she left him for the artist Henry Wallis; that relationship did not last, and Mary Ellen died two years later, in 1861. Meredith put the pain of his marriage, and his wounded pride, into the sonnet-sequence *Modern Love* (1862). This was a direct challenge to Victorian pieties, and Meredith was one who could appreciate Gissing's rebelliousness about sexual mores in *The Unclassed*.

Both men had experienced the damage caused by a collision between sex and class, though Gissing's problems came from marrying down, Meredith's from marrying up. New evidence about Meredith's first marriage gives it what might be called a Gissingesque flavour. It used to be taken for granted that Mary Ellen had fled because of emotional conflicts with her younger husband; now it seems that she was bitterly offended by his lying to her about his social origins. He had hinted that he came from a Welsh aristocratic background, but Mary Ellen opened by mistake a letter from his father in South Africa, asking Meredith to forward some of his tailor's bills.[50] In 1884 Meredith also was living with another secret: for some years he had been suffering from *tabes dorsalis*, a syphilitic infection of the spine.[51] Probably this came from consorting with prostitutes in his youth, which would give him a personal interest in Gissing's treatment of prostitution in *The Unclassed*. Behind the polite exchanges in Chapman's office lay Meredith's perception that here was a young man of talent whose path in crucial ways coincided with his own.

None of these affinities had any effect on the miserly £30 that Frederic Chapman gave Gissing for his novel, but the proofs came swiftly and Gissing could say to Algernon, 'literary life begins in earnest at last.'[52] He finished the proofs by the end of May, and kept working on 'The Graven Image'. He had also decided to leave Oakley Crescent, telling Algernon that there were too many lodgers in the house and he could not get the quiet he needed for his work. After he had left, he admitted something closer to the real reason: 'I had grown too friendly with the people in the house, and found it increasingly difficult to force myself to solitary work after the other day's work was over.'[53] A rumour has survived that Gissing's landlady had become too fond of him.[54] She had a husband on the premises, and Gissing had a wife in the offing, so it would be prudent for him to flee the situation.

Gissing's new home, at 62 Milton Street, was near his old lodgings at Blandford Square.[55] Here he took on another pupil, Walter Grahame, for ten hours of tutoring a week at the excellent rate of five shillings an hour. Once he had made the move (on 10 May 1884), Gissing predictably felt lonely and depressed, and he abandoned 'A Graven Image', on which he had worked so doggedly. *The Unclassed* was ready in mid-June and Gissing sent out two of his precious six free copies, to Algernon and to Frederic Harrison. He was looking for reassurance from those close to him, before the expected mud-throwing of the critics. Instead, the mud started to arrive immediately. Algernon and Harrison seem to have hated everything about the novel, but especially the nihilism of Waymark (the novel's hero) and the frank treatment of prostitution. Gissing argued that he portrayed Waymark as a contemporary type, not a mouthpiece for his own views. Waymark was an English equivalent to Bazarov, in Turgenev's *Fathers and Sons*. But Turgenev had given Bazarov a strong opponent in the novel, Arkadi; even so, there was a storm of protest in Russia and Turgenev had to exile himself to France. Gissing tried to get out of the line of fire:

You evidently take Waymark's declaration of faith as my own. Now this is by no means the case. Waymark is a *study of character*, and he alone is responsible for his sentiments. . . . If my own ideas are to be found anywhere, it is in the practical course of events in the story; my characters must speak as they would actually, and I cannot be responsible for what they say. You may tell me I need not have chosen such people; ah, but that is a question of an artist's selection. You see, I have not for a moment advocated *any* theory in the book.[56]

An artist, in Gissing's view, just decided whether a tiger or a cow would make the better picture; it was not a question of whether he was bloodthirsty or peaceful. But Frederic Harrison complained that *The Unclassed* was full of an anti-social spirit: 'My ideals involve war to the knife with those which are professed by the hero of the Unclassed. I have known something of social revolt in many forms, and have had not a little sympathy with very many of its champions. . . . That of Waymark is to me mere moral dynamite.'[57] Faced with Harrison's disapproval, Gissing did not show himself in his best light. First he cringed, saying that it was unpardonable of him to expose Mrs Harrison to his book, and that he would never see the Harrison boys again. Then he admitted that, yes, Waymark did speak for him:

It is true, as you said, that I have a quarrel with society. . . . ever since I can remember I have known this passionate tendency of revolt. It has sought for satisfaction in many schools and many modes of life. I write these social passages in a fury; but I scribbled in precisely the same temper when I was ten years old.

His misfortunes had made him a social cripple, Gissing said: 'I live so much alone that I habitually think too much of myself, and am always in danger of giving offence where I feel most anxious not to do so.'[58] He wanted to write novels of passionate revolt against the social order, but also to claim that the artist was a mere observer, with no stake in the game he described. Yet individual passion was really his subject as a novelist; the nuts and bolts of urban reform never greatly interested him.

Fortunately, Harrison calmed Gissing's self-torture. He knew that the actual Gissing was different from the characters in his books, and could go on teaching Harrison's children and being a friend of the family. Still, Gissing had told Harrison abut Nell's rape, and there remained the awkward question of why *The Unclassed* was so knowledgeable about prostitution. Waymark insists to his friend Casti that he has 'absolutely no social purpose' when writing his novel. Casti shrewdly replies that 'Granting that this is pure art, it is a kind of art only possible to an age in which the social question is predominant.' Waymark has to agree, and goes further:

> every human situation is interesting to me in proportion as it exhibits artistic possibilities, and my temperament is especially sensitive to the picturesque in what is usually called vileness. Thus, for instance, prostitution and everything connected with it is my highest interest. In the prostitute you have the incarnation at once of the greatest good and the greatest evil, the highest and the lowest, that which is most pure associated with that which is most foul – using all these words in the conventional sense.[59]

When Gissing revised *The Unclassed* in 1895 he removed most of the flagrant passages about prostitution. He had realised by then that the dangers of confessional writing outweighed its benefits.

It had taken Gissing four years to get a novel published after *Workers in the Dawn*, and the appearance of *The Unclassed* was anticlimactic in that he attracted some attention from the critics but not enough to give him a real foothold in the literary world. The *Evening News* gave the novel a long review, and praised Gissing for his pure-minded English treatment of prostitution, so unlike those dubious French novels:

> Mr Gissing has succeeded in lifting the veil from the life of a section of the world of London concerning which serious novelists have too long kept silence, and he has done his work with so much good feeling and good taste that no reader will be offended, while all will be the richer for some authentic information, much needed in these days of social reform.[60]

Gissing did not understand prostitutes, though, said the reviewer: 'the notion that the mind of a prostitute can remain pure and unsullied in the midst of her profession is simply contrary to fact, however well it may fit in with this or that theory.' This was a subject on which critics were ready to show their expertise; Arthur Barker, in *The Academy*, commented that 'a long-continued platonic attachment between a normal young man – even of aesthetic tastes – and a London prostitute is an incident hardly within the range of probability, to say the least'.[61] Yet Gissing's actual attachment to Nell had been more improbable than that.

The Unclassed appeared, was advertised and reviewed, and sold only a few copies more than *Workers in the Dawn*. Probably some two or three hundred copies went to the libraries before the rest of the print run was remaindered.[62] At some point Mudie's realised that the book was likely to offend its members, and they withdrew it. Gissing was no closer than before to making a living from his books; but he at least had Meredith on his side (and Thomas Hardy, who was impressed by the novel). He patched up his differences with the Harrisons, too, and was invited to go on holiday with them at Ullswater for two weeks in August. Gissing could walk on the hills, and visit Wordsworth's grave. Wordsworth 'requires to be read amid his own scenes', he told Algernon. A free holiday as a house guest suited Gissing well, and he boasted to Algernon that he got on to 'a perfectly natural footing of polite intimacy' with the Harrisons' friends in the Lakes.[63] He was about to advance further into good society than ever before, and on to uncertain ground.

4

Love With a Lady

When Gissing returned from the Lakes at the end of August, Harrison put more work in his way. He was to visit the David Gaussen family in the Cotswolds, examine their three boys (aged nine, thirteen and fifteen), and advise on their further education. The pay was three guineas, train fare, and two nights of lodging at Broughton Hall, a grand Tudor mansion near Lechlade. As a side benefit, Gissing hoped to pick up material for his novels. 'I am getting to like the atmosphere of cultured families,' he told Algernon. 'I study the people, and they are of use.'[1] They studied him, too. James Gaussen, the oldest boy, remembered that Gissing turned up in a rented frock-coat and top hat, and was 'terribly shy'. Mrs Gaussen's daughter Ellen gave him a pear, which he was too nervous to eat. He put it in his pocket, and then sat on it at tea.[2]

In *Born in Exile*, Godwin Peak is invited to lunch with the upper-middle-class Warricombes, and strenuously watches his ps and qs:

> No less introspective than in the old days, though he could better command his muscles, Peak, after each of his short remarks, made comparison of his tone and phraseology with those of the other speakers. Had he still any marks of the ignoble world from which he sprang? Any defect of pronunciation, and native awkwardness of utterance? Impossible to judge himself infallibly, but he was conscious of no vulgar mannerism. . . .
>
> Heaven be thanked that he was unconcerned on the point of garb! Inferiority in that respect would have been fatal to his ease.[3]

Gissing was doomed to anxious monitoring of his own performance, while also striving to assert his intellectual superiority. No wonder he lacked ease! He did get a novel out of his encounter with the Gaussens; but he also got heart-sickness, a nervous breakdown, and a lesson about his exact place in English society. He was delighted to stay at a house built for Ann Boleyn, now held by a wealthy member of the country gentry. David Gaussen, the head of the family, was an Irish landowner of Huguenot descent, a lawyer who had never practised, a lazy man interested in little but hunting, shooting and fishing. His wife Elizabeth had adapted herself to life among the squirearchy, but her origins were more exotic. She was born in India to English parents, then adopted as a girl into the Apcar family, Armenians who had become the most powerful commercial dynasty in Calcutta.[4]

Mrs Gaussen struck Gissing as 'one of the most delightful women imaginable'.[5] She was thirty-eight when he met her, the mother of three sons and three daughters. Ellen, the eldest child, had just 'come out' as a debutante; she amused Gissing by dressing up as the famous Pre-Raphaelite beauty Jane Morris, who lived nearby at Kelmscott. Gissing was only nine years older than Ellen, but his romantic interest seized on her mother, who was eleven years older than him. When he made her into the heroine of his novel *Isabel Clarendon* she became a widow who had suffered from a hateful husband. For her part, Mrs Gaussen took a shine to the clever and sympathetic young man she had engaged, and set about improving his prospects. Gissing was asked to tutor her son James for five and a half hours a day, to get him ready for a public school. This would give Gissing an income of about six pounds a week, and more if he could squeeze in other pupils. To receive James in London he needed better lodgings, and within five days of returning to town he had taken two rooms off Hampstead Road, near Euston Station.[6] The rent was eleven shillings a week, which now he could easily afford.

Mrs Gaussen 'has utterly transformed my room', Gissing told his sister Ellen, 'new chairs, tables, lamps, flower-vases, cushions. . . . I have just had an etching of one of Rossetti's heads framed and hung.'[7] The head may have been of Jane Morris; it would help to create a soulful atmosphere to go with the new furniture. Gissing bought a new dress suit to help his climb up the social ladder. His only care was the usual grim burden of work. Apart from a full day of tutoring, he was revising 'Mrs Grundy's Enemies' at a great rate, in the hope of making it acceptable to George Bentley. The job was done in six weeks, by the 12th of October, and he felt that it was now 'six times as good as before'.[8]

Gissing was now free to resume work on his political novel, *Demos*. 'There will be nothing offensive in it,' he had said, back in June. He wanted to ensure that his future books would have a smoother path to publication than 'Mrs Grundy's Enemies'.[9] If he could get a conventional novel published on good terms, he could enter the drawing-rooms of Bayswater with confidence. He boasted to Algernon of his 'Astonishing accession of acquaintances of late', whom he had met thanks to the patronage of Mrs Gaussen.[10] A private tutor to the gentry, by definition a university man

with a classical education, would be assumed to have a good family background and have prospects of taking orders or getting a fellowship at
Oxford or Cambridge. Gissing's two published novels would add to his
standing, so long as no one actually read them and discovered their far
from genteel subject-matter.

But Gissing was never one to take good fortune in moderation. Instead
of returning to *Demos* and working-class London, he decided to write a
novel based on Mrs Gaussen and her family and friends. This was not a
prudent undertaking, and within a month of starting the book he had
plunged in deeper, by giving up his Rutland Street rooms and taking a
more expensive modern flat. Cornwall Residences (since demolished) was
at the top of Baker Street, near Regent's Park. Living there would nearly
double his housing costs, but for the first time in his life he would have a
home of his own: 'There is a sitting-room, bed-room, kitchen, pantry, &
W.C. – in fact a complete house. At last I shall be free from the thraldom
of landladies, &, what is more, be settled for a good long time. ... The
access of respectability will be enormous, & the comfort is really astonishing.'[11] Apart from the quality of the flat itself, Gissing was moving into
a better neighbourhood, closer to Bayswater, where Mrs Gaussen had her
London house. 'These places are quite aristocratic in character,' he told
Algernon. 'There are carriages at the door all day long.'[12] The great question is: how often did Mrs Gaussen come to the door, and for how long did
she stay?

Morley Roberts claimed that there were many visits, which did not
increase Gissing's respectability:

> A certain lady not without importance in society, the wife of a rich husband
> ... allowed her curiosity to overcome her discretion. She visited him very
> often in his chambers, and though he told me but little I gathered what the
> result was. ... This woman of the upper classes had come to him like a star,
> and had been a lamp in his darkness.[13]

The landlady at Rutland Street would surely not have tolerated such visits
to her lodger. James Gaussen said later that it was his mother who found
the flat for Gissing; perhaps she also advanced him the money for his lease
and moving costs? Was Gissing's talk about moving up in the world a
cover for his primary motive: to have a place where he and Mrs Gaussen
could be alone?

Pierre Coustillas calls Roberts an 'evil-tongued biographer' who made
'innuendos' about an affair for which there is no other evidence.[14] John

Halperin assumes that *Isabel Clarendon* can tell us what we need to know about any encounters at Cornwall Residences:

> Isabel Clarendon is an idealized version of Mrs Gaussen, fitted out with all the usual paraphernalia of Gissingesque wish-fulfilment applied to sexually unattainable women. The novelist was fond of tormenting himself with the proximity of superior women beyond his sexual reach, and for several years in the mid-eighties Mrs Gaussen was the chief of these.[15]

Roberts, the Victorian, takes it for granted that a woman who visits a man alone in his rooms has agreed to go to bed with him. Halperin, the contemporary critic, takes it for granted that Mrs Gaussen could not have gone to bed with Gissing because he was her social inferior. In their opposite ways, both views are simplistic. But what *did* happen at Gissing's flat, in bed or out of it?

No letters from Mrs Gaussen to Gissing have survived, and only two letters from him to her. They date from 1886 and 1888, and give no hint of intimacy with the recipient. But in 1885 Gissing had written to his sister Ellen: 'I want to remind you of the fact that [Mrs Gaussen's] letters are always subject to the possibility of being opened. No doubt you will bear that in mind when you write to her.'[16] The only person who might feel entitled to open her letters would be her husband (in *The Odd Women*, Monica Widdowson gets an accommodation address because she fears that her husband will read her letters). Mrs Gaussen would have been free to send letters to Gissing, so long as she posted them herself; but did he act like Bernard Kingcote in *Isabel Clarendon*, who burns all his letters from Isabel once he has decided that their affair is doomed?

Those who think there was no real affair can argue that Roberts lied in his book, or that Gissing lied to Roberts, by falsely taking credit for the conquest of a society lady. Nine years later, in *In the Year of Jubilee*, Gissing wrote about 'the rules' of how Victorian ladies and gentlemen might meet without chaperones. Lionel Tarrant receives a visit in his lodgings from Nancy Lord, to whom he is secretly married. After she has been there for several hours, she asks why no one ever knocks at the door. Because his male friends know better than to disturb him, Lionel says, unless they have an appointment. Nancy replies that she wouldn't like to be seen coming or going from the flat, because if one of his friends saw her, they would assume that she was a woman of easy virtue. Lionel gives her a lecture:

> 'Do you suppose for a moment that any friend of mine is ass enough to think with condemnation of a girl who should come to my rooms – whatever

the circumstances? You must get rid of that provincialism—. . . .'

'They wouldn't think it any harm – even if—?'

'My dear girl, we have outgrown those ancestral prejudices. . . . We have nothing to do with Mrs Grundy's morals.'[17]

Gissing might have boasted to Roberts that he had made a 'conquest' of Mrs Gaussen, and that his possession of a self-contained flat made it safe for her to visit him. But means, motive and opportunity do not necessarily add up to guilt.

Bernard Kingcote, the intellectual hero of *Isabel Clarendon*, encounters a woman dissatisfied with her empty upper-class life, and who is eager for love after having been mistreated and deceived by her late husband. She is the one who first declares her love to Kingcote. Mrs Gaussen's husband was still alive, but was often away in pursuit of fox or pheasant. Perhaps he had wounded her with infidelities.[18] If dissatisfaction with her husband caused her to want an adulterous affair, the sexual code of the day would almost compel Gissing to oblige her. No gentleman should humiliate a lady by refusing her favours once she has offered them.[19]

I am inclined to accept Morley Roberts's claim that Gissing and Mrs Gaussen had some kind of affair in the early months of 1885. The existence of *Isabel Clarendon* is strong evidence in itself that Gissing was deeply smitten by the beauty, charm and prestige of Mrs Gaussen. For the first half of the novel, Isabel is an ideal figure, seen from afar. We hear of her wounds from a difficult marriage, and of her awkward relations with her late husband's illegitimate daughter, Ada Warren. Bernard Kingcote, a man not unlike Gissing, has taken a cottage in Isabel's neighbourhood, where he leads a quiet, scholarly life. Then Isabel suddenly makes a declaration of love to him. If art followed life, Gissing wrote those pages around January 1885, when he was in his first month of possession at Cornwall Residences, and Mrs Gaussen was helping him with his furniture and decoration. In the novel, Kingcote is at first filled with delight at Isabel's love for him, but he soon retreats into jealousy and complaints. He cannot bear Isabel's society friends, or the society manners that she affects even when they are alone: 'She was impulsively affectionate, but there was an absence in her manner, a shade of intermittence in her attention, a personal restlessness, an almost flippancy in her talk at times, which kept him uneasy. The atmosphere of the town and of the season was about her.' Kingcote realises that Isabel loves him, but he cannot love wholeheartedly in return because he is possessed by a spirit of disapproval. He recognises where this comes from: 'a certain stiffness of moral attitude derived from his mother. His prejudices were intense, their character being determined by the refinement and idealism of his nature.'[20]

Kingcote suffers from Gissing's own social and moral dilemma. The lower middle class wants to be accepted by the more leisured classes above it; at the same time, it feels morally superior to them. It wants to climb the social ladder but, once arrived, it fears being seduced away from its original values. What the lower middle class has achieved through hard work and self-denial, its superiors enjoy as a birthright. Unable to tolerate Isabel's sense of privilege, Kingcote suppresses his love for her. Isabel cannot soften his disapproval, and eventually marries someone of her own class. Kingcote is left isolated, though with some hope of marrying Ada Warren, his social equal. Yet he fears that his sense of being superior to Isabel is a sham, since what she really wants from him is superiority of a different kind:

> She . . . longed to arouse in him the energy which should make her subject. A woman cannot be swayed against her instincts by mere entreaty, but she will bow beneath the hand that she loves. Had he adored her less completely, had the brute impulse of domination been stronger in him, his power and her constancy could have defied circumstances. But he would not lay on her the yoke for which her neck was bowed in joyful trembling.[21]

The Victorian male has a Darwinian duty to overpower his mate. In passages like this, Gissing steps out of his novelistic character and simply preaches a doctrine, yet one that he also turns against himself. By Darwin's law, he seems to be a failure. One might even read the passage as a veiled confession that when Mrs Gaussen took him as a lover he found himself impotent.[22] Certainly he could not enter an affair just for the pleasure of it. H. G. Wells put it this way: 'Poor Gissing. He thought there was a difference between a woman and a lady. There isn't, you know, there isn't.[23]

In *Isabel Clarendon*, Kingcote's failure with Isabel is entirely due to his internal conflicts. Her husband has died, and she is free to marry her lover. In real life, Mrs Gaussen had a husband, six children, and a social position that she would have lost for ever if she ran off with her son's tutor. She could only have lived with Gissing in France or Italy; had she done so, the English courts would have forbidden any further contact with her children. Nor could Gissing marry her, because he was married already and had no hope of being able to divorce Nell.

By the time Gissing was introduced to Mrs Gaussen he had told Harrison about his imprisonment and his attempt to divorce Nell after she was raped in 1883. It is unlikely that Mrs Gaussen would have been able to accept the knowledge that Gissing was secretly married to a prostitute. Since she continued to be friendly with him for some years, most likely she never knew of Nell's existence, hidden away in her slum room. Yet Gissing was living a lie by mixing with society people and tutoring their children, when Nell could turn up at his flat and expose him at any time. Mrs Gaussen may have felt that Gissing rejected her love, as Kingcote does in *Isabel Clarendon*, when in fact he was first of all afraid to reveal himself to her. He could not be truly close to any woman so long as the threat of his secret marriage hung over him.

By the end of *Isabel Clarendon*, being Isabel's lover has literally made Kingcote into a sick man:

> It was nothing less than an illness which fell upon him, an illness of the nerves and the imagination. There were intermissions of suffering, mostly the results of exhaustion; his torment rose to the point at which a mental catastrophe seemed imminent, then came a period of languor, in which he resumed strength to suffer again. Later, these three months became all but a blank in his memory.[24]

Gissing's own crisis came in March 1885, while he was writing the last pages of the novel. Mrs Gaussen's son James came to stay with him, sharing the flat's single bedroom. After the day's lessons, James went to bed and Gissing took up work on his novel. One night, James heard noises from the bathroom:

> I woke with a start and with horror saw him standing in front of the mirror in the act of cutting his throat with a razor. I called out 'Mr Gissing! Mr Gissing!' and he closed the razor and handed it over to me, saying:- 'Boy, boy. Keep it safely.' Next morning I slipped the razor quietly onto his table.[25]

All that Gissing told Algernon was: 'I have been in a sadly dyspeptic state of late; it threatens to become chronic. Yesterday I went to see a doctor about it, a man to whom Mrs Gaussen recommended me.'[26] Dyspepsia for a Victorian meant primarily depression, along with digestive troubles and insomnia. When Gissing used the term he was admitting to a full-blown nervous breakdown. That he found himself in such a state is evidence of his passionate and thwarted feelings towards Mrs Gaussen.

Whatever the state of his nerves, Gissing finished *Isabel Clarendon* on 26 March and sent it off to Chapman & Hall. While he was waiting for their verdict, he tried to launch his sister Ellen on the world. She was eighteen, intelligent, sympathetic, and quite pretty. Gissing brought her up to London for two weeks at the end of May 1885, staying for the first week with him and for the second with Mrs Gaussen in Bayswater. She had to buy an evening dress, and received much nervous coaching from her brother. Mrs Gaussen was kind and Ellen greatly enjoyed herself; but the people she met would have immediately sniffed out her provincial background, and also have seen where Gissing himself came from. No gentleman suitor attached himself to Ellen, and she went back alone to Wakefield to feed on her memories. Gissing could only imagine a different outcome for her through creating the character of Emily Hood in *A Life's Morning*.

Gissing himself was finding social life at the Gaussens' a terrible strain. He needed to do seven hours of teaching a day to cover the increased expenses of his new flat. When he was called away to dinners or concerts by Mrs Gaussen he was tormented by thoughts of the work he was not doing. To keep on writing novels was his only hope of escape from poverty and obscurity. Authorship was the one ladder he could climb; but until he *did* climb it, he was simply driving himself to the point of exhaustion, night after night, for little reward. In addition, the more Gissing saw of Mrs Gaussen's friends, the less he liked them. This started with an outburst against the Harrisons, at the end of January 1885: 'I fancy intercourse with the Harrisons is as good as over. Nor could it well be otherwise, we were so little akin. I never met more conventional people than those, in the purely social matters. ... Of course such an attitude is incompatible with any real interest in one of my views: to them I am an enemy of society, & no more.'[27] Frederic Harrison's distaste for *The Unclassed* was still rankling with Gissing. When he began writing *Isabel Clarendon*, he was still infatuated with upper-middle-class society, and with Mrs Gaussen as its female embodiment. But as the novel progressed he showed Kingcote becoming bitterly critical of Isabel's world and, by contagion, of Isabel herself. At the end, Kingcote even returns contentedly to a life that was Gissing's own point of departure: he becomes a shopkeeper in a provincial town. But that was no plausible solution for Gissing himself.

Chapman took more than two months to give Gissing an answer on *Isabel Clarendon*. Finally, in early June 1885, he told Gissing that his reader, George Meredith, suggested that it be cut down into two volumes rather than three. Gissing readily agreed. He started to revise the manuscript on 15 June, and finished on 9 August:

Chapman tells me he much prefers two vols., and one vol. is becoming commonest of all. It is the new school, due to continental influence. Thackeray and Dickens wrote at enormous length, and with profusion of detail; their plan is to tell everything, to leave nothing to be divined. Far more artistic, I think, is this later method, of merely suggesting; of dealing with

episodes, instead of writing biographies. The old novelist is omniscient; I
think it is better to tell a story precisely as one does in real life, – hinting,
surmising, telling in detail what *can* so be told, and no more. In fact, it
approximates to the dramatic mode of presentment.[28]

The three-decker did not die so easily; it held on for about ten more years.
But Gissing cut *Isabel Clarendon* down to about 125,000 words, some 50,000
less than a standard three-decker.

Even the task of cutting and restructuring the novel brought Gissing
close to another fit of despair:

> I have all but made up my mind to give up this fruitless struggle & misery
> ... & go again to America, where it is possible I might get literary work,
> though I had rather end all that & work in a healthy way on a farm. .... The
> fact is that this kind of life is too hard, I can't endure it. I grow more and
> more low-spirited & incapable of continued work. Suddenly in the middle
> of writing I am attacked by a fearful fit of melancholy, & the pen drops; I
> get nothing done. For hours I walk round & round the room & sicken with
> need of some kind of variety in my life.[29]

Eduard Bertz had gone to America to be a farmer in 1881, but had succeeded
only in bankrupting himself. Morley Roberts, Gissing's other close friend,
was now driving spikes on the Canadian Pacific Railway in the mountains
of British Columbia. Gissing still had enough common sense to know that
he could never do such work. America had no attraction for him, except
that if he went there he would no longer be hemmed in by relationships that
wore him down. His brother Algernon was a constant drain on Gissing's
nervous energy, as he either failed to get a job, or failed at the job once he got
it. Gissing told Algernon that although Eduard Bertz was full of schemes, 'It
is as deadly certain as fate that he will never do anything at all, but I suppose
he cannot see that. There are certain men of whom one predicts that with
terrible security.'[30] He could not say it outright, but knew that his brother
was moving towards a similar fate.

At the beginning of July, Gissing told Algernon he would see very little
of Mrs Gaussen from now on. She had forty people to lunch one day, and
thirty-five the day after, for the Oxford and Cambridge cricket match. He
could not feel special in her eyes when he was only one among so many.
Later that month he gave her the first volume of the revised *Isabel Clarendon*
to read in manuscript. She was on the point of giving up the lease of her
London house and going to live permanently in the Cotswolds at Broughton Hall. No direct evidence has survived of her response to the novel. 'I
believe she really thinks the novel very poor,' Gissing told Ellen, '*but* of

course she would not say so.'[31] She must surely have found the novel embarrassing, with its thinly disguised and worshipful portrait of her as Isabel. The more she had opened herself to Gissing in real life, the more the novel would have been an unwelcome gift.

When Mrs Gaussen went off to the country at the end of the 'season', Gissing no longer had to deal with the conflict of trying to fit into an upper-class society that he secretly despised. He had no pupils for the moment, just the daily appointment with the blank page. 'I do not go out,' he told Algernon, '& have nothing to tell. ... Regularity of work has a singular way of making time at the same time long and short. The days go by with amazing rapidity.'[32] In completing *Isabel Clarendon* he spoke to no one for three weeks, except for shopkeepers and his daily help. 'Yesterday I wrote for nine hours and at last in that peculiar excitement in which one cannot see the paper and pen, but only the words. I kept choking, and had my eyes painfully moist. I don't think the result of this can be worthless.'[33]

What enraptured Gissing was the next-to-last chapter of the novel. Ada Warren is jilted by the worthless Vincent Lacour. Instead of being heart-broken, she goes off to the country and is mystically transformed into a passionate beauty who plans to become a writer. Just over the horizon lies a romance with Kingcote, who has left Isabel behind. If Gissing was in tears as he wrote this, some deep fantasy was working within him. Kingcote renounces Isabel in favour of a woman who seems to be a projection of Gissing himself: a social misfit, a lover of nature, wounded by the lack of a father, confident of a renewed literary vocation. He no longer yearns for an upper-class beloved, but for a woman like himself. Together Kingcote and Ada could hold out against conventional society, supported by Ada's income of £300 a year from her father's estate. With that security, Kingcote can return happily to his origins, and become a bookseller in Norwich.

The roots of the Gissing family were in East Anglia, so Kingcote's flight there was a significant detail. When Gissing was welcomed into Mrs Gaussen's circle it was seven years since his return to England, as a penniless young man with a criminal record. He had climbed the social ladder almost to the top, only to feel wretched and insecure once he arrived. *Isabel Clarendon* was a fantasy of achieving sexual and social success, then giving it up. The new fantasy with which the novel ended should have been something within Gissing's reach: to achieve a settled life in the provinces, with a cultured young woman of his own class as a partner. But the free-thinking Ada Warren was an exception; Gissing's sisters were closer to the true provincial type, with their piety and sexual repression. Nor could

Gissing expect to share his life with any respectable young woman, so long as he remained married to Nell.

Algernon Gissing's engagement illustrated the sexual politics of his milieu. He fell in love with Catherine Baseley, the daughter of a Southampton hosier, in 1884. Her uncle and aunt lived in Wakefield and she had spent much of her childhood with them. Catherine's family had serious misgivings about Algernon as a suitor: he had not been able to settle into a steady job, and showed signs of agnosticism. Eventually they accepted him, and the couple were able to marry three years later. But George remained unable to find companionship in London with a young woman whose position resembled his own: someone intellectual, emancipated, and rising in the world through education or creative work. These 'new women' were appearing here and there, and would be recognised as a distinct social type by the 1890s. Gissing would brush shoulders with them at the British Museum reading room, at lectures or concerts, or browsing at second-hand bookstalls. They would figure prominently in his novels, young women like Marian Yule in *New Grub Street* or Rhoda Nunn in *The Odd Women*. Some of them, living away from their families in London, might have been willing to enter a 'free union' with Gissing, or at least to visit him alone in his flat. Why were Gissing's sexual interests always aimed either below or above the social level where he himself lived? He might have suffered much less from loneliness and sexual deprivation if he had chosen women whose status was closer to his own. But such women seemed to have little appeal for him. They had neither the coarse sexuality of a work-girl nor the glamour of a society lady. Another hindrance was his difficulty in seeing any woman as his equal; or, more precisely, if he had an equal relation – with Clara Collet, for example – it seemed to exclude a romantic attachment.

Gissing's infatuation with Mrs Gaussen, whether or not it included a sexual affair, lasted only a year. He had no regular partner, and perhaps no sexual fulfilment at all, for five full years after the completion of *Isabel Clarendon*. When he did find someone, in 1890, it would be a woman of low status and with no intellectual interests. Apart from his general awkwardness with women, there was always a sense in which his true partner was not another person, but his writing-desk. One sees this devotion to the task in his advice to Algernon:

> I cannot say how strongly I would dissuade from any abrupt change of occupation; it is almost always the case that men whose lives turn out failures date the beginning of failure from some such abrupt departure. One loses hold of life, and becomes a waif. My own unspeakable sufferings are largely due to the fact of my never having had a beginning in life, such as you have;

with but one foot on the lowest rung of the ladder, I could have risen to something definite. To cast oneself afloat is madness, only possible indeed to one utterly lacking experience of the hardships of a sundered lot.[34]

It was not just professional failure that Gissing feared; worse was the loss of connection that came with the 'sundered lot'. To call his sufferings unspeakable had a literal sense: he might go for weeks without exchanging a word of friendship with anyone. There was the brute fact of failure, and then the further torture of feeling it locked up within one's breast, unspoken, unshared.

The remedy for dangerous impulses, and the only way to find safety in an indifferent world, was the path of discipline:

> Often and often I am tempted to read a book instead of writing my day's chapter, and the only thing that helps me is the recollection that only perfect regularity bears results, that what is not done to-day only becomes an extra burden for to-morrow, that there is immense satisfaction in a task accomplished, and, lastly, that it is just the missing of odd days which makes the difference between attaining your end in time and arriving too late.[35]

Gissing saw being a writer as in essence a problem of production, in the narrowest sense of being able to meet a self-imposed quota of words. He rarely speaks of inspiration as a problem; nor, as he writes, does he concern himself with how his words may be received by his readers. When he started to write *Isabel Clarendon* it never seemed to occur to him that a novel about romantic infatuation should be produced in any different way from his two previous works, *The Unclassed* and 'Mrs Grundy's Enemies'. There was no need to read love sonnets or wander in a daze by the river. The task was the same as usual, to fill up his quota of blank sheets. At this point in his career, Gissing paid little attention to the terms on which his books were published, and he did not even read his reviews if he could avoid them. The production of the book was his real task, in the teeth of hardship or the temptation to shirk each day's duty. To come up to scratch was enough, and he was remarkably untroubled by Chapman & Hall's refusal to publish 'Mrs Grundy's Enemies'. At the same time, he recognised the difficulties brought upon him by his peculiar sense of the writing profession. In five years' time he would produce the definitive account of every writer's difficulties, in *New Grub Street*.

Gissing finished his revision of *Isabel Clarendon* on 9 August 1885, and started his next novel two days later. The setting of *A Life's Morning* was the Wakefield of his youth.[36] Critical opinion has not been kind to the novel, sometimes even writing it off as one of Gissing's pot-boilers. This is unfair. It was written very quickly – in less than three months – but this was because Gissing was so excited with the idea of revisiting his early years, and describing a familiar town and countryside. Even so, he approached the issues of his youth indirectly, without giving the novel a male protagonist who represented his own experiences. That would come later, with *Born in Exile*. Gissing was still working on his encounter with Mrs Gaussen and her social world. *A Life's Morning* traces the path from the provincial lower middle class to higher levels of society, and from north to south. The novel's hero, Wilfred Athel, is loosely based on William Summers, Gissing's wealthy friend from Owens College. Like Summers, Athel goes to Oxford and becomes an MP. He has to choose between Beatrice Redwing, who comes from his own class, and Emily Hood, an idealistic lower-middle-class governess. Emily is a projection of Gissing's concern about his sisters, especially Ellen, whom he had tried to launch in London society. In the novel as he wrote it, Emily both succeeds and fails: she wins the love of Wilfred, but dies before her wedding day. Gissing was indignant later when his publisher insisted that Emily had to survive.

A Life's Morning also had a characteristic subplot that allowed Gissing to tiptoe around his own brush with crime. Emily's father is a clerk who finds a ten-pound note in his employer's files, money that was put there on purpose to tempt him. Before he can return the money he loses his hat, and must get a new one so that he can deliver a message to another company in respectable style. Then he runs into a needy old friend and lends him a pound. When his employer accuses him of holding back the money and dismisses him, Mr Hood kills himself. Gissing could not speak plainly of how Nell had made him a thief. What he could speak of was how law and conventional morality could crush a decent man, one who firmly believed in the rules that destroyed him.

When he met Mrs Gaussen, in August 1884, Gissing had been a writer for eight years and had written at least a million words of fiction, financially at a net loss. Although 1885 was a disappointing year for his personal life, his relation with Mrs Gaussen began a period that brought the first signs of critical and financial success. The writing of *Isabel Clarendon* and *A Life's Morning* occupied Gissing from October 1884 to November 1885. Once he had finished the books, he was largely finished with Mrs Gaussen, and he reverted to making his writing the sole focus of his existence. Nonetheless, breaking with her meant the return of Gissing's old agony, solitude. He was caught between the failure of his relationships with Nell and Mrs Gaussen, and the failure of having no relationship at all:

London is deserted; only some three million and a half people remain to await the coming of next season. All the houses round Regent's Park are shut up, and the sight of the darkened windows does not make one cheerful. I myself live in utter solitude; it is more than three weeks since I opened my lips to speak to anyone but the servant. This is a dolorous state of things, and I fear is likely to last till October, when my pupil will come back again.[37]

Morley Roberts had been away in the US since the spring of 1884, and Eduard Bertz had gone back to Germany around the same time. Gissing had not found any close companions to replace them, and he always needed male friendships as a respite from his inevitable troubles with women.

Gissing had almost finished *A Life's Morning* when he received George Meredith's opinion of the revised *Isabel Clarendon*. 'Meredith tells me I am making a great mistake,' Gissing told Algernon, 'in leaving the low-life scenes; says I might take a foremost place in fiction if I pursued that. Well, the next will in some degrees revert to that, though it will altogether keep clear of matter which people find distasteful. I shall call it *Demos* and it will be rather a savage satire on working-class aims and capacities.'[38] Meredith clearly preferred the East End slums of *The Unclassed* to Kingcote's country cottage in *Isabel Clarendon*. Gissing had tried to write more respectable novels after the abuse directed against him for his treatment of prostitution in *The Unclassed*, and Bentley's squeamishness about 'Mrs Grundy's Enemies'. His family and his patron Frederic Harrison had scolded him too. Now Meredith was telling him to return his fiction to the underworld.

Meredith's opinion that *Isabel Clarendon* was a wrong turn in Gissing's career cannot have raised his stock at Chapman & Hall; but Frederic Chapman needed no outside help to do his worst by his authors. Known as 'the liar' in the trade, Chapman had offered £50 for *The Unclassed*, then brazenly sent a cheque for £30. Now he told Gissing that he would publish *Isabel Clarendon* on the half-profit system, which meant no profit for the author. Gissing extracted a promise from Chapman that he would get £15 on publication, but apparently even this was not paid. In the end, Gissing got nothing at all. At least he had enough sense to send the manuscript of *A Life's Morning* to a different publisher, Smith, Elder. Within three weeks he had a firm offer of £50 from their reader, James Payn. Soon another £50 was promised, for periodical rights in *The Cornhill Magazine*. One hundred pounds for three months' work was a much better reward than for any of Gissing's previous efforts. Smith, Elder would become Gissing's bread-and-butter publisher for a while, though the butter would always be thinly spread.

In writing *Isabel Clarendon* and *A Life's Morning*, Gissing had hoped to turn out a safer product than *The Unclassed:*

> You misunderstand Meredith. He merely urges me to keep to low life, which is of course open to any man, though certainly it is difficult to treat it with the amazing laws which govern literature in England. Alas, alas, if one had been born a Frenchman! They alone understand the dignity and the claims of art.[39]

When Gissing wrote this letter, Bentley had had the revised manuscript of 'Mrs Grundy's Enemies' for more than a year. Gissing rightly feared that the novel would never appear, though parts of it had been set in type nearly three years ago. What if he became labelled an indecent writer, so that future novels faced the same fate? Even if he followed Meredith's advice, he faced the problem that *Workers in the Dawn* and *The Unclassed* were frankly autobiographical novels, which placed their author in a milieu that he now wanted to leave behind him. If he had to return to the lower depths, he needed to view them from a safer perspective. Gissing's solution was to map out the territories where the working-class world was being infiltrated by the classes above them. Philanthropy and socialism were the motives behind these intrusions. Gissing wanted to show that life in the slums could not easily be changed by the good intentions of outsiders. Further, he believed that the workers had their own forms of resistance and their own pleasures, which the reformers would do well to leave alone. His return to low life would be on his own terms, different from almost anyone else who was trying to write novels of protest.

5

Low Life

A week after Gissing started to write *Demos*, Algernon moved into Cornwall Residences, on 11 December 1885. Gissing was amused by the differences between them: 'With him the *first* idea is domestic comfort; with
me it is a matter of indifference, freedom to work being everything. He
does not as yet know what real hard work means, and I fear such work as
I have to do would make him ill.'[1] If work didn't sicken Algernon, Gissing's
awful cooking could have done the job. 'I get tinned meat,' he reported to
Wakefield, 'and mess it up with potatoes which I cannot trouble to peel.
The flavour is rather fishy, but it satisfies appetite, and a dinner of this kind
only costs a little more than sixpence.' This might be followed by 'amateur
pudding', a Gissing invention made by putting bread in a saucepan, boiling
it with condensed milk, and putting jam on the result. There were also
experiments with vegetarianism, which saved money and also provided a
better fuel to work on. Less time for cooking meant more time for writing;
and the more cheaply Gissing could live the less teaching he had to do.
Algernon was expected to live on the same regime while he studied for the
Civil Service exam. That two could live more cheaply than one was part of
the plan, except that this was true only if Algernon had an income to pay
his share, and there was no sign of that.

Gissing did find money to furnish a study for Algernon in the flat, with
a new carpet, bookcases and pictures. The brothers would live together for
more than a year, without any real quarrels. Algernon studied fitfully and
also tried his hand at writing a three-decker novel, called 'A Dinner of
Herbs'. The Civil Service exam would not be passed, and the novel would
not be published, though not because of any lack of support from George.
He had considered himself the head of his family since he was thirteen and
did everything he could, without complaint, to get his brother and his
sisters launched on the world. In addition, a pound a week had to go to
Nell. When Algernon eventually left, Gissing felt relieved that he had one
less burden to carry. 'I have felt very great difficulty in doing good work

during the past year,' he would tell Ellen, 'though I have never liked to admit it: it is a strange thing that I require solitude in order to get on well.'[2]

Demos was Gissing's first truly political novel, where he considered the social question in a systematic way, rather than just testifying to his own fall into poverty. He had shown a little group of radicals around Mr Tolladay, the socialist printer of *Workers in the Dawn*, but they were either Tolstoyan figures of simple benevolence or embittered cranks. It was not credible that such people were fit to exercise power. *The Unclassed* also focused on individual acts of generosity: its idea of social reform was that Mr Woodstock should decide to be a more generous landlord. In both novels, Gissing remained in the moral universe he inherited from Dickens, keeping to a pre-ideological vision of England's social problems.

By 1885, Gissing's relations with Mrs Gaussen had given him a lesson on his position in the class hierarchy, or rather his lack of position. Since his college days he had been pushed far down the ladder of class through his liaison with Nell. Frederic Harrison had done a great deal to restore Gissing's status, and Mrs Gaussen had given him a further boost. But he was still handicapped by his prison record, his marriage to Nell, and the failure of his novels to sell decently. It was much easier to rise in the world if one had a wife who was socially presentable and who provided emotional support. Gissing knew well the close ties between marriage and ambition, but *Isabel Clarendon*, *New Grub Street* and *Born in Exile* all showed how a failed relationship could lead to failure on every other front, and even to death. Gissing's personal experience also made him cynical about the working-class ideal of solidarity. Middle-class reformers might boast that they stood shoulder to shoulder with the workers; Gissing knew what it meant to lie side by side with one. Nell was a dead weight on her husband's aspirations. Gissing had to console himself with the fantasy of *The Unclassed*, where Ida transforms herself, through education, from a girl of the streets to a genteel wife.

Another kind of stake in social reform came from Gissing's poverty. Being culturally eligible to join the middle class meant little if one didn't have the necessary income. His novels had never brought in much money. He was a successful tutor, but the most he could make in this way was five or six pounds a week, and when his pupils went on holiday they didn't pay. In a good year Gissing might make a bit more than £200 a year from all sources. He now had fixed expenses of £50 a year for Nell and £50 for his rent and the daily cleaner. That left about £100 a year for food, clothing, books and everything else. If he took fewer pupils his literary career might go on faster, but there was no guarantee that he would make more money by it. With his very small disposable income, Gissing was holding on to respectability with his fingertips. He could keep up a middle-class façade only by eating the cheapest food and hiding in his flat for most of the time. He was trapped in a particularly English kind of shabby-genteel poverty. Culturally he could put up an impressive front; economically he was less secure than any skilled working man with a regular job. He was well aware of how the scholarship system had produced a new, uneasy class of social misfits. His experience had also cut off any line of retreat. Though he retained some core lower-middle-class values, he could never return to a settled provincial existence, or to the sexual repression and narrow piety that his sisters had embraced. Within the British class system, Gissing was like a stateless person; for the rest of his life he would dream of finding a home, and know that a dream was all it could be.

Much critical ink has been spilled over the exact politics of Gissing's 'proletarian' novels, from *Workers in the Dawn* to *The Nether World*. For a biographer, these discussions are largely beside the point. Gissing's politics were rooted in his immediate personal situation; he cared little for political philosophies beyond what he himself had seen and suffered. He firmly believed that for the social question there could only be individual solutions; and believed just as firmly that for most people there was not going to be any solution. For his own problem, the solution was to have a private income that would make him independent of the world's 'beastly scrimmage', as Lionel Tarrant calls it in *In the Year of Jubilee*. If he could ever achieve that, he would retire to the English countryside to live cosily and read the classics. Gissing anticipated the Bloomsbury ethic of seeing money as no more than a means. The valuable ends were leisure, modest comfort, and cultural pleasures. He had little interest in progress for its own sake, still less in Britain's ambition for world power. The sufferings of poor people touched him, but he believed that most of them were not capable of living on a higher plane than what they were used to.

Gissing's explicitly political phase, beginning with *Demos*, can be framed as a debate with William Morris. He admired both Morris's poetry and the values of the Arts and Crafts movement.[3] When Morris began his political agitation, Gissing saw it at first as a kind of conservatism:

> I would make a chief point of the necessary union between beauty in life and social reform. Ruskin despairs of the latter, and so can only look on bygone times. Younger men (like W. Morris) are turning from artistic work to social agitation, just because they fear that art will be crushed out of the world as things are.[4]

Still, Gissing wondered whether struggling to improve the condition of the poor would do anything for art and beauty. Not only that, would those who were capable of creating beauty be improved by entering the struggle, and taking on the daily grind of political propaganda? 'I grieve to see Morris in the companionship of Secular Review,' Gissing told Algernon, 'and of men like Ingersoll and the rest. It is deplorable. I confess I get more and more aristocratic in my leanings, and cannot excuse faults of manner in consideration of the end.'[5] He was distressed to see Morris descending into the twilight zone of cranks and half-educated devotees of absolute causes.

When Morris joined the socialist Democratic Federation in 1883 it had only about two hundred members. Its leader was H. M. Hyndman, who came from a wealthy family and went to Trinity College, Cambridge. But most of the rank and file were closer to Edward Pease's description: 'characteristically democratic men with dirty hands and small heads, some of them obviously with very limited wits, and mostly with some sort of foreign accent'.[6] This did not prevent Pease joining their cause, even though he was a stockbroker. Hyndman, Morris and Pease were all upper-class idealists who believed that a revolution was at hand, never mind how unpromising their fellow recruits might appear. In Morris's poem 'The Pilgrims of Hope', he describes how a short, shabbily dressed worker welcomes him to the movement:

> He spoke like a friend long known; and lo! I was one of the band.
> And now the streets seem gay and the high stars glittering bright;
> And for me, I sing amongst them, for my heart is full and light.
> I see the deeds to be done and the day to come on the earth,
> And riches vanished away, and sorrow turned to mirth;
> I see the city squalor and the country stupor gone.[7]

For Morris this was like a religious conversion, and he called himself 'born again' into the revolutionary cause. He was possessed by a dream of fellowship with the workers, who appeared to him as types rather than individuals. Their particular failings or differences of outlook scarcely counted for Morris, or for others like him. Gissing, on the other hand, was well acquainted with the mixture of characters to be found in the slums; he also had the lower-middle-class concern to distinguish between the poor who were worthy and those who were not. It is precisely his eye for difference that enlivens his brilliant account of the socialist meeting in chapter 6 of Demos.

Another divergence from middle-class radicalism lay in Gissing's

instinctive support for law and order. This was not because he identified
with state power, but because he hated any kind of physical violence. He
was not impressed by William Morris's arrest in September 1885:

> Do you see the report of the row the Socialists have had with the police in
> the East End? Think of William Morris being hauled into the box for
> assaulting a policeman! ... alas, what the devil is such a man doing in that
> galley? It is painful to me beyond expression. Why cannot he write poetry
> in the shade? He will inevitably coarsen himself in the company of ruffians.
>
> Keep apart, keep apart, and preserve one's soul alive, – that is the teaching
> for the day. It is ill to have been born in these times, but one can make a
> world within the world.[8]

Anyone who descended into the streets of the East End, Gissing felt, would
be defiled. To do so was to contradict what Morris himself had preached in
bygone years, for example in *The Earthly Paradise:*

> *Forget six counties overhung with smoke,*
> *Forget the snorting steam and piston stroke,*
> *Forget the spreading of the hideous town;*
> *Think rather of the pack-horse on the down,*
> *And dream of London, small, and white, and clean,*
> *The clear Thames bordered by its gardens green*

No political movement could order its followers to forget and to dream.
Morris was able to produce art, so he should preserve the conditions that
allowed him to do so. He should leave politics to those who were coarse
enough to succeed at it. Contact with the London masses could only bring
Morris down to their level; he had no chance of raising them into the higher
life of culture.

As he started *Demos*, Gissing was absorbing another great poet's view
of the political realm. He was teaching himself Italian by working through
Dante's *Divine Comedy* at the rate of a canto a day. The political lesson of
the poem seemed to be that the superior man must expect isolation and
betrayal; he could only take revenge through a work of his imagination.
Exile was a benefit to the poet, if not to the man, because one had to separate
oneself from the political arena in order to pass judgement on it. When
Gissing said that he had 'gained a new sense, a new power' from reading the
Inferno, this confidence carried through to his writing of *Demos*.[9] However,
Dante was hardly the right model for 'writing poetry in the shade'. The
Divine Comedy came out of Dante's furious obsession with the Florence
that had rejected him. If Gissing really believed in 'writing in the shade' he

would not have written his own bitter novels. Nor did he believe in Morris's medievalism, that society should return to artisan modes of production and an organic sense of community. In any case, his disposition was that of a novelist, whereas Morris and, later, Hilaire Belloc and G. K. Chesterton were all drawn to forms based on the romance. Gissing's method in *Demos* was to show how various individuals reacted to the social crisis of the 1880s, according to their different class positions and intellectual histories. One of these characters, Mr Wyvern the vicar, seems closest to Gissing's own views; but even Wyvern changes from leftism to quietism in response to his personal experiences.

In 1884–5 Gissing was deeply impressed by the riots in the West End and the rise of socialism, but from the perspective of the interaction between mass phenomena and individual choice. The ideal place to observe this was the political meeting, from huge gatherings in Trafalgar Square to a handful of zealots meeting in private. The small meetings interested him most, revealing politics at the most personal scale. In November 1885, when Gissing was already well started on *Demos*, he went to a meeting at William Morris's London residence, Kelmscott House:

> The arrangement is this: there is a shed next to the house, and this is the meeting place of the Hammersmith branch of the League. Positively I felt *en plein roman*. There was Miss Morris – the secretary of the Branch – talking familiarly with working men. She is astonishingly handsome, pure Greek profile, with hair short on her neck; wore a long dark fur-trimmed cloak, and Tam O'Shanter cap of velvet. Unmistakeably like her mother, – the origin of Rossetti's best type.[10]

The shed was a former coach-house, later a workshop where young women sat knitting Morris's 'Hammersmith Carpets'. It was a long, narrow room with seats for about a hundred people; rough tapestries and pictures covered the walls. The centre of Gissing's attention, evidently, was not Morris and his lecture, but his twenty-three-year-old daughter May. When Gissing used the French phrase to say that he felt he was in the middle of a novel, this was literally true. He immediately started to write May Morris into *Demos:* not as the daughter of Mr Westlake (the William Morris figure) but as his wife:

> In listening to anything that held her attention her eyes grew large, and their dark orbs seemed to dream passionately. The white swan's down at her throat – she was perfectly attired – made the skin above resemble rich-hued marble, and indeed to gaze at her long was to be impressed as by the sad loveliness of a supreme work of art.[11]

Later, the narrator says that Mrs Westlake's eyes 'dreamed against a distant goal'. This was a quotation from Rossetti's sonnet-sequence *The House of Life*, love poems inspired by both his own wife and Morris's wife Janey. No doubt Gissing was romanticising the revolutionary struggle; but he was using *Demos* as a projection of his personal history, where his longing for love and a home had encountered the harsh realities of Victorian society.

An intriguing question about Gissing's interest in William Morris and his family was how much he knew about the Pre-Raphaelite choice of lower-class women as objects of desire. Morris had met his wife in 1857 as an artist's model in Oxford. She was the daughter of a stable hand and of a mother who could not sign her own name. Rossetti's Lizzie Siddal was probably a shop-girl when he discovered her, and Ford Madox Brown married the illiterate daughter of a farmer. Holman Hunt fell in love with a barmaid and paid for her to have lessons in elocution and deportment.[12] When Morris, Rossetti and Burne-Jones lived together at Red Lion Square they made their house a refuge for prostitutes; Rossetti also took a former prostitute, Fanny Cornforth, as his mistress and model, and wrote the poem 'Jenny' about a prostitute. Why did none of these amours end in shipwreck, when Gissing's relations with Nell Harrison and Edith Underwood ruined his life? The Pre-Raphaelite women had the kind of beauty that made them celebrities, with power and status in their own right. More important, the Pre-Raphaelite men, unlike Gissing, were already established in the middle class or higher, so that they could marry beneath themselves with relative safety. Gissing's class position, and his finances, were already so shaky that an unpresentable wife tipped the balance against him. He also made the mistake of taking the Pre-Raphaelite myth too much to heart. He kept a romantic view of Nell, and tried to educate her, long after it should have been obvious that there was no hope for their marriage. The Pre-Raphaelites loved within their means; Gissing always loved beyond them.

Gissing mistrusted alliances between aspiring workers and conscience-stricken middle-class intellectuals. In *Demos* Richard Mutimer stands for the first class, Mr Westlake for the second. Mutimer's grandfather was a Chartist agitator, killed in the Midland riots of 1842; his grand-uncle an 'iron-willed' capitalist who 'early discerned the truth that a man's first object must be to secure himself a competency, seeing that to one who lacks money the world is but a great debtors' prison'.[13] Mutimer inclines to the workers' cause, and becomes a leader when his speech goes over well at a socialist meeting. Such private motives are central to Gissing's idea of politics. Alfred Waltham, for example, is a businessman–Radical who 'hated the aristocratic order of things with a rabid hatred. . . . Never trust

the thoroughness of the man who is a revolutionist on abstract principles;
personal feeling alone goes to the root of the matter.' Westlake's radicalism,
similarly, comes from his passion for his wife: 'She is a tenth muse, the
muse of lyrical Socialism. From which of them the impulse came I have no
means of knowing, but surely it must have been from her. In her case I can
understand it; she lives in an aesthetic reverie; she idealises everything.
Naturally she knows nothing whatever of real life.'[14]

Equally important, for Gissing, are those who stand aside from the fight.
The vicar Mr Wyvern seems to express Gissing's own views, though he
has taken a different road to arrive at them. When he was a curate in a slum
parish he was furious at social injustice; then he fell ill, inherited some
money, and went to live in Italy for two years. When he came back, he
realised that he 'was no longer of those who seek to change the world, but
of those who are content that it should in substance remain as it is'. He
moved to a quiet country parish, and decided that rich and poor are equally
likely to be happy, or to be miserable. The fundamental error of middle-
class radicals, he concludes, is to believe that the poor as a class are unhappy
and in need of help:

> It is a mistake due to mere thoughtlessness, or ignorance, to imagine the
> labouring, or even the destitute, population as ceaselessly groaning beneath
> the burden of their existence. Go along the poorest street in the East End of
> London, and you will hear as much laughter, witness as much gaiety, as in
> any thoroughfare of the West. . . . A being of superior intelligence regarding
> humanity with an eye of perfect understanding would discover that life was
> enjoyed every bit as much in the slum as in the palace.[15]

This argument doesn't take into account that the poor could be better fed
and housed and still have their old enjoyments.

Gissing certainly mistrusted the do-gooders. He had been pushed down
into the working class and was still struggling to get out; people like Morris
were just down there on a visit. Morris could give his socialist speeches
while enjoying an income of over £2,000 a year, most of it from his profitable furniture business. He also had a beautiful daughter whom Gissing
could never imagine possessing.[16] Yet it is too simple to say that Gissing
could have become a leader of the workers among whom he had lived, but
rejected socialism out of pique. Wyvern predicts that even if 'progress'
makes everyone richer, they will be less happy in the future. They will
expect more of life, but industry and commerce will have destroyed the old
sources of happiness. Those who suffer most will be the class of which
Gissing himself was a forerunner:

8

7

'It is a class created by the mania of education, and it consists of those unhappy men and women whom unspeakable cruelty endows with intellectual needs whilst refusing them the sustenance they are taught to crave. Another generation, and this class will be terribly extended, its existence blighting the whole social state. Every one of these poor creatures has a right to curse the work of those who clamour progress, and pose as benefactors of the race.'

Wyvern pities this class, but he hates the capitalists: 'Monstrously hypocritical, they cry for progress when they mean increased opportunities of swelling their own purses at the expense of those they employ, and of those they serve; vulgar to the core, they exalt a gross ideal of well-being, and stink in their prosperity.'[17]

For Wyvern, the only classes with a hope of contentment are the workers and the uncommercial middle and upper class. The capitalists destroy nature, intellectual life, and those they employ; the lower middle class are tantalised by desires that they don't have the means to fulfil. One might say that Gissing's view of politics is self-centred, founded on the discontent of the scholarship boy who found that there was no room at the top for him. Yet everyone in *Demos* is enclosed in a position determined by their temperament and their class; and temperament is usually the more important. Hence the fundamental disunity even of the socialist meeting in Islington:

> He rose half-way down the room, – the man who invariably rises on these occasions. He was oldish, with bent shoulders, and wore spectacles – probably a clerk of forty years' standing. In his hand was a small note-book, which he consulted. He began with measured utterance, emphatic, loud.
> 'I wish to propose to the lecturer seven questions. I will read them in order. . . .'
> The debate is opened. Behold a second inevitable man; he is not well-washed, his shirt-front shows a beer-stain; he is angry before he begins. . . . He is that singular phenomenon, that self-contradiction, that expression insoluble into factors of common-sense – the Conservative working man.[18]

And so the question period rolls on, with its arguers, its jokers, and the man who has a fit and has to be carried off. All are workers or small tradesmen, but their personalities make them disagree, and disagreement feeds on itself. Politics becomes a Punch and Judy show; there can be no 'correct' position, and one can only find peace by walking out.

One could point out that Gissing's own political views did not come from sober analysis, but from deep personal frustrations. Yet if politics was determined by class, how could one explain the conservative working man at the meeting, or Mr Westlake's hatred of the capitalism that had made him rich? Politics was not scientific, and those who tried to make it so must fail – whether economic liberals, Marxists, or rationalists like Sidney and Beatrice Webb. In any case, Gissing was not writing a treatise, but a novel; he wanted to show how different people lived out their political beliefs, and to understand his own position in the political arena. He still felt pity for those crushed by the world, 'poor girls in London garrets and . . . men who perish prematurely to support their children'. But his own solution had to be some kind of escape, beginning with psychic detachment from the worldly struggle.

The final justification for Gissing's political stance in *Demos* was that the novel was better than anything he had written before. 'I believe the turning-point has come at last,' he told Ellen. 'In my private opinion, "Demos" is distinctly ahead of anything since George Eliot ceased to write, I see that in reading the proofs.'[19] Eliot had died five years before, in December 1880. Others were starting to recognise the size of Gissing's talent. The greatest strength of *Demos* was its epic vision of London: beyond the birth-pangs of socialism lay the greater struggle for existence of the city's anonymous masses. The end of that struggle was the subject of one of Gissing's great set-pieces, the description of Manor Park Cemetery where Jane Vine is buried – one of the 'poor girls in garrets':

> Not grief, but chill desolation makes this cemetery its abode. A country churchyard touches the tenderest memories, and softens the heart with longing for eternal rest. . . . Here on the waste limits of the dread East, to wander among tombs is to go hand in hand with the stark and eyeless emblem of mortality; the spirit fails beneath the cold burden of ignoble destiny. Here lie those who were born for toil; . . . Indistinguishable units in the vast throng that labours but to support life, the name of each, father, mother, child, is as a dumb cry for the warmth and love of which Fate so stinted them. The wind wails above their narrow tenements; the sandy soil, soaking in the rain as soon as it has fallen, is a symbol of the great world which absorbs their toil and straightway blots their being.[20]

The final wielder of power, Gissing suggests, is London itself. Whatever the political hopes of its inhabitants, London always exacts its human tribute in the end. Gissing's pessimism is not just about whether the poor can hope to better their condition; it is about the new phenomenon of the urban mass. No political philosophy is adequate to the sheer scale of modern life, so a wise man will retreat as far from modernity as possible. Gissing would write about politics again, but *Demos* was both his first and his last word on the political possibilities of his time; and Manor Park Cemetery had the last word of all.

Gissing worked ferociously on *Demos* and completed it in four months, from 5 November 1885 to 6 March 1886. Three weeks after he started work, Smith, Elder's reader James Payn had accepted *A Life's Morning*. Fired by his approval, Gissing sent him the first two volumes of *Demos* on 3 February 1886, hoping to have the novel accepted before he had even finished writing it. Five days later, riots broke out after a workers' demonstration in Trafalgar Square: 'For myself,' Gissing commented, 'it is rather a good thing than otherwise, for I am writing a book that deals with Socialism, and it may prove more interesting on account of the attention that is being drawn to the subject. I did not myself see anything of the uproar. In fact we knew nothing of it till we saw about it in the papers next morning, – such is London.'[21] It seems typical of Gissing that he went on quietly writing *Demos* in his flat at the top of Baker Street while an angry crowd of the unemployed was filling Trafalgar Square, a couple of miles away. William Morris was not involved this time, because he had split from the Social Democratic Federation, which had organised the meeting; however, he supported the demonstration after the fact. The crowd had set off along Pall Mall for Hyde Park; servants at the Reform Club threw shoes and brushes at the mob, and they then started to smash windows at the clubs along Pall Mall and St James's Street. They rampaged on through Mayfair, breaking into shops, and ran out of steam at Oxford Street. If they had gone a little further, they could have looted the shop that sold William Morris's furnishings.

The riots helped Gissing in several ways. Two weeks later, Payn offered him £100 for *Demos*, twice as much as he had offered for *A Life's Morning*. There was still time for Gissing to write current events into volume III, giving him the chance to express his own views on the mob. Finally, he had a publisher knocking at the door demanding his manuscript, instead of having his books rejected or suppressed as had happened so often in the past. Payn did want to be reassured that volume III would not have any provocative sexual content, which had caused trouble for *The Unclassed*; and he also wanted a cheerful ending. In the final pages of *The Unclassed* four characters die, by smallpox, TB, falling down stairs, and suicide. Gissing promised to avoid sex and another massacre, though he said Richard Mutimer would have to die according to poetic justice. He liked the idea of writing up to the minute and being in the public eye, but there was one more snag: Payn wanted *Demos* to appear anonymously. This may have been because Gissing already had two very different novels in press; or Payn may have thought that an anonymous novel about the political turmoil of the day would arouse the public's curiosity. Gissing felt he had to agree, but pointed out that if *Demos* failed to go into a second edition – where he could be identified as the author – he would have £100 to show for his work and nothing more. In the event, a second edition of *Demos* would appear later in 1886 with Gissing's name on the title page, and his next three published novels identified him as 'author of *Demos*'.

Gissing had a more substantial worry, too: that Payn might pressure him into writing novels that were closer to journalism than literature. Payn was a best-selling author with an assured position in the world. By the time of his death in 1898 he had published a hundred novels. It was good to have him as a patron, but Gissing needed to draw his own lines:

> you have not forgotten what an advantage it would be to me to have the help of *actuality* in my subject. I could not forget that I owe you my best work. But I may repeat that I have never considered the book save from an artistic standpoint. Perhaps the events of the day may aid me, but I had far rather they did not aid *too much*.[22]

Payn wanted Gissing to see political events at first hand, but that was not his method. He did not go back to Kelmscott House, just as he had not attended the great Trafalgar Square meeting. When he wrote about it in *Demos* he relied on newspaper accounts. His scrapbook shows how much he relied on the popular press for inspiration, cutting out items of all kinds, pasting them into his book to make a little archive for use in his novels. These clippings were his preferred link between his imaginative work and the turmoil of the London streets, the brute actuality. In any case, Gissing was not much interested in the large political issues behind the uproar. Rather, he wanted to imagine why someone decides to throw a stone through a window, or what it feels like to be the target of one.

One firm article of belief in Gissing's politics was that it was wrong both to throw stones, and to condone those who threw them (as Morris did).[23] Gissing's socialist hero, Richard Mutimer, never panders to the mob. But he gets caught up in a street battle between his political faction and one that follows his rival Roodhouse.[24] On the surface, the fight is about accusations that Mutimer has stolen money from the movement (false) and that he has abandoned his work-girl fiancée for a lady (true). But the real instigators are a group of mindless onlookers, 'a large element of mere drifting black-guardism, the raff of a city, anticipating with pleasure an uproar which would give them unwonted opportunities of violence and pillage'.[25] When

Gissing said in his letter to Payn that it was 'justice' for Mutimer to die at the hands of this mob, he meant that Mutimer should have known who he was dealing with when he started urging the workers to rebel: 'Demos was roused, was tired of listening to mere articulate speech; it was time for a good wild-beast roar, for a taste of bloodshed. Scarcely a face in all the mob but distorted itself to express as much savagery as can be got out of the human countenance.'[26] This is the *demos* of Plato's *Republic*, the enemy of reason, the many-headed monster for which throwing a stone is the best argument.

Between his visit to Kelmscott House and the Trafalgar Square riots, a period of two months, Gissing certainly hardened his attitude towards the working class. But he was also judging Mutimer as someone who crosses class lines, and as a result is first isolated and then destroyed. The fatal attack on him comes because the workers hate him for trying to become someone better than them. His upper-class wife Adela has also disowned him, because of: 'those faults of the working class which are ineradicable in any one generation. . . . she was getting to appreciate with a thoroughness impossible hitherto, the monstrous gulf between men of that kind and cultured human beings.'[27]

Some of these sentiments may reflect Gissing's prejudice against the class below him. Those who called themselves 'lower middle' were identifying with those above them; never would they say 'upper working'. At the same time, Gissing was always sceptical about those who tried to leave their origins behind. His fiction is full of self-defeating characters who are able to rise in the world, but cannot live comfortably with the false self they have constructed to make that rise possible. They fail, typically, because of their relations with women. The man who is trying to rise socially either cannot meet the expectations of a superior woman, or is pulled down by an imprudent tie with a woman who is his inferior.[28]

Why should women be represented as the Achilles heel of ambitious males? Gissing's woman problem has two sides. One kind of woman destroys by being too easily possessed, the other by being unattainable. Male rivals are generally no problem for Gissing: in youth he took it for granted that he would be the cleverest among his peers and carry off armfuls of prizes. Times were harder when he was trying to establish himself as a novelist, but his relations with publishers or with other writers were not neurotic or self-defeating; nor does he dramatise such situations in his novels.[29] More typical is the male solidarity between Julian Casti and Osmond Waymark in *The Unclassed*. Two men sitting in front of a fire, smoking their pipes and discussing the classics, is Gissing's model of happiness. In *Henry Ryecroft*, this narrows down to a man alone.

Gissing's difficulties, and those of his heroes, reflect the interaction between class and gender in the Victorian system of opportunity. A scholarship boy could qualify for a middle-class job more easily than he could qualify as suitor to a lady. Nor could he look for a woman who shared his experience because, effectively, there were no scholarship girls. Someone like Emily Hood in *A Life's Morning* would come closest: she has been well educated (though not at university), and her career chances are limited to being a governess or a schoolteacher. This was also the situation – not a cheerful one – of Gissing's two sisters. Still, this was the natural level for Gissing to seek a mate, assuming that he could free himself from Nell. But the miserable fate of such educated young women in his novels – Emily Hood, the Madden sisters in *The Odd Women*, Marian Yule in *New Grub Street* – suggests that Gissing found them anti-erotic. They are lonely yearners, often victims of unrequited love for a man who is more powerful or successful than they are. Typically, they are prisoners of their own idealism, or of narrow provincial piety. Because they lack sensuality they either attract no suitors, or frustrate the ones that do come forward.

As Orwell pointed out, Gissing's problems originated at the intersection between poverty, ambition and sexual desire. Ambition was starting to find some reward at the beginning of 1886, thanks to the promising outlook for *Demos*. To be earning better money from his writing lifted Gissing's spirits, even if he still had to put in long hours of tutoring to make ends meet. He had more confidence in his future as a novelist, and that made it easier for him to accept invitations: 'Thank Heaven,' he told his sister Ellen, 'I can go without the torture of feeling myself *nobody*.'[30] That he was still at heart a pessimist had most to do with the brute fact of Nell's place in his life. Even if he never saw her, she absorbed a large chunk of his income. He kept his address secret, but she could turn up at any time and destroy his respectability, that lower-middle-class treasure; and just to know the kind of life she must be leading made it impossible for Gissing ever to enjoy real peace of mind. He felt he had to cut her off, but could not escape his guilt for doing so. Having failed to divorce her, his release could come only by her death; and this may be why, in his novels, death comes so frequently to resolve situations that otherwise would be unbearable.

Work-girls could never satisfy Gissing's cultural needs; lower-middle-class women were puritanical; genteel women were beyond his reach. That was the basis of his female mythology, and of his continued loneliness and sexual misery. Bohemia might have provided an escape, but in the 1880s it was still very restricted in Britain and under the thumb of the established order. The periodical press, for example, was ferociously opposed to all forms of 'immorality'; once tarred with that brush, Gissing would find it impossible to make a living as a writer in English. For someone like him, lacking the protection of class or independent wealth, there was really only one escape route: to cross the Channel. In France or Italy he would be beyond the surveillance of English propriety. In the end, that would be the closest Gissing could come to liberation, living in a 'free union' with his French companion. Even there, he still would be constrained by what was acceptable in the English literary marketplace.

Once he had finished *Demos*, Gissing had time and means to make his first foray to the Continent: two weeks in Paris, from 20 March to 2 April. After a stormy crossing where he froze on the open deck, he was delighted by the beauty of the city. It seemed far superior to the muddle and grime of London. In *Demos*, Adela Waltham had expressed the respectable English view of Paris:

> 'Dissipation' too; to her pure mind the word had a terrible sound; it sketched in lurid outlines hideous lurking places of vice and disease. ... With the name of Paris she associated a feeling of reprobation; Paris was the head-quarters of sin – at all events on earth. In Paris people went to the theatre on Sunday; that fact alone shed storm-light over the iniquitous capital.[31]

Gissing might consider himself superior to this kind of fantasy, but his Paris was a fantasy too, constructed from two of his favourite French novelists: Henri Murger, author of *Scènes de la Vie de Bohème*, and Alphonse Daudet. He knew also Eugène Sue's collection, *Mystères de Paris*. The Hôtel Cujas, where Gissing stayed, was in the Latin Quarter, the home of Murger's Rodolphe and Mimi. He started his first day with a visit to the Morgue, near the Gare de Lyon. This was a gruesome choice, and also a popular one; up to a million people visited it in the course of a year. Dickens had gone there regularly when he lived in Paris in 1846, until he found the corpse of a drowned man too much even for him.

Gissing surely had read about the Morgue in Zola's *Thérèse Raquin*, where Laurent goes every day to look for the corpse of the woman he drowned, Camille. Ostensibly the corpses were on display so that they could be identified, laid out behind large windows that have been compared to that other Paris invention of the time, the department store:

> When [Laurent] reached the last row of slabs and there were no cases of drowning, he sighed with relief and his disgust lessened somewhat. He then became a mere sightseer, and found a strange pleasure in looking violent

death in the face, with its lugubriously weird and grotesque attitudes. It was
an interesting show, especially when there were women displaying their
bare breasts. This brutal display of naked bodies spattered with blood,
sometimes with holes in them, held him spellbound. . . . When the slabs are
occupied and there is a nice show of human flesh, the visitors jostle each
other and indulge in cheap thrills, shudder with horror, crack jokes, applaud
or whistle just as they would at the theatre, and finally go away satisfied,
declaring that the Morgue has been a good show today.[32]

The day that Gissing went was a quiet one, with only two bodies. It was
'at once very horrible and very simple', he told Algernon. 'Most ghastly
were the photographs of unrecognized dead and buried hung up on the
entrance.'[33] This was a step beyond even the bleakness of the Mile End
cemetery, to see a great city so indifferent to individual fate that they no
longer even had names.

   Gissing made the tour of the expected sights, but he prided himself on
how differently he was seeing Paris from the way Englishmen usually did.
He ate in cheap restaurants with ordinary folk, and was still amazed at how
much better the food was than in London. He imagined that he could live
in Paris for about fifteen shillings a week, less than half of what he paid at
home. Because he could read and speak French well, he could absorb the
nuances of French social life and perhaps even write novels about France
like the ones he already admired. When he objected to being called 'the
English Zola' it was not because he disagreed with Zola's morality, or with
his aim of giving a panoramic view of life in a great capital city. Rather, he
was more committed than Zola to the particularity and autonomy of his
fictional characters. Zola's starting-point was to consider society as a
complex system, in which individuals were secondary to the collective
forces that shaped them. Gissing was interested in how people could be
subjected to the same forces, and still be different from each other.

   Nonetheless, Gissing made a Zolaesque pilgrimage to Belleville, 'the far
East End of Paris'.[34] It was the Paris equivalent of Whitechapel or Stepney,
with an unsavoury reputation and a distinctive accent. A drinking-den
there was supposed to be the model for the one in Zola's *L'Assommoir*. It
had a still for producing its own cheap liquor and a room where its customers
could pass out on heaps of straw. The rue Monjol was the bottom of the
barrel for the sex trade: in its filthy little bars, with filthier rooms upstairs,
bargemen or sewer workers could get an ageing prostitute at the lowest
possible price.[35] In his first two novels Gissing had described the people
who lived in the dirtiest corners of the East End, like the beggar called
'Slimy' in *The Unclassed*. But one of his deserving prostitutes, Lotty Starr,

Ida's mother, lives a relatively clean and respectable life, and looks after her daughter well. 'In the profession Lotty had chosen,' Gissing observed, 'there are, as in all professions, grades and differences.'[36]

Intellectuals, following the lead of Baudelaire, felt the need to explore the most sordid bars and brothels. Gissing joined these connoisseurs of the horrible: the Morgue was the place to really know death, Belleville the place to know sex. Walking the streets of great cities, especially at night, one could expect to find the most amazing sights. In the very worst of them, like rue Monjol or 'Elm Court' in *The Unclassed*, some kind of deep truth about modern life seemed to be revealed. In 1886 Gissing still felt that this was the frontier of the novelist's territory, even if Mrs Grundy prevented him from giving a full report of his travels.

There may have been a more personal compulsion in Gissing's expeditions to places like Belleville. Going there would only intensify the loneliness and depression to be felt by anyone finding himself on his own in a strange city. Gissing had to cope with the shock of a new culture, the noisy streets that made it hard for him to sleep, and the fact that he was an author of some modest repute in London but in Paris a nobody. The people of Belleville would accept you if you accepted them, and be willing to speak to a stranger. It was by going to such places, when he was a student in Manchester, that Gissing had launched himself – disastrously, to be sure – into a radically different life. The one thing he did not visit the slums to do was to indulge in sympathy for the downtrodden. In Paris as in London, these were the 'dangerous classes', who needed first of all to be kept in their place.

One question remains open. In his letters from Paris, Gissing says much about the sights he saw during the day, but very little about what he did by night. He mentions in detail only several visits to the Théâtre Français, where he saw Sarah Bernhardt in a play by Sardou. His surviving letters are only to his brother and sister, where prudence was required. So did Gissing go to Paris for the obvious reason a single Englishman might want to visit: to enjoy cheap sex in relatively pleasant surroundings? H. G. Wells said that Gissing was too poor to frequent prostitutes when living alone in London in the 1880s; but in Paris one could go to a modest brothel for five francs (about four shillings), and a luxurious one for ten francs. Gissing certainly had that much to spare. If he was afraid of venereal disease, the health regulation in French brothels was much stricter than anything existing in England.

It comes down to whether Gissing was desperate for sexual relief, after three years of living apart from Nell, or whether he had learned to keep himself apart from women. The Gissing-like protagonist of 'A Lodger in Maze Pond' says that he does not have 'a sensual or passionate nature'. Jacob Korg sees in this evidence for Gissing's relative chastity; Halperin, on the other hand, takes it for granted that Gissing resorted to prostitutes during his separation from Nell, and slept with Edith Underwood before he married her.[37] I suspect that Gissing went to the Paris underworld to look, but not to touch. If Paris was a chance for him to enjoy sex freely, why did he wait two years to go back, and then take a male companion who shared his room? He loved to read about *la vie de bohème*, but at no time in his life did he ever really live like a bohemian. He was supposed to spend three weeks in Paris, but packed up and went home after a fortnight.

There had also been some intellectual work to do in Paris. Gissing had a single introduction, to a Comtean acquaintance of Frederic Harrison. Gissing called him a 'distinguished French communist', but he was no more than a self-educated house painter, the kind of artisan intellectual who figures in *Demos* and *Thyrza*. Now that *Demos* was about to appear, Gissing had to worry whether the reading public would take to a novel largely about people at that social level. His novel was both realistic and sceptical, with its emphasis on the weakness of working-class character and intellect. Would its topical interest carry it through to success? Smith, Elder helped by launching a major advertising campaign, far beyond any publicity for Gissing's previous novels. He cut short his trip to be present when the book was published, arriving in London on Friday 2 April. In the next day's *Times* there was a long anonymous review of *Demos*. It began with praise of the novel's literary qualities, quoting from Gissing's description of the Manor Park Cemetery. Then the reviewer started to complain about the lack of a clear message:

> But *Demos*, though a tale of English Socialism, is not a Socialistic novel. Perhaps it would pique curiosity more deeply if it were. Sometimes the author seems to preach the doctrines of Saint-Simon, and sometimes to scoff at them. . . . If *Demos* suggests a practical moral, it is that the modern Socialist is insincere. But on the general problem we get but negative results, leading us nowhere, and sadly bidding us despair of the future of the human race.[38]

The Spectator came out with a long review a week later, whose conclusion attached a label to Gissing he was never able to get rid of: '*Demos* is the book of a pessimist with no belief in the power of what are called progressive ideas, but also with little or no spiritual faith which might prove a higher motive-power than that of which equality and fraternity are the favourite watch-cries.'[39] The *Guardian*, a church magazine, suggested that if Gissing had any positive creed it was aestheticism, which was just as bad as Social-ism. The critics were right to sniff out Gissing's lack of belief in three standard remedies for England's troubles: Socialism, Toryism, or spiritual renewal. Aestheticism rejected orthodox religion, but could only be the creed of a cultural elite (creating problems that William Morris was never able to resolve). As for Gissing, he had many of the impulses of an aesthete; all he needed was a sufficient income to satisfy them.

One political option remained: the Gladstonian Liberalism that had been the firm conviction of Gissing's father. The problem there was Gissing's implacable dislike for commerce and industry, ignoble activities that de-spoiled the countryside and destroyed culture. The critics had rightly noticed that Gissing had written a novel about political problems that, in his quirky perspective, had no political solution. He was not going to put his own shoulder to the wheel. To be a pessimist, an individualist and a fatalist was what made sense to Gissing; but who else could rally to such a banner?

Gissing still looked to Mrs Gaussen to help launch his book: 'By just mentioning the name among your friends, and saying that the book deals with Socialism,you will be able to help me appreciably, and I shall be very grateful.'[40] It was odd to assume that Mrs Gaussen's upper-middle-class circle could make the novel a success, when it did so little to support their prejudices. There was plenty in *Demos* to offend Whig, Tory and socialist alike. Payn still assured Gissing that it would be a success, and it sold five hundred copies in the first five weeks after publication, a good deal better than Gissing's two previous novels. But Mudie's did not send in repeat orders. George Moore believed that Mudie boycotted naturalistic novels that had any hint of 'Zolaism'. 'The novel of observation, of analysis,' Moore complained, 'exists no longer among us. Why? Because the librarian does not feel as safe in circulating a study of life and manners as a tale concerning a lost will.'[41] *Demos* was certainly a novel of analysis, even if it contained a lost will too, which took away Richard Mutimer's fortune.

Gissing had tried to steer clear of Mudie's dislikes, such as any sym-pathetic treatment of prostitution; but he had failed to provide a happy ending or a simple and positive message for readers. That had prevented him becoming a truly popular writer. Still, *Demos* had drawn critical attention and could raise his hopes for future books. More straws in the wind were that the book was published in Germany by Tauchnitz, for Continental English readers, and that his publisher, George Smith, invited him to dinner. Gissing realised that £100 was not a very good price for *Demos*, and he should try to get more in future. The modest success of the novel when first published reflected its limited appeal to the conventional middle-class readers who got their fiction through Mudie's. When Smith, Elder started to issue *Demos* in cheaper editions, it did better. A one-volume edition at six shillings came out in November 1886 (still without Gissing's name on it). Two years later there were separate editions at 3/6d, 2/6d and 2/-, reaching down to the bottom level of the fiction market, 'yellow-backs' for people who read on trains and buses. Smith, Elder also arranged for Gissing's first publication in the US, a cheap edition by Harper, printed in two columns.[42]

This complex publishing history was something completely new for Gissing. *Workers in the Dawn* had 277 copies printed, then never appeared again in his lifetime; *The Unclassed* was not reprinted until 1895 (in a shortened version), eleven years after its first edition. But Gissing's poverty and lack of business sense had led him into a trap that he could never quite escape. He got into the habit (with a few exceptions) of selling the copyright of his books for a flat sum, usually just enough to live on until he had another book to sell. He did not get a penny from the later success of *Demos*, once he had cashed his first and last cheque for a hundred pounds. The royalty system was starting to make inroads in Britain, and Gissing realised early on that he might do better to take an advance against future sales, and gradually build up a steadier income as he published more books. But he had no reserve of capital to carry him through the lean years, and he wanted to give up teaching and write full-time as soon as he could. Nor could he set his principles aside, at this point anyway, and write a popular novel to the standard formula. He was left with what we might call a strategy of hope.

The considerable success of *Demos*, with its respectful reviews, made Gissing optimistic that his next books might get a higher price. The £100 for *Demos* might rise to £150 or £200, and on up the ladder of success. Unfortunately, publishers did not share this rosy vision. If they could buy a Gissing novel for £100, they expected to go on buying them at the same price, or at most £150. They knew that he was in a weak bargaining position, and in the commercial culture of the time it was hard to get one publisher to bid against another for a book. Gissing did try to get off the treadmill by accepting £50 for his next book, *Thyrza*, against a 10 per cent royalty on sales. But what if the novel did not sell more than *Demos*, so that he still ended up with only £100 or less? He would have to write two novels a year to make ends meet, and continue to do some tutoring. For him, that meant producing four thousand words a day once he had thought out the plot and the characters. This was an output twice as great as Trollope's, that monster of literary industry. And at a comparable stage of his career, Trollope was already getting £350 per novel (at his peak, he would get £3,000 or more).

Another problem was that Gissing's next two novels, *Isabel Clarendon* and *A Life's Morning*, had been written before *Demos* and on very different themes. *Isabel Clarendon* finally appeared in early June 1886 from Chapman & Hall. Once he had his bound copy, Gissing told his sister Margaret that 'it is not quite so feeble as I thought. On the whole it may very well take its place among my writings, and – some day – be read by intelligent people in an intelligent way.'[43] The reviews were not glowing, but they did not lack intelligence, and Gissing was compared to Meredith, George Eliot and Henry James. His portrait of his heroine came in for praise, as a fine study of her social type.

In representing Isabel, all Gissing needed to do was draw on his close observation of Mrs Gaussen in London and in the Cotswolds. His problems with the novel lay more on the side of his hero and alter ego, Bernard Kingcote. Reviewers complained of the novel's scrappy and unresolved plot, but its flaws were inseparable from the character of Kingcote. One reviewer saw him as a Hamlet, 'a mind of peculiarly fine fibre afflicted with a morbid taint'.[44] The *Saturday Review* had less patience: 'His hero is one of the dyspeptic persons who, instead of going into a monastery, as in former days (where at least they plagued nobody but each other), mope and moan about the world without the pluck to do or the power to enjoy anything.'[45] Gissing certainly had created a pusillanimous hero who failed to bring the novel to the expected happy ending, and his private reasons for making his hero so inert were not evident to *Isabel Clarendon*'s readers. They did not see any objective barriers to his successful courtship of Isabel, so that lack of vigour seemed to be the only reason for his romantic failure. In real life, being poor, married and lower-middle-class were much more adequate reasons for his failed love affair with Mrs Gaussen.

The reviews for *Demos* and *Isabel Clarendon* identified Gissing – labelled him, in fact – as a gifted novelist who had something wrong with him. 'Morbid' was a Victorian term of suspicion, more damaging than just calling him a pessimist. A kind of vague critical dissatisfaction would haunt Gissing's career until at least the mid-1890s, when he started producing deliberately cheerful works of more popular fiction. Yet there was little true morbidity in the content of Gissing's novels, of the kind that critics might discern in Dickens, Zola or Dostoevsky. The morbidity of which Gissing was accused by the critics was really his persistence in exploring the dark corners of Victorian society, places thought fit to be visited only by those who were obliged to do so. For a French novelist, such morbidity would just be business as usual; Gissing had to suffer for the myth that

England was a cleaner, more moral nation than its neighbour across the Channel.

By the time Gissing was reading such reviews he had put *Isabel Clarendon* behind him, and claimed that he was too busy to mingle with people like the Gaussens. Probably this was no more than a half-truth; the other half was that the appearance of the novel was an embarrassment both to Mrs Gaussen and to himself. He made no more money from it, and it was never reprinted in his lifetime. Characters like Kingcote would turn up again in his novels, but they would not spend hundreds of pages mooning after some high-born lady. *Isabel Clarendon*, like the relationship with Mrs Gaussen that inspired it, had to be written off to experience.

Thyrza

Gissing knew that he wanted to write another working-class novel; but what approach could he take, after his critique of socialist ideals in *Demos*? His answer was to focus on a heroine this time, an idealised work-girl. Her lover would be a middle-class intellectual who wanted to bring culture to the people. In both *Demos* and *Thyrza*, though, the lover would betray his work-girl and turn back to a woman of his own class. The background for *Thyrza* would be Lambeth, a new district for Gissing to explore, south of the river. As he began the novel, Gissing told his sister Margaret that he had to visit a hat factory and a lunatic asylum (probably Bedlam), and wander about in the slums. The asylum did not get into the novel, though the hat factory did: the heroine, Thyrza Trent, works there for a pound a week. Gissing took his title from Byron's 'Elegy to Thyrza', about a beautiful and gentle girl who dies young.[1] The lover who betrayed her lives on, tormented by guilt but consoled by the idea that Thyrza will never lose her beauty to age and decay. Behind Byron's Thyrza was the young woman in the Old Testament who asked Moses for the right to inherit from her father, since she had no brothers. She was the first person to speak up for the rights of women, and Jahweh told Moses to grant her request.[2]

Gissing spent the month of April 1886 mulling over his ideas for *Thyrza*, then began writing in May with his usual speed, in spite of still having to tutor Walter Grahame for two hours each morning. 'In parts it will be rather grim,' he told Ellen, 'and the ending tragical enough.'[3] He had decided to nail his colours to the mast, defying the critics who wanted happy endings at all costs. When he met Thomas Hardy for the first time, a month later, Hardy backed him up: 'It is a great pleasure to me to find from what you say that you are bent upon high artistic aims, and not merely striving for circulating-library popularity.'[4]

Gissing's visit to Hardy at his lodgings in Upper Bedford Place began a wary but continuing friendship. Hardy was seventeen years older than Gissing and a solidly established author. Gissing was familiar with his novels and gave them a grudging respect, but did not see Hardy as a writer at his own level. The novels that Hardy would write over the next ten years, culminating with *Jude the Obscure*, did not change Gissing's judgement. He had a shrewd appreciation of Hardy's achievement, but could never see anything extraordinary in it. This misjudgement may have been founded on his own similarity to Hardy, rather than on his differences from him. They had both grown up lower-middle-class in market towns. Both had pious mothers, studied the classics, knew and loved the countryside. They had struggled to survive in London in their twenties while trying to establish themselves as writers. Both had suffered from unhappy marriages, and from an insecure social position. Hardy and Gissing both defined themselves through hostility to the emotional values of their lower-middle origins: sexual repression, piety, the cult of respectability. Both had replaced those values with a bleak determinism, put forward bluntly in their novels in a way that regularly annoyed their critics.

With so much in common, there was still a great difference in the places where they sought inspiration. In July 1887 Hardy sent to Gissing a copy of *The Mayor of Casterbridge*, and added the recommendation: 'Do not be induced to write too fast.' If anyone else had said this to him, Gissing probably would have given a sharp reply; but to Hardy he laid out his agenda as a novelist:

> Yes, I know too well the danger of writing too fast, and I fear I shall not be able to shun it altogether. It is my misfortune to be obliged to make literature a business, – a very poor one in sooth, – yet it shall go hard with me but I will follow your example and give my books that individuality which comes of their being heart-felt. And then indeed the question is how to get into a lifetime the work suggested by this myriad-voiced London. Every year I hate it more and more, longing for the pure sky, yet every year I see in it more opportunity for picturing.[5]

Instead of the pure sky, the impure smoke of London inspired Gissing. Hardy, conversely, found everything he needed in the fields and cottages of Wessex, and left London almost entirely out of his novels. It was not that Gissing disliked country life; he longed to live there in peace and comfort, like the 'Henry Ryecroft' of his late book. But the huge vitality and variety of the capital remained Gissing's obsession, and the well-spring of his creativity. What he did not have yet was a comprehensive vision of London, like Balzac's or Zola's visions of Paris.[6] Perhaps it was Gissing's hating the city more and more that prevented him doing it full justice.

Whatever their differences, it was an important step for Gissing to gain

Hardy's recognition, and to exchange copies of their recently published novels.[7] They stood together as two serious English novelists who did not have the standing of 'gentlemen', and who held to their vision of the world without fear of unpopularity. That alliance was what Gissing affirmed to Hardy after their first meeting:

> in your books I have constantly found refreshment and onward help. That aid is much needed now-a-days by anyone who wishes to pursue literature, as distinct from the profession of letters. In literature my interests begin and end; I hope to make my life and all its acquirements subservient to my ideal of artistic creation. The end of it all may prove ineffectual, but as well spend one's strength thus as in another way. The misery of it is that, writing for English people, one may not be thorough; reticences and superficialities have so often to fill places where one is willing to put in honest work.[8]

In less than ten years, Hardy would find the demand for 'reticence' so oppressive that he would give up novel-writing altogether, after the abusive reception of *Jude the Obscure*. Gissing had to struggle on with his misery. Not only did his ideal of literature doom him to failure in the marketplace, Victorian prudery would not let him write to his full capacity about the dark issues of his life: crime, sex and economic survival. Each book he wrote would have its shadow, the book he would have written if he had been free to tell everything he knew. Gissing expressed the pain of this suppression in a letter to Margaret, where he said that he read very little of Scott, Thackeray or Dickens:

> the writers who help me most are French and Russian; I have not much sympathy with English points of view. And indeed that is why I scarcely think that my own writing can ever be popular; a few intelligent people will come to look out for it, but the mob will go to other people who better suit their tastes. Day by day that same mob grows in extent and influence.[9]

By 'the mob' Gissing meant the new reading public that was replacing the compact group of circulating library subscribers; it was at least ten times as large, and would gravitate towards the new mass media of daily newspapers and cheap magazines.

Gissing went on with *Thyrza* in accordance with his own principles, knowing that his rewards were likely to be modest. Until now he had always placed his stories of working-class life in places like Clerkenwell and Islington, north and east of the city centre. For his drama of the work-girl Thyrza Trent and her friends, living around Walnut Tree Walk in

Lambeth, he wanted to bring out a new aspect of London life. Charles
Booth had found it difficult to define south London, except negatively:
'There seems to be a lack of spontaneous social life among the people,
perhaps due to the want of local industries. There is altogether less going
on. . . . The very public-houses do not seem to exhale so genial a spirit as
elsewhere. . . . Their doors do not so frequently emit that cheerful buzz of
talk within, which surely is, of all sounds known to man, the most attractive.'[10] Perhaps that was what interested Gissing about south London: it was
a vast expanse of generic urban life with very few landmarks. There were no
great churches, monuments, hotels, department stores or public buildings
south of the river. More than two million people lived there without even
an identifiable town centre. From Lambeth you could see the Houses of
Parliament across the river, but it might as well have been in a different
world.

By this time Gissing's wife was living in Lambeth, off Lower Marsh near
Waterloo. Gissing was fearful of any direct contact with her, but perhaps
he wanted to play with fire by wandering around streets where he might
run into her by chance. In his novel he was again imagining alternative
pasts: his cultured young hero, Egremont, falls in love with a pure and
warm-hearted work-girl, and tries to educate her. It seems that Gissing
wanted to reassure himself that such relationships could succeed (though
at the end the one in *Thyrza* fails, too). Once again he was fascinated by
how much difference there could be between young women born into the
same class and circumstance:

> The women with the babies grew thirsty in the hot, foul air of the street,
> and invited each other to refreshment of varying strength, chatting the while
> of their most intimate affairs, the eternal 'Says I, says he, says she,' of vulgar
> converse. They stood indifferently by the side of liquor-sodden creatures
> whose look was pollution. Companies of girls, neatly dressed and as far
> from depravity as possible, called for their glasses of small beer, and came
> forth again with merriment in treble key.[11]

Nell Gissing was now one of those drink-sodden creatures. They are
not included in the company of the respectable women, but neither are they
driven away; they have their drink, in the warm and noisy pub, and each
other's company. It was Gissing who had ostracised Nell. For *Thyrza*, he
would at least keep company with the common folk of Lambeth. 'I have a
book in my head,' he told Ellen, 'which no one else could write, a book
which will contain the very spirit of London working-class life. . . . it will
be a stronger and profounder book than "Demos".'[12] Even if in *Demos* he

had given up on the socialist movement, he still cared deeply about women workers, and the many ways in which they were exploited. Not being able to vote, they had no direct voice in the political struggle; the long-suffering work-girl was Gissing's emblem of political injustice. Here, his indignation was not diluted by other doubts he may have had about the capacity of the working class for cultural improvement. However, the indignation also came from his continued loyalty to the Victorian double standard: even a work-girl had an innate weakness and innocence that deserved society's protection.

At the end of July, Gissing decided that everything he had done so far should be scrapped. Nearly four months of work had produced nothing that he wanted to use. The new start meant returning to the streets of Lambeth where he went daily in search of inspiration, sometimes not returning home until two in the morning. He made good progress with rewriting the first volume, but then suffered another of his brief nervous breakdowns and had to flee London for a few days. Hot weather always disturbed Gissing, and made it hard for him to work. 'To-day I am in exceeding dumpishness,' he told Catherine Baseley. 'A growing biliousness and semi-fever has culminated, and work is at a standstill. Unfortunately that is too often the case with me, and I verily believe that in a year or so my life's business will be practically over, through sheer decay of health.'[13] Catherine was his brother Algernon's fiancée. She had complained of troubles with her health; somewhat thoughtlessly, Gissing responded that his health was worse than hers – putting him at death's door, in fact. What he was really suffering from might be called 'writer's depression', a combination of troubles with his current book and the emotional isolation that was the product of his burying himself in routine. 'Biliousness', of which he regularly complained, meant a combination of intense irritability and anxiety. When it became acute, he became physically unable to complete his daily quota of writing, and the only remedy was to leave home until he felt better.

On this occasion, Gissing was lucky in his choice of a refuge. He went first to Brighton, and loathed it: 'simply a lump of wealthy London put back to back with a lump of Whitechapel and stuck down on a most uninteresting piece of coast. . . . a more hideous and vulgar sea-side town the mind of man has not conceived.'[14] The next day he walked twenty miles along the shore, until he arrived at Eastbourne: 'Surely there is no more beautiful watering-place. It is handsomely built, with broad, clean streets, almost all of them avenued with fine, thick chestnuts. I could not discover a dirty thoroughfare, and saw no single blackguard, – yet there is a population of twenty-thousand or so.'[15] Eastbourne was an almost brand-new seaside resort, dating from the arrival of the railway in 1849. There was an old Eastbourne village, a mile and a half inland, and beyond that endless walks on the Downs. He could only stay three nights before returning to London, but he had marked Eastbourne as his favourite seaside town, and would keep returning there.

Gissing was also forming a plan to move his mother and sisters down to within reach of London. Now that Nell was out of the picture, day-to-day relations with his family were much easier. It would be a comfort to visit without the substantial cost of a railway ticket to Yorkshire. Gissing felt that his mother could live much more pleasantly on her modest capital somewhere on the South Downs, say between Guildford and Dorking. Ellen meanwhile had taken a job away from home, as governess to some small children. She was only nineteen, and suffering from homesickness, children who didn't want to learn, and urchins who hooted at her as she walked through the village. Gissing offered sympathy, but urged her to stick it out: 'What you are just now suffering, I have gone through for some eight years, – practically the same, and with an outlook far less encouraging. Resolve to laugh it all away, my dear sister. Will can do very much in such situations.'[16] Gissing was worried about his sisters, and thought he would be less lonely if he could visit them regularly. The lease on the Wakefield house was due to expire, and Mrs Gissing and her daughters would have to move, wherever they went. A few months later, Gissing had decided that Eastbourne was an even better choice than Surrey: 'If soberly you all decide to come down here, I am at any time ready to seek a house for you. I think very anxiously of those beautiful Sussex sea-places. It would be such a thing for me if there were a house by the sea that I could go to with little more expense than the railway journey.'[17] When Gissing felt particularly ill or depressed he hankered for his sisters to come and cheer him up, especially Ellen. But it would be hard for them and their mother to leave behind all their Wakefield friends. Gissing went on nudging them to move until it turned out that they could renew their lease after all, and the whole scheme was dropped.

Gissing's own home had once again become a solitary one, when Algernon left in mid-December of 1886. He had found a place in Northumberland, and gave various reasons why he would be better off there than in London. Like his brother, Algernon was given to vague illnesses and fits of depression (though he lived to be seventy-seven). Country living would be healthier and cheaper, he argued, and the Borders would be a good setting for the novel he planned to write. Perhaps his mother and sisters could move north rather than south, and the four of them could settle down in the old market town of Alnwick.

There were deeper reasons for Algernon's departure, however. One was the chronic restlessness he felt after five or six years of failure. Then there was the discomfort of trying to start a writing career himself, just as George was beginning to enjoy some real success. He was getting reviewed in the main journals, was meeting George Meredith and Thomas Hardy, and finding his novels accepted as soon as they were finished. Algernon could only look on enviously. He did not manage to write anything substantial during the year he lived with George, nor did he find any employment to help with the household expenses. The real problem, George felt, lay within Algernon himself: 'Every year makes it more impossible for him to settle to any occupation; indeed he has a constitutional inability to pursue any work that is in the least repugnant.'[18] With the eternal exasperation of the ant for the grasshopper, Gissing asked what would become of them all if he refused to teach because he didn't like it. It was as impossible for George *not* to buckle down to a task as it was for Algernon to do what the world demanded of him. In one degree or another George had to carry all four of the other members of his family, not to mention supporting Nell as well. If Algernon had ever come forward to share the load, George's fate might have been a much easier one.

As Algernon was preparing to leave Cornwall Residences, an old companion returned, much to Gissing's pleasure. Morley Roberts had left for Texas in March 1884; now he was back in London after his wanderings around the American and Canadian West. Before going away he had slaved as a copyist in the India Office at tenpence an hour; now he was determined to become a writer, on ten shillings a week given him grudgingly by his father. He took a single room in Chelsea and settled down to live even more frugally than Gissing. When he saw Gissing's flat, though, he found it 'a horrible place of extraordinary gloom, and its back windows overlooked the roaring steam engines of the Metropolitan Railway'.[19] Roberts had little money for buses and it was a good hour's walk from Chelsea to Baker Street, but he and Gissing exchanged visits every Sunday afternoon. They drank beer, ate each other's peculiar cooking, and feasted on such subjects as the scansion of Greek verse:

> As [Gissing] could not afford two fires he usually cooked his pot on the fire of the sitting-room. ... [His] idea of cooking was fatness and a certain amount of gross abundance. He would put into this pot potatoes, carrots, turnips, portions of meat, perhaps a steak, or on great days a whole rabbit, all of which he himself had bought, and carried home with his own hands.

We used to watch the pot boiling, and perhaps about seven or half-past he would investigate its contents with a long two-pronged iron fork, and finally decide much to our joy and contentment that the contents were edible.[20]

Gissing's friendship with Roberts was like an immediate return to their college days, ten years before, as if nothing had happened to them in the meantime. Gissing was impressed by Roberts's ruffian-like appearance and adventures in the wild West. Bertz and Roberts were the only two real friends Gissing had found in all those years. Like many men, he had difficulty being intimate with his own sex; he might get closer to women, but all too often that meant getting closer to trouble. The pleasures of food and drink, and of intellectual conversation, were an escape from troubles that seemed to have no solution, and therefore were best swept under the carpet. One thing the two men completely agreed on was the need for literary production. Gissing told Roberts to write down his tales of hard times in the West, and he responded by writing ninety-three thousand words in less than a month. Roberts's book was *The Western Avernus, or, Toil and Travel in North America*. Like all his books it was no masterpiece, but a glib and lively account of his adventures. Gissing put him in touch with James Payn at Smith, Elder; the book was accepted quickly and published in March 1887.[21]

While Roberts was getting such a good reception from Payn, Gissing sent him the first volume of *Thyrza* and received a terrible blow to his hopes:

> even though there should be a great improvement afterwards in the matter of movement ... the novel will not suit 'Cornhill'. There is too much of what the vulgar call 'preachment' in it, and I fear Egremont would by some readers be thought priggish. The 'poor' scenes are infinitely the best; some indeed are very good; but even these seem to me to lack the 'go' of those in *Demos*. I by no means say that we will not publish the novel, but only that it will not suit the Cornhill.[22]

This news was not quite as disastrous as Gissing thought. Smith, Elder would publish *Thyrza* on similar terms to *Demos* – £100 outright – provided that Gissing completed the novel in reasonable style. He would not get the further £50 or so that *The Cornhill* would have paid for serial rights, as they had done for *A Life's Morning*.[23] Nonetheless, Gissing was knocked sideways by Payn's letter. His first reaction was to abandon *Thyrza*, feeling that it would only harm his reputation after the success of *Demos*. He could quickly write another novel, and meanwhile scrape by on what he had saved. In response to Payn's criticism he sent a despairing letter; Payn wrote back at once telling him to calm down, and making a firm offer of £100 for the copyright of *Thyrza*. Before long Gissing's mood swung back again, and he spent the Christmas of 1886 alone in order to finish the novel. 'It is good,' he told Ellen, 'better in many respects than "Demos". Last night I cried myself into illness over a chapter as I wrote it, and this cannot be balderdash. I value the book more than anything I have yet done.'[24]

Gissing's tears were shed for old Mr Boddy, a one-legged man who had taken care of Thyrza and her sister when their parents died. As Christmas approached he could not pay his rent, and slowly starved in his room. His landlady wanted to evict him and send him to the workhouse, just as Gissing feared he would end up in the Marylebone workhouse across the street from his flat. In the novel, Mr Boddy goes out to pawn his violin, in order to pay his rent, but then cannot struggle home:

> But the cold and the weakness and the anguish of dread grew upon him. . . .
> He stumped on, fancying that he recognised this and that object, and at length knew that he had reached Westminster Bridge Road. The joy of drawing near home supported him. . . . He reached the grave-yard, walking for the most part as in a terrible dream, among strange distorted shapes of men and women, the houses tottering black on either hand, and ever that anvil-beat of the blood at his temples. Then of a sudden his wooden limb slipped, and he fell to the ground.[25]

This overwrought scene suggests how much Gissing himself felt at the end of his tether. If he made himself ill by writing the passage, it was through identification with Mr Boddy's ordeal. The old man's pawned violin stands in for the novelist's pen, about to fall from his grasp.

Gissing wallowed in his own misery as he nibbled on his Christmas turkey, which lasted him until the new year. Frederic Harrison asked him to dinner after Christmas, and Gissing chose to take offence that the invitation came from his fifteen-year-old son: 'They do things very indecently,' Gissing complained to Algernon, 'getting Bernard to write for them. I shall go in evening uniform, though it is not necessary, but merely to indicate that the invitation must be a proper one or none at all.'[26] Dinner at a comfortable Bayswater home would be the only pleasure of his holiday season, but he would only accept in a way that preserved his dignity. Did it occur to him that acting in that way would lead to fewer invitations in future, and that dignity hardly existed when one was alone?

In spite of Payn's rebuff, Gissing completed the last volume of *Thyrza* in less than four weeks. 'Thyrza herself is one of the most beautiful dreams I ever had or shall have,' he wrote to Ellen. 'I value the book really more than anything I have yet done. The last chapters drew many tears. I shall be glad when you know Thyrza and her sister. The vulgar will not care for them, I expect.'[27] What the vulgar surely would not care for was the way Thyrza dropped dead at the end of the novel for no apparent reason, other than to draw tears over another deathbed scene. However he may have conceived her at the beginning of the novel, Gissing ended by making Thyrza another of his negative heroines, a queen of renunciation. Walter Egremont, the bourgeois do-gooder, falls in love with her beauty and her singing, but decides to give her up: 'He knew what miseries had again and again resulted from marriages such as this, and he feared for her quite as much as for himself.'[28] Thyrza agrees to sacrifice herself to her faithful working-class suitor, until that marriage is prevented by her maidenly death. When he renounces Thyrza, Egremont also abandons his dream of raising up the workers through education; instead, he enters into a passionless marriage with Annabel, a woman of his own class. Egremont starts out as Gissing's alternative to William Morris: instead of stirring the workers up to revolt, he wants to give them the benefits of culture. Unfortunately, his mission runs into another dead end. Gissing seems unable to find a positive destiny for Thyrza either: she is an exceptional woman who cannot safely marry up, but neither will she be content with an ordinary man of her own class. It is the talented and idealistic people who try to cross the barriers of class, only to find that the barriers are there for everybody, without exception.

When Gissing sent *Thyrza* off to Payn, he told him that he would rather not take the same £100 for which he had sold *Demos* outright. Instead, he accepted an advance of £50 and a royalty of 10 per cent on the wholesale price after that. He told Algernon that he knew this was risky, but it was worth trying as an experiment. Smith, Elder printed only 500 copies of the first edition, compared with 750 for *Demos*. The circulating libraries had pushed the price at which they bought three-deckers down to less than a pound, just over half the official price at which the novel sold. This meant that Gissing could do no more than cover his advance on sales of the first edition; in fact it sold only 412 copies, on which royalties earned would have been about £40. So his experiment failed, since Smith, Elder did not issue *Thyrza* in any cheaper edition, as they had done with *Demos*. Perhaps they were trying to resist the coming of payment by royalty, and wanted to teach Gissing a lesson. If he was unhappy with selling his novels for £100, here was a way for him to get £50 instead. That might also teach him not to kill off his heroine in volume III.

Smith, Elder waited four years to reissue *Thyrza* in cheaper formats, after the success of *The Nether World* and *New Grub Street* made it a more valuable property. On their 6/- edition Gissing would be due a royalty of about 4½d; this meant about £2 for each hundred copies sold at 6/-, £1 for the 3/6d edition, and so on. But all this became moot when, in early 1891, Gissing accepted a miserable £10 from Smith, Elder for the entire copyright. He even volunteered to revise the text as part of the deal, feeling that it might sell better if it were shortened. If he was going to lose at the publishing game, he might as well lose in style. Adding insult to injury, Smith, Elder advertised a new edition as soon as the ink was dry on Gissing's acceptance, and published three more editions at various prices in the year after.[29] Smith, Elder squeezed Gissing out of his pennies per copy because they could; Gissing let himself be squeezed because he did not know how to resist, and because he hoped that getting his earlier books back into print might help him get more money for his new ones. Had Smith, Elder been a bit less penny-wise, they would have realised that Gissing would move to a less miserly publisher as soon as he could, which is exactly what happened before 1891 was out. In 1887, meanwhile, Gissing had to acknowledge that he had failed with his first royalty deal, and had to fall back on the bird in the hand of outright sale – no matter how skinny the bird.

There seemed no choice but to write another novel of similar kind, and do so as quickly as possible. He did some more of his prowling around London, with Roberts for company, then went off to Eastbourne for a few days. His holidays had to be taken at awkward times, whenever he had just finished a book. A cheap room at the seaside in January was too much even for him to bear:

> I can't say that I am much enjoying myself, for I have a cold and comfortless bedroom and no sitting-room, so perforce must stay out of doors whatever weather it is. I don't feel exactly well, and of course have no peace of mind. . . .
> I can't write more, as my hands are getting frozen in this bare room.[30]

After four days of this Gissing moved to a place where he paid 10/- a week instead of 6/6d, so that he could begin his new novel. The problem now was that too much comfort was making him uncomfortable: 'There is something gross in entering a stranger's house and taking the best room and saying do this and do that. . . . It is monstrous to ask people to do this. . . . I feel ashamed of myself every time the woman enters the room.'[31] At least he didn't need to have a guilty conscience about the pleasures of walking twenty miles every day across the Downs:

in every wooded hollow you come upon old, old hamlets, warm, peaceful, sheltered with old trees. Each has its little Norman church, generally built of flints, and with church-yards that make one always think of Gray's Elegy, – all the head-stones overgrown with lichen and fungus, so that you can seldom read the inscriptions. Never have I seen such quaintness and old-world beauty.[32]

Gissing was never happier than in a country churchyard, and such musings would fill out his greatest popular success, *The Private Papers of Henry Ryecroft*. Yet his real talent lay in the opposite direction, in describing the East London cemetery of *Demos*. Thomas Gray had already said it all about the yew-tree's shade; Gissing was called to be the poet of London's chimney-smoke and drizzle.

Gissing returned to London on 9 February to face a new round of work for which he would be as hard-pressed as ever. Having accepted so little for *Thyrza*, he expected to be 'harassed through all the next book and do poor work'.[33] He was quite taken aback to be asked by the *London Figaro*, a middle-brow review, for a photograph. It was a magazine that gave close attention to Gissing's career, and regularly praised his novels. He had just been identified as the author of *Demos* in an advertisement, so publicity linking the two novels would be helpful; but publicity was not something that Gissing was ready for. 'It would be painful to me,' he told the *Figaro*, 'to see any likeness of myself put before the public at this very early stage of my literary career.'[34] Perhaps he feared that a photograph might uncover news of his prison term, now eleven years in the past, or his marriage to Nell. But the more he succeeded, the more those risks were bound to increase.

Algernon was now trying to get his start as an author while living in lodgings in the small town of Wooler, in the Cheviot hills near the battle-field of Flodden. He was writing a novel called 'A Dinner of Herbs', with regular encouragement from George, who said they would both do a great deal of work in 1887. What George could not anticipate was that all his work would be a complete waste, making 1887 the most futile year of his entire literary career. He would work on no fewer than three novels: 'Clement Dorricott', 'Sandray the Sophist', and 'Dust and Dew'. None of them would be published, and no manuscripts have survived. Gissing had abandoned several other novels, and had another – 'Mrs Grundy's Enemies' – suppressed. But given the reputation that *Demos* and *Thyrza* were starting to gain for him, it was an extraordinarily barren year that he now had to suffer through.

Some of that suffering came from Gissing's determination to help his family. He was very anxious about Algernon's idea of renting a house for his mother and sisters in Alnwick, and about his seemingly hopeless engagement to Catherine Baseley, who still lived with her family in Southampton:

> Everything is made so difficult by our want of money. I suppose there is no doubt that, if I live, five years will see the worst of these embarrassments over. But what of the intervening time? ... In London I can and shall make a living. Marvellous thing of all, – for years I have not only made a living, but have dispensed considerable sums upon other people; I believe that, for the last three years, I have been able to devote to various other people not less than eighty pounds a year! I know not how I have done it.[35]

His mother seemed to consider him 'unstable and untrustworthy', Gissing went on, but Algernon was the one who really couldn't be trusted. If we deduct Nell's £50, most of the balance must have gone to Algernon, supporting him while he lived at Cornwall Residences and giving him enough to move to Northumberland. Up north, he could get food and lodging for six shillings a week; probably Gissing paid that too. His teaching and writing combined had been bringing in about £200–250 a year, so a third of that had been going to his family and Nell. Without these obligations he could have led a much easier life.

Gissing began writing the successor to *Thyrza* in March, working from eight in the morning to eleven at night; when he went to bed, he lay awake thinking about the book. He could work so intensely because his pupil Walter Grahame was away with his family for three months. Gissing's working title was 'Clement Dorricott: A Life's Prelude'. All we know for certain is that he wrote it in only ten weeks for three volumes, that he was very pleased with it while he was writing it, and that it dealt 'almost entirely with theatrical life'.[36] Gissing advised Algernon that *his* novel should have plenty of incident: 'In "Dorricott" I have managed that no single chapter is without its incident, and therefore the writing is so easy.'[37] The other way to make writing easy was to lay out the whole story in one's head before starting to write:

> If I write laboriously, it either means that the subject is not properly clear to myself, or that I am ill; and in either case it is necessary to suspend effort. At present I write 21 printed pages a day, but only because I am well advanced with the story, and characters and incidents are perfectly clear. Pray try a day of mere thinking.[38]

Gissing seems to have put in about three weeks of 'mere thinking' before starting to write 'Clement Dorricott'. His idea that writing a novel became easier as you went along is confirmed by the number of times he tore up the beginnings of a novel and started again. A good active plot was what helped to build momentum and carry a novel through.

As Gissing was hurrying on to the conclusion of 'Clement Dorricott' *Thyrza* appeared, with plentiful advertising by Smith, Elder. The reviews consolidated Gissing's reputation as an authority on working-class London. 'Mr Gissing writes gracefully and in good taste,' said the *Whitehall Review*, 'with plenty of vigour and strength of a most promising kind. We have few novelists in the present day who outrival him in quiet power and intensity, or who can approach his perfectly level method of thought and feeling.'[39] This was a solid testimonial for a novelist who, after all, was not yet thirty years old. But then the reviewer came up with a bizarre speculation, based on the anonymous publication of *Demos:*

> we would like to relieve ourselves publicly of the firm conviction that 'George Gissing' is of the feminine gender, in spite of his swashing and martial outside, but, if we are mistaken, we offer humble apologies, at the same time that we intend to rest on our conviction until we have very good proof afforded us of its truth or the reverse.[40]

Apart from having the same first name as George Eliot, it is not clear why Gissing should give an impression of femininity. The reviewer seems to have seized on the sentimental treatment of Thyrza's dreams, and assumed that the author identified with her; in fact, he only sympathised.

All the reviewers showed respect for Gissing's seriousness and the quality of his mind. 'It is not as a novelist,' wrote William Stead, 'in the narrow sense of the word, but as a social reformer and as an eager student of social life, that he occupies so important a place among contemporary writers.'[41] But the reviewers also underlined Gissing's continued difficulty in gaining a popularity matching his achievement. 'Thoughtful novels have to be very good to achieve success,' the *Whitehall* noted sagely.[42] Gissing understood his problem, but reacted to it by belittling his reviewers and extolling his artistic mission:

> So very much of my own culture derives from foreign literature, that I cannot be my real self when unable to refer familiarly to the foreign authors I value. . . .
>
> How sluggish-minded are the few people whom I know in England! I do not think over-highly of my own attainments, but certainly, compared with them, I am a very Casaubon. I keep up steadily my reading in Greek, Latin, German, French; and I do not know a soul – save yourself – who ever reads

anything but English – at all events for pure pleasure. Hence their terrible narrowness.— ...

Trollope? Ah, I cannot read him; the man is such a terrible Philistine. Indeed, of English novelists I see more and more clearly that there is *only one* entirely to my taste, and that is Charlotte Bronte. A great and glorious woman! George Eliot is miserable in comparison.[42]

Miserable or not, George Eliot was the English novelist closest to Gissing for her intellectual and social background, and her analytical mind. When complaining in this way he was fluffing up his self-esteem to console himself for his lack of readers. He knew, too, that displays of erudition were not what the Victorian novel was about. If he wanted to be a sage rather than a novelist, he could have written philosophical articles for the reviews, or even tried to revive his academic career. In any case, he believed that he could be true to himself regardless of how the literary world valued him: 'I think of very little but Art, pure and simple, and all my work is profoundly pessimistic as far as mood goes. Never mind: if I live another ten years, there shall not be many contemporary novelists ahead of me; for I am only beginning my work.'[44]

'Clement Dorricott' was Gissing's next offering to the literary marketplace. Payn's meagre offer of £50 advance for *Thyrza* was an obvious incentive to look elsewhere. Five years before, George Bentley had paid fifty guineas for 'Mrs Grundy's Enemies', and then never published the book. One would expect Gissing to hold a grudge, yet he still spoke of 'owing' Bentley a novel in exchange for the money he had paid. He may have come to feel that 'Mrs Grundy' was inferior work, and he was better off keeping it in the drawer (and eventually destroying the manuscript). More shrewdly, he may have realised that Bentley might have a guilty conscience about the episode, and be ready to pay well for another Gissing novel.

In March 1887 Algernon had his eye on Bentley as a likely publisher for 'A Dinner of Herbs', and asked George if that would interfere with *his* plans to market 'Clement Dorricott'. George told him that he saw no conflict, but also warned him that 'A Dinner of Herbs' would be too moralistic for Bentley's taste: 'The fact of the matter is, that, spite of all his personal moralizing, Bentley is notorious for the sensational character of his publications, – witness Rhoda Broughton, Mrs Wood and others. He is a typical instance of half-unconscious English hypocrisy.'[45] Bentley had a talent for finding and promoting best-selling novelists, soon to include Marie Corelli. He had money to spend on authors, and also edited *Temple Bar*, which Gissing considered 'by far the broadest of the magazines'. Gissing wrote 'Clement Dorricott' with *Temple Bar* in mind; a plot in which something happened in every chapter was well suited to serial publication.

As Gissing had predicted, Bentley duly rejected 'A Dinner of Herbs'. George sent in 'Clement Dorricott' a month later; Bentley took seven weeks to read it, and ended by telling Gissing that it was not suitable for *Temple Bar*. But he said it would do well as a regular three-decker, and he would pay a good price for it. Gissing believed that this meant a minimum of £150, three times what he had received from Smith, Elder for *Thyrza*. Yet he flatly refused Bentley's offer. He wanted 'Clement Dorricott' to run as a serial, and if not, he would put it on the shelf. One day, Gissing told Ellen, it would make him even more money; but that day never came, and at some unknown time he destroyed the manuscript.

Why did Gissing sabotage himself so thoroughly with 'Clement Dorricott'? Part of it was his tendency to go to pieces when his work was criticised. He had set his heart on getting the novel into *Temple Bar*, and failure there outweighed any other possible success. He told Ellen he was lonely and depressed, but in this condition he often had a stubborn belief that he knew exactly what his writing was worth and everyone else had it wrong: 'I cannot and will not be reckoned among the petty scribblers of the day, and to avoid it, I must for a time issue only one novel a year, and each book must have a distinct character, – a book which no one else would be likely to have written.' 'Clement Dorricott', he felt, 'will not do for my next staple work.'[46]

Once again Gissing had fallen into the trap of despising other people's opinions of his work, then being shattered when those opinions were less than totally approving. The sensible thing would have been to take Bentley's offer for 'Clement Dorricott'. He would have £150 or more to live on for the coming year, and could write his next novel in the best of circumstances. He seemed to fear that it would be obvious that 'Clement Dorricott' had been written as a serial, and he would be considered one of Bentley's stable of popular writers. In May he had turned down a dinner invitation by George Smith, the publisher of *Thyrza*, with the same kind of haughtiness:

> It is my rule henceforth to dine with no one. My solitude makes me more and more unfit to mix with people who are light-hearted, and it is better not to make pretence. So henceforth I shut myself from all acquaintances, and simply work on. I cannot get to know the kind of people who would suit me, so I must be content to be alone.

The day after this complaint, he told Ellen that his next novel, to be called 'Sandray the Sophist', would 'deal with the representative "literary man" of our days, – a contemptible creature'.[47]

The publication of *Thyrza*, with the usual fuss about advertising and reviews, was Gissing's cue to stand on his anti-social dignity. Yet when George Smith renewed his invitation, two months later, Gissing accepted and was almost childishly pleased with his evening. He met the eighty-eight-year-old widow Mrs Anne Procter, who had known all the great English writers back to Byron and Shelley. His host George Smith had published the Brontës, and Charlotte was said to have hoped to marry him until he chose a society heiress instead. Gissing was eager to hear at first hand about the novelist he so much admired:

> It was a wonderful evening. The Smiths' house has a large balcony, and a lot of us (we were some twenty altogether) sat out there, smoking, drinking coffee, hatless, shawl-less; a glorious moon in the sky right before us. I felt thoroughly well and content and hopeful for the future, and answered people's questions merrily about 'Thyrza'. Then old Smith came and sat down by me, and I said: 'Come now and tell me all you can about the Brontes.' So he began his stories. It was a wonderful thing to think that this man had entertained Charlotte in his house some forty years ago, just as he was now entertaining me. . . . he hints that he is the original of 'Dr John' in 'Villette'. . . .
>
> Well, all this is glorious. A happy thing that I have not come too late to talk with these people: if I live thirty years more, the memory will be interesting.—[48]

It is significant that Gissing speaks of feeling 'thoroughly well' at this party, because he so often complains of being laid low by his nervous illness. He half-recognised that his reclusiveness was becoming pathological: loneliness made him ill and illness made him lonely. When he did go out into the world he made a good impression and felt warmed by people's attention; yet he convinced himself that he had neither time nor money to support a social life. His inability to convert the reputation of his books into social success was a chronic handicap in building his literary career.

Part of Gissing's social awkwardness was his difficulty in separating business from friendship. Bentley made his offer to publish 'Clement Dorricott' as a three-decker the day after Smith's dinner party. 'It would seem very ungracious to Smith,' Gissing told Ellen, 'to give the next book after "Thyrza" to another publisher, and yet "Clement Dorricott" must not appear through Smith, as I do not think it *characteristic* enough; I wrote it for a magazine.' What was Gissing thinking? Smith had taken two proletarian novels, *Demos* and *Thyrza*, and also *A Life's Morning* (though the latter was not yet published). 'Clement Dorricott' might upset the idea that Gissing wrote mainly about the London poor; but all he had to do to settle the question was offer the novel to Smith, Elder. If it was accepted, that would show that Smith thought it worthy to stand with Gissing's other novels; if it was refused, he could take Bentley's £150 without feeling disloyal. Perhaps the deep reason for Gissing's failure to do the sensible thing was that he didn't want *anyone* to see 'Clement Dorricott'. Such a failure in artistic self-confidence threatened all his work in 1887. As he was completing 'Dorricott' in April, he spoke optimistically to Algernon about his next novel, 'Sandray the Sophist': 'I shall put into it all of culture that I have got up to this time. It will be mainly a satire on the modern cultivation of literature, and more particularly periodical literature.'[49] By the beginning of July, though, he had given it up. This may have been for the best, for if he had completed 'Sandray' he might never have written what may be his masterpiece, *New Grub Street*.

While ruminating on 'Sandray', Gissing was also witness to events that would inspire another of his best novels, seven years later. Victoria's Golden Jubilee, the fiftieth anniversary of her coming to the throne, was celebrated at the end of June. The centre of the city was closed to traffic, and enormous crowds washed through it on foot. Thanks to the growth of the city and improvements in public transportation – the Tube, railways and trams were all Victorian innovations – these must have been the biggest crowds since the beginning of the world. Gissing walked among them, separate in spirit. His feelings show the paradox of calling him a 'Victorian' novelist:

> after all it is something to have seen the most gigantic organized exhibition of fatuity, vulgarity and blatant blackguardism on record. Anything more ignoble can scarcely be conceived. ... What has this woman Victoria ever done to be glorified in this manner? The inscriptions hung about the streets turn one's stomach. It is very clear to me that England is very far indeed from the spirit of republicanism. Well, I don't object to that, but it certainly degrades humanity to yell in this way about a rather ill-tempered, very narrow-minded, and exceedingly ugly farmer's daughter, just because she cannot help having occupied a *nominal* throne for half a century. But the vulgarity of the mass of mankind passes all utterance.[50]

Gissing never met a mass emotion that he liked. He was ahead of his time in understanding that ideas of mass defined where the world would go in the next century, from mass media to mass production, mass consumption, and mass mobilisation in war. Mass murder too, of course.

As he was going through his troubles with Bentley and Smith over 'Clement Dorricott', Gissing hit on a subject for his third novel of the year, to be called 'Dust and Dew'. It would be 'Tragical strong in parts, but jubilant at the end: the triumph of strong natures amid hateful circumstances'.[51] The title seems to name things to be struggled with on a journey, as in a poem by Bret Harte.[52] For the rest of the book we have only a few hints. Gissing went to Surrey and Essex to scout some locations for it, and it had a hero named Peake, like the later *Born in Exile*. He told Thomas Hardy in July that it was 'a story that has grown up in recent ramblings about Clerkenwell, – dark, but with evening sunlight to close. For there may occasionally be a triumph of individual strength; a different thing from hope for the masses of men.'[53] In October he warned Ellen that 'Dust and Dew' would be less entertaining than *Thyrza*: 'It is very serious indeed, and deals with some of the wretchedest problems of this huge London. One cannot always be showing the pleasant sides; there will be very little indeed that is pleasant in this story.'[54]

It sounds as if Gissing had tried to move on from *Demos* and *Thyrza* by having a more positive hero, someone who could fulfil himself apart from the class struggles that could not have any good result. But the one thing certainly known about 'Dust and Dew' is that Gissing had a terrible struggle just to get it written. He was well into the third volume by the end of the year, but also had to go back constantly to rewrite earlier passages, six or seven times for the first chapter alone. The title was changed in the new year, too, from 'Dust and Dew' to 'The Insurgents'. Gissing was feeling even more isolated from the English collective, whether it showed itself in the Jubilee mobs of June or the radical mobs of November (protesting the arrest of an Irish nationalist MP). Novels were supposed to be social documents, but what if the novelist lost his faith in any kind of group action? Gissing's pessimism was reinforced by the illness of the German Crown Prince Frederick, who had promised to be one of the few wise and moderate European leaders:

what unspeakable fools are the masses of mankind, who confess that they cannot do other than be led into quagmires by any ruler who happens to find a pleasure in seeing them there. Civilization! With all the European peoples desiring to live in peace and comfort, the mere fact of one man's death and his son coming to a throne might in all probability lead to wars of incalculable duration.[55]

This was Gissing prophesying with a vengeance. Frederick died of his illness, his son came to the throne as Kaiser Wilhelm II, and he led Germany into the quagmire of the First World War. The socialists of the time believed that the masses would be emancipated, under the guiding hand of rational and unselfish leaders. Gissing had looked hard at the movements of the left, and turned away in disillusion. One could call it a symptom of his depression that he expected Europe to be drenched in blood, with psychopaths ruling most nations, except that his predictions about the twentieth century were so terribly accurate. He judged the future by what he knew of the past: gullible masses and crazed leaders were the norm in the culture he loved to study, that of Imperial Rome. The Kaisers or Tsars of his time were much like the Caesars of the past; their names had just been translated into another language.

Gissing's life in the second half of 1887 and on into 1888 centred on his painful struggle to complete 'Dust and Dew'. He supported himself by continuing to teach Walter Grahame; in November Bernard Harrison, who was now sixteen, came back to him also. Walter came every morning, and Bernard in the evenings from six to seven. It broke up Gissing's day and made it very difficult to write steadily, but he felt unable to refuse Frederic Harrison's request, and he needed the money. To have accepted only £50 for *Thyrza* now had the direct result of cutting down on his time and energy for writing.

Meanwhile Algernon decided to get married, much to Gissing's dismay. Algernon had been engaged to Catherine Baseley for three years, and had known her long before that. She was an intelligent and sensible young woman; Gissing's worries were not about her, but about what kind of husband Algernon could make. He had never held down a job for very long, and had now embarked on a far from promising career as a writer. Gissing told Ellen that he was very depressed that Algernon had no definite prospect of any income, which meant he would continue to be a dead weight on his family, and have a wife to be looked after too. After six months or so in the Cheviots, Algernon went down to visit his cousins in the Cotswolds: Mrs Emma Shailer, and Tom and Mary Bedford. Life in a Cotswold cottage was more attractive than shivering in a boarding-house on the Scottish border. Algernon took a lease on Smallbrook Cottage at Willersey, near Broadway, and persuaded Catherine to marry him almost immediately, on 8 September 1887. The cottage was actually quite a sub-stantial two-storey house, in beautiful countryside. Most likely Catherine had some money of her own to set up house, because Algernon can have had little to spare.

Catherine had a plain, square face with blunt features; but she had some education, and other qualities suitable for becoming the wife of an unsuccessful writer. Her steadiness allowed Algernon to launch his career in much better conditions than George had ever enjoyed. Algernon had a sympathetic companion, a small library, and a charming country cottage. He scrounged enough money that he didn't have to work as a tutor. Nonetheless, George held to the fixed idea that any marriage contracted in poverty was bound to end in disaster. This was his excuse for refusing Catherine's invitation to the wedding:

> You will not, I trust, think it any unkindness on my part that I do not make an effort to see you and Alg. on that day. If I can help it, I shall never be present at any wedding of any person whatsoever at any time whatsoever. But that has nothing to do with my feelings to those who have made up their minds to face life together; very heartily indeed do I wish to all such as full a measure of content as life has to give.[56]

Gissing had been present at one wedding, at least: his own, to Nell Harrison eight years before. But whether he was dragged to the altar by the inconveniences inflicted on unmarried couples, or by Nell's demand that he marry her, he felt that it was one of the great mistakes of his life. Yet it was another of his quirks that he at once boycotted marriage, and believed that it imposed solemn duties on those who entered into it. No one takes marriage lightly in his novels, except for outright liars and cheats. Gissing might scorn a social convention, but he could never just laugh at it or propose evading its requirements. The debate between Rhoda Nunn and Everard Barfoot (in *The Odd Women*) about entering a 'free union' is Gissing's set-piece exposition of why marriage really counts, even for those who profess to despise it. What Rhoda ends up saying — and Gissing surely agrees — is that a free union is no more possible than a free lunch.

The other implicit message of Gissing's letter to Catherine was that she and Algernon were to be envied for seeking their ideals together in a country cottage, while he remained stuck in his world of 'bricks and mortar'. He still believed that his novels needed raw materials, the actuality of crowded streets and little events recorded in newspapers. This was partly the idea that his best niche in the literary marketplace was in offering the middle classes a kind of conducted tour of the lower depths. Perhaps he also feared that his brutal schedule of work had dried up his imagination, so that he could only write of things he regularly saw for himself. It made a great deal of sense for Gissing to follow Algernon's example and live more quietly and cheaply in the countryside that he loved. But so long as he felt dependent on the daily stimulus of life in the metropolis, he could not leave for more than a week or two at a time.

Before Christmas Gissing made a couple of forays into middle-class society, though without settling into any more regular social life. He went to an evening at the house of George Bradley, the Dean of Westminster, because he greatly admired *A Village Tragedy*, a novel just published by Bradley's daughter, Mrs Margaret Woods.[57] The Dean lived in a fine old house attached to Westminster Abbey. Gissing relished the comfort and the educated company; he even set out to impress a young lady, telling his sister that 'when I am really in good spirits I can talk consumedly'.[58] As usual, he liked to warm his hands at the fire of good society, but then stayed away for fear that he might get used to it. He also spotted Oscar Wilde at a lecture: 'I looked at him with no little curiosity. He is growing enormously fat, and is conforming, in attire, to conventional standards. Also, he has even shortened his hair.'[59] Gissing appreciated Wilde, and would feel sorry for him when he fell, but did not try to speak to him. Their common ground was limited to being three years apart in age and lovers of the classics. Gissing was earnest, all too earnest. To the lower-middle-class world from which Gissing came Oscar had nothing to say, except: 'It is only by not paying one's bills that one can hope to live in the memory of the commercial classes.'

After his usual blank Christmas, Gissing had nothing to look forward to in 1888 except driving 'The Insurgents' to a conclusion, a task that became harder as it went along and threatened to bring on another nervous collapse. There was some good news on 20 January, when Algernon's novel was accepted by the publishers Hurst & Blackett. Called *Joy Cometh in the Morning*, it was a two-volume story of love in a cottage. The terms were a straight royalty of four shillings a copy, beginning after 280 copies had been sold. This was at least better than publishing at his own expense, as George had had to do with *his* first novel. But Algernon's books sold even fewer copies than George's, and he would find himself stuck at a price of about £40 or £50 for his future novels: enough to let him think of himself as a professional writer, not enough to support his family. Gissing felt 'miserably ill' at the end of January, which was his term for feeling miserably depressed. He set off on impulse for Algernon's cottage, and was much impressed by the cosy home he found there. 'If a man cannot do good work in this house,' he told Ellen, 'and amid these surroundings, he never will do it.'[60] A week with Algernon and Catherine did him good, as relief from his losing battle with 'The Insurgents'.

From this time on, until a year before he died, we have the daily record of Gissing's life in his diary. The first entry is for 27 December 1887, but pages of the manuscript notebook are torn out before that and it seems likely that there were entries in the notebook going back to 1885.[61] Whether Gissing kept a diary before 1885 is unknown, but an entry for 7 April 1902 gives some idea of why he kept a daily record:

> Yesterday chanced to open the first vol of my Diary, and found it such strange and moving reading that I have gone on, hour after hour. – Who knows whether I may not still live a few years; and if so, I shall be sorry not to have a continuous record of my life.[62]

If the diary is 'strange and moving' it can only be through its cumulative impact, because thousands of its entries could belong to a *reductio ad absurdum* of literary naturalism. Like the imaginary novel 'Mr Bailey, Grocer' in *New Grub Street*, the diary might be called 'Mr Gissing, Writer'. On 17 January 1893 Gissing's entry was: 'Sunshine and rain. Corrected proofs. Wrote 2½ pp.' This might be the template for innumerable other days: first the weather, last the number of pages written, in between whatever life there was in the day. Not every entry was so dry, certainly; but the core of Gissing's diary is the record of his output, and the circumstances of its production.

This is probably the fullest record we have of a Victorian writer's life from day to day. One of Gissing's motives was simply to register his complaints, to show in grim detail what it cost him to get his books written. Another concern was to create a text about his texts, more monumental than any individual novel but stripped of anything that might leave the reader entertained, amused or pained. Finally, the diary was the place where he could confess, and also prove, the words he wrote there: 'Few men, I am sure, have led so bitter a life.'[63] There was no one to whom he could safely say this, day after day after day; but he could say it to himself, and leave behind the evidence. When he made his will, he asked that his diary be preserved, and given to his eldest son when he was twenty-one.

The Death of Nell

Gissing came back to London from his visit to Algernon and realised that he might have to abandon 'The Insurgents':

> Two days of blank misery; incapable of work; feeling almost ready for suicide. This evening a little light comes to me. Will it be credited, that I must begin a new novel? I am wholly dissatisfied with the plan of what I have been writing. This terrible waste of time. I dare not tell anyone the truth; shall merely say that I am getting on very slowly.[1]

After a few more barren days, he decided to return to Eastbourne in the hope of shifting his depression. His spirits did not pick up after his arrival on 13 February, so he begged Morley Roberts to come down and keep him company. Roberts came at once, though he had no patience with Gissing's idea that Eastbourne was the great good place. The boarding-house was draughty and shabby, the landlady incompetent. Roberts tramped gamely over the Downs with Gissing, in deep snow and a full gale. They were kept going by thoughts of the rich apple pudding that Gissing had ordered for dessert. When it arrived, they found that the landlady had put it under the shelf where she kept her lamps, and it tasted not of apple but of kerosene.

Roberts went back to London after four days. He had done his best to cheer Gissing up, but he had no money to spare for boarding-house living. Gissing's room was too cold to work on 'The Insurgents'; instead of writing novels, he could only read them. He took out a library subscription and started working his way through popular novels by Hall Caine and Rhoda Broughton. Romance in Mrs Broughton's pages brought on a taste of romance in real life. Gissing found himself smitten by a Miss Curtis, who worked in a tobacco shop around the corner in Church Street. As he moped in his freezing room for ten days after Roberts left, all he had to look forward to was a few words with Miss Curtis across the counter each day.

On the afternoon of 29 February Gissing broke his routine by taking the train to Lewes and wandering around in the snow. When he got back to his lodgings there was a telegram saying: 'Mrs Gissing is dead. Come at once.' Nell's landlady had found the Eastbourne address on an envelope in Nell's room. Even as she lay dying, Nell had not dared to ask her husband to come to her. Or perhaps she did, and he turned a deaf ear. Morley Roberts recalled that 'at intervals she used to send him heart-breaking messages asking to be forgiven, messages that even his unwisdom at last could not listen to'. Gissing still suspected a trick; but he set off for London, and asked Roberts to meet him at his flat. He arrived late at night, so there was nothing to do but sit up with his friend and let the news sink in: 'We sat silently for hours, and I knew that he was going back over the burning marl of the past. Sometimes he did speak, asking once and again if it could be true, and I saw that while he was still uncertain he was bitter and pitiless. Yet if only she were really dead.'[2]

In the morning they set out for 16 Lucretia Street, Lower Marsh. Still suspicious, Gissing waited at Waterloo while Roberts went to the house to see if Nell really was dead. He came back to say that the news was true and they went back together to Lucretia Street. Gissing went upstairs to see Nell's body, Roberts could not face it. Then they saw the doctor who had come to Nell at the end. The death certificate gave 'acute laryngitis' as the cause of death, but Roberts claims that this was a euphemism, since Nell had been treated for syphilis earlier.[3] Tertiary syphilis often attacked the larynx, with swelling and deep ulceration. There was no treatment, and death could come very quickly – by suffocation, unless a tracheotomy was performed. Gissing's diary says that Nell's 'last struggle' began at six in the morning of 29 February, and she died three and a half hours later. Her thirtieth birthday had been four days before.

After seeing the doctor Gissing went back to sort out Nell's possessions, a grim enough experience in itself, but also one that he felt compelled to record in his diary. The scene he viewed in her room – inventoried might be a better word – was one that defined his entire life; but just for that reason, no one else could read his words until after he was dead. Yet to whom was Gissing speaking when he began with those chilling five words: 'Let me describe this room'? Perhaps the same imagined companion he addressed in the first words of his first book: 'Walk with me, reader, into Whitecross Street.' More than a reader: a friend, a beloved, a witness, a judge? What strikes the heart unbearably can be exorcised by being written down:

It was the first floor back; so small that the bed left little room to move. She took it unfurnished, for 2/9 a week; the furniture she brought was: the bed, one chair, a chest of drawers, and a broken deal table. On some shelves were a few plates, cups, etc. Over the mantelpiece hung several pictures, which she had preserved from old days. There were three engravings: a landscape, a piece by Landseer, and a Madonna of Raphael. There was a portrait of Byron, and one of Tennyson. There was a photograph of myself, taken 12 years ago, – to which, the landlady tells me, she attached special value, strangely enough. Then there were several cards with Biblical texts, and three cards such as are signed by those who 'take the pledge', – all bearing date during the last six months.

On the door hung a poor miserable dress and a worn out ulster; under the bed was a pair of boots. Linen she had none; the very covering of the bed had gone save one sheet and one blanket. I found a number of pawn tickets, showing that she had pledged these things during last summer, – when it was warm, poor creature! All the money she received went in drink; she used to spend my weekly 15/- the first day or two that she had it. Her associates were women of so low a kind that even Mrs Sherlock did not consider them respectable enough to visit her house.

I drew out the drawers. In one I found a little bit of butter and a crust of bread, – most pitiful sight my eyes ever looked upon. There was no other food anywhere. The other drawers contained a disorderly lot of papers: there I found all my letters, away back to the American time. In a cupboard were several heaps of dirty rags; at the bottom there had been coals, but none were left. Lying about here and there were medicine bottles, and hospital prescriptions.

She lay on the bed covered with a sheet. I looked long, long at her face, but could not recognize it. It is more than three years, I think, since I saw her, and she had changed horribly. Her teeth all remained, white and perfect as formerly.

I took away very few things, just a little parcel: my letters, my portrait, her rent-book, a certificate of life-assurance which had lapsed, a copy of my Father's 'Margaret' which she had preserved, and a little workbox, the only thing that contained traces of womanly occupation.

Came home to a bad, wretched night. In nothing am I to blame; I did my utmost; again and again I had her back to me. Fate was too strong. But as I stood beside that bed, I felt that my life henceforth had a firmer purpose. Henceforth I never cease to bear testimony against the accursed social order that brings about things of this kind. I feel that she will help me more in her death than she balked me during her life. Poor, poor thing![4]

Was Gissing to blame? Fredric Jameson calls Nell a 'proletarian woman tormented by a middle-class marriage and drinking herself to death'.[5] The grain of truth in this is that Gissing saw his wife as a character in need of correction, rather than an identity in need of respect. But Nell was not a figure of proletarian virtue, nor did any proletarian helpmeet come forward to save her after she left Gissing. She wanted him to take her back because she knew that without him she would perish. It was one of Gissing's lost illusions that he could make Nell his intellectual companion, and he thought he had failed utterly. Yet in her room he saw that she had kept her icons of culture, in which she saw a power to be respected. Raphael's Sistine Madonna, with Jesus in her arms, looked down at Nell in her bed; and Nell looked up at her. There was one book: Thomas Gissing's *Margaret and Other Poems* (1855). The title poem had contributed to the catastrophe of Gissing's marriage, but it said the right thing here: Forgive! Yet it was not so simple. Gissing left Nell's room holding on to three beliefs not easily reconciled: that Nell was a victim, that he was not to blame, and that society was.

The few things that Gissing took from Nell's room, including his letters to her and his photograph, have been lost. They were probably destroyed by Gissing himself; if not, by Gabrielle Fleury after his death. He went back the next day for two things more: 'A daughter accompanied me to a low public house, where the landlady had a pawn-ticket for Helen's wedding-ring, security for a debt of 1/9. I paid the debt, and redeemed the ring, from the broker's. – Cut a little hair from the poor head, – I scarcely know why, alas!'[6] Gissing arranged for a simple funeral, costing six guineas; he gave another £3 to Nell's landlady and her daughter, to buy mourning and attend the funeral in his place. When Nell was laid out, she looked more familiar. 'I saw her yesterday in the coffin,' Gissing told Algernon, 'and had a wonderful sense of rest and peace in looking at her. No more wretched blind struggling for her, no more suffering under the world's curses.'[7] Whatever Nell had done, society should not have punished her as cruelly as it did. 'Outcasts always mourn,' the most famous victim of Victorian hypocrisy would write; Gissing and Nell had both, in different ways, been made outcasts by their relationship. Gissing's sister-in-law Catherine was reading *Workers in the Dawn* at this time, where the idealist Arthur Golding marries Carrie Mitchell in a futile attempt to save her from alcoholism and prostitution. 'That book was a singular piece of detailed prophecy,' Gissing told Catherine.[8] But should it be called prophecy when one already knows what lies at the end of the road, and takes that road regardless?

However distraught he might be as a husband, as a writer Gissing felt curiously vindicated by the manner of Nell's death. 'For me there is yet work to do,' he told Algernon, 'and this memory of wretchedness will be an impulse such as few men possess.'[9] For the past year his imagination had failed him, with his three unsatisfactory and unpublished novels; now, Nell's death told him what to write. For some days he could not begin. He asked Ellen to come and stay with him, and she arrived at King's Cross an hour before Nell was buried in the Lambeth Cemetery at Tooting. This was a place of lawns and trees, much less bleak than the Manor Park Cemetery described in *Demos;* but Gissing was not going anyway. The Victorians often sent hired mourners to the graveside rather than the immediate family, though in *Demos* Jane Vine's two sisters go to the cemetery with her coffin. At Lambeth there was a ceremony in the chapel before each interment, and that may have been part of what Gissing was determined to miss: the ceremony beginning his brother's marriage last September, the one at the end of his own in March.

Ellen was the one person Gissing most wanted near him, even if there was much that she could not understand about her brother's suffering. At twenty she was studious, provincial, pious and a virgin, which she most likely remained all her life. Her experience of woman's condition was as far from Nell's as could be imagined; perhaps that was more comforting to Gissing than to talk openly about the twelve-year-long sexual disaster he had just finished living through. After five days Ellen had to go back to her work in Wakefield, and Gissing was plunged back into despair, to the point of thinking he might die. 'I speak very seriously,' he told Ellen, 'when I say that I feel to be growing weaker and weaker. I cannot reconcile myself to the thought that my life's work is over – there is so much I still want to do: I have so much to say.'[10] His real illness was the loneliness that Nell's death only made worse: 'Do you think it comes from the fact of my release from that long burden, that I feel my loneliness far more than hitherto? Hitherto I have reconciled myself to it as being inevitable; now I fail before the prospect of months and months, years perhaps, of absolute solitude.'[11]

As usual, Gissing was a shrewd self-critic. So long as Nell was alive, he could blame her for his inability to find a companion and sexual partner; now he had no one to blame but himself. He blamed himself in advance for the lonely years ahead of him; he recognised his own irrational pessimism, and blamed himself for that:

> You will get so used to this kind of querulousness that you will pay no attention to it – which perhaps will be the best thing that could happen. What *is* the use of complaining, when there is no remedy? Yet it seems so miserable that a man at my age, with my (I suppose I might say) reputation, and, now, with absolute freedom, should be so utterly companionless. What I want is domestic society; I want to know a family of people, with whom

to have restful intercourse. If that were gained, it would matter little where
I lived. It will never benefit me to take change of air, or anything of the
kind, so long as I am a hermit wherever I go: I merely carry a desert with
me.[12]

Gissing even suggested that he would be better off if he gave up his flat
and went back into lodgings, where he could at least sit by the fire with his
landlord in the evenings. But companionship with those he felt to be his
inferiors could never really satisfy him. He saw also that his frustration was
not peculiar to him; he felt just as badly for Ellen, stuck with a dreary job
and without anyone to love or be loved by:

> There must be few, very few – if indeed there is anyone – who understand
> you and value you aright. The commonplace consolation is: 'Remember
> what multitudes of people are in the same position.' That is no solace at all;
> it merely intensifies the misery of the particular case by making it seem more
> hopeless.[13]

That dilemma of the thwarted soul was at the heart of Gissing's early
fiction, and it was insoluble so long as he rejected the two possible ways of
escape from it. One was to leave conscience behind and seize whatever he
could get in the world; he was too much in thrall to the morality of his
youth to break out in that way. The other solution was to see his suffering
as typical of a whole class, and look to socialism for salvation; he had
examined that choice in *Demos* and found it wanting. He was left with a
personal consciousness that was incapable of enjoyment, and a collective
consciousness that he could not trust. If happiness or a social mission were
both ruled out, one thing was left for him to do. 'When I am writing,' he
told Ellen, 'I can partly forget myself in the world I create. Write I must; it
is the only refuge.'[14] A ray of hope was that Fanny le Breton wrote from
Paris, asking if she could translate *Demos* into French. Following on the
American edition of *Demos* in 1886, a French publication would help Gissing's ambition of becoming an international author, known beyond the
parochial world of the English reading public. The translation went ahead
and appeared with Hachette, though not until 1890.

Gissing now had to make good on the pledge he had made in Nell's
room, that he would draw up an indictment against the society he held
responsible for her death. Two weeks after her funeral, on 19 March, he
shook off his depression and wrote six pages of a new novel, later called
The Nether World. The novel he had worked on for the past nine months,
'The Insurgents', was abandoned for ever. He took up his old regime of

visiting workshops and walking the streets, this time in Clerkenwell, where his novel would be set. Meanwhile Algernon's novel, *Joy Cometh in the Morning*, appeared from Hurst & Blackett. It was a Cotswold romance set in the 1820s, centring on a young blind woman kept prisoner in an old manor house by her villainous uncle. Algernon had written a competent piece of pulp fiction, with cardboard characters and rustics commenting on the action in Cotswold dialect. Gissing told him that he would soon write better, and less sentimentally; but Algernon was just good enough to get published, not good enough to write a novel that anyone would take seriously.

When he had put in a month's work on *The Nether World*, Gissing had another crisis. After he had been unable to write a line for four days, he went down to Eastbourne and presented himself on Miss Curtis's doorstep. He spoke to her for nearly two hours, and sent her a copy of *Thyrza* when he got back to London. Miss Curtis may have been an orphan, like Annabel Newthorpe in the novel, since she lived with her aunt; perhaps Gissing thought she might be a real-life Thyrza, a clever and pure-hearted work-girl. He suffered for twelve days while waiting for a reply: '[I] paced my rooms in an agony of loneliness. This becomes intolerable; in absolute truth, I am now and then on the verge of madness. Thought of Miss Curtis, and longed, longed that she too might have thought of me. This life I *cannot* live much longer; it is hideous.'[15] The next day he went down to Eastbourne to see Miss Curtis again. 'All gone off in smoke,' he wrote in his diary. 'Never mind; the better perhaps.' Gissing appeared to be a gentleman; he was quite handsome and ever polite. This was not enough to capture the fancy of young ladies in tobacco shops or any other such places. He could write with insight about their lives, but never enter into those lives on a human level. The day after Miss Curtis turned him down, Mr Gladstone mentioned *The Unclassed* in a review in *The Nineteenth Century;* Gissing could get respect from the former prime minister, but not from an Eastbourne shop-girl. With Nell gone, he was free to seek love from someone else – and to find that they were free to reject him.

Just before this, another kind of rejection would have equally painful consequences. Gissing had given Ellen a novel by Alphonse Daudet, one of his favourite authors. *Fromont Jeune et Risler Aîné* dealt with love affairs in Parisian society; perhaps Gissing gave it to his sister because she was approaching her twenty-first birthday. He recognised, he said, that some novels belonged 'to the *studio* not to the *drawing room*', and should not be read by young ladies; but he did not think that *Fromont Jeune* was in any way offensive. He had been helping Ellen with her Latin and Greek, and his hope was that she might be a real intellectual companion for him. Unfortunately, Ellen started reading *Fromont Jeune* and was deeply shocked by its treatment of love and sex. Gissing's first reaction was to be appalled that she was so narrow-minded; then he realised that he should not have expected anything different:

> My dear, dear Nelly,
>
> Do, I pray you, throw the book into the fire, and let it go to perdition rather than cause you half a moment's trouble; no book in the world is worth that. . . . The fact of the matter is, I have lost all perception of the ordinary prejudices; I offend people when I had never dreamt of doing so, merely because my whole view of life is at variance with that usually accepted. We cannot help this; and I do not for a moment believe it makes me a scoundrel and a ruffian. . . . Pack the book up and have done with it, and let Daudet of the flowing locks be excommunicated, – only never let me have letters such as this from my dear sister, who is the truest and nearest friend I have.[16]

Gissing had already created attractive, intellectually independent female characters, such as Ada Warren in *Isabel Clarendon*; later there would be Rhoda Nunn in *The Odd Women*. When it came to his favourite sister, though, he at once threw in the towel. If Ellen could only be happy by being conventional, all he could do was tell her she was right. In the long run, following the old rules did not make Ellen happy either; by the time of *The Odd Women*, four years later, Gissing had decided that most women of his sister's type were simply doomed to live unfulfilled.

Ellen's response to Daudet told Gissing that she was capable of learning, but not of thinking for herself. If he moved to a provincial town to escape the misery of Cornwall Residences, he would be at the mercy of Ellen's world: 'lack of religious conformity shuts one out from the society of such places.'[17] Within a couple of months after Nell's death, Gissing had decided to go away for a year, as soon as he had finished *The Nether World*. He still had no idea *where* he might go to be more content. But he no longer had to pay for Nell's keep, and he was confident that he had a strong novel in hand, after his failure with three manuscripts over the past year. All he had to do was buckle down to the task of finishing it. Morley Roberts went off to Cornwall for three months in May, leaving Gissing without a friend. But his worst days, paradoxically, were his days off: the Sundays when he was too depressed to work, but unable to enjoy his freedom from the daily quota of pages:

> I have lived in London ten years, and now, on a day like this when I am very lonely and depressed, there is not one single house in which I should

be welcome if I presented myself, not one family – nay, not one person – who would certainly receive me with good will. I wonder whether any other man would make such a statement as this with such absolute truth.[18]

No doubt part of Gissing's misery came from the awful circumstances of Nell's death; yet neither in his diary nor in his letters did he say a word about her, once she had been buried. Nor was *The Nether World* a directly autobiographical book. Gissing fulfilled his pledge to Nell by examining the general condition of the poor in Clerkenwell, rather than by creating a character whose story ran parallel with Nell's. Perhaps the character of the abused little girl, Jane Snowdon, owed something to Nell's stories about growing up as a stepchild in Shropshire. If so, Gissing changed the outcome, since Jane ends up redeemed, rather than on the streets like Nell. And if he wanted to lay blame for the sufferings of the weak, why is the instrument of Jane's torment a healthy and good-looking young woman, Clem Peckover? Clem is a working-class girl like Jane, who inflicts pain because she enjoys doing so, not because anyone has done evil to her. Victorian society cannot be blamed for the existence of Clem; the only determinism prominent in the novel is the taint of bad heredity, not the injuries of class.

From the beginning of *The Nether World*, Gissing was deflected from trying to make the case that women like Nell were victims of the social order. Gissing had tried to save her, and the temperance people had made her take the pledge; but she had always returned to the flaring gaslight of cheap pubs, the smell of beer and tobacco, the easy money from selling her body to all comers. It came back to the power of will: Nell could not save herself and now she lay underground. Gissing could not, finally, substitute his will for hers. Nor did his own force of will bring him any happiness; he could only drive himself on to finish *The Nether World*, and then look around for some new way of escape. He was halfway through the third volume when he went to two meetings in support of striking match-girls. Middle-class radicals like Mrs Besant and R. B. Cunninghame Grahame made speeches, though few of the actual strikers were present. Gissing gave two shillings to the strike fund because he was 'ashamed to give nothing, in [his] bourgeois costume'.[19] On the way home he realised that he could not wind up the plot of *The Nether World* in the way he had planned, and would have to rewrite some earlier passages to fit with a new ending. Perhaps he felt that the poor turnout at the strike meetings meant that if work-girls would never be able to stand up for themselves, neither could Jane Snowdon recover from the oppressions of her childhood: 'As humble now as in the days of her serfdom, Jane was incapable of revolting against the tyranny of circumstances. Life had grown very hard for her again, but she believed that this was to a great extent her own fault.'[20] Where, though, was the tyranny to be situated? Gissing could not accept the socialist concept of evil; to blame 'circumstances' for the sufferings of the poor was very different from blaming their exploitation by the ruling class. The relations between labour and capital showed only part of human nature; circumstances included much more than that. In his larger view of circumstances, also, Gissing was now taking a more explicitly Darwinian view than he had done in his previous political novels.

Halfway through *The Nether World* is a chapter called 'The Soup Kitchen'. As winter comes to London, people must perish, just as animals and plants do when overcome by cold. Winter is a warning to the denizens of the city that they can survive only by engaging in a struggle with their own kind: 'Day after day the stress becomes more grim. One would think that hosts of the weaker combatants might surely find it seasonable to let themselves be trodden out of existence, and so make room for those of more useful sinew; somehow they cling to life; so few in comparison fail utterly.'[21] Why do the weak persist in their hopeless struggle? What was most terrible in Nell's room were the letters and photograph that she still clung to, in the hope that Gissing would save her. The plot of *The Nether World* revolves around the question of whether people can be saved from outside when they cannot save themselves. Michael Snowdon wants Stanley Kirkwood to use his fortune to relieve the poor. Kirkwood resists such a duty: 'there arose in him a struggle between the idealist tendency, of which he had his share, and stubborn everyday sense, supported by his knowledge of the world and of his own being.'[22]

The struggle for existence in the social world is re-enacted in the mind of the intellectual: do you try to soften the world's harshness by helping the weak, or allow that harshness to do its cleansing work without interference? The lower depths of London are full of people who are like crippled birds; if they are beyond help, as Gissing seems to believe, then why torment yourself with the hope of saving them? Stanley Kirkwood's choice then seems to be best:

'I am no hero,' he said, 'no enthusiast. The time when my whole being could be stirred by social questions has gone by. I am a man in love, and in proportion as my love has strengthened, so has my old artist-self revived in me, until now I can imagine no bliss so perfect as to marry Jane Snowdon and go off to live with her amid fields and trees, where no echo of the suffering world should ever reach us.'[23]

Love and art may be private pleasures, but they are the best compensation for the world's wrongs. To enjoy them, one must first move off, to where one cannot hear the cries of those who are freezing or drowning. Stanley is not Gissing, of course, nor does he follow through on his own beliefs. But in the process of writing *The Nether World* Gissing paid off his debt to Nell's memory, and decided that he need no longer walk the streets of outcast London. Rather, he should go far away, out of Cornwall Residences, out of London, out of England. Nell's death allowed him to give up tutoring for ever. Much as Gissing had chafed under the burden of teaching – which he had done for seven and a half years – he never took it out on Walter Grahame:

> He was a wonderful teacher, and the quality of his teaching was never affected by ill health or depression. He was always equally patient, helpful and interested, and always ready to be carried away by his enthusiasm for the glorious literature of Greece and Rome. That made his pupils' work intensely interesting, and, realizing my interest, he formed expectations of me which I never fulfilled in any way. If I made unusual progress under his tuition, it was owing to his zeal and ability as a teacher, and not to my aptitude as a pupil. As I look back now, knowing what he often suffered at that time, his courage and unvarying good humour seem amazing.[24]

In June Gissing went up to Oxford for the first time to speak with Walter Grahame's future tutor, Smith of Balliol. He was impressed by the 'monastic feeling' of the colleges. 'Is the future England growing up here?' he wondered. 'No, no; but in poor London lodgings. Ah, but the sense of rest! To forget modernism, and read Greek!'[25] He told Eduard Bertz that 'The life of a Fellow at Oxford or Cambridge is, I should think, almost ideal. He has his man-servant, his meals either in private or at the public table, an atmosphere of culture and peace.'[26] He had lost his chance for such comforts in the cloakroom at Owens College.

Gissing finished *The Nether World* on 18 July and sent it off to Smith, Elder the next day. He was due a lump sum for his tutoring, on which he could live until he sold *The Nether World*. The remaining anvil around his neck was the rent for Cornwall Residences, about which he constantly complained. The cost to him was about £52 a year, and he hoped to sublet it furnished for £60. In spite of all efforts, no tenant came forward; the noise and smoke from the railway may have been to blame. Gissing was determined to take the road, regardless. He would spend the next two months visiting his family, then be off. Seascale, in Cumberland, offered both the seaside and walks in the hills behind. Gissing had been there twice

before, as a boy of eleven or twelve, just before his father died. Now he
went with his mother and sisters, for a fortnight in August. He enjoyed the
dramatic landscape, and would make good use of Seascale as a setting for the
romance between Rhoda Nunn and Everard Barfoot in *The Odd Women*.
Whatever the limitations of his mother and sisters' company, Gissing
always benefited from the relief of his chronic loneliness.

After the Seascale holiday Gissing went back to Wakefield for three
weeks, to visit his old haunts. He had no impulse to start another novel,
noting that: 'The atmosphere of Wakefield would soon make the completest
dullard of me.'[27] He took to reading Crabbe, whom he saw as a forerunner
for the kind of novels Gissing himself wrote: 'he delights in the dreary and
depressing scenery of the Suffolk coast, in squalid streets, in poverty-
stricken chambers.'[28] From Wakefield Gissing completed his family tour
by going to see Algernon and Catherine in the Cotswolds. Algernon was
working happily enough at his next novel, but George was still impervious
to the idea of marrying someone of his own class and settling in the country.
His hopes were fixed on Paris, where he could live more cheaply than in
England. Ernst Plitt would go with him, a German artist whom Gissing
had known slightly for a couple of years. From Paris they might go to
Naples, where living would be even cheaper.

Gissing had effectively laid down his pen after finishing *The Nether
World* in July 1888. He made no attempt to start a new novel until he
returned to England from the Continent in the spring of 1889. He did reply
to a request from the Reverend George Bainton for an account of his 'art
of composition'. Some people, he said, could write 'good, nervous, lucid
English' without even thinking about how they did it. Gissing was not one
of them, however: 'My own attempts at authorship . . . have had the result
of making me constantly search, compare, and strive in the matter of style.'
If he did write with any skill, it came from his close study of authors he
admired, such as Ruskin, Landor and Charlotte Brontë.[29] Just before
leaving, Gissing was asked by the editor of the weekly *Dispatch* for a
short novel, to run in ten instalments at five guineas each. This was reasonable pay for a piece of literary journeywork, but Gissing refused the
commission. He would rather buy his freedom by living on less money,
which he could do in Paris or Naples. 'I shall come back,' he told Ellen, 'if
all go well, stronger in mind and body. Indeed, I feel as if life were only
beginning.'[30]

He left with Plitt on 26 September, taking the night ferry from Newhaven
to Dieppe. The Hotel Cujas, where he had stayed before, had been pulled
down; but he was soon comfortably installed at the Hotel de Londres on

rue Linné. Paris, he wrote back to England, was 'the city which, in spite of all things that make one shake one's head, must still remain the metropolis of modern art'.[31] The only problem was one he had brought with him, his companion Plitt. He was 'a good and honest fellow, only stupid, very stupid. I have never known intimately so stupid a man.'[32] Not too stupid to take advantage of Gissing, though. Plitt's room was 25 francs a month (about £1) and Gissing's was 35; Plitt said that he couldn't afford to stay unless Gissing paid 5 francs towards his rent. Gissing still only had to pay 32 shillings a month; but he also had £4 to pay at Cornwall Residences. He could save money by cooking simple meals for himself and Plitt over the fire in his room; Plitt got on his nerves, but at least he kept the devil of loneliness at bay.

While Plitt worked at his paintings, Gissing was free to wander Paris by day and go to the theatre by night. He went back to his favourite place, the Père Lachaise cemetery, and to see the rising up of the new Eiffel Tower. 'Of course did not impress me,' he sturdily observed; 'mere artificial bulk cannot do so.'[33] He bought an English newspaper to read about the two latest Whitechapel murders, by the man to be known as Jack the Ripper. The victims were women much like Gissing's Nell: past their youth, occasional prostitutes and fond of drink. One victim, Mary Kelley, was killed in the same kind of room where Nell had ended her days; her mutilated body was found lying on her bed. For a French newspaper, Le Petit Journal, the murders were proof of English sexual hypocrisy; Gissing copied the piece into his diary to prove the contrary, that the French were vulgar and ignorant.[34]

A week after arriving in Paris, Gissing finally heard from Smith, Elder. They complained about the slow sales of Thyrza, but nonetheless offered £150 for the copyright of The Nether World. Gissing was happy to take the money. In his eight-year career as a novelist, he had now climbed from paying for his first book to be printed, to £100 a novel, and now £150. That was just enough to support a single man in shabby-genteel style, without needing extra income from teaching. Still, Gissing was gaining more respect than popularity; and by selling off his copyrights he left himself completely dependent on being able to turn out a new novel at least once every year.[35]

Gissing was not a penny-pincher like Plitt, but he strictly kept his expenses down to what he could afford. He never borrowed from his wealthy friends or found himself completely without money. On the Continent he could live on £5 a month and stretch out his payment for The Nether World for at least a year ahead. He had set out with Plitt for reasons of economy, not because he was a real friend; after three weeks with him in Paris, Gissing had learnt a lesson about himself:

> Strange thing that I, all whose joys and sorrows come from excess of individuality, should be remarkable among men for my yieldingness to everyone and anyone in daily affairs. No man I ever met *habitually* sacrifices his own pleasure, habits, intentions to those of a companion, purely out of fear to annoy the latter. It must be a sign of extreme weakness, and it makes me the slave of men unspeakably my inferiors. Now, here is Plitt . . . I never dare say what I think, for fear of offending him, or causing a mis- understanding. And this has so often been the case in the course of my life. – Therefore it is that I am never at peace save when alone.[36]

On the face of things, this was a true account of Gissing's temperament; and what he said about Plitt also held true of Nell and other women yet to enter his life. Yet one wonders if Gissing was really as passive as he claimed to be. He had trouble standing up to others, but he nourished resentment when put upon, and eventually made that resentment plain. He did not have a sunny disposition, and his obsessiveness about his work had to appear selfish to those who wanted a bigger share of his attention. To feel resentful towards other people's needs, and to hide that resentment behind a grudging compliance, was bound to end in the breakdown of relationships. Gissing had no ability to strike a compromise between his own needs and the needs of others. Instead he would give in 'for the sake of peace', then find himself living in a false peace that gave no real satisfaction either to himself, or to the person he was with.

With the daily burden of Plitt, Paris was becoming a burden too, and Gissing became eager to depart for Italy. Regular trips to the Louvre were a preparation for the art he would see in the south, on its native ground. He found on a stall a copy of Goethe's *Italienische Reise*, the classic intro- duction for a journey from the north to the land of lemon blossoms. At the same time, Gissing was letting go of the passions that had driven him to write *The Nether World*:

> I experience at present a profound dislike for everything that concerns the life of the people. Paris has even become distasteful to me because I am living in this quarter, in a house thronged with workpeople, and where, to get away, I must always pass through dirty and swarming streets. All my interest in such things I have left behind in London. On crossing the Channel, I have become a poet pure and simple, or perhaps it would be better to say an idealist student of art.[37]

A nation is like a family: we know too much about our own people, as they do about us. The French poor did not trouble Gissing's conscience as the London poor had done; when he arrived in Naples, the poor offered him a pleasing spectacle. By the time he returned to England, Gissing would have detached himself emotionally from the working class, and they would never again be a central concern of his novels.

Gissing went to visit his French translator of *Demos*, Mme le Breton, and was disappointed to find that she was actually two spinster sisters, elderly and plain. A later translator would be more appealing, but that lay ten years in the future. He and Plitt took their leave of Paris on 26 October, by an overnight train to Lyon. As they went on the next day, Gissing 'began to understand what is meant by the South; by sunlight and air! The valley of the Rhone marvellous in autumn foliage. The poplars a sort of old gold, flashed upon by the sun; such a colour I never beheld and it cannot be described. . . . Little white-shining towns perched on top of hills; old castles. Just before Avignon noticed the first olive-trees.'[38] To encounter the real South, after living there in his imagination through studying the classics, was the greatest adventure of Gissing's thirty-one years. Every mile he covered took him further away from the nether world of London, where Jack the Ripper prowled the foggy courts of the East End. He travelled the more hopefully because of what he was leaving behind.

From Marseille Gissing and Plitt boarded a French boat for Naples, a voyage of three days and two nights.[39] The boat stank intolerably, but to sail along the Mediterranean coast was for Gissing a huge delight. 'Let no one tell me that I am in the 19th century,' he wrote to Ellen. 'These are the mountains that the Greek colonists saw. . . . The sea and the shore have in nothing altered since the times when Carthage was the great empire of the Mediterranean.'[40] In the afternoon of 30 October they steamed into the Bay of Naples, with pink smoke rising from Vesuvius. The passengers were ferried off the *Durance* in small boats, which landed them in the middle of a howling mob of porters and touts; but this fearsome introduction to the city did not deter Gissing from finding what he had already decided would be there. He had been reading Goethe on his journey, who had written a century before:

Everything one sees and hears gives evidence that this is a happy country which amply satisfies all the basic needs and breeds a people who are happy by nature, people who can wait without concern for tomorrow to bring them what they had today and for that reason lead a happy-go-lucky existence. . . . [Naples] is a paradise, and everyone lives in a state of intoxicated self-forgetfulness, myself included. .... It is strange for me to be in a society where everyone does nothing but enjoy himself.[41]

This was the myth, still alive in the teeth of any evidence to the contrary, of Naples as the Queen of the Mediterranean, a place of supreme beauty and universal joy. For Gissing it was something he was determined to find: the shortest way out of Clerkenwell. But he also had a more positive reason to delight in Naples. The classical world, here, had never really died.

That Virgil was buried almost within sight of Gissing's *pension* meant more to him than any part of Naples's tortured recent history. At the beginning of the nineteenth century Naples ruled over nearly half of present-day Italy, and was third in population after London and Paris. But in 1861 the Kingdom of the Two Sicilies merged with Italy, and Naples ceased to be a capital. It was a city in rapid decline, like Vienna after the First World War. Then, in 1884, it was struck with a terrible epidemic of cholera. When Gissing arrived a great effort was being made to clear the worst of the city's slums and rebuild its sewers. But typhus was still endemic, spread through the city by rats and fleas. A third of the population still lived in underground hovels called *bassi:*

> Imagine the doorway of a cave where on entering you must descend. Not a ray of light penetrates into it except by the one aperture you have passed through; and there, between four black battered walls and upon a layer of filth mixed with putrid straw, two, three, and four families vegetate together. The best side of the cave, namely that through which humidity filtrates the least, is occupied by a rack and manger to which animals of various kinds are tied; a horse it may be or an ass, a calf, or a pig. On the opposite, a heap of boards and rags represent the beds. In one corner is the fireplace and the household utensils lie about the floor.[42]

Gissing established himself comfortably in a room with a view on Vico Brancaccio 8, for which he paid nine shillings a week. Wine and food were laughably cheap compared with London. He saw the wretched dens of the poor and the animals that shared with them; but what would have horrified him in London gave him pleasure in Naples. It is not that Gissing was a fool or a hypocrite in his response; rather, being a foreigner allowed him to stop caring about poverty and squalor. In England he had to care. Not only that, he was now comfortably off, and free from the shadow of the class system. He could mingle on equal terms with any middle-class English tourists he met, and have the advantage of his deep knowledge of art and the classics. Finally, he had exchanged the grimness of London streets for the magical beauty of the city and bay of Naples. The city was being transformed by what was called the 'disembowelling', the clearing of slums and widening of streets. But it still had an incomparable setting, and, in its buildings, two thousand years of palpable history. 'No, I don't think I shall do any writing in Italy,' Gissing told Eduard Bertz. 'I have so much to see, so much to learn.'[43] For the remaining four months of his stay in Italy, he kept to his plan. On 15 November he noted in his diary that *A Life's Morning* was published in book form, after having been serialised since January. 'I rejoice unspeakably that I am out of the way,' was his comment.[44]

Gissing became a different man in Italy. In London he brooded constantly about completing his quota of work, and about his loneliness and lack of social position. Italy gave him so much immediate pleasure that he could free himself from the torment of his usual regime. One pleasure was absent, though: his erotic life seemed to be suspended while he was in the south. Except for comments in his diary on the ugliness of Neapolitan women and the beauty of Roman ones, he recorded no further sexual interest, whether in prostitutes or respectable women. His life became one of receiving impressions, rather than actively pursuing any of his desires.

Having walked all over Naples – including, of course, the main cemetery – Gissing planned to spend the second half of November in excursions near the city, before going on to Rome. He went down the coast to Amalfi, impressed both by its dramatic setting and by the great number of beggars: 'The number of soldi I had to give away, surprising. Men, women, and children, – all begged, and seldom one that showed good will, that did not laugh jeeringly, – I note here that the Italian people have the *vices of poverty;* that explains all.'[45] The poverty came from agricultural depression and the decline of Naples. Southern Italy was being emptied out by emigration to America. Gissing understood this well enough, but did not want to be distracted from his classical reveries. The beauty of the great temple at Paestum was more important to him than any sufferings by the people of today. Nor did he care about his own comfort. He made a hair-raising climb to the summit of Vesuvius, almost incinerating his clothes and boots. Compulsive travel had taken the place of compulsive writing, except that travel gave him deep and spontaneous pleasure. To see Naples and Rome was a chance to be seized with both hands.

If Gissing was so content in Italy, why did he not go further, and settle there to live? He could live comfortably on half of his English income, and he knew the precedent of writers like Shelley, Byron, the Brownings, or Fanny Trollope. His main reason for returning to England was probably the belief that his novels about London needed to be written in London.

Even so, his next novel would have an Italian setting and would sing the praises of expatriate life. That Gissing did not embrace it himself may also be because he met in Pompeii an expatriate of about his own age, and from his own part of England. John Shortridge was a nephew of the Gissings' family doctor in Wakefield. He had run away to sea as a boy, and had been living in Italy for the past seventeen years with his Italian wife and brood of children. Gissing accepted an invitation to stay with Shortridge in Massa Lubrense, at the tip of the Sorrento peninsula facing Capri. The house lacked sanitation and was run in completely higgledy-piggledy fashion. Apart from his wife and children, Shortridge hosted his peasant in-laws and an alcoholic brother who was dying of consumption. Shortridge had some talent as an artist, but all he did now was try to keep his unruly household under control, and complain about his fate. Gissing took all this in his stride, and Shortridge became a good friend. He had enough inherited money to keep his ramshackle family going, so that he had the kind of artistic freedom Gissing always dreamed of – except that Shortridge never produced much art. Nor was the way of life he had chosen one that could ever suit Gissing's temperament. He was not shocked by the disorderly house at Massa Lubrense, but neither did he envy it.

Gissing liked to tackle Italy in a regular way: a month in Naples would be followed by a month each in Rome, Florence, and Venice. He left for Rome by the night train on 28 November 1888, happy to be rid at last of Plitt's company. Rome struck him as astonishingly different from Naples: 'They are not the same nation. Here no noise, no pestering to buy, etc. – all grave and quiet and dignified. In that respect a change vastly for the better.'[46] He found lodgings at Via Margutta 59, near the Spanish Steps, and made a beeline for his usual first stop: the Protestant Cemetery, where Keats and Shelley were buried. Gissing revered Shelley; Keats he knew by heart. 'To like Keats is a test of fitness for understanding poetry,' he had told Ellen, 'just as to like Shakespeare is a test of general mental capacity. ... If you do not *revel* in Keats, – put all poetry aside forever. There is no medium.'[47]

As Gissing came to know Rome, it became for him the supreme place in the world. He was a tireless viewer of painting and sculpture, devoting days at a time to just the Sistine Chapel; but Rome meant most to him as a scene of past action. Since childhood he had studied the classics; now they were transported from printed texts to the actual stones where Horace walked or Caesar's body was burnt. 'Roman life and literature becomes real in a way hitherto unconceivable,' he wrote to Margaret. 'I must begin and study it all over again; I must go to school again, and for the rest of my

life. Ah, if only I could have come here years ago!'[48] Gissing drew strength
from the Eternal City, whereas London only took his strength away:

> It is a great and wonderful thing to me that Rome is no longer a name. The
> Forum I know as well as I know 7.K. . . . The Tiber is an old friend. – My
> life is richer a thousand times – aye, a million times, – than six months ago.
> Now I can talk with any man as an equal, for I am no longer ignorant of the
> best things the world contains. – It only now remains for me to go to Greece,
> and a matter of £50 or £60 will at any time manage that. Then I shall have
> all the ground-work of education.[49]

In Italy, Gissing felt that travel and study were enough for a good life in
themselves, a life whose aim was perfection of the self rather than literary
production. One might object that this ideal led only to the attenuated life
of a Henry Ryecroft, or of the perpetual tourists in *The Emancipated*. But
Gissing had earned his sunny Italian days by his nights of toil in London,
and he knew that he would have to return to his desk in the New Year.
Meanwhile he was discovering a new and strange sensation: 'Woke early
this morning and enjoyed wonderful happiness of mind. It occurs to me –
is not this partly due to the fact that I spend my days solely in the consideration of beautiful things, wholly undisturbed by base necessities and
considerations? In any case the experience is most remarkable.'[50] The only
flaw in Gissing's life at Rome was his failure to meet any congenial people.
Yet he was wary of other tourists, and if he heard a commonplace remark
by English people in a gallery, he would steer clear of them hereafter. He
refused Eduard Bertz's offer of an introduction to Frau Kurz, a well-to-do
German writer who lived in Florence. With such attitudes it was not
surprising that Christmas was just another solitary day for Gissing, except
for some talk with an American studying for the priesthood. He observed
closely the masses at St Peter's, though he had no strong feelings about
Catholicism, one way or the other. Only the ancient Romans counted for
him.

When Gissing moved on to Florence he appreciated the beauty of the
town, but thought it inferior to Naples and Rome in every other way.
'Florence is the city of the Renaissance,' he told Algernon, 'but after all the
Renaissance was only a shadow of the great times, and like a shadow it has
passed away. There is nothing here that impresses me like the poorest of
Rome's antiquities.'[51] He felt that he was already in northern Europe,
including the bitter cold of unheated rooms. The one advantage that Florence had over Rome was in the cheapness of Gissing's lodgings at Borgo
Santi Apostoli 17. He calculated that if he could get rid of his London flat

he could return and live comfortably on about £65 a year. He went so far as to go and see the villas where the Brownings and Landor had lived; but what kind of social life could he have, whether with Italians or expatriates? On New Year's Eve Gissing went to a restaurant for a special dinner of wild boar, and found himself 'in vast discomfort, owing to the place being full of Italians in exuberant spirits . . . It made me feel wretched.'[52]

Wretched as it may have been to be left on the fringes, Gissing still felt that Italian social life was vastly better than its English equivalent. After three weeks in Florence he received the proofs of *The Nether World*, to be published in April. This was a good occasion for Gissing to compare English manners with those he saw in Florence. In the Uffizi, Gissing was delighted to see the 'low-class girls' of the city on Sunday, when admission was free: 'They are fat-faced and ruddy-cheeked, cheerful but never noisy, and they come to the gallery because it is a *festa* and they really find pleasure in looking at the pictures.'[53] The Italians might have their faults, but Gissing liked them more than the French, and vastly more than his countrymen:

> I shall come back home strengthened in my conviction that the English, as a people, excel all others in vulgarity and coarseness. . . . Amid my own various little difficulties here and there . . . I have often thought with horror what must be the experiences of a Continental man living in England under corresponding circumstances. Here everything is made simple by the *suavity* of the people, high and low; in England every difficulty is heightened by native boorishness. As regards average intellect, as regards culture in individuals, England is above all other countries, far; but I never felt so strongly as now the general brutality of the populace.[54]

The English were coarse, Gissing believed, because they were isolated: 'On the continent you never for a moment lose sight of the fact that there are other nations in the world besides your own; the average Englishman has to reflect before he can sincerely admit this. I mean that, in practice, he *never* reckons with reference to other nationalities.'[55] These thoughts had momentous implications for his future writing. He was correcting the proofs of *The Nether World*, and starting to work out the novel he had to write as soon as he returned to England in six weeks' time. Wandering around Florence in bitter weather was painful, but he saw that the Florentines lived through their winter in quite a different way from Londoners. What if the 'nether world' of English society had more to do with nation than with class? If Italian workers were gentle with each other, and had a sense of beauty, one had to look beyond just their poverty and oppression. Gissing had long been sceptical of the leftist belief that everything that was wrong with working-class life could be blamed on the selfishness of the rich. Florence suggested that the evils described in his novels might be more geographical than political. Perhaps the English were still northern barbarians in their fundamental habits, while the Italians still kept the civic humanism of the old Romans. If one looked only at England, it would seem that poor people got drunk because they were miserable; but in Italy, where they were poorer yet, they enjoyed their cheap wine without turning into beasts.

For the past few years Gissing had been criticising the approach of middle-class reformers, who both pitied the poor and assumed that they could be encouraged to practise middle-class virtues. In spite of his scepticism, he still believed that working-class life in London was an immensely significant subject for an English novelist. Dickens had shown the way, and others – himself included – needed to follow it. But once he stepped back from the English scene, Gissing's perspective shifted; as he said to his sister-in-law, 'England is a strange country to look at from a distance.'[56] His place in English society would remain the same, when he returned; the change would be in the kinds of lives he chose to examine in his novels. Having reclaimed some freedom in his own life by going to Italy, he would write about characters with more room to manoeuvre, which meant placing them higher on the social ladder. His contact with the Italian poor had alienated him permanently from the poor of England. They effectively disappear from Gissing's novels after *The Nether World*, except for shabby-genteel characters like the Madden sisters in *The Odd Women* or Biffen in *New Grub Street*. The Gissing who would return from Italy was a different man from the one who had left four months before.

As the days went by in Florence, though, Gissing no longer felt any of the euphoria that had possessed him in Naples and Rome. Apart from the harsh weather, he was tormented by a flare-up of haemorrhoids, which sent him to various doctors in search of relief.[57] He was fretting about the work that awaited him on his return to London, and was as lonely as ever. The masterpieces of the Renaissance did not make up for his mundane discomforts, but he dutifully made the rounds of Florence before leaving for Venice on 29 January. His lodgings, very much to his taste, were in the Palazzo Swift on the Grand Canal. Ruskin had written *The Stones of Venice* there. Gissing admired everything about the incomparable city on the Adriatic, with the reservation that he did not care deeply about any architecture since classical times. Paestum was the supreme building for him, until he could get to Greece itself. Renaissance painting was another matter, and he spent hours with his two favourites, Bellini and Tintoretto. He was upset by letting himself be talked into visiting a glass factory, where he felt obliged to buy a worthless neck-pin and globe; as soon as he escaped he threw them into the canal, lamenting the loss of 3/6d. At least the passing show was free, and it confirmed the ideas he had been mulling over in Florence:

> Again I notice the democratic character of Italian society. Here promenade, side by side, the gentleman and the gondolier, the lady and the girl who makes wax-matches. There is no feeling in the poor people that they are out of place. And it is the more remarkable in the case of women, seeing that here the work-girls have a distinct costume; they are, of course, bare-headed, and wear invariably a long shawl, which reaches the ground, generally of grey colour. Heavens! The beautiful faces that I pass every hour. They are magnificent, these Venetian work-girls![58]

Two months later, back in London, Plitt came to see Gissing. He had just returned from a long stay in Rome. 'By telling me of an Italian girl who lived with him there,' Gissing wrote in his diary, 'he made me so wretched in my loneliness that work was impossible.'[59] Gissing had lived with an English work-girl, and would do so again. His troubles came from needing to idealise such relationships, and make them legitimate. One could say that this was to Gissing's credit, since Plitt discarded his Roman work-girl when it suited him to return to England. But why did Gissing feel wretched about Plitt's affair? Probably because he realised how incapable he was of seizing a sexual opportunity, as Plitt had done, and enjoying it. An affair with an Italian girl might have turned out badly for both of them, like Shortridge's cat-and-dog life in Massa Lubrense. But at least Plitt had taken his chance. Gissing felt vastly superior to Plitt, yet he had spent four months in Italy without any real contact with the Italian people. For all his love of the country, he had allowed no one to take him by the hand.

8

The Emancipated

Gissing left Venice on 26 February 1889 for a grim seventy-two-hour journey to London, with only one night of three in a hotel bed. He crossed Germany on the first anniversary of Nell's death, though he put down no word about it in his diary. His arrival in London was in character, with snow falling and slush in the streets. The next day he went up to Agbrigg, a suburb of Wakefield. It was good to have contact with his family, even if none of them were achieving any great happiness or success. Algernon had been there for a month, with Catherine and their daughter Enid, who had been born while Gissing was in Naples. Algernon's first novel, *Joy Cometh in the Morning*, had sold a modest 329 copies; his payment for it was fifteen guineas, and he was working himself up to make another rash move. Neither of Gissing's sisters had much to look forward to beyond their tutoring of children in the neighbourhood. Ellen was now twenty-one, and pestered by an unwelcome suitor; she felt guilty about not liking him, and needed some tough-minded advice from George:

> Even an apparent *mutual* liking is anything but a proof of genuine
> sympathy; still less is it possible to argue as you do when the liking is
> only on one side. Indifference would be bad enough, but you speak of
> repulsion; and to try to overcome anything of that kind – unless on most
> solid grounds of reasoning – I should consider utterly wrong. You need
> not think that there *is* anything in yourself answering to the other's
> feeling; as likely as not, nothing of the kind exists. As a matter of
> experience, this is quite certain. Belief in the contrary is constantly leading
> to utter calamities.[1]

How good was this advice? By this time Gissing knew that his next novel was going to be, in part, a portrait of his sisters. It would be a critique of pious Northerners who were blind to the sensuous charms of Italy. Neither Ellen nor Margaret Gissing ever married, and perhaps they would have felt repulsion for any man who wooed them. But Gissing encouraged

Ellen to think of her distaste as absolute, something she need not even begin to examine. His own experience warned him that love did not beget love. Nell's love for him, he seemed to suggest, did nothing to make him feel even affection towards her. Gissing's argument was grimly solipsistic: how you feel about another person has nothing whatever to do with how they feel about you. It followed that two people were very unlikely to be equally in love with each other. There are a few such couples in Gissing's novels, such as Everard Barfoot's friend Micklethwaite and his fiancée in *The Odd Women*; but almost all his main characters follow the rule that there is always one who kisses, and one who turns the cheek. Gissing's advice to Ellen boiled down to saying: protect yourself, since all relationships are unequal.

Gissing spent only four days at his mother's house. Wakefield was dull and provincial, but returning to Cornwall Residences was not easy. 'I don't know how I shall face a year of it again,' he told Ellen, 'I have resumed all the old habits – precisely as if I had never left London. – My dinner at the dirty eating-house, my purchase of the *Star*, my walk round the park, &c &c. But fortunately I have made a beginning of work, and that is the only help.'[2] To ease his gloom he went to visit John Shortridge's sister in Acton, a Mrs Jolly, and found her unmarried sister Ellen staying with her. He found both women 'refined and distinctly sympathetic. . . . How such people come out of Barnsley, I can't understand.'[3] The visit went swimmingly, and Gissing was invited to stay for dinner, where he enjoyed Ellen's stories about her recent visit to her brother's bohemian household. Gissing went home well pleased, and sent Mrs Jolly a copy of *Thyrza*, the same novel he had sent to Miss Curtis of Eastbourne. Perhaps he saw a similarity between Ellen Shortridge and Annabel, Egremont's middle-class beloved in the book. Alas, another fiasco followed. Six weeks later, Gissing presented himself on the Jollys' doorstep in Acton; Mrs Jolly was out, and her husband and Ellen were 'not particularly cordial'.[4] Either they disliked *Thyrza*, or were surprised to find Gissing turning up, even though he had written a few days before to ask if he could come. He vowed not to see the Jollys again, unless they sent him an invitation! Having been snubbed by them, he was ready to snub back when George Smith, who had just published *The Nether World*, invited him to dinner. 'I explain to [the Smiths],' he told Algernon, 'that I have made a rule against all social intercourse. And indeed after this I accept no invitation of any kind.'[5]

Gissing had recently seen Mrs Gaussen a couple of times in London. The first visit 'put him out of gear', and his comment on the second was:

'Found idiots there.'[6] Once again, he narrowed down his social life to his family, and Morley Roberts. He made an exception for a group of Roberts's friends, who met regularly in Chelsea for dinner and literary talk; they included the painter Alfred Hartley and the writer W. H. Hudson, whose work Gissing had long admired. He liked this cosy group of outsiders, who had talent without the curse (in his eyes) of worldly success. Another reason for shunning company was the need to get his new novel under way. Unfortunately, Gissing was suffering one of his fits of self-doubt, in which he would start the novel, tear up what he had written, then start again and destroy that. It took him three and a half months after his return from Venice to see his way clear.

While Gissing was struggling with his Italian novel, *The Nether World* appeared, on 3 April 1889. It was nine years since *Workers in the Dawn*, and Gissing had now published a total of five novels with working-class themes. His two novels of a different kind, *Isabel Clarendon* and *A Life's Morning*, had been less successful than the others, and Gissing was firmly identified by the reading public as a novelist of the slums. *The Nether World* was the most unrelenting of these novels. Its focus was on the immediate miseries of poverty, rather than on the attempts at remedy of middle-class reformers. Imagined political solutions counted for little when Gissing faced the horror of Nell's tenement room. This singleness of purpose made *The Nether World* more acceptable to Gissing's reviewers than had been the case with *Demos* or *Thyrza*. *The Court Journal* praised him as a guide for his middle-class readers to:

> some horrible region of damned souls, such as a modern Dante might imagine as the final punishment of the most degraded types of humanity. We move, shuddering, with the author, through an atmosphere fetid with all the abominations of life in the slums. The writer is sufficiently realistic for us to easily fill in the blanks which he must perforce leave. ... Mr Gissing's shoulders may yet grow broad enough for the hitherto unappropriated mantle of the great novelist.[7]

The comparison with Dante removed Gissing from contemporary fears of socialism; it also hinted at the comfortable doctrine that those who lived in London's underworld were there because of their sins, not because of any fault in respectable society.

Gissing thought that F. W. Farrar's review of *The Nether World* was cold and condescending, yet it helped to raise Gissing's moral standing. Farrar, the Archdeacon of Westminster, had become rich by writing biographies of Jesus and St Paul:

I have called the book realistic, but happily it is an English book, and the reader will find in it none of that leprous naturalism which disgusts every honourable reader in the works of Zola and his school. There is nothing in it which is loathly, nor malignant, nor cynical, though it deals throughout with the ruin and shipwreck of human existence, the catastrophe and horror of hopeless degradation.[8]

Gissing had his differences with Zola, but this kind of praise he could do without. That *The Nether World* was an English book did not make it pure, except in the sense that Gissing had to observe the rules of English prudery in order to publish anything. Farrar offered another back-handed compliment by praising Gissing for not proposing any political solution to the evils he described; that, Farrar said, showed that Gissing agreed with Gladstone's words:

'It is against the ordinance of Providence, it is against the interests of man, that immediate reparation should be possible when long-contained evils have been at work. For one of the greatest safeguards against misdoing would be removed if at any moment the consequences of misdoing could be repaired.'[9]

In fact, this kind of moralism would have infuriated Gissing. The last thing he wanted to say in *The Nether World* was that the poor needed to be punished for their sins, otherwise sin might become too popular. He did not expect the poor to change their ways, and neither did he expect that the social system would provide them with a decent living. His bitterness at the life and death of Nell had helped to make *The Nether World* the most artistically effective of his early novels. Yet how could he go on writing in this vein, now that he had lost all faith in the possibility of progressive change? Meanwhile, his stay in Italy had opened the door for another kind of novel altogether. It was typical of Gissing that he would go through that door, with no fear that he might lose the reputation he had built up, or fail to please a new kind of reader.

Writing an Italian novel did not, however, do anything to cheer up Gissing's return to his old routines at 7.K Cornwall Residences. He was discouraged, also, by the way Algernon seemed to be enacting an even gloomier version of the writer's career. After the fifteen guineas he made on his first novel, Algernon was offered £20 for his next one by Hurst & Blackett, with a royalty after 300 copies sold. He settled for a payment of £25 outright.[10] In mid-May, he decided that he could not write at all in his Cotswold house. Within a few days he had sold up, sent Catherine and the baby to stay with relatives, and moved to lodgings in Harbottle,

Northumberland. This was part of his old scheme of becoming a 'northern writer', but as usual those around him had to pick up the pieces and lend him money for his move. Before long he was talking of moving again, this time to London. Apart from the annoyance that Algernon had chosen to be an unsuccessful writer, rather than an unsuccessful anything else, Gissing was once again trapped by his own weakness. He could not quarrel outright with Algernon, nor could he even set conditions for continuing to support him.

A few days after Algernon's plan to move up north, Gissing himself made an odd and impulsive decision. In the struggle to get his Italian novel under way, he had many fits of discouragement with what he had managed to write. When the weather turned hot at the end of May, and painters were coming into his flat, Gissing decided to go and stay with his mother and work on the novel there. He was writing about northerners in Italy, so why not go where he could observe them in the place they came from? He should perhaps have anticipated some friction with his sisters, whom he was using as inspiration for some of his characters. Nonetheless, Gissing found refuge, of a kind, in the home at Agbrigg. He had tried to make his sisters more tolerant and worldly, and had introduced Ellen into Mrs Gaussen's circle in Bayswater. But he did not challenge their beliefs directly (though they did not hesitate to challenge his). On the surface, life went along smoothly enough. Gissing had his meals looked after, for which he paid 15 shillings a week. He walked in the countryside with his sisters, and made steady progress on his novel in an attic room. This seemed to be the happy state he had enjoyed on a visit years before: 'Good gracious, what a life I should have, and what work I should do, if I had always my wants so cared for, and all bother cleared out of my way! What a comfort it was to be called to regular meals, at regular hours, without having to think about them previously!'[11]

Yet Gissing was storing up trouble for a year ahead, when the book would be published. He was never one to invent a novel out of whole cloth, and he was building a psychic bomb in his mother's attic. The novel would be a relentless critique of provincial morality, especially as practised by young women not unlike his sisters. When he spoke facetiously to Bertz of living in 'this home of Puritanism', he meant both the nonconformist heritage of Wakefield, and the family home in which puritanism still ruled.[12] Indeed, the working title for the novel he was writing was 'The Puritan', before he changed it to *The Emancipated* (which still meant, those who had liberated themselves from puritanism). One chapter of the novel would contain a savage description of Sunday in the provinces, a day that Gissing could hardly bear even when he was in London. Miriam Baske, in her Neapolitan villa, muses on the Sundays of her childhood in a Manchester suburb:

> Half an hour later than on profane days, Mrs Elgar descends the stairs. She is a lady of middle age, slight, not ungraceful, handsome; the look of pain about her forehead is partly habitual, but the consciousness of Sunday intensifies it. She moves without a sound. Entering the breakfast-room, she finds there two children, a girl and a boy, both attired in new-seeming garments which are obviously stiff and uncomfortable. The little girl sits on an uneasy chair, her white-stockinged legs dangling, on her lap a large copy of 'Pilgrim's Progress'; the boy is half reclined on a shiny sofa, his hands in his pockets, on his face an expression of discontent. The table is very white, very cold, very uninviting.[13]

Mr Elgar writes business letters in his room, dating them as 'Saturday' or 'Monday'. 'The vast majority of English people are constantly guilty of hypocritical practices,' the narrator comments.[14] Having grown up in such a world, Miriam as an adult is still unable to think:

> By reason of her inexperience of life, it was impossible for Miriam to analyse her own being, and note intelligently the modifications it underwent. Introspection meant to her nothing but debates held with conscience – a technical conscience, made of religious precepts. Original reflection, independent of those precepts, was to her very simply a form of sin, a species of temptation for which she had been taught to prepare herself.[15]

This was a crushing judgement on the mentality of Gissing's sisters. He was fond of them, especially Ellen, and relied on them to relieve the loneliness of his London life. But he felt that they were part of a misguided religious culture, and that it was more important to expose that culture than to respect their privacy. Gissing kept hoping that his sisters would see things more clearly if they saw more things, in particular through foreign travel. He could not afford to take them to Italy, like Miriam Baske and Cecily Doran in *The Emancipated*, but France was within reach. Eventually, though, he would have to accept that he could not change his sisters' opinions, nor the lives they would lead. He was not the only stubborn member of the Gissing family.

In June, Gissing received a letter that opened up another perspective on the position of educated women. Edith Sichel had written an article a year earlier on *Thyrza* and *Demos*.[16] 'She shows a certain insight,' Gissing had commented, 'but . . . avoids all *literary* criticism. I suppose she meant to do so. .... This is the great instance of the superiority of the French over the English public, as a whole. The French are instinctively artists; the mass of English understand nothing in literature save the matter.'[17] When Sichel finally wrote to Gissing, asking if he had read her piece, he replied that he respected her work for the poor, but was himself without any 'philanthropic motive':

> It is my misfortune as a writer of fiction that English readers have so long been taught to look for the moral of such works, and especially in the case of stories which deal with the poor. .... Now, were I, in a Preface, to say that 'the philanthropic movements of the day are nothing to me save as artistic material, and I care not in the least whether my books promote or discourage those efforts', the result would be much surprise and more indignation. Yet I should have told the truth, and a truth which I had fancied self-evident.[18]

Sichel assumed that it was the writer's duty to make the world a better place, which meant that 'an artist has no right to be a pessimist'.[19] Gissing's usual response to such criticism was irritable and dismissive, but he did not want to be rude to a lady to her face. He preferred to start a conversation with her. He found out that she was five years younger than he was, unmarried, and comfortably off (her father, an East India merchant, had left her more than £20,000). Her family had converted from Judaism to Christianity. Gissing took note of Sichel's Jewish features, though without showing either prejudice or particular interest in Judaism. When she asked him to visit her in London he said he was too busy with his novel to leave Agbrigg; he turned down a similar invitation from Thomas Hardy. London in June was a social maelstrom, which inspired both fear and fascination. 'I do not come in contact with the "Season",' he told Sichel, 'but its proximity always depresses me, – for complicated reasons with which do not fear that I shall trouble you.'[20]

Apart from the social advantages of knowing Edith Sichel, there was also the ever-tantalising chance of a romantic liaison. Sichel was an educated woman with private means, who wrote articles and was an active reformer – the kind of woman who might frequent Mrs Lessingham's London salon in *The Emancipated*. Why should not Gissing enter such a world in reality, through a fortunate marriage? His reputation as a writer certainly stood high with Sichel, and other writers like Meredith and Hardy had married up on the strength of their achievements. Nonetheless, Gissing thought it prudent to stay home and write. He had received £150 for *The Nether World* nine months before, and needed at least as much to carry him through the coming year. Sichel could wait until he had finished *The Emancipated*.

What drove Gissing in his daily work was fear of what he might become if he stopped. At Agbrigg he had a frightening breakdown after writing one page of his daily quota. The next day was also black and hideous: 'Not a line of writing. Too horrible to speak of.'[21] The day after he was back in his right mind, and able to work; he finished the novel in just over ten weeks, on 13 August 1889. 'Quick work,' he noted in his diary, 'of course too quick. But needs must.'[22] Still, Gissing had spent seven months thinking about the novel before he put pen to paper. He was not the kind of novelist who revised meticulously on his way to a final text, though he did make cuts and corrections when a new edition gave him opportunity to do so. Gissing always wrote with an eye to the market for fiction, but even if he had had unlimited leisure his aim would not have been to write richly textured 'art novels'. Nonetheless, *The Emancipated* did achieve a more complex treatment of character and motive than his previous novels. This was not because it was written under different conditions, but because its focus on middle-class artists and intellectuals required a fuller account of their inner life.

As he was writing *The Emancipated* in the summer of 1889, Gissing had several signs that he was extending his literary reputation. The translation of *Demos* into French by Madame le Breton was announced for autumn publication; in the US there were respectful reviews for *A Life's Morning* and *The Nether World*.[23] Gissing's friend Eduard Bertz was made secretary of the German Society of Authors and editor of its journal, *Deutsche Presse*. He wrote an enthusiastic article on Gissing, for publication there in November 1889. A German translation of *Demos* was also in hand by Clara Steinitz, a friend of Bertz's.[24] Finally, Gissing wrote a commissioned article about Christmas in Rome, for the newspaper syndicate Tillotson's. This was something he did in a week and received £10 for, which was three months' rent of his flat.[25] The print mass media were expanding, and any author with an established reputation could pick up many little jobs like this. Gissing needed to enter that market so that he was not staking everything on his annual novel. He would never have the commercial talent of authors like Arnold Bennett or H. G. Wells, but at least he was starting to diversify his literary offerings.

Once he had finished *The Emancipated*, Gissing took Margaret off for a month's holiday in the Channel Islands. They went first to London, where Gissing left the manuscript of *The Emancipated* at Bentley's. Gissing was dissatisfied with Smith, Elder, who seemed unwilling to pay more than £150 for any of his novels. The sensible thing would have been to try and get the two publishers to bid against each other, but Gissing never managed to be sensible when selling his books. Smith, Elder had now reissued three of his novels in various cheaper formats: *Demos*, *A Life's Morning*, and *The Nether World*. The combined sales of these editions ran into several thousands, but Gissing did not receive a penny for any of them. Now he said nothing to Smith, Elder about having a new novel, but simply left the manuscript at Bentley's and went off on holiday.

After a stormy crossing to Guernsey, Gissing and Margaret were happy with the island, and decided to save money by staying there rather than going on to Brittany. The visit to Guernsey was for them a pilgrimage to Victor Hugo, who had moved there in 1852 after Louis Napoleon seized power in France, and stayed until the Republic was restored in 1870. At Hauteville, looking out over St Peter Port and the sea, Hugo wrote romantic novels like *Les Misérables* and *The Toilers of the Sea*. Gissing and Margaret read these on their holiday, as well as Hugo's novel of the Revolution, *Ninety-Three*. Gissing had his doubts about Hugo, but not about *Les Misérables*: 'a great book, in many senses of the word'.[26] But after Hugo, his taste in reading diverged from Margaret's: 'Of course troubles and annoyances about church-going; fitting in of meals, etc. In morning Madge went to Forest church. Afternoon we sat on the rocks, and I read Ovid, – Madge some dirty little pietistic work. Evening she went to St Martin's.'[27] Gissing's Ovid was the *Amores*, full of seduction and adultery. Margaret did not have enough Latin to see what it was about, nor could she make any real intellectual contact with her brother. 'My poor sister is a Puritan,' Gissing told Bertz, 'and we can talk of nothing but matter of fact.'[28] In justice to Margaret, she found her brother a gloomy and silent companion; they shared only a love of the natural beauty of the islands, especially Sark. Margaret's invalidism improved with their long walks and sea-bathing, and Gissing felt better too. Obsessively tied to routine as he was, he followed the rituals of holiday as faithfully as the rituals of work.

While on Sark, Gissing had a curious exchange about homosexuality. Eduard Bertz had become very enthusiastic about Whitman's poetry; he corresponded with him, and promoted his work in Germany. But Whitman's open homoeroticism made Bertz uneasy. What did Gissing think?

> I do not go so far as the writer in the *Gentleman's;* these passages do not strike me as 'disgusting'; but, on the other hand, I am inclined to think that Bucke's enthusiasm makes him wilfully blind to this writer's meaning. In fact, the passages in which Whitman speaks in this way of male friendships awaken no sympathy in me; it is my habit to regard such language as a tender exaggeration. Far *truer* to me would it sound if he talked of hearty

grasp of hands. I have always felt, indeed, that some of Tennyson's language
in 'In Memoriam' went beyond my sympathy.

But would this be so to a member of the Latin races, of to-day?[29]

Gissing's reply seems deliberately obtuse. He describes the seemly way of
expressing male friendship as if sexual love between men had never existed.
Yet from his classical studies he knew well what 'Greek love' was, and he
discussed it later when Oscar Wilde was on trial. In *The Unclassed* he had
given an ideal picture of the friendship between Osmond Waymark and
Julian Casti. Waymark takes Casti away from his shrewish wife and looks
after him as he is dying of TB. At the end, Casti 'clasps his friend's hand'
before saying good night; in the morning, he lies dead. Gissing often uses
the motif of a man trying to save his friend from a destructive relationship
with a woman, as Morley Roberts had tried to do for Gissing in real life;
but the homoerotic potential of such interventions is something that he is
determined to avoid.

Gissing and his sister left Sark on 14 September, well pleased with their
holiday if not with each other's company. While on holiday he had thought
about a novel to be called 'A Man of Letters'; this was the one he eventually
wrote as *New Grub Street*, but only after a number of false starts. Though
Gissing is often thought of as a journeyman writer who produced a steady
stream of novels, his output was intermittent, especially in the earlier part
of his career. In the phase of trying to launch a book, he might often be
paralysed by fits of depression, illness, sexual frustration, or anxiety about
money. Once he was able to write regularly, attacks of self-criticism might
cause him to tear up everything he had done. All of this was more like a
roller-coaster ride than an ox-like ploughing of the same furrow; or one
could say that Gissing passed various Stations of the Cross in his writer's
Calvary, and then visited them again for each successive book.

There was one Station that Gissing managed to escape, though he constantly feared that it would be the end of his line. This was the Marylebone
workhouse, across Marylebone Road from his flat. Gissing was haunted
by failure, and the workhouse was Victorian society's tribute to Social
Darwinism, failure made into an institution. It was a huge complex housing
1,500 paupers, and in September 1889 Gissing was given a tour by the
Assistant Master:

The terribly obsequious rising and hat-doffing of the old people as we
passed. ... A ruffian just out of prison for thrashing wife and children will
make complaint that they have been neglected in the House. ... Peculiar

bloodlessness of the old people; their white seamed faces. Looked like
respectful automatons.

The Casual Ward has 3 baths. People when admitted sit in the outer shed
for 2 hours. Then they give their names, occupations, whence and whither.
Admission refused to those who have 4d or more. First they have supper,
then a bath. Oakum picking in the cells; no stone-breaking at Marylebone.
... Almost all regular tramps carry a 'lip', which is the steel off a boot; it
helps them with the oakum. The pervading smell of oakum.[30]

George Orwell and Gissing saw the workhouse with much the same eye;
the difference between them was that Gissing would never have dreamed
of *choosing* to live like a tramp.

Keeping out of the workhouse depended on selling *The Emancipated*.
Gissing hoped for a good price, but when Bentley asked him about the
commercial success of his previous books he was quite unwilling to answer.
He considered it vulgar to reveal how much money his books had made;
in any case, having sold the copyright he had no further share in any profits.
Nor did the publishers have any duty to report sales to him. It was in their
interest to keep quiet if sales were good, because that might strengthen
Gissing's hand when he had a new manuscript to offer. He could see,
though, that *Demos* had been issued in five editions in England by 1889, plus
the US and Continental editions and French and German translations.[31] Did
English publishers pass the word around that Gissing would always accept
£150 for a book? When he eventually got up to £250 – in 1898 for the
English edition of *The Town Traveller* – the contract was negotiated by his
agent at the time, William Colles. Gissing asked Bentley for £250 for *The
Emancipated*, but the best he would offer was £150 for sales up to 850 copies,
£50 for the next 150, and a final £50 if sales went over 1,000. For a three-
decker first edition selling at a guinea and a half, 850 was a difficult target,
and sales never reached that point. Not only did Gissing fail to get a higher
price than for his previous books, he got no commitment from Bentley to
follow up the three-decker with cheaper editions. This was a fatal mistake.
By now, Gissing's novels were certain to get respectful reviews in the major
journals, which created a demand for the later editions that Smith, Elder
always produced. With Bentley's failure to provide a follow-up, *The Emancipated* would not have its proper impact on Gissing's reputation. But when
he received the offer from Bentley, Gissing wrote the usual words in his
diary: 'I shall accept.'[32]

Gissing had written to Edith Sichel from Sark proposing a visit, and on
28 September he went down to see her at Chiddingfold, Surrey. When he

arrived he found that she was living with Emily Marion Ritchie, a sister-in-law of Thackeray's daughter Anne Ritchie:

> Miss Sichel did not greatly interest me, but she is intellectual and sharp-witted. A very Jewish face. Miss Ritchie – about forty, I suppose, – is a woman of much refinement, and highly educated. She knows everyone; impossible to mention a man or woman prominent in to-day's literature or art with whom she has not personal acquaintance.[33]

Although Gissing spent an enjoyable day with Sichel, and would see more of her, he could not bring himself to join the social circles to which she offered him a key. With Mrs Gaussen he could make the excuse that she was not an intellectual, but Sichel was a respectable critic and historian. Virginia Woolf would call her 'That talented Jewess'.[34] Gissing was impressed by the cultured atmosphere of Sichel's household, though he told his sister Ellen it had as much to do with advantages of birth as with native talent:

> They have always lived in intellectual society. It is not remarkable brain-power that distinguishes them, but *opportunity*. Had you lived in the same way, your attainments would be no less than theirs. These people learn most of what they know in *conversation*. They live much in foreign countries, and so acquire languages with comparative ease. ... They live at the *centre* of things.[35]

Soon after meeting Sichel, Gissing decided to call his next novel 'The Head-Mistress'. He started a course of reading in the British Museum on what he called 'all sorts of queer scholastic and woman's-rights literature'.[36] Sichel belonged to a social group, upper-middle-class feminists, that was as clearly defined as the leisured Italian tourists of *The Emancipated* or the work-girls of Lambeth. Gissing always had his eye open for such novel-sized groups, where a network of personal relationships was conditioned by some wider social context. Unlike Zola, though, he was not just looking for 'representative' characters; he observed individuals who wanted their own fulfilment, but ran up against the iron laws of society and of nature. In *The Emancipated*, Cecily Doran faces the brute fact that 'nature herself had dealt cruelly with women. Constituted as she is, limited as she is by inexorable laws, by what refinement of malice is she endowed with energies and desires like to those of men?'[37]

Gissing's attitude to the women's movement resembled his attitude to the London poor. He felt deep sympathy for what women endured, and deep scepticism about their chances of escaping from bondage. Their fate

was unjust – and unavoidable. He too had suffered, so that he identified
with them; but he considered himself morally and even physiologically
different. With the imagined Head-Mistress of his next novel, Gissing was
interested in the relative success such women could achieve, even within
their subordinate condition. They had more hope than the poor, since a
woman with independent means could create her own little world of
comfort and respect. Olive Schreiner was Gissing's model for such success;
he had heard about her from Sichel and Ritchie:

> I was told that she has quarrelled with her family because they do not share
> her Socialism, and has gone to live alone in the New Forest. Though well-
> to-do, she will not have a servant, because she cannot bear to have a woman
> in her house who is not leading the intellectual kind of life she deems proper.
> She does everything for herself. A remarkable person; I should like to know
> her.[38]

Gissing had already enjoyed Schreiner's feminist novel, *The Story of an
African Farm*. He went on with his research into careers for women, but
abandoned 'The Head-Mistress'. The material he had gathered was
reworked in *The Odd Women*, three years later.

After his visit to Chiddingfold, Gissing told Eduard Bertz that he would
use Sichel as no more than a stepping-stone: 'I cannot say that she strongly
interests me. But at present it is my business to make acquaintances. Naturally, this becomes easier for me now that, wherever I go, my name is
tolerably well known. – *I cannot stand obscurity*.'[39] The next time he saw
Sichel was in London, at her luxurious flat in Barkston Gardens, Earls
Court. Gissing invited himself to tea and discussed his books with Sichel;
his feelings about her were changing: 'Miss Sichel interested me; for some
reason her face pleased me more than when I first saw her down in Surrey.
I half think she is beautiful. .... Spent evening in a troubled frame of mind,
occasionally glancing at Darwin's "Origin of Species". – a queer jumble of
thoughts.'[40] One could give a cynical explanation for Gissing's turmoil:
when he wrote to Sichel saying he wanted to come and see her, he had just
learned about the £20,000 she had inherited from her father. With her as
his patron, he could escape the iron cage of always having to write for
money. She would understand what he was trying to do in his work, and
she was the first 'lady' to take an interest in him since he had met Mrs
Gaussen five years before. Unlike Gaussen, though, Sichel was unmarried
and mistress of her own destiny.

Gissing left for Greece two days after seeing Sichel at her flat. He wrote
her a letter on the journey, and in a dream he 'talked much with Miss Sichel

and grew very intimate with her'. Her reply took more than a month to arrive, and was 'Very cold and uninteresting'.[41] Neither letter has survived, but Gissing may have made another of his sudden plunges towards a woman, and have been rebuffed again. In any case, Sichel's reply ended her friendship with Gissing: she sent him a couple of invitations when he was back in London, but he refused them. In approaching Sichel, Gissing seems to have been oblivious to her intimate relationships with Emily Ritchie and with the poet Mary Coleridge. None of them married; they shared an intense piety, literary interests, and concern for the work-girls of the East End.[42] In considering marriage to Sichel, Gissing failed to see that her emotional and even sexual interests might lie elsewhere – that she and Ritchie had what was called at the time 'a Boston marriage'. Mary Barfoot and Rhoda Nunn live together in *The Odd Women*, but the personal issue between them is that both are attracted to the same man. A jealous triangle is common in Gissing's novels, with two women or two men in competition for someone of the opposite sex. Same-sex intimacy does occur, but only as ideal friendship.[43]

Gissing's interest in Sichel had in any case taken a back seat to his desire to get out of England as soon as he had his £150 from Bentley for *The Emancipated*. He had done the same thing the year before with his money for *The Nether World*. 'I should like to go to Athens,' he told Algernon, 'but it would be expensive. On the other hand, I cannot stay here through these black months.'[44] Gissing had always believed that a cultured person needed to know at first hand both classical Rome and Greece; now he had his chance. As soon as he had corrected the proofs of *The Emancipated*, he would be off to Athens. His only lament was that his closest friends, Bertz and Roberts, were too poor to join him:

> I am beginning to feel that it is a disagreeable thing to have any measure of success, when those about one do not share in it. Yet have I not gone through enough misery? Who has experienced more – other things being equal? ... it is not always heartlessness that makes a successful man shun the unsuccessful; it may be sheer inability to bear the strain upon his sympathies. – I should have twice the vigour if I were surrounded by people whom success made cheerful. Half my time I am groaning uselessly on others' account.[45]

Since Gissing wrote this to Ellen, it would have been tactless to say that much of his groaning was also for his sisters and for Algernon.

Gissing left for Greece on 11 November, and soon stopped worrying about those he had left behind. He had a six-day voyage from Marseille to

Piraeus, sailing around the Peloponnesus to the most southerly point in Europe, Cape Matapan. Mount Taygetos, in the land of Menelaos and Helen, was a 'marvellous vision':

> Such a view is not of this earth, as *we* understand it; more wonderful, I think, than even South Italy. The astonishing barrenness of the coast is transformed into loveliness by effects of colour. This is indeed the land of Apollo. . . . Well, I think I shall never spend another winter in England. I had rather live in the South on 2d. a day. Here, life is worth living. I am well and hopeful – whereas in England I am neither.[46]

Athens, however, was a much less pleasing city than Naples. It was dusty, windy, cold and rainy; and there were soldiers everywhere – 'This continental curse of militarism.'[47] Gissing was thrilled by Greek as a living language, but not by those who spoke it. 'As far as I am able to judge the Greeks,' he told W. H. Hudson, 'I don't like them. In appearance they are – in the mass – singularly ignoble, and their manners lack both vivacity and suavity. What can one expect, after ages of varied slavery?'[48] Still, Athens was crowned by the Acropolis, and Gissing spent many days there. He walked to Eleusis and back by way of Salamis, where he sat at the vantage point where the Emperor Xerxes looked down at the destruction of his fleet in 480 BC. Greece completed Gissing's education, as he walked around Athens with Aristophanes as his guide. But he could find no friends among the people, and was frustrated by not being able to travel outside the city:

> I shall not be able to see anything of the further parts of Attica. To do so would involve, I find, too much expense. And the kind of accommodation offered you at country houses is too fearful; – rooms with unglazed windows, horrible stenches, livestock without end, and food that no man can digest. Had I but a companion, I shouldn't mind facing these inconveniences; alone, it is too much. – Always the same trouble with me; my solitude spoils everything.[49]

Solitude might be more tolerable in Naples, so Gissing took ship from Patras to Brindisi on 17 December, and arrived in Naples on the 20th after a stormy crossing. He was delighted to walk its streets again, and stay at his old lodgings on Vico Brancaccio. Perhaps he would write something serious about Naples, which would mean learning the Neapolitan dialect. An invitation from Shortridge to go and stay again at Massa Lubrense was a chance to see how many troubles an Englishman could bring on himself when he 'went native'. He went to Shortridge's on New Year's Eve 1889, and stayed for a week. The household was 'a splendid opportunity of studying the life of the lower Neapolitans. The family live in dirt and discomfort and misery, – all this in the midst of glorious scenery.'[50] Since Gissing's last visit, Shortridge's son Jack had died of meningitis, leaving him with four daughters, his wife, his father-in-law, and his sick brother Herbert. Shortridge blamed most of his troubles on his wife, Carmela; but Gissing could see her side too. She 'is not bad', he told Bertz, 'only foolish, and animal-like, and – Italian. . . . She almost made me cry, telling of her sorrows in the foolish sing-song Caprese dialect.'[51] For the sake of watching this family drama, Gissing was willing to put up with the dirt, the horrible food, and the brandishing of knives. When he went back to Naples Short-ridge followed him and they explored the medieval districts where whole streets were being torn down to modernise the city. Gissing thought of returning to England with foreboding: 'To my mind, it is all embodied in the Marylebone workhouse, towards which I am drifting.'[52] But to stay out of the workhouse he had to go back, and write.

Gissing hoped to leave Naples on 6 February, taking a ship directly to London; but he fell ill with influenza and had to stay another fortnight. The doctor he saw also found some congestion in his right lung, which added to his general sense of doom. His brother William had died of TB at the age of twenty-one, and it was believed that TB ran in families. A month before falling ill, Gissing had been living in a dirty house with Herbert Shortridge, who was in the terminal stage of TB (he died in March). Koch had identified the TB bacillus in 1882 but there was no clinical test for it yet, still less any effective treatment. Gissing was already fond of saying that he would be dead in a year or two; now he had good reason to fear that his lungs were failing him. But he could not live as an invalid: he had £77 in hand to keep himself until September, by which time he had to finish another book.

Gissing sailed for London on the *Orient* on 20 February 1890. The minute he went on board he was back in England, with English food – no coffee or wine – and English company. 'I don't like English people,' he told Bertz, 'and just as little do they like me.' He got into conversation with the ship's clergyman, who said he'd been told by someone in first class that Gissing was a famous author. 'This has a symbolical significance,' Gissing com-mented. 'It is my fate in life to be known by the first-class people and to associate with the second class – or even the third and fourth. It will always be so.'[53] He might come to live in Germany, he told Bertz; the country would be 'politically and socially of extreme interest for some years', though he detested its 'military atmosphere'.[54] Gissing had the German question exactly right, but his idea of moving there and becoming an expert on the country remained a pipe dream.

By 28 February Gissing was back in the 'desperate solitude' of Cornwall Residences. He needed fifty shillings a week to live, which meant he would run out of money by the end of September. Allowing time for the publisher to read the manuscript, that meant that he had six months to finish a novel. Algernon, meanwhile, managed to get £40 for his third novel, *A Village Hampden*. This was twice as much as for the one before, and created a faint hope that he might become self-supporting. Gissing put his nose to the grindstone at 7.K, but soon ran into his usual difficulties. In spite of all the research he had done, he decided that 'The Head-Mistress' would not work, and started on another subject. All we know about it is that much of the action was to take place on Guernsey and Sark; after writing thirty-one pages Gissing abandoned it, on 7 April. The next day he started yet another novel, 'A Man of Letters'. Having spent so much time at the British Museum in the autumn, he now decided to write about the kind of people who read there in order to regurgitate what they had read into more books and magazines. This was a perfect subject for Gissing, requiring no further research at all, though writing the novel would inflict on him the usual agonies.

'The Head-Mistress' and 'A Man of Letters' were both conceived as novels in Gissing's new manner, focused on middle-class protagonists. Much depended on the success of his first major offering in this line, *The Emancipated*. Gissing received his six free copies on 20 March, and sent one off to his sisters. He soon got a letter back from Ellen, telling him that she disliked the novel 'from beginning to end'. 'Naturally,' was Gissing's comment.[55] Ellen believed that Gissing had based the character of Miriam Baske on herself. Certainly the novel pilloried the evangelical and pro-vincial way of life, with Miriam an example of the human cost of holding such values. The first half of *The Emancipated* lays out the indictment, while the second half, somewhat implausibly, shows Miriam abandoning her beliefs and becoming a happy, open-minded wife. Both parts would have been equally offensive to Ellen. First her brother showed that he despised her world, then that he hoped she would renounce it. His defence of the novel cannot have made things better. 'The one thing that grieves me,' he wrote, 'is the thought that, owing to lack of experience, you imagine me singular in my way of thinking. Whereas the fact is that I only represent the prevalent views of our day.'[56] Gissing also tried to give her lessons in theology: 'I never attack spiritual faith in itself, – but I shall never cease to use all my power against such illusions as, for instance, that which imagines

Sunday to be different from any other day (in plain defiance of the New Testament and ecclesiastical history, as strong Christians have again and again pointed out).'[57] Why, then, did Gissing never write on Sundays? He claimed that the English Sunday made him too depressed to do anything; but if he didn't believe in it, why should it affect his mood? In fact, Gissing's best writing was inspired by what he most feared, things like cemeteries, poverty, difficult women, loneliness, religion – and Sunday.

Gissing tried to convince Ellen that he was criticising both sides, the emancipated as much as the orthodox:

> But no, you will not like my future books. I have been waiting until my position with the publishers enabled me to write with freedom. Even you must recognise that hypocrisy in literature, however mild, is not admirable. My part is with the men and women who are clearing the ground of systems that have had their day and have crumbled into obstructive ruin. To those who live in quiet corners of the earth, where those systems still seem solid edifices, and who know nothing of the true state of things in the greater part of the world, – we seem mere reckless destroyers. This is an inevitable misconception.[58]

By Gissing's reasoning, the way for his sisters to change their ideas was to change where they lived, preferably by moving to the south of England. Instead, they decided to stay in the area, but move from Agbrigg to a house at 8 Westfield Grove, just north of the centre of Wakefield. They would hold on to their views, and stay in Wakefield until they died, many years ahead.

In spite of all this friction over *The Emancipated*, Gissing still wanted to take his sisters to Paris, and they agreed to come. He was spending money he could ill afford, but he cared for his sisters whether or not they cared for his work. They left London on 17 April and stayed for ten days, enough to see all the most famous sights. Gissing escorted his sisters to the English church on rue d'Aguesseau on Sundays (duty), and refused to go inside himself (conviction). He had no objection, though, to attending a Catholic service with them on Sunday evening (research?). Ellen and Margaret were delighted to have seen everything they should, from the Mona Lisa to the Eiffel Tower; with George as their guide they saw cemeteries too, both Montmartre and Père Lachaise. Rain and sea-sickness were the only hazards of the trip.

The trouble over *The Emancipated* must have been smoothed over, because Gissing decided to spend the summer with his family, as he had done the year before. It would eke out his remaining money a few months longer, and help him to push his next novel through to a conclusion. In 1889 he had paid his mother fifteen shillings a week for his board; this year the agreement seems to have been that he would not have to pay anything until his book was sold. The reviews of *The Emancipated*, meanwhile, were not altogether encouraging. Critics could no longer complain about having to read about poor people in sordid settings, but they still objected to an 'undercurrent of pessimism' and a book 'more calculated to give pain than pleasure'.[59] Everyone recognised that Gissing was a novelist of ideas; the trouble was that most of the ideas went against the grain of conventional wisdom. He presented a group of men and women who, he thought, were clearing a way into the future; the critics saw a collection of morbid types and harbingers of decadence. They remained set on patronising Gissing and instructing him on how to be a more popular writer. The *Saturday Review* was typical:

> If Mr Gissing aspires to popularity he must condescend to human infirmity by endowing some, at least, of his *dramatis personae* with those graces of character which conduce to attractiveness, and inspire the reader with feelings of interest and affection. Novels, no less than poems, should obey the Horatian mandate to be 'sweet'.[60]

The best that can be said for such criticism is that it was accurate in its predictions. *The Emancipated* sold fewer than four hundred copies of its first edition, and Gissing remained stuck halfway up the stairs, a hundred-and-fifty-pound novelist who was more respected than read. He knew this all too well, and hated his critics all the more for constantly reminding him of it.

9

Second Wife

Three days after returning from Paris at the end of May 1890, Gissing left Cornwall Residences to spend the summer in Wakefield. Through May and June he worked steadily, if unhappily, on what would become *New Grub Street*. Edith Sichel invited him to an 'at home' in June: 'Of course must refuse,' he wrote in his diary, 'and should in any case. English society is no more for me.'[1] At the end of the month he decided to scrap the novel he was working on and start another, which he called 'Storm-Birds'. This was probably about a group of people who challenge conventional ideas about politics and religion (storm-birds gave warning that a storm was on the way). Gissing may have been inspired by Marie Bashkirtseff, the singer and painter whose diary he was reading. She had lived passionately and rebelliously, dying of TB in 1884 at the age of twenty-five. But after a month Gissing broke down again, overcome with wretchedness and 'profound misery'.[2] He now had worked on three or perhaps four novels since he came back from Italy at the end of February, and his prospects, he felt, were as black as they had ever been. 'If another five years such as the last is before me,' he told Ellen, 'I shall either end in the Asylum or the Thames (I say it in all seriousness).'[3]

In his despair, Gissing fell into another of his romantic follies when his sister Margaret invited a friend over for the evening. Connie Ash was twenty-five, the daughter of a Wakefield corn merchant. She was a pretty young woman with a good singing voice. Three days later, Gissing gave her his inevitable courtship present: a copy of *Thyrza*. He was invited to supper at the Ashes, where Connie sang again; his sister Margaret told him to watch his step:

Madge . . . has amused me by insisting on the girl's slatternliness at home – as warning to me, I fancy. Well, these warnings are useless. The faults you have noticed are curiously like some of my own, and, if anything, they have helped to increase my feeling of sympathy with her. But I don't try to explain it; from the first, I have simply fallen in love with her, and there's an end of it.[4]

Gissing's feelings for Connie Ash left him completely bewildered and unable to write. He realised that he had to get out of Wakefield, and left on 19 September. Ash may never have known about his infatuation, but it is certain that he quickly gave up any hope of marrying her. He had fallen in love out of what he called, in one of his short stories, 'that need in me – the incessant hunger for a woman's sympathy and affection'.[5] But Connie Ash, he realised, was not likely to meet that need:

> I have come to my senses, and again understand, as I always do after a time, that my lot is one of hopeless solitude and struggle. I shall never have any money, and, worse than that, I shall never be able to make a place in any social circle. To ask anybody to share such a life as this would be absurdity – I should only excite astonishment and ridicule. Poverty with society some people will face, but poverty *without* society, not one in a million. It is useless for me to look upwards; a rare chance may perhaps enable me to meet some day with a companion much lower than myself. That is the only glimmer of hope.[6]

Gissing's despair over Connie Ash makes one wonder how much was known in Wakefield about his imprisonment, fourteen years before. The obvious place to look for a wife was among his sisters' friends. Having £150 a year did not make him a poor man, in the provinces at least, and perhaps he could find a wife with an income of her own. Many young women in Wakefield were pious and narrow-minded, but surely not all. Gissing may have feared that Connie Ash's father already knew about his disgrace, or would find out if he and Connie became engaged. But he always seemed to foresee the worst, examining society's rules and assuming that there could never be an exception to them. 'Marriage, in the best sense, is impossible, owing to my insufficient income; educated English girls *will* not face poverty in marriage, and to them anything under £400 a year is serious poverty. They remain unmarried in hundreds of thousands, rather than accept poor men.'[7]

Gissing wrote this to Bertz in Germany; he believed that writers were more respected on the Continent, and he would have a better chance of marrying across the Channel. His later relation with Gabrielle Fleury suggested that he was not wrong. In England, though, he was convinced that he was a victim of the mercenary middle-class approach to marriage. His next novel would present a different case: a well-brought-up young woman *does* marry a poor man, trusting that he will succeed as a writer.

But when she experiences poverty in marriage she cannot bear it for long, and discards her husband. Gissing believed that this would also be true for him, leaving only one solution: 'In London I must resume my search for some decent work-girl who will come and live with me. I am too poor to marry an equal, and cannot live alone.'[8] In little more than a month, he had found her. But a decent work-girl would not live with him; she would insist on marriage. Gissing knew how dangerous this was, for he had already experienced the disasters of marriage to Nell. But neither English morals, nor the values of his family, nor his own temperament, allowed for anything else.

Gissing returned to London from Wakefield on 21 August, feeling very shaky and with no clear path to finishing a novel and getting some money. Somehow he had to patch a book together from the many false starts of the past year. His first attempt was 'Hilda Wolff', perhaps a new version of 'The Head-Mistress' with a Jewish theme suggested by his friendship with Edith Sichel. After three lonely weeks he had finished the first volume, but felt it would never do. 'I know that I shall never do any more good work till I am married,' he wrote in his diary.[9] He left off 'Hilda Wolff' and began another novel, 'Victor Yule', without any confidence that he could carry it through. The 24th of September was a day of 'extreme misery' when Gissing could write nothing. At last he rushed out of his flat and spoke to the first young woman he came across, in the Marylebone Road around the corner from his flat; she agreed to walk down Baker Street with him to the Oxford Music Hall, on Oxford Street. Her name was Edith Underwood and she lived with her father, a stonemason, in Camden Town. So Gissing's second marriage was launched: a disaster that he foresaw, and even planned. This was what he told Morley Roberts, and so the story appeared in *The Private Life of Henry Maitland* after Gissing's death.[10]

Let us consider an alternative version. Gissing had thought about writing a novel about London music halls a year earlier, so he knew them well. The Oxford was one of the leading halls; it was also known as a place where prostitutes could be found.[11] Seven years later, in a letter to Clara Collet, Gissing declared firmly: 'Against Edith's character not a word can be said. The marriage was regular as that of any grocer.'[12] But in the same letter Gissing lied about Nell. He said that she was a drunkard, but not that she was a prostitute; that she died in 1881 or 82, when it was actually 1888. Even if we believe that Edith was faithful to Gissing while she was married to him, we may wonder about her sexual conduct before then. Or he may have intended to pick up a girl of the streets, only to find that Edith was more respectable than she seemed.

After the music hall, Edith agreed to meet Gissing on the weekend and go to Richmond with him. In *The Unclassed*, Osmond Waymark goes on a day's outing to Richmond with Ida Starr, a prostitute with whom he has fallen in love, and her friend in the same trade, Sally Fisher. The town girls become different people as they walk in the park: 'Ida talked less, but every now and then laughed in her deep enjoyment. She had no reminiscence of country life; it was enough that all about her was new and fresh and pure; nothing to remind her of Regent Street and the Strand.'[13] These were streets known for prostitution. Gissing's fantasy was that a girl of the London streets could be made into a different creature by exposing her to country air. Edith Underwood, whatever her character, was a Londoner through and through. She was the youngest of six brothers and sisters; her mother had been dead for ten years. The men in her family were all artisans, which put the Underwoods a step below Gissing's social level. She was an ordinary-looking young woman, to judge by a surviving photograph, and ordinary in every other way as well. But Gissing's old Pygmalion complex was at work: he believed that Edith was a woman of 'extreme quietness and docility', whom he could mould into the kind of companion he so desperately needed.[14]

The two people closest to Gissing, his sister Ellen and Morley Roberts, immediately told him that he was deluding himself. Gissing's response to Ellen was that he could not be making a mistake, because this was his only chance of survival:

> My demands are very humble. I ask for nothing but good temper and sincerity. You must remember that I have ample experience of what it means to live with an uneducated wife and I never felt *that* fact unbearable, never. A cultured woman has always seemed hopelessly above me. . . . Things have gone ill with me since boyhood, and there is no setting them altogether right. It will be a great thing to secure for myself a very simple, quiet home, after all I have passed through.
>
> In my books I have pictured ideal things. I have to live in the plain, bald reality. Successful grocers, and such people, are able to win good and beautiful women; – not the men who make the world understand what goodness and beauty mean. . . .
>
> If this girl prove but faithful and kindly disposed – that is not asking much – I shall feel such passionate gratitude as ordinary people cannot conceive. Of *in*gratitude under such circumstances I am by nature incapable.[15]

Gissing's heartfelt cry was also an evasion of his first motive for choosing Edith: sexual frustration. He recognised the 'innate puritanism' of his family, which made it impossible 'to hint at anything like sexual relations. ... One result is that Nelly and I, when we endeavour to talk intimately, get into the most ridiculous game of cross-purposes, and exhaust our ingenuity in devising vagueness of speech.'[16] He could not say that if a work-girl could give him physical comfort, he would expect little in terms of positive qualities.

Morley Roberts saw through Gissing's rationalisations. 'It was a strange thing,' he wrote, 'that [Gissing] did not seem to know what love was.'[17] It was not just that Gissing wooed Edith for convenience rather than love. In Roberts's view, neither Gissing himself nor the male characters in his books ever loved a woman because they passionately desired her. Such men are 'essentially too reasonable'; they start by imagining – in solitude – the *kind* of woman who might save them. 'They suffer physically,' Roberts wrote, 'or they suffer to a certain degree from loneliness, but one never feels that only one woman could cure their pain. ... At times Maitland seemed, as it were, to be in love with the sex but not with the woman.'[18] Few women could have understood this on first acquaintance. If Gissing courted them, they would naturally assume that he desired them as an individual. What he really desired was a particular set of female attributes; and he believed also that he could make the woman in front of him fit the shape he had in mind. This was a sure recipe for anger and disappointment on his side, and wounded vanity on hers.

What Edith Underwood could see was that an older gentleman was interested in her, and that he had money for trips to Richmond and dinners in restaurants. The second time they met, when they went to Richmond for the day, she agreed to come into his flat and sit with him for an hour. They soon fell into a pattern of going to Richmond or Kew on Sundays, and seeing each other at Cornwall Residences or Edith's home in Camden Town on Wednesdays. But what went on, when Edith was at Gissing's flat? He read poetry to her, for one: Tennyson's 'The May Queen', which is about a cruel flirt who is taught a lesson. John Halperin, Gissing's most recent biographer, says that they obviously went to bed together; what else could they have in common? Morley Roberts just says that Gissing would have done better to pick up a prostitute, since before long he would have tired of her and could then send her on her way.

I suspect that reading Tennyson was as far as Gissing got in making love to Edith. In 1890 – the year he met Edith – he made a note about Henri Murger's creations, Mimi and Musette: 'With the English character the "Vie de Bohème" is impossible. In English girls there is first conscience, and secondly stupidity, keeping them from this ideal.'[19] In January 1891, four months after he and Edith had met, he wrote to Eduard Bertz: 'Our relations are as yet platonic. She lives with her father, brother and sister; the family is a respectable one, and if anything is to come of our connection it will have to be marriage.'[20] Marriage it was, a month later; and nine and a half months after the ceremony, Edith gave birth to a child. It was in her best interest to refuse intercourse until they were married, and Gissing was not the kind of person to seduce or bully her into changing her mind. In his novels, there are no free-spirited lower-class girls who enjoy sex for its own sake; there are good girls, and there are prostitutes. Even the New Woman Rhoda Nunn will not go beyond an academic belief in sexual freedom.[21] In the absence of reliable contraception, any young woman who yielded to premarital sex was running a fearful risk.

Just before Gissing met Edith, Morley Roberts had approached two of his female cousins, marriageable young ladies who had met and liked Gissing when he was a student at Owens College. Would they be willing to take Gissing on, to save a man of genius from folly? They agreed to meet him, but when Roberts went to tell him this good news, Gissing said that it was too late. He had already proposed to Edith.[22] This resembles the plot of 'A Lodger in Maze Pond', a short story Gissing wrote three years later. It seems likely that Gissing proposed to Edith less than two weeks after their first meeting.[23] At the beginning of December he turned down a dinner invitation from Edith Sichel, saying: 'I suppose I shall never again sit at a civilized table.'[24] Yet two days later he told the publishers Smith, Elder that he planned to go abroad in a month. In 'A Lodger in Maze Pond', Shergold's friend Harvey Munden carries him off to the Continent to prevent him marrying his maid. Roberts tried to do this for Gissing, but could not persuade him.[25] What made Gissing go through with the marriage to Edith Underwood was largely the fear that he might be completely unable to write if he stayed on his own, and so become penniless. He was penniless already, in the sense that he had spent the money he had received for *The Emancipated* and was now living on credit from his mother and £6.5 from selling many of his books. In November he had to sell another £5 worth – the equivalent, for Gissing, of burning his furniture in order to keep warm.

However disastrous Gissing's choice of Edith may have been in the long run, in the short run it helped his work. Over the two years before he met Edith, Gissing completed two novels and abandoned at least six others. In the year after he met her he completed three novels, of which two count among his major works. One week after taking Edith to the Oxford Music Hall he settled on *New Grub Street* as the novel to complete, and he wrote a new version from beginning to end in just over two months. Edith was the spur for him to produce at the manic rate of which he was capable: up to twenty-four thousand words a week, the equivalent of seven or eight three-decker novels a year. If Halperin is correct, Gissing was able to write *New Grub Street* because he was getting sexual satisfaction from Edith; but it might have been enough that he had Edith's companionship and the prospect of marriage. *New Grub Street* argued that marriage must have a foundation of money. In the world, Gissing wrote the novel to have the money to be able to keep the woman whom he needed in order to be able to write.

For a wife Gissing needed to have a home, and he had decided that it would not be Cornwall Residences. He had now lived there for six years, but had never been able to sublet it, and it cost him about a third of what he was paid for his annual novel. His next novel was going to be set in a provincial town, and he needed to go and live in one in order to write it. Any town other than Wakefield, that is. He decided that Exeter would suit him, without ever having been there. It would be much cheaper than London, and he could walk in the countryside. Before, he had always feared to live in the country because he thought that loneliness literally might kill him.

Gissing finished *New Grub Street* on 6 December 1890. Like so many Gissing heroes, Edwin Reardon dies at the end of the novel. Gissing had read up on pneumonia to make sure that he died authentically. After Bentley's failure with *The Emancipated*, Gissing felt that he had no choice but to crawl back to Smith, Elder, where he was treated in just the way one would expect. The previous August he had asked them to make him an offer for the copyright of *Thyrza*, which they had taken for an advance of £50. They had not had to pay any royalties, by the simple method of not publishing any editions in cheaper format, which they had done for the Gissing novels that they had purchased outright.[26] Their offer to purchase the copyright of *Thyrza* was an insulting £10, and even Gissing realised that he had to refuse. Now he left the manuscript of *New Grub Street* with them and waited, in freezing weather, for their verdict. 'Very low spirits,' he wrote in his diary, 'dreading the future.'[27] There was tension with Edith's father over the proposed marriage, so Gissing and his future bride ate Christmas dinner alone in her room. Underwood's two daughters were keeping house for him, and perhaps he opposed the marriage because it threatened his comfort.[28]

On 7 January of the new year, Smith, Elder made their offer for *New Grub Street*. They found the book 'clever and original', but too gloomy;

they would give the same amount as for *The Nether World*, £150. Gissing groaned, and accepted. He also caved in on *Thyrza*, saying he would now take £10 for the copyright. When Smith, Elder did not reply, he thought they must be ashamed of their paltry offer. Then a cheque for £10 arrived in the post. 'They are not ashamed after all,' Gissing recorded.[29] Neither were they ashamed to bring out a new edition, now that Gissing would have no share in the proceeds. He had advertised in the Exeter paper for rooms to let, and the day after getting his £150 cheque he took the train down and reserved three rooms on the outskirts of the city, at 24 Prospect Park. The rent was six shillings a week, less than half of what he had been paying in London. Like almost all the places where Gissing lived, the house was completely without charm, just a recently built semi-detached villa. He liked the rooms, but would have to live cheek-by-jowl with his landlord and bride. Two newly married couples sharing a kitchen was a recipe for trouble, and it did not fail to come.

Gissing quickly packed up at Cornwall Residences and moved down to Exeter. He now had to persuade Edith to join him, against the delaying tactics of her family. His method was to send one ultimatum after another: she must marry him by this or that date, or he would have nothing more to do with her. Edith finally gave in, but a pattern was set. She must do what Gissing thought best, and so allow him to make her better:

> When I have accustomed her to speak without the vile London accent, she will have a reasonably refined mode of speech. I can say with certainty that her instincts are anything but vulgar. . . . The girl is peculiarly gentle and pliable, with a certain natural refinement which seems to promise that she might be trained to my kind of life.[30]

It is extraordinary that nowhere in his diary or letters does Gissing really say anything about Edith as an individual; nor does there seem to be any portrait of her in his fiction. He speaks only of the kind of person she is, and of what such a person might be made into. Everything about the new household had to be arranged by him, using his furniture from Cornwall Residences. This was largely unavoidable, since Edith could not in decency come down to Exeter until they were married; but it meant that she had to leave everything she knew and put herself entirely into Gissing's hands. For him the question of Edith's autonomy did not arise: he was raising her from a lower condition to a higher one, and that was the end of it. As he waited for her to arrive, Gissing read Montaigne's essay 'Of Cruelty'. Did he notice the author's ultimate test of virtue? 'Socrates, it seems to me, tested himself still more roughly, keeping for his exercise the malignity of his wife, which is a test with the naked blade.'

Gissing was lonely in his new lodgings; he filled the time by going for long walks in the countryside and studying Darwinism, which would be at the centre of his next novel. He also revised and shortened *Thyrza* for the cheap edition now forthcoming from Smith, Elder. There was grim humour in his visit to the Exeter registrar for a marriage licence: 'He said his occupation was "literary man",' and the registrar told the clerk, 'Put gentleman.'[31] As late as 20 February Gissing still did not know if the marriage would go ahead; but Edith at last said she was ready and on the 24th he went up to London. He went with Edith to buy her a wedding ring on Tottenham Court Road, then took a room for himself at a Covent Garden pub, the Bedford Head. They were married the next day at the Pancras Registry Office. Edith's father and sister signed as witnesses, but there were no friends or family on Gissing's side. Over the next few years Gissing wrote constantly to one of his two closest friends, Eduard Bertz, and never told him he was married.

From the Registry Office Gissing and Edith went straight to Paddington, and they were home at 24 Prospect Park for their wedding night. Something else made the day memorable for Gissing: *The Times* published his letter on Greek prosody (a pet subject), with examples from Homer, Apollonius Rhodius and Milton. Fewer than a thousand people in England can have had any idea what Gissing was talking about. That didn't matter to Gissing; but he was concerned that Edith was baffled by ordinary English prose: 'My own books will of course be for ever out of the question for her; I shall not even let her pretend to read them. An attempt with "The Nether World" was a dismal failure, as might have been expected. It is not for everyone that my books are written.'[32] True enough, both then and now.

Whether Gissing and Edith enjoyed anything like a honeymoon period cannot be known. Walter Grahame, Gissing's former pupil, went to see him in Devon two years after his marriage and reported that he was happy and 'His wife was evidently devoted to him.'[33] Gissing himself said virtually nothing about his domestic life in its early months. His physical health became much better; it had always been affected by his emotional state. Exeter had many amenities for a town of its size, including a very good library system. Gissing had money in hand from the sale of *New Grub Street*, and two could live more cheaply in Exeter than one in London. To have someone to share his life, and his bed, was certainly what Gissing had said he longed for; but to have Edith was also to give up everyone else. 'Whether the solitude of two will eventually be more endurable than that of one,' he told Mrs Frederic Harrison, 'I cannot foresee. But I shall never again meet with educated people, so that I must perforce live in silence and be very grateful for the mute companionship that is granted me.'[34]

There was nothing to prevent Edith making friends among people of her own sort, once she had adapted to the difference between Exeter and London. But the diary records no social life for Edith at all. Gissing was almost as isolated. He believed that being married to Edith disqualified him from contact with the middle class, and he had neither time nor inclination to mix with people at Edith's level. 'Of course we have not a single acquaintance,' he told his sister Ellen, 'and I suppose never shall have.'[35] It is not surprising that his next novel, *Born in Exile*, has a hero who lives a lie because he is so desperate to find a secure place in society.

At the end of April it became clear that Edith was pregnant, with the baby due at the beginning of December. Gissing expressed no joy about the pregnancy, and he told no one about it until Edith was a month away from giving birth. That there was a child on the way added to Gissing's financial worries, since he did not yet have another novel to sell. Perhaps there was another trial, too, since the orthodox medical view was that a husband should have no intercourse with his pregnant wife.[36] If Gissing followed this rule, he may have had only two months of sexual satisfaction with Edith in the fifteen months between his meeting her, and her giving birth.

New Grub Street was published on 7 April 1891. It was both an autobiographical novel and an important event in Gissing's life, consolidating his literary reputation. The novel's hero, Edwin Reardon, may appear to be a projection of Gissing's own beliefs and desires. Yet the book is not a direct autobiography, but rather a counterfactual fantasy. In real life, Gissing was getting ready to marry a work-girl as he wrote the novel, believing that this was his only chance to survive. Reardon takes the opposite path: he marries a lady, and perishes. His wife's disappointment with the marriage, and his writer's block – who can say which is cause and which effect? – combine to destroy him. The novel suggests that you can't beat either the marriage market, or the literary one. You can only succeed by giving consumers what they want. Women want a husband who has money, readers want trivial entertainment. If a writer can provide the entertainment, like the unscrupulous journalist Milvain, he will be able to 'buy' a desirable wife. Reardon gets it backwards: he wins Amy by promising her literary success, but then cannot deliver it. He loses both his marriage and his ability to write at all.

New Grub Street still stands as the most acute analysis of the literary marketplace in English fiction. Yet in writing it Gissing argued himself into burying himself in a provincial town with a wife who would do nothing to help his career, and much to hinder it. He believed that the literary world had become a system in which individual writers counted for little. This was plausible to him because he undervalued Hardy, and all the other Victorian giants – from Tennyson to George Eliot – were now dead. The nature of the system was Darwinian: individuals could not fight it, they could only try to adapt. Reardon, in *New Grub Street*, says that he understands the system, but he uses that understanding only to rationalise his own defeat. The logical way to behave is shown on the first page of the novel, where Jasper Milvain finds that his breakfast egg tastes all the better because he knows that a man is being hanged as he is eating it.

Despite Gissing's hatred for the literary market, by 1891 he had made his own niche in Grub Street. He would never become rich, but neither was he one of the wretches who were slowly being starved out, like Biffen in *New Grub Street* or his brother Algernon in real life with his forty-pound novels. Gissing was steadily raising his status: each new novel was quickly accepted by a publisher and then greeted with respect by the critics (subject to the usual complaints about pessimism). *New Grub Street* gave him a definite step up in reputation, and was a steady earner for Smith, Elder as they reissued it in several cheaper editions through the 1890s. Gissing earned nothing from these reprints, and his only recourse against Smith, Elder was to find a more generous publisher. But he had succeeded in the market to the extent of being able to live entirely on his writing after he gave up tutoring in the autumn of 1888. The argument of *New Grub Street* is that anyone who is sensitive and loyal – like Edwin Reardon or Marian Yule – will fail both economically and in the market for love. Yet both of these characters are aware that their own weakness and indecision are largely to blame for their failures.

The reviewers of *New Grub Street* helped to raise Gissing's market value too, in part by arguing about whether he had given an accurate picture of the literary world. Gissing cared very little for Walter Besant, seeing him as the promoter of a commercial approach to authorship; but Besant admired *New Grub Street*'s sympathy for those that the market trod underfoot:

> Because a man follows the calling of letters, he must, by other followers of that profession, be slated, scarified, torn to pieces. Every other profession has its unwritten laws of decency and politeness. That of literature, none. I do not suppose that Mr Gissing's book can become popular, but from my own knowledge I can testify to its truth. I know them all, personally, – two

or three of each – Mr Yule – Jasper – Edwin – and the fidelity of Mr Gissing's portraits makes me shudder.[37]

Andrew Lang replied to Besant by saying that Gissing's 'realism' was in fact 'a perverted idealism, idealism on the seamy side. In Grub Street there are many mansions; they are not all full of failure, and envy, and low cunning, and love of money, and hatred of success.'[38] The *Saturday Review*, however, lined up with Besant:

> The book is almost terrible in its realism, and gives a picture, cruelly precise in every detail, of this commercial age. The degradation of art by the very necessity of its 'paying its way' is put forward with merciless plainness. The bitter uselessness of attempting a literary career unless you are prepared to consult the market, and supply only that for which there is a demand, forms a sort of text for the book. Art for Art's sake is foredoomed to financial failure.[39]

The problem was that Gissing did consider himself an artist, not a sociologist or an economist, and still less a social reformer. *New Grub Street* had already taken account of these disagreements between reviewers; it showed that the literary world could appear as a heaven or a hell, depending on whether it was Reardon or Milvain who was looking at it. It became a literal hell for Reardon because he began with such a gloomy view of the marketplace. If you are a pessimist the market will confirm your gloom, if an optimist you have a good chance of prosperity. Temperament is fate. Gissing's cross was that he felt unable to change a temperament that would always leave him trapped in a sense of failure and unhappiness.

Nonetheless, Gissing did get *New Grub Street* on to paper, whereas Edwin Reardon remained blocked. The novel was out there in the world and critics, such as the anonymous writer for the *Whitehall Review*, were recognising Gissing's stubborn integrity:

> Mr Gissing's newest literary triumph is a singularly skilful piece of work, and proves how true a prophetic vision was ours when, on reading his first book a few years ago, we proclaimed him to be a man of no mean parts, with a great future, if he never deviated from the course he was commencing to hew for himself in the path of fame. Since then he has never disappointed us, and each fresh work he has published has been better and stronger than the one which preceded.[40]

Critics would always complain about Gissing's pessimism, but it had also become part of his 'brand' in the literary marketplace. They were ready to drink any wine of his making, provided it was not sweet.

There was little danger of sweetness, given Gissing's life at Exeter. He was married on a Wednesday, and by Monday he was up in his study planning a new novel, called at this point 'Raymond Peak'. There was no money or time for a honeymoon, so Gissing got to know Edith by taking her for long rambles around the countryside. He certainly enjoyed these outings, but there is no record of Edith taking any interest in nature. Her previous walks had been from Camden Town to Baker Street. When the doctor pronounced Edith pregnant, Gissing took her to Budleigh Salterton for a weekend. He liked the little town, and would return there under different circumstances in 1897. The early months of Edith's pregnancy were 'constant sickness and misery'; Gissing kept on writing through it all, feeling that he had no choice:

> Look at my position, with a novel succeeding as 'New Grub Street' has done. I cannot buy books, I cannot subscribe to a library; I can only just afford the necessary food from day to day; and have to toil in fear of finishing my money before another book is ready. This is monstrously unjust. Who of the public would believe that I am still in such poverty?[41]

Having a child on the way made Gissing's finances look truly desperate. But Edith had cause for desperation too. She was sick, without friends or family, taken from London to a strange city. Worst of all, she had become a writer's wife without any resources for coping with the role. Some days Gissing wrote in his diary just 'thinking' or 'did nothing'. That meant he either spent the day in his study with the door closed, pondering some problem with his novel, or, as Edith would experience it, ignoring her even when he was physically present. When he was not wrestling with his novel, Gissing read for hours each day. For *Born in Exile* he needed to know the main work in geology and evolutionary biology of the past fifty years. Edith tried to read an occasional book, but there is no record of her actually finishing one. Gissing's plans to educate her were soon dropped. He liked the idea of spending some time on the Continent, but there would have to be English people around because Edith was incapable of learning a foreign language. The people with whom they shared the house were, he reported, 'extremely vulgar and selfish beyond belief'.[42] In all of this, there is no hint that Gissing gave any thought to Edith's emotional needs. Thinking about the book he was writing was a full-time job, and the only one he could not neglect. He believed he was Edith's superior, and had the right to control her; what he remained blind to was how to win her affection or love.

At the beginning of July, Gissing and Edith set off on their summer holiday. He had chosen Clevedon on the Somerset coast, after seeing an article which praised it as 'Good for Tired Brains'.[43] Gissing had not quite finished *Born in Exile*, so for the first ten days he was closeted with his manuscript. When he sent it off to Smith, Elder he told them that he wanted £250 for British and American copyright; this was more assertive than his usual practice, though it did not benefit him in the outcome.[44] He was now stuck in seaside lodgings, in cold and rainy weather; it was up to him to entertain Edith, and vice versa. This cannot have gone well, because he started going on day-long excursions by himself, to Minehead and Glastonbury. His excuse, presumably, was that Edith was too pregnant to go with him; but what was she to do when left alone? After three weeks at Clevedon they moved to Burnham-on-Sea. Ten days was all they could stand, as Gissing found it 'deadly dull'.

Gissing returned to Prospect Park to receive a double blow. Mrs Rockett, the young wife downstairs, told him that she wanted the use of their rooms and they should look elsewhere. Perhaps she did need the space, but her real motive was that the Gissings and the Rocketts were approaching open warfare. The shared kitchen experiment had failed, as might have been expected. Then Gissing received an infuriating letter from James Payn, the reader for Smith, Elder. In tiny, illegible handwriting Payn said that he couldn't read the manuscript of *Born in Exile* for another month, because he was going on holiday. But he could say in advance that there was no chance Smith, Elder could give £250, because *New Grub Street* had been 'a financial failure'. This can hardly have been the case, because in 1891 alone Smith, Elder issued the book in two printings of the three-decker edition, a one-volume edition at 6 shillings, and a Tauchnitz edition for which they received £30. For good measure, Payn told Gissing that his 'pessimism' was to blame for the book's failure.[45] Gissing finally did what he should have done long before: he retrieved the manuscript of *Born in Exile* and sent it off to A. P. Watt, the pioneering literary agent (he had been in the business since 1875). It would take some years, but this was the first step Gissing took towards getting a decent price for his books. Having written *New Grub Street*, it was time for him to learn its lesson.

Meanwhile, relations with the Rocketts were quickly going downhill. They were behaving 'with every kind of vulgar malice . . . It makes me ill; I pass the time in sick, trembling rage unable either to read or think.'[46] Gissing could think enough to imagine a book of short stories called 'At a Week's Notice', about the horrors of living in lodgings. He was furious enough to do more than write a book: within ten days he had found somewhere else to live and moved out of 24 Prospect Park. Their new home was a self-contained house at 1 St Leonard's Terrace, Wonford Road.

This was a leafy suburb with many attractive Regency houses, much nicer than the dreary terrace the Gissings were leaving. For £19.10 a year, less than half of what Gissing had paid at Cornwall Residences, he got eight rooms, including a study for his work.[47]

On his first day at St Leonard's Terrace Gissing received bad news from A. P. Watt. Chatto & Windus offered only £120 for *Born in Exile*, out of which Gissing would have had to pay £12 commission to Watt. Gissing could not settle for such a small sum, but now had more worries than ever about how to pay his rent and look after his pregnant wife: 'I should perhaps have done better if I had let S. and E. do as usual. But I have gained knowledge. I know that my books have still no solid market value, and that I must continue to work for small sums. . . . it is now proved that S. and E. have not dealt so badly by me.'[48] That one publisher offered less than Smith, Elder for a novel did not really exonerate them. They advertised Gissing's books widely, but this was a business decision to capitalise on the five books they owned outright, all of which were in print in various editions in 1891. Gissing was a solid long-run property for any publisher willing to support him, even if he would never be a major best-seller. He suffered both economically and psychologically from Payn's dislike of the tone of his work, and Smith, Elder's hard bargains over rights. Gissing was the only serious living novelist on Smith, Elder's list; they were a middlebrow firm whose best seller was Mrs Humphrey Ward, the anti-feminist novelist. By 1891, for Gissing to break with Smith, Elder was long overdue.

Gissing's money was running low and once again he had to get another novel on the market as quickly as he could. He decided to set the first chapter in Clevedon, and spent September thinking out the plot. Then a stroke of luck intervened. Morley Roberts had persuaded a new publisher, A. H. Bullen of Lawrence & Bullen, to take on no fewer than three of his books. On Roberts's recommendation, Bullen wrote to Gissing on 26 September saying he would commission a one-volume novel from him on a royalty of 1/- on a 6/- price, and pay him £100 advance on delivery of the manuscript. Bullen's eagerness for his work jolted Gissing into action. He could not give Bullen *Born in Exile*, because it was too long; but he thought of a political novel, to be called 'The Radical Candidate'. Within ten days he had made a plan for the novel and started writing. Two weeks into the book, Gissing could write in his diary: 'Am writing with extra-ordinary ease just now. Scarcely remember a like period. Means vastly improved health, I suppose.'[49]

Gissing never made much distinction between his physical and his mental health. He may have lived in a healthier way in Exeter than in London, but the simpler explanation of his burst of productivity was that A. H. Bullen was the first publisher to show real confidence in his work. When Gissing was close to finishing 'The Radical Candidate', Bullen came to Exeter to promote his publishing house to provincial booksellers. He invited Gissing to dinner at the Clarence, the fine old hotel in the Cathedral Close. Bullen was a well-known scholar and editor of Elizabethan literature, but Gissing found him 'rather less intellectual' than he had expected. 'How consistently I am disappointed,' he wrote in his diary, 'when I meet men of whom I have heard!'[50] This was a comment that probably said more about Gissing than about those he met. Nonetheless, Bullen gave him attention, the promise of quick money, and a good dinner. All of this was welcome, and the next day Gissing wrote seven sheets, more than five thousand words. He finished 'The Radical Candidate' on 12 November, having written about 100,000 words in just over five weeks.

The ease of writing 'The Radical Candidate' did not make it one of Gissing's best novels. Over his career, the more agony a book cost him, the higher the quality when it was finished. Nonetheless, Bullen's encouragement was the best thing that had happened to Gissing in his long struggle with English publishers since 1880. When Bullen received the manuscript he was disappointed, telling Gissing that he expected him to do stronger work in future. He also persuaded Gissing to change the title to *Denzil Quarrier*, after the novel's hero. Booksellers had said that female readers might be put off by 'The Radical Candidate'. Still, Bullen came through with his advance against royalties, and even raised it to a hundred guineas (£105). He also arranged for Colonial, Continental and American editions, for which Gissing received another £30 and a trickle of royalties.[51]

Apart from the immediate lift to his finances, Gissing's idea of himself as a professional writer was changed by the arrival of Bullen. It was just two months from the day he received Bullen's first letter, to having a cheque for a hundred guineas in his hand. This experience of quick rewards encouraged Gissing to write two short stories in just over a week: 'A Casual Acquaintance' and 'A Victim of Circumstances'. The first was rejected by *Macmillan's Magazine* and nothing more was heard of it, but 'A Victim of Circumstances' was accepted by *Blackwood's*.[52] All of Gissing's writing at this time was concerned with fatal mistakes and secret sins. In 'A Victim of Circumstances' a talentless artist passes off his wife's watercolours as his own, and then is trapped by his lie. When demand increases for the pictures, his wife finds that she cannot go on producing them: 'Even if her nature were equal to the strain, it was obvious that discovery and disgrace would sooner or later befall the perpetrators of so singular a fraud.'[53] In *Denzil*

Quarrier, disaster comes through the concealment of a shameful marriage. Lilian Northway, one of Gissing's idealised heroines, was married at seventeen; as they left the church her husband was arrested for forgery and sent to prison for three years. She then falls in love with Denzil Quarrier and lives with him pretending to be his wife. He has rejected the idea of living openly in a 'free union' because 'We are face to face with the world's immoral morality. To brave it would be possible, of course; but then we must either go to a foreign country or live here in isolation.'[54]

Quarrier has convinced himself that he can safely become a public figure in the provincial town of Polterham: 'The risk of betraying himself in an unguarded moment was diminished by the mental habit established during eighteen months of secrecy in London.'[55] He has not counted on being betrayed by someone else: his closest friend, the artist Eustace Glazzard. In this character Gissing created a curious double for himself, perhaps inspired by his recent reading in Dostoevsky. When Gissing stayed at Eastbourne in 1888 his landlady had called him 'Mr Gizzard'.[56] Glazzard finds Lilian's husband and bribes him to denounce Quarrier as an adulterer. Lilian kills herself, even as Quarrier is winning his election as a Liberal candidate.

Denzil Quarrier might be considered a relatively slight work, yet it reveals Gissing's continuing turmoil over his disgrace at Owens College, fifteen years before. Lilian is destroyed by the guilty secret of her unworthy marriage. Glazzard, her betrayer, sees himself as 'a man whose existence had always been loveless – who, with passionate ideals, had never known anything but a venal embrace'. Gissing, in a letter, said of him: 'I thought the man painfully human.'[57] At the end of the novel Glazzard sculpts a head of Judas, evidently a self-portrait, which he then destroys. *Denzil Quarrier* may be an emotionally incoherent novel, but having to write it so fast forced Gissing to use the psychic materials that were closest to hand. His attack on the religious hypocrisy of the Polterham evangelicals shocked his sister Ellen again, yet Gissing insisted that the book was 'a strong defence of conventionality'.[58] At the beginning of the novel, Quarrier believes that individuals have no duty to obey collective rules: 'Social law is stupid and unjust, imposing its obligation without regard to person or circumstance. It presumes that no one can be *trusted*. I decline to be levelled with the unthinking multitude. You and I can be a law unto ourselves.'[59]

Because society cannot appreciate the pure and true love that Quarrier and Lilian have for each other, they feel justified in lying to society. Quarrier's mistake is to think that he can achieve authority in the community while secretly flouting its rules. When Lilian's sin is about to be exposed, she chooses death over living with the shame. Instead of taking revenge on

Glazzard, Quarrier says, in the last words of the book, 'Now I understand the necessity for social law!' Conventional morality is vindicated, because those who violate it will suffer. This is a masochistic response on Quarrier's part, and the plot of the novel seems to reflect Gissing's remorse and self-hatred for his own crime. *Denzil Quarrier* is a novel whose characters are unable to be true to themselves, which makes it both a lesser work, and one that is very revealing of its author's inner conflicts.

Father and Son

Whatever its literary worth, *Denzil Quarrier* provided Gissing with a large cheque just when he needed it. He spent twenty-five shillings on a set of china for the table, a long step towards respectability. 'Hitherto,' he noted, 'we have made shift with kitchen utensils.'[1] This conjures up a gloomy scene of Gissing and Edith eating their dinner out of the frying pan. Perhaps things were not so bad, but during their entire marriage they seem never to have entertained a guest to dinner. Now they had to prepare for Edith's confinement, which required a live-in nurse as well as their regular servant. Edith's labour began on the morning of 9 December 1891 and lasted nearly twenty-four hours. The doctor gave her chloroform just at the end, but Gissing called it a 'blackguard business'. In almost the only reference in the diary to Edith's feelings, he wrote: 'the poor girl's misery is over, and she has what she earnestly desired.'[2] But Edith's difficult labour was just the beginning of her troubles, as the marriage deteriorated after the birth of Walter Leonard Gissing. He arrived with a large and ugly birthmark over his right eye; human nature being what it is, pretty babies are easier to love. Gissing had this to say when his second son, Alfred, was born:

> Edith cares infinitely more for him than she ever did for Walter. When she said to Walter, in her rage, 'I always hated you,' there was a measure of truth in it; from the boy's birth onwards, scarcely a day on which she has not loudly regretted his existence. The baby receives very different treatment; she is really very fond of it, and does not grudge just the little trouble it exacts.[3]

A month after her delivery, Edith still could barely stand and was suffering from mastitis, which made it too painful for her to breast-feed Walter. He was a colicky baby, hard for parents to cope with at the best of times. On top of all, Edith suffered a severe post-partum depression. Gissing described Edith as 'violently bilious', which in Victorian terms meant extremely irritable and aggressive. She quarrelled constantly with the baby's nurse. At times the baby had to be kept away from her, with either the nurse or Gissing feeding him prepared food. 'Perhaps the most uncomfortable Christmas I have ever known,' Gissing wrote. 'E. downstairs, but not able to walk. Much quarrelling with nurse, who is vulgar, meddlesome, and conceited.'[4] Gissing could not look to his family, or Edith's, for help since none of them had shown their face at Exeter since the marriage. The only cheerful news was that A. P. Watt had finally sold *Born in Exile* to the Edinburgh publishers Adam & Charles Black for £150. Of this Gissing had to pay £15 in commission to Watt, and half the payment was held back until the book was published. Selling the novel through Watt had not been a step forward. Since Bullen promised to give good terms for future work, Gissing decided that he would deal with him directly, rather than through Watt.

Gissing did his best to help with the baby, but domestic chaos continued. A month after Walter's birth the nurse left, richer by £7 for her work. Edith immediately broke down, both physically and mentally. The only solution Gissing could find was to have the baby boarded out. The vicar of Brampford Speke, four miles from Exeter, recommended a farmer's wife who would take Walter for six shillings a week. He was bundled off to Mrs Phillips, and fed milk straight from the cow. During the next three months he was looked after in rough-and-ready fashion, and thrived well enough. His parents went to see him from time to time. Edith recovered her health, and Gissing was able to return to some creative work.

Gissing's first project was to revise *Born in Exile*, which he was not satisfied with – 'the end especially is very feeble.'[5] He retrieved the manuscript from A. & C. Black and spent eighteen days on intense revision. Before sending it back he changed the title from 'Godwin Peak' to *Born in Exile*, one of his most evocative titles.[6] As soon as that was done, he went off with Edith for a week's holiday in Cornwall. They took lodgings in Penzance, and Edith was now well enough to walk seven miles over the moors to St Just. Gissing was delighted with the scenery and the warm climate of Cornwall, and especially liked St Ives. While he was at Penzance he heard from Adele Burger that she had translated *New Grub Street* into German and it was now appearing in a Budapest newspaper. There was no money in it, but Gissing was delighted to be read on the banks of the Danube.

Cornwall might have been a chance for Gissing and Edith to get on better terms, but new misfortunes arrived. Edith developed a toothache, which led to painful and expensive dental work. It was followed by chronic neuralgia, pains in the face and neck that made her life a misery. At the beginning of April she went up to London for four days to see a doctor but had little relief. Gissing had some time to read and to make a number of starts on a new novel, without being able to settle down to steady work. Not much had changed for the better in the Gissing household when, after three months, Walter came home from Brampford Speke. His parents found it impossible to keep him quiet and contented, or to get proper sleep for themselves. Edith told her sister-in-law Catherine Gissing about her troubles:

> From morning till night we are both of us worn out. ... The difficulty is not to get the boy to sleep in the evening, for he generally goes off after his last bottle; but he has to be fed twice in the night, and will not sleep after five in the morning. ... things are made worse just now by the beginning of teething, and he has been utterly spoilt at Brampford Speke where they fed him every half hour.[7]

Neither scheduled nor demand feeding seem to have worked with little Walter. Sleepless nights continued, nurses came and went, neuralgia reigned, and Gissing and Edith lived permanently at the end of their tether. Not surprisingly, it was hard for them to look at Walter with any fondness:

> The poor little chap is deplorably ugly. His great mole over the eye seems to increase in size, and will forever be a deformity. Then, his face is frequently in a rash, and he scratches his nose and cheeks till they are a sad spectacle. People look at him in the street and marvel at his unsightliness.[8]

In Gissing's story 'A Son of the Soil', a syphilitic father has three children who are 'miserable, puny creatures, burdened with an unutterable curse'.[9] Perhaps Gissing feared that Walter was such a cursed child.

At least Gissing's literary reputation was still on the rise, with two novels coming out in quick succession. *Denzil Quarrier* was published in February 1892, and got the usual frosty reception in Wakefield: 'Letter from Nelly, expressing dislike of *Denzil Quarrier*. Of course.'[10] We can guess that Ellen was particularly upset by Gissing's satire on the evangelical party's hypocrisy and political meddling. He was not going to give up his hostility to religion, so all he could do was ask Ellen to keep an open mind: 'The new spirit in fiction is pretty sure to repel you; yet never cease to reflect that there are a great many people of substantially your own way of thinking who welcome the new movement as a vast improvement upon the old worn-out processes.'[11] Ellen may have reflected, but not enough to make her soften her views.

The anonymous reviewer of *Denzil Quarrier* in the *Chicago Tribune* was a good prophet: 'The future historian of English fiction may possibly regard this novel as more truly significant and representative, more genuinely a product of the age than many a finer and more famous work. For Mr Gissing swims with the stream.'[12] Bullen had good publishing connections in the US, and as the 1890s went on Gissing sold more and more in that market. The Americans did much to pull him out of Grub Street. In England, the clerical magazine *Guardian* disliked Gissing's 'unpleasant' view of sexual morality; it did not take into account Quarrier's recanting his radicalism at the end of the novel. *The Times* saw the recanting, but objected to it: 'We are afraid it is becoming too common a trick among novelists to take refuge in the incalculable in human nature as a substitute for intelligible motive.'[13] But it was not that Quarrier's motives were incalculable; rather, he was divided, like Gissing himself, between rebelling against social convention and feeling that he had transgressed and deserved to be punished.

Born in Exile followed in May. It had a more coherent message than *Denzil Quarrier*, and so was more easily understood by readers and critics. This did not mean that they were charmed by the book; the old complaints about pessimism returned in full force. But even those who found little pleasure in reading *Born in Exile* recognised its solid worth. 'Mr Gissing has skill,' said the *Daily Chronicle*, 'and he is becoming popular. He has gone on steadily from strength to strength, and this, his latest achievement, is also his best.' This critic also perceived how Godwin Peak embodied Gissing's self-division, rather than just expressing a set of fixed beliefs:

> We don't like him, of course, nor does his creator, but so masterly is the characterisation that, in spite of ourselves, our dislike of him is softened down by more than a dash of genuine pity. . . . But Mr Gissing never loves his heroes. His analysis is the analysis of cold intellect, not of warm sympathy, and that is why we close his books a little sadder than we opened them.[14]

The *Times* critic again attacked the lack of a plausible motive for Godwin Peak's trickery:

> It does not seem to us that there is any adequate motive for Peak's unpremeditated treachery to himself. To a strong, self-contained, and proud character . . . such a sudden and violent deflection from ordinary straightforwardness appears well-nigh impossible. However, it could hardly have failed to occur to Peak that in the nineteenth century he was far more likely to attain the social position he coveted by persevering in his own work than by masquerading as a clergyman. Nor does society receive every clergyman with open arms.[15]

This was all solid common sense, except that irrational self-destructive acts are what Gissing is about. 'Peak is myself – one phase of myself,' Gissing wrote. 'I described him with gusto, but surely I did not, in depicting the other characters, take *his* point of view?'[16] There was a Gissing who, like Peak, had compulsively ruined his own prospects; but also a Gissing who judged his follies from outside, according to the conventional standards of his society. The trouble was that neither rebellion nor convention could give Gissing a stable identity, one that would allow him both to write coherent novels and to believe in himself.

Gissing's identity included shadow-selves, the persons he might have been if his fate had been different. In *New Grub Street*, a lady falls in love with the hero, but then is alienated by the failure of his literary career. If you marry a work-girl you will be able to write (so Gissing himself reasoned); if you marry a lady, your pen will fall limply from your hand. In *Born in Exile*, Peak says he longs to possess Sidwell Warricombe, but manages to sabotage his heart's desire. His friend Christian Moxey accuses him of not being capable of love:

> 'Sincerely, do you care for women at all?'
> 'Perhaps not.' ...
> 'If you had ever been sincerely devoted to a woman, be assured your powers would have developed in a way of which you have no conception. ... If only you knew the desire of a woman's help. ... There's no harm in repeating what you have often told me – your egoism oppresses you. A woman's influence takes one out of oneself.'[17]

Peak does not even try to refute Moxey's criticism. In a novel about the conflict between Darwinism and Christianity, it is appropriate that Peak should be a sexual egotist. Once he has climbed the social hierarchy, he should have a desirable woman as his reward; conversely, she will not respond to him as an individual, but as a male of high status. Peak is possessed by:

> A craving for love capable only of a social (one might say, of a political) definition. The woman throned in his imagination was no individual, but the type of an order. ... The sense of social distinction was so burnt into him, that he could not be affected by any pictured charm of mind or person in a woman who had not the stamp of gentle birth and breeding. If once he were admitted to the intimacy of such women, then, indeed, the canons of selection would have weight with him; no man more capable of disinterested choice.[18]

The last sentence means that Peak could love a woman as an individual
provided that she belonged to the class of woman he desires. It is true that
Gissing said Peak represented only one side of his own nature; but Peak is
only an extreme case of Gissing's inclination to treat women as means
rather than ends. It is just as well that Peak fails in his pursuit of Sidwell
Warricombe, because one cannot imagine how they might live together
happily as man and wife.

Gissing's programme of finding an obedient work-girl had now culminated in the daily miseries of life at St Leonard's Terrace. The baby
Walter was endlessly sick and troublesome, and Edith's neuralgia had
become chronic. There was a long procession of servants who either proved
to be incompetent, or suddenly walked out. Gissing believed that it was
Edith's job to keep the house running smoothly, so if anything went wrong,
it was her fault. It was one of his fixed ideas that only upper-class women
knew how to handle servants, and that servants only respected mistresses
who were clearly superior to them. There was certainly a big cultural divide
between a working-class Londoner like Edith and the young Devonshire
women who worked for her. Gissing too was not the person to have an
easy human relationship with a servant. But servants probably left mainly
because they didn't like living in an unhappy household. They were speeded
on their way by crockery-smashing rows with Edith.

Gissing's vision of a peaceful, well-ordered domestic life never had a
chance of fulfilment in Exeter. In *New Grub Street* he shows how a disappointed and egocentric writer, Alfred Yule, tyrannises over his long-
suffering working-class wife. Edith had not turned out to be like Mrs Yule,
as Gissing had hoped; and he himself might end up like Mr Yule, if his
novels stopped selling. There was also the problem of how to produce them
in the midst of domestic uproar. Gissing went off on solitary outings, or
sent Edith away. She spent a few days with Walter and his old nurse at
Brampford Speke in March, and five weeks with her sister in London in
October and November 1892. The rest of the time, Gissing had to do his
best at home, and it was probably the worst struggle of his career. He had
finished *Born in Exile* in July 1891, before Walter was born. In August
1892 he started his next novel to reach publication. In the thirteen months
between, he started and then abandoned at least nine other novels. Even
for someone who found writing as painful as he did, this was an extraordinary spell of futile effort.

Gissing did not lack ideas: again and again he would plan out a novel
and write several chapters of it. Then misgivings would come, and what he
had written would be set aside. He was caught in a vicious circle; he forced

himself to write under miserable conditions, then came to believe that nothing written under such conditions could be any good. Like most writers, once a book came newly printed into his hands he was surprised by how good it was. The trick was to remain convinced of its worth during the horrid struggle to get it written. Each book that Gissing abandoned deepened his despair of ever writing a decent novel again; yet each failed attempt also moved him closer to judgement day, when his money would run out and he would have nothing to offer a publisher.

Gissing's crisis of sterility in 1891–2 has to be attributed to his unhappy marriage, because his friendship with A. H. Bullen gave him the kind of support from a publisher that he had long needed. If he could only write a book, he knew that Bullen would publish it and do his best to make it a financial success. On 15 August 1892 Gissing made his last desperate move to provide Bullen with a manuscript. In fifty days it was finished, a three-decker of some 150,000 words. He had written like a machine, working every day of the week including Sunday. Money was running out, and he had to come up to the mark or perish. He recorded his success on 4 October: 'Shall call the book "The Odd Women". I have written it very quickly, but the writing has been as severe a struggle as ever I knew. Not a day without wrangling and uproar down in the kitchen; not an hour when I was really at peace in mind. A bitter struggle.'[19] The manuscript went off to Bullen the next day, and nine days after that he had accepted the novel. 'I am inclined to agree with you,' Bullen wrote, 'that it is your best book. Whether it will be popular I, of course, cannot say; but I am sure that it will be far more successful than *Denzil Quarrier*.'[20] He offered an advance of a hundred guineas against royalties, and also enclosed a cheque for £13.2.6 – Gissing's half of the sale of Continental rights to *Denzil Quarrier*.

The Odd Women was not outstandingly popular during Gissing's life-time; but it is indeed one of his four best novels, and probably the one that is most frequently taught today. Orwell thought it was 'one of the best novels in English'.[21] On the face of it, the novel does not seem directly relevant to Gissing's unhappy existence with Edith in Exeter. He had been thinking of a novel on the position of women since at least the autumn of 1889, when he was doing research for 'The Head-Mistress'. It was typical of Gissing that he learned about the women's movement mainly from books and newspapers. The only New Woman he knew was Edith Sichel, and he had only met her twice. For the Madden sisters of *The Odd Women* he could look to his own sisters, though the Maddens lead a grimmer life. Mrs Cosgrove, the sexually liberal society hostess, probably owes something to Mrs Gaussen. But the central milieu of the novel, Mrs Barfoot's feminist business school, comes entirely from Gissing's imagination rather than any direct experience of such a place.

Gissing's treatment of the 'woman question' is extraordinarily comprehensive and sympathetic, given his daily Calvary at home. The most unfortunate odd women in the novel are Virginia and Alice Madden, who have no chance of marriage and who scrape a living from teaching children and a tiny inheritance. Margaret and Ellen Gissing were twenty-nine and twenty-five at this time. They were part-time teachers whose hopes of marriage were almost gone. Monica Madden, the youngest sister in the novel, has prettiness without brains or ambition. She settles for a conventional marriage because it is easier than working in a department store and is punished by getting Mr Widdowson, one of Gissing's most grotesque and compelling characters. Mrs Barfoot and Rhoda Nunn are the New Women, but also opposed in their views: Barfoot is a liberal humanist, Nunn a puritanical extremist. Finally there is Mrs Cosgrove: a feminist, but one who shuns confrontation and encourages the companionate marriage of equals.

In the relation between Rhoda Nunn and Everard Barfoot, Gissing showed an understanding that he seemed quite unable to achieve in his personal dealings with women. Everard agrees to marriage with Rhoda, rather than a 'free union', but then has misgivings:

> Her energy of domination perhaps excelled his. Such a woman might be unable to concede him the liberty in marriage which theoretically she granted to be just. ... how miserable to anticipate a long, perhaps bitter struggle for predominance. ... Need he entertain that worst of fears – the dread that his independence might fail him, subdued by his wife's will?

Rhoda's fears mirror Everard's: 'Was he in truth capable of respecting her individuality? Or would his strong instinct of lordship urge him to direct his wife as a dependant, to impose upon her his own view of things? She doubted whether he had much genuine sympathy with woman's emancipation, as she understood it.'[22] Each is caught up in a struggle for mastery where only one can prevail. Legal marriage would strengthen Rhoda's hand, free union would strengthen Everard's. They love each other, or at least feel passionately, but cannot resolve their clash of wills and eventually separate. Gissing suggests that egotistical conflict between lovers inevitably creates jealousy, which is destructive of love. In spite of her feminist belief in personal freedom, Rhoda cannot free herself from jealousy of Monica Widdowson; both she and Mr Widdowson suspect Monica of having an affair with Everard. A feminist and a male supremacist find common ground in their fear of Monica's sexual appeal to others. Rhoda is driven to renounce sexuality altogether; Monica dies, innocent of adultery. Everard will marry the wealthy and free-spirited Agnes Brissenden. Once again, their union shows that for Gissing happiness requires every blessing: high status, plenty of money, and freedom to enjoy the world's culture.

Gissing rightly said of *The Odd Women*: 'I have written it at a great speed, but I think it equals anything I have done yet.'[23] Nonetheless, he was feeling that he could not produce novels regularly in Exeter. He needed the use of the British Museum library, and had also come to realise that in Exeter he could never have any social life. In a year and a half, one member of his family had come to visit, his sister Margaret. She got on badly with Edith, and no one would come from Wakefield after that. The best Gissing could hope for was an absence of conflict, which meant being apart from Edith. They would go for a week's holiday at Weymouth, on the Dorset coast, to celebrate having finished *The Odd Women*. Then Edith would go to London for the winter with Walter, staying with her sister in Camden Town. Edith would have company, whatever pleasures she could find in London, and perhaps a doctor who could cure her neuralgia. Gissing, meanwhile, would go into lodgings in Birmingham to do research for an industrial novel, to be called 'The Iron Gods'.

Everything started out according to plan. Gissing was reading *Tess of the d'Urbervilles* (published in November 1891). He and Edith would pass through Dorchester on their way to Weymouth, and in happier circumstances Gissing could have renewed his friendship with Hardy. He had just been quoted in the press as having a special admiration for Gissing's books. Gissing, however, did not return the compliment. 'Tragic power is hardly his attribute,' he told Algernon; later he commented that the ending of *Tess* was 'an entire artistic mistake'. Turning a criticism often made against himself back against Hardy, Gissing said that he preferred Hardy's earlier novels, 'when the idyllic spirit was unaffected by fierce pessimism'.[24] The one contemporary that Gissing wholeheartedly admired was Tennyson, who had just died at the age of ninety-three:

> Well, we have lost our one indisputably great poet; for my own part, I agree with those who think him a worthy successor of Theocritus and Virgil. He had not much to say, but his utterance is consummate, the very perfection of language. His place among the Immortals is far more certainly assured than that of Byron – perhaps than that of Shelley.[25]

The week in Weymouth was a holiday of sorts, though Gissing complained that they did little but push Walter up and down the front in a hired

pram. They set off for London on 21 October; at Swindon Gissing veered
off to spend two weeks with Algernon in the Cotswolds. When Gissing
arrived he found his mother there too, keeping house. Gissing enjoyed
roaming the hills with Algernon in fine autumn weather, and tried to cheer
him up over his flagging literary career. Cheering up had always required
regular loans of £10 or £20, which Algernon never paid back. His family
was important to Gissing, but there often seemed to be more duty than
pleasure in his seeing them.

Only a week after Edith had gone, she wrote to say that she was not
getting on with her sister and might have to leave soon. 'No dealing with
these low-class Londoners,' Gissing wrote in his diary.[26] He went on to
Birmingham anyway, on 3 November, and set to work on his research.
Part of his time was spent at the Central Library, part wandering around
industrial districts like Dudley and Walsall. The focus of his novel would
be Aston, known for its grim back-to-back houses where people worked at
home on small items of ironware (Aston also produced two working-class
staples, beer and vinegar). Gissing was in Birmingham to get away from
Edith and be able to work, but he did not like solitude either. That did not
mean that he was willing to go to a pub in the evening, like other men on
their own; during his three weeks in Birmingham he spoke to no one except
his landlady.

Gissing's Birmingham novel was never finished, though he recycled
parts of it in *Eve's Ransom*, which he wrote in 1894. It is a pity he did not
carry it through, because it might have taken him back to the industrial and
social concerns of his earlier novels. What we know of his plan for the book
comes from his response to another request for money from Algernon:

> This ceaseless trouble about money, all around me, has made me strike a
> rather clearer note on socialistic matters in my new book. The name I
> propose is 'Gods of Iron', – meaning Machinery, which is no longer a
> servant but a tyrannous oppressor of mankind. One way or another this
> frantic social struggle must be eased. I have a few people who work their
> way to an idea on the subject: – that the intellect of the country must
> proclaim for Collectivism, but by no means for Democracy unrestrained.[27]

Gissing's solution to the Condition of England problem sounds rather like
the Fabian Society, which had been active since 1884. But he had never
moved in those circles, and his stay in Birmingham was probably the last
time that he imagined any political means of ending the 'social struggle'.
While he was there he had a personal stroke of luck in the trouble about
money. His story, 'A Victim of Circumstances' had not appeared in *Black-*

wood's after a year, so he wrote to the editor asking for the return of the manuscript. Instead, he got a letter of apology, a promise to publish it in the January issue, and a cheque for £20. Gissing had not expected more than £6 or £7 for the story; William Blackwood had raised the fee by way of apologising for his delay. Twenty pounds was enough to pay Gissing's house rent in Exeter for a year. He had written the story in three days, which opened up a much better commercial prospect than agonising for months over a novel. The Education Acts of 1870 and after were now doing their work of greatly expanding the English reading public. There were many more magazines, and all Gissing needed to do was study his market and then meet the demand for material. He became more proficient at this as the 1890s went on, and by the middle of the decade his struggle for subsistence was over. To succeed, he had to become more like Milvain of *New Grub Street*, less like Reardon. Gissing knew what was happening, and worried about the effect of this transition on the quality of his work. But the easy money was on the table, and he could not resist picking some of it up.

Gissing returned to Exeter from Birmingham on 24 November, and Edith and Walter came four days later. Instead of spending the winter in London with Edith's married sister, they had only stayed there a month. Gissing had the material he needed for 'The Iron Gods', and could get down to work as soon as the house was in order. But his stay in Birmingham had convinced him that it was time to leave Exeter. His health was better than in London, but in every other way he felt he could only stagnate if he remained. 'I should fancy no town in England,' he told Ellen, 'has a more unintellectual population. And the country people are ignorance embodied.'[28] Although Gissing encouraged Algernon to write novels about country folk, he never had much inclination to do so himself; he loved the countryside, but not the people in it. He had heard about a fine new library that Henry Tate, the sugar millionaire, had donated to Brixton. 'I simply must not go anywhere,' Gissing told Algernon, 'if there is not a good reading room at hand, as, in my personal isolation, I am so greatly dependent for material and suggestion on the daily and weekly papers.'[29] Brixton, in due course, it would be.

Morley Roberts wanted to come and see Gissing, but was told that 'our domestic confusion makes it impossible to receive visitors'.[30] The confusion arose from the servant problem, which in Gissing's mind was the Edith problem. He was fond of Walter, and tried to be a good father to him, but in the circumstances he could not be a professional writer and cope with a one-year-old at the same time. Three weeks after Edith and Walter came

back from London, Gissing rented a room to write in, a few minutes' walk
away off the Heavitree Road. There he could get started on his Birmingham
novel, and also heavily revise the proofs of *The Odd Women*. There was a
roast goose for Christmas, but on New Year's Eve the plumber had to be
called in for burst pipes, and the reckoning for the past year was a grim
one:

> The year 1892, on the whole profitless. Marked by domestic misery and
> discomfort. The one piece of work, 'The Odd Women', scribbled in 6 weeks
> as the autumn drew to an end, and I have no high opinion of it. Have read
> next to nothing; classical studies utterly neglected. With my new plan of
> having a study away from the wretched home, may hope to achieve more
> in year to come.[31]

Domestic misery seemed to be unavoidable, but in the early months of
1893 Gissing was at least able to work in his rented room. He wrote another
story for *Blackwood's*, 'The Minstrel of the Byways', in the hope of making
another £20. Unfortunately, Blackwood turned this one down, and Gissing
sent it nowhere else. He forged ahead with his novel, 'The Iron Gods'; his
trouble lay in leaving his study for the house where Edith lay in wait. 'On
way home, at night,' he wrote in his diary, 'an anguish of suffering in the
thought that I can never hope to have an intellectual companion at home.
... Never a word exchanged on anything but the paltry everyday life of
the household. ...'[32] He was finding an ally in his son, though this would
foster more trouble with Edith in the long run. When Edith scolded Walter
one night, 'I went and fetched him up, and when his mother came I saw
him fix his little eyes on her for a long time with look of grave resentment,
sad and impressive. Evidently he had felt the injustice.'[33]

In March Gissing heard from his former pupil Walter Grahame, who
was now reading Classics at Balliol College, Oxford. When he had gone
up to the university, two years before, Gissing had written to a friend: 'I
hope he will no longer trouble to write to me, for it would only be disagreeable to have to tell him that our intercourse is at an end.'[34] Yet after
much pondering, he now invited Grahame to lunch. They enjoyed two
roast chickens, an apple tart, and a bottle of Burgundy, the kind of solid
English fare that Gissing would have eaten regularly if he could afford it.
Long afterwards, Grahame gave a glowing account of the day: 'He seemed
busy and happy, was in good health and getting on well with the work he
had in hand. His wife was evidently devoted to him, and he was very proud
of his baby son.'[35] Either Grahame did not have a sharp eye for what was

happening at Prospect Park, or there were happier times in Exeter than Gissing was willing to admit.

There was also some pleasing recognition for Gissing from the literary establishment. When Tennyson died in November 1892, Gissing had written to Edmund Gosse agreeing with him that most English people had little appreciation for poetry. Gosse replied that he admired Gissing's 'powerful and mournful studies of life'; in March he asked Gissing to contribute some thoughts on poetry to a collected volume of Gosse's essays.[36] Gosse, eight years older than Gissing, was by this time one of England's leading men of letters. He was a largely self-taught intellectual, who got his start as a cataloguer at the British Museum. But most people, Gissing thought, could not be taught anything:

> To love poetry is a boon of nature, most sparingly bestowed; appreciation of the poet's art is an outcome of studious leisure. Even an honest liking for verse, without discernment, depends upon complex conditions of birth, breeding, education. No one seeks to disparage the laborious masses on the ground of their incapacity for delights necessarily the privilege of the few. ... Everywhere there are the many and the few.[37]

Much as he loved poetry, Gissing's own verse was never more than sentimental and derivative.

In April 1893 *The Odd Women* was published. The critics were now more willing to treat Gissing on his own terms, rather than just complaining about his pessimism. To some extent he had succeeded in educating his critics and readers; they were coming to realise that he was 'profoundly interested in the phenomena of the civilization round him', and therefore was justified in flouting Victorian conventions of how a novel should be written. 'His book represents the Woman question made flesh,' the *Pall Mall Gazette* continued, 'his people live it instead of talking it.'[38] *New Grub Street* had also been a social issue personified, but sociology was only background to Gissing's cry of pain about the writer's life as he had experienced it. In *The Odd Women* his mind could move more freely between different kinds of lives, doing justice to each. This brought qualified praise from the critic of the *Saturday Review:*

> Curious to state, Mr Gissing's women are far truer to nature than his men. Their conduct is intelligible from their varied points of view, but the personality and the behaviour of Mr Everard Barfoot, for instance, would baffle the understanding of most people. He is meant to be a charming and aristocratic (though rather wild) person: in reality he is a very pronounced cad.[39]

Gissing identified with the exclusion of his female characters from power and comfort. If they succeeded at all (like Mrs Barfoot and Rhoda Nunn), they did so through self-discipline and education, which Gissing saw as the best help for any subordinated group. Most were still doomed to be cast adrift, and Gissing felt that they needed some piece of wreckage to cling to: religion for Alice Madden, brandy for Virginia, a loveless marriage for Monica. Gissing's feminism was not a positive call for emancipation, like John Stuart Mill's; it was much more a feeling that the sufferings of Victorian women had much in common with his own. For the male characters of his novels, Gissing's quarrel was mainly with their optimism. Any positive, self-confident male is likely to be callous and exploitative: Milvain in *New Grub Street*, Barfoot in *The Odd Women*, Lionel Tarrant in *In the Year of Jubilee*. But Gissing's selfish heroes had found the secret of success that had eluded their creator.

The *Pall Mall Gazette* showered Gissing with back-handed compliments:

> *The Odd Women* falls short of genius only through its author's characteristic limitations – the complete lack of dash, the strange occasional flatness of the writing, the curious blindness (effective too, in its way, and especially in this book) that refuses to see any colour in the world but grey. But to a modern mind it is, for all that, the most interesting novel of the year.[40]

For those willing to see it, Gissing's novels were specially interesting because they dramatised contemporary issues without trying to fit them into the Procrustean bed of the conventional Victorian plot. The critical complaint against Gissing for most of his career had been that he would not give his readers what they wanted. In *New Grub Street*, *Born in Exile* and *The Odd Women* he had assumed that plots had to change in order to accommodate new social realities. *New Grub Street* showed how a new literary marketplace was destroying old myths of the writer as a romantic individualist. *Born in Exile* showed that there could be no happy ending to the conflict between evolutionary science and religious dogma. *The Odd Women* showed that the Victorian doctrine of 'separate spheres' for men and women had broken down; the prospect was for decades of conflict until women and men reached equality through education. Gissing still believed in a role for individual self-fashioning, and cared more for the fate of each character than for the impersonal workings of the social machinery. However, his characters would not be wrapped up and put away in a traditional happy ending, with distribution of rewards and punishments. Gissing was doing much of the demolition work for the twentieth-century English novel.

The cold eye with which Gissing surveyed late Victorian society disturbed readers and critics. Nowhere is his stance more isolated, or more
prophetic, than in his expectations for feminism:

> My demand for female 'equality' simply means that I am convinced there
> will be no social peace until women are intellectually trained very much as
> men are. More than half the misery of life is due to the ignorance and
> childishness of women. The average woman pretty closely resembles, in all
> intellectual considerations, the average male *idiot* – I speak medically. . . .
> Among our English emancipated women there is a majority of admirable
> persons; they have lost no single good quality of their sex, and they have
> gained enormously on the intellectual (and even on the moral) side by the
> process of enlightenment, – that is to say, of brain-development. I am
> driven frantic by the crass imbecility of the typical woman. That type must
> disappear, – or at all events become altogether subordinate. And I believe
> that the only way of effecting this is to go through a period of what many
> people will call sexual anarchy. Nothing good will perish; we can trust the
> forces of nature, which tend to conservation.[41]

Gissing was free to speak his mind because he was writing to his trusted
friend Bertz in Germany. But what did he mean by 'sexual anarchy'? Mrs
Cosgrove, in *The Odd Women*, had said that: 'We shall have to go through
a stage of anarchy, you know, before reconstruction begins.'[42] She meant
that some brave women needed to defiantly live in sin, in order to discredit
the institution of marriage. How would anarchy of this kind promote the
disappearance of the typical woman who upset Gissing so much? Perhaps
he was toying with the idea of having an affair with a free-spirited woman,
as relief from the daily miseries of his life with Edith. Under present
arrangements, most women might be idiots but they still had institutional
power within marriage. Even the feminist Rhoda Nunn had seen the advantage of having such protection against the wayward inclinations of Everard
Barfoot. Marriage protected the wife and punished the adulterous husband.
Did Gissing mean that in 'the coming anarchy' women would give up that
protection in exchange for the right to education and a career? A few
women had that freedom already, if they were educated and financially
independent: Constance Brissenden in *The Odd Women*, for example, or
Edith Sichel in real life. Yet Gissing himself remained close to Edwin
Reardon: still entangled in social convention, still doomed to defeat in his
relations with women.

If he could not yet escape his marriage to Edith, Gissing could at least
escape Exeter. On 25 March he gave his six months' notice to his landlord,

and soon began looking for lodgings in Brixton. 'I fear that I have wasted two years here in Devon,' he told Algernon. 'It is obviously in London that my material lies, and I must work hard to recover lost ground.' To Bertz he said simply: 'I want the streets again.'[43] He went to London and rented a room in Kennington for a week; after roaming the streets for hours every day he felt as if he had never left the city at all. Clement Shorter, the editor of the *English Illustrated Magazine*, had asked him for a bank-holiday short story, like chapter 12 of *The Nether World*. Gissing went to the working-class resort of Rosherville Gardens, near Gravesend, and made it the setting for his story 'Lou and Liz'. He had encouraging visits with his publishers, Arthur Bullen and Henry Lawrence; one of Gissing's reasons for returning to London was that he could have a social life there by accepting invitations and leaving Edith at home. In his diary he said he was driven back to London by 'perpetual rows in the house'. London gave him a better chance to be out of the house when the rows happened. Gissing may have hoped that Edith's temper would improve if they moved; Morley Roberts said that she was 'a girl of the London streets and square, [who] loathed the country, and whined in her characteristic manner about its infinite dullness'.[44]

Gissing went back to Exeter to finish up the remaining months of his lease. He went right to work on his story for Shorter, completing it in three days. Another, 'How a Misfortune Made a Philosopher', was written against future demand.[45] But his novel 'The Iron Gods' ran into the sand; with only twenty pages left to write, he was so dissatisfied that he set it aside and it was never published. For the three months remaining in Exeter, Gissing did almost no writing. He did not have the nervous energy to start another novel, and knew that once he was in London new material for a novel would arrive of itself. He went to the seaside at Paignton with Edith and Walter for a week at the end of April. Morley Roberts turned up unexpectedly just before they were due to leave, and spent a few days with Gissing. He was making five or six hundred pounds a year from his writing, and encouraged Gissing to write more short stories. Then Gissing's mother came and stayed with them for a fortnight. As usual, Gissing had nothing to record of his feelings for his mother – or hers, except that she liked to drink stout. They all went to Burnham-on-Sea for a week, where Gissing was able to slip away with his mother to his two favourite places, Wells and Glastonbury. Then it was time to pack up, after two and a half years in Exeter.

Gissing had written two major novels in Exeter, *Born in Exile* and *The Odd Women*, and had held his own financially. He had £116 in the bank, and the prospect of raising his income if he could find a good market for his short stories. His troubles with Edith made him unhappy about his Exeter life, but it was an illusion to think that a change of scene would bring him any greater marital contentment. Finally, Gissing had tried out his idea of living in a provincial town and realised that it would never suit him. From now on, his only settled homes would be either in the London area, or across the Channel.

Brixton

Gissing took his next home sight unseen, the upper floor of a terraced house in Brixton at 76 Burton Road. His landlord was C. W. Tinckam, who worked for the publishers Sampson, Low, and the rent was £32.10 a year. Burton Road was not a fashionable district, but this did not matter because Gissing planned to keep up his general rule from Exeter: No Visitors. He was creating a household much like that of the man of letters Alfred Yule and his working-class wife in *New Grub Street*. He saw himself as weak and put upon, yet like Mr Yule he believed it was his natural right to rule the roost. Edith and Walter were sent off to stay at Brampford Speke while Gissing bought new furniture and arranged everything at the Brixton end. After he had toiled in the heat for five days, he had done enough for Edith and Walter to join him, on 30 June 1893. There was still the eternal problem of finding a servant. Within another couple of weeks Gissing felt sure he could not work at home, so he took an attic room at 38 Cranmer Road, Kennington, for three shillings a week.[1] His room was a ten-minute walk from Burton Road and there he sat alone with one chair and a table for company. Soon he was turning out short stories at a steady rate.

Brixton was far from Camden Town where Edith had her relatives. Perhaps this was by design (in *New Grub Street* Mr Yule becomes apoplectic when his wife's relatives appear at his house). Gissing could get to central London easily, by bus, tram or the recently opened Tube station at Stockwell. In recent months he had received several letters from admirers wanting to meet him. Charles Stewart, a member of the Athenaeum Club, even asked him to come for a long weekend at his country house in Kent. Gissing listed these signs of recognition to Algernon, and added to each: 'Of course refused.'[2] His position was like Rhoda Nunn's in *The Odd Women*: she did not want to marry, but was proud to receive a proposal that she could turn down. Later in the year Gissing gave his justification for living as a hermit in London:

The very truth is that I have made up my mind never again to mix in the society of educated people. It is a necessity of my circumstances. I find it a wretched discomfort to pretend social equality where there can be none. My acquaintance can only be with a few individuals; in a gathering I am at once set in a false position – I cannot talk, cannot listen, and become a mere silent misanthrope.[3]

In fact, within a year or so of returning to London he did start to mix with educated people, especially writers. His dislike of society before that was a neurotic trait, rooted in his imprisonment, his sense of class inferiority, and the stigma of his marriages. Gissing even claimed that he could find enough 'human interest' material for his novels just by reading the daily newspapers. It may be to his credit that what most troubled him was the need for some kind of play-acting in casual social encounters. His awkwardness in the drawing-room hindered his literary career, if we compare him with more gregarious novelists like Dickens, Thackeray or Trollope. Yet his reclusiveness contributed to the sociological and analytic power of his books. If much was to be lost by his isolation, his works were not necessarily the worse for it. Their astringent and obsessive quality reflect Gissing's enclosure in a prison of his own making.

Gissing at least had his family and his little circle of male friends like Roberts and W. H. Hudson. Soon after he moved to Brixton he gained another friend who would greatly smooth his path for the remainder of his life. Clara Collet was three years younger than Gissing. She was the middle-class daughter of a Unitarian family; her father was a radical journalist. Clara was a typical New Woman: educated at the North London Collegiate School for Girls, she was one of the first women to receive a degree from the university of London. She had been a schoolteacher for several years, then a researcher for Charles Booth. When she met Gissing in 1893 she had just become the first woman to hold a professional job in the Civil Service. At the Board of Trade she collected statistics on female employment and was paid £300 a year, which gave her a home of her own in Richmond, near the river.

Collet was small and genteel but she went into some of the worst houses in London to do her research for Booth's *Life and Labour of the People in London*. For three months in 1888–9 she lived in the East End – a brave undertaking for a single young woman of her background. She became an enthusiast for Gissing's novels, especially *The Nether World*, because she felt they gave a true picture of actual conditions for the poor. In October 1891 she published an article on 'George Gissing's Novels: A First Impression' in the *Charity Organisation Review*. The following February she lectured on Gissing at the South Place Ethical Society, which pleased him very much. 'I have heard nothing of this lecture,' he told his sister Ellen, 'but it is very important indeed, and I must find out about it. The Ethical Society is known to me; the lecturers are people of very good standing.'[4] In the lecture, Collet had defended Gissing against the old charge of bleak pessimism, though she thought he was too critical of working-class women.

In early May of 1893 Collet wrote to Gissing in Exeter, asking him to call on her. She probably made the approach because she had just read *The Odd Women*, which was published on 10 April. It was as if Gissing first created Rhoda Nunn as a character, then found her real-life equivalent knocking at his door. He wrote back to say that he was too far away to see her, and was also married. But a correspondence began, and Collet persisted. She was a 'very independent and clever woman', Gissing told Ellen – a woman of the future, evidently. She was the third such woman to seek him out, after Mrs Gaussen and Edith Sichel; Eliza Orme, Rosalind Williams and Gabrielle Fleury would follow. Except in the case of Gabrielle, he would treat these privileged women with caution. He felt unquestionably superior to Nell and Edith; he could imagine a relationship of equals in his novels, but to actually live one was much more threatening.

It was part of Clara Collet's emancipation that she readily developed an intimate friendship with a married man – a friendship, not an intrigue. Before Gissing had even arrived in London she had invited him and Edith to spend a long weekend with her in Richmond (he declined), and had sent him her photograph. Collet was a small, energetic woman with a pleasant, if not beautiful, face. She fought hard for women's rights, without being hostile to men as such, and was attracted to several men; unfortunately, none of them fell in love with her. She never married, and may well have remained a lifelong virgin. Her attachment to Gissing was certainly profound, though not at the expense of what she considered due to Edith. As soon as he had finished moving in at Burton Road, Gissing went to visit Collet at her house in Richmond. They rented a boat and he rowed her to Kingston and back. In *The Odd Women* Mr Widdowson woos Monica Madden by rowing her up the Thames from Chelsea Bridge, while Monica holds the tiller. After this decorous Victorian ritual, Collet told Gissing that she would like to meet Edith. Two weeks later, she came to tea at Burton Road; then Edith went to Richmond for the day, while Gissing stayed home and looked after Walter.

Collet was playing a curious game, though not necessarily a dishonest one. She admired Gissing's work, and enjoyed discussing French literature with him, or the social questions of the day. Edith, on the other hand, was the kind of working-class woman that Collet had devoted her professional life to 'raising up'. Collet went off to Leicester in August to stay with Charles Booth; when she wrote to Edith from there, Gissing replied on his wife's behalf: 'My wife wishes me to give you her best thanks for the long and interesting letter.' In October he wrote: 'Do not think that Edith disregards your letters. But she has long since given up the hope of learning to write. So I will answer for her.'[5] When Gissing had first gone down alone to Exeter he had received letters from Edith, and coherent letters in Edith's handwriting survive in the archives.[6] Edith could write, just not to Gissing's satisfaction. He accused her of opening his letters, so certainly she knew how to read them.

By September 1893 Gissing and Collet were effectively conspiring together, and Collet had given up on the task of making Edith into a socially acceptable wife. One afternoon she took Edith to the theatre and arranged for Gissing to receive a letter while she was out. The letter pledged that if Gissing should die, Collet would become Walter's guardian and pay for his upkeep, since Edith, on her own, could not be a fit mother. Gissing was deeply moved by the offer. He told Collet that he had been only thirteen when his father died: 'I know only too well the miseries and perils of a child left without strong, wise guidance. . . . Your letter eases my mind, though, I repeat, far more with reference to the moral, than to the material, aspect of the matter.'[7] Still, a strong-minded woman with a secure £300 a year could protect Walter against all dangers. Having this guarantee made Gissing much less anxious, and helped him with his writing. Collet was now a steady friend and a companion on family outings. Gissing told her that he was still determined to refuse all the social invitations that kept coming his way; but with her to rely on, his intellectual loneliness was no longer absolute.

Part of Gissing's reason for moving to Brixton was to research a south London setting for his next book. He wandered all over the neighbourhood, but before settling down to the novel he took up Morley Roberts's suggestion that he should turn out a batch of short stories. Clement Shorter got Gissing started by commissioning the story 'Lou and Liz' and publishing it in the August 1893 *English Illustrated Magazine*. Shorter was a hyperactive literary entrepreneur who also edited the *Illustrated London News* and *The Sketch*. In 1915 he would lead the hue and cry against D. H. Lawrence's *The Rainbow*, but now he was very useful to Gissing by helping him to meet the market's steady demand for formulaic short stories. These needed to have ingenious plots and lively, recognisable characters; each story would have several illustrations and provide half an hour of entertainment.

Gissing could learn the knack by studying back issues of Shorter's magazines at the public library. He also met Morley Roberts at the Authors' Club on 21 July, and probably got another earful about writing stories. Roberts followed up by sending Gissing some Maupassant, Zola's *L'Argent*, and some of his own work. On his own account, Gissing read Henry James's 'The Real Thing'.

Once he recognised the opportunity in writing stories, and that he had the skill to take advantage of it, Gissing plunged in with a will. By the end of 1893 he had written no fewer than fifteen that were eventually published. One reason he was so productive may have been that he was no longer so painfully isolated as he had been in Exeter. He could see friends like Roberts and W. H. Hudson regularly; even more valuable was the deep loyalty and understanding he could count on from Clara Collet. Roberts despised Edith, which made it impossible for Gissing to confide in him about his domestic troubles. Collet gave Gissing something he had always lacked, a shoulder to cry on. He was no longer alone in his marital foxhole. Visits to the British Museum could resume, where Gissing must have had some casual acquaintances, and he had to make business calls on publishers and editors. Before long such contacts led to invitations that Gissing felt he had to accept, and that he actually came to enjoy.

Gissing's other great motive for writing stories was their vastly shorter production cycle, which relieved his chronic problems with self-criticism and writer's block. In the middle of April 1893 he had written 'Lou and Liz' in three days; by July he received a copy of the *English Illustrated Magazine* with his story in it. Clement Shorter then asked Gissing for a story to go into the Christmas number of the *Illustrated London News*; he began 'Fleet-footed Hester' the next day and finished it in three days. While writing it, he received a cheque for eleven guineas for 'Lou and Liz'; he complained that it wasn't enough, but three days' work had paid for four months' rent on his lodgings. Between 27 July and 27 August Gissing wrote six stories that he sold for publication, plus two that he abandoned. One of them, 'Under an Umbrella', he wrote in a single session of six hours. When he was working on a novel he might write as many words in a day, but the difference was that two days at three thousand words a day produced a saleable story, with no time to fret about its worth. If Gissing had doubts, he could just put the story aside and start another.

Gissing's short stories are not fundamentally different from the world of his novels. They deal with the lower-middle range of English life, the everyday rather than the melodramatic, but with an extra dose of misfortune. The stories are packed with events: marriage proposals, con-

frontations, disappointments, sudden death. Some of the stories are
tragedies of common life in London. In 'The Day of Silence' a working-
class family is happy in the morning, and by the end of the day they are all
dead. Even in such a story, there is little room for philosophy; Gissing
could indulge his pessimism, but not develop it into a systematic view of
London life. His quick success as a short-story writer came because his
stories were rapid, lively and full of familiar types, with no room for the
ponderous meditations of his novels. Two of the stories, 'A Capitalist'
and 'A Lodger in Maze Pond', provide biographical interest through the
presence of 'Harvey Munden', a detached observer who is in part a mouthpiece for Gissing's views.[8] In both stories Munden is set against a more
active and passionate figure who is moving towards a wilful marriage. The
capitalist is a rich money-lender who now wants a quiet life in the country.
He tries to wipe out his past by becoming engaged to the daughter of the
local squire. The lodger is a medical student with literary interests who
foolishly proposes to his landlady's daughter. Munden carries him off to
Italy, but he goes back to the girl, marries her, and dies soon after. 'What's
the good of advising a man born to be fooled?' Munden says to him.[9] The
story is a debate between Munden, the cynic, and his friend Shergold, who
is a fool about women. Munden speaks for the contemplative Gissing,
Shergold for the active one; action prevails, and leads to disaster. In his
stories, Gissing frequently suggests that people cannot learn by trying to
be wise, only by suffering the consequences of their actions.

At the beginning of September Gissing looked in at his old building,
now called Cornwall Mansions, and learned that the next person to rent his
flat had killed himself (though not at home). 'The atmosphere I left behind
me, some would say, killed the poor man,' Gissing noted.[10] At least he *had*
left it behind, as he was making the transition from a writer starving in his
garret to one whose work was in demand. On the same day as he heard
about the suicide, Gissing spent £1 for six photographs of himself in his
best suit and tie. Clement Shorter wanted a picture for *The Sketch*, and
there would be other occasions when the public wanted an image to match
with Gissing's growing reputation. In the portrait, Gissing put up a good
front, with his impressive moustache and head of curly hair; but his eyes
seemed to convey a different message, of remoteness and defeat. He convinced himself that Shorter was not paying him enough for his stories, and
asked for a raise from twelve to eighteen guineas for world rights. Typically, he backed down when Shorter refused.

Gissing did realise that he needed the help of a literary agent to widen
the market for his work. He had given up on A. P. Watt, who had not been

able to sell *Born in Exile* at a better price than previous novels. There were many possible buyers for Gissing's short stories, and the obvious expert in the field was W. H. Colles, who was an agent, the director of the Authors' Syndicate, and legal counsel to the Society of Authors. Gissing wrote to Colles, and got an enthusiastic reply; he met him, and found 'a fat, red-faced, vivacious man, and a great talker'.[11] Colles said that Gissing should get three guineas per thousand words for a story, and Gissing left five stories with him, to see what he could do.[12] All were eventually placed, at close to the price Colles had named. The rate per word was equivalent to about six hundred guineas for a three-decker novel, so for the same effort Gissing would be paid about four times as much.[13] Not only that, the amount of creative agony was much less. When Gissing engaged Colles, it was a year since he had finished *The Odd Women;* he had written most of the novel about Birmingham, but then abandoned it. Short stories became the main focus of his creative efforts in 1893, and he would go on writing them until the end of his life.

Gissing was well aware that he had come to a fork in the road of his literary career. 'I am entered upon the commercial path, alas!' he told Eduard Bertz. 'But I shall try not to write rubbish.'[14] Colles had told Gissing that Walter Besant admired his books – a dubious endorsement, because Besant was beating the drum for making literature less of an art and more of a business. Colles gave him a J. M. Barrie story as an example of how to be a popular success.[15] One could say that Gissing used the writing of *New Grub Street* to convince himself that the literary marketplace ruled all, and a book was ultimately just a commodity: 'For my own part, I am growing less thin-skinned in this matter of literary scruple. It is an age of vulgarity, and the terrifying examples before our eyes make us fear to exercise even a legitimate freedom. But if one's spirit be not vulgar, it is surely safe to obey the dictates of literary instinct.'[16]

Unless Gissing was willing to accept commercial failure and die, like Reardon and Biffen, his task was to produce an honest commodity of good quality. He did not have a Jamesian love of form for its own sake, nor was there any appeal in joining the aesthetes of the Nineties. If Gissing had lived to see the Modernists, after 1908, he surely would not have joined them either. After writing so many books about the miseries caused by lack of money, how could he spurn money now that it was coming within his grasp? When his friend Bertz complained about depression and his stagnant literary career, Gissing was blunt about the remedy: 'Now do keep it clearly before your mind that you *can* earn money if you like. Finish your book as soon as possible, and see the result. Of course you must get into a less depressing sphere, and money alone can help you to do so. Money – remember – means *health* as well as liberty.'[17] Still, for a writer there were better and worse ways of making money, and Gissing knew that he should put his best efforts into another serious novel, the one that he had moved to Brixton to write.

Gissing's first title for this novel was 'Miss Lord of Camberwell'.[18] His publisher later convinced him to change it to *In the Year of Jubilee*, but Gissing's original idea was a significant one. He did not call earlier novels 'Thyrza of Lambeth' or 'Miss Snowdon of Clerkenwell'.[19] Camberwell was in his new title because it was not just a district of London, it stood for a new form of life, lower-middle-class suburbia. South of the Thames, an ocean of red brick was swallowing up old villages. Population in the over-spill areas was growing at some 50 per cent every ten years. An army of clerks and shop assistants went up to town each day by bus, train and tram, reading en route the new mass media targeted to their interests, from the *Daily Mail* to *Tit-Bits*. South London might be considered a cultural wasteland, with hardly any monuments, museums, theatres or great public buildings. Yet that made it a distinctively modern place, defined by new kinds of housing and transportation, and by the emerging soft culture of mass media, advertising and consumer credit. Gissing chose to live in south London because he was both fascinated and appalled by it.

In his early novels, what appalled Gissing was the poverty, immorality and dirt of the London slums; what appalled him now was lower-middle-class success. Their frantic house-building was destroying the Surrey countryside. They had enough money to buy mass-produced consumer goods, to enjoy a 'life-style' based on brand names and advertising, and to transform journalism and entertainment. The lower middle class had traditionally been pious, frugal, and subservient to their betters; in south London there were no betters to restrain a prosperous and self-confident new civilisation. It was no accident, either, that Gissing chose a female protagonist for 'Miss Lord of Camberwell'. South London was a com-mercial rather than an industrial culture. Tens of thousands of shops and small businesses catered to female purchasing power and provided employ-ment opportunities for women. In *The Odd Women*, Rhoda Nunn is an ideological feminist who wants to improve the status of women by raising their consciousness. In the new novel, Beatrice French starts her own business and raises her income. What do women want? Cheap and fash-ionable dresses. Most of the characters of *In the Year of Jubilee* make their money from small businesses, unlike those crushed by sweated labour in the proletarian novels. The spirit of Camberwell in the 1880s is very far from the narrow evangelical beliefs of Gissing's childhood days in Wake-field. These south Londoners may be considered more emancipated, yet they almost all use their freedom badly. The expanding urban economy is dissolving many of the fixed points of the old social order but not, in Gissing's view, to replace them with anything better.

Gissing found plentiful materials in his walks around Camberwell and Brixton, and read books on advertising as background for his character Luckworth Crewe. But he had the usual difficulties in getting his book written. He began producing his daily quota of words on 12 September 1893. Work went on in fits and starts for three months, with constant worry about whether he was on the right track. On 4 December he went to see Clement Shorter, and found that his brusque manner concealed a great faith in Gissing's talent. Shorter suggested that Gissing should write a short novel to be serialised in the *Illustrated London News*, and commissioned six more stories at twelve guineas each. He also invited Gissing to dinner (he refused). Gissing had already written eight stories for publication in 1893, most of them since his return to London at the end of June. It was easier to produce more for Shorter than to continue struggling with his novel, especially since Shorter had agreed to pay for the stories on delivery rather than on publication. Gissing sat down to work in his grubby Camberwell room the day after his meeting with Shorter, and finished the six stories by Christmas Eve, a rate of one every three days.[20] To earn £75 in such a short time was an eye-opener for Gissing, especially since he could boast to Clara Collet that 'some of [the stories] are not bad'.[21] He told Ellen that he should be able to earn £200 a year if he was left in peace. This would place him on the lower steps of the middle class; in fact, he would earn considerably more in every year from 1894 to the end of his life.

From the material point of view, at least, his 1893 Christmas at Burton Road was much more hopeful than the previous one at Exeter. He told Clara Collet that he had decided to take a house in north London, near Regent's Park, and live more like a gentleman:

> This is the result of much brooding. Why should I go on struggling wretch-edly against adverse conditions, when, in all likelihood, a bold change might greatly add to my success in literary work? I must have a quiet room of my own. I must have two servants, one of them able to cook a potato and roast a joint. I must have an end of squalid troubles, largely, I believe, the result of my own lack of courage.[22]

Gissing might well brood, because he was wrestling with the old question of whether a writer produced because he had comfortable working conditions, or because of his imaginative contact with the outside world. He told Bertz that there was nothing left for him in life but steady work; yet he did not want to become a mere writing-automaton, like Zola or Walter Besant. 'The least defect of health,' he wrote, 'and the least domestic trouble, puts an end to that machine-like regularity. Nor do I think such regularity a very desirable thing. An artist, after all, should live very differently from a mechanic.'[23] Yet even when he was free to do so, in the interval between separating from Nell and marrying Edith, Gissing had never really lived as an artist. The only exception was when he had been a wanderer in Italy and Greece. He may not have thought 'regularity' to be desirable, but that is how he had survived as a writer for fifteen years or more. He had worked obsessively to meet his quota of words, at the expense of freedom and pleasure; he only stopped working when he was depressed, or on equally regular holidays.

The Christmas season showed no great change in Gissing's life routine. His brother Algernon came and stayed with him for a month, recuperating from one of his fits of discouragement about his writing career. That he stayed so long means that he at least kept on civil terms with Edith; and he must have been alone with her much of the time because Gissing would be away in his rented room, grimly writing. Gissing now had three patrons, where before he had none; not surprisingly, he vacillated between them. He remained loyal to Arthur Bullen, the first publisher really to have faith in him; Shorter was eager to make Gissing a kind of staff writer for his magazines; William Colles was the literary agent who was sure he could manage Gissing's career much better than he had managed it himself. But Gissing would not let Colles handle his novels, or the stories he placed with Shorter. For the proposed short novel to run in the *Illustrated London News*, Gissing negotiated his own terms, which were better than anything he had managed before. The novel, *Eve's Ransom*, was to be only sixty thousand words, the equivalent of a single volume of a three-decker. For this Gissing would get £150, without having to pay an agent's commission, and he could then sell the novel again in book form for whatever he could get. When all the money was in he would be paid more than four times as much per word as for any previous novel.[24] Most of this income came from Gissing's appearance in a mass-circulation magazine, even if it was at the more snobbish end of such periodicals.

Colles was now putting pressure on Gissing to let him handle the sale of *In the Year of Jubilee*, which had been coming along steadily since 1 January. Gissing said he wanted the book published as soon as possible, which meant giving it to Bullen and accepting whatever he offered. Colles insisted that he could get a better price for the novel, to which Gissing responded: 'But I have promised my friend A. H. Bullen that he should have this book, and, what is more, our personal relations preclude any thought of injustice on his side or of discontent on mine. This will explain the matter.'[25] Bullen was an Oxford man, the son of the head of the British Museum library. It was important to Gissing to have such a man as a friend; even more important, fair dealing between friends was an antidote to the terrible impersonality of the market. Over the past few months, paradoxically, Gissing had become a much more marketable writer, and was starting to enjoy the financial rewards that followed. His friendship with Bullen helped him to believe that his most valuable artistic work – his novels – would continue to be circulated in a more gentlemanly fashion. Bullen told him in January 1894 that *Denzil Quarrier* had done very poorly in the US, so that he had had to reimburse Macmillan of New York £53 for printing costs. He still sent Gissing a cheque for £25 as an advance on royalties for the English edition. 'This seems absurd,' Gissing wrote in his diary. 'Nothing can possibly be owing to me, and I can't take the money.'[26] When his books failed to sell as well as he had hoped, Gissing felt guilty towards Bullen. Colles had to convince Gissing that he should get the best price for his books, and not worry about how much his publishers might benefit. The underlying problem was that Gissing had no great faith in himself: 'Since 1886 I have managed to *live* by literature – or, let us say, by writing; and the fact seems to me rather wonderful, for never have I tried to please the public, and I have, in fact, pleased only the minutest fraction of it.'[27]

If only the life that Gissing had managed to earn had more pleasure in it! At home, Walter was chronically ill with bronchitis and swollen tonsils; the doctor recommended that he should be taken out of London. What if he had a weak chest like his uncle William, who had died at twenty? At least Gissing had enough money coming in from his stories to be able to move his family to the seaside until the spring. On 7 February 1894 they arrived at comfortable lodgings in Hastings, at a place Clara Collet had recommended. Walter, Gissing believed, 'shall not lose all his strength and get pale among streets'.[28] This meant that the family could not continue to live in London after their lease at Burton Road ran out in June. Gissing also had got all the south London material he needed for *In the Year of Jubilee*. Three weeks after arriving in Hastings, he sent the first two volumes off to Bullen, and he doggedly worked on volume III while living in lodgings with a sick child. Those crowded conditions may have had something to do with Lionel Tarrant's insistence in the novel that he and his wife should live separately until they can afford a spacious house, and perhaps stay apart even then.[29] Edith, of course, had almost nothing to do on her supposed holiday except look after Walter, while Gissing spent hours each day working at his book. For two weeks at the end of March they moved from Hastings to Eastbourne. Gissing was confirmed in his belief that it was the best seaside town in England, and he could get away from Edith on long walks across the Downs to his favourite villages. What could not be escaped was the need to keep writing: Gissing would go and lie on Beachy Head to think out his next book, the serial he had promised to deliver to Shorter by June.

As soon as he returned to Burton Road at the beginning of April, Gissing began scouting around for a new home, either in Streatham or on the fringes of London near the North Downs. He completed *In the Year of Jubilee* on 13 April, though he considered the last pages 'very slovenly'. There, Nancy prostrates herself before her selfish and mediocre husband, unlike Rhoda Nunn in *The Odd Women*, who rejects her suitor and keeps her self-respect. Perhaps Gissing gave in to wish-fulfilment, imagining domestic peace instead of his own marital battleground; perhaps he could not imagine any better ending than female subordination to 'Nature's Law'. He had tried to assert his masculine prerogative at home, without gaining any submission from Edith, and his search for a house showed one of the reasons why: his chronic difficulty in making a decision.

Gissing was too restless to wait for the end of the Burton Road lease; he put the furniture in storage and took Edith and Walter to Clevedon in Somerset. The business in hand was to meet his deadline for the *Illustrated London News* serial. In April and May he had written about two-thirds of it, using as much as he could of his Birmingham novel, 'The Iron Gods', which he had abandoned a year before. None of this work satisfied him, and at the end of May he seems to have suffered another of his creative breakdowns. He told Clara Collet that his literary career was over, and he would have to support himself in some other way. What he had done was 'more complete trash than any living author has yet done. I sometimes have to hold my right hand with my left, to get letters shaped.'[30] He arrived in Clevedon on 2 June and took three rooms, one of them a study, at 84 Old Church Road. With a string of four-thousand-word days he got it done, sending off the manuscript on 30 June; he told Collet that it was 'unutterable rubbish'.[31] Fortunately, Clement Shorter did not agree; he sent the manuscript straight to the printer, and proofs started to arrive at Clevedon within ten days. Gissing had put in a thoroughly professional month at his desk — which was part of why he was so disgusted with what he had produced.

Eve's Ransom was far from being trash, though few would agree with H.

G. Wells that it was the 'best and least appreciated' of Gissing's novels. If it had been a three-decker, as Gissing originally planned for 'The Iron Gods', there would have been scope for it to be a novel of ideas, like all of Gissing's works up to then. Stripped of ideology, and broken into short chapters for serial publication, the texture of *Eve's Ransom* was closer to a series of short stories than a panoramic novel.[32] Its protagonist, Maurice Hilliard, is an industrial draughtsman who longs to develop the artistic side of his nature. He unexpectedly receives £436 that was owed his dead father, and decides to quit his job and live 'like a human being' for as long as the money lasts. A large share of his capital goes to rescuing and wooing Eve Madely, after he has fallen in love with her photograph. Love needs comfort and trips to Paris in order to thrive; Eve shows she has learnt that lesson by agreeing to marry Hilliard's best friend, Narramore, who is seriously rich.

Gissing gives Eve a typically feminine motive for her betrayal: fear of poverty. A man has at least the chance of wealth through success in the marketplace; most women can only hope to attach themselves to a 'good provider'. When he meets Eve, Hilliard has no prospects, except to enjoy his legacy. Like Amy Reardon in *New Grub Street*, Eve is bound to lose faith in a man who has no faith in himself, but who nonetheless tells Eve that a man must always rule his wife:

> He is simply a man with a will, and finds it necessary to teach his wife her duties. Emily knows no more about the duties of life than her little five-year-old girl. She thought she could play with a second husband as she did with the first, and she was gravely mistaken. She complained to me of a thousand acts of tyranny – every one of them, I could see, merely a piece of rude common-sense.[33]

It is important to see that Gissing the narrator does not quite align himself with Hilliard the male supremacist. When Hilliard hints that Eve might also need 'a strong man to take her in hand', she 'pays no attention'. Hilliard might speak for Gissing; but one might also view him as a self-deluded blusterer, who is outmanoeuvred by Eve. He complains that she 'in the manner of her sex, could like him better for his love without a dream of returning it'.[34] At the end of the novel he renounces Eve, resumes his friendship with Narramore, and delights in being free of desire. No doubt Gissing unloaded some of his personal frustrations as he rushed through the writing of *Eve's Ransom*; yet the book also shows how men defeat themselves through their foolish attitudes towards women. Standing next to the hero who suffers is the author who says: 'What did you expect?'

Gissing's identity is divided between them. *Eve's Ransom* has no space for large theoretical speculations; it presents starkly the conflict between how Gissing acted in his sentimental life, and how he believed he should act. At least he was trying to purge himself of the illusion he had held for so long, his sentimental idealism about women.

After his frantic labours in June, Gissing was eager to get away from Edith for a while. He went to stay with Algernon at Willersey for a week, and found a complete contrast with his own domestic life:

> This is the only civilized dwelling I have entered for a very long time. On an income less even than my own, these people manage to keep up a really beautiful little house, excellent taste with great simplicity – a contrast indeed to my hovels at Exeter and in London. I sit down to meals without feeling ashamed of the necessity of feeding – so delicately is everything arranged, and so skilfully prepared.[35]

At least Gissing could feel that the money steadily trickling from his pocket to Algernon's was well spent.

Back at Clevedon, Gissing devoted five days to a final revision of *In the Year of Jubilee*. Once that was done, he did no writing for more than two months, a long interval for him. Some of his hesitation about getting back to work may have come from the outbreak of a great literary row over the fate of the three-decker novel. Mudie's had announced that from now on they would pay only four shillings a volume, instead of five; that was less than 40 per cent of the list price at which novels were sold to individual purchasers. Authors and publishers fought back, threatening to drop the three-decker altogether and make the standard a shorter, one-volume novel. It would sell for six shillings in the first edition and reach a much wider book-buying public. Gissing's three-deckers had not done particularly well; the £150 or so that he received for them reflected first-edition sales of about five hundred copies. A three-decker needed to sell at least a thousand first-edition copies to make it worth the publisher's while. Now, if a novel sold for six shillings – including a one-shilling royalty to the author – it needed to sell three thousand copies for the author to earn £150. In 1894 it was not clear if three thousand or more people would regularly be willing to buy a novel outright for six shillings, when they could subscribe to Mudie's for a guinea a year. 'My own interests in the matter are entirely dubious,' Gissing noted in his diary.[36] As it turned out, his income would increase substantially over the next nine years. Even before the end of the three-decker he was beginning to diversify his output, into the short novels and stories for which there was a rapidly growing demand in the new mass media. *In the Year of Jubilee* was the last three-decker he would write. It could be argued that all of Gissing's best novels are three-deckers, in which case Mudie's self-interested move may have been bad news for Gissing's literary career.

On 27 August Gissing, Edith and Walter left Clevedon for London. They separated at Paddington: Edith and Walter went off to stay with her married sister, while Gissing made another house-hunting trip into Hertfordshire. He spent two uncomfortable nights at Berkhamsted, and disliked it. The problem with Hertfordshire was 'a certain squalor of the towns and villages, due, doubtless, to influence of London'.[37] Gissing did not encounter a young classics master at Berkhamsted School, Charles Greene; his son Graham would arrive ten years later. Greene and Gissing were both novelists who found their material in the seedy side of life, and who agreed that Berkhamsted was mortally depressing. Gissing gave up on the neighbourhood and moved on to Surrey. After two days he found a stop-gap, furnished rooms at 3 Clifton Terrace, Dorking. The house had a high position and was built on dry, sandy soil, features that met the Victorian obsession with whether a particular spot was healthy or not. Gissing moved Edith and Walter there for a fortnight, and renewed his search. He quickly found a house in Epsom that he thought would suit, and agreed to take it on a year's lease for £40. As usual, he made the decision without Edith even seeing the place.

'Eversley', Worple Road, was a semi-detached two-storey house with two large bay windows at the front. It was on the south side of town, within reach of Epsom Downs (though Gissing considered the Derby 'blackguardism at its height', and left town on the day of the race).[38] The soil was chalk and gravel, and the house had a separate bathroom, for Gissing a new and welcome luxury. If it lacked charm, that was no worse than every other English house that Gissing managed to find. He also seemed to attract domestic disasters: toxic vapours, water pouring through the kitchen ceiling and, in time, a gas-pipe explosion. In *The Private Papers of Henry Ryecroft* the ideal is a 'plain little house amid its half-wild garden, the cosy book-room with its fine view across the valley of the Exe to Haldon'.[39] Gissing had been inside many fine dwellings and loved domestic comfort, but he was incapable of creating it for himself. His choice of houses to live in had something in common with his choice of women to live with. Driven by his stubborn and usually self-defeating will, he would not allow himself to be seduced, but carried out a set plan in an obsessive way. Like many of his temperament, he also combined decisiveness with a tendency to 'buyer's remorse'. In the case of lodgings, there was a cycle of wanting to move but quickly becoming dissatisfied with the new place, which was supposed to be an improvement on the old place, but wasn't. The more Gissing was vexed by his actual housing, the more he longed for the stable and comfortable home that always receded beyond his grasp.

Gissing at least had many of the external things he needed for contentment at Epsom. He was close both to the Surrey hills, and to central London; there was hope that Walter's health would be better in the winter, away from London pollution; he had a garden, and a study to work in at home. The cheque for the serialisation of *Eve's Ransom* had just arrived, £150. Clement Shorter wanted more stories for his magazines, and by the end of the year Gissing had done three for him. Soon after moving in he also wrote a three-thousand-word story for Colles, 'Simple Simon', in two days. Colles told him it was just what was in demand, and launched Gissing on another sideline, writing sketches. These were miniature short stories with no more than two or three characters and a single, pithy point. 'Simple Simon' is about two clerks who are keen vegetarians and teetotallers. One of them, Simon, is in love with a publican's daughter who will not give up her roast beef and ale. When his friend shows himself to be a drunken hypocrite, Simon denounces him and goes off to find happiness with his carnivorous beloved. Having been half-starved at various times in his life, Gissing was sure that health and happiness depended on being well fed, in the traditional British way. He loved nature, but had no qualms about killing animals for food (a point of difference with Hardy).[40]

A new phase for Gissing began in September, when he finally accepted an invitation from Shorter to go out to dinner with him. He also agreed to dine with his publishers, Harry Lawrence and Arthur Bullen. After his constant complaints that he was unfit to have a social life, and did not enjoy it when dragged into it, it is unclear why Gissing changed his mind. There were practical reasons for him to circulate in the London literary world, but they were just as relevant when he was living at Cornwall Residences or in Brixton and refusing to go out. People like Shorter and Bullen persisted with their invitations because they admired Gissing, and because his stock was going up as a literary 'lion'. He had often argued in his novels that being successful brought friends; and in spite of his melancholy temperament he could be very good company. He was an unusual literary man in that he never seemed to acquire any enemies – in part, no doubt, because he never wrote reviews.

Gissing's first outing was to Shorter's dinner at the National Liberal Club on 26 September. He met H. W. Massingham, the political editor of the *Daily Chronicle*, and found – to his surprise – that he enjoyed the evening very much. A month later he invested in his social career by buying a new dress suit and an Inverness cape. The latter may have been inspired by the Sherlock Holmes stories, which were hugely popular at this time, though Gissing passed on the deerstalker hat. At the Lawrence & Bullen dinner, he met another important figure in his life, Eliza Orme. She was nine years older than Gissing, and close to Clara Collet in her interests. Orme was the first woman to receive a law degree from London University; she was active in feminist causes, and had family connections to many Victorian writers and artists. When the company went back to Bullen's rooms to smoke cigars, Orme had a cigar too. She never married, apart from a 'Boston marriage' with Harry Lawrence's sister. In future years she would be an indispensable helper to Gissing in his marital troubles.

Gissing dined at the Authors' Club in November, where his dress suit started to earn its keep. His neighbour was Walter Besant, the personification of the literary businessman:

> A little insignificant man, talking with a commonplace diffidence. Never a word that might not fall from the lips of a respectable draper.
>
> To mingle with these folk is to be once and for ever convinced of the degradation that our time has brought upon literature. It was a dinner of tradesmen, pure and simple. . . . literature is now on all fours with the butter-trade, and one must be glad that one's goods are sought in the market. . . . I must use the people, just to make a living; but I certainly shall not join their Club.[41]

Gissing praised Hardy for keeping clear of such company. Yet they liked Gissing, even if he did not care for them. Besant wrote a puff for Gissing in the January 1895 The Author, and invitations continued to show up in his post.

Being sought after in London helped Gissing to bear with turmoil at home in Epsom. Just before Christmas their servant fled the house in secret, as soon as she had her month's wages. Gissing had asked Edith to stay out of the kitchen and not quarrel with her, to no effect. But there is also something suspicious in his failure even to name his servants when he writes about them in his diary, or to show any interest in them beyond how well or badly they did their work. It is little wonder that servants constantly fled, caught between the two fires of Edith's bad temper and Gissing's chilly indifference. He was himself guilty of awkwardness with servants, stemming from his own feelings of insecurity. For good measure, he had rigid and perfectionist standards, often berating servants in his diary as totally incompetent.[42]

Worse than any servant trouble, though, was Gissing's bitterness towards Edith over her treatment of Walter. In October he made a desperate entry in his diary:

> Today, the little boy has not been very well, owing to wet weather. At eight o'clock tonight, as E. did not come down to supper, I went quietly to the bedroom door, to listen, as I often do, whether the boy was asleep. To my amazement I heard E. call out 'Stop your noise, you little beast!' This to the poor little chap, because he could not get to sleep. And why not? Because the flaring light of a lamp was in the room. I have begged – begged – again and again that she will *never* take a lamp into the bedroom, but she is too lazy to light a candle, and then uses such language as I have written.
>
> But for my poor little boy, I would not, and could not, live with her for another day. I have no words for the misery I daily endure from her selfish and coarse nature.[43]

Gissing had entered the marriage because he found it unbearable to live alone; now he was finding it unbearable to live in company. With the improvement in his financial prospects, he could afford to separate from Edith, but for the moment he felt that the most important thing was to stay together in order to protect Walter from his mother.

In February, while writing *In the Year of Jubilee* at Hastings, Gissing had imagined what it would be like to walk out and take Walter with him. In the novel, Arthur Peachey dotes on his little boy, whom his mother rejected from the day of his birth. Arthur blames the failure of his marriage on the nature of lower-middle-class wives: 'In his rank of life married happiness was a rare thing, and the fault could generally be traced to wives who had no sense of responsibility, no understanding of household duties, no love of simple pleasures, no religion. Yes, there was the point – no religion.'[44] Gissing's view of religion was brutally pragmatic. He hated the sound of bells on Sunday; but those who were below him on the social ladder needed religion. They needed a consolation for sufferings that had no remedy on this earth; and they needed an external source of moral authority. In Gissing's eyes, Edith was a barbarian who refused his authority as her husband, but had no values of her own. He was too desperate to consider the flaws in his own position. Why should Edith, or any other lower-class person, be expected to believe in a God that Gissing did not believe in himself? Beyond this, Gissing simply could not imagine that Edith might have any valid reason to be dissatisfied with her marriage, or that she had been provoked by his own self-righteous rigidity. When he was thinking as a novelist, Gissing excelled in creating couples who are blind to each other's values and needs: Monica and Widdowson in *The Odd Women*, Amy and Edwin Reardon in *New Grub Street*. But in his marriage to Edith he could only react instinctively, like an animal with its leg caught in a trap. Even if the marriage was doomed from the start, it could have ended with less damage to everyone concerned if Gissing had not lost so much of his imagination and intelligence when he crossed the threshold of his home.

For the moment, Gissing let off steam in his diary but took no concrete steps either to improve or to escape his marriage. Whatever his misery, he had at least been able to keep working through 1894 in his little rented room. When he looked over his accounts on New Year's Eve he saw that he had 'earned by literature in 1894 no less a sum than £453-12-5. Bravo!'[45] Gissing's living expenses for the year had been £239, so he had taken the first step towards his long-held dream: to accumulate enough capital to draw an independent income. Novelists like Scott or Balzac might be trapped in debt by their social ambitions, but Gissing always kept his caution about money. His financial success in 1894 may have been a mixed blessing, because it encouraged him to follow the market by writing more short stories and commissioned novels. The market preferred cheerfulness and, except for his unhappy marriage, Gissing was no longer suffering the pains of poverty and lack of recognition. He was not the Biffen-like recluse of old, starving in his garret while clinging to his artistic principles. Between the writing of *In the Year of Jubilee* and *The Whirlpool*, Gissing came close to being a strictly commercial writer.

In the Year of Jubilee was published just before Christmas of 1894. Gissing had finally educated some of his critics to the point that they would accept him on his own terms. L. F. Austin, in *The Sketch*, set out something close to a mainstream position on Gissing's work:

> There may be a good deal of exaggeration in this pessimism, but it is the honest belief of a skilled observer, and it gives to Mr Gissing's novels an intellectual quality, an austere sincerity in the face of shallow optimism, a moral weight, entirely lacking in the mass of current fiction. More than that, the book before me is extremely good reading, with all its grimness, and the character of Nancy Lord is a study of which any novelist, whatever his eminence, might be proud.[46]

The Sketch was one of Clement Shorter's magazines; in addition to this long and favourable review, it ran one of the photographs Gissing had sat for a year earlier. Perhaps the main thing that prevented *In the Year of Jubilee* selling in large numbers was the unattractive personality of its hero, Lionel Tarrant. Those readers who admired Nancy Lord's vitality and independence were brought up short by her complete submission to Tarrant in the novel's conclusion. The reviewer for the *Manchester Guardian* made this case bluntly:

> The weakness of this situation is that while Nancy emerges a fine and pure if too docile character, Tarrant, in his marital fireside philosophy, becomes self-complacent and priggish. The author does not observe that his assertion of his superior greatness, sense, and intellect is, after all his currish conduct, ludicrous.[47]

In response to another review of *Jubilee*, Gissing said that 'the most characteristic, the most important part of my work is that which deals with a class of young men distinctive of our time – well educated, fairly bred, *but without money*'.[48] Lionel Tarrant does excuse his caddish behaviour by saying that 'There's no villainy, no scoundrelism, no baseness conceivable, that isn't excused by want of money.' But he says this to a Gissing surrogate-figure, Harvey Munden, who makes a sceptical reply. Want of money can scarcely justify Tarrant's obnoxious arrogance, nor his particular treatment of Nancy – first abandoning her, then taking for granted that he is morally superior to her because she is a woman. Tarrant, like Everard Barfoot in *The Odd Women*, exploits his social privilege in the hope of dominating a woman he is attracted to. Gissing seemed to realise that he was grinding a personal axe with the ending, rather than letting his characters act according to their nature and situation. The plot of *Jubilee* repeats that of *New Grub Street*, but with the balance of power between husband and wife reversed. Even though Tarrant is morally inferior to Reardon, he prevails in his marriage; Nancy is a superior person to Amy Reardon, but chooses to submit.

Another curious aspect of *Jubilee* is that Gissing cut from the novel an episode that would have made Tarrant more understandable, if not any less objectionable. Tarrant has a dream in which he is a penniless outcast; he sees Nancy's face and reaches out for help, but she laughs at him and disappears:

> He plunged on through fern and bramble, and came to a spot of smooth turf; and there, beneath a bush which somehow he recognised, lay a naked, crying child. And by an instant transference of identity, that naked, crying child became *himself*, and he was conscious only of self-pity, for his parents had forsaken him, and he cried in vain for help.[49]

If the child is Tarrant, then Nancy becomes his mother-substitute. His real mother died when he was young, and that loss caused him to grow up into a cold and prickly adult. Tarrant keeps Nancy, and everyone else, at arm's length because of this hidden wound. If readers knew this, they might see him as pitiable, not merely selfish. Gissing cut from his manuscript another secret: that Tarrant is a bastard. Since he was raised as a gentleman, perhaps he was taken from his mother in infancy and given to his father's relatives (a plot device used for the background of Ada Warren in *Isabel Clarendon*). In the novel as finally published, Tarrant's arrogance appears as simply the privilege of being male and upper-class, with no vulnerable childhood to excuse it.[50]

Unhappy Family

Gissing's literary prospects continued to improve, helped by his building up of connections in London. Bullen advertised *In the Year of Jubilee* widely, and photographs of Gissing appeared in magazines. *Eve's Ransom* had been delayed because Fred Barnard, its illustrator, had an alcoholic breakdown. He was replaced, and the novel started to appear in the *Illustrated London News* on 5 January 1895. The more Gissing's name appeared in the press, the more commissions came his way. Jerome K. Jerome, the author of *Three Men in a Boat*, decided to give Gissing regular work on the weekly he edited, *Today*. In December 1894 he asked Gissing for a series of six sketches on 'every-day lower-middle-class London folk'.[1] They started to appear in May, under the title 'Nobodies at Home'. Just pot-boilers, perhaps, but such work would have been a godsend to Gissing in his lean years. He could write one of these sketches in a day, and receive £3 for it. Then, much to his surprise, Smith, Elder came crawling back to ask Gissing for a one-volume novel. Now he could have the pleasure of replying that he was too busy to do anything for them. Gissing told Colles that he wanted to keep his 'solid' books together at Lawrence & Bullen, who had been faithful to him in 'the evil days'.[2]

Less than solid was a short novel for a new series by Fisher Unwin. Gissing got to work on it at once, calling it eventually *Sleeping Fires*. He wrote thirty-three thousand words in less than two months, for a flat payment of £150. In the first three months of 1895 he had already earned £180, more than he had made in a year in the old days. In addition, he received at the end of January fifty guineas from Bullen for the book version of *Eve's Ransom*, having already had £150 for the serial. Methuen had wanted to make a rival offer for the book but Gissing refused, much to Colles's frustration. Gissing could only promise that he would give Methuen some future novel (as eventually he did, with *The Town Traveller*). He naively told Colles that he was impressed by Smith, Elder continuing to advertise his novels; of course they did this because they owned the copyright and the books were profitable. The more Gissing became known, the more Smith, Elder profited from books they had bought from him at very sharp prices. Another drag on Gissing's success was that others were eager to share it. Algernon got £10 from him in January to soften his literary failure, and Morley Roberts got £5. Gissing was never anything but a soft touch with friends, family or publishers; he only survived because he was so frugal with his own needs.

In February Gissing was surprised and pleased to receive a letter from Martha Barnes, his student when he was teaching high school in Waltham, Massachusetts, in the winter of 1876–7. Probably she wrote to him because of the publication in the US of *In the Year of Jubilee*. 'It seems she has read some of my books,' Gissing wrote in his diary, 'writes very nicely, and like an intelligent woman. Replied to her. Strange, strange!'[3] What was strange, perhaps, was that a buried episode of his past had now risen up again, as happens so often in his novels. Martha was a year younger than Gissing, and still unmarried at thirty-seven. From now on Gissing wrote to her regularly and sent her copies of his books as they were published, but none of their letters have survived (Martha had Gissing's letters burnt after her death). The depth of feeling on either side remains a mystery.

Gissing's renewed connection with Martha Barnes was a symptom of his general restlessness. He went for a week in March on a working holiday in Eastbourne, with Edith and Walter. When he came back, he visited Father Osborne Jay in Shoreditch. This was a curious step, because in September 1893 Gissing had written to *The Times* complaining that Jay had plagiarised from *The Nether World* in his book *The Social Problem*. Jay claimed that he greatly admired Gissing, and had only forgotten to put quotation marks around his excerpts. In Shoreditch, Jay was trying to alleviate the distress of 'darkest London', as he called it. With his usual softness towards those who had wronged him, Gissing was willing to be friendly with Jay; after visiting him, he noted: 'Think I see my way to a big book.'[4] This was probably 'The Spendthrift', a serial novel that Gissing started in April, but soon abandoned. He also went up to Wakefield in search of material, visiting old acquaintances and wandering around scenes from his youth.

Perhaps Gissing was thinking of an openly autobiographical novel, of the kind he had never risked in the past. He went from Wakefield to see his old college haunts in Manchester, and to Alderley Edge where he had been at school. From there he went to nearby Wilmslow where, for the first time, he saw his brother's grave. When William died in April 1880, Gissing had not gone to the funeral. He wrote to his mother that the grave was well kept, and that he had climbed Alderley Edge 'and sat there for a long time looking over the fields I used to know so well. It is *twenty years* gone by.'[5] In ten days he had made a complete survey of his youth: Wakefield, Manchester, the slums of London. After all this, though, the novel was not written. Gissing may have feared that a book about his youth would uncover the story of his prison term and destroy his literary reputation. Or perhaps it was not a book he was looking for, but an answer to how he had arrived at his present unhappiness and failed marriage. If this was the case, the past had no real answer to give him. The only possible solution was to be found in his house at Epsom.

A buried life in the suburbs with Edith at least meant small expenses. In May 1895 Gissing could report that he had £436 in the bank, and hoped to reach £1,000 to invest as a safeguard for Walter's future. His great fear was that his son might be left poor and at Edith's mercy. He told Clara Collet that she was welcome to come and visit them at Epsom, but Edith would not go to visit her. Perhaps Edith was developing agoraphobia, avoiding contact with others because she felt anxious or humiliated in social situations. Alternatively, she was just becoming more hostile to outsiders, especially Gissing's relatives, but also servants or landladies. The most worrisome aspect of her behaviour was her ill-treatment of Walter, now three years old, and her lack of any deep affection for him. Gissing was still able to go off and visit his trusted friends and confide his troubles to them. Edith, for whatever reason, could not find support outside the home; she made no friends, and stayed in the house, stewing in discontent. Yet one tie remained: at just about the time Gissing was complaining abut her agoraphobia, she became pregnant again. As with Walter, Gissing recorded nothing about it in his diary until just before the baby was born. It is unlikely that either he or Edith was pleased by the prospect of another child.

At the beginning of April *Eve's Ransom* was published as a book, three days after its last instalment in the *Illustrated London News*.[6] It was the first of Gissing's short novels to appear, and sold briskly at six shillings. Within three weeks of publication a second edition was called for. Gissing had insisted on staying with Lawrence & Bullen; he was hoping for a bigger sale than usual, and agreed to a flat 20 per cent royalty on each copy sold. This proved a poor gamble; after the first flurry sales dropped off, and Gissing made only about £80 in book royalties by the end of 1895 (against the £150 he got for the serial version). Eighty pounds meant sales of about 1,300 copies. Colles surely could have got Gissing more than that, since Fisher Unwin had paid £150 for the copyright of *Sleeping Fires*, a much shorter book. Still, Gissing's star was on the rise, and *Eve's Ransom* improved his literary chances. Instead of being typecast as someone who wrote only long, gloomy sociological novels, Gissing now had two other strings to his bow: lively novellas, and short stories designed for general-interest magazines. The reviewer of *Eve's Ransom* for the *Manchester Guardian* said that the book 'is not only fully up to the intellectual level of Mr Gissing's former work, but it is for the first time ... possessed of just that subtle power of arresting the attention and arousing the sympathies of the reader which such work as *In the Year of Jubilee* or *The Emancipated* lacked'.[7]

The most substantial review of *Eve's Ransom* appeared in the *New York Times*. It was by Harold Frederic, an American novelist living in London:

> [Gissing] has been known to the few for ten years. Suddenly, within the last six months or so, there have risen indications that the many have at last heard about him. ... You begin to hear his name mentioned in those conventional talks about books which pass for literary conversations at dinner tables of non-bookish people. Very often now it happens that, when the names of Meredith and Hardy are quoted, that of Gissing is bracketed with them.

Frederic argued that George Moore's *Esther Waters* (1894) had 'turned the tide in Gissing's fortunes' by arousing interest in society's nether world:

> The public, having discovered that after *Esther Waters* Mr Moore had nothing better to offer than the sickly rehash called *The Celibates*, began to hear vaguely that there was a man who for ten years had been doing work of the same sort as *Esther Waters* – who had indeed made that whole humble and squalid milieu of London's basements and cellars and reeking taprooms his own long before George Moore ever thought of taking it up.[8]

Frederic helped greatly to boost Gissing's status in the US, though he did not grasp Gissing's intellectual disillusion with the socialist movement. Nonetheless, he had assessed Gissing's achievement as far back as *The Unclassed*, and made the case that he was one of England's three leading novelists. This was no small signal of recognition.

Rising fame drew Gissing into more intense social relationships than he had been willing to accept before, and he surely realised that this was a counterweight to life at home, necessary for his emotional survival. He made contact with his childhood friend Henry Hick, now a doctor in Kent, and invited him over for a day to Epsom. Gissing would value Hick's advice on his own health, and on Edith's. Another new friend was Edward Clodd, a banker with intellectual interests who was seventeen years Gissing's senior. Clodd was a strong supporter of T. H. Huxley. His circle of friends were believers in Darwinism who favoured moderate social reform, people with whom Gissing could feel comfortable. Clodd had a country home and a yacht at Aldeburgh, Suffolk, where he hosted all-male intellectual house-parties. Gissing accepted Clodd's invitation for a long weekend at the end of May 1895. The other guests were the literary journalists Clement Shorter and L. F. Austin, the novelist Grant Allen, the solicitor George Whale, and Sir Benjamin Ward Richardson, who was the physician of the Royal Literary Fund. Richardson was an eminent figure in anaesthesia and public health.[9] Grant Allen was a notorious figure at the time of the party. *The Woman Who Did*, a novel that advocated 'free unions' and the right to have two lovers simultaneously, was bringing him £25 a week and a torrent of abuse. His next novel had just been turned down by two publishers because of the backlash from the Oscar Wilde trial.

Wilde had just been convicted of sodomy in his second trial, and sentenced to two years' hard labour. Gissing revealed his feelings to Morley Roberts, his most trusted friend:

> The Wilde business is frightfully depressing. I have a theory that he has got into this, not through natural tendency, but simply in deliberate imitation of the old Greek vice. He probably said: go to, let us try the paederastic pleasures, and come to understand them. No doubt whatever he justified himself, both to himself and to others, by classic precedent. But the catastrophe is awful, and one tries not to think of it overmuch.[10]

From his Oxford days Wilde had believed in the ideal love of boys, as practised by the Greeks; but he does not seem to have become actively homosexual until he was thirty-one, when he was seduced by the seventeen-year-old Robert Ross. Gissing passionately admired the Greeks too, though his paganism stopped at the bedroom door. Sex of any kind could not be for him a merely pleasurable or aesthetic experience, as it tended to be for the ancients. In his dealings with women he remained an uneasy mixture of puritan, idealist and male supremacist, though he was reasonably tolerant of those who behaved differently. Gissing felt compassion for Wilde (and, later, for Dreyfus), rather than the hatred that so many British intellectuals indulged in.

Grant Allen also became a friend after this meeting at Clodd's. *The Woman Who Did* was a silly and shallow book, completely outclassed by *The Odd Women*.[11] It managed to promote sexual freedom in language that would make no maiden blush. In person, though, Allen made a good impression. 'Very talkative,' Gissing wrote, 'and, with me, confidential about his private life. Says his wife suits him admirably, and shares all his

views of sexual matters. Showed me a letter just received from her, beginning "My darling Daddy".'[12] Gissing could make no confidences in return
about his wife's seductive ways.

The masculine pleasures of eating, drinking and gossiping were just
what the doctor ordered for Gissing; he told Clara Collet that the weekend
had done him more good than any holiday in years. He could also transact
some literary business. Shorter asked him to write six more stories for the
Illustrated London News, and twenty short pieces for *The Sketch*. When he
dealt directly with Shorter, Gissing was not obliged to pay any fee to Colles.
He had both enjoyed a luxurious holiday and booked 132 guineas' worth
of commissions. Gissing felt guilty about taking on another packet of pot-
boiling work, but the chance to build up his savings was not to be missed.
As soon as he got home he started on the stories, and decided to make them
into a series on provincial lower-middle-class life, called 'Great Men in
Little Worlds'. Before going to Suffolk he had also signed a contract with
Cassell for a short novel, to be delivered by October; another plan was to
write a one-volume novel that could be sold as a serial, like *Eve's Ransom*.
In June he had four stories published, in different magazines. Yet success
seemed to create almost as much anxiety as failure:

> as I work very slowly – far more slowly than of old – I am in constant fear
> of not being able to meet my engagements. Then again, hardly a day goes
> by but I receive some sort of invitation. . . . All this kind of thing is pleasant
> enough, but ruinous to work. . . . The small stories are, for the most part,
> poor stuff, but they keep me alive. My long novels simply *will not* sell; they
> disappoint everyone connected with them.
>
> It is strange how many letters I get from women, asking for sympathy
> and advice. I really can't understand what it is in my work that attracts the
> female mind.[13]

One of these women was Miss Rosalind Travers of Dorney House,
Weybridge. Gissing grumbled when she wrote to him in March; but he
accepted a gift of asparagus when it came into season, then went to visit
Miss Travers and her parents at the beginning of July. The connection
turned into a real friendship. There was, of course, a great deal to attract
the 'female mind' in novels like *The Odd Women* or *In the Year of Jubilee*.
Rhoda Nunn and Nancy Lord illuminated the conflicting passions of
women in the 1890s, and it was not surprising at all that women should
write to Gissing in the hope of sympathy and understanding. The sad thing
was that by the time Gissing became well known and eligible for a good

match, he was already imprisoned in his wretched marriage to Edith and his bland villa in Epsom.

Gissing dipped his toe in the waters of society, but put his literary production first. In June, after he came back from Suffolk, he wrote four of the short stories he had promised Shorter. He then turned to his short novel for Cassell's, which he had decided to call 'The Paying Guest'. This was to be only twenty-five thousand words, but still Gissing wrote it amazingly fast, in the fifteen days between 2 and 16 July. Of these days two were Sundays, when he wrote nothing, and one was a day off. This was Saturday 13 July, when Gissing was invited to a dinner of the Omar Khayyam Club, of which Clodd was president. The club followed Fitz-gerald's *Rubaiyat* in its devotion to wine and philosophising; it differed in being for men only, with no pleasure-girls to fill the cup. The gathering was at the Burford Bridge Hotel, near Box Hill, and it honoured George Meredith, whose house was just up the road. Editors and critics made up a large share of the club, but members also included Thomas Hardy, Edmund Gosse and Theodore Watts-Dunton (the guardian of Swinburne). Mere-dith himself only came in after the meal, and Gissing thought him 'griev-ously aged; very deaf and shaky, but mind clear as ever'.[14] In fact, he was only sixty-seven, but suffering from *tabes dorsalis*, a degeneration of the spinal cord caused by a syphilitic infection in youth. Nonetheless, he would outlive Gissing. When people were called on for speeches, Gissing rem-inisced about how, unknown to him, Meredith had been the publisher's reader for *The Unclassed*. The dinner was written up in the newspapers, and Gissing was mildly embarrassed to see himself named as one of the three leading contemporary novelists, with Hardy and Meredith. But his two peers seem to have agreed with the ranking: Meredith asked Gissing to visit him at his home, Flint Cottage, and Hardy invited him to Dorchester soon after. Gissing could even be said to stand alone, since neither Hardy nor Meredith would write another novel.

From the heights of dining with Hardy and Meredith, Gissing came down to the depths of going on holiday with Edith and Walter. They went into seaside lodgings at Gorleston, south of Yarmouth, for ten increasingly uncomfortable days. Edith sulked, and their landlady, Mrs Bunn, was a terrible cook and 'outrageously coarse and brutal'. They decided to move, but Mrs Bunn said they must pay for the three weeks they had originally booked, and locked up their luggage as hostage. After a great row at the police station, Gissing had to go back to their lodgings with a policeman to get the luggage, which he retrieved while the Bunns screamed insults. 'The constable tells me,' Gissing noted, 'that these Bunns are Salvation Army people, and *therefore* worthless.'[15] The Gissings spent the balance of their holiday at Yarmouth; when they returned home, their servant had again abandoned them. 'How am I to write,' Gissing asked himself, 'in our life here without a servant?'[16] To a modern ear the question sounds absurd; yet in every lower-middle-class villa up and down the country either there was a servant living in, or the residents were looking for one. A house where heating and cooking were done with coal was intrinsically dirty and labour-intensive; beyond that, domestic work was apportioned according to a complex system of expectations and taboos. The master might work in the garden, but touch nothing in the kitchen; the mistress might dust, but not bring in the coal. The great servant question held its interest because, in the way it was posed in 1895, it was a question without an answer.

After the Box Hill dinner Gissing went over twice to see Meredith (where, also, the servants were 'awkward and careless'). On the first visit, things went well until the appearance of Lady Lawrence, the wife of the local Conservative MP. 'M's manner to Lady L. extremely deferential,' Gissing noted, '"yes, my lady", and so on. This jarred upon me.'[17] Before this intrusion, Gissing was intrigued by Meredith's 'strong interest in women'. On the same day as his first visit to Meredith, Gissing wrote to Hardy about books he was reading, the hooting of owls, and the education of his young son. Walter was off for his first day of school (though still only three). Meredith was looking back at it all, as someone who had 'fought through life and looks quietly back upon all its pleasures and miseries'.[18] The childless Hardy did not share Gissing's concerns about Walter, but agreed with him about owls – 'birds which always interest me by their quaint solitary habits'.[19] Like certain writers, owls sat alone in their tree and hooted plaintively. Gissing went down to Max Gate, Dorchester, for a long weekend on 14 September. Apart from their difference in age – Hardy was seventeen years older – they were close enough in social background to be friends. But they could not be truly cordial, perhaps because Gissing instinctively belittled Hardy, both as a man and as a writer. There was an element of snobbishness in his critique, a trait evident in the book he had just completed, *The Paying Guest*. Gissing took the distinctions of status even within the lower middle class very seriously, and he applied them to Hardy:

> Thomas is of course vastly the intellectual inferior of Meredith. I perceive that he has a good deal of coarseness in his nature – the coarseness explained by humble origin. . . . He seems to me to be a trifle spoilt by success; he runs far too much after titled people, and, in general, the kind of society in which

he is least qualified to shine. . . . Born a peasant, he yet retains much of the
peasant's views of life.[20]

In fact, Hardy's father was a small builder. Hardy learnt Greek and Latin
as a boy, and trained as an architect. Meredith, the son of a tailor, never
went to university. If one extends the list of lower-middle-class novelists –
Defoe, Richardson, Dickens, George Eliot, Joyce, D. H. Lawrence – one
wonders why Gissing was so uncomfortable with his own class, so insistent
on finding the stigma of inferiority in even its most talented members. At
the same time, he wanted Hardy and Meredith to value him more, and titled
nonentities less.

Gissing also needed to belittle Hardy as a writer about nature. 'I admire
Hardy's best work very highly,' he told Bertz, 'but in the man himself I feel
disappointed. To my great surprise, I found that he did not know the names
of flowers in his own fields!'[21] What they most shared was something that
they were least able to talk about, the unhappiness inflicted on them by
their wives:

> In a short private talk with Mrs Hardy, she showed me her discontented
> spirit. Talked fretfully of being obliged to see more society than she liked
> in London, and even said that it was hard to live with people of humble
> origin – meaning Thomas, of course. She then scolded her servants noisily
> for being late with lunch – oh, a painful woman! . . . It is disagreeable to see
> a man like Hardy so unsettled in his life. . . . Of course all this is the
> outcome of misery in his marriage. I suppose he has done his best work; the
> atmosphere of success does not suit him. Vastly better, no doubt, if he had
> married an honest homely woman who would have been impossible in
> fashionable society.[22]

Gissing had married two women who were impossible in fashionable
society, though comfort and peace of mind had not followed. Nor was it
obvious that Hardy would have been happier if he had married someone
like his own restless and wilful rustic heroines. Hardy's strong point in
coping with life was his sense of resignation, a trait that Gissing never
managed to develop.

Seeing the flaws in Hardy's domestic life may have been the spur for
Gissing to make a resolution about his own. While his work was in demand
he would make as much money as he could, and he would relieve the strain
of living with Edith by going away regularly: to Clodd at Aldeburgh, to
Hardy in Dorset, and to his old friend Henry Hick in Kent. Gissing finished
his twenty short pieces for *The Sketch* (usually doing each one in a day),
and took on three more stories from Shorter on top of the six already

commissioned. He made drastic cuts to *The Unclassed* for a new edition
from Lawrence & Bullen, removing material about prostitution that now
seemed too inflammatory.[23] His only policy towards Edith was to try and
subject her to his will. He asked Clara Collet to be joint guardian with
Algernon of his children, in the event of his death. She agreed, but only if
Edith was made a guardian too. After coming to Epsom to talk things over
with Edith, Collet wrote a letter (which has not survived) asking him to
soften his position. Gissing's response was to dig in deeper. He said he was
battling against 'deathly tendencies', and was like the captain of a ship that
was headed for a wreck. In such a situation, the only way to prevent a
disaster was for everyone to follow the captain's orders:

> My great mistake has been in living a life utterly subordinate to Edith's
> short-sighted wishes. . . . for nearly four years I was shut up at home, and
> bore most patiently – out of regard for Edith – with things which would
> have frenzied almost any other man. I was wrong; that kind of life is
> done with. It meant a prolongation of my narrow circumstances, and so an
> embitterment of the domestic difficulty.[24]

Only if the household was run in exactly the way he wanted would
Gissing be able to write well and earn enough for them all to live comfortably. Edith should accept that he had to sit alone in his study, quietly,
for so many hours a day. Instead, he had been 'living in the kitchen' – that
is, constantly dragged into scenes of domestic uproar. Things were going
badly in the house because Edith refused to do things in the right way,
preferring to do them in her way. This brought Gissing to the point of
complete exasperation:

> I will do my best to be gentle and forbearing; more than that I cannot
> promise, until Edith exerts herself to be worthy of more. Utterly unmerited
> abuse, slander, obstruction – day after day, year after year – has worked its
> natural effect. You do not know what these years have been; you would not
> believe the story were it faithfully told. I have done marvels; a weaker man
> (and I am not a very strong one, in will) would have sunk very low.
> All Edith has to do is not to quarrel with her bread and butter.[25]

Collet found herself in two minds. As a feminist, she tried to make
Gissing see that even if he was objectively right in his domestic requirements, he was treating Edith oppressively. He wanted her to do what he
wanted without question, and expected her to obey, in large part because
he was a man and she was a woman. But Collet was not ready to confront
Gissing on this. She liked and admired him, and she believed that a working-

class woman like Edith was in fact inferior, and in need of guidance if not subjugation. For his part, Gissing expected Collet to validate his outrage at Edith's disobedience:

> When we were at Yarmouth . . . I told Edith that the boy was not to be taken to hear the blackguard singers on the beach. As thanks to me for my concessions on other points, she deliberately took the child and sat with him for an hour listening to low songs and the words to this day are humming in the poor lad's head. . . . No man could, or ought to, endure such behaviour as this. After it – what becomes of affection?[26]

Gissing could not imagine that listening to comic songs on the beach might be a welcome relief for Edith from a gloomy and irritable husband. In Naples he had been delighted to hear the street-singers everywhere. In England, he feared that they might infect a three-year-old with working-class tastes.

Gissing had now been with Edith for five years, and she was pregnant with their second child. He had married her out of loneliness, but also in the hope of making her into a docile and helpful companion. Even if she was a flawed person to begin with, Gissing's treatment of her was not designed to bring out her better qualities. The intellectual concepts of feminism may have been beyond her, but she was in a state of inarticulate revolt against the yoke her husband had placed on her. Gissing never loved her in the way he had loved Nell. For a time he had blinded himself to Nell's faults, but with Edith the faults were most of what he saw from the beginning. He married her because he expected to reconstruct her to his own specifications. We can never know if the marriage might have been happier if Gissing had been more affectionate and less demanding. Edith's later excesses, and her complete loss of sanity by 1902, suggest some organic process driving her mental symptoms. Still, she might have functioned better if she had married someone closer to the class she had been brought up in. Bernard Shaw had not yet written *Pygmalion*, but in the 1890s Gissing was acting out a tragic parody of the story. He entered the affair believing that women were, by nature, ready to be moulded by a firm masculine authority. Instead, the more he tried to impose his will on Edith, the more she resisted him. In his novels he was well able to understand the perverse consequences of seeking absolute control over another person, as Widdowson does with his wife Monica in *The Odd Women*. Yet in his own house Gissing kept tightening the screws on Edith until the final catastrophe, now not far off.

In the midst of this domestic uproar, Gissing resolved to put his writing career on a more lucrative track. He had a solid backlog of commissioned stories and sketches, and could expect to get more requests from editors so long as he continued to deliver reliably. His income from writing in 1895 would be more than £500, the most he had ever made, and when he made up his accounts for the year his savings had increased to £560, because he always managed to spend less than he earned. Algernon was another story: he kept on with his novels, moaned and fussed about his prospects, and seemed to get less for each successive book. His latest, *The Sport of Stars*, was a two-volume novel that went for only £25 to Hurst & Blackett. Algernon was becoming more openly dependent on his family to keep going, and all George could do was limit his requests: if he asked for £20 as a loan, George would send him £10 as a gift. There would be respite while Algernon made his rounds elsewhere, to his sisters and to his wife's relatives; then it would be George's turn again. The more his brother succeeded, the more justified Algernon felt in getting his share of the rewards.

In October Gissing accepted an invitation from John Lane to write a long short story for *The Yellow Book*. After the Wilde trial this periodical had been purged of its Beardsley illustrations and other whiffs of decadence. Gissing could help return it to a safer middle way. He wrote 'The Foolish Virgin' in a week, earning £25. It was on the topical question of 'the great servant difficulty', and Gissing wrote from the heart. He was in as much difficulty as anybody, in spite of offering what he considered a high annual income – by coincidence, that same £25. That was for a live-in servant who received room and board; many got only £15, or even less. In the story, a selfish and idle middle-class woman is forced to make a living by becoming a servant to a young wife with three children. She becomes a healthier and better person through hard work. The husband shakes his 'dreamy and compassionate head' over his servant's loss of status, but his wife disagrees:

> 'Of course I'm sorry for her, but there are plenty of people more to be pitied. Work she must, and there's only one kind of work she's fit for. It's no small thing to find your vocation – is it? Thousands of such women – all meant by nature to scrub and cook – live and die miserably because they think themselves too good for it.'[27]

Miss Jewell, this genteel 'odd woman', has to scrub floors because her suitor, Mr Cheeseman, has failed in the masculine arena of business. The story suggests that society is breaking down because neither men nor women are able to do what nature designed them for. Under the pressure of his unhappy marriage, Gissing was falling back on a vulgarly Darwinian

Thomas Waller Gissing (1829–1870), 'the good father'.

Margaret Gissing (1832–1913), 'My mother has lived a very narrow life in a little provincial town; she is purely domestic, and religious in a very formal way.'

Ellen Gissing (1867–1938), the youngest of the family, and Gissing's favourite of his four siblings.

Gissing in 1884, by Naudin. Probably taken for the publication of *The Unclassed*.

Bellevue Prison, Hyde Road, Manchester (since demolished).

Domenichino, *The Hunt of Diana* (Palazzo Corsini, Rome), detail. 'The loathsome "Susanna" ... where the woman props herself on her back in shallow water, and is a mere prostitute at play.' Gissing's memory slipped; he remembered the subject as Susanna and the Elders, rather than Diana at her bath.

Marianne Helen ('Nell') Harrison (1858–1888), Gissing's first wife.

Mrs Sarah Gaussen, the inspiration for *Isabel Clarendon*.

Rosalind Williams, sister of Beatrice Webb, in 1889. Gissing had a brief affair with her in 1898.

Clara Collet, feminist civil servant, staunch friend of Gissing.

The Marylebone Workhouse, one of Gissing's bugaboos. 'Peculiar bloodlessness of the old people; their white seamed faces. Looked like respectful automatons.'

'The Home Quartett: Mrs Vernon Lushington and Children', by Arthur Hughes (1883). Gissing tutored the girls; the eldest, Catherine (playing the cello) became Kitty Maxse, a model for Virginia Woolf's Mrs Dalloway.

Edith Underwood (1867–1917), the 'work-girl' who became Gissing's second wife.

Gissing in September 1893, by Alfred Ellis.

Gissing in Rome, 1898, with the makers of late-Victorian popular culture. *l to r*: Gissing, E. W. Hornung, Arthur Conan Doyle, H. G. Wells.

Queen Victoria's Diamond Jubilee, 1897. Of the Golden Jubilee, Gissing wrote: 'after all it is something to have seen the most gigantic organised exhibition of fatuity, vulgarity and blatant blackguardism on record. Anything more ignoble can scarcely be conceived.'

Gabrielle Edith Fleury (1868–1954), in the 1890s.

Camille Brion MARSEILLE

Anna Fleury (1839–1910), 'Maman'.

Gissing at Trient, Switzerland, in August 1899. His mother or sisters have cut Gabrielle out of the picture but her skirt is visible.

Gissing, May 1901, by Elliott & Fry. The lesion on the right side of his forehead is visible.

LEFT *Our Friend the Charlatan*, 1901, illustration by Launcelot Speed. The hero Dyce Lashmar (with moustache) witnesses the death of Mr Robb, MP. Lashmar will run for his seat, unsuccessfully.

ABOVE The sanatorium at Nayland, Suffolk, where Gissing was a patient in the summer of 1901. Now converted into flats.

view of gender roles. *The Paying Guest* made a case similar to 'The Foolish Virgin': a silly young woman needs to be tamed by the rough common sense and physical force of her lover, Mr Cobb. She hates being bullied, but on a deeper level knows that she is born to submit.

The Paying Guest appeared at the beginning of January 1896, a month after *Sleeping Fires*. Both books were well received. They were relatively light and cheerful, and Gissing was now in favour with the critics. These lesser works were given a better reception than their weightier predecessors. H. G. Wells reviewed both of them and hailed Gissing as a rising talent. His judgement of *The Paying Guest* seemed to turn Gissing's message on its head. The Mumfords, who try to teach Louise Derrick common sense and good manners, are taken by Wells to be the villains of the book:

> In and about London there must be tens of thousands of Mumfords, living their stiff, little, isolated, pretentious, and exceedingly costly lives, without any more social relations with the people about them than if they were cave-dwellers, jealous, secluded, incapable of understanding the slightest departure from their own ritual, in all essentials savages still – save for a certain freedom from material brutality.[28]

The great joke of the book, Wells said, was 'The grotesque incapacity of everyone concerned to realise for a moment [Louise's] mental and moral superiority to the Mumfords'. Louise may have shown plenty of vitality in challenging the rules of genteel suburban life; nonetheless, Gissing clearly sees her as a loose cannon, good for nothing until tied down. Wells had a constant need to rebel and to deride; Gissing wanted to have more order in his suburban household, rather than less. Wells believed that the grimness of Gissing's previous novels had been a strategy to impress the critics. Now he was showing flashes of his true self – which turned out to be rather like Wells's own:

> He has shown beyond all denial an amazing gift of restraint, a studious avoidance of perceptible wit, humour or pathos that appealed irresistibly to their sympathies. Now if he will let himself go, which he may do with impunity, and laugh and talk and point with his finger and cough to hide a tear, and generally assert his humanity, he may even at last conquer the reading public.[29]

Gissing could be a good companion, as Wells would find out when they met; but the iron had gone too deep into his soul for him to become the jolly madcap that Wells was calling for. Gissing did not feel safe enough to indulge his antic tendencies – life was too desperate an affair for that – and in his books he kept his emotions in fetters. No one in a Gissing novel lets himself go without discovering harsh consequences.

Another reason to doubt Wells's reading of *The Paying Guest* was Gissing's own judgement on the book: he said it was a 'paltry story'.[30] In part this came from his frustration at spending so much of his time on short commissioned works, which had to please a mass readership. Gissing was a classicist who believed a philosophic life was best, and that it required leisure and peace of mind to be enjoyed. But his imagination was preoccupied with what made contemplation impossible: the grim struggle for economic survival. It followed that his characters ceased to interest him – or his readers – once they had their safe thousand pounds a year. Like most obsessive characters, Gissing had a problem with pleasure. Now that he was earning twice as much money as ever before, he just saved half of it and wrote faster. When he imagined characters with ample money, education and leisure, they usually had some form of 'Ryecroft syndrome': an inclination to withdraw from the world and find the highest good in not being bothered.

Gissing's great hope for 1896 was that he could finish off his minor commissions and concentrate on a serious and substantial novel. Serious, however, did not mean anything like *Jude the Obscure*, which Hardy's publishers sent to Gissing on 2 November:

> This is a sad book. For one thing, Thomas has absolutely lost his saving Humour – not a trace of it. The bitterness which has taken its place is often wonderfully effective – certain passages go beyond anything I know in vehement illustration of pessimism. But the book as a whole is wearisome. ... There are great and fine things in the book, but it suffers from Hardy's determination to arraign life.[31]

Gissing had placed his characters in situations just as bleak as anything in Hardy. What he objected to was Hardy's philosophy and his quarrel with God. Gissing agreed that individual hopes would always be blighted by the vast indifference of both nature and the social system. But to 'arraign life' was to assume that someone or something could be blamed for human suffering. Hardy felt that he knew enough about the universe to hold it to account for the pain it inflicted. Gissing, as he told H. G. Wells later, was not sure that there was anything available for us to judge:

> By the bye, you speak of 'God'. Well, I understand what you mean, but the word makes me stumble rather. I have grown to shrink utterly from the use of such terms, and, though I admit perforce a universal law, am so estranged

by its unintelligibility that not even a desire to be reverent can make those old names in any way real to me.[32]

Whether God was cruel or kind, he had to be personal first, and Gissing could not imagine that any such person existed. It followed that individual misfortune had no larger significance. Gissing's denial of a tragic sense of life may have been a defence mechanism that helped him to endure his own unhappiness. Still, he held to his belief that Hardy's sunnier early novels were his best work, and that the more he took things too hard, the worse he wrote.

For all his disappointment with *Jude the Obscure*, Gissing realised that it had weight, and if he wanted to write something comparable he needed to change the pattern of life he had slipped into over the past two years:

> Seeing that my books yield very little, and journalistic work a fair sum, it is doubtful whether I ought to refuse invitations to write; but there seems to be a fear that my reputation will suffer if I don't presently turn out something solid. So I am taking the serious step of living upon capital for a year or so. The worst of it is there will shortly come two or three months during which I shall not put pen to paper.[33]

The period when he could not write was the time of Edith's giving birth, from January on. Gissing was extraordinarily reticent about the intimate side of his marriage, and gave no clue as to why Edith became pregnant again in 1895. Contraception was inconvenient and unreliable, but it did exist. Perhaps there was some reconciliation between Gissing and Edith in April, when the child was conceived; perhaps Edith wanted a daughter and Gissing agreed, in the hope it would make her happier.

Gissing's sexual life remains obscure, since he almost never spoke or wrote openly about it. There may be some clues in his response to Morley Roberts's *A Question of Instinct* (1895). In this novel, a man of bigamous temperament has a child with an idealistic new woman, but wants her to accept his having a mistress too. Roberts peddled the curious mixture of Darwinism and feminism that was popular at the time with people like Grant Allen or H. G. Wells. Motherhood should be supported by the state, so that women could love freely without putting themselves at the mercy of a male provider. Men would also be freed, to express their need for promiscuity. The heroine of *A Question of Instinct* speaks of allowing men 'to live their natural lives without cramping themselves to provide for others'. Gissing agreed, he told Roberts: 'My own experience teaches me how terribly cramping it is for a father to take keen interest in the child from the very first, and to have much to do with it.'[34] By allowing himself to become attached to Walter, Gissing had added more chains to his imprisonment within marriage. This was a different problem from the one treated in Roberts's novel, which was that marriage frustrated male desires for promiscuous sex. Gissing was not worried about having several women at once, he was worried about how to live with one. The only solution he could see was the one offered in both *A Question of Instinct* and *In the Year of Jubilee*: 'some day husbands and wives, or whatever name they have, will live in entirely separate houses.'[35]

The period leading up to Edith's confinement was a particularly gloomy one for Gissing, with servant troubles, domestic quarrels, and not much written except for a few short stories. He was still casting about for the consolations of friendship, and met up again with his college friend John George Black, now working at the Public Record Office. They had gone whoring together twenty years before; now Black was a married man with numerous children. Another pair of old friends from America turned up in London: Dr Marie Zakrzewska and her friend Julia Sprague. Dr Zakrzewska was the founder of the New England Hospital for Women and Children; she and her friend were characters out of Henry James's *The Bostonians*, 'Boston marriage' included. Gissing saw as much of them as he could, and introduced them to Clara Collet. He had no nostalgia for his American days, but still felt grateful to those who had befriended him in that lonely year.

Edith gave birth to a son, Alfred Charles, on 20 January 1896. Although she had hoped for a girl, she became much more fond of Alfred than of Walter. Again she had trouble with her breasts, but Gissing was determined that she should feed Alfred regardless. 'Walter was all but starved on beastly bottle food,' Gissing told Collet, 'and of course screamed ceaselessly for six months.'[36] Things were a little more peaceful this time: Edith stayed upstairs with Alfred and her nurse, while Gissing spent his whole day looking after Walter, who was now four years old. The morning was lesson time, and before long Walter knew how to read. Gissing himself had no chance to work until Walter went to bed at half-past six, and he was so tired that he could only read after that. He felt that working as a nursemaid was making him 'nervously ill'; nonetheless, it was work that he believed in:

> One of my misfortunes in boyhood was that my father had exceedingly little time to give me. His leisure was devoted, mostly, to municipal business. Now, I have often asked (not in the wrong spirit) whether he was justified

in giving those hours to the public good, when I and his other children would have benefited so greatly by more of his companionship. Seriously, I count this one of the causes of my wasted life. I needed discipline more than most boys, and had next to nothing of it – that is to say, of the *kind* by which I should have benefited. So, now I ask what right I have to refuse myself to the little lad. If this sacrifice of days will help him to get sanely through the terrible years of youth – heaven forbid that I should grumble! For I would rather the boy died straightway than that he should plunge through dark solitude, at the most critical time of life, and suffer as his father did.[37]

As usual, Gissing found it difficult to distinguish between what he felt and what he ought to feel. Thomas Gissing was another obsessive type, who filled up all his spare time with self-imposed civic duties. George wanted more love from his father, to make up for the love his mother was unable to give. But now he complains, not of too little love, but of too little discipline. Sometime in his formative years, he converted his need for fatherly affection into the conviction that he was full of bad impulses, from which his father should have saved him. In the present, Edith seemed to be an even more inadequate mother for Walter than Mrs Gissing had been for George. The worse Edith treated Walter, the more Gissing felt he needed to do to make up for it. But he was taking on more than he could handle, and starting a chain of events that would break up his family within a year.

If caring for Walter made it hard for Gissing to write, the arrival of Alfred was another reason why he had to write. Algernon was always there with his hand out; Margaret and Ellen were starting a little school in their house at Wakefield, and Gissing sent them £5 to help with the launch. He may have had a sinking feeling, though, in seeing them follow the path of the hapless Madden sisters in *The Odd Women*. Then there was Edith's nurse to be paid. Gissing had to go back into his study, shut the door, and start meeting his quota of pages. Meanwhile, an accident with the oil lamp in the hall had convinced him that he needed to install gas lighting. On 2 March, while Gissing was away in London, a workman had the bright idea of testing the new pipes with a candle. This set off an explosion that blew down the drawing-room ceiling and started a fire. The workman suffered burns, but Edith and the children escaped injury. While repairs were being done, Gissing sent Edith and the boys to stay in furnished rooms at Dorking for a week. This allowed him to start writing short stories as quickly as he could, to bring in money. In less than a month he wrote five stories, of which four were eventually published.[38] The easiest way to produce so fast was to use little anecdotes about the world he knew best, playing the role defined for him by H. G. Wells, a 'minute and melancholy observer of the lower middle-class'.[39] Gissing's own melancholy was not in doubt: Edith came back early from Dorking, workmen were in the house, and there was 'utter misery' in the life he was leading. 'I try to keep off insanity by planting cabbages,' he told Clara Collet.[40] When he planned to take Walter on a visit to his family at Wakefield, Edith told the boy 'that she never wished to see him again, – that she wished he had died in one of his illnesses, – that he was a little wretch'.[41] Gissing decided to take her at her word. He and Walter left for the north on 8 April; Gissing was at the end of his tether, and knew that unless he could find some peace and quiet he would have a complete breakdown.

Gissing was not the only one at the end of his tether. Walter, at Wakefield, was also showing the effects of growing up in an unhappy family:

> At night tremendous scene with the boy, over his bath. Madge bathing him, and of course he refused to come out. He fought and shrieked – a worse outbreak than I ever knew. I had to seize him and carry him to bed. ... A doleful business altogether, and showing that it would be criminal to take him back to the old life in our home which is no home. He must stay here, evidently, and be tamed.[42]

Gissing seems to have seen only the symptom, not the disease. He charged Margaret and Ellen with curbing Walter's outbreaks, and went off alone for a week in north Wales. A photo taken at this time shows him looking shockingly haggard and aged beyond his thirty-nine years. He had been ground down by life with Edith, and desperately needed a respite. He went first to visit his old headmaster at Lindow Grove School, James Wood, who was now retired and living at Colwyn Bay. From there Gissing went to stay at Nefyn on the Lleyn peninsula, a beautiful setting where he walked on the beach and the hills, and calmed his soul. As his spirits rose, he took notes on the Welsh setting for his new novel, *The Whirlpool*, where Wales would become a refuge from the horrors of fashionable London.

When he got back to Wakefield, Gissing was resolved about Walter's future. The boy would live with Margaret and Ellen, and attend their new school where he would have friends to play with. Gissing would pay £10 per quarter for his keep. Walter's behaviour was already much better, Gissing told Algernon, and he would be 'as sweet-tempered as he is naturally affectionate'. Edith had told Walter 'I always hated you'; now Gissing would take her at her word.[43] He would return to Epsom and when Edith said 'Where's Walter?' she would learn what he had done. He expected a terrible scene, and there was one; but for once he had drawn his line in the sand:

> *I* am responsible for his future, and I *know* I am doing the right – the only right – thing.
>
> Impossible to make you believe the treatment – the ceaseless insult – to which I have been subjected for a year or two. ... It has come to Edith's opening my letters (from relatives), that she may find new forms of vulgar abuse. In the presence (or hearing) of servants (even, I should think, of neighbours) she brings revolting charges against me, and prays fervently (her one prayer) for misery to befall me and mine. No one could bear it.
>
> I must live here for the present. I don't know how things will go on. But the boy never comes to be permanently at *home* again. Rather I will go with him to a foreign country.[44]

Clearly, Gissing's marriage to Edith was dead; yet he felt that his least worst option was to stay on at Worple Road, if only to protect Alfred. Beyond this, Gissing felt that he had won a victory over Edith by removing Walter, and could now consolidate his gains. It was his old *idée fixe* that he had ruined his life by giving in to everyone around him: 'Entreaty and reasoning having proved vain – indeed ruinous – I find that savage determination works, for the present, fairly well. There is a calm.'[45] Gissing now started a routine of going into his study at nine in the morning and staying there until bedtime; he expected the house to be quiet, and he made it a rule that there would be no discussion at all of the problems in their marriage. That allowed him to get started on his new novel, of which he had great hopes; he wrote the first page on 28 April, four days after his new policy of giving Edith the silent treatment. His working title for the book was 'Benedict's Household'; eventually it would become *The Whirlpool*.

With quiet at home, if not peace, Gissing was able to work steadily through May and June. He wrote long and affectionate letters to Walter once a week, and Walter wrote back in four-year-old style. He was becoming more tractable under Margaret and Ellen's care, so Gissing was willing to let them make a little Christian of him. 'Let the little fellow think as a child during his childhood,' Gissing told Clara Collet, 'and let us hope that some moral good may result from it.'[46] Gissing felt the pain of being separated from Walter, but felt that he could not protect him from Edith so long as he stayed at home. When he wrote to Walter he said not a word about Edith, as if the boy had no mother at all. Edith wrote to him too,

without mentioning his father, and sending a confusing mixture of endear-
ments and threats: 'I hear you enjoy your days now and you don't want
your mother at all. . . . dear Walter you are not a bad boy now I am so glad
because you will be able to teach your brother to be good. . . . With much
love and many kisses and no beatings.'[47] Edith still distressed Gissing by
getting into screaming rows with the servants, but life at Worple Road
went from being agonising to merely painful.

Gissing took advantage of the relative calm to get out more often, with
three dinner parties in one week. His acquaintances now included most of
the leading writers of the day: he went again to see Meredith at Box Hill,
and on 20 June met J. M. Barrie at an Omar Khayyam dinner at Marlow.
Barrie was a surprise for Gissing: 'I had imagined [him] rather tall, rather
elegant; I found a small, slouching, boyish fellow, carelessly dressed.'[48]
Gissing did not like Barrie's *Sentimental Tommy* at all, when he read it later
in the year; but he got on well with Barrie himself, and was invited to his
house. It often seems that Gissing's lack of popular success helped to win
him the respect of more commercial writers. He also struck up a friendship
with Israel Zangwill, the popular novelist, playwright and Zionist. *Children
of the Ghetto*, which Zangwill had published in 1892, was a kind of sequel
to *The Nether World*, though with a less bitter taste. 'It is not only a
remarkable, but in certain respects, a grand book,' Gissing felt. 'It is not
only a story, but a page of the world-history, and written in a noble spirit.'[49]
Unlike Trollope or George Eliot, Gissing never showed any special interest
in Jewish life. His common ground with Zangwill was an interest in
working-class London, and that they had both made their way to dinner at
the Savoy through scholarships and literary talent. A week after that dinner,
Gissing went to Zangwill's house for an intimate talk:

> The mysterious Gissing has come within my ken at last and sitting in my
> study poured out his sad soul. He is a handsome youthful chap but seems to
> have bungled his life in every possible way, and after a terrible uphill fight
> to be still burdened with some woman who, I suspect, breaks out in drink.
> He hates woman and is not in love with life. From another source I hear
> that the cloud on his career had its origin in imprisonment for stealing
> money from overcoats &c when he was *the* pride of Owen's College,
> Manchester. This statement being 'libellous' please do not 'publish' this
> letter. He is now making a fair income but unfortunately he has no interest
> in his old books and he will probably never write anything again as good as
> *Thyrza* or *New Grub Street* or *Demos* or the *Nether World*. Still I encouraged
> him to go on, in his old groove and not now to knuckle under to the popular
> demand.[50]

Zangwill probably learnt of Gissing's conviction from Frederic Harrison, who was also at the Savoy dinner. Since Zangwill passed the story on to his friend Montagu Eder, one wonders how many people in literary circles knew Gissing's secret by 1896. Whatever was known, not a word was published about it until after Gissing's death, though people surely gossiped about Gissing behind his back. He knew that a professional writer had to live by his reputation, and all he could do was try to keep his private life as quiet as possible, and hope that his two unsuitable marriages would never become fodder for the popular press.

Gissing's reputation was going up another step, thanks to a perennial quirk of the literary world: reviewers decided that he deserved more respect, so they praised highly two books – *Sleeping Fires* and *The Paying Guest* – that were much weaker than novels published earlier. In the US, six of Gissing's novels were published between April 1895 and April 1896. *In the Year of Jubilee* was the one that started a minor Gissing boom. Kate Michaelis spoke of it as 'that strong and masterful book that a few months ago set the world at large to reading the previously neglected works of Gissing'.[51] She looked forward to the new novel on which Gissing was at work (*The Whirlpool*), 'which will take all his time for the coming year, and which he considers his greatest book'.[52] In England, the two most significant reviews of *Sleeping Fires* and *The Paying Guest* were by H. G. Wells, writing anonymously in the *Saturday Review*. Wells liked the way in which Gissing was starting to reveal his own prejudices in these two novels; his earlier books had suffered from the 'colourless theory of fiction', in which Gissing, like George Moore, had concealed his own judgement of his characters.

There had been no shortage of strong emotions in Gissing's earlier novels; Wells's real complaint was that Gissing did not get up on the stage with his characters and speak in his own voice. Gissing's novels were dramatic productions, in which the reader was not told directly where to look for the truth. Some of Gissing's self-effacement had come from the need to conceal his private life; but he also chose to have different characters speak for one side or the other of his internal conflicts. These practices were part of Gissing's strength as a novelist, and it was not good advice for Wells to ask him to step forward as an egotistical presence in his future books. That strategy suited Wells's own taste for the limelight, and his talent for making himself into an attractive public personality; but Gissing was best advised to follow his own path.

Breaking Away

When Gissing started work on *The Whirlpool*, he was very conscious that since he had moved to Epsom in September 1894 he had not produced any major work, just short stories and three lesser novels. All had been written on commission, to keep the pot boiling; but he also felt that his life with Edith had been too disordered for him to be able to write at his highest level. Gissing was able to start writing *The Whirlpool* once he had removed Walter into his sisters' care, and he knew that it was crucial for his reputation to carry the novel through. It would be a panoramic novel of upper-middle-class London society, doing for that world what Gissing's proletarian novels had done for the lower depths. By the end of June 1896, though, he was again so nervous that work on the novel was grinding to a halt. He felt that it was his duty to have his usual kind of family summer holiday; he also knew that there was no chance he would enjoy it.

Gissing reserved three rooms on the Lincolnshire coast at Mablethorpe, and they set off on 22 July, with a nursemaid for Alfred, and a beach tent that Gissing had paid £5.10 for. As soon as they were settled in, he went over to Wakefield and brought Walter back with him to Mablethorpe, reuniting the family for the first time in four months. Walter was only four, but Gissing already had definite plans for him:

> I grow more and more determined that he shall grow up away from London, and I will take very good care that he has either trade or profession very clearly cut out for him, if I live long enough. The grievously unhappy men are those who have no definite place in society, and in consequence no regularity of income, no social intercourse of the wholesome kind. On that very account, I don't grieve much at the thought that I shall leave him no money.[1]

These were not tactful words to address to Algernon, since his own life was exactly the kind that Gissing was warning against. Gissing's formula for happiness was somewhat bleak: discipline in childhood, regular employment once one grew up. He was unable or unwilling to recognise that the key to happiness was love, and that Walter was already suffering from lack of it:

> Nothing could be more difficult than my position as regards the boy Walter. All but every statement made to him he answers with a blunt contradiction; to all but every bidding he replies 'I shan't'. As I sit in the room, where the nurse-girl is present, he calls me all manner of abusive names. . . . He knows there is no harmony between his mother and me, and he begins to play upon the situation . . . The poor child is ill-tempered, untruthful, precociously insolent, surprisingly selfish. I can see that Wakefield *may* have a good influence, but only the merest beginnings show as yet. – I should like to know how the really wise and strong father would act in this position. But no wise and strong man could have got into it. Talk of morals! What a terrible lesson is the existence of this child, born of a loveless and utterly unsuitable marriage.[2]

In his letters to Margaret, Gissing did not dare tell her how much he despaired of Walter. No doubt his ugly birthmark made it less likely that he would get the spontaneous affection that he obviously needed. Gissing's sense of duty made him do his best for his son; but he was a novelist with a sad lack of insight into the boy's inner life (in his novels, also, there are few memorable child characters). Walter needed to be improved by order and discipline, and that was that. There may have been a streak of vulgar Darwinism in Gissing's attitude, identifying Walter as the son of a degenerate mother. His despairing cry – 'Talk of morals!' – seems to have meant: 'This is what happens when the need for sexual fulfilment can only be satisfied by marriage.'

Gissing found Mablethorpe a nice, quiet little resort, and was pleased that it was near Somersby: Tennyson had grown up there, and had often played on Mablethorpe sands. But keeping Walter busy and happy was a challenge, and it gave Gissing an appreciation of what it meant for his sisters to look after a whole pack of boys in their home:

> If you feel able to bear this toil, you are doing something a thousand times better than all the scribbling of journalistic women. This work of education – especially with the very young – is the highest of our time; no labour is more worthy of respect, or – if rightly done – half so fruitful of vast results. . . . To lay the solid foundations of one worthy life is greatly more than to 'succeed' in this or that 'career' which people chatter about.[3]

Perhaps Gissing was regretting his treatment of the Madden sisters in *The Odd Women*, old-maid schoolteachers who look pitiful next to the vital feminist Rhoda Nunn. He did not seem concerned, though, that female teachers were preparing boys for careers that were still not open to women. And no matter how important it was to raise Walter well, Gissing had no intention of raising him himself.

After the holiday Gissing soon went off again, to stay with his old patron Frederic Harrison at Haslemere. He had not seen his former pupils, Austin and Bernard, for ten years. They were now young men starting their careers – one in the diplomatic service, one a painter – though Gissing was not greatly impressed by their talents. On the train coming back he sat across from a young woman who looked familiar: it was Kitty Maxse, whom he had tutored when she was Kitty Lushington. Her husband Leopold was now editor of the *National Review*, which had recently printed three of Gissing's stories. Kitty was twenty-nine and very much the fine lady; she was a close friend of the Stephen sisters, and Virginia would use her as a model for Mrs Dalloway.

Kitty Maxse may have given Gissing some ideas for *The Whirlpool* too, which was a tract on the destructive effects of fashionable life in London. There is Mrs Bennet Frothingham, for example, 'a good-natured, feather-brained, rather pretty woman, whose sprightliness never passed the limits of decorum, and who seemed to have better qualities than found scope in her butterfly existence'.[4] Gissing had worked on the novel for four months, but in the holiday season had come to a full stop. The day after meeting Kitty Maxse, he started to rewrite the novel from the beginning. It was to be a major work of 180,000 words, the equivalent of a three-decker in one volume. Gissing shut himself in his study at Epsom and buckled down to his task for eight hours a day. For relief he gardened or read in English and Greek (he was working his way through Plutarch's life of Pericles). This relatively tranquil existence was possible because of Walter's removal to Wakefield. Edith tried to keep in touch with him, but when she signed a letter 'With much love and kisses' Walter drew next to it a picture of a woman holding a stick![5] She was still bitter that Gissing had taken him away and put him into the care of the hated Wakefield relatives. Clara Collet went to see Walter at the end of October, and wrote Gissing that she would come to Epsom to report on her visit. Edith flew into a rage, and Gissing had to flee the house and meet Collet in London.

Algernon was now suffering another of his breakdowns. He left his family at Willersey and went off to Richmond, Yorkshire. Gissing sent him a cheque, probably for £10 or £20, which was all he could afford. He could

count on at least £150 once he finished *The Whirlpool*; what worried him
was whether he could go on writing a novel a year for much longer. 'I don't
like the cough which has troubled me this last half year,' he told Clara
Collet, 'it is very like that from which my father suffered just at my age,
and which killed him at 42. As soon as I have done my work, I shall have a
talk with the doctor.'[6] Gissing had just had his thirty-ninth birthday, and
his gloom about his health was justified. His constitution, he believed, 'was
ruined in garrets and basements, some fifteen to twenty years ago' (perhaps
it was ruined in Nell's bed).[7] In the years that were left to him, his main
hope was to build up some capital for Walter and Alfred.

These worries raised the stakes on the success of *The Whirlpool*. Gissing
wrote the last words on 18 December: his hero, Harvey Rolfe, walks home
happily, holding the hand of his seven-year-old son. When Gissing took
the manuscript to Bullen three days later, he got a warm reception. Bullen
offered 150 guineas in advance for the book; for the last Gissing book he
published, *Eve's Ransom*, the advance had been 100 guineas. He gave
Gissing a cheque for seventy-five guineas on the spot, with the rest on
publication. Gissing had not used Colles's services for *The Whirlpool*; that
saved him the agent's 10 per cent, except that Colles probably could have
got him better terms for his first major novel since *In the Year of Jubilee*.
Bullen would publish the book at six shillings; of this Gissing's royalty was
a shilling, so a first printing of two thousand copies would earn him £100.
He needed a large second printing to get past his advance.

Bullen received the manuscript of *The Whirlpool* on Monday 21 December, and Gissing received the first proofs on Thursday of the following
week. Bullen suggested substantial cuts, amounting to twenty-five or thirty
printed pages, and Gissing accepted most of these.[8] He knew that the book
would appear early in 1897, and with a good advertising campaign behind
it. Christmas Day was as cheerless as usual, with only Gissing, Edith and
the baby to celebrate it; he went off on a six-mile walk by himself, and read
Arthur Morrison's novel A *Child of the Jago*. This was a sensational account
of life in the East End slums. Morrison knew what he was talking about,
having grown up there himself, but Gissing thought his book 'poor stuff'.[9]
After Christmas Gissing went to see Dr Beaumont, the local G P who
had delivered Alfred. His symptoms were chronic cough, bronchitis and
shortness of breath, which had persisted for some months. Beaumont told
him that there was a suspect patch on one lung; he prescribed painting the
chest with iodine and regular doses of syrup of hypophosphites. This was
a patent medicine containing strychnine and hypophosphorous acid. Both
were poisons, though strychnine, in small quantities, stimulated the nervous

system and improved appetite. Gissing's immediate trouble was emphy-sema, caused by twenty years of heavy smoking and six years living in the railway smoke at Cornwall Residences. The only real treatment in 1896 was to live a healthier life, with no smoking, clean air and fewer worries. This would require some care and sympathy from Edith; what Gissing got was the reverse:

> This feeling against [Dr Beaumont] dates from the moment when he told me that one of my lungs was out of order. This she has fiercely resented – of course purely on her own account; and hardly a day has passed without abuse of me because my health has failed. 'You knew it all along, but what did *you* care. I wonder what my father was thinking of to let me marry such a man – the old idiot!'[10]

Bad news may bring people together, or drive them further apart. Gissing's realisation that he was seriously ill, and Edith's response to his condition, ended their marriage in less than a year. To Gissing, life now appeared as a struggle for his survival, and that of his children. Edith had shown that she would do nothing to help him keep his head above water.

Survival included economic survival, the writing of more books for as long as Gissing had strength to do it. In the same week as he completed *The Whirlpool*, he received a letter from J. H. (Holland) Rose, a friend from Owens College days. Rose was editing a new series on the Victorian era for Blackie, and asked Gissing to write a critical book on Dickens. After Owens College, Rose had gone to Cambridge and become a historian. Here was another person on the London literary scene who knew about Gissing's crime, but was happy to do him a favour. Gissing agreed by return of post to do the Dickens book, feeling that it would be a 'change from fiction-grinding'.[11] He would become known as a steady supplier of Dickens criticism, with many commissions over the next six years.

As his marriage was dying at the end of 1896, Gissing found someone who seemed to be an ideal friend and supporter. He met H. G. Wells on 20 November at an Omar Khayyam dinner at Frascati's, Oxford Street. Wells rushed up to Gissing after dinner and said that when he first read *New Grub Street* he had been poor and ill, with a wife named Amy, and living on Mornington Street. Wells had things mixed up – it is Jasper Milvain who lives on Mornington Road, not Reardon and Amy – but his enthusiasm was welcome. 'I rather liked Wells's wild face and naïve manner,' Gissing wrote in his diary. 'As usual, not at all the man I had expected.'[12] Wells already had his eye on Gissing, having written his two anonymous reviews earlier in the year, and five days after the dinner he invited Gissing to have dinner at his house in Worcester Park. They had both just been 'paragraphed' in the *Echo*; Gissing was said to have a 'pleasant Epsom home', and Wells 'a charming house and picturesque surroundings'.[13] Gissing had snubbed a multitude of invitations, but could not reject one written like this:

> Mr George Gissing will be recd. At the c & p.s.h. at any hour or season he may find convenient, he will be fed and given drink, tea, lemonade, or alcoholic fluids as he may prefer, and he will be conversed with in a genial but respectful tone. But as Mr H. G. Wells rarely washes, is commonly unshaven and dirty about the cuffs, it will be refined behaviour on the part of Mr Geo Gissing if he abstains from any aggressive neatness of costume. ... Mr H. G. Wells is painfully aware that in writing to this effect he commits a gross breach of etiquette, for which he takes this opportunity to apologize.[14]

Gissing found this 'most amusing', and told Wells that he came near to Gissing's 'ideal of the brotherly man of letters'.[15] It was three weeks before he could take up the invitation, but on 16 December he went over to Worcester Park to meet Wells, his wife Amy Catherine, and his mother-in-law. Gissing liked Wells immediately, and was also impressed by his fund of knowledge and his intellectual vitality. Their standing in the world was closely matched in 1896; the difference between them was fundamentally a matter of temperament. At first sight, Gissing might seem to overshadow Wells: he was better-looking, a head taller, and nine years older. Both had clawed their way up from the lower middle class by hard study, followed by teaching jobs; both had suffered years of poverty and ill-health. The literary success they were both starting to enjoy had not yet changed their dispositions. In Gissing's case there never would be change, but Wells was on the verge of becoming a public man, the sort of culture hero who would live in the glare of celebrity, and would come to depend on it. In 1896 their personal difference could be summed up in their experiences with women, above all the two marriages that each had already contracted.

Wells had been immeasurably more fortunate than Gissing in the women he married, but fortunate is not really the right word because Wells loved women – often not wisely, to be sure – and received love in return. He was short, sickly, skinny, and not blessed with looks that would turn anyone's head. Success came to him because he adored women, impressed them, and made them laugh. His romantic history was the reverse of Gissing's: he fell in love with two extremely pretty and good-natured women, who appreciated his talent and supported his career. He married Isobel Wells, his first cousin, after a long courtship dragged out by lack of money. They were at last wed in 1891, when Wells was twenty-five and had just got his B.Sc. A year later he fell in love with Amy Catherine Robbins, a science student whom he was tutoring at the London Correspondence College.[16] Isobel agreed to let Wells go, and he married Amy Catherine in 1895 when his divorce came through. She stuck with him until her death, propping up her husband's career in every conceivable way, in spite of the constant infidelities he allowed himself after ten years of marriage. In 1902 Beatrice Webb gave one of her typically acid assessments of the Wells marriage:

> His wife is a pretty little person with a strong will, mediocre intelligence and somewhat small nature. She has carefully moulded herself in dress, manners and even accent to take her place in any society her husband's talents may lead them into. But it is all rather artificial, from the sweetness of her smile to her interest in public affairs. However, she provides him with a charming well-ordered home, though I should imagine her constant companionship was somewhat stifling.[17]

One reason why Wells's second marriage had gone forward so smoothly was that H.G. started to be financially successful from the beginning of it. In the year that he married Amy Catherine, Wells published *The Time Machine*, an instant best-seller. The following year, when Wells and Gissing met, Wells made a thousand pounds from journalism alone. He was an immensely prolific writing machine, and Amy Catherine's first concern was to provide favourable conditions for him to churn out his books and articles. He could emerge from his study boasting that he had made £10 before lunch, and no doubt Amy Catherine cried 'Bravo!' as she brought the food to the table. She admired his writing, and served him as a highly efficient secretary. Edith Gissing saw only that George locked himself away all day, refused to speak to her, and was tormented by his task. Even if she had been willing to help with his literary work, there was nothing she could do because there was nothing she understood. Amy Catherine was there to give her husband a pleasant home, encouragement, and sexual comfort, even if his conduct towards her, in that department, was far from perfect. 'The brute fact,' he wrote to her later in the marriage, 'is that I am not and never have been – if there is such a thing – a passionate lover. I am affectionate and need only interesting things and brief interludes and I want a healthy woman to stay my needs and leave me most free for real things.'[18] A convenient kind of sex for a writer, no doubt.

Wells's feminism may have been self-serving, and deficient in other ways; but he had been able to find an accomplished woman, of a somewhat higher class than his own, who loved and admired him. Gissing had completely failed in this aim. He rationalised his failure in the way Edmund Reardon did in *New Grub Street*, by saying that one needed worldly success to succeed with women. But Wells had found love with both his first and second wives while he was still poor and struggling. They took him as he was while judging, rightly, that he would become successful before long. Gissing was just as talented, and there was no external reason why he should not have found a loving young woman who could have helped him up the ladder. The blame for his marital disasters lay first with himself, rather than in the systemic problems of Victorian sexuality. Many couples could find happiness in spite of that system; that Gissing could not was because of his own perverse choices.

Gissing began 1897 trying to cling to some kind of regular personal and professional life. He told Colles that he wanted to write an eighty-thousand-word novel before Easter, suitable for publication both as a serial and as a book. The title would be 'Polly Brill' and there would be two plots. One concerned a rich man who disappears, leaving rival claimants to his property; the other was about an Anglican mission in the East End, probably based on Gissing's friendship with the Reverend Charles Anderson in 1887. Gissing hoped to get the book done in two or three months, but domestic troubles forced him to abandon work on it after writing only four pages.

The other remedy for miseries at home was to visit friends as often as possible, even if it made Edith all the more angry. Gissing walked over to Box Hill to enquire after Meredith, who had just had an operation; he visited J. M. Barrie and his wife in London, and spent an evening with the Wellses, where he could compare a happy marriage with his own. None of these escapes provided any cure for the downward spiral at Worple Road. England was experiencing some of the worst weather of the century, freezing pipes and making everyone in the house ill. Edith was the first to crack, saying that she wanted to leave Epsom and live on her own with Alfred. Gissing got her brother Herbert, who was twenty years older than her, to come down and give her a talking-to. On 10 February Edith raked Gissing over the coals with a string of accusations: he had lied about letters sent to her, he had brought TB into the house, he had measured out two inches of bacon for her breakfast. It was more than Gissing could stand; he left the house with nothing but the clothes on his back and went to stay at Previtali's Hotel in Piccadilly.

Shortly before, Gissing had written a letter to the *Westminster Gazette* on the subject of reviewing. 'It is still too common,' he wrote, 'to find a reviewer quoting sentences uttered by a character in a novel as though they came from the author himself – a particularly irritating form of mis-representation.'[19] But what about an author acting out, in real life, some-thing previously done by one of his characters? *In the Year of Jubilee* shows Arthur Peachey walking out on his harridan wife, taking his three-year-old son with him. He takes the train out of London to 'the broad sunny meadows and the sweet hop-gardens of Kent'. Gissing, the day after leaving Edith, took the train down to stay with his friend Henry Hick in New Romney, Kent. He could not take Alfred because he was not yet weaned, though Gissing was deeply worried about Edith's ability to take care of him. All novelists make use of their past experiences in their books; Gissing also used his books to imagine what a future experience might feel like. Having written about it, he was ready to do it. Of course, before he married Edith he had written about intellectuals marrying work-girls, as if the whole course of his marriage needed to be foretold.

Gissing's fixed idea was that he needed only to find the courage to be an egotist, and then everyone else would bend to his will. But Clara Collet had seen how Gissing's obsessiveness made him unable to tolerate any deviation from a fixed household routine. Edith could not appreciate a writer's needs, and knew only that her husband was making her live the life of a prisoner. Coldness and rigidity were Gissing's weapons; care-lessness and bad temper were hers. Blindly, they were smashing the mar-riage up because they could no longer bear to live within it. Gissing feared that the marriage had literally been killing him. Henry Hick saw that he was seriously ill, and persuaded him to see a leading lung specialist, Philip Pye-Smith of Guy's Hospital. Gissing and Hick came up to London together for the consultation, on 16 February 1897. Pye-Smith told Gissing that he did not yet have active TB, but would get it soon if he stayed in Epsom for the winter and suffered the nervous strain of living with Edith. He should go to some country place with a milder climate and without air pollution. Gissing was happy to take the advice, because it also gave him a reason to stay away from Edith.

While in London, Gissing invited H. G. Wells to dine with him at Previtali's and meet Henry Hick. The two got on well, and Hick would become both Wells's personal physician and a lifelong friend. Two days later, on 18 February, Gissing went down to spend the rest of the winter at Budleigh Salterton, Devon. He had stayed there with Edith in the spring of 1891, and liked the town very much. When he arrived the weather was mild, flowers were in bloom, and a beautiful countryside was nearby for him to walk in. Gissing had found a refuge where he could calm his nerves, and hope to heal his lungs. Two weeks after he had left, Gissing could report to Algernon that Edith 'laments and repents; but what is the good of that after six steady years of outrageous ill-behaviour!'[20] She was completely dependent on Gissing, and it was not surprising that she wanted him back, just as Nell had wanted him to return also. Edith found herself caught in a familiar marital paradox: she needed Gissing to be there in order to have someone to complain to about her life. Quarrelling with servants was not as satisfying as quarrelling with a husband. She apologised, and waited for him to come back; once he did, the old habits would return for both of them.

Gissing's women friends came forward to limit the damage of his flight from Epsom. Clara Collet kept an eye on Alfred, and for legal advice Gissing turned to Eliza Orme, whom he had met two years before through his publisher H. W. Lawrence. Orme was a new woman, but not militant in her personal relations, and she sided with Gissing in his marital troubles. She went down to Epsom and convinced Edith to forward Gissing's mail, and to remain at Worple Road rather than follow him to Budleigh Salterton. Miss Orme used the white lie that Gissing was under doctor's orders and would return home when he was better. She made herself responsible for Edith, and without her help Gissing's later years might have been truly disastrous.

Clara Collet was also an indispensable friend, though she was not willing to put all the blame on Edith. Gissing confessed all his follies to Collet, and also tried to justify everything he had done by listing Edith's misdeeds. Very occasionally, he tried to look at the situation objectively and take his share of the blame: 'Here is the explanation: not once, but twice, have I made an ass of myself. My first wife was a hopeless drunkard, and died miserably in 1881 or 1882, I forget the year. This will seem to you incredible. Is there another such imbecile walking the earth?'[21] Once he was settled at Budleigh Salterton, though, Gissing upset Collet by telling her how easy he found it to be alone:

> Something in my nature seems always drifting me away from ordinary human intercourse; I feel it a strange thing when I frequently see and talk with people. The bad beginning of it was when, at 16 or so, I was most foolishly sent to live alone in Manchester in miserable lodgings. Hence all subsequent ills and follies. . . . And now it is difficult to see how I shall ever manage to live together with my boys, in the ordinary human way.[22]

Collet replied to this with a 'severe letter', and Gissing admitted that there was 'much truth in your accusations'.[23] None of Collet's letters have survived, but their gist seems to have been that Gissing had treated Edith in a cold and rigid way, and that his social isolation had made the problems in their marriage worse. Although Collet and Eliza Orme were both strong feminists, they did not really blame Gissing for behaving as a typical male. He was willing to concede that Edith was an ordinary woman who might have been happy if married to someone like herself. But if so, why did Walter draw that picture of his mother carrying a stick? There is little doubt that Edith abused her children, and constantly provoked rows with servants and landlords. Victorian male writers often treated their wives miserably, and Gissing must take his share of guilt for his tiresome habits. He certainly could have treated Edith with more tenderness and understanding. But her later history suggests that not even a domestic saint could have made her a happy or an emotionally stable person.

Gissing was in desperate need of some peace and solitude, away from the battlefield of Worple Road (where he had been embarrassed by his neighbours overhearing the sound of strife). He still felt ill and slept badly, but his cough got better and he slowly gained weight. The troubles of January had left him too nervous to do any writing, and for a few months he even stopped keeping his diary. The last entry was made the day before he left home; he had left in a rage and without luggage, so probably the diary was left behind. Edith may not have known of its existence, and he certainly would not have wanted her to read it. How could he get the three notebooks out of the house and sent to Devon without alerting her? He could have continued the diary in a new notebook; one suspects that he did not do so because his central concern in keeping the diary was to record his writing as he did it. In Devon he could not write, and it would be painful to note this day by day.

What Gissing could do to fill out his days was read, once he had done his regular five-mile walk. Having agreed to write the critical book on Dickens, he now had the pleasurable task of going through all his novels again:

> Dickens has not wearied me; far from that. I think more highly of him than ever. In this book, 'Little Dorrit', which I have often foolishly abused, I find most admirable things on all but every page. I am much less inclined to charge him with exaggeration in his characters. I see all his artistic faults, but there remains such splendid power, and such bright energy of temper! No man writing today has a shadow of claim to speak contemptuously of Dickens. He belongs to a greater race.[24]

At times in the past Gissing had said that he preferred Thackeray to Dickens. He admired above all Dickens's courage and vigour as a writer, but could be very critical of individual novels. Of *Little Dorrit* he had said in 1882 that it was 'Dickens's poorest work. There is not even a well-drawn character in the book, and the story is very wearisome.'[25] Now it was twenty-seven years since Dickens had died; as Gissing reread the novels in Devon he was taking one of the first steps in the great Dickens revival, and in particular the revaluation of Dickens's later novels. Things in Dickens that had seemed careless, melodramatic or cheaply popular were now, in a longer perspective, taking their place in Dickens's great panoramic vision of life.

Having time on his hands, Gissing naturally turned to the classics, and from this reading another novel would emerge six years later. The late Roman Empire had long fascinated him. In Devon he found an old edition of Cassiodorus, the sixth-century historian and statesman who at the end of his life turned his country estate into a monastery. Gissing started to dig deeply into the period when the Goths overran the Empire, and saw great possibilities in a historical novel about those events. He would have to master all the details of everyday life at the time; this was the kind of work he enjoyed, but could never settle into while he was living with Edith. The question was, could he find a way to a more peaceful and scholarly existence in the future? By mid-April, he had the dubious satisfaction of having Clara Collet come round to his view of Edith. 'I am glad,' he wrote to her, '(if gladness there can be in such a matter) that you understand something more of Edith's mental and moral peculiarities.'[26] When he went to work at the British Museum, Edith had accused him of getting up to some other mischief: how could he need to go to a library when he had so many books at home? But having Collet and Miss Orme agree that Edith was a Tartar did not give him any better way of dealing with her.

Gissing was also wondering whether living in Devon was the way to a better future, or a form of exile:

> I feel a miserable certainty that I shall never again be allowed to live in or near London. That complicates everything, and makes the future very dark. I need London for my work; in very truth, I can do little away from it; in the country, idleness oppresses me – especially when I miss my desk, my books &c. Well, I can but spend the days in the open air, and try to hope that my symptoms are not so serious as I believe them to be.[27]

This was not just hypochondria. For someone with diseased lungs, the pollution from London's millions of coal fires could be deadly. At best, Gissing could spend part of the summer in London and the rest of the year in a better climate, either in the countryside of southern England, or in the

Mediterranean. Algernon had survived as a writer outside of London, but only with the support of others; now he was restless again, and adding to Gissing's worries. First Algernon decided that he must go back to living in the north; a week later, his plan was to study for the Church of England ministry. How would he support his family while he was at a theological college? Gissing asked. However, he had no objection to using religion as the path to a more comfortable and secure life:

> It is very evident that rural parishes are falling into the hands of the merest boors; I constantly see country parsons who have no claim whatever to be called gentlemen, and I marvel how they got into the church. By sheer contrast, your personality would at once make itself a place of some distinction. As for dogma, why, the Church of England cannot be said to insist on any whatsoever; it is becoming ... merely a moralizing and civilizing force, acting in a thousand different – and nearly all secular – ways.[28]

Gissing was sufficiently despondent about Algernon's future that he felt any kind of regular job was worth pursuing, but he also felt that the dilemmas of *Born in Exile* belonged to the past. Godwin Peak, in that novel, was born in 1856 and went through his crisis of belief as a young man. The battles over evolution and Christian orthodoxy that shook the Victorian Church had now burnt themselves out. There would be no more Godwin Peaks. For Algernon it did not matter anyway, since his dream of wearing a clerical collar soon faded.

Sometimes the success of one sibling seems responsible for the failure of another. As Gissing steadily climbed up the literary ladder, Algernon could only watch in frustration. *The Whirlpool* was published on 6 April 1897, seventeen years after Gissing's first book. It was in a one-volume edition of two thousand copies at six shillings, and soon had to be reprinted. There were another 1,500 copies for Bell's Indian and Colonial Library (perhaps sales were helped by Hugh and Sibyl Carnaby's voyage to Australia in the novel).[29] Gissing's royalty on the English edition was a shilling per copy, £100 for each 2,000 sold. He was entitled to 'half-profits' on the US edition published by Stokes. They issued five printings of the book in 1897 alone, but half-profits provided only a tiny return to the author. The only way to make money on US editions was by getting a substantial advance, and Gissing did manage this with his next book, *The Town Traveller*. Stokes paid £100 for that. With *The Whirlpool*, Lawrence & Bullen now had seven of Gissing's novels in print at six shillings, finally giving him a small but steady flow of royalty income.[30] It was much better for Gissing's reputation to sell four thousand copies in a six-shilling edition than four hundred in the expensive three-decker format. Both in England and else-where, he was making the transition to being a known quantity with the growing novel-reading public. The better he did, of course, the more it grated on him to have sold so many of his major copyrights to Smith, Elder.

With bigger sales came bigger reviews, and the publication of *The Whirlpool* inspired long, respectful surveys of Gissing's career. By far the most acute of these was one he probably never saw – a pity, because it might have made him reconsider his fundamental approach to writing novels. In his 'London Letter' for *Harper's Weekly*, Henry James used *The Whirlpool* as an occasion to speak of Gissing's work as a whole:

> For this author in general, at any rate, I profess, and have professed ever since reading *New Grub Street*, a persistent taste – a taste that triumphs even over the fact that he almost as persistently disappoints me. I fail as yet to make out why exactly it is that going so far he so sturdily refuses to go further. The whole business of distribution and composition he strikes me as having cast to the winds; but just this fact of a question about him is a part of the wonder – I use the word in the sense of enjoyment – that he excites. ... It is form above all that is talent, and if Mr Gissing's were proportionate to his knowledge, to what may be called his possession, we should have a larger force to reckon with.[31]

James went on to illustrate Gissing's problems with form, especially in his handling of dialogue, where he did not sufficiently differentiate one voice from another. But Gissing's true gift, in James's eyes, was his knowledge, his 'saturation' or 'possession' by his material. He had a great theme, almost unique to his novels, which was the nature of life among the English lower middle class:

> He reeks with the savour, he is bowed beneath the fruits, of contact with the lower, with the lowest middle class, and that is sufficient to make him an authority – *the* authority in fact – on a region vast and unexplored.
>
>   The English novel has as a general thing kept so desperately, so nervously clear of it, whisking back compromised skirts and bumping frantically against obstacles to retreat, that we welcome as the boldest of adventurers a painter who has faced it and survived. We have had low life in plenty, for, with its sores and vices, its crimes and penalties, misery has colour enough to open the door to any quantity of artistic patronage. We have shuddered in the dens of thieves and the cells of murderers, and have dropped the inevitable tear over tortured childhood and purified sin. We have popped in at the damp cottage with my lady and heard the quaint rustic, bless his

simple heart, commit himself for our amusement. . . . We have recognised the humble, the wretched, even the wicked; also we have recognised the 'smart'. But save under the immense pressure of Dickens we have never done anything so dreadful as to recognise the vulgar.[32]

Gissing deserved huge credit for opening up a new prospect for the English novel. His limits were 'the lack of intensity in his imagination' and, in a word, 'distinction'. One can soften James's judgement, but not deny it. Gissing could never have the formal distinction of James himself; his talent was not on that scale. Then there were the conditions under which Gissing wrote, his literally exhausting life. Nor, finally, did Gissing ever try to achieve the final polish that distinguished the 'art novel', as James had invented it in English. Gissing's virtue lay elsewhere, James concluded:

> It is impossible not to be affected by the frankness and straightness of Mr Gissing's feeling for his subject, a subject almost always distinctly remunerative to the ironic and even to the dramatic mind. He has the strongest deepest sense of common humanity, of the general struggle and the general grey grim comedy. He loves the real, he renders it, and though he has a tendency to drift too much with its tide, he gives us, in the great welter of the savourless, an individual manly strain.[33]

James was perhaps the first serious critic to ignore the question of Gissing's pessimism. To live is to be caught up in the 'general struggle', and it is Gissing's virtue to have a deep sense of what that involves. The other reviewers of *The Whirlpool*, however, kept on blaming Gissing for the bleakness of his vision. The shorter novels that had preceded *The Whirlpool* had been lighter in tone, milder in their judgement of contemporary society. In trying to write a more substantial novel, Gissing again felt that he had to write a darker one. He could have drawn a grim enough picture by showing the horrors of his own failing marriage; instead, he turned to the failures of marriage among the upper middle class. The reviewer for the *Manchester Guardian* blamed these troubles on 'the relentless clutch of Mammon upon the lives of all'.[34] This was true enough, but perhaps the relentlessness itself is the deeper point, stronger than just the destructive effects on marriage of money and ambition. Although Gissing stayed far away, in *The Whirlpool*, from the literal circumstances of his own life, his starting point was that most marriages were scenes of discord. Alma Rolfe, a discontented upper-class woman who seeks a career as a violinist, is as different from Edith Gissing as can be imagined. Yet she is the same in that she sets her will against her husband, and from that first clash they grind each other down into misery and ruin.

It is a weakness of *The Whirlpool* that the materialism of life in London carries the responsibility for every conflict between, and within, its characters. In *The Way We Live Now*, Trollope was genuinely appalled by England's decline from aristocracy to plutocracy. The same forces of greed and speculation are at work in *The Whirlpool*, twenty-five years later. But Gissing had no emotional attachment to the aristocratic order, and little interest in the actual workings of the financial world. To him it was just one great swindle. The disagreements about money, in his novel, are merely symptoms of some more fundamental wrongness about marriage as an institution. The *Pall Mall Gazette* reviewer saw that particular social arrangements had little to do with the outcomes of Gissing's plots:

> In *The Whirlpool* his art almost convinces us that it does not much matter what you do, since everything is certain to turn out badly. If you marry your life will be wrecked, and if you do not marry that abstention will probably wreck your life as completely as the most reckless love-match of them all. That your life is going to be wrecked is a foregone conclusion, and not worth bothering about; it is the question of how the wreck is going to be accomplished that lends to life its interest.[35]

This reviewer disliked in Gissing precisely the grimness that would arouse the admiration of George Orwell, some thirty years later.

Gissing's new friend H. G. Wells pushed the pessimism aside by making *The Whirlpool* into a sociological critique, rather than its author's own cry of pain:

> In the early novels it would seem that the worst evil Mr Gissing could conceive was crudity, passion, sordidness and pain. But *The Whirlpool* is a novel of the civilised, and a countervailing evil is discovered – sterility. This brilliant refinement spins down to extinction, it is the way of death. London is a great dying-place, and the old stupidities of the homely family are, after all, the right way. That is *The Whirlpool*'s implication, amounting very nearly to a flat contradiction of the ideals of the immature *The Emancipated*.[36]

Wells was determined to find something positive in Gissing's turn towards conservatism. There are two ways to overcome the sterility of contemporary London, Wells argues: 'the old idea of refined withdrawal from the tumult and struggle for existence, and the new and growing sense of the eternity and universality of conflict'.[37] Wells seized on a scene in *The Whirlpool* where Harvey Rolfe reads from Kipling's *Barrack-Room Ballads*:

'The brute savagery of it! The very lingo – how appropriate it is! The tongue of Whitechapel blaring lust of life in the track of English guns. He knows it; the man is a great artist. ... We may reasonably hope, old man, to see our boys blown into small bits by the explosive that hasn't got its name yet.'[38]

'Here,' Wells wrote, 'in the mouth of a largely sympathetic character, is a vigorous exposition of the acceptance, the vivid appreciation of things as they are.'[39] But Wells had misread Gissing's intention. Rolfe was parodying popular enthusiasm for imperialist adventure; he saw nothing good in the jingoism that would soon touch off the Boer War. Two months after that war began, Gissing made his position crystal-clear in a letter to his German friend Bertz: 'No man living more abhors the influence of Kipling than I do; and I cannot endure to have it thought that I glorified him in "The Whirlpool".'[40] Wells liked the idea that the times called for battle; Gissing never wavered from his internationalist and pacifist convictions. Nor was he ever enthusiastic about scientific progress, which he expected to make wars more bloody and destroy the countryside. Gissing saw what was coming in the twentieth century, and looked about for a place to hide from it.

Wells's article on Gissing was not yet written when he and Amy Catherine arrived at Budleigh Salterton on 26 April. They had come down from London on their tandem bicycle, a formidable six-day journey over unpaved roads. For Wells, bicycle-riding meant pedalling into the future, and he rolled along with his usual bouncy enthusiasm. He and his wife spent three weeks with Gissing, who wrote in his diary: 'their company did me a great deal of good.'[41] For the first week, the Wellses overlapped with Margaret and Walter, who had come down from Wakefield for the Easter holidays. The Wellses had their own lodgings, up the hill from Gissing; they went for long walks in the countryside and became fast friends:

> We got on quite astonishingly well; this is the only case in which I have been able to make friends with a new writer. Wells's sole defect is his lack of a classical education; he makes up for this by singular sweetness of disposition, a wonderfully active mind, and a ceaseless flow of merriment. I believe he will do fine work, for he has a literary conscience and no touch of vulgarity in his views of life.[42]

Gissing was able to appreciate Wells, and the reverse was also true. Wells would not have spent so much time with Gissing had he been no more than a morbid obsessive. Taken away from his marital hell at Epsom, Gissing could laugh and be a good companion. Fears about his health had convinced him that he was in Devon to eat well and enjoy the fresh air, not to write four thousand words a day. This made a place in his life for real friendship. Most of the time, he felt it was a luxury he could not afford.

After three weeks at Budleigh Salterton, the Wellses went off to walk across Dartmoor. Gissing had never had a woman he could walk with across the countryside, or enjoy any kind of light-hearted companionship. Spending time with a happy young married couple like the Wellses might have set Gissing to thinking about how he might find such happiness for himself. Instead, he was now mulling over another disastrous step, to return to his old married life at Worple Road. He felt that he could not stay indefinitely at Budleigh Salterton. He was now supporting three house-holds: himself in Devon, Edith and Alfred at Epsom, Walter at Wakefield. Living in lodgings, and with no library at hand, he had not been able to do any writing. For all his dislike of literary London, he seemed to need its stimulus in order to work. Finally, he had turned against Devon, as he had done before when he lived at Exeter: 'I hope never to come to Devon again. As I think I told you before, I can't like the country, with real liking, and the people are very antipathetic to me. It always was so.'[43]

Towards Edith he had taken the path of least resistance: she kept upset-ting him by demanding that he come back, and he fudged the issue by saying that he would come back once he was better. She would not agree to a formal separation, and if Gissing refused to return she would go off on her own with Alfred. Gissing could not face this, because he feared – rightly – that Edith would end up treating Alfred as badly as she had treated Walter. Gissing's only shred of hope was that Miss Orme had been seeing Edith regularly, and was trying to teach her to be a better mother and housekeeper. Perhaps he could return to some kind of domestic truce that would allow him to work. At least Devon seemed to have restored his health: he had gained twenty pounds, and his cough had almost gone. So he agreed to return to Worple Road at the end of May, and to go on another family holiday with Walter in the summer. But he forced another decision on himself by letting the lease on his house expire. In the middle of Sep-tember, there would have to be another change.

Gissing returned to Epsom on 31 May 1897, and started to keep his diary once again. He went up to be examined by Dr Pye-Smith the next day, and got a fairly positive report. There did not seem to be any active TB, just asthma and the shortness of breath caused by compensatory emphysema.[44] He could continue to live within reach of London, provided he found somewhere high and dry to move to before the winter. The family reunion started out on a good note. 'Things are going very much better here,'

Gissing told Algernon, '– a better spirit altogether. Miss Orme has been vastly useful.'[45] With Edith reined in for the moment, Gissing could get down to a short novel he had been planning for some time, one that could be sold both as a serial and as a book. It would be a lower-middle-class comedy about shopkeepers and salesmen, *The Town Traveller*. It was the most light-hearted of Gissing's books, with the smallest load of ideology. Probably this was why he could say of the writing: 'Never got on so quickly with anything.'[46]

When the day of Queen Victoria's Diamond Jubilee came, Gissing was offered a good seat to see the procession. He took pleasure in thinking that millions of people would like to have his place, and pleasure in refusing to go and sit there. Roman emperors interested Gissing, but not the Empress of India. He wrote in his diary: 'Thank heaven, possessed my soul in quiet and did 3pp. as usual.'[47] Three pages were close to three thousand words, and in thirty working days the novel was done. Having written it strictly to put money in his purse, Gissing sensibly gave it to his agent, Colles, with instructions to sell it to the highest bidder. The result would show that he could do better through an agent than through just turning over each book to Lawrence & Bullen. However, Bullen had asked him to put together a collection of his short stories, which Gissing agreed to do. When he sent in the texts in July, twenty of the twenty-nine stories were brief portraits of London characters, originally published in *The Sketch* and paid for at three guineas each. Bullen offered only seventy-five guineas as an advance, and Gissing accepted a low offer because he had already been paid £120 or so for the stories when they appeared in magazines. If the Eighties were the decade of Gissing as a struggling novelist in a garret, in the Nineties his work would be shaped by opportunities that came with new media for the mass reading public. He had many more stories that could be collected and sold again in book form. Bullen gave his collection the unappealing title of *Human Odds and Ends*. He hoped to issue a follow-up volume in 1898, but no more story collections appeared until after Gissing's death.[48]

Eager to produce commercial work after his long stay in Devon, Gissing mostly stayed away from London. In June he went up to sit for two drawings by William Rothenstein. Max Beerbohm came to lunch, and impressed Gissing as a 'remarkable youth'.[49] Once *The Town Traveller* was done, his mind was set on the sacred summer holiday. Gissing's long and painful experience of seaside landladies had convinced him to go inland this year. In the Yorkshire Dales there would be beautiful countryside for walking and, he hoped, plenty of fresh milk and butter, thought to be good for the lungs. He took lodgings, sight unseen, at Castle Bolton, near Leyburn in Wensleydale. Gissing, Edith and Alfred set off in great heat on 24 July, braving riotous crowds at King's Cross. They picked up Walter at Northallerton, and arrived at Mrs Mason's cottage by pony trap in the evening.

Gissing could find no fault with Castle Bolton. There were magnificent views of Wensleydale, no shops or pubs, and it was a perfect place for the children to enjoy themselves. The lodgings were a problem, though; only twenty-five shillings a week, but primitive and with a reeking earth-closet in the garden. The bedroom doors had to be left open for ventilation, so Gissing lay awake at night worrying that a tramp might break in. After two months back with Edith, he was suffering from 'excessive nervousness, and dread of catastrophes'.[50] For a few days they could all rejoice in the moors and the old, half-ruined castle, but soon Edith's discontent and anger at the children broke out again. The lodgings were kept by a widow and her daughter, which made Gissing even more nervous. 'Unfortunately, there is no *man* in the house,' he wrote in his diary, 'and to be given over to the care of women is always dreadful.'[51]

This was both a characteristic remark, and a peculiar one. Whenever Gissing had been at home in Wakefield for the past twenty-seven years there had been no man in the house. He did not count himself or his brothers: they were male, but not *men* – patriarchs who provided for the house, and ruled it. When there was no man you became like a child, ruled by female will. Even in his own marriages, Gissing felt he had not played a man's part. The women at Castle Bolton were beyond masculine control; Gissing had no idea what they might do, but knew that he feared it. Another fear was that, with no man to keep them in order, the women would fight with each other. Strife soon began, as it always did when Edith was on the scene. On 24 August she joined battle with the landlady's daughter, accusing her of having taken Edith's tin-opener. When the tin-opener turned up, Edith wanted to keep quiet about it; Gissing, of course, insisted on apologising. By this time he had given notice that they were leaving early, and had made up his mind to take drastic action about Edith. The next day, Alfred was playing with Gissing's shaving brush and the handle fell off and rolled into a corner. Edith accused Gissing of hiding it deliberately:

'There's no knowing how nastiness will show itself,' she declared. ... at length she said to Walter: 'Why, your father jumped up as the thing rolled into the room, and I *saw* him take it up.' This was too much. I answered 'That is a deliberate lie' and asked Walter whether he thought me capable of lying on such a subject. ... I was very angry, and told her I would not be accused of lying before my own son. Thereupon she screamed, with a violent gesture: '*Hold your beastly noise, or you'll have this plate at your head*!' Hating the odious necessity of what I did, I turned to the boy, and said quietly, 'Walter, repeat to me the words your mother has just used.' He did so, poor little chap, with tears, and I wrote the sentence at once in my pocket-book.[52]

Gissing wrote it down so that Edith could not deny later on that she had said it. She alternated between storm and sunshine; when she got into a better mood, Gissing noted, 'she is astonished that I do not forthwith forget the outrages thrown upon me'. Edith's side of it was that she might throw plates, but she could be cheerful too, whereas Gissing was 'never in a decent humour'.[53]

A marriage where one partner screamed threats and the other wrote them down in his notebook was not doing well. In fact, it was effectively dead. Gissing wrote long letters (now lost) to his sister Margaret and to Miss Orme, justifying what he had decided while lying awake at night. The Worple Road lease would not be renewed, the furniture would go into storage, Edith and Alfred would go into lodgings, and Gissing would go to Italy.

The Shores of the Mediterranean

'In a sleepless night,' Gissing told Algernon, 'last week, the thought flashed upon me – "My boy, your path lies to the shores of the Mediterranean. Go, in the name of all that is sensible and hopeful, and work there till next spring."'[1] Gissing told his friends and his family, but he did not tell Edith. For two weeks he delayed and dodged about, staying with friends overnight when he could. Worple Road had to be vacated by mid-September, but it was not until the 6th that Gissing told Edith what was going to happen. 'Fury and insult, of course,' Gissing recorded, 'but quiet afterwards.'[2]

Behind all her bluster, Edith must have been terrified of what lay ahead of her. Once again, Miss Orme came forward to help: she offered to find rooms for Edith and a nurse for Alfred. 'My gratitude to this admirable woman beyond words,' Gissing noted. 'What toil and misery she is taking off my hands!'[3] Not just that, but taking on her own hands. Orme proposed that, rather than going into lodgings, Edith and Alfred should come and live with her in Tulse Hill. Orme had been a social worker, and saw Edith as a challenge. Money was also a factor: Gissing would pay £50 a quarter, a pretty steep price. He was now committed to paying £200 a year to Miss Orme and £50 a year for Walter's keep. How long could he go on doing that, if Lawrence & Bullen were paying him only £150 for a novel? A great deal rested on whether Colles could sell *The Town Traveller* at a better price, but Gissing would have to wait for many months before he found that out.

What remained was to pack up Worple Road – furniture and fifteen cases of books – and to pack off Edith and Alfred. 'Domestic misery to the very end,' Gissing recorded, '– rage and ill feeling.'[4] The van came for the furniture on the morning of 17 September, and the unhappy little family went to catch the train at Epsom station. Edith and Alfred got off at Clapham Junction to join Miss Orme at Tulse Hill; Gissing went on to Victoria, then to Paddington and the Cotswolds to stay with Algernon and Catherine. After three days at Willersey he went on to Wakefield to say goodbye to

Walter. He could look forward to two things, both of which he would enjoy: solid work, and solitude in a quiet town in Italy. As soon as his book on Dickens was finished, he would go down to Calabria, the Magna Graecia of antiquity. His friend Henry Norman, the literary editor of the *Daily Chronicle*, had said he might publish some sketches from Gissing's travels. Gissing expected two more books to come from his journey: one an account of his travels, the other his novel about the break-up of the Roman Empire.

Gissing's wheel had come full circle. It was just seven years since he had met Edith Underwood and crawled into marriage to escape the unbearable loneliness of his life. Now he was crawling out of the marriage, covered with domestic scars. He was deeply worried about Walter and Alfred, and it might seem that he should have stayed in England in order to be near them. Part of his reason for fleeing to Italy was his conviction that he would not live for many more years. If so, his first duty was to make enough money for his sons to have a middle-class education. He was afraid that another London winter might kill him. In Italy he could write the three books he had in mind, and write them quickly. His only way of dealing with Edith was to hide, and in Italy he could be sure that she would never find him.

Gissing started his run to cover from Charing Cross on the morning of 22 September 1897. Henry Hick met him at the station and rode with him to Dover. From Calais Gissing took the line to Basel, and on over the St Gotthard through the night. On the Italian side melons were ripening in the fields and there was tropical heat. Gissing spent a night in Milan and one in Florence, arriving at Siena on the 25th. He found a pleasing room with a view of the cathedral, and settled down to write about Dickens. 'An old, old city, this,' he told a friend, 'one lives in the middle ages still. Streets very narrow and high; no side walks; magnificent white oxen drawing carts. People very quiet and kind.'[5] The only local event to draw Gissing's interest was the display of the head of St Catherine of Siena, who had been dead for five hundred years. His lodgings were extremely cheap, less than £4 a month, and seemed ideal to him at first. There were excellent meals and he spoke Italian constantly with his hostess. Only later did he find that her husband was on his deathbed downstairs. 'An unfortunate thing for me,' Gissing wrote in his diary, '— I always come in for such things.'[6] But he was truly sad, and sent flowers, when the man died three days later.

Gissing was thinking seriously about his own death, and the risks of his planned journey to Calabria. He wrote to Clara Collet about making a new will that would prevent Edith having control of the boys if he died. 'There is a doubt in my mind,' Gissing wrote, 'whether she is really quite sane. . . .

she will always be a hopeless person. No one would act unkindly towards her. It is merely that she must not have it in her power to damage the boys' hopes in life – as assuredly she would, one way or another.'[7] Gissing's solution was to name three guardians – Edith, Algernon and Clara Collet – and say that if there was disagreement the majority would rule. Collet pointed out to him that by the 'Mother's Act' of 1886 a widow would automatically become guardian of her children. But the father still had the right to appoint guardians, so Gissing went ahead with his new will anyway. It also said that if Edith became sole guardian, an application should be made to have additional guardians appointed by the court. Edith would get one-third of the income from Gissing's estate, Walter and Alfred the rest.[8]

Gissing found that writing literary criticism could not be done as quickly as writing a novel. Nonetheless, he managed two thousand words a day and finished his study of Dickens in five weeks. One can see why he was such a star in the examination room: he produced the most impressive study of Dickens to date with little or no access to the novels. Gissing had read them earlier in the year and remembered them. He praised, above all, Dickens's 'idealization of English life and character. ... To be truly and profoundly national is great strength in the maker of literature.'[9] From his rooms Gissing could go out into the hot, dark streets of Siena, and flinch at how alien they were to the cosy haunts of Mr Pickwick, Mr Cheeryble, and the rest of Dickens's 'beneficent gentlemen':

Does one *like* Italy? The fact is, I always feel it a terrible country; its unspeakable beauty is inseparable from the darkest thoughts; go where you may, you see the traces of blood and tears. To be sure, this will apply to the whole world; but here one *remembers* so much more than in other countries. Age after age of strife and tyranny, of vast calamities, of unimaginable suffering in the palace and the hut. You feel something pitiless in the blue sky that has looked so tranquilly on all this. And the people – you see centuries of oppression in their faces, hear it in their voice. Yes, yes, one likes Italy; but in a very special sense of the word.[10]

Italy was in a troubled state, with rioting in Rome, where a man was shot dead. 'Italy is being very quickly ruined,' Gissing told Algernon, 'owing to the crazy effort to be a first-class power.'[11] He had heard that peasants were dying of hunger in the south, and a revolution might be imminent; these were things to be seen at first hand, if he could manage it. As soon as he had finished the Dickens book he would leave Tuscany, for which he cared little. Before he left, he received a request from *Who's Who* to update his entry and made a characteristic reply: 'As for my recreations,

I cannot call to mind that I have any, except travel. Yes, *Travel* might be set down.'[12] To travel further south and deeper into the past was his aim, and in doing so to put even more distance between himself and everything he had been living through with Edith.

Gissing finished his study of Dickens on 5 November 1897, and sent it off to Colles with a request that he try to get some more money by selling it in the US. Colles succeeded, and Gissing got another £50 for the book.[13] Colles also sold a story that Gissing had written two and a half years ago and forgotten about, 'A Despot on Tour'. The *Strand Magazine* bought it for the excellent price of six guineas a thousand words. This run-of-the-mill story fetched £23.10, equivalent to six months of board and lodging in Siena, and it had taken Gissing two days to write. Here was another reminder that short stories were a very good commercial proposition. In the New Year, Gissing would turn to them again.

Gissing left Siena as soon as he was free to do so, on 8 November. At Rome he was met by BrianBorú O'Dunne, a young Irish-American journalist who had befriended him in Siena. He stayed only two nights in Rome, then went on alone to Naples – 'The most interesting town (modern interest) in the world!' he told H. G. Wells.[14] His business here was to get letters of introduction for his journey south. Gissing wanted to catch the last of the autumn weather. Everyone knew that Calabria was too dangerous for foreigners in summer, due to the prevalence of malaria. He probably realised that it was dangerous at any time, because at the Consulate he signed the will that his solicitor had sent over from England. As soon as his business was done, Gissing wanted to get off to the sea and the mountains. He took it as an ill omen that when he went to a restaurant he knew, on his first night, he found it closed because of a death in the family. 'A superstitious man would flee from Italy,' he wrote in his diary. He did not flee, but that didn't mean he was not superstitious.

On 16 November Gissing left Naples on a steamer that was going down the coast to Messina, stopping on the way at the little town of Paola. From there he could go inland over the mountains to Cosenza. In *By the Ionian Sea*, Gissing tells why he became a traveller:

Every man has his intellectual desire; mine is to escape life as I know it and dream myself into that old world which was the imaginative delight of my boyhood. The names of Greece and Italy draw me as no others; they make me young again, and restore the keen impressions of that time when every new page of Greek or Latin was a new perception of things beautiful. The world of the Greeks and Romans is my land of romance; a quotation in either language thrills me strangely, and there are passages of Greek and

Latin verse which I cannot read without a dimming of the eyes, which I cannot repeat aloud because my voice fails me. In Magna Graecia the waters of two fountains mingle and flow together; how exquisite will be the draught![15]

Gissing longed to escape the modern world, and especially that corner of it where he had been suffering in the suburban cage of his marriage to Edith. But he was also eager to encounter Magna Graecia as it existed in his own time, with its ruins, its dispirited inhabitants and its filthy inns. The hosts of his lodgings in Naples were appalled that Gissing wanted to explore such a backward region as Calabria. But he was the classic type of English Victorian traveller, not just undeterred by hardship but encouraged by it. That also meant travelling alone. He would be forced to find companionship among the local people, and at the same time be free to do just as he wanted. Whatever the dangers and inconveniences of going south of Naples alone, once he left the city he was utterly cut off from all obligations. In Calabria he could expect the complete negation of the life he had led, until recently, at Worple Road, Epsom, Surrey.

Gissing was undeterred by Baedeker's warning against his adventure:

> The whole district bore the name of *Magna Graecia;* but the traces of that prosperous epoch are now scanty. The fields once extolled by Sophocles for their richness and fertility are now sought for in vain, and the malaria exercises its dismal sway throughout the whole of this neglected district. The soil belongs to the nobility, who let it to a miserably poor and ignorant class of farmers. The custom of carrying weapons is universally prevalent here, and brigandage was carried on until the year 1870. The villages are generally wretched and filthy beyond description. No one should therefore attempt to explore the remoter parts of this country unless provided with letters of introduction to some of the principal inhabitants.[16]

When he was in Athens, Gissing had feared to venture alone into the countryside. Now he was ready to take his chance, even though he mostly stayed in the towns and carried the letters recommended by Baedeker. Being fluent in Italian was indispensable in making such a journey; nonetheless, a solitary Englishman ran all kinds of risks. The only English person Gissing met in his month in the south was the Consul at Taranto. It is possible that at the time Gissing was the only English tourist in the whole of Calabria. His aim was to forget his English life and project himself back sixteen hundred years; the local people did not hamper his imagination, but hordes of English idiots would have done. Emotionally, he was travelling light; literally, he took a large and heavy portmanteau. He had the

three-volume guide of François Lenormant, *La Grande-Grèce*, and enough
other books that on rainy days he would always have something to read.

Gissing began his tour of Magna Graecia at Cosenza, where Alaric
was buried. The Visigoths came from present-day Bulgaria and Romania;
Alaric led them on a trail of pillage through the Roman Empire, ending
with the sack of Rome itself in 410 CE. From there he marched down
towards Sicily, but at Cosenza he fell sick and died. Legend held that he
was buried with his treasure in the bed of the river Busento, after which
everyone who knew the exact place was killed. Why was Gissing fascinated
by the rapine and terror of the late Roman Empire, when in the present he
detested Kipling and everything to do with war or imperialism? The classical world possessed the beauty of decay and silence. No cry of pain could
now be heard, and that appeased Gissing. All suffering was placed out of
reach by death. That the ancient world was more horrible than the nether
world of the London slums he took as a consolation. Even such terrible
power had entirely disappeared, leaving only a few weathered ruins. In
Magna Graecia one saw that history might equally well be of advance, or
decline; that confirmed Gissing's disbelief in the myth of progress recently
trumpeted through the streets of Victorian Britain. In London he jeered at
the Jubilee, at Cosenza he mused on the hidden tomb of a far more fearsome
monarch, Alaric the Goth.

Gissing spent only two days at Cosenza on the trail of Alaric, probably
because he was so appalled by the Hotel Leonetti, where he stayed. He
wrote home that the hotel 'would have dismayed a decent English pig'.[17]
As he continued his journey, neither food nor lodging would get any better.
From Cosenza he went on by train to Taranto, a little port that delighted
him and where he would spend several days. Everything that was backward
about the south, and was scorned by those northern Italians who came
there on business, gave pleasure to Gissing. 'The worse the better' might
have been his motto. 'This great plain between the hills and the sea,' he
wrote, 'grows very impressive; so silent it is, so mournfully desolate, so
haunted with memories of vanished glory.'[18] In the harbour there were
fishermen who pulled in their nets just as they had done under the eye of
Plato or of Hannibal. Outside the town there was a ploughman who filled
Gissing with a rapture he could never have felt in an English field:

> I could not but approach the man and exchange words with him; his rude
> but gentle face, his gnarled hands, his rough and scanty vesture, moved me
> to a deep respect, and when his speech fell on my ear, it was as though I
> listened to one of the ancestors of our kind. ... The donkey's method of
> ploughing was to pull for one minute and then rest for two; it excited in the

ploughman not the least surprise or resentment. .... They were not driver and beast, but comrades in labour. It reposed the mind to look upon them.[19]

At Taranto Gissing was invited to dinner on his birthday by Wilfred Thesiger, the young English Consul, who complained that he had nothing whatever to do. From Taranto Gissing headed south on the railway line that skirted the Ionian Sea. He spent a day in the ruins of Metaponto, where Pythagoras had died, and arrived at the Hotel Concordia in Cotrone on 26 November. Before he could see much of the town he fell ill with a high fever and stomach trouble. He would spend a week in bed in this gloomy inn with its unspeakable meals, a week that might easily have been his last.

What was Gissing's illness at Cotrone? Riccardo Sculco, the friendly doctor who treated him, gave him large doses of quinine, the specific for malaria. If Gissing had malaria it would have come from mosquito bites a week or more before, perhaps at Cosenza. Gissing himself thought he had got sick by going out while the *tramontana* was blowing – the old belief that the disease came from 'bad air'. Just three months before, Ronald Ross, an army doctor in India, had proved that malaria was a parasitic infection of the blood transmitted by mosquitoes.[20] Gissing mentions that he met travellers who were suffering from malaria, but he never calls his own illness that. Apart from fever, malaria can have a great variety of symptoms, and can interact with existing illnesses. It can also recur, even when the person infected is no longer in a malarial zone. Whether he had malaria or not, Gissing was seriously ill at Cotrone and came closer to death than ever before in his life. The journey to Calabria was a step downwards in the fundamental deterioration of his health.

Sculco was a conscientious doctor, but Gissing had nothing palatable to eat and no proper nursing. There was no English person that he could call on for help, and he survived by drawing on his own resources. Not only did Gissing resist his illness, he took pleasure in a strange night of hallucinations when his fever was at its height:

I soon after fell into a visionary state which, whilst it lasted, gave me such placid happiness as I have never known when in my perfect mind. Lying still and calm, and perfectly awake, I watched a succession of wonderful pictures. First of all I saw great vases, rich with ornament and figures; then sepulchral marbles, carved more exquisitely than the most beautiful I had ever known. The vision grew in extent, in multiplicity of detail; presently I was regarding scenes of ancient life – thronged streets, processions triumphal or religious, halls of feasting, fields of battle ... The delight of these phantasms was well worth the ten days' illness which paid for them. I

shall always feel that, for an hour, it was granted me to see the vanished life
so dear to my imagination.[21]

These hallucinations came from Gissing's longing to escape into the classical world, a longing that would recur on his deathbed.

After ten days, Gissing left 'terrible Cotrone'. He was eager to reach
higher ground at Catanzaro, but never considered cutting short his tour
and returning to the comforts of civilisation. He did decide that a later hotel
at Squillace was too filthy to stay at, though not to eat lunch there: 'Peperoni
cut up in oil came as antipasto, then a stew of *maiole* (pork) and potatoes.
Nothing but *maiole* to be had in these places – Homeric food. The bread a
sort of flat round cake, with hole in middle – consistency of cold pancake.
Wine poisonous.'[22] To know that such food was eaten in Homer's day
would please hardly anyone, but it pleased Gissing. He drew the line at
another discovery: that people in the ancient world lived with the smell of
excrement constantly in their nostrils.

Catanzaro was the one oasis in Gissing's journey. It was beautifully
situated in the hills, above the malarial coast, so that the people were
healthier and more prosperous than those below. He received twenty-three
letters there and the typescript of his Dickens book, which he corrected
and sent back to Colles before he left the town. There was good news
about money, too: £78 had come in from the publication of his short story
collection *Human Odds and Ends*, and Colles had sold the Dickens book
for £50 to Dodd, Mead in New York. Gissing would have that money as a
cushion when he returned to Rome, and the sale of *The Town Traveller* was
still to come. At Catanzaro Gissing felt his strength returning, and that the
worst of his journey was behind him. On his way to Reggio he visited
the place where Cassiodorus had withdrawn from the world to found a
monastery on his family estate, around 540 CE. Everything had since been
destroyed by the Lombards, but Gissing was moved just to walk in the
footsteps of Cassiodorus, one of his intellectual heroes.

Gissing's own dream of retirement would find expression in *The Private
Papers of Henry Ryecroft*. Cassiodorus retired on a grander scale. As a
senator, he tried to reconcile Roman values with the new hegemony of the
Goths. When he realised that Roman civilisation was crumbling away, in
spite of any effort he could make, he left public life. On his estate he tried
to create a little enclave of order and prosperity; he wrote a history of his
time and gathered much information on everyday life, religion and peasant
customs. Gissing saw such a life as a model. Cassiodorus turned his back
on a violent public world; he lived peaceably for study and contemplation;

he had no wife or family to distract him. Like the poet Horace, another favourite of Gissing's, he found peace within his own soul when society preferred strife.

The last stop on Gissing's tour was Reggio. It was beautifully situated overlooking the Strait of Messina, but its location was also its misfortune. Every invader, from the Goths to the Turks, had both coveted Reggio and destroyed what they found there. In this city of endless war, Gissing was moved by a memorial to a young soldier who died at the age of twenty, fighting with Garibaldi to liberate Reggio from the Bourbon monarchy:

> The very insignificance of this young life makes the fact more touching; one thinks of the unnumbered lives sacrificed upon this soil, age after age, to the wild-beast instinct of mankind, and how pathetic the attempt to preserve the memory of one boy, so soon to become a meaningless name. ... In the days to come, as through all time that is past, man will lord it over his fellow, and earth will be stained red from veins of young and old. That sweet and sounding name of *patria* becomes an illusion and a curse; linked with the pretentious modernism, *civilization*, it serves as a plea to the latter-day barbarian, ravening and reckless under his civil garb. ... In our day there is but one Italian patriot; he who tills the soil, and sows, and reaps, ignorant or careless of all beyond his furrowed field.[23]

In forty years' time, Italian soldiers under the fascist banner would be marching into Ethiopia, trying to restore the Roman *imperium*. The flaw in Gissing's lament, though, was that the young soldier of 1860 was a volunteer. Soldiers were not just sacrificed; they sacrificed themselves. But perhaps Gissing was consistent: he did not deny the bloody inclinations of his species, he only insisted that true happiness lay in solitude and withdrawal from what most men desired. That was the concluding note of his journey to the south:

> Alone and quiet, I heard the washing of the waves; I saw the evening fall on cloud-wreathed Etna, the twinkling lights come forth upon Scylla and Charybdis; and, as I looked my last towards the Ionian Sea, I wished it were mine to wander endlessly amid the silence of the ancient world, to-day and all its sounds forgotten.[24]

In his diary, Gissing's thoughts were more brutal: 'Mood of anger with modern Italians, who ruin all the old associations. These countries ought to be desolate. Over there in Sicily, barbarism trying hard to hold its own – the Mafia at Palermo.'[25] Gissing wanted to see one more survival from the old world, the monastery of Monte Cassino between Naples and Rome. He spent the night there and enjoyed its splendid isolation on the mountain top.[26] Gissing admired St Benedict as a preserver of culture, but never responded to the glamour of Catholicism. A Greek temple, no matter how battered, could be relied on to give him a thrill.

Gissing arrived back in Rome on 15 December 1897. His lungs were still weak, so he was afraid to return to England before the spring. Rome was the best place for him to pass the winter; he could live in comfort there, and have libraries to research his novel on the time of Cassiodorus. Still, the months he spent there proved to be a relatively barren period. His historical novel did not get beyond the research stage, and neither could he get down to writing the story of his journey to the Ionian Sea. That would not be completed for another year and a half. Gissing was intermittently ill, perhaps recurrences of malaria from Cotrone. In addition he was burdened by a stream of letters from Miss Orme, telling him how badly things were going with Edith. He was terrified of seeing her again, and could only hope that Miss Orme could manage to keep her in hand. But after three months at Tulse Hill, Edith had caused so much trouble that she clearly would have to be sent somewhere else.

What was wrong with Edith? She was now thirty years old, and Miss Orme thought she behaved more like a child than an adult, throwing tantrums whenever people failed to give her what she wanted. Her letters show no obvious cognitive impairment up to this point, nor had she displayed symptoms of major psychosis. When Gissing first met her he thought she was quiet and eager to learn. Much of this may have been his wishful thinking, but to the casual eye she had a normal, stable personality. When Walter was born Edith suffered from post-partum depression. After that, the obvious signs that something was going wrong were her lack of close friends, her quarrelling with servants and landlords, and her abusive treatment of Walter. However, none of this added up to madness. Edith became much more extreme in her anti-social behaviour after Gissing left her in September 1897, and would be committed to a mental hospital less than five years later, at the age of thirty-four. Fifteen years after that she died, still hospitalised.

Edith's cause of death was reported as 'organic brain disease', which meant some kind of degenerative process in her brain. There could be many reasons for this, from a tumour to Alzheimer's disease, but for a nineteenth-century doctor probably the first diagnosis to come to mind would be tertiary syphilis. Was that the cause of Edith's erratic behaviour and subsequent breakdown? If Gissing had latent syphilis when he married Edith he could still have been contagious, and the infection might have led to her being certified with dementia eleven years later. Gissing commented on marital syphilis in *The Whirlpool*:

> Cecil Morphew ... showed a face which was growing prematurely old; a fatigued complexion; sunken eyes; ... His declaration in a letter, not long ago, that he was unworthy of any good woman's love, pointed to something which had had its share in the obvious smirching of his character; something common enough, no doubt; easily divined by Harvey Rolfe, though he could not learn how far the man's future was compromised.[27]

Nonetheless, the course of Edith's illness does not seem typical of syphilis. Her behaviour – in the early years of the marriage, at least – was more bad than mad. The modern diagnosis might be borderline personality disorder, with symptoms such as poor impulse control, difficulty in forming or sustaining relationships, lack of empathy, and abusive confrontations with people around her. The roots of Edith's troubles probably lay in her childhood, but little is known of it except that her mother died when Edith was eleven. In adult life she was shunned by her family, for no known reason other than that they found her difficult. A borderline personality often becomes more disturbed after an external shock to the self, such as Gissing's decision to walk out of his marriage in 1897. The marriage was unhappy, but it gave Edith a certain stability, even in antagonism. After five years on her own with Alfred, her personality seems to have completely fallen apart.

This is not to absolve Gissing of his faults as an individual and as a Victorian husband. With all his extraordinary intelligence and imagination, he was profoundly lacking in empathy, especially where women were concerned. As his marriage was ending, he created a memorable portrait of a talented and discontented woman, Alma Frothingham in *The Whirlpool*. But he could not imagine any real dialogue between Alma and her husband Harvey: she is trapped by her impulses, he by clinging to the letter of a proper marriage rather than its spirit. Gissing was a typical obsessive-compulsive in his rigid insistence on rules and standards. Rather than trying to understand the person across the kitchen table from him, he preferred to break off all connection with her. 'But this one thing is determined,' he told Clara Collet, '– that I shall not resume the pretence of domestic life. I will have a shadow of peace during the years that remain to me.'[28]

To Herbert Sturmer, a new literary friend, Gissing explained that social life was as unsatisfactory as life at home had been:

> Do not for a moment suppose that I attach undue importance to dining-clubs, and so on. .... I think I know, too, exactly what weight is to be given

to the friendly advances of certain people in certain spheres – experience is not lacking. No man of letters is, in reality, further apart from circles and cliques than I am. I have *never* asked for a notice, or a paragraph, or anything of the sort, and never shall. Everything of that kind is done without my knowledge; and I do not even see the newspapers. ... For twenty years I have worked and struggled in absolute independence, and so it will be to the end.[29]

Literary London was its own kind of whirlpool, enticing but ultimately treacherous. Gissing would try to stay aloof from its gossip and back-scratching. He was not a tradesman, but a gentleman.

Of course, being Gissing, he had trouble with gentlemen too. Sturmer gave him an introduction to Robert Swinton-Hunter, who lived in some style on Via due Macelli. Gissing went to Swinton-Hunter's tea parties, but was baffled that anyone could be content with such a life: 'I do not pretend to understand him. He has settled in Rome indefinitely, together with his Italian friend; he lives in luxury, and seems to have no particular aim; but I like him, and I think he is a thoroughly good fellow. If you can help me to comprehend his *soul*, pray do.'[30] Swinton-Hunter's Italian friend was nominally his secretary, but surely more than that. Was Gissing being deliberately naive about the relation between the two men, and the reason why Swinton-Hunter chose to live abroad? Another society lady, Mrs Lambart, shocked Gissing by saying that Oscar Wilde was the author of 'The Ballad of Reading Gaol'. Ladies were not supposed to utter that name.[31] In Rome Gissing could pass as a full member of polite English society; once accepted, he complained that it was not polite enough.

Brian Ború Dunne gives us some hints about how Gissing looked from the outside. Dunne was a nineteen-year-old American, the son of a judge, educated in the classics. He had met Gissing at their boarding-house in Siena, and spent a good deal of time with him both there and in Rome. His memories are valuable because Gissing had so few close friends, though Dunne had little psychological insight, or knowledge of Gissing's troubled earlier life. Dunne was also a devout, even a bigoted Catholic. Gissing liked 'men who had studied and starved, and who liked Latin and Greek – and who minded their own business by not asking personal questions'.[32] Dunne met all these requirements, except that he had never starved.

Dunne was much impressed by the way Gissing slaved away at the writing of *Charles Dickens: A Critical Study* in Siena. His manuscript was phenomenally clean, because of Gissing's ability to compose in his head. 'I know everything I am going to do when I write a novel,' Gissing told

Dunne. 'I have all the characters before me, and I proceed from the first chapter on to the end of the novel.'[33] Perhaps this was part of why he found writing such a strain. It was not in his nature to just let the words flow and then return to improve them. Anything he put on paper had to be close to finished work.

Dunne presents Gissing as an eccentric, shy and prudish figure, a misfit among the jolly tourists in Italian boarding-houses. Gissing never spoke an immodest word; he would not speak to his fellow guests, except at meals; he would blush like a schoolgirl when contradicted. Some of this behaviour may have been self-protection: Gissing was in Italy to work, not to amuse himself. Some was snobbery: he would sing for his supper when invited to dinner by a baron, but hold aloof from tourists he considered ignorant. To Dunne, Gissing occasionally revealed himself – for example, his disgust at prostitution: 'The sale of contraceptives on the street corners of the large cities and the flood of scarlet women let loose exactly at the noon hour up and down the Corso, Rome's famous business and social thoroughfare, angered Gissing. ... [he] hated the name, the thought, the presence, the descriptions, the suggestion of prostitution, which was gaily discussed by Latins at luncheon.'[34] Gissing also delivered a tirade one night about going to the theatre in London, where afterwards gentlemen could be mobbed by prostitutes, their hats knocked off and their clothes rumpled. Female sexual aggression upset Gissing's belief in the natural modesty of women. The other side of the coin was his mistrust of feminine wiles, as with the damsel in 'The Fate of Humphrey Snell' who pretended to be in distress in order to entrap a male protector. In Gissing's world, men are sexually vulnerable to boldness and modesty alike.

What seemed to Dunne to be Gissing's eccentricity was perhaps just a symptom of great nervous strain. He was under severe financial pressure, followed by the near-fatal illness at Cotrone. In Rome Gissing fell ill again, with some kind of toxic combination of malaria, flu, TB, emphysema and pneumonia. Illness always made him depressed; now he felt that his health was truly broken and he was entering old age, having just passed his fortieth birthday. He told Collet that he was planning to seek refuge with Algernon's family when he went back to England:

I am too ill and miserable to write more. It is bitterly cold here. – This winter has been a monstrous mistake. In England I should have done better for health and everything else. – The solitude is terrible.

But when have I been anything but solitary? As no doubt you understand quite well, it was *that* that led to my insane marriage seven years ago. I have fifty times been on the point of frenzy from sheer loneliness. When I had

my flat near Regent's Park, I used sometimes to walk about the room really
crying with misery because I had no one to speak to for days and days.[35]

Why then was Gissing so aloof at his boarding-house? He wanted
company; but he also found fault with the company that was available.
Nonetheless, once he got over the worst of his depression he established a
busier social life for the remainder of his stay in Rome. He had an introduction to a Mr Lambart, who was a gentleman 'with lords as common as
blackbirds among his acquaintances'. Gissing became quite friendly with
the Lambarts, except that social success made him almost as miserable as
social failure:

> They swarm with aristocratic acquaintances of the great Catholic world.
> Just a little bitterness in associating with them. How can I help thinking that
> my brains ought to have given me a place in this world of refinement long,
> long ago? It would have been so, but for the first fatal mistake. Why had I
> not some sensible friend to look after me when I was a boy of seventeen? –
> Can you *think* yourself into my place, at that age? Or can you imagine what
> it means to me *now*, to know that life is over, yet never to have lived as I
> might so easily have done, with my intellectual kindred?[36]

Gissing considered himself an artist, but he did not look back on his life
and consider it justified by his artistic achievement. Rather, he saw only an
immense labour and an inadequate reward.

Two months after Gissing's arrival in Rome, those rewards began to
improve. Colles was still unable to place *The Town Traveller* as a serial, but
after seven months of trying he got an offer of £250 from Methuen for book
publication, and another £100 from Frederick Stokes for the US edition.
This was a lesson to Gissing on using an agent and giving him time to
work. He would receive more for *The Town Traveller* than for any previous
book, and it had taken him only five weeks to write it. Another encouraging
sign was the step up in income from a US edition. The International
Copyright Agreement was consolidating the English-speaking world into
a single market, in which authors received proper payment from all editions.
Frederick Stokes seems to have done well with his edition of *The Whirlpool*,
for which he paid an advance of only £50; now he was doubling his offer.
It helped, too, that the US editions of Gissing's books mostly had a more
attractive format than the English ones. The US population was now nearly
double that of the UK, and books were generally cheaper on that side of
the Atlantic. From about 1895, Gissing was probably selling more copies
of his books there than in his home country. *The Town Traveller* is not a
trivial book, but it is one of the most cheerful and least ideological of

Gissing's works. That probably helped Colles to get a good price for it.

The news from Colles encouraged Gissing to get down to work on a short story he had promised to *Cosmopolis*, and for which he was to receive £25.10. 'The Ring Finger' is about hotel life in Rome. Miss Kerin, an 'almost pretty' young woman from Ulster, falls in love with Mr Wrighton, who takes her sightseeing. She says nothing to him about her love. One day he tells her that he has received a letter from England, accepting his proposal of marriage. Miss Kerin will go back to Ulster with her aged uncle, and lead an empty life in a country town; Mr Wrighton will never know that she longs for him as she looks at her ringless third finger. Gissing wrote the story from the viewpoint of the disappointed woman. Perhaps he suspected that someone at his boarding-house in Siena or Rome had been in love with him; perhaps he was simply reversing his own experiences of rejection. What was certain was that, in Gissing's world, lovers were likely to be ill-matched and victims of their illusions about the other.

Miss Orme's reports about Edith convinced Gissing that she would have to find a home somewhere else. 'With people of the educated class she cannot live,' he told H. G. Wells, '—their proximity simply maddens her, in spite of every effort to win her good-will. I foresee that it will be necessary to take the child away; he might just as well be in the care of a drunkard or a lunatic, as of this furious and hateful woman.'[37] Wells's reply to this letter has not survived; perhaps Gissing was upset by it and threw it out. In his autobiography, Wells was caustic about Miss Orme's efforts to patch up Gissing's second marriage:

> The helpful lady was meddling with things beyond her experience and the poor wife, perplexed and indignant beyond measure by this strange man who had possessed himself of her life, was progressing through scenes and screams towards a complete mental breakdown; she was behaving very badly indeed, and letters would arrive at the Hotel Aliberti in Rome, that left Gissing white and shaking between anger and dismay for the better part of a day.[38]

Wells offered to go to Tulse Hill and sort things out, but Gissing declined. Wells seemed to think that Edith was first a victim of Gissing's peculiar way of life, and then of Miss Orme's attempt to make her conform to middle-class expectations. This assumed that Edith's many confrontations with servants, landlords and the police were somehow caused by the way Gissing had treated her. The case that Edith might have been a happy person if she had not been mistreated by her misogynistic husband can never be proved. One could argue just as plausibly that Edith's mental state became much worse after her husband left her, so that the marriage, unhappy as it may have been, had done her some good. All that can be known for certain is that Gissing and Edith had blundered into marriage without knowing either themselves, or their mates.

H. G. Wells still considered Gissing a firm friend and was happy to accept an invitation to come to Rome, for his first journey out of England. When he arrived, with Amy Catherine, he proved the rule that tourists to Italy are of two kinds. Gissing was there for the art, the history and the literary associations. Wells wanted a holiday from writing (he was finishing *When the Sleeper Wakes*), and from English weather:

> I'm not coming to Rome a sight seeing. I don't care a triturated damn for all the blessed oil paintings in the world, and precious little for the sculpture, and I'm not going to be made to go and see places I shouldn't go to see if I lived in Rome. . . . I'm coming to see Rome and yourself, and I don't mean to fall into the snare of the tourist and not see the city for its sights.[39]

Above all, Wells wanted to observe Roman society, and be part of it himself. Gissing's instincts were rather to stand apart; but with his wide experience of the country and his fluent Italian he was an invaluable guide to his friend.

Even before he came, Wells was dreaming of a sociable utopia rather different from the Devonshire retreat of Gissing's 'Henry Ryecroft':

> I am sick of this damned climate and of my perpetual catarrh. . . . Do you think of coming back, or settling on some Mons of Rome? If so we will be with you in five years time. I mean to lead a great multitude of selected people out of this reek, sooner or later, artists and writers and decent souls and we will all settle in little houses along and up a slope of sunlight all set with olives and vines and honey mellowed marble ruins between the mountains and the sea. There we will sit in the evening of our days dressed in decent blouses talking talking of this and that.[40]

Gissing did manage to live his last years in the south, though in a much more restricted style than Wells's fantasy. When Wells arrived for his month in Rome, on 9 March 1898, he made sure to assemble a congenial band of male chums. Apart from Brian Ború. Dunne, the core group was Wells, Gissing, E. W. Hornung and Arthur Conan Doyle. Hornung, the creator of the gentleman-thief 'Raffles', was married to one of Conan Doyle's sisters. Gissing already knew Conan Doyle through the Omar Khayyam Club. He considered him an overrated author, perhaps because of his melodramatic treatment of the London slums in the Sherlock Holmes

stories. Nonetheless, Hornung reported that he and Doyle got on well with
Gissing in Rome:

> We have seen quite a lot of Gissing and Wells during the last fortnight. ...
> We like them both quite immensely. Wells is a very good little chap when
> you know him, humorous, modest, unaffected. As for Gissing, he is really
> a sweet fellow. ... He has charm and sympathy, humour too and a louder
> laugh than Oscar's. That man is not wilfully a pessimist. But he is lonely –
> there has been a great sorrow and ill-health too.[41]

Gissing enjoyed being with a lively group of writers, all younger than
himself, though it must have irked him that they had all achieved huge
commercial success, while he had the fatal label of 'pessimist' hung around
his neck. Their work failed to interest him deeply because he did not see any
value in what they were doing: creating the great myths of late-Victorian
popular culture. For Gissing, popular culture was an oxymoron.

Ladies, too, were happy to send invitations to Gissing and use him as
their guide around Rome. Caroline Fitzgerald was one, a beautiful American heiress who had been painted by Burne-Jones when she was nineteen.
She was a poet and scholar; Gissing's verdict on her was 'clever but shallow'.
At his hotel he met Rosalind Williams; like Fitzgerald, she had a disastrous
marriage behind her. Gissing's first impression was not favourable: 'loud;
bullies waiters; forces herself into our conversations'.[42] Mrs Williams was
eager for sexual adventures; she would tip head waiters in order to be seated
next to likely Englishmen at meals. Gissing beat her off at first, but soon
gave in and started guiding her around Rome.

Gissing and Mrs Williams were in contact for only eight days, and then
she left with her eight-year-old son Noel for Venice. Some kind of a bond
was created in that time, enough that they would meet again in the summer
in England. There may not have been any sexual connection in Rome,
though Mrs Williams did not believe in long courtships. They were certainly having an affair by the summer. What was the attraction between
them? Mrs Williams was eight years younger than Gissing, good-looking,
soulful, nervous, and impulsive. She had a private income of about £1,000
a year. She was the youngest of nine daughters of Richard Potter, a wealthy
railway investor from Liverpool; unlike her brilliant sister Beatrice (by
now married to Sidney Webb), she had no academic pretensions. From the
time of puberty, she wrote, 'my thoughts were largely occupied with the
other sex. ... I was secretly violently in love with all my sisters' admirers,
and also with the heroes of the novels I read.'[43] Rosalind suffered from
anorexia and depression as a teenager; when she was twenty-three she

married a barrister, Dyson Williams. On their wedding night, Williams confessed that he was suffering from syphilis; they had a son, but he died in 1896.

When Rosalind met Gissing she was recovering from a nervous breakdown and restlessly travelling on the Continent, having affairs here and there. Her sister Beatrice said that she was 'not sure that *sanity* and *celibacy* are both within her capacity'. But there was nothing insane in Rosalind's attraction to Gissing:

> Since my first great affection and intimacy with my father I have had a great longing to understand and enter into the mind of some man who was my intellectual superior and to make my mind as if it were a mirror of his. I have little or no independent intellectual life or originality of my own and am, in fact a sort of mental parasite.[44]

Gissing was a well-known writer, and a brilliant guide to the ruins of ancient Rome. Rosalind was infatuated with him, though not necessarily in a sexual way. She had recently fallen in love with George Dobbs on Capri, and said that it was only with him that she experienced 'the ecstasy of physical love'.[45] Eventually she married Dobbs, and had several children with him. One can think of reasons, on both sides, why Gissing and Rosalind might go to bed together and have the experience fall short of ecstasy. Gissing had always been full of inhibitions and resentments about sexual relations with a 'lady'. Rosalind's sisters had warned that they would ostracise her in England if she lost her reputation, so that she was 'quite unable to contemplate the consequences of setting up house with a man to whom she was not married'.[46] Edith was adamant that she would not divorce Gissing and even wanted to get a court order forcing him to come home. Rosalind saw that Gissing was not free to marry and probably never would be.

The English residents of Rome in 1898 could not live and love just as they pleased. They still had their ties to England through their professions, their families, and their past histories. The only way for Gissing and Rosalind Williams to live together would be as expatriates, and neither of them was willing, at this point, to consider such a life. Gissing's life in Rome did not satisfy him; he felt that he had lost the ability to work, and wanted to go back to England. Wells and his wife went south, to Naples and Paestum, while Gissing, on 12 April 1898, took the train north. Before returning to England, he wanted to visit Eduard Bertz in Berlin. He had not seen him for fourteen years, though they had exchanged hundreds of letters. Bertz had a house at Potsdam, where Gissing stayed for four nights. He found

Bertz looking old and grey-haired (he was forty-five), and no doubt Bertz saw Gissing in the same way. By day Gissing walked around Berlin, finding signs of wealth and ambition, but little beauty. He knew German well and admired German culture; unfortunately, there was 'rampant militarism everywhere about'.[47] The same thing was happening in Italy and it was clear to Gissing that, as each European power flexed its muscles, the end of it must be war.

15

Gabrielle

Back in England, Gissing needed a place to work, which was also a place to hide. He saw Rosalind Williams in Chelsea, then went up north to see his sisters and Walter. To keep Edith off his track he asked Algernon to spread the rumour that he was living in Worcestershire, while he looked for a hideaway south of London. Algernon, in a muddle as usual, squeezed £25 out of his brother in exchange. Gissing soon found a semi-detached house in Dorking at 7 Clifton Terrace, which he took on a one-year lease for £42. It was the most attractive of his English houses, with a steep garden at the back and a fine view across to the Surrey Downs. 'I have now to write for dear life,' he told Hick, 'and for some time must live like a hermit.'[1]

Gissing moved into his hermit's cell on 14 May 1898 and engaged a young widow with four children, Mrs Boughton, as his housekeeper. He found her 'dry and distasteful', but she was competent and a good cook. Her wages were £18 a year – about the price of a short story, which Gissing soon began writing. Edith, meanwhile, had been moved out of Miss Orme's house and put in four rooms at 90 Mansfield Road NW, not too far from where she had grown up. Miss Orme's former nurse lived in the same house, and could keep an eye on her. Edith was far from content, though, and was determined to find Gissing and claim her marital rights. In early June she made her way with Alfred to Willersey, where she tried to get Gissing's address from Algernon. With the threat of Edith's return hanging over him, Gissing could think only of selling what he wrote at the highest price. He had felt disloyal to Lawrence & Bullen in giving *The Town Traveller* to Methuen, but more disloyalty was going to be necessary:

> I am in a serious position. My expenses are far heavier than they used to be, and I *must* make money – a difficult thing for an unpopular author. What's more, I must make it speedily, and for the moment I can think of nothing but this vile necessity. . . . Of course I must go hard for the magazines. Only in that way can some hundreds a year be hoped for. The problem is, how to do it without degrading oneself.[2]

Gissing knew that he had failed as a father, with both his sons living away from him. He was deeply worried about their future, but felt that he needed to be alone in order to build up capital for them. If he made enough money, he would at least succeed as a provider. At the end of May he got down to work in Dorking and wrote four stories in three weeks. Two of the stories returned to the theme of marriage as fate. In 'The Peace-Bringer' a poet has become sick and retired to the country with his wife (some of the details are reminiscent of Meredith at Box Hill). He becomes infatuated with a young woman and pays her to come and sing for him. When she leaves England to meet another man, the poet turns back to his wife and begs for her love, only to get a dusty answer: 'I feel only a certain duty to you. How should I feel more? I was never able – never in my life – to have affection for any one who had none for me. I don't reproach you, of course. Love exists, or it does not. If you turn from me to someone else, I can say nothing.'[3] The poet has to die without the love that he craves. In 'The Elixir', conversely, a man restores himself by finding love. Mr Orgreave was once a Gissing-like outcast; after wooing a rich young woman he becomes a successful manufacturer and politician. His elixir was marital happiness:

> That's what transformed me, gave me a new life, a clean soul! In my case there was no other salvation. My ideal woman, and a solid income. Pretty large demands, I'm aware; but it was my destiny, you see. I'm the one man in a million who gets what he wants, and, having got it, I had drunk the elixir of life. ... On the one hand, death blaspheming in a gutter; on the other, a life of health and splendid happiness, with philosophy enough to face the end. No third possibility in my case.[4]

Both of these stories end with the death of their protagonists, and both take a fatalistic view of how a life can be summed up. The value of life is determined by marriage, which is something separate from the two persons who blindly enter into it. At the end of 'The Peace-Bringer', the poet tries to console his wife by saying that, once he is dead, she can have a new beginning with another man:

> 'Dear,' Mrs Jaffray answered, through her tears, 'the new beginning would have the old end. Ten years of marriage teach one all one has to learn about that side of life. I know you, and I know myself. The one is just as much and just as little to blame as the other. Only the foolish embitter life with reproaches.'[5]

For Gissing, fatalism was both a philosophy, and a defence against taking any blame on himself for the failure of his two marriages. Marriage was a roll of the dice, and the dice were loaded. Yet his luck in love was about to turn, in a way that would force him to reconsider his beliefs.

Having rattled off his short stories, Gissing decided that he should solve his financial problems by writing some plays, preferably comedies. This was a dubious enterprise, since dialogue was not a strong point in his novels. It was three years since Henry James had been humiliated by the failure of his play *Guy Domville*. Gissing never got near an actual stage, which was just as well. He spent three weeks on becoming a playwright, then abandoned the idea. Methuen asked him to write eleven prefaces for a set of Dickens novels, at ten guineas each; he was happy to take on this piece of steady work. Then he received a proposition from Grant Richards, a young man of twenty-six who had gone into publishing with enough capital to snare some major authors for his list. Richards told Gissing that he would pay him more than any other publisher for the rights to all his work for the next five years, perhaps as a set annual income. Gissing jumped at the idea of distancing himself from the literary marketplace:

> Now, it is quite certain that an arrangement such as this, provided it worked well for the publisher, would have the effect of putting my mind greatly at ease, and so enable me to do better work than when disturbed by thought of bargainings. . . .
>
> I want to write (I think you know that I write to please myself) two kinds of novel: one running to about 150,000 words, the other to some 80,000. I want also to write short pieces of between 3,000 and 10,000 words. As to character of work, that must be entirely my own affair. For twenty years I have written what I thought good in spite of every difficulty, and I cannot imagine myself being induced by any circumstances to do otherwise.[6]

Gissing proposed that Richards should give him £1,000 a year, and tell him how many books he should write for that money. That was about twice what he had earned in his best year, so he would have done well if Richards had taken the bait. But they came to no agreement, and Richards never published a Gissing book. He would soon go bankrupt, anyway; he got back into business, but remains most famous for tormenting James Joyce over the publication of *Dubliners*. A thousand a year, that nice round sum, stayed for ever beyond Gissing's reach.

If lack of money contributed to Gissing's nervous state in June, the other factor was his usual trouble, his relations with women. For once, though, trouble came from having too many women in his life rather than too few. Since January 1898 Clara Collet had been hinting that she would like to take Edith's place. She urged Gissing to get a legal separation, and told him that if he became seriously ill she would come to Italy and nurse him. He turned that suggestion aside, but hinted that other doors might be open once he returned in the spring:

> Have no fear but that I shall come and see you in London. The old fetters – which had begun at length to poison the wounds they made – no longer hold me. To live in utter solitude, just because that poor, silly creature wished me to do so, would be mere foolishness. I shall move about, in future, with perfect liberty, and get what help I can from anyone who is capable of helping me.[7]

It would be natural for Collet to read this as a promise that Gissing would be more intimate with her on his return. What he meant was rather different: yes, he was available, but not just to her. In fact, he would be available to someone instead of her. Collet kept telling Gissing in Italy that he was attractive and worthy of a good woman's love. This only encouraged him to try his luck with women who were younger and more sexually appealing than she was.

The details of Collet's disappointment remain hidden, because she destroyed Gissing's letters to her for a crucial year, and all of her diary for the 1890s.[8] When he got back to London he went to dinner with Rosalind Williams in Chelsea, then to see Collet on the following afternoon. The next we hear of Williams in Gissing's diary is three months later when he goes to see her at a cottage she has rented for the summer at Holmwood, three miles from Dorking. It cannot have been a coincidence that she turned up there; we can safely assume that Gissing encouraged her to come and live nearby. Williams was five years younger than Collet, with enough charms to attract two husbands and many other lovers; Collet did not marry and may have remained a virgin all her life. In a sexual competition, Collet had no chance against Williams.

Rosalind Williams remained a close friend of Gissing's from their first meeting in March 1898 to at least the autumn of that year. By coming to stay at Holmwood she was making herself available for an affair. She believed in free love and Gissing could take from her what he wanted, or was capable of. Rosalind could be considered a Godwin Peak fantasy come true: she was rich, beautiful, and upper-class. But she was not willing to live openly with a married man, nor could Gissing face the social ostracism that would have followed a union with Rosalind. He also disliked her small son, Noel. So there was still a place open in his heart when, on 23 June, he received a letter from Gabrielle Edith Fleury asking if she might translate *New Grub Street* into French. *Eve's Ransom* had recently been translated by

Georges Art, and Gissing was always pleased by recognition from a country whose novelists he admired much more than English ones. A French lady writing to him was even better, and Mlle Fleury proposed coming over to England to see him. Gissing could not give her permission to translate *New Grub Street* because he had sold the rights to Smith, Elder, but he certainly could invite her to tea at Dorking.

When Gabrielle came over, two weeks later, Gissing was staying for several days with the Wellses at Worcester Park. He had rented a bicycle and Wells was teaching him how to ride it; he thought he was doing well, and Wells thought he was doing badly – 'far too nervous and excitable to ride'.[9] Both of them had a point. Gissing bought his own bicycle for £14 and rode it around Dorking, but he complained of being black and blue from falling off. On Wednesday 6 July Gabrielle Fleury came down to Worcester Park for lunch, and Gissing went to meet her train:

> I was looking this way and that, on the station platform, wondering what sort of lady I had to expect. Suddenly my eyes fell on a figure which, in the same instant, I *hoped* was hers. And (I have never yet told you of this little experience) so strongly did I hope it, that the hope excited a corresponding fear lest I should be mistaken. Though finding myself near you, *I deliberately turned and moved away.* . . . It was as though an instinct made me tremble in your presence; I could not approach with a matter-of-fact readiness to the woman who, so mysteriously, was about to take possession of my life. Another glance from a distance, and I drew near again. Then – your voice – your voice—[10]

What Wells saw was 'a woman of the intellectual bourgeoisie, with neat black hair and a trim black dress, her voice was carefully musical, she was well read, slightly voluble and over-explicit by our English standards, and consciously refined and intelligent'.[11] Wells was conscious of Gabrielle's feelings, Gissing was conscious only of his own, that here before him was his 'ideal of womanhood'. As always, the ideal would come to be tempered by the real.

Who was Gabrielle Edith Fleury? Her father had been treasurer of the company that ran the Marseille docks; she was raised in a comfortable home and had relatives who were rich industrialists and landowners. She had not gone to university – very few French women had, at that point – but she was well read, spoke several languages, and was a good pianist. She moved in literary circles, and was friendly with the aged sister of the romantic poet Alfred de Musset, and with the first wife of Leopold von Sacher-Masoch. There were other ladies Gabrielle knew who loved or helped writers, and

Gabrielle wanted a writer of her own. It seems revealing that she was an eager collector of writers' autographs. Gabrielle had never worked at any profession and never would, except for her occasional translations. Before she met Gissing, the defining event of her life had been her engagement to the eminent poet and man of letters René Sully-Prudhomme. She became attached to him as a teenager and broke off her engagement in 1892, when he was fifty-three and she was twenty-four. As Gabrielle told the story, 'a very serious illness led to the severance of their poetic engagement and caused the remainder of the poet's life to be one of grief'.[12] Another version was that her parents objected to her marrying someone more than twice her age, and managed to prevent it. The engagement may have been devoted, but was unlikely to have been passionate. Sully-Prudhomme had wanted to become a monk in his youth; he suffered a stroke in 1870 that left him partially paralysed below the waist. He was already an invalid when Gabrielle met him, and did not marry after she left. Sully-Prudhomme was awarded the first Nobel Prize for literature in 1901, though his reputation has fallen low and his doleful lyrics are little read today.

Gabrielle had first become interested in Gissing when she attended a lecture on his work given by Yetta Blaze de Bury in Paris in December 1894. Gabrielle's friend Alice Ward, the Paris correspondent of *The Author*, then pointed Gabrielle towards *New Grub Street* as a good novel to translate. When she got off the train at Worcester Park she was already an admirer of the English writer who had come to meet her. Gissing was ready to do more than admire her back:

> At the first moment of beholding you, I thought you the most beautiful woman I had ever seen. . . . I, who was destined to love you, naturally saw in you my ideal type of beauty. . . . After that, need I insist on the obvious fact that my love has more in it than passionate desire? Loving you for the beauty of your face, I came to love you for the perfection of your mind.[13]

Gabrielle seems to have avoided the camera, for few photographs of her have survived; but it is hard to see in those pictures anything but a young woman of commonplace appearance, self-conscious and with a letter-box mouth. Her dresses are neat, but not particularly fashionable. Gissing was so worn down by his years with Edith that he was bowled over by the first woman who was presentable and appreciated his work. There was a great gap in his being, and infatuation came to fill it.

Infatuation meant that a quart of fantasy boiled over from an ounce of actual knowledge of the beloved. Gissing had a few hours of conversation with Gabrielle at the Wellses on 6 July, after which she went back to stay with friends in Suffolk. Smith, Elder gave her permission to translate *New Grub Street,* and she then sent a copy to Gissing to make cuts for serial publication in France. He made these cuts in only a day or two, though he also supervised Gabrielle as she worked on the translation in 1898 and 1899. For three weeks after their first meeting they exchanged rather stilted letters, making arrangements for the translation and for a second meeting in Dorking. Gissing explained that it would be improper for her to stay at his house, and recommended a local hotel. Eventually, Gabrielle just came down for the day. She spent nine hours with Gissing on 26 July, talking about his novels and the lives they had lived before they met. By the end of the day Gissing was deeply in love, though all he did to show it was kiss Gabrielle's hand in the evening.

Gissing started to reveal his feelings in the letter he wrote to Gabrielle the next day, and when he received an encouraging reply he poured out his love in a stream of letters. It was a literary wooing in which each partner pushed the other to new heights of emotion.[14] The way Gissing signed successive letters shows how he climbed the ladder:

Always sincerely yours
Affectionately yours
Yours ever
Yours ever devotedly
Ever and ever yours, my heart's darling
Yours heart and soul, my beloved
For ever yours, my beloved

Gissing had idealised Nell, a girl of the streets, and written sentimental sonnets about his love. With Gabrielle there was no limit at all to the wonders he saw in her. In his story 'The Peace-Bringer', he had suggested how affection from one partner could set off an escalation, with each outbidding the other in love. By offering Gabrielle his passionate love, he might hope to get even more passionate love in return. Another of his gambits was to say: I have always loved a certain kind of woman, but could never find her. He had gone through adult life with a specific pair of shoes dancing in front of him; now Gabrielle, miraculously, had appeared to fill them:

Let me sketch the woman whom, for so many years, I have vainly imagined. I saw her, to begin with, a much nobler being than myself; I saw her, before all, a true woman, endowed with every grace of mind and heart which is characteristically feminine. Her face represented my own ideal of personal beauty – each man has his vision of the perfect face; she had very gentle eyes, eloquent of sympathy, bright with intelligence. And her voice – woman's voice is perhaps the first thing that attaches one to her; her voice was soft and varied, always musical. Then, she was capable of passion; one divined in her an infinite tenderness. Her mind was open to the world of art; she loved music especially. And with all that, she had the domestic instinct, so seldom found with the other qualities.[15]

Gissing saw nothing wrong in falling in love with a pre-existing idea of a person; he thought that was how love worked. In *The Crown of Life*, Piers Otway likes to gaze at the beautiful women displayed in shop windows:

He could not satisfy himself with looking and musing; he could not pluck himself away. An old experience; he always lingered by the print shops of the Haymarket, and always went on with troubled blood, with mind rapt above familiar circumstance, dreaming passionately, making wild forecast of his fate.

Piers goes home to the middle-class family with whom he lodges, outside of London, and finds that their niece has come to stay for a week:

Even had her features been hidden, the attitude of this stranger, her admirable form and rapid graceful gestures, must have held the young man's attention; seeing her with the light full on her countenance, he gazed and gazed, in sudden complete forgetfulness of his half-opened letter. Just so had he stood before the print shop in London this morning, with the same wide eyes, the same hurried breathing; rapt, self-oblivious.[16]

Instead of going down to meet this Irene, Piers stays in his room for the evening. Whether at the print shop or at home, he prefers to stay on the other side of the glass from his ideal, so that he can indulge his fantasy without the restraint of actuality. It is the positive counterpart of that other experience of Gissing's: gazing through the glass at the corpses in the Paris Morgue. Piers stands and gazes for two reasons: because fantasy is more satisfying than engagement, and because by the time he actually encounters the object of his gaze, everything that will happen has already been decided. 'I am a determinist,' Gissing told Gabrielle, 'I know that nothing *could* happen but that which did, for every event is the result of causes which go back into eternity.'[17]

If Gabrielle was not everything that Gissing imagined – no woman could be – she was at least closer to his ideal than any other woman he had yet wooed. But she was out of reach in Paris for the next two months after their day together, and to develop his fantasies in letters was rather different than actually getting to know his beloved. Gabrielle, for her part, seems to have been happy to encourage Gissing's rhapsodies about her. Before she came to Dorking he had told her that he lived apart from his wife and had two children. He was not ready to tell her about Nell, though he did say that if he had not met Gabrielle he would have got into trouble with a woman again:

> I am not made to live in solitude, and it was only too likely that I should have sought the companionship of some woman, who, sooner or later, would have involved me in new unhappiness. You need not tell me that this would have been ignoble. I *know* that it is ignoble to seek anything but the ideal in love. But be patient with me, dearest; I was so weak until I knew you, and so hopeless.[18]

One woman with whom he had been weak was Rosalind Williams, whom Gissing did not mention to Gabrielle until November, and then only in neutral terms. Gissing had lunch and dinner with Rosalind at Holmwood on 31 July, five days after Gabrielle's visit to his house. He cycled over to see her regularly in the following weeks. Could he have continued an affair with Rosalind while writing his daily love-letters to Gabrielle? In *The Crown of Life*, which Gissing started writing in October, Piers cherishes an ideal love for Irene and tries to preserve his chastity by cold baths and exercise. But when his business takes him to Russia for long periods, he sleeps with other women: 'The truth was, of course, that though imagination could always restore Irene's supremacy, and constantly did so, though his intellectual being never failed from allegiance to her, his blood had been at the mercy of any face sufficiently alluring. So it would be again, little as he could now believe it.'[19] If Piers could do it, and justify it to himself, perhaps Gissing could too. It would not be the first time in his life that he was living a lie, though his syrupy love-letters to Gabrielle appear in a different light if, at the same time, he was making love of another kind to Rosalind.

Let us give Gissing the benefit of the doubt, and assume that after he told Rosalind about Gabrielle she agreed to be his friend rather than his lover. That would be consistent with what Gissing told H. G. Wells about the relationship:

> I am not sorry that Mrs Williams has come to Holmwood. She is not at all likely to interfere with my working hours, and at other times I am very glad to be saved from melancholy madness. She is a good and sensible and honest woman; I like her better the more I know her, and respect her not a little. Her weaknesses are amiable – a great thing. And, as I begin to see, she has a quite unusual loyalty and right feeling in her friendships.[20]

Gissing's phrase 'quite unusual' would refer to the assumption, in many of his novels, that you cannot care for someone without being jealous of them too. Rosalind's feelings may even have been the reverse: that Gissing's infatuation with Gabrielle was no obstacle to Rosalind's sleeping with him too, in accordance with her belief in free love. Gissing, of course, found it hard to say no to a woman in any circumstances. Certainly Wells felt that Rosalind's steadiness and generosity would have made her a much better partner for Gissing than Gabrielle, not to mention her £1,000 a year. Gabrielle's private income was only £100. But Rosalind wanted to have a respectable life in England and rejected a 'free union'; Gabrielle finally accepted it.

Whatever the extravagant hopes he placed on Gabrielle, Gissing had plenty of immediate troubles for which Rosalind could offer advice and comfort. A week after Gabrielle's visit to Dorking, Gissing heard from Miss Orme that Edith had attacked her landlord and his wife with a stick, and the police had been called in. Edith moved to other lodgings on the same street, leaving her furniture behind. Gissing then told his solicitor to get the furniture removed and put into storage; Edith saw this happening and tried to prevent it, destroying her former landlord's front garden in the process. She wrote a threatening postcard addressed to 'Bad Eliza Orme', and demanded a house and furniture of her own, custody of both Alfred and Walter, and a separation agreement. Gissing struck back by putting the furniture beyond her reach: he brought some down to Dorking, and sold the rest. He had been paying her rent at Mansfield Road, but now that she had moved he started to pay her a flat sum of 35s a week through his solicitor, S. N. P. Brewster. At the end of the year this was raised to £2.[21] Having quarrelled with her husband, with Miss Orme and with her own relatives, Edith was now adrift in the world, with Alfred as her little hostage.

Not surprisingly, Edith turned back to Gissing in the hope of having a home. She tracked him down through the movers who had taken the furniture to Dorking, and arrived on his doorstep on the afternoon of 7 September:

> Happily, there was no scene. I gave her to understand that our parting was final, but that I should not take Alfred away from her as long as she keeps well. The poor little child is now in knickerbockers; he looked bright, but pale; had walked all from the station on this day of terrific heat, but did not seem overtired. I spoke not a word to him, and he hardly looked at me. They had tea, and set off for the station again. – So, this event I have so feared is over. She promises not to come again, but—[22]

Alfred was now two and a half; did he even remember his father after not seeing him for a year? Gissing's failure to even speak to his son is hard to forgive. As he had done with Nell, Gissing would send money to Edith but never speak or write to her if he could avoid it. He felt that this was the only way he could survive. Nonetheless, his actions showed the enormous bitterness he felt towards both his wives. Poor little Alfred was just collateral damage. He was also a victim, probably, of Victorian ideas about heredity. Edith resented Walter as 'his father's child', Gissing saw Alfred as Edith's.[23] However he justified it, Gissing looked on with relief as Edith and Alfred set off, hand in hand, on their long, hot walk back to the station. He would live for another five years, but never see either of them again.

This dismal afternoon would make trouble for Gissing with Gabrielle too. He told her nothing at the time, but three years later she added her own bitterness to the toxic brew. Complaining to H. G. Wells about Gissing's treatment of her, she spoke of Edith's visit to Dorking:

> You say that woman would not possibly find us out in England, but how did she discover G's abode when he was at Dorking and so carefully concealed his address, and how is it that she came down straight to the place and asked for him and was admitted and he gave her tea, and so on, – at a moment we were already engaged together?[24]

In Gabrielle's mind, any contact Gissing had with Edith was a kind of adultery, a betrayal of his new beloved. That a two-year-old might need to drink and have a rest, after walking a mile and a half, did not cut any ice with her.

At first Gabrielle assumed that Gissing would get a divorce from Edith and then they could have a civil marriage in France or England. But they soon faced the realisation that Gissing had no chance of escaping his marriage:

> Having no personal knowledge of the woman from whom I have parted, you cannot of course understand how improbable (I may say impossible) it is that she will ever give me a chance of obtaining a divorce. ... As long as she lives, she will be lonely and embittered, – her *one* consolation the thought that *I* cannot marry again. ...
>
> I should be mad if I thought you ought to put yourself in conflict with received ideas, and sadden all your friends. I do not look for *that*. Only tell me that you understand the real hopelessness of our position, and then, if you can still bear it ... I too will strive against my nature, and for your sake live on in solitude.[25]

We do not know how Gissing and Gabrielle negotiated their problem, because Gabrielle's letters have been destroyed and she later went to work with scissors and ink to censor Gissing's letters to her. If a divorce was not possible, they faced a crisis that Gissing saw in classic Victorian terms:

> And now, when at last I meet the woman I have sought, I am forbidden to think of her as a wife . . . forbidden to enter into the Paradise which has been set before my eyes.
>
> My darling, a woman (the high-minded woman) is content with love afar off – with its spiritual gifts; she can live her whole life long on imagination. Alas! It is not so with a man.[26]

Gissing may have known of John Stuart Mill's platonic relations with Harriet Taylor, until her husband died and she was free to marry Mill. Gabrielle seems to have made some such pledge to Gissing. She would come to stay with him in October, but not sleep with him until they were free to marry. 'I shall soon hold you in reality –,' Gissing wrote to her, 'your very self – and look into your beautiful eyes, and give you the kiss which puts a seal upon our union. That our perfect life is still in the future, cannot be helped; you shall never hear me complain of that.'[27]

Gissing's mother came to him at Dorking in mid-August, and stayed for a month. He tried to explain his mother to Gabrielle:

> The relations between my mother and myself would seem to you rather strange. We are excellent friends, but – as is so often the case in England – we have very little in common, mentally or morally, and *never* talk in a confidential way. My mother has lived a very narrow life in a little provincial town; she is purely domestic, and religious in a very formal way. Often I have lamented the lack of sympathy between us. . . . Well, this is English, you know.[28]

Gissing did not feel able to take Walter for his summer holidays; work came first. Dr Hick generously agreed to take Walter at New Romney for seven weeks from the end of July (Gissing paid something for his board). Soon after Walter arrived there, Hick took in H. G. Wells, who was recovering from a kidney abscess, and his wife. Hick was doing a lot for the cause of literature. Gissing finally went down to New Romney on 16 September; Walter came back with him for four nights at Dorking, then returned to Wakefield with his grandmother. Gissing's project at this time was to do the Dickens prefaces for Methuen as quickly as possible. He could do one in three or four days and earn ten guineas, except when paralysed by worries about Edith. A proper start on his next novel, *The*

Crown of Life, would have to wait until his emotional state had settled down.

A fortnight after his mother had left, Gissing met Gabrielle on the platform of East Croydon station. H. G. Wells said that Gabrielle spent her week in Dorking 'under circumstances of extreme decorurm'.[29] Mrs Boughton lived in, and was very proper in her ways; in any case, the decorum was as much an internal as an external form of discipline. Gabrielle had not come to sleep with Gissing, but to discuss the terms on which she might sleep with him in the future. Gissing's idea was that, at this point, they should do no more than kiss. He wanted his relation with Gabrielle to be completely different from any sexual experiences he had had before:

> Darling, one troublesome thought mingles with my delight. I look back on my by-gone life, and I contrast it with the purity of yours. Gabrielle, will you forgive me everything? Can you forget, my darling, my beloved? Indeed, I have all but forgotten; it is only now and then that the dark thought comes back. ... Believe that my love of you is unshadowed by anything unworthy![30]

It seems almost certain, then, that Gissing and Gabrielle did no more than what he recorded in his diary: that they walked on the Downs by day, and he read poetry to her – Browning and Tennyson – in the evenings. They saw no one except Mrs Boughton, and by the end of Gabrielle's stay they had decided, as Gissing wrote, 'that our life together shall begin next spring'.[31]

What kind of life together, and why next spring? Gissing was tied to the lease on his Dorking house, and was too anxious about money to imagine living in France while continuing to pay rent in England. Meanwhile, Gabrielle had the delicate task of explaining to her parents and friends in France that she planned to live with an English author in the new year. She was part of a circle that was highly respectable and religious, but also willing to recognise the claims of art. Her friend Madame de Musset's brother Alfred had enjoyed a spectacularly erratic love-life, which had not prevented him being enrolled in the Pantheon of French poets. Madame Sacher-Masoch was divorced, yet not disgraced by the notorious works of her former husband. By the end of her visit, Gabrielle had almost committed herself to live with Gissing in spite of his still being married to Edith. She still had to sell the idea to her family, and that would take time.

Gissing did not have to sell the idea of a free union with Gabrielle to anyone, and he told few people about it. H. G. Wells had been somewhat acid about Gissing's previous misadventures, so Gissing chose not to tell him what he and Gabrielle planned to do. Morley Roberts came down for a visit on 13 November, and Gissing told him everything. He told Algernon only that he planned to move to France in the new year, because it was cheaper to live there. Eduard Bertz was told of developments on the French side:

> Well now, her mother knows the whole truth of the matter, and has given full consent. I have had a beautiful letter from her about it. Her father, being so ill (and hopelessly) is merely told that Gabrielle is going to marry an Englishman. Moreover, her French friends will learn the story in the same shape – simply a marriage in England.
>
> As explanation of this rather extraordinary state of things, you must remember that I am at present almost as well known in Paris as in London, . . . Of course all this has affected the mind of Mme Fleury, a woman of great intelligence, well acquainted with English.[32]

Gabrielle's mother agreed to a sham marriage between her daughter and Gissing because he was such a well-known writer; unusual reasoning, indeed! Gissing's hope was that the French would not know he was already married in England, while the English would not know that he was pretending to be married in France. That he did get away with it suggests that he was not as well known as he thought.

For the remainder of 1898, Gissing had to wait for complications to be resolved in Paris, and get on with writing *The Crown of Life*. The day after Christmas, he received an anonymous letter hinting that Edith was having adulterous relations with someone. Who could have written such a letter? It had to be someone who knew Edith, and also knew Gissing's address in Dorking. Could Edith have arranged for the letter herself, hoping to make Gissing jealous? The episode unfolded like something in Gissing's novels. He advertised in the *Daily Mail* and received no reply. He knew that Edith had now moved to Brighton with Alfred, so he made plans to have her watched by a private detective. If he could get proof of Edith's adultery he would have grounds for divorce, and could have a proper marriage with Gabrielle. Alternatively, he might be able to get a divorce in the US or Germany. But Gissing fell ill with the flu, and gave up on his hopes for any kind of divorce. This, in turn, gave Gabrielle second thoughts about whether she should go through with a sham marriage.

Gabrielle's father died on 13 January 1899 after a long illness, leaving her about £2,000 worth of investments. If she pretended to have married Gissing, a *lettre de faire part* would have to be sent out to her friends and relatives – a formal announcement that she was now Madame Gissing. But to receive the income from her investments she would have to sign her legal name. If she signed as Gabrielle Gissing it might be considered a forgery; if she signed as Gabrielle Fleury, it would reveal that she was not really married. Gabrielle threw Gissing into despair by proposing that they should put off their marriage for a year or two, and hope that somehow he could get a divorce. Fortunately, she soon changed her mind and said they should go ahead and marry for love, without paying attention to worldly conventions.

Gissing had to wait seven months for Gabrielle, in all, and he had little to do but make money by writing. His health improved for a while after he met her, though she was still very concerned about his weak lungs. She was ahead of her time in trying to persuade him to stop smoking. Healthy or not, his task was to stick at his desk until *The Crown of Life* was finished, and sell it for a good price. As soon as Gabrielle left in October he was fuelled by the hope of marrying her, and wrote the whole novel over the next three months. While he was still working on it, he decided to drop W. M. Colles as his agent in favour of James B. Pinker. Gissing knew Pinker socially as a friend of the Wellses; he considered him more enterprising than Colles, and Wells had encouraged him to make the switch. Nonetheless, Gissing treated Colles shabbily by giving *The Crown of Life* to Pinker without even telling Colles what he had done.

When Colles wrote to ask how his new novel was coming along, Gissing said blandly: 'I was unfortunately obliged to make separate arrangements about it some time ago.' Colles sent a furious reply, and Gissing's response did little more than whine about his lack of success:

> Now *why* should you be deeply hurt? Pray look at the matter from my point of view, and what can be simpler? I have always held myself absolutely free as regards disposing of my work; indeed, otherwise I should not be able to work at all, for restraints harass me. . . .
>
> Consider the peculiarity of my position – the ridiculous contrast between my reputation and my income from literature. It is only natural that I should try this, that and the other method of selling my work; a more energetic man (and one less afraid of hurting people's feelings) would have made ten changes to my one. . . . In a word, the case is abnormal; there is no comparison between my own peculiar harassments in the literary career, and those of any other writer; and it results from these circumstances that I must have an absolutely free hand.[33]

Some of Gissing's new-found aggressiveness about selling his work came from H. G. Wells, who treated all publishers and agents as thieves and liars. But it was hardly fair to unload on Colles all of Gissing's pent-up grievances over the constant difficulties of his literary career. Colles could point out that if Gissing's stories sold slowly, it was because they often had to go to five or more magazines before anyone would take them. Colles had done a lot for Gissing, especially in making him a successful short-story writer. That Gissing was a novelist 'considerably more talked about than read' was hardly to be blamed on Colles.[34]

Gissing appeared in a much better light in the troubles over Harold Frederic, the American author of *The Damnation of Theron Ware*. Frederic had died at his second home in Surrey on 19 October 1898. He had a legal wife with whom he had five children, and a mistress, Kate Lyon, with whom he lived openly and had three more children. Lyon was charged with manslaughter because she was a Christian Scientist who kept doctors away from Frederic in his last illness. She was not convicted, but the two wives and eight children were all in need, and Gissing joined Frederic's friends in trying to help them. A fund was set up to help the legal Mrs Frederic, and Gissing wrote in to say that it would be 'hugely unjust' if Kate Lyon were not helped too. He then sent two guineas for the benefit of each wife, saying that he 'had to give to both or to neither'.[35]

As the scandal developed, Gissing became furious about the usual British hypocrisy. He wrote to Mrs Stephen Crane, who was looking after Kate Lyon's children: 'I feel that everyone who has read with understanding and pleasure any of Frederic's recent work owes to *her* [Lyon] a vast debt of gratitude. But for his true companion, his real wife, this work would never have been done. I cannot express the loathing with which I regard any man or woman who speaks slightingly of her.'[36] Gissing probably did not realise that he was preaching to the choir. 'Mrs Stephen Crane' was formerly the madam of a brothel in Florida, and she was not legally married to Crane, just pretending to be so. The discrimination against Kate Lyon and her children stirred Gissing's hatred of respectability:

> They have the brute world against them – and it has shown its bestiality in ways that make me rage up and down the room. Of course no public subscription can be opened for them. ... The children are away in the country, in good hands, and we want to secure them there for a year or two, till it can be seen what Kate Lyon can do. Of course their identity has to be concealed – else the sweet neighbours would make life impossible for the people who take care of them.
> Grrr![37]

Gissing was letting off steam because he would soon be in Harold Frederic's position, with one legal wife, one 'true wife', and two small children suffering from lack of a regular home. For all his defence of Kate Lyon's 'free union', he could not imagine exposing Gabrielle to insult by living with her openly in England. He was a quiet, but not a vigorous open supporter, of both Oscar Wilde in England and Dreyfus in France.[38]

Gissing told Gabrielle that he had rejected Clara Collet's suggestion that they should just act like George Lewes and George Eliot:

> Speaking of our difficulties, she asked 'Why not declare the truth, like George Eliot?' (You know that George Eliot made a free marriage with a man of letters miserably married already, and that English society forgave it out of consideration for her genius?) I replied that it seemed impossible, because of your numerous connections with the 'respectable' world.[39]

To put all the responsibility on Gabrielle was less than honest. Ever since he had sailed for the US in 1876, at the age of eighteen, Gissing concealed whatever he thought discreditable in his life, rather than avow it and live freely with the consequences. He was not of the stuff of which martyrs are made, any more than the various figures in his novels who choose to deal with the world through deceit. Denzil Quarrier ended up a sincere believer in conforming to 'social law'; Gissing did not believe in it, but he felt that he had better observe it in externals. He knew that with his nervous temperament he probably would have been unable to write if he became a target for the gutter press of his day. His angry defence of Harold Frederic's free union came, in part, from the knowledge that he himself could never be so bold.

Even before he finished *The Crown of Life*, on 16 January 1899, Gissing was sending parts of it to Pinker. The inconclusive negotiations with Grant Richards had given Gissing great hopes of getting a breakthrough price for his new novel. He also felt that his supreme love for Gabrielle had helped him to write a supreme book:

> Under the guise of fiction, this book deals with the most solemn questions of life, and in no light spirit. I have not felt a disagreeable contrast between this work and the sad realities which have fallen upon us. For it has never been my habit to write flippantly, idly; I have never written only to gain money, to please the foolish. And my reward is that – however poor what I have done – I do not feel it ignoble.[40]

Gissing was also excited by the idea that *The Crown of Life* was a highly topical book, because it coincided with Tsar Nicholas II's campaign for world peace. But having his characters talk about contemporary issues was not the same as making those issues part of the substance of the novel (something that H. G. Wells was spectacularly good at). Grant Richards understood this. Pinker had told him that *The Crown of Life* would make Gissing into a best-seller, and he asked for £800 for a five-year copyright. Richards refused the bait, and commented that 'a few strictures on War . . . are very much of a side issue of the book, however, and don't lend it any particular opportuneness'.[41]

At the end of the day, Pinker could not do much more than Colles. *The Town Traveller* had drawn a £250 advance from Methuen, *The Crown of Life* went to £300, for a much longer and more ambitious book. Each brought in another £100 from the US. Gissing even insisted on returning the £25 that Grant Richards had paid for an option on *The Crown of Life*. He did not realise the ceiling that he was bumping up against; instead, he told Gabrielle that 'I have no doubt at all that I can count on £500 quite certainly, every year – probably much more – oh, much more! When I am rich, I will give my Gabrielle such presents!'[42] Gissing had always been generous when he had the means. Algernon had another breakdown in January 1899; his sister Ellen promised him £100 to help him recover, and Gissing added another £50.

With all these commitments, and married life ahead to pay for, Gissing had to return to his desk, if only to finish up the Dickens prefaces for Methuen. But towards the end of February the English winter laid him low again, with flu, pleurisy, laboured breathing, insomnia and general weakness. His lungs were slowly giving out; he was prescribed quinine by his local doctor, so there may have been a recurrence of malaria too. The insomnia was perhaps the most disabling of all. Gabrielle mentions his 'long quite sleepless nights spent in pacing his room with such shouting and shrieking that his housekeeper thought at first he was mad and was frightened'.[43] Gissing had been telling Gabrielle that her love had made him better; now that he was clearly worse, he could only blame Edith:

> I am so glad you have learnt that emphysema can be produced by mental suffering. One reason why I think of my past life so bitterly, is because I *know* that my health was destroyed by the moral torments I underwent. Up to the age of 39, I had *not a trace* of weakness of the lungs. But my sufferings at that time would have *killed* a weaker man.[44]

Gissing was referring to his diagnosis of lung disease early in 1897, after which he left Edith for several months. But he had been warned about the condition of his lungs by an Italian doctor in 1890, and emphysema was hardly a psychosomatic disease. It came from smoking and living in London's polluted air. Gissing made women the cause of everything that happened to him. Wicked Edith had almost killed him; beloved Gabrielle would restore him to health. Gabrielle did her best for him, but he would be dead in less than five years, regardless.

While waiting in France, Gabrielle was also busy trying to raise Gissing's literary profile there. Apart from her work on *New Grub Street*, she wanted to get some of his short stories translated and published. Gissing saw her as what she herself aspired to be: 'the ideal *femme d'artiste*'.[45] This was a concept that distinguished France from England. The *femme d'artiste* was at once a secretary or model, a creative inspiration, and a woman who furthered an artist's social interests by presiding gracefully over his salon. If Gabrielle could not be a legitimate wife, she could have other satisfactions.

Now Gissing had only to survive the miseries of ill-health, and prepare for a marriage of his and Gabrielle's own design. He went up to London to buy two rings and a black suit. Financial arrangements would be old-fashioned: 'I do not wish you to spend any of your money after our marriage,' he told Gabrielle.[46] In other words, she should hold on to the £2,000 she had inherited from her father and reinvest the income. Gissing would pay for all. Gabrielle said she wanted to bring Walter over to France to live with them; Gissing wanted to leave him where he was. He was doing well with his aunts, and they needed the £40 a year that Gissing sent them for the boy's lodging. Walter had just had a successful operation to remove his birthmark, which would improve his prospects in life. The idea of re-creating part of Gissing's family by having a household of himself, Gabrielle and Walter soon faded away. Margaret and Ellen detested Edith, but they also thought that any connection with another woman would be immoral. They would not want Walter to live in such an establishment. On Gabrielle's side, there was an absolute commitment to her newly widowed mother, who was sickly, demanding, and unlikely to fit in comfortably with a seven-year-old boy. In choosing Gabrielle, Gissing was effectively discarding Walter, except for an occasional brief reunion.

As he came closer to living with Gabrielle, Gissing suffered from frustrated sexual desire, and from anxiety about having such feelings. Gabrielle was a virgin; she may even have expected that her marriage to Gissing would be a spiritual union rather than a physical one. Gissing had to tiptoe around Gabrielle's maidenly expectations:

> And the truth is, sweetest, I felt a wish, when I was ill, that I might always love you with that calm, passionless love, that worship of your soul in mine.

I could not help, girlie, feeling a little ashamed of my restless desires, when I contrasted them with *your* placid tenderness, your pure love. – And yet, is it not true that, if I really *did* lose my passion for your beauty, something would be lost of our perfect union? You would not really be glad; I *know* you would not, my loved one! For indeed it is Nature's bidding that I should love you in this way. You will understand it all, afterwards, and, when you understand, you will *wish* me to love you in every way – not with the spirit alone.[47]

Gissing felt guilty about his previous sexual experience, and sentimental about women who were not slaves of desire. At the same time, he had a vulgar Darwinian belief that a woman would submit to her man's will when the time came for her to do so. With Gabrielle, his problem was how to justify having a physical relationship with such a superior being.

In any case, Gissing's relation with Gabrielle was now to become reality, rather than fantasy. He had only to put his books and furniture into storage, and visit Walter, before joining Gabrielle in Normandy. Margaret and Walter were staying with Algernon at Willersey, so Gissing went there rather than to Wakefield. Before going, he shared with his sister Ellen his years of frustration with Algernon's spendthrift ways:

I wonder how much I have 'lent' him altogether? It began long years ago, when, living in London, he borrowed sovereigns of me to run down to Southampton. And ever since – £5, £10, £20 – always increasing. He has grown into the fatal habit of dependence. And I terribly fear the time is gone by for his getting any sort of employment.

But for Alg., we should now never need to speak of money; we should all have become decently self-supporting. I greatly fear that he will make this state of things forever impossible to us.[48]

To abandon Algernon was to abandon his wife and children too, which his helpers could not bring themselves to do. But he had become a parasite before he had wife or children, and Gissing had never managed to confront him about it. Nor was he ready to confront him now: Algernon would keep on with his unsuccessful novels, while Gissing stood surety for him at the bank. 'When people can't support themselves,' Gissing said to Ellen, 'the burden always falls on somebody else.'[49] He might have added that if he had refused to help Algernon, a bigger burden would have fallen on his sisters. Gissing's only way of laying down the burden was to die himself.

When Gissing was too ill to write in February and March, H. G. Wells wrote that he had £1,000 to spare if Gissing needed it. Unlike his brother, Gissing found it easy to refuse the offer, albeit gratefully. He had no time to visit the Wellses, and did not tell them about his plan to live with Gabrielle. Still less would he confide in his family, knowing how shocked they would be by what he was going to do. But he was sure that a new life with Gabrielle was his only hope of survival. Everything he had suffered up to now had loneliness at its root, and Gabrielle would save him from that:

> In spite of all the passion which at times torments me, I find myself in these last days of expectation, most often thinking of the companionship of heart and mind which will enrich my life henceforth. That is the enduring blessing promised by our marriage, the deep satisfaction which nothing can deprive us of. To have lived as long as I have without knowing the intimacy of true marriage is a grievous misfortune, yet it makes me all the more capable of appreciating the priceless thing which has been granted me at last. ... We know that each is the other's destined mate, and that no such thing as sorrowful disillusion can ever come between us. But what infinitudes of mutual revelation still remain.[50]

Gissing's miserable experiences with Nell and Edith seem to have taught him nothing about himself, except how much he longed for a different relationship with a different woman. Yet his choice of Gabrielle resembled his two earlier marriages in that he was raising a lofty structure of fantasy on a slender foundation of actual knowledge of the woman he was taking into his life.

From Willersey, Gissing went to stay at the White Hart, an Elizabethan coaching inn in Lewes. He waited there five days for Gabrielle to tell him when he could come and meet her in Normandy. William Rothenstein, who had done two portraits of Gissing in 1897, turned up for dinner one evening. His companion was Walter Sickert, the painter, who was living in Dieppe while getting a divorce from his first wife, Ellen. No doubt Gissing and Sickert chatted politely, without revealing the cross-Channel business that each was engaged in.[51] The next day, 6 May 1899, Gissing crossed over from Newhaven to Dieppe, to claim his crown of life.

The Private Life of Monsieur Gissing

From Dieppe Gissing took the train to Rouen, where he was reunited with Gabrielle and met her mother for the first time. They all stayed at the Hôtel de Paris, a modest place that may have been chosen because they were unlikely to run into anyone they knew. Gabrielle and Maman shared a room, Gissing had his own next door. On the evening of the next day he and Gabrielle plighted their troth and exchanged rings; it was a ceremony of their own devising, with no clergyman and only Maman as witness. 'Dear Maman's emotion,' Gissing wrote in his diary, 'and G.'s sweet dignity.'[1] The next day, Maman went back to her flat in Paris, while Gissing and Gabrielle went to the Normandy coast for their three-week honeymoon.

St-Pierre-en-Port was a pretty little fishing village near Fécamp, hemmed in by dramatic white cliffs. It had a small casino and the Hôtel des Terrasses, where Gissing and Gabrielle stayed looking out over the sea. There were only two other people staying at the hotel – Englishmen, whom Gissing avoided – and there was cleanliness and excellent food for only 4/6d a day. Here Gissing and Gabrielle walked along the cliffs, talked day and night (in French only), and started to truly know each other. Gissing wrote in his diary that they heard 'a few notes of the nightingale'.[2] After a few days, he went back to work on his Dickens prefaces, finishing the one for *Nicholas Nickleby*. The preface gave no sign of the romantic circumstances of its composition, except perhaps for a criticism that Gissing might also have applied to himself: 'Dickens never succeeded in depicting an ordinary well-bred and charming girl – unless in his very last book.'[3] Gabrielle, in the flesh, was more than charming: 'Absolute perfection of mind and character,' Gissing wrote to Eduard Bertz. 'For the first time in my life, I am at ease in mind.'[4]

In the early months of Gissing's 'marriage' to Gabrielle he told only a handful of people that the union existed. He also became very reticent in his diary entries, perhaps because he feared that Gabrielle or even her mother might read them. On the scanty evidence we have, the couple seem to have been very happy on their honeymoon at St-Pierre-en-Port, and later down the coast at Veules. Nonetheless, trouble in the marriage began soon after they went from Normandy to Paris, and it came from a predictable quarter, Gissing's mother-in-law. Anna Fleury had agreed to her daughter's marriage to Gissing because he was a distinguished writer, and perhaps out of a genuine desire for Gabrielle to be happy. But with the death of her husband 'Maman' became the head of the Fleury household, and she had no intention of giving up control of it to her daughter's mate. Her picture suggests a formidable, tight-lipped personality, who much resembled Gabrielle in appearance. She professed to be weak, on the verge of dying at any time from a 'bad heart'; but that weakness made her the centre of attention, and a fomenter of guilt in those she expected to look after her.

Two years later, Gabrielle told Amy Catherine Wells about life with her mother: 'From the age of 14 I have had my mother, an invalid, always with serious matters, at first the chest, then the heart, and she has never had another nurse than myself, so that, without having made special medical studies, I have got a too good medical knowledge of illnesses, treatments, nursing, etc.'[5] When Gabrielle first met Gissing she had been serving her mother in this way for sixteen years. Maman had taken on the identity of the *'femme souffrante'*, whose needs had become other people's obligations. It was taken for granted that Gabrielle must continue to live with her, at her flat in Passy or wherever they might travel. All plans depended on her state of health. Gissing expected that after Normandy they would go on to spend summer in the Alps, which would be good for his lungs. But Maman was not well enough, so he had to wait for six weeks in the summer heat of Paris before they could go. What kind of illness was it, anyway, that lasted for twenty-eight years and allowed her to outlive Gissing, who was eighteen years her junior? Gissing soon came to realise that he had married a wife whose first loyalty was not to him, but to Maman. It was Maman who ruled the roost and especially the dining-table, and who would frustrate Gissing's third attempt at having a happy married life.

The roost to which Gissing and Gabrielle went after their honeymoon was a bourgeois apartment at 13 rue de Siam in Passy, a highly respectable but not very lively quarter of Paris. Gissing never liked the apartment, finding it dull and gloomy. He complained of the cost of living there, so presumably he paid a good share of the expenses. Apart from Maman, Gabrielle and himself there was Gabrielle's younger brother René. After a year he moved out, and Gissing took over his room as a study. Gabrielle had her £100 a year from her father's estate, so presumably Maman and

René had several hundred more between them. Whatever money they had, they acted as if they were short of it, running a cheese-paring establishment with only one overworked maid. Gissing felt that he still needed his own £500 a year, and in the early months of his marriage he was well on his way to getting it. In Paris he turned out three more of the Dickens prefaces and wrote a short story, 'The Scrupulous Father', for which Pinker got him £34.[6] But his main project was to write *By the Ionian Sea*, a year and a half after his travels in Calabria. His troubles with Edith and uncertain health had kept him away from writing up his adventures. At the end of June 1899 he got down to work in the rue de Siam and progressed with phenomenal speed, even for him. Gissing wrote the first three chapters in two days – about seven thousand words – and in twelve days he had written half the book, nine out of eighteen chapters. He sent those chapters to Pinker to see if the book could be sold as a serial; then he, Gabrielle and Maman left for a summer in the Alps.

In Paris Gissing had been given a taste of the mildly intellectual circles to which Gabrielle belonged. He met Mme Lardin de Musset, the eighty-year-old sister of the poet, and Mme Emma Herwegh. Through these ladies he was a step away from having known Balzac and Heine. Then it was his turn to encounter the French bourgeois idea of a summer holiday. They left in mid-July for Samoëns, a quiet resort in the next valley from Chamonix. It was believed dangerous to go directly to high altitude, so they spent a week of acclimatisation at seven hundred metres. From Samoëns they had to travel all day in a great circle to get to Trient in Switzerland, just across the border from Chamonix. This was at 1,300 metres, a picturesque Alpine hamlet with a scattering of chalets and *pensions*, and a noisy stream rushing down through the meadows. Gissing and his companions spent five weeks there, enjoying the mountain walks. After ten days Gissing tackled the walk up to the Col de Balme, getting to the top in three hours to see the superb view of the Mont Blanc massif. For a man with advanced emphysema this was impressive, climbing more than a thousand vertical feet per hour – all the more so because Gissing did his mountaineering in a three-piece suit and tie, and street shoes. The scenery put him in an expansive mood and he wrote much more in his diary than usual, probably intending to use his impressions in a novel or travel book: 'Remember the wooden barn partly filled with new hay – exquisite scent. ... To left, in Chamonix direction, valley closed by the double-peaked Buet, glaciers on its sides; to right, Fin Haut, seeming to cling on the midside of its great mountain, with white torrents leaping past it into profound gorge. Its white hotels and church tower.'[7] Still, Gissing respected the Alps rather than loved them, as he explained to Walter (who had been boarded out to a clergyman's family for his summer holiday):

> I do not care so much for Switzerland as for Italy, and the reason is because I never care very much for scenery, however grand or beautiful, unless something happened there in by-gone times; I love Italy because of its history, because every town and every river reminds me of things I have read about. Rome is the most interesting place in the world, because of the wonderful people who have lived there, and the wonderful things done within its walls.[8]

Gissing described the mountains in his diary, but not his daily life with Gabrielle and Maman. He told Clara Collet that he could not say anything to her about it, because 'The contrast with things gone by is too great. I have perfect intellectual companionship – a vast help to me in my work.'[9] This was tactful, in that Collet may have envied Gabrielle her place at Gissing's side; but he did not speak of his love to anyone else either. Even the intellectual companionship must have been somewhat one-sided. If Gabrielle had respect for literature and art, she also had a thoroughly conventional mind, without any spark of originality or curiosity about where the world was going. She gave emotional support to Gissing's writing, but it is hard to see any direct inspiration from Gabrielle in his work after 1898, apart from the sentimentality about romantic love in *The Crown of Life*. Her main role, it seems, was to save him from the paralysing breakdowns caused by loneliness.

At Trient Gissing finished the remaining nine chapters of *By the Ionian Sea*. It was one of his most attractive books, and a brilliant piece of travel writing, yet he had worked on it for only twenty-five days in all. Once that was done, he had the proofs of *The Crown of Life* to correct; he found it, on this reading, 'My best book yet for style'.[10] Then there was time for another pot-boiling short story, 'Humplebee', about a schoolboy who saves a friend from drowning and gets little reward from the friend's rich father. In three months since starting to live with Gabrielle, Gissing had written a book, four Dickens prefaces, and two short stories, work for which he would be paid more than £350. Professionally, his marriage was certainly doing him good. Working alongside, Gabrielle finished her translation of *New Grub Street* at Trient. Not everyone would accept their partnership, though. Gabrielle sent to Eduard Bertz a picture of herself and George, side by side among the rocks at Trient. After Gissing's death, Bertz returned his letters to Wakefield; Margaret and Ellen scissored Gabrielle out of the photograph, leaving only a ghostly fragment of her dress.

Gissing made some friends at Trient: the parish priest, and a Swiss philologist from Lausanne, Ernest Bovet. He had with him his newly married wife and her brother, who was a sculptor. Bovet was a professor of French and German at the university of Rome, though he was only twenty-nine years old. Gissing would always enjoy having someone with whom to discuss fine points of syntax or Roman history; Bovet was also congenial as a political idealist and pacifist. He would become a prominent figure in the League of Nations after the First World War. It was a happy and enlightened little group that came together at Trient, apart from the wet blanket of Maman and her ailments. Adding in the good food and the mountain walks, there was a stark contrast to previous horrid summer holidays with Edith at seaside boarding-houses. Madame Bovet became pregnant during their stay, and Gissing and Gabrielle kept up a friendly correspondence with the Bovets over the next year.

When the evenings started to get chilly, Gissing and Gabrielle set off for the southern slopes of the Alps, spending most of September in the Ticino at Airolo and Lugano. Gissing enjoyed speaking Italian again, and feasting on peaches and grapes. He did no more work, but was mulling over a novel to follow *The Crown of Life*. As soon as they were back at the rue de Siam he got down to work on 'The Coming Man', later changed to *Our Friend the Charlatan*. The novel's hero, Dyce Lashmar, is an ambiguous figure: he often talks like Gissing, but ends up as a devious rascal. The original title has a double meaning; Lashmar is a man on the rise, but also a man of the future – a bleak future.

As Gissing was starting the book, the Boer War broke out, on 12 October 1899. Swinburne had a war poem in *The Times*, howling for the British army 'To scourge these dogs, agape with jaws afoam,/ Down out of life. Strike, England, and strike home.'[11] Gissing had been asked to write a column for a new magazine, the *Review of the Week*, so he sent in a piece attacking Swinburne. 'Noble verse,' he wrote, 'may no longer raise the battle-cry.' Even Kipling, he thought, would be on the side of 'those who hope that men will some day no longer cut each other's throats and explode each other's heads off'.[12] Gissing was encouraged to get a letter from Thomas Hardy praising his article; someone, at least, shared his gloom about the century to come.[13]

The Crown of Life was published a week after the Boer War began, which put it completely at odds with the belligerent spirit of the moment. Gissing blamed this timing for the novel's lack of popular success. It was not a pessimistic book, but its positive values were just of the kind to alienate many readers. Gissing's practice as a novelist had shifted again, after the early proletarian novels and the middle phase of books about problems of middle-class life. In *The Crown of Life* he put forward solutions to the two problems that haunted his earlier books: politics and sex. He had solved them to his own satisfaction, but in ways so idiosyncratic as to make it difficult for his readers to grant him approval, or even understanding.

'The Crown of Life' is ideal romantic love, which Piers Otway finds with Irene Derwent. After eight years of setbacks and misunderstandings, they are able to admit their love to each other, and look forward to marriage at the end of the book. So far, *The Crown of Life* might be seen as just an expression of wish-fulfilment, written at the time when Gissing was separated from Gabrielle but full of hopes about their future life together. Irene, like Gabrielle, exists as little more than a figment of Piers's desires. Piers himself is another matter. Gissing was not in a position to fully reveal his sexual history with Nell and Edith, but from the beginning of the novel he uses Piers to expose the mystifications created by masculine desire. Piers has dreamed Irene into existence before he even meets her. He falls in love, but has to reconcile his idealisation of Irene with the sensual appetites of a single, lonely young man:

> He feared the streets at night-time; in his loneliness and misery, a gleam upon some wanton face would perchance have lured him, as had happened ere now. Not so much at the bidding of his youthful blood, as out of mere longing for companionship, the common cause of disorder in men condemned to solitude in great cities. A woman's voice, the touch of a soft hand – this is what men so often hunger for, when they are censured for lawless appetite.[14]

Piers needs both the hand to touch, and the image to worship – and each attached to a different woman. *The Crown of Life* is Gissing's most blatant presentation of the sexual self-division of the Victorian male. Piers is ashamed of his sexual lapses, but he argues that a man's need for physical relief, and for an ideal to worship, are equally urgent, contradictory as they may be. Yet when Irene accepts him at last, Piers expresses no rapture at their forthcoming union; the book ends short of any reconciliation of spirit and sense in a loving marriage. With Gissing, sexual choice cannot be separated from the issue of class. From his uneasy lower-middle-class perspective, he looks down at the women of the streets, and up at the women of the drawing-room. In *The Crown of Life*, Piers is troubled by his evenings in society: 'Brilliant women awed him a little at first, but it was not till afterwards, in the broken night following such occasions as this, that they had power over his imagination; then he saw them, drawn upon darkness, their beauty without that halo of worldly grandeur which would not allow him to forget the gulf between them.'[15] Such women are different beings by day and by night, clothed and naked. But the consciousness of their difference is in Piers rather than in them; and one suspects that Gissing was deeply affected by the same kind of splitting. On the evidence of *The Crown of Life* one would not expect Gissing to achieve an easy, sensual intimacy with a refined woman like Gabrielle.

What actually occurred between Gissing and Gabrielle in their time alone remains obscure. *The Crown of Life* ends with Piers and Irene doing no more than holding hands. After Gissing's death, Wanda von Sacher-Masoch wrote venomous letters to Eduard Bertz and said she was writing a book to expose the mistreatment of Gissing by Gabrielle and her mother (the book never appeared). Wanda was a close friend and secret enemy of Gabrielle's. She claimed that Gabrielle shared the best bedroom at rue de Siam with her mother, and that Gissing either had no sexual relations with Gabrielle or only what her mother permitted.[16] Against this we can put what Gabrielle wrote to Bertz in May 1904: 'My great regret is not having had a child myself, as I should have done four years ago – perhaps you knew that.'[17] This suggests either that Gabrielle became pregnant and miscarried, or that she wanted a child and Gissing insisted on contraception. Whatever happened, it seems certain that Maman was a great obstacle to any easy closeness between Gabrielle and Gissing.

Gissing's political stance in *The Crown of Life*, and the novels that followed, is also somewhat contradictory. Piers dislikes the rising spirit of imperialism in England, and admires the pacifist Doukhobors that he meets in Russia:

> They uphold the ideal above all necessary to our time. We ought to be rapidly outgrowing warfare; isn't that the obvious next step in civilisation? ... Yet we're going back – there's a military reaction – fighting is glorified by everyone who has a loud voice, and in no country more than England. ... And it seems to me that this is the world's only hope – peace made a religion.[18]

Traditional religion is in decline, Piers believes, and science, its natural successor, has been put in the service of 'money-making and weapon-making'. Socialism means the rule of the crowd, 'at its best, a smiling simpleton; at its worst, a murderous maniac'. Piers has come to hate London, 'a huge battlefield calling itself the home of civilisation and of peace'.[19] Once he has made enough money to marry Irene, he gives up his business to become a writer. Through Piers, Gissing expounds a view of society that seems entirely without hope. One might condemn Gissing for his political pessimism, except that he saw exactly where European civilisation was heading in the twentieth century.[20]

Gissing expected *The Crown of Life* to be a big step towards the commercial success that had eluded him for so long. As soon as he returned to Paris from the Alps he could pocket a cheque for £254, the balance of his English and American advances on the novel. This took care of his immediate worries, but *The Crown of Life* did not bring in anything significant beyond its advance. Reviews of the novel were not more enthusiastic than for previous works. The *New York Tribune* headed its review 'An unexpectedly Cheerful Book', but that was not enough to present romantic heroes and heroines with whom the public could identify. 'It is very doubtful,' Morley Roberts wrote, 'if Mr Gissing ever loved this heroine of his at all.'[21] That was a cutting thing to say, given that Roberts must have known how much Irene Derwent owed to Gabrielle. Reviewers complained about Gissing's politics, too: 'There is also a good deal of unpatriotic sentiment in the book, and much petulant protest against the expansion of England.'[22] The most significant review came from Arnold Bennett in *The Academy*, except that he devoted most of his space to a discussion of why Gissing's earlier novels had not been more successful in the marketplace:

> His novels contain less of potential popularity than those of almost any other living novelist of rank. They have neither the prettiness which pleases, nor the outward beauty which subdues, nor the wit which dazzles, nor the thematic bigness which overawes. And they are not soiled by any specious lower qualities which might have deceived an innocent public into admiration. ... Yet Mr Gissing is renowned. He stands for something. ... The fact is, he has that peculiar moral significance and weight which exist apart from mere numerical popularity, and which yet have an assessable value in the commercial market.[23]

Bennett was ten years younger than Gissing, and was just getting his career as a novelist under way with *A Man From the North*. His social origins were a little higher than Gissing's – his father was a provincial solicitor – but he was close enough to sympathise with Gissing's lower-middle-class preoccupations:

> Mr Gissing by no means accepts the idealistic theory that the rank is but the guinea stamp and a man's a man for a' that. He may almost be said to be obsessed by social distinctions; he is sensitive to the most delicate *nuances* of them; and it would seem that this man, so free from the slightest trace of

snobbishness, would reply, if asked what life had taught him: 'The importance of social distinctions.'[24]

In theory, Gissing now had enough literary distinction to have left
worries about his class position behind him. Literature, like the Anglican
Church, was supposed to be an institution where you left your origins
at the door. Yet Gissing's heroes never stop thinking about those social
distinctions. It takes Piers Otway eight years to make himself worthy of
Irene, by overcoming the stigma of his illegitimacy and his lack of inherited
wealth. Gissing's position in 1899 presented him with a new kind of
problem. Now that he had come to live in France, his status depended
considerably on that of Gabrielle's family. On the face of it he was well
placed to shine in Parisian intellectual society, but things did not work out
so happily. His first priority was to meet his quota of writing, which left
little time for cafés and salons. And when was the 'English Zola' going to
meet the real Zola? In July 1898 Zola had fled to England after having
been convicted of libel for his writings in support of Captain Dreyfus. He
returned to Paris in June 1899 but was still in the thick of the battle. Dreyfus
would not be fully exonerated until 1906. Gissing was a keen supporter of
Dreyfus and would have liked to meet Zola, but was reluctant to intrude
on his busy life. Gabrielle wanted them to meet too, not least because it
would have been a confirmation of Gissing's status in France. Yet somehow
the meeting never happened.

That Gissing and Zola never met was a measure of where Gabrielle
stood in the literary hierarchy of Paris. She was not close to the big dogs
of the cultural scene, only to a few academics and hangers-on. There is no
record that she and Gissing entertained at rue de Siam, probably because
Madame was too ill, or too stingy, to put on a dinner party. The rich
relatives of the Fleurys were not intellectuals. Gissing might complain that
his social life in England was limited by his two unpresentable wives, but
he sat at table with almost all the major English writers of his time. In
France, Gabrielle would not embarrass Gissing, but there was nothing
brilliant about either her looks or her intellect. The woman who had seemed
to him a goddess in anticipation was, on her home ground, a somewhat
dowdy and neurotic figure; and she was completely under the thumb of her
mother, who was worse. Gabrielle's efforts to promote Gissing's literary
standing had no significant result. The publication of her translation of *New
Grub Street* in 1901 was really her first and last success; the next translation
she did, *The Odd Women*, failed to find a publisher.

It has to be said that Gissing himself did little to seek out opportunities in Paris. From the rue de Siam he could have been in the centre of the city in twenty minutes, but he disliked noise and crowds and mainly chose to stay home and write. Gabrielle confided to Clara Collet, two years later, that he was much more awkward as a husband than she had expected:

> Perhaps you are aware of the strange, quite peculiar, and I believe morbid disposition of my husband to get discontented of his present circumstances very quickly, to imagine he would be so much happier and healthier in others, to want frequent changings. And then to get strange fancies in his head. ... George, with regard to practical, everyday life, is like a child. As soon as he meets one of the many little worries inevitable in every existence, he attributes it to his actual conditions of life – not to life itself – and imagines he would avoid it in changing his circumstances.[25]

People with chest trouble were advised by their doctors to try one place or another for the climate or altitude. This often led to chronic restlessness, and the conviction that if they could only find the right place they would get better. In fact, climate had almost nothing to do with the progress of TB or emphysema, so that all this moving about amounted to chasing a will-o'-the-wisp. Gissing was profoundly fearful and anxious, both about his health and about what would happen to his family if he could no longer write. Gabrielle quickly lost patience with his invalidism, even though for seventeen years she had been dancing attendance on Maman, who may not have been a real invalid at all. No doubt Gissing was exasperated that Gabrielle took her mother's complaints so much more seriously than his own.

Gissing's fussiness about small matters of everyday life annoyed Gabrielle because she saw every such incident as a symptom of her husband's loyalty to Wakefield rather than to his relationship with her and Maman. This annoyance had nothing to do with Gissing's actual presence at Wakefield. He had gone there in late January 1899 for five days, to see Walter and to have a family conference about Algernon's financial troubles. Apart from a brief visit with Algernon at Willersey, he did not see his family again until April 1900, when he spent nine days at Wakefield, without being able to tell his mother or sisters that he had been living with Gabrielle for a year. His family could not interfere with the household at the rue de Siam because they did not know it existed. What Gabrielle objected to was the presence of Mrs Gissing at second hand: Gissing seemed to use the way things were done at Wakefield as a standard by which to judge Gabrielle, and to find her wanting.

Wakefield was also the place where Gissing's elder son lived. At heart,

Gabrielle resented Gissing's children. They belonged to Wakefield, and they were a reminder of Gissing's sexual tie to Edith. Beyond that, she was simply jealous of them, judging by her outburst to H. G. Wells in 1901:

> And once, quite in the beginning, when he said to me he knew he was quite right in doing what he did in marrying me, 'because he had to live *for his children*'? – And some unhappy words like that, which I succeeded of removing from my mind, but which come back in the hours of solitude and misery. I know he would not have said them now – or I think so – and yet![26]

What Gissing was trying to say was that Gabrielle had saved his life, and that if he had died his children would have been in a desperate state. He was worried enough as it was: Walter was not thriving with his sisters, and Alfred had disappeared into the custody of his disturbed mother. Perhaps Gissing had not expressed himself tactfully; but even though Gabrielle had him with her all the time, she resented his concern for his sons and begrudged the money he sent for their support.

Did all or any of Gabrielle's complaints have worth? Gissing was an obsessive-compulsive who needed to control everything in his surroundings, from the attic to the kitchen sink. His marriage to Edith had failed, in part, because she would not conform to his precise instructions on how to run a household. In Paris, what Gabrielle called 'Wakefield' was really the domestic habits and values that Gissing had acquired in his childhood, traits that lay below the level of conscious choice. Conflict in the rue de Siam was most intense around the question of food, where our idea of a good meal is usually what we liked as children and it is futile to argue about tastes. But Gissing did argue, and the argument started at breakfast. He wanted bacon, Maman wanted to deny him bacon (leaving aside the question of where in Paris one could hope to find it). Maman's food was not what he liked to eat, and there was not enough of it either. Nor, in his view, was it properly served. The breakfast table was covered with oilcloth, and set with cheap knives and forks. This was even worse than the absence of bacon, eggs, and a proper cup of tea: 'Poor as I have been,' Gissing wrote, 'I generally managed to sit down to a white table, spread with very simple, but not ungraceful gear; as a matter of fact, I had rather eat poorly at a table so equipped than plenteously at a rude board.'[27] The French way of setting the table showed 'an aesthetic, even a moral, deficiency'.

Gissing's anxiety about food had one source that he could not admit to anyone, and perhaps not to himself: the deliberate starvation inflicted on him in prison. The flat in the rue de Siam was a kind of soft prison, where

Maman set the rules and doled out Gissing's rations. Miserable as his two marriages may have been, he at least felt that he was in charge of his own house, even if he had to fight to get his orders obeyed. Living alone was miserable too, but he set the terms of his own misery. The ghastly concoctions that he made for himself – the lentils, the unpeeled potatoes, the pudding made by boiling together bread and jam – could not be blamed on anyone else. In fact, he was proud of them. Even better was the splendid breakfast table at Wakefield, laid on for Gissing by his mother, his sisters and their servants. That was the satisfying way for a Yorkshireman to start his day. Paris, alas, was a foreign country; they did breakfast differently there.

All of these conflicts only grew worse for being hidden under a formal politeness. Both Gabrielle and Gissing were unhappy with their life together, but they could not bring their grievances out into the open. Neither of them was willing to admit that their great love story had taken a bad turn. In spite of the tension, Gissing did make one step towards permanence: he ordered the furniture he had stored in Dorking to be sold, and got £16 for it. In November he wrote a short story, 'Snapshall's Youngest', about a man who auctions off his furniture and then decides he wants to get some of it back from the dealer who bought it.[28] In real life the furniture was gone for ever, a recognition that Gissing was unlikely ever again to have an English home. His imagination was not going to move, though: neither 'The Coming Man' nor any of his later writings would show any sign that he was a permanent resident of France.

Gissing began writing 'The Coming Man' on 29 September 1899, only four days after returning to Paris from the Alps. He produced more than half of a draft in six weeks, then lost faith in the book and stopped work.[29] There had been illnesses and servant problems, but Gissing's main worry was how to ensure a steady income from the books he had written over the past seven years. Lawrence & Bullen had plenty of money and confidence when they published *Denzil Quarrier* in 1892, and six of Gissing's books after that. Now they were on the verge of bankruptcy, though Bullen would struggle on with his own imprint for a few more years. Pinker suggested that they should try to get Gissing's titles back from Lawrence & Bullen, and from some of his other publishers, in order to have a uniform series of his novels issued by Methuen. Gissing had his doubts. He only got about £10 a year from Lawrence & Bullen, but if Methuen bought the titles he would get nothing for a few years, until the books showed a profit for their new owner. Smith, Elder continued to make money on the five Gissing novels of which they owned the copyright, so there was no reason for them to give the books to Methuen, except at a good price. In any case, all these schemes collapsed when it became clear that Methuen was no more than lukewarm about supporting Gissing. There was no point in making them the primary custodians of Gissing's literary property if they weren't willing to put up the necessary money. The elusive publisher who could end Gissing's financial worries would never turn up.

When he set aside 'The Coming Man' in mid-November, Gissing started another novel, on 'the restless seeking for a *new religion*, which leads people into Theosophy, Spiritualism, and things still more foolish. . . . I feel sure I can make this a striking and rather an exciting book.'[30] Perhaps he thought that the coming turn of the century would make the book more topical. He was discouraged by the tepid response to *The Crown of Life*, though there was some consolation that Robert Buchanan quoted from it as an antidote to the jingoism of Kipling: '[Buchanan's] article is a violent attack on Kipling and I strongly approve of it. Indeed, nothing too severe can be said against the brute savagery of Kipling's latest work. I wish you could read 'Stalky & Co.' . . . Such a book ought to be burnt by the hangman! It is the most vulgar and bestial production of our times.'[31] That was all very well, but Kipling was speaking for England in the summer of 1899. His poem 'The Absent-minded Beggar' helped to raise £250,000 for the families of soldiers sent to South Africa, and Lord Salisbury offered him a knighthood (which he refused). While Gissing stayed in Paris and lamented the madness of war, Kipling went to South Africa and wrote poems glorifying the Tommies. When the war was over he had a £9,000 manor house in Sussex and a 1,200-guinea motor car. His response to the war was to jump in and write about it; Gissing's, to feel that there was no point in writing at all:

> How anyone gives himself to literature just now with any sort of courage, I can't understand. It seems to me that only very few novelists will earn more than dry bread for years to come. I have a feeling that – owing to the curse of capitalism – we are simply rushing towards a period of wild confusion, when every man who wants to live quietly will be kicked into the gutter, and bidden enjoy himself *there*. . . . I wish I had died ten years ago; I should have gone away with some hope for civilization, of which I now have none. One's choice seems to be between death in the workhouse or by some ruffian's bullet. As for those who come after one – it is too black to think about.[32]

A Boer bullet would kill Charles Gaussen in December 1901; the fifteen-year-old boy that Gissing met at his mother's in 1884 had grown up to be a professional soldier. Gissing thought of sending Walter to some place where there was no military service and he could grow up an 'honest farmer. ... I would greatly rather never see him again than foresee his marching in ranks, butchering or to be butchered.'[33] But where in the world could one be sure of safety? History would have its way with Walter, and his father could do nothing to protect him.

It was in this gloomy spirit that Gissing pressed ahead with 'Among the Prophets' and finished it by the beginning of February 1900. It seems significant that in all his dark predictions about the future he never said anything about having the love of Gabrielle as a consolation. It was the ball and chain of writing for a living that determined his mood, not the rewards – such as they were – of domestic life with Gabrielle and Maman. He complained in one of his letters to Walter that 'in Paris one has often to do without a fire, even when it would be pleasant, for coals and wood cost twice as much here as in England. Everything – except wine – is dearer here than at home, and people do not know what is meant by real comfort.'[34] For two and a half months Gissing stopped writing in his diary, usually a sign that things were going badly with him. He felt that his novel was 'poor stuff', but sent it off to Pinker to see what it might fetch, and also finished his Dickens prefaces for Methuen. *By the Ionian Sea* did well: the *Fortnightly* took it for a serial, paying £120, and in May Chapman & Hall offered another £130 for the book. Travelling in Calabria had almost killed Gissing, so it was good to be paid well for a book he had written in four weeks. 'What I am at,' Gissing told Roberts, 'is to get a couple of thousand pounds safely invested for my two boys.'[35]

If Gissing was to get money, it would not be by going back to the subjects that had first made his reputation. When *The Cornhill* asked for an article, he firmly refused:

> I reluctantly come to the conclusion that I should not be able to write a satisfactory article on the subject you suggest. It is now ten years at least since I had any opportunity of observing the life of the lower classes in London. At one time I knew that world pretty well, and I managed to make some use of it in fiction; but I have not only long lost touch with it as a living subject – it has so far ceased to interest me that I am not likely ever again to use working-class life in my books. ... Several younger writers have dealt very well indeed with the London poor of late (their names will at once occur to you), and with much more genuine sympathy than I ever had.[36]

Gissing was thinking of such books as Arthur Morrison's autobiographical *A Child of the Jago*, or Somerset Maugham's *Liza of Lambeth* (which was about factory girls). The bitterness against the social order that he had felt at Nell's deathbed had long burnt out; here he even claims that he never felt it. He wrote two stories in March 1900, 'The House of Cobwebs' and 'The Pig and Whistle'. Both of them dealt with decent lower-middle-class folk who made the best of the narrow world they found themselves in. To the extent that Gissing still had any interest in politics, it was with issues like pacifism or the defence of culture. His creative works were now focused on the middle-class conscience and the search for a refuge from capitalism and war.

As he wrote his English stories, Gissing suddenly decided that he needed to go over to England. His announced reason was that he needed to transact some literary business face-to-face; but more important, he confided to Edward Clodd, was his need to visit Wakefield. No doubt he had heard again from Margaret and Ellen that Walter was causing problems. Their usual complaints against him were that he was conceited and disobedient. Gabrielle probably saw him as the 'bad seed' of his mother Edith. Gissing was caught in the middle. He had not shown his face in Wakefield for more than a year. Why was he living in Paris, instead of in London, where he could be sent for if his sisters needed help? Gissing was afraid to tell his sisters the real reason, that he was living in sin with a French woman. He felt he had to go to England to see what he could do for Walter, even if there was nothing he could do for Alfred, who had completely disappeared from sight. It was impossible for Gabrielle to go with him to Wakefield; his best course was to go alone for a brief visit, and tell Gabrielle as little as possible about his family problems.

Gissing crossed the Channel on 2 April; he saw Pinker the next day and went on to Wakefield. He stayed there for nine days, catching a bad cold and fending off questions about how and where he was living in Paris. He went on to Lincoln and St Neot's for a week, probably for research on a historical novel, since he visited houses connected with the Cromwell family. There was no immediate result from these wanderings, other than to satisfy Gissing's taste for poking around in old country towns. He then stayed for a week with Edward Clodd at his house in Tufnell Park. Clodd was a well-to-do banker, and Gissing enjoyed staying in the kind of style that he could never possess for himself. His business in London was to try and get his novels consolidated under the imprint of Smith, Elder. Pinker did his best, but Smith, Elder were content with their profits from the five novels they already had. They did not want to increase their investment in Gissing. At least Gissing could enjoy himself running around London and seeing all his closest friends. He went down to Box Hill to dine with George

Meredith, and brought the hard-up W. H. Hudson to dine with Clodd at the Savile Club. Gissing canvassed his literary friends and in 1901 Hudson got a Civil List pension of £150 a year, so Gissing had saved at least one writer from the workhouse. H. G. Wells was at the other end of the wealth spectrum: Gissing went down to see him at Sandgate, where he was building a large and luxurious mansion by the sea.

The cold that Gissing had caught at Wakefield lingered on, and Gabrielle noticed when he got back that he had lost weight and was out of sorts. His left eye became swollen after the cold, and an inflamed patch of skin appeared on his right forehead. It became entrenched, grew, and would plague him for more than two years. Gissing had started to have a chronic problem with eczema in June 1898, first on his arms and then spreading over his body. These skin troubles may well have been the first signs of tertiary syphilis. However, neither Gissing nor Gabrielle seems to have had any suspicion of where his eczema was coming from. All they could see was that Gissing was plagued by one chronic ailment after another. He was again laid up with rheumatism when he got back to Paris, though he was able to have an enjoyable dinner with H. G. Wells, his brother Frank, and Henri Davray, the translator of *The War of the Worlds*. It was a brief escape from the rue de Siam, even if Davray saw a sick man across the table from him:

> I see again his shapely head with its black, thick and short moustache, his finely shaped nose, his high forehead, from which his long, flat hair, already going grey, receded down to the occiput, round the ears and clear of the temples, brushed back without a parting. I also see the expressive look of his eyes dilated by fever, for disease had been gnawing at him for a long time, and he had that hectic thinness of people who are dying of consumption.[37]

Gissing was not dying of consumption, and the strange look of his eyes may have been Argyll-Robertson pupils, a symptom of syphilis.

Ill or not, Gissing went back to his desk. 'A Daughter of the Lodge' was one of his best short stories, about the daughter of a head gardener who educates herself and becomes a feminist. After she refuses to kowtow to the daughter of the big house, her parents are threatened with eviction. To save them, she must go back and make a craven apology. She has to learn the lesson of 'the importance of social distinctions'. 'The Pig and Whistle' is one of Gissing's few comically optimistic stories. A country landlord ruins himself by getting the fixed idea that he must meet the Prince of Wales. His death by misadventure creates an opportunity for a shabby-genteel schoolmaster, who would much rather run a pub. Social distinctions only do harm when we believe in them too much.

On Gissing's return from England, Gabrielle and Maman were ready to sublet their flat and go to the country for the summer. The Alps were now considered to be too far away and too strenuous for someone in Maman's delicate state of health. For £50, she had taken a six-month lease on a house in St Honoré les Bains, in the Nièvre. St Honoré was a thriving spa town with a casino and theatre, popular with the *haute bourgeoisie*. It was beautifully situated at the edge of the Morvan hills, so Gissing and Gabrielle could enjoy long walks in the countryside. There was no large town within reach, and social life consisted mainly of gossiping about the ailments for which people had come to take the waters. Such a place suited Maman perfectly; and it also suited Gissing surprisingly well, if one judges by the writing he was able to do there. The Villa des Roses (now demolished) was typical of the French houses Gissing would stay in during the last four years of his life, and typical of the English houses too, if one takes its first quality to be a lack of charm. The Villa was large and four-square with a mansard roof, probably built around 1855 when St Honoré first became a resort. In France, medieval farmhouses were still occupied by peasants, living in near-medieval conditions; there were no tastefully renovated stone houses available to the English middle class.

Gissing was content in St Honoré, at least for his first months there. He liked the large garden with its fruits, vegetables and flowers, and the countryside was superb:

> St Honoré is a most beautiful place; a hilly country, magnificently wooded – some of the finest oaks and chestnuts I ever saw, making woodland glades of unutterable delight in this summer time. ... After sunset a peculiar feature is given to the place by certain sounds strange to England – the ceaseless shrilling of crickets, the clamour of frogs, and the queer hooting of *toads*—[38]

Apart from the hooting, Gissing was pleased by the resemblance of the countryside to the west of England, and delighted by the 'blessed country stillness' after the noise of Paris. For more than three months he and Gabrielle went nowhere, a hermit-like existence that suited Gissing well. There was no risk here that Edith could turn up, or that they might run into awkward questions about their marriage. Gissing was heartsick about the way the world was going, with the Boxer rebellion in China and the Boer War; though the worse things were, the greater his relief at being so far away from them:

The newspapers lately have made me ill. It is to be feared that never again in our lifetime shall we see peace and quietness. Of course the outlook of literature is very gloomy. . . . No *great* writer can be looked for, I am quite sure, nor, indeed, any great artist of any kind. A period of struggle for existence between the nations seems to have begun, and indeed it will obviously soon be a struggle for the very means of life. This may very well result in a long period of semi-barbarism, until – perhaps by immense slaughter, perhaps by famines and epidemics – the numbers of the human race are once more reduced.[39]

In the 1890s Social Darwinism was extended from the struggle between individuals to the struggle between nations. Like an individual, a nation struggled blindly and ruthlessly for what it needed in order to survive. Paradoxically, Herbert Spencer, the intellectual father of Social Darwinism, had come to resist this idea. In 1882, with Gissing's friend Frederic Harrison, he founded the 'Anti-Aggression League'. In 1902 he opposed the Boer War in his *Facts and Comments*. It never seemed to occur to Gissing that if some people were opposed to war, imperialist expansion could not be a universal impulse, like a biological drive. He only knew that the barbarians were in the saddle, and any sensible man would look for an individual refuge. Indeed, the modern barbarians were worse than the ancient ones, because as the Roman Empire declined people like Cassiodorus and St Benedict were building new institutions to protect culture. Gissing's radically individualist pessimism led to *The Private Papers of Henry Ryecroft*, which he wrote at St Honoré. He liked the retired life for its own sake, but also because the Great Powers were turning public life into a blood-soaked arena.

In a sense the Boer War did Gissing good, by making him content to avoid great cities and their intellectual strife. The values of *Our Friend the Charlatan* and *Ryecroft* came in part from Gissing's longing to find a refuge from the struggle for survival in the literary marketplace. In addition, the struggle between the nations now seemed to destroy all the hopes for social improvement of the 1880s and 1890s. The Reverend Lashmar, in *Charlatan*, says to his son Dyce: 'You *cannot* believe in [Christianity]; for you were born a post-Darwinian.' Unfortunately, he continues, Darwinism is both true, and socially destructive: 'To me your method of solution seems a deliberate insistence on the worldly in human nature, sure to have the practical result of making men more and more savagely materialist. . . . From my point of view, a man becomes noble *in spite* of the material laws which condition his life, never in consequence of them.'[40] Gissing had abandoned socialism because it had an ideal rather than a real understanding of the working class. Social Darwinism had the virtue of describing how people actually behaved, but all it showed was selfishness and aggression as far as the eye could see.

As soon as he arrived at St Honoré and planned his summer's work, Gissing told Pinker that he had become very doubtful about the novel he had sent him two months before, 'Among the Prophets': 'I want you to tell me with entire frankness whether you find any difficulty in disposing of this book. That which I am now engaged upon, "The Coming Man", will be incomparably better, and I have had grave thoughts of withdrawing "Among the Prophets" altogether.'[41] Gissing could live for a while on his advance from Chapman & Hall for *By the Ionian Sea*, while completing 'The Coming Man', and he may have felt that a serious novel about contemporary political life was more relevant than a satire on cranks. Pinker agreed with Gissing's doubts, and 'Among the Prophets' was withdrawn and eventually destroyed. *Our Friend the Charlatan* pleased Gissing as he wrote the early chapters, and he thought it was the best thing he had done since *New Grub Street*. He finished it on 29 August, after three more months of work, and sent it to Pinker. Certainly the conditions under which he had written it were the best he had enjoyed for a long time. But the contradictions within the novel's exponent character, Dyce Lashmar, were not well resolved.

Lashmar is a variant on a familiar Gissing type, the superman with a moral flaw. Like Godwin Peak of *Born in Exile*, Lashmar is haunted by a guilty text – in his case, a sociological treatise that has helped to make him a 'coming man', but which he plagiarised. The problem with the novel is that Lashmar is first presented as a fearless intellectual pioneer, but then is compromised by his own cynicism. Or is it that cynicism appeals to him because it suits his innate dishonesty?

> He recognized in himself a tortuous tendency, not to be overcome by reflection and moral or utilitarian resolve. He could not, much as he desired it, be an entirely honest man. His ideal was honesty, even as he had a strong prejudice in favour of personal cleanliness. But occasionally he shirked the cold tub; and, in the same way, he found it difficult at times to tell the truth.[42]

Gissing had been reading Jean Izoulet's *La Cité Moderne* (1894), and Lashmar reads it too. Social life is a biological phenomenon, Izoulet argued, in which we strive to assert ourselves and are drawn to the power that will further our interests. What does it mean to speak of honesty when we observe the interactions of a swarm, whether of insects or of people? People who value honesty are simply deluded about the way the world works.

Society embodies a tension between elites and the crowd: the mob has to understand that they are part of a 'vast organism', and progress comes from association rather than antagonism. Lashmar and his friend May Tomalin are part of the elite, yet *Charlatan* also leaves open the possibility that they are defective rather than clear-sighted, 'incapable of romantic passion, children of a time which subdues everything to interest, which fosters vanity and chills the heart'.[43]

If Lashmar and Tomalin are products of their time, there still might be better people at different times, or in different places. Gissing's ideas of escape were either to live imaginatively in the past, or to remove oneself from imperial centres like London, Paris or Berlin. As Dyce Lashmar becomes more dogmatic and self-centred, the reader's sympathies in *Charlatan* shift towards Lord Dymchurch, an impoverished aristocrat. He blames himself for chronic lack of ambition and actually admires the lower middle class, 'That busy and aspiring multitude'. When he meets an old gardener in Somerset, Dymchurch realises that the best way of finding meaning and satisfaction in life is to restore a garden. 'Neglect your garden for a few weeks, and it becomes a wilderness; nature conquers it back again. Think what that means; how all the cultivated places of the earth are kept for men only by ceaseless conflict with nature, year in, year out.'[44]

Dymchurch's musings derive from T. H. Huxley's famous distinction between human purpose and the blind forces of evolution:

> Not only is the state of nature hostile to the state of art of the garden; but the principle of the horticultural process, by which the latter is created and maintained, is antithetic to that of the cosmic process. The characteristic feature of the latter is the intense and unceasing competition of the struggle for existence. The characteristic of the former is the elimination of that struggle, by the removal of the conditions which give rise to it.[45]

Man is both part of nature, and someone who tries to subdue it. The existence of universal struggle does not justify mere egoism and aggression in man, because man also has the potential to create a little sphere of order around himself. For Dymchurch, the right calling is to grow food for humanity on a farm he owns in Kent. 'I will cultivate this ground,' he tells himself, 'because it is mine, and because no other way offers of living as a man should – taking some part, however humble, in the eternal strife with nature.'[46]

Dymchurch's return to the soil is part of Gissing's farewell to Dyce Lashmar and all power-seeking idealists of his ilk:

And how many preachers of socialism – in this, that, or the other form, had in truth the socialistic spirit? Lashmar, with his emphasis on the universal obligation of social service – was he not simply an ambitious struggler and intriguer, careless of everything but his own advancement? Probably enough. And, on the whole, was there ever an age so rank with individualism as this of ours, which chatters ceaselessly of self-subdual to the common cause?[47]

This was for Gissing a final criticism of socialism. Dymchurch can achieve a virtuous life on his farm because it is a *private* life. He need persuade or control no one but himself. Anyone who attempts a collective solution must enter the political arena, where any success will have the side-effect of inflating the politician's ego. By this point in his life, Gissing is a cynic about politicians: they want above all to feel self-important, and anything they achieve for the common good is likely to be incidental. Politicians of both the left and the right have similar personalities, greedy for power and applause. In *Charlatan*, Lashmar stands for Parliament as a Liberal because he needs the support of Lady Ogram; he complains that if he had been able to stand as a Conservative, he would have won.

The Dymchurch critique of politics in *Charlatan* leads to the complete withdrawal from the public sphere presented in Gissing's next book, *The Private Papers of Henry Ryecroft*. It seems an extreme position to say that politics are bunk because politicians are in it for self-gratification. But to support that view Gissing only needed to point to the Boer War, which showed him that the peaceful cultivation of their garden was the last thing politicians were interested in. *Charlatan* also suggested that the war between the nations had its counterpart in the war between the sexes. After Lady Ogram's death, Constance Bride unexpectedly has £70,000 and Dyce Lashmar has nothing. Naturally he wishes to marry Constance and use her money to support his political ambitions. He is flabbergasted by her reply to his proposal:

'I always knew that you despised women, that you looked upon them as creatures to be made use of. If you ask: why, then, did I endure you for a moment? – the answer must be that I am a woman. . . . You mustn't lose heart; I have little doubt that some other woman will grasp at the opportunity you so kindly wish to reserve for me. . . . There are plenty of women, still, who like to be despised, and some of them are very nice indeed. They are the only good wives; I feel sure of it. We others – women cursed with brains – are not meant for marriage.'[48]

Constance needs to feel this way in order that poetic justice be inflicted on the arch-cad Lashmar. But even allowing for the requirements of plot, there is a definite shift of mood between *The Crown of Life* and *Our Friend the Charlatan*. Each novel has its clever, independent heroine: Irene Derwent and Constance Bride. In the novel written before Gissing had started to live with Gabrielle, the woman gives up that independence in order to enjoy a love supreme with the hero. After Gabrielle, Gissing reverts to his earlier themes, that marriage is always a struggle for power, and romantic love is only a deluded form of self-surrender. He could not really complain about the externals of his life at St Honoré, since it was so much more comfortable than either his solitary days in London or his cat-and-dog days with Edith. But had he not submerged his identity in that of Gabrielle and Maman? They had determined what country he lived in, what house, and in what way. In time, Gissing would say openly that petticoat rule had deprived him of his proper standing in his household. In *The Private Papers of Henry Ryecroft*, his next book, he removes women from the equation altogether, except for a housekeeper who has no character beyond submissiveness. To the eternal questions of domestic life, Gissing proposes a Robinson Crusoe solution, complete with Woman Friday.

Looking Homeward

Three days before finishing *Our Friend the Charlatan*, Gissing finally went to see a physician in St Honoré, Dr Cornoy, about the lesion on the right side of his forehead. Cornoy prescribed bathing in the local hot sulphurous springs and drinking the water. Not surprisingly, this had no effect. When caused by tuberculosis such a lesion was called a lupus; but a contemporary French authority noted that syphilitic and tuberculous lesions were in some cases impossible to distinguish.[1] Gissing certainly had TB by this time, but he could have had syphilis as well, with the two diseases producing similar symptoms. Syphilis, after all, was called by physicians 'the great imitator'. Whatever the cause, Gissing's health was steadily deteriorating. He had complained often enough that his health was broken and he would die before long; now he really was on a steady downward slope. 'Henry Rye-croft' dies five years after he retires to Devon. Gissing, as he wrote the book, had just over three years left.

Gissing finished *Our Friend the Charlatan* on 29 August, and the next day Gabrielle finished her translation into French of *The Odd Women*. Unfortunately, she could never find a publisher for it, nor could she make any significant literary income to supplement her £100 a year.[2] It was up to Gissing to keep writing as fast as he could. For one day after sending off the manuscript of *Charlatan* he wrote in his diary the single word: 'Idling.' The next day he had begun work on 'An Author at Grass', the musings about his twilight years that would become *The Private Papers of Henry Ryecroft*. Gissing did manage to make a day's excursion to Autun, an hour or so away, with Alice Ward. She was a friend of Gabrielle's of about Gissing's age, an English journalist and translator who lived in Paris. Gissing was very taken with Autun, a beautiful and historic town that was much larger than St Honoré, and much more interesting too. His visit led to renting a house there for the following summer of 1901. When Gissing wrote about Autun in his diary he listed all the Roman remains but said nothing about the Romanesque cathedral of St Lazare, with its magnificent sculptures by Gislebertus. Nothing medieval had much resonance for Gissing, apart from his love of Wells and Glastonbury in England.

'An Author at Grass' can be seen as an alternative happy ending to *New Grub Street*. When a racehorse is retired, it is put out in the meadows to eat grass, rather than the high-octane fuel of oats. Henry Ryecroft, Gissing's imagined author, has toiled in Grub Street for thirty years when, at the age of fifty, he is bequeathed a life income of £300 by a friend. He takes a country cottage near Exeter and lives peacefully on his own, meditating on his past struggles, until his death five years later. It is easy to see why Gissing's fantasy took this particular shape, given his profound disillusion with politics and equally profound fatigue with the demands of the literary marketplace. But one looks also at what is missing from Ryecroft's little paradise – the absences that *make* it a paradise for him. In real life Gissing had fifteen people who depended on him to some extent: Edith, Walter and Alfred; Gabrielle and Maman; his two sisters and his mother; Algernon with his wife and five children. He had to keep writing for them, and write until he literally dropped. His union with Gabrielle forced him to do his work in France, a country he appreciated but never really loved. Ryecroft has no dependents at all (his daughter is well married), so he can live precisely how and where he likes. His choice of place is simple: a cottage in the English countryside. When Gissing looked out from his window at St Honoré he saw a landscape similar to parts of Devon; but where he wanted to be was the real Devon.[3] He seems to have forgotten that when he last lived in Devon he complained and said he never wanted to go back. Though he had a French wife and spoke fluent French, he never got over being homesick for England. Ryecroft's way of life can be called bookish, exiled or contemplative, but its essence is to be independent. He has complete control of his income and his environment, without having to consider anyone else's views. His only companion is a housekeeper whose one aim in life is to please him.

Obligations and connections may often cause pain, but they also give shape to a life; many would say that they are what we live *for*. Gissing was conscious that a life like Ryecroft's might appear selfish and empty. Eduard Bertz made this suggestion, and in his reply Gissing carefully drew a line between Ryecroft as an imaginary creation, and how he himself had chosen to live:

> There is some force in your objection to the picture of such tranquillity of mind in a quite solitary man aged only 50. . . . I prefer to regard his happiness as quite possible, and I will tell you why. Had he been merely a booklover,

I admit that the picture would be improbable, but a booklover who is at the same time a passionate lover of nature can, I believe, more easily and happily live quite alone than any other kind of man. Ryecroft, it is obvious, was at no time fond of *much* society, and at 50 he *was* (as you say) decidedly cool of temperament. Books and nature, taken together, I think suffice to a man of that stamp.[4]

What Gissing means by coolness is a lack of sexual desire for women. In *Ryecroft* Gissing was imagining how much happier his life might have been if he had not been driven by lust to get involved with Nell and with Edith.

Gissing found 'An Author at Grass' easy to write, and he finished it in less than two months. 'In style,' he noted, 'it is better than anything I have yet done.'[5] He had written the closest thing he would ever achieve to a bestseller, though by the time it was really making money, Gissing would be dead. For all his confidence in the book, he was going through another period of financial panic. From the time he sent the manuscript of *Our Friend the Charlatan* to Pinker, at the end of August, it would be five months before he got an offer from an English publisher. That made him anxious about going back to Paris for the winter, where he never had enough coal for his fire. No doubt Maman counted every piece as the servant carried it up.

The deeper problem was Gissing's lack of income from his backlist. By the autumn of 1900 he had published twenty-one books, but everything before *The Crown of Life* was bringing in no more than £20 or £30 a year. *Workers in the Dawn* and *Isabel Clarendon* he wanted to be forgotten, and they were not reprinted. The five novels sold to Smith, Elder brought him nothing. Heinemann had offered to take over the Lawrence & Bullen titles, but neither Gissing nor Pinker wanted to do business with them. Gissing felt that they had treated Algernon shabbily when he submitted *A Vagabond in Arts* to them in 1894. Pinker's objection was probably that they were hostile to literary agents and to the Society of Authors. No other publisher came forward. Gissing called himself a 'library author': people took his books out of the library, but did not particularly want to buy their own copies.[6] In 1900, as his health was failing, Gissing's prospects had not changed. If he could write more books, Pinker could sell them at a reasonable price, such that his income might be £400 or £500 a year. But there was no way of guaranteeing a steady income at this level for the future, if he became too sick to write or died. To enjoy Ryecroft's £300 a year without working, Gissing would have needed a capital of about £7,500. That was more than he had earned in his whole career to date. His marriage to Gabrielle had not improved his financial position; he was chained to his oar, and could only keep rowing until his final collapse.

Before returning to Paris, Gissing had a taste of the kind of life he would have liked to have. Gabrielle had two sets of well-to-do cousins living not far from St Honoré, so she went with Gissing and Maman to pay them an extended visit. They went first for a week to Robert Eustache and his wife, who lived at the Château de Chasnay, just outside Nevers at Four-chambault. Mme Eustache was half-English, her mother having married an upper-class Englishman called Walter Crawshay. The Eustaches were landowners, living in an imposing nineteenth-century château that had a fine park of two hundred acres, overlooking the Loire. Gabrielle had a host of uncles, aunts and cousins at Nevers; perhaps the only pea under her mattress was that she and Maman were poorer relatives, unable to live in thirty-room style like the Eustaches. From the Château de Chasnay they moved to the nearby Château de Tazières for two weeks. This was a smaller château, more like an English country house. It had been built by Alfred Saglio, who owned a foundry at Fourchambault. Gissing appreciated the comfort and good food at Tazières, but that was as far as it went; he never found the French *haute bourgeoisie* worth writing about.

From Tazières, Gissing returned to Paris with Gabrielle and Maman on 19 November. Gabrielle's younger brother René had left the flat; he was something like Algernon, unable to settle on a career and sponging off his relatives. He had left his room in a great mess, but once that was cleared up Gissing would have a proper study to work in, and could have his books sent over from storage in Dorking. He was now thinking hard about his Roman novel, and needed his histories and classical texts to provide him with background. Still, the coming winter in Paris offered a dreary prospect. The weather was rainy and foggy, there was no getting away from Maman, and he feared that his books might become even less popular. 'The truth is,' he told Eduard Bertz, 'you know, people are rather forgetting me, and I shall have a hard struggle to keep myself alive, with all my expenses. It is a disagreeable thing to feel that, at my age, I am beginning to lose even what little public I had.'[7] Gissing often complained about 'paragraphing', the publication of little items of gossip about authors. But gossip and publicity are necessary fuel for the literary world, and it did Gissing's career no good when he removed himself from the London literary scene. He had been away from England now for a year and a half, and before then he had been lying low in case Edith got on his track. There was only one way to keep his reputation going, he told Pinker: 'to publish and publish and publish yet again'.[8] But it was hard to get his pages done when he was again penned up in Maman's flat, and dining at her skimpy table. He told Hick he wished that 'an honest bit of English roast beef' could be sent in a letter – gravy included.[9]

One of Gissing's motives in taking up his Roman novel was that he might revive his fortunes by publishing something completely different from any that he had written before, perhaps even under an assumed name. He spent a month after his return to Paris in making a plan for the book, under the working title of 'The Vanquished Roman'. As soon as he was ready, Gissing set pen to paper – on Christmas Day! 'The first Christmas Day in my life on which I worked,' he noted.[10] It was less a day of celebration in France than in England but, even so, Gissing was taking his vow of ceaseless labour all too literally. Summing up his position at year-end to Clara Collet, he spoke of little but money worries on all fronts.

Money matters, at least, took a turn for the better in the New Year of 1901. Holt of New York offered £150 for *Our Friend the Charlatan;* three weeks later, Chapman & Hall offered £350 for five years of English rights.[11] This was the most Gissing had ever received for a novel, and he seemed to be climbing a regular ladder: £250 for *The Town Traveller*, £300 for *The Crown of Life*, and now £350 for *Charlatan*. Sixteen years before, Chapman & Hall had given Gissing £30 for *The Unclassed*, his first payment for a novel. He wrote to Clara Collet that his time of stress was over and he could now continue 'The Vanquished Roman' in a good spirit: 'the first really honest piece of work I have offered to my readers, for it represents the preparatory labour of years, and is written without pressure'.[12] *By the Ionian Sea* was in production too, with illustrations that Gissing liked and a large, luxurious format.

There was hope that Gissing might make a somewhat better living from his books than before, but the real question was whether he could remain healthy enough to keep producing. When the cold weather set in, he soon came down with a bad cold. Maman could not go outside at all, and Gabrielle caught the flu more than once. This might be written off as the usual discomforts of winter, except that Gissing had been coughing for nearly a year and was steadily losing weight. If Gabrielle had her way, she told Clara Collet, she wouldn't let Gissing work at all:

> I think it is very wrong to try so to force himself to labour in such a state, because that weakens him still more; he is certainly no longer able to do, in that respect, what he formerly did. Often enough you can see in him signs of being overworked, of wanting rest, and this brain tiredness does not improve his general health, already so uncertain! And he gets then so nervous and so anxious looking![13]

Gabrielle's belief was that Gissing had picked up a cold when he visited Wakefield a year before; now he had a chronic weakness in the chest. He needed to stop working and put himself in the hands of a good French doctor, who would prescribe a strict regime, such as Maman followed. Gabrielle would keep both of them alive. But a month earlier the Wellses had come to dinner at rue de Siam, and they had a different story: 'We found him in a state of profound discontent. The apartment was bleakly elegant in the polished French way. He was doing no effective work, he was thin and ailing, and he complained bitterly that his pseudo mother-in-law, who was in complete control of his domestic affairs, was starving him.'[14] Wells firmly believed that his friend was being deprived of the diet and comforts that he needed. Gabrielle just as firmly disagreed. Gissing had come from the defective culture of Wakefield, and needed to appreciate French medicine and French refinement. Once he did, he might get better.

The underlying truth in this tug of war was that Gissing's health had broken down and he was going to die in less than three years, whether he died in an English way or a French way. Emotionally, though, he had to be on Wells's side. Wells came from a similar background; he was trained as a biological scientist; and he had gone from his sickly and tubercular youth to triumphant vitality and success. Jealousy was not one of Gissing's vices, but he did compare himself with Wells, who was, Gissing thought, 'one of the happiest and most fortunate men living. . . . He has built himself a beautiful house on the cliff at Sandgate (near Folkestone), where, sitting at his ease, he communicates with London by telephone! That kind of thing will never fall to me.'[15]

Through March and April Gissing struggled on in Paris, working on 'The Vanquished Roman' when he could, but writing little in his diary and often feeling too ill to do anything. At the beginning of April Margaret wrote to him saying that she and Ellen could no longer cope with Walter's behaviour, and they wanted him sent away to boarding school at once. Gissing would have to pay twenty guineas a term for three terms, instead of the £40 a year he was paying his sisters. It upset him that Walter would become homeless at the age of nine, when Gissing himself had suffered so much from that loss even in his late teens and twenties. In June Margaret found a Miss Rickards at Ilkley who said she would take Walter for £40, and also provide his clothes. Walter was immediately packed off to her, and Gissing had too many other troubles to be able to protest.

Gabrielle finally got Gissing to agree that he would put himself under the care of a well-known Paris doctor, Anatole Chauffard. His consultation with Chauffard, on 26 April 1901, was a critical point in Gissing's life and in his relation with Gabrielle. After that day he wrote nothing in his diary for almost a year. Chauffard did not find anything new, but Gissing's general condition was alarming. His lung troubles were severe, with chronic bronchitis, emphysema, and a spot on the right lung. For the lesion on Gissing's forehead Chauffard prescribed hypodermic injections of sodium cacodylate, an arsenic compound. Chauffard apparently did not tell his patient that this had been a standard treatment for syphilitic lesions since the 1840s.[16] The injections had to be given daily, and Gabrielle did this when they were away from Paris.

Another painful directive from Chauffard was that Gissing should go nowhere near the sea — which meant he could not travel to England, as he longed to do:

> I had lived, positively lived, on the hope of seeing an English field, and walking in an English lane, this summer. . . . Now I must go to the centre of France (I don't think the Alps are possible) and vegetate amid things which serve only to remind me that here is *not* England. Then again, I had thought night and day of a boiled potato — of a slice of English meat — of tarts and puddings — of tea cakes; night and day had I looked forward to ravening on those things.[17]

It was not just English food, but the Yorkshire food of his childhood that Gissing was ravenous for. Hunger and homesickness went together, and they came from the same source: Chauffard had, that day, given him something close to a death sentence. For Gabrielle, though, England was the cause of her husband's illness, and France his hope of a cure. She may even have asked Chauffard privately to tell her husband he couldn't go there. Only seven months later, Chauffard was telling Gissing to spend the winter by the sea — in France.

Since Maman could not go to the Alps, Chauffard's advice meant spending the summer in the same general region as the year before. Gabrielle rented a house at Autun, which Gissing already knew and liked, and they would all move down there in June. Meanwhile, Gissing was fretting about being tied down. 'My great trouble,' he told Clara Collet, 'is that I am possessed by a ceaseless longing for movement, and above all (of course) for the sea. . . . Upon this summer — the use I make of it — clearly depends whether I live or die. I am not in the least nervous, but very resolute to act on my own instincts if I find myself steadily growing worse.'[18] He was not yet ready to defy Gabrielle by rejecting Chauffard's advice, but was plucking up courage to do so. Then, the magazine *Literature* asked if he would come to England to have his portrait taken by Elliott and Fry. It was flattering to appear in a portrait series with writers like Hardy, Tolstoy and Whitman, and here was the perfect excuse to cross the Channel.

Gabrielle agreed that Gissing could go, provided that it was only for four days (not long enough to go to Wakefield) and she came along to look after him. The plan was to take the Folkestone ferry on 27 May and spend the night with the Wellses, who lived only a couple of miles from the harbour. Then they would go and stay for two nights with J. B. Pinker at Worcester Park, while Gissing took care of his literary business in London. One more night with the Wellses at Sandgate, and they would return to Paris to prepare for the summer move to Autun. Hal Way, the photographer for Elliott and Fry, would come to Sandgate to take Gissing's picture. Everything went according to plan, and Way took his picture of a haggard-looking Gissing. The lesion on the right side of his forehead is clearly visible, unusual at a time when a studio retoucher would usually remove such blemishes. Wells had seen Gissing in Paris only three months before; now he was so shocked by his appearance that he told a friend Gissing was 'palpably dying'.[19] He got Hick to come over from New Romney to examine Gissing, and persuade him to spend a few more days at Sandgate. He could stuff himself with English food and enjoy the luxuries of the Wellses' new house. Gabrielle, worried about Maman, went back to Paris on 3 June, expecting Gissing to follow her shortly. But Wells and Hick were ready for a coup: once they had got rid of Gabrielle, they knew that they had a good chance of making Gissing do what they wanted.

Hick convinced Gissing to have another consultation with Dr Philip Pye-Smith, the lung specialist who had examined Gissing at the beginning of 1897 and sent him off by himself to Budleigh Salterton. He now gave the same advice: Gissing should go to a sanatorium in the south of England. Gissing did not particularly want to go to a sanatorium, but the knock-down argument for him was that, now that he could eat what he liked, he was rapidly gaining weight. He put on eight pounds in his first two weeks in England (he was 139 pounds when he arrived), and he believed that if he stayed in France starvation would kill him. With the Wellses guiding his pen, he wrote to tell Gabrielle that instead of coming home he was going to stay on at Sandgate for at least a couple of weeks:

Pye Smith has said *privately* to Hick that it would be most dangerous to incur the least risk of losing weight again, and that it is simple madness of me to undertake long journeys whilst I am benefiting so greatly here. . . . Last night I hardly slept, thinking about you, and longing for you, and hoping you would not misunderstand me.

Which is better – to have a short separation that I may become strong and live for years, or to spend the summer together and perhaps never see another. Hick says: 'It is life or death.'[20]

Gabrielle gave in for the moment – she had no alternative – but she fired off a fifteen-hundred-word letter to Amy Catherine Wells, reproaching her for keeping George in England. 'Of course no French doctor,' she wrote, 'would never dream of taking away an invalid from his wife – provided his wife is decent enough – to put him in the care of strangers.'[21] Gabrielle had four points to make, which she drew out at exhausting length. France had not been fatal to George; he had got better there rather than worse. She could not come back to England now and nurse him, because Maman might die at any moment. If Gabrielle did come, Edith might track them down and confront her, which would be unbearable. Finally, if they were in England Gissing's family would want to come and see him, and he had not yet been able to tell them that he was living with Gabrielle:

> You know it would be impossible for me to meet them, they do not even know of my existence, George having never dared to hurt their feelings and incur their remonstrances on this point. For them, I should be an object of unspeakable contempt, and *that* I shall never be able to bear. – I cannot bear humiliations like that, I am too proud. – I have certainly made great sacrifices, of half the natural joys of every married woman, but I cannot bring myself to be treated with scorn and contempt, assimilated to a low and vulgar creature.[22]

Gabrielle might indeed find herself in a sticky position in England; yet there were people like the Pinkers, the Wellses and Clara Collet who would treat her with as much respect as if she were Gissing's legal wife. The real reasons for her refusal to come were unwillingness to leave her mother, and fear of being treated rudely by Gissing's family. In fact, during this whole visit Gissing would never see his Wakefield family or Walter, thanks to Gabrielle's opposition to his doing so. She feared that his family might get control of him; the corollary was that she and Maman needed to keep tight hold of the control they already had. Backed up by the Wellses, Gissing had come to believe that Maman was the sole cause of his failing health:

> The only trouble (except my lung) arises from the fact that Mme Fleury, despite her grave illness, holds with fierce authority to the rule of the household, treating G. and me like little children. The result of her dictation as to my diet is that I have all but starved into downright consumption.[23]

Away from Gabrielle and Maman, Gissing could take a firm view of his situation. He explained to Gabrielle that she would be much happier once he had reclaimed his masculine power (as several of his fictional characters stiffen themselves up to do):

> Looking back over the past two years, I see myself as a rather poor creature, living in querulous subjection, without courage to rebel and to say: 'No, this is not the life of a *man*!' I am going to be more worthy of respect in the eyes of my wife. After all, the old predominance of the *man* is thoroughly wholesome and justifiable, but he must be *manlike* and worthy of ruling. Most contemptible is the man who lets himself be dominated even by the most beloved woman.[24]

Once Gissing had taken control, Gabrielle would admire him and love him more than ever. Nancy Tarrant of *In the Year of Jubilee* responds in that way to her husband's dictates, but Gabrielle had no taste at all for submission. Perhaps there was a sexual subtext to Gissing's proclamation that 'you are going to be my wife, my real, true wife!'[25] He might have become impotent, or Gabrielle may have been unwilling to sleep with him. He certainly felt that he had not been acting as a man should. Gissing felt that masculine self-assertion would revive his marriage; unfortunately for him, it was not a belief that Gabrielle in any way shared.

Three weeks of comfort and good food with the Wellses had put Gissing back on his feet, but he could not stay longer because Amy Catherine was now a month away from giving birth to her first child. Before going, he and Wells went to stay overnight at Rye with Wells's friend and neighbour Henry James. They were an odd couple of friends, and would eventually fall out; at this point, James was still very taken with Wells's humour and vitality. In his review of *The Whirlpool*, James had praised Gissing as the voice of the English lower middle class. But when Gissing and Wells knocked on the door of James's exquisite Georgian house in Rye, and his maid opened the door to them, we can be sure that both host and guest observed every rule of upper-middle-class domestic behaviour. Yet none of the three properly belonged to that style of life; what they did together they chose consciously to perform. All that Gissing told Gabrielle about the visit was that James had spoken of having known Turgenev in Paris. Later, James spoke of Gissing as being 'worn almost to the bone (of sadness). . . . quite particularly marked out for what is called in his and my profession an unhappy ending'.[26] Gissing gave James a copy of *New Grub Street*, with its unhappy ending for Reardon. Once his guests had left, James returned to putting the final touches on *The Ambassadors*. But he invited Gissing to come again and restore himself at Lamb House: 'I further much feel your allusion, in your note, to the element of worry in your life; so that, please, I'm not indulging in a mere form of speech when I hope you may before too long again give me a chance to see, *here*, if I mayn't a little bedim for you that consciousness. Nothing would give me more pleasure than to try.'[27] It is pleasant to imagine Gissing opening his heart to the Master, and taking his advice about Gabrielle and Maman. The household at rue de Siam, seething with tensions, could easily have provided material for one of James's stories. But the best of advice makes no impression on the deaf and Gissing hardly ever did what he was advised to do. He did what he was driven to do.

Gabrielle and Maman had now arrived at the rented house in Autun. Gissing had a good excuse for not joining them: his English doctors wanted him to enter a sanatorium. On 24 June he went to Dr Jane Walker's brand-new sanatorium outside Nayland, Suffolk.[28] It was deep in the countryside, to keep its patients totally removed from any of the concerns of everyday life. The 'treatment' was very simple: long hours in the open air, absolute rest, and heavy feeding to build up the patient's strength. Gissing had taken to heart his doctors' warnings, but there was also a clash of wills in progress with Gabrielle. Her strategy was to keep Gissing starved for her letters, while sending long, complaining letters to the Wellses and to Clara Collet. Gabrielle held to her claim that it would be too expensive and inconvenient to come and see Gissing at Nayland, so they were stalemated. Gissing sat tight in Suffolk, Gabrielle and Maman in Autun. His thank-you letter to Amy Catherine Wells said: 'I live only for one hope, that you and [H. G.] may some day sit with Gabrielle and me at our own table under an English roof. That will never be, most likely, but it would be an honest joy.'[29] Behind Gabrielle's concerns about the dangers of being in England lay a fundamental reluctance to adapt to Gissing's tastes and values; rather, she expected him to adapt to hers. Her conventionally feminine manner covered an inflexible will and rigid views on proper behaviour. In the long run, Gissing's force was completely outmatched by Gabrielle's. Being away from her that summer helped him to build up his physical strength. It did not make him any more capable of standing up for the kind of home that would make him happy.

Gissing stayed at Nayland for a month and a half. He hoped for a dramatic cure in his early days there; later on, he became sceptical of Dr Walker's medical skills. A long succession of doctors had found spots on Gissing's lung, starting twelve years ago, but his health had failed gradually, and with a host of symptoms unrelated to TB. Some of the symptoms associated with emphysema – palpitations, shortness of breath, fatigue – might also come from the aortic insufficiency that was a common result of tertiary syphilis. A TB sanatorium was not going to cure that. Still, Gissing was well nourished and relieved from the harsh discipline of writing. If he had stayed on as an invalid at Nayland he might have lived a few years longer.

In his everyday life, Gissing had always felt the obsessive's need for a rigid routine; the sanatorium imposed one on him from outside, and he did not find it irksome. He also found a friend among the patients in Rachel White, a young classics scholar. She later became a lecturer at Newnham College, Cambridge, and in 1906 married Nathaniel Wedd, a fellow of King's. There is no hint of Gissing's taking a romantic interest in Miss White, but she was an ideal companion for the empty days at the sanatorium. Gissing would use her as the model for the strong-minded schoolteacher of 'Miss Rodney's Leisure', who whips her slatternly landlady into shape: 'For the first time in her life the flabby, foolish woman had to do with a person of firm will and bright intelligence; not being vicious of temper, she necessarily felt herself submitting to domination, and darkly surmised that the rule might in some way be for her good.'[30] This resembled Gissing's old fantasy of making Edith into a dutiful wife and housekeeper by force of will, a project that had no hope of succeeding. Miss Rodney, though, holds to her course and gets the job done. Gissing's friendship with Miss White was no more than that, but it suggested his constant failure to fall in love sensibly. Instead, he had dreamed Gabrielle into existence as an ideal beloved, and only gradually discovered how little life with her would suit him.

Apart from his friendship with Miss White, Gissing could report that 'I am regarded with much interest and curiosity here. It is curious, this feeling of being an important person.'[31] Although he had been too ill to produce any significant writing for some months, it happened that in May and June Gissing had two books published that were widely noticed: *Our Friend the Charlatan* and *By the Ionian Sea*. Many of the patients at Nayland were the sort of people who read *The Times*, and on 29 June they could glance across the breakfast table at the new patient Gissing as they read this:

Although *Our Friend the Charlatan* is rather like Mr Gissing's earlier work in essence it is 'like, but oh! How different.' There is as much satire, but it is amused and not indignant satire. He still shoots folly as it flies, still holds up to ridicule the peculiar vices and absurdities of the hour; but he does it with the calm curiosity of a scientific investigator, and no longer in the 'woe!

woe!' vein of a minor prophet. Mr Gissing is still, too, it may be noted, more interested in ideas than in men and women.[32]

The *Times* reviewer finished by saying that Gissing's readers were still waiting for a 'work of genius' from him. Still, most of the reviewers felt that *Charlatan* was on a level with Gissing's other major novels, and better than most of what he had published since *The Whirlpool*. What remained the same, though, was a modest level of sales. Gissing could continue to make a middle-class income from his books, but could only dream of the kind of prosperity enjoyed by H. G. Wells.

By the Ionian Sea was not cut out to be a best-seller either, though it received – as it deserved – glowing reviews. It also prepared the way for the success of *The Private Papers of Henry Ryecroft* by showing how versatile Gissing could be as a writer:

> We know now that his aesthetic and moral pre-occupations are of the widest. We know that the painter of modern squalor, sadness, gloom, and heroic futility, has had eyes continually on other scenes and other ages. We know that if he has chosen to deal artistically with much that is ugly and repulsive, it was from no morbid inability to discern a more obvious and a more sublime beauty than dwells in the domesticity of London.[33]

Gissing suddenly appeared to have the kind of snob-appeal that he had never enjoyed before. That appeal came, oddly enough, from the spectacle of an English gentleman coping with malaria, bedbugs and unspeakable food, all the while rhapsodising about the sunset of the Roman Empire. It helped that the book was appearing in a de luxe illustrated edition, selling for sixteen shillings – more than twice as much as a typical novel. Gissing had good reason to be pleased with the book's reception, and reviewers even praised his black-and-white drawings; this was a belated fulfilment of his youthful ambition to be an artist rather than a writer. To crown all this attention, Morley Roberts's survey article on Gissing appeared in *Literature* in July, with the photograph taken at Sandgate.

In his own country, Gissing was being honoured; the problems in his life lay further off, in France. Nayland was too expensive for a long stay, and Gabrielle was fretting to have him back with her at Autun. After two weeks at Nayland, Gissing told Clara Collet that he would go to Wakefield for a week at the end of July, before returning to France. He had not seen Walter for more than a year, and he was resolved to tell his sisters face-to-face about his liaison with Gabrielle. Meanwhile he was sending Gabrielle a stream of what must be called soppy letters, telling her how much he

loved and missed her: 'Kisses, kisses, endless kisses to darling girlie sweet –
to dear, dear wife.'[34] If Gissing thought that words of love would soften
Gabrielle's dislike of Wakefield, he was wrong. Her letter to Amy Catherine Wells shows Gabrielle completely walled up in her own ideas about
her marriage. Gissing had announced that he planned to be master in his
own house, and Gabrielle would come to respect him for it. Well, not
exactly:

> I shall certainly do my best to please George in everything, but I entreat
> you not to think his strange complains about not being master in his house-
> hold and I not mistress etc, quite justified. Good G. has the faculty of getting
> strange fancies in his head and to be easily wrong in things of that kind. He
> has no idea whatever about the realities of domestic life, but thinks he has,
> and as his criterium in that as in every thing is Wakefield, if something is
> different, it is immediately condemned.[35]

Gabrielle's ideas of right and wrong were her own, and entirely justified;
Gissing was a puppet of his mother and sisters. There was no need to take
him seriously, since he didn't even realise where his so-called beliefs were
coming from. In this way Gabrielle defined her husband as incorrigibly
weak, vacillating and deluded. Wakefield was another matter: that was an
enemy worthy of respect, so it was crucial that Gissing not be allowed to
set foot there:

> Of course I quite understand his wish to see his boy and people and in
> another year and circumstances I should quite approve of his going to see
> them ... but *this* year, I think, is exceptional. ... Of course I extremely
> dread the results of this stay and increased intimity between him and his
> people, just before his intended returning to me, knowing as I only too well
> know his extreme, astonishing submissiveness to them. That will lead to
> troubles, I am afraid. And I know their loving of exercising their authority
> over him, and their natural animosity against everyone who appears to have
> some influence on him![36]

It never seems to have occurred to Gabrielle that she was completely under
the thumb of her own mother, even as she prevented Gissing spending
even a week with *his* family. For the last three and a half years of his life he
would never see his family or his sons at all. If Gabrielle could keep Gissing
away from Wakefield, and neutralise the influence on him of the Wellses,
she could get him to return speedily to Autun. Indeed, within a few days
he wrote to her: 'It shall be done as you wish with regard to Wakefield.'
The only drop of acid he allowed himself was to sign the letter 'Ever yours,

G. G.' – instead of 'For ever yours, sweetheart, Old G.', which was his usual style.[37] Nonetheless, he had made an unconditional surrender.

If he could not go to Wakefield, he had to break the news about Gabrielle by letter. Ellen was away in Switzerland, so he wrote to Margaret, and left it up to her whether she would tell their mother or not:

> Well now, dear Margaret, you know two things – that my marriage was a horrible failure, and that, on all such subjects, I hold views quite apart from those which are called orthodox. Let me tell you, then, that, about a year and a half ago, I contracted a new marriage – one which is to me perfectly sacred and valid, though of course it cannot be made legal. It came about through an acquaintance with a French lady who was translating my books. Her name was Gabrielle Fleury, her age about 30, and she was in possession of an income of about a hundred pounds a year. . . . Her family is more than respectable, for she is related to both French and English people of very good social standing, and associates with the best world in Paris. . . .
>
> I know, my dear and good sister, that you cannot regard it with any approval, but the fact of the matter is that I could not live on in my state of helpless misery. By this time I should have succumbed to lung disease, and my boys would have been left a burden to other people. . . . Were it *possible* for you to see the thing as my friends do, need I say how glad I should be. But I leave you to your own judgement and own conscience – which, indeed, is all I ask of others myself.[38]

When Margaret replied, Gissing thanked her for 'a very good and kind letter', though he told Clara Collet that the result of his letter was as he expected: 'misery and pain and a future only of gloom'.[39] More than ever, he was caught between his loyalty to Wakefield and to Gabrielle. It was never likely that his sisters and mother would approve what they considered an adulterous or even a bigamous relationship. When Gissing kept Gabrielle a secret from Wakefield, she resented it; when he told Wakefield the truth, they resented her.

Death in Exile

Gissing stayed on at Nayland two weeks longer than he had planned, then left without going to Wakefield or seeing any of the friends he had wanted to visit.[1] His last sight of England would have been Beachy Head, where he had loved to walk in the days when he stayed at Eastbourne. As the headland sank below the horizon, England was lost to him for ever. At Autun, Gabrielle and Maman were ready to welcome him, and to make sure that he would not go off to England unsupervised again. The Chalet Feuillebois that they had rented was a large and modern country house, surrounded by meadows and with a fine view down to Autun. 'This place is delightful,' Gissing told H. G. Wells, 'from our garden, a view over the picturesque old town, with a far horizon of great hills beyond. Out of Italy, I know no town so mediaevally attractive.'[2] He had some elbow-room to get away from Maman, and the sanatorium seemed to have built up his strength. Gabrielle proposed a simple solution to the diet problem, too: Gissing could have plenty of food, so long as he was willing to pay for it. His weight continued to go up, and by October he reached 169 pounds – thirty pounds more than when he had left for England in May. The only fly in the ointment was that Gissing was living in Burgundy, but forbidden to drink wine.

Unfortunately, the two main ideas for the treatment of TB at the time were mistaken. One was the belief that patients should be stuffed with food, and this would somehow arrest the progress of the disease. The other will-o'-the-wisp was the search for some particular place where the disease would spontaneously retreat. Gissing thought at first that Autun was a fine place, with the right kind of altitude and fresh air. Later it was seen as 'very damp, and did me much harm'.[3] Before his health failed, Gissing usually spent at least two or three years in whatever place he lived; after he left Epsom in 1897 the longest he spent in any one place was a year. His restlessness in the last years of his life came either from the search for the right, healthy, place or, conversely, the failure of Gabrielle and Maman to provide the kind of cosy home (by his standards) in which he could be content.

The previous summer at St Honoré had been a productive one for Gissing, and at Autun he was also able to get back to his desk, after having done very little in the first half of 1901. His first task was to thoroughly revise 'An Author at Grass', though he could only manage to work for two hours a day. He made it into a more tranquil book by cutting many of the bitter memories of Ryecroft's previous life on Grub Street, and emphasising the happiness of his life in retirement. Gissing also removed his grumblings – directed at Maman – about the lack of comfort in French bourgeois life. The softening of tone made 'An Author at Grass' into a more consistent work, in the sense of reflecting Gissing's conviction that our feelings are the product of our circumstances. A man who is comfortably off will become a comfortable person. In turn, the cosiness of Ryecroft's situation made Gissing's readers more comfortable with him.

Much of the appeal of Ryecroft's way of life came from his renunciation of any duty to be productive. The image of the reclusive man of letters, in his picturesque country house, is a powerful one in this period: Henry James at Rye, Rilke at Duino, and many others. But Ryecroft has not retired from the world to commune with his muse; he retires because he is exhausted by his struggle with the literary marketplace. It is not a question of producing literature, but of recovering from what the production of literature has inflicted on him. Gissing was well aware that he probably would never become a Ryecroft himself: 'I hope too much will not be made of the few autobiographic pages in this book. The thing is much more an aspiration than a memory. If I live a few more years, I hope to find a corner of England where I can await my end in peace, somehow as did Ryecroft. But in the meantime I have to keep myself as fit as possible for continuous work.'[4] Work was one half of what Ryecroft was in flight from; the other half was the duties of marriage. He had done his part, but now his wife was dead and his only daughter married. Gissing was still caught on both flanks: by the need to work, and the need to care for wife (or wives), children and mother-in-law.

Gissing dispatched 'An Author at Grass' to Pinker on 23 September. While he was waiting for it to be typed up and sent to publishers he wrote 'The Riding-Whip', a short story about a defiant scoundrel who is dealt with by being given a good thrashing. The story was taken by the *Illustrated London News*, and a bigger stroke of luck was that 'An Author at Grass' was quickly accepted as a serial by the *Fortnightly Review*. 'I am unspeakably glad that the thing seems so acceptable,' Gissing told Pinker. 'As a bit of style, it is better than anything else of mine – but style, you know, goes for so little nowadays.'[5] W. L. Courtney was both the editor of the *Fortnightly* and the chairman of Chapman & Hall, who had published Gissing's two most recent books. They followed up their offer of £150 for the serial of 'An Author at Grass' with £100 for the book, against a 20 per cent royalty. Gissing hoped for more, and told Pinker to try other publishers. Then Courtney made a third offer to Gissing, to write a biography of Dickens. Gissing replied that he could not possibly do this while living in France, without access to English libraries. But he agreed, for £150, to do an abridgement of John Forster's massive *Life of Charles Dickens* (1872–4). This could be a literal scissors-and-paste job, with Gissing cutting up a copy of the book and adding bits of his own criticism of the novels. It was quick and relatively easy money, much easier than writing another novel.

After sunny beginnings at Autun, the skies opened for an unrelentingly wet autumn. As one cold and rainy day followed another, Gissing's cough worsened, and he found it more and more difficult to breathe. He could walk no further than the kilometre or so into town and back. It seemed unlikely that he could survive another winter in Paris, and England was out of the question. In the middle of October he and Gabrielle went again for a long stay with Mlle Saglio at the Château de Tazières. They might have remained there until the New Year, enjoying the comfort of a wealthy household; but soon Fourchambault started to freeze. Gissing was convinced that cold air made his shortness of breath much worse. He and Gabrielle went up to Paris in early November for another consultation with Dr Chauffard, who found that the emphysema was progressing, and the lesion on Gissing's forehead was still growing. His report to Ellen in Wakefield was a gloomy one:

> I seem to have got at the truth about my lungs. I am threatened with gradual hardening of all the surface, which, if it went on, would of course stop all breathing, and so extinguish me. . . . My case seems to be rather a singular one, and puzzles doctors a good deal. I keep in good flesh and look very well indeed, but I cannot walk a mile, and pant terribly if I have to go upstairs.[6]

Whatever was going on in Gissing's body, his doctors could do nothing about it. Chauffard only suggested his usual remedy: a rest cure in the south.

Arcachon, on the Atlantic coast near Bordeaux, was another purpose-built health resort for the bourgeoisie. It had no special attractions for Gissing, and few resources for a writer, but it was better than being cooped up in the rue de Siam under the eye of Maman. He had made some progress at Fourchambault on his abridgement of Forster, and had also written an article for *Literature* on 'Dickens in Memory'. At Arcachon he would be able to go on with the Forster, though only while taking the fresh-air cure in a chaise longue. He and Gabrielle went down to Arcachon on 3 December, and she stayed with him for two weeks at his *pension*, the Villa Souvenir. After that, as she explained to Clara Collet, she had to go back to Paris: 'One very sad part of the business is that we do not see how I can possibly remain here, having that rent of the flat going on at Paris. So that I shall have to leave G. in about a week's time and the idea of that long separation, so full of anxieties, makes me dreadfully miserable. He will have to stay here till the weather is settled in spring.'[7] As usual, Gabrielle was making what she wanted to do into what had to be done. If it was a choice between spending the winter with her mother or her husband, she chose her mother. Gabrielle was still fond of Paris and had a circle of friends there; once she had returned, she paid no further visit to Arcachon. It would be five months before she would see Gissing again.

At Arcachon you could stay in a sanatorium or in a private *pension*, according to your means. Gissing, ever worried about money, chose a modest *pension* (though the food was good, so at least he did not have to worry about losing weight). Arcachon was a curious and interesting place, he thought:

> Along the flat sea-border from Bordeaux to the Pyrenees, wind and sea have, from time immemorial, heaped up several ranges of immense sand hills, more than 100 ft. high, and these are covered with a forest of great pines – a forest which stretches over more than 80 miles along the coast. Between two ranges of these hills, and amid the pine trees, is built the 'winter town' of Arcachon – which consists of some hundreds of villas, each apart in its garden; no streets, no shops. . . . Our position in the forest is an absolute security against wind. . . . The odour of the pines is said to be good for one; the sandy soil of course absorbs moisture at once.[8]

The invalid's Arcachon was a new town of gingerbread villas, built over the past forty years as a haven against TB. Gissing's Nayland friend Rachel White was now high up in the Alps at Davos; Gissing was on the flat, but supposed to be healed by calm and the fragrance of the pines. He lay out on his chaise longue in the garden, hearing the distant roar of the sea, and nourishing dreams of recovery. For a while, he was content to be where Chauffard had sent him.

From Arcachon Gissing sent a friendly letter to Henry James, saying that he was doing well, but only able to work for two hours each day when formerly he had been able to do ten. 'Your muffled Arcachon sounds rather terribly in the minor key,' James replied, and then gave some curiously testicular advice on a writer's hours of work:

> If you can work 2 hours *cherish* your 2 hours, for it isn't the given quantity – or the wasted occasion – that does the job, but the little hoarded continuity, the few forged links. They – the daily links – make the chain, which grows by *each* successively. I never in my life have been able to write more than 3 or 4 hours a day. . . . And for that matter, I think I should never have been able, at best, to squeeze out *quality* at a stretch of more than 3 or 4 hours and I don't see how it's done. It's after all by quality that we live – and when I've distilled my few drops I must wait for new secretions.[9]

For Gissing, alas, it was by quantity that he had had to live. Although James was not independently wealthy, and had wrested a living from the literary marketplace as Gissing had, he had enjoyed a far more comfortable existence. As a bachelor, he had avoided Gissing's disastrous entanglements with women. He was also an American citizen, with the advantage of earning the full returns on his books both in England and in the US (it was the latter that provided two-thirds of his income). Towards Gissing he showed both kindness and appreciation; unfortunately, Gissing was not able to give him much appreciation in return:

> *Henry James* was an example of the misfortune of a *déraciné* novelist. He has lost his Americanism, without ever acquiring as a novelist the Eng[lish] nationality, so that his novels have something *factice*, untrue, uncharacterized. – Very subtle psychology – even too subtle sometimes – his personages not living. – He thought H. James was not to be compared with Meredith.[10]

Gissing was consistent, at least. Though he lived a good part of his life in France and Italy, he never tried to write novels, or even short stories, about Continental society. Unlike James, he did not believe in the autonomy of a person's moral life. Everyone is hemmed in by social forces that leave only a narrow space for self-assertion. This does not mean that Gissing's characters cannot make moral choices; but they cannot do so through the kind of sensitive interior adjustments that make up the life represented in a Jamesian novel. While at Arcachon Gissing wrote 'Christopherson', a story about a poor book-collector who sacrifices his library to give his wife a chance of happiness. He is free to do that, but not to escape the poverty and illness that have given him an unhappy fate. It is a weakness of Gissing's later novels that they continue to show individuals to be determined by their place in the social structure, yet society itself is no longer scrutinised as carefully as in earlier novels. Gissing was endangering his own particular talent when he first withdrew to the outskirts of London, and then out of England altogether.

At Arcachon, Gissing's social observation was as limited as it had ever been. He took all his meals at the *pension*, and saw few people other than those who lived there with him. He had some contact with Charles and Alice Williamson, well-to-do journalists who were friends of J. B. Pinker. The abridgement of Forster was finished by the middle of January, but after that Gissing entered his usual season of discontent when the latest change of place had not improved his health. The company at the *pension* grated on him more and more:

> Villa Souvenir in the Ville d'Hiver – badly managed and decayed house, the mistress, Mlle Gatineau, deaf as a post, and at the mercy of insolent servants. All my days have been passed on chaise longue in the galerie de cure, where, somehow, I have managed to write now and then. Companions two young Frenchmen – Cognat, a Normalien, and Anthier, in business; a few weeks ago came another, Ferronault, a commercial traveller. Never have I lived so long in the company of blackguards. Cognat is an educated peasant; Anthier only to be described as a cad. Impossible to give an idea of the filthiness of their minds and the grossness of their talk. They are petty, envious, malicious; always jeering or sneering at someone or other.[11]

Gissing told Gabrielle in January that she should not come down to see him, because the Villa Souvenir was too cold and uncomfortable; she should wait until February or March, when spring would have begun. But somehow conditions were never favourable. Gabrielle preferred Paris and the company of Maman; Gissing perhaps preferred being on his own. Still, boredom and irritation plagued him by day, and insomnia by night. For the last three months of his stay at Arcachon he produced very little, just two short stories and a review of Frederick Kitton's biography of Dickens for the *Times Literary Supplement*.[12] The review had three points of interest. One was Gissing's comments on how a novelist uses people he knows in creating characters: 'direct portraiture is very rare in the best imaginative work. On the other hand, every living figure in fiction owes its origin to the author's observation of life.' Gissing left open the question of whether, in journeyman work, copying from life might be a useful short cut. Then he praised Kitton for saying as little as possible about Dickens's separation from his wife and his infatuation with Ellen Ternan. This came in part from Gissing's puritanism, in part from a deep belief in the right to privacy (including, of course, his own). Finally, there was Gissing's positive idea of what a literary biography should contain: 'this is for us the root of the matter – how Dickens taught himself to be a writer of books, and how, one after another, those books were written.'[13]

In January, Gissing heard from Miss Orme that Edith had got herself into deep trouble. She had been living in lodgings with Alfred in Brixton, with Miss Orme trying to keep an eye on her, and Gissing's solicitor doling out £2 a week for her to live on. Alfred was now six, and his life for the past four years had been one of wandering from one set of lodgings to another with his increasingly disturbed mother. Edith's landlady in Brixton reported her to the police for beating Alfred. The police took Edith and the boy to the Lambeth Workhouse Infirmary in Kennington – the only place that would treat poor people without charge. At the Infirmary Edith was diagnosed as insane and removed to a private asylum. This would cost Gissing 25 shillings a week for her keep, but it was discovered that she had saved nearly £120 from her allowance, which would cover her expenses for some time. Later, Miss Orme had Edith transferred to a County Asylum.

There was no question of sending Edith to trial for her treatment of Alfred, given her mental state:

> You will remember that Miss Orme years ago declared that E. was not of sound mind, and doubtless she was right. I should feel more sorry for her, were it not that she has so cruelly treated the child. It was because she behaved in the same way to Walter that I had to send him away from home. – By the bye, the police state that she has constantly threatened to kill Miss Orme and her sister, and that she has been known to hang about the neighbourhood of Tulse Hill.[14]

Edith's breakdown was not altogether unwelcome to Gissing. He would save money, and one of Gabrielle's objections to living in England was no longer valid, since Edith would be safely locked away. If he were free to do so, he would like to live in Devon or Cornwall with Gabrielle, where winters were mild. Gissing soon realised, though, that Maman would never agree to live outside France. But at least he could now feel that he had no responsibility for anything that had gone wrong in his second marriage. A mad wife was a guilty wife, and that was that:

> I regard this as a good thing for the poor woman herself, who was merely leading a brutal life, causing everybody connected with her a good deal of trouble. She will now be taken care of in a proper way, at less expense to me than before. Little Alfred ... is to be sent, to recover his health, to a farmhouse in Cornwall, where he will be close to the residence of a sister of

Miss Orme. My mind, on *that* score, is enormously relieved. I always felt myself guilty of a crime in abandoning the poor little fellow. He will now have his chance to grow up in healthy and decent circumstances. I cannot tell you how greatly I am relieved. Indeed, I believe that this event is already having a good effect upon my health.[15]

Gissing was firm that his mother and sisters had too much work already, with the care of Walter and their school. There was no chance that they could take Alfred too. Nor did Gissing even consider bringing Alfred to live with him and Gabrielle, since he was already afraid that Gabrielle would break down under the strain of caring for her mother. Alfred went to live with the Alfred Smith family, on their farm at Treverva, Cornwall. The cost would be £20 a year. Miss Orme's elderly married sister lived nearby, at Falmouth, and would look out for him. Gissing felt later that she had been very kind to the boy, though it was hardly like having a loving parent to look after him. But Gissing convinced himself that life on a farm was the best thing for Alfred. 'I should be rather glad than otherwise if he grew up a stolid countryman,' he told Henry Hick, 'interested in turnips.'[16] That he was in Cornwall helped to soothe Gissing's conscience: health and happiness, he felt, were largely a matter of geography. At least Alfred had been saved from Edith, and Edith saved from responsibility for herself. Gissing could manage no more salvation than that.

Once he got out of Arcachon, Gissing did not want to return to Paris. Capri was attractive, except that Maman would not go to Italy. That left southern France, and Gissing's physician at Arcachon thought highly of Cambo, a spa town near Biarritz. Gissing proposed to Gabrielle that he would go down to the Basque country by himself and find a small furnished house where they could spend both the summer and the following winter. There he could have his books and a study, and write the novel he had been pondering, *Will Warburton*. Gabrielle and Maman would give up the flat in the rue de Siam and find something much cheaper on the outskirts of Paris, where they could keep their furniture and have a place to stay when they were in town. For once, everything went according to plan. Gissing paid off Dr Festal, who had charged only £8 for a whole winter's attendance, and happily said goodbye to Arcachon at the end of April.

Gissing went south to St Jean de Luz and stayed at the Pension Larrea facing the sea in Ciboure, a commune adjacent to St Jean. After five months enclosed in the flat pine forests of the Landes, St Jean was a delight to the eye, with the great Atlantic breakers on one side and the Pyrenees on the other. This was the right place for them to make a home, Gissing told Gabrielle:

The whole place is extremely beautiful. It combines sea and mountain and rural scenery. A wonderful richness of vegetation. Lovely little gardens scattered everywhere in the town itself, and these gardens already a mass of *roses* – just like St Honoré in June. The architecture is very curious – unlike anything I know; Spanish, in part, I suppose. Very strange to hear the people talking basque everywhere.[17]

Gissing explored the countryside, and soon decided that they should look for housing in St Jean de Luz rather than in Cambo or one of the villages in the foothills. He was afraid of the deadly boredom of another winter in some sleepy backwater. St Jean had an English colony, good postal service to England, doctors and shops. Gabrielle worried about the wind from the sea, dangerous to Gissing or to Maman; they should not live in any exposed place – that is, anywhere with a view. Gissing dutifully picked out a furnished apartment in a large villa on the town square of Ciboure. They could rent it for six months from July 1 for 1,200 francs (£48), or for a year for 1,500 (£60). Living was cheap in Ciboure, so Gissing could feel less deprived at the dinner table. It all looked promising except that, as usual, Gissing had managed to comb over one of the most beautiful regions in Europe and find living quarters that were completely without charm. He engaged a Basque servant girl for thirty francs a month, and lingered on at Ciboure rather than return to the hated rue de Siam. He had corrected the proofs of his abridgement of Forster, and had no other work on hand. This brought on a severe case of what Freud called 'Sunday neurosis': anxiety caused by the lack of a set task:

> Having nothing to read, and nothing to do, passed the day in utter idleness – heaven knows, indeed, how the hours have gone by. And how often in my life have I spent such a day as this, – blank, wearisome, wasted! A sort of destiny of idleness and wasted time seems to oppress a great part of my life. Each time a day such as this comes, I make a resolve that it shall never happen again. But circumstances are too strong for me. Indeed, the only way in which I could avoid this miserable folly of barren hours would be to live always in reach of a large library – the impossible thing for me, now and ever.[18]

Having almost worked himself to death, Gissing still reproached himself for not having worked harder.

Gissing returned to the rue de Siam on 23 May 1902. The next month was taken up with moving, something that he disliked at the best of times, and no doubt made more tiresome this time by the fussing of Gabrielle and Maman. The new pied-à-terre was in Boulogne-Billancourt, on the western edge of Paris, at a rent of only £27 a year. However, they would make little use of it over the next year and a half. Gissing's check-up with Dr Chauffard was inconclusive: he was a little stronger, but there was no improvement in the state of his lungs. If St Jean de Luz suited him, he might be well enough to produce another novel by the end of the year. Meanwhile 'An Author at Grass' had begun to appear in the *Fortnightly Review*. It made an immediate impression, though Gissing was frustrated that the editor had decided to publish it in four instalments, each three months apart. The book had four sections – Spring, Summer, Autumn, Winter – and the editor wanted them to appear in the appropriate season. That delayed publication as a book until the spring of 1903. In June Gabrielle's translation of *New Grub Street* came out in book form, and Gissing hoped that it would be widely reviewed in the French press. Unfortunately, it received little notice, and Gabrielle's hopes of getting more of her translations published came to naught. Gissing had been either too sick or too reclusive to establish his personal presence on the French literary scene, and Gabrielle remained a small fish with no prospect of getting any bigger.

On 2 July Gissing, Gabrielle and Maman left Paris for St Jean de Luz. Gissing was still telling his friends that he hoped to visit England in the summer of 1903, and even to find a way of living there. But this was a one-way journey to the south from which there would be, for him, no return. A week after arriving at Ciboure he was hard at work on his new novel, *Will Warburton*. Yet he rejoiced to hear that his friend W. H. Hudson had been granted a Civil List pension, and told his friend Edward Clodd that he should retire too:

> I shall rejoice – quite sincerely rejoice – when I hear that, like Lamb, you have gone home for ever. No man can make a better use of tranquillity than you.
>
> There was a praetorian prefect under Hadrian, a fine old fellow called Similis. Permitted at length to lay down office, he retired to his country estate, where he died seven years later. On his tomb he had graven: 'Here lies Similis, who existed for sixty-four years, and *lived seven*.'[19]

Gissing himself would surely have received a Civil List pension if he had become too sick to write. After his death, his two sons received small grants from the Civil List for their education. Nonetheless, idleness was no blessing to Gissing; it was a torment. He might write lovingly about Ryecroft's life of leisure, but in real life he probably could not have tolerated it for more than a few weeks.

Gissing realised that his resources of invention were draining away. He could only work in the mornings at *Will Warburton*, and was troubled by how slowly it was coming along. 'The intellect threatens decay, I fear,' he told Morley Roberts, 'for a long time now, I have been losing my interest in life – a bad pass for a novelist.'[20] In the afternoons he read *Don Quixote* in Spanish; he had bought his copy in 1886 and was now fulfilling an old ambition by using it to master the language. Gissing worked at his Spanish for months with 'profound enjoyment', perhaps the only Ryecroft-like pastime that he managed in his life. When Cervantes made himself a character inside the book, in the second part, the literal-minded Gissing strongly objected:

> What devil was it suggested to Cervantes that most fatal idea that ever occurred to a great writer – the introduction into the story of the *book itself*? ... Alas! Could not Cervantes see that, at a blow, he destroyed the credibility of his story. If he thought it a touch of Realism, he was strongly misguided; for how *could* the adventures of D. Q. be supposed to have become known to an author, and to have been written and published and become popular in *one month's* time?[21]

The Spanish language gave Gissing much pleasure for its own sake, as he compared it with languages he knew well already: Latin, French and Italian. Like many visitors, he was fascinated to hear Basque spoken around him, a language unrelated to any other (though it contains many loan-words from Latin and French). Gabrielle even tried to learn it, though she soon gave up. The Gissings became friendly with Wentworth Webster, a scholar of Basque language and culture who lived near St Jean de Luz. There were many English people living in the area, and Gissing was happy to have some social life after having been penned up for so long at Arcachon. He met H. Butler Clarke, an expert on Spanish literature who was a fellow of St John's College, Oxford, and Jean-Baptiste Gentz, a retired professor of Classics. These were the sort of people with whom Gissing could enjoy long talks about history and philology. He and Gabrielle made expeditions into the countryside, and across the border into Spain. If he had had a more philosophical temperament, Gissing might have been quite content with his life, but he still dreamed of a better one, in a country cottage in Devon.

Gissing had taken up his diary again at Arcachon in April, but he only kept it intermittently during the year, and stopped altogether in November. Evidence for the last year of his life is restricted to his letters, and Gabrielle's later reminiscences. Everything now had to be measured out: his work on *Will Warburton*, his times of rest, his correspondence, and his exercise. 'I can walk for an hour at a time,' he told H. G. Wells, 'with not more than a dozen pauses to labour agonizingly for breath at the wayside.'[22] There was one gleam of hope, when he went to see Dr Jean Blazy in October at St Jean de Luz. Gissing passed on the good news to Dr Hick in England:

> By the bye, you remember that patch of skin-disease on my forehead? Nothing would touch it; it had lasted for more than 2 years, and was steadily extending itself, when at last, a fortnight ago, I was advised to try *Iodide* of *Potassium*. Result – perfect cure after week's treatment! I had resigned myself to being disfigured for the rest of my life; the rapidity of the cure is extraordinary. – I am thinking of substituting Iodide of Potassium for coffee at breakfast and wine at the other meals. I am also meditating a poem in its praise – which may perhaps appear in the *Fortnightly Review*.[23]

Since the Wassermann test would not come into use for another four years, the most reliable diagnostic indicator of syphilis in 1902 was rapid improvement after the administration of potassium iodide. Hick's reply to Gissing has not survived, but he left a note about it: 'I wrote suggesting that much said about Potass Iod would lead the half-educated to diagnose syphilis. At no time when I saw George Gissing did he show signs of any specific disease.'[24] By 'specific' Hick probably meant a disease caused by a known pathogen, such as *Treponema pallidum*, the infectious agent for syphilis. Almost certainly, his colleague Dr Blazy had decided that Gissing's skin lesion *was* specific – a syphilitic gumma – so potassium iodide treatment should be applied. He didn't tell Gissing because many doctors considered it more humane not to tell syphilitic patients what their diagnosis was. When Gissing naively boasted about the results, Hick of course told him to shut up.

The episode shows that Gissing probably had tertiary syphilis, roughly from the time of the 'eczema' on his arms in June 1898, and he either did not know, or did not admit, what he was suffering from. After Hick's warning it would have been hard – though not impossible – for him to remain in denial. In any case, what could not be denied was that his health was on a relentless downhill slope, and he was not going to make old bones. He was afraid of the coming winter, and to Morley Roberts made his old complaint, that one could not be really comfortable in France:

> I wish to heaven I could ask you to come and stay with me, but that is one of the satisfactions I shall never have as long as I live; for life will always be for me a matter of grinding economies and pinched comforts. We are not very well housed, and suffer a good deal from cold in the bedrooms – for not only is fuel costly, but the strength of one servant has its limits.[25]

Gissing wanted to live on a more generous scale, both for himself and for his guests. But he could not break his lower-middle-class habits of economy, even when he had a few hundred pounds in the bank. His children needed to be saved from the workhouse, and who could tell how much money would be needed to make them self-supporting? He felt sure, also, that he would never break out into becoming a popular author, despite the praise he was getting as 'An Author at Grass' came out in the *Fortnightly Review*. Then there was Gabrielle, with her £100 a year income and the mentality that went with it. If anything, she made Gissing's economic horizon even narrower.

Towards the end of 1902 Gissing developed a literary friendship that might have had a great influence on his career if it had happened sooner. In 1898 he had read one of Joseph Conrad's stories, and admired his style.[26] He met Conrad in June 1901 while staying with the Wellses at Sandgate; Conrad was then living at Pent Farm, Postling, about five miles away. At St Jean Gissing found the latest Conrad story being serialised in *Blackwood's*, and recognised his extraordinary gifts: 'No man at present writing fiction has such grip of reality, such imaginative vigour, and such wonderful command of language, as Joseph Conrad. I think him a *great* writer — there's no other word. And, when one considers his personal history, the English of his books is something like a miracle.'[27] The *Blackwood's* story was 'The End of the Tether', about an old sea-captain who struggles on in order to leave some capital for his daughter. 'No fiction has so moved me for years,' Gissing would tell Conrad later.[28] He surely identified with Captain Whalley, an unappreciated man who finds meaning in holding to the code of his profession:

> To keep the ship going he had been involving himself deeper every year. He was defenceless before the insidious work of adversity, to whose more open assaults he could present a firm front; like a cliff that stands unmoved the open battering of the sea, with a lofty ignorance of the treacherous backwash undermining the base.[29]

Like Captain Whalley, Gissing felt it his duty to earn money, for the good of others, until he could do it no more. His praise of Conrad was in a letter to Edmund Clodd, who promptly forwarded it to Conrad himself:

> I — who had always had a very human affection for you — am no longer young enough to accept with proper self confidence all that you may think right to give. After forty it is easier to spurn away blame than to embrace the fair form of praise. There is a talking spectre, a ghostly voice whispering incessantly in one's ear of the narrow circle circumscribing all effort, of the

shortness of one's vision and of the poverty of one's thought. . . . And I am my dear Gissing, as I've been always (but only now encouraged to set down the very words) admiringly and affectionately yours.[30]

They could both meditate on the trials of life after forty, but did they realise that they had been born eleven days apart? Conrad knew how bad Gissing's health was; even so, what he sent him was an impressive show of affection and respect. And it was not just Conrad: similar tributes had come from Meredith, Hardy and Henry James. What a contrast, though, between the warmth directed to Gissing by the finest creative minds of his time among men, and his poor success at gaining the love of women! Conrad sent Gissing a copy of his newly published *Typhoon* in May of 1903, and Gissing responded with rapturous praise of the four stories in the book. Sadly, though, Gissing never received 'The End of the Tether' when it was collected in *Youth*, so he missed reading the third story in that volume, 'Heart of Darkness'. Gissing by now was highly critical of Hardy's pessimism, which he saw as pointless railing against the nature of things. But he found Conrad's pessimism positively congenial. Conrad believed that a tight-lipped fidelity to one's duty was the best response to the cruelties of fate; Gissing admired Conrad's ethic of endurance, though what he most admired in Conrad was his style. 'He is the strongest writer – in every sense of the world – at present publishing in English,' Gissing told Clara Collet.[31]

If faithfulness to a task was what made a man, Gissing's great trouble as the winter came on was how little he could do at his own vocation:

In the days gone by, I used to imagine for my later life all the evils of poverty; what I never foresaw was inability to work through failure of health. Here have I been pottering at a novel since midsummer, and it is not yet half done, owing to constant breaking-down. . . . We have made a good many acquaintances, one or two of them very pleasant people. But of course my inability to do serious work takes away from every kind of enjoyment.[32]

To put it another way, Gissing could not enjoy himself unless he had 'paid' for his pleasure with a quantum of work. He could work even less in early January when he began to suffer from sciatica, rheumatic pains in the hips and legs that made it difficult even for him to walk around the house. The doctors told him that this was 'only a symptom of [his] generally ailing state'.[33] It could hardly be a symptom of emphysema, but rheumatic pains often accompanied late-stage syphilis. Gissing's life force was ebbing away, and he must have known it. The only question was whether he could struggle on for a few more years, and set his house in order. Psychologically, his situation resembled that of Henry Ryecroft, just before he inherits his annuity:

> In moments of depression he spoke of his declining energies, and evidently suffered under a haunting fear of the future. The thought of dependence had always been intolerable to him; perhaps the only boast I at any time heard from his lips was that he had never incurred debt. It was a bitter thought that, after so long and hard a struggle with unkindly circumstance, he might end his life as one of the defeated.[34]

Then, in a development thick with irony, *The Private Papers of Henry Ryecroft* was published as a book in January 1903. Gissing found himself neither defeated as an author, nor pensioned off, but – a popular success. A success that came too late, and was marred by Gissing's failure to have sold the book on decent terms. He had already been given clues to the book's potential when it was appearing in the *Fortnightly*, and many friends and strangers had written to him to praise it. When the book came out, the praise increased, including the notorious clergyman who wrote asking if Ryecroft's housekeeper was available for employment, now that her master had died! Gissing's contract meant that he needed to sell about 1,900 copies just to cover his advance of £100 (and Pinker would get £10 of that in commission). The book's first printing was 2,500 copies for the British market; they sold out, and new printings followed in March, April and October. When Gissing got his first royalty statement at the end of September 1903, it included a cheque for £75, suggesting sales up to that point of between 3,500 and 4,000 copies.[35] The difference between *Ryecroft* and all of Gissing's other books was that this one had legs. There were six printings by the end of 1904, and innumerable further editions for thirty-five years after that. The US proceeds were small at first, but became substantial after Gissing's death.

Gissing was left with his glowing reviews for *Ryecroft*, and a cheque for £75. The next royalty statement from Constable would bring more money; but that was in six months' time, and Gissing would be dead. *Ryecroft* did improve the prospects for his last two novels, though again nothing would be reaped during his lifetime. If he had lived longer, *Ryecroft* might not have been the best thing for his career, because on a superficial reading it seemed to present a Gissing quite different from the author of all his other books. W. L. Courtney, reviewing *Ryecroft* enthusiastically in the *Daily Telegraph*, made it seem that Gissing was a typical *Telegraph* reader himself. Of course he was not, and especially in his hatred of war and imperialism –

though it was not a socialistic hatred either: 'Democracy is full of menace to all the finer hopes of civilization, and the revival, in not unnatural companionship with it, of monarchic power based on militarism, makes the prospect dubious enough. There has but to arise some Lord of Slaughter, and the nations will be tearing at each other's throats.'[36]

Ryecroft is no Tory, but neither has he any hope for the masses. He will do no harm, because he will join in no collective endeavour. There is no guilt in his wealth because he has no capital, only a leasehold house and an annuity that will end at his death. Although he delights in traditional country life, Ryecroft has no ambition to be a squire, going to church on Sunday and demanding deference from his tenants. He bears the marks of high status, a classical education and a love of books. But he is separated from the class to which he might otherwise belong by his lack of any power over others. Perhaps the most purely English person is the Englishman abroad; Ryecroft lives like an expatriate in his own country.

The reviewer for the *Pall Mall Gazette* took it for granted that Gissing was using Ryecroft to express his own deepest longings: 'His hero, of whose latter life the book is an imaginary diary, praises many things, and denounces many things, from one point of view – the supreme beauty of solitude.'[37] Ryecroft may have reached this stage of stoic tranquillity, but we have to remember the younger Gissing who would run out into the London streets howling with loneliness, and who would make the worst of marriages just to escape the horrors of solitude, not the beauty of it. His distance from Ryecroft would have become evident if he had lived to write a sequel to it, which he described to Gabrielle in the last months of his life:

> A second book in the style of Ryecroft, though quite different in spirit: Ryecroft being the outcome of his past life and experiences, – this second one – the expression of his *present* life. And this book he was to dedicate to me, and said I should see how he would find a way of saying everything he wanted in that dedication. Said often he had that book already quite ready in his mind, and would write it immediately after the few months of good rest he was going to take when he had completed 'Veranilda'.[38]

Gissing wrote *Veranilda* first because he needed the money and thought the novel would sell well. The sequel to *Ryecroft* would not be about the joys of solitude, but the joys of union with Gabrielle. It was probably a good thing for Gissing's reputation that the book was never written. In any case, what *could* Gissing write about life with Gabrielle, given his attitude to speculations about the unconsummated marriage of Thomas and Jane Carlyle?

One had suspected such secrets, but why the 'many-headed beast' should be allowed to gloat upon them, I cannot understand. The affair is grossly indecent, in every sense of the word. In the case of such a man as Carlyle, it is inevitable that the external facts of his domestic life should be written about, but no one has any business to go beneath the surface in such a matter. Sufficient to know that his marriage was, like most marriages, half a blessing and half a burden. His wife's view of the matter has absolutely no relevance for the public.[39]

Nor could Gissing write about the joys of nature in his present life because, as he told George Williamson, the Basque countryside did not enchant him: 'The address upon your letter stirs me to envy. To live at Guildford, and to see Spring coming up over the heaths——! Here we have primroses and violets, yes; even hartstongue and spleenwort; but these things on the slopes of the Pyrenees are not the same as in a Surrey lane.'[40]

Like the longing he expressed for English food in *Ryecroft*, not to mention English weather, Gissing's emotions were fixing themselves on his childhood and youth.[41] This may have been a symptom of his ill-health, a search for comfort in earlier days. The more certain it became that he would never see England again, the more he longed for it. On the Continent, he could love cities or landscapes only when he could connect them with history, above all ancient Greece and Rome. In the Basque country he was moved by the pass of Roncesvalles, with its nostalgia of victory in defeat. But his loss of connection with England was a creative problem too. His new work was suffering from his having come to live in a country that did little to inspire or to sustain him. As he worked on *Will Warburton* in St Jean de Luz, he put in snippets of the Basque country, and of the holiday he had spent in the Alps at Trient. But most of the novel's action took place on the streets and in the shops of London, where Gissing had scarcely set foot for years. London had been the deep root that nourished his fiction; now that he had severed himself from it, his prose was bound to become thinner and more schematic. Gissing would not let Gabrielle read the typescript of *Warburton* because he thought it a poor novel. 'He wanted badly to go back to England for a time,' he told her, 'in order to renew his materials.'[42] In *Ryecroft* he was lamenting his loss of the English countryside, but London was the greater loss to his art.

Will Warburton was almost entirely a London novel, and Gissing's farewell to the great city. He complained of taking a full eight months to write it – from July 1902 to March 1903 – though that was not so long for a novel of medium length. What made it seem long was the struggle with so many kinds of ill-health while he was writing it. It is not surprising that

Warburton is one of Gissing's less impressive works. Its themes went back to the beginnings of his career, and showed that living in France had done little to dilute his obsessions. 'The importance of social distinctions' is once again combined with 'the guilty secret'. *Warburton* reverses the action of *Born in Exile*. In the latter novel a lower-middle-class hero strives to become a gentleman; in the former a gentleman willingly declines into the lower middle class. In *Warburton*, Gissing sets aside much of his old bitterness: the guilty secret resolves into a happy ending, and a partial escape from the oppressions of class.

Why should Gissing choose the relatively optimistic plot of *Will Warburton* at that particular stage of his life? The story was one that only he could have thought up. Warburton, a gentleman of scholarly inclinations, is cheated out of his capital by an aristocratic friend. In order to survive, he becomes a grocer in South London. He assumes the name of the existing business, and conceals his new life from all his old friends. The business does well enough, thanks to a sensible working-class partner, but Warburton still has a problem: 'what rendered his life intolerable was its radical dishonesty. . . . Grocerdom with a clear conscience would have been a totally different thing from grocerdom surreptitiously embraced.' By the end of the novel, Warburton is earning a middle-class income from his shop, yet to the genteel it is dirty money. 'Why should retail trade be vulgar,' Warburton asks plaintively, 'and wholesale quite respectable?' He is reconciled to his loss of status, but would a woman from his previous life be willing to share his stigma? 'One may be content to be a grocer, but what about one's wife?'[43] Warburton is infatuated with Rosamund Elvan; when she finds out that he has become a grocer she flees and marries his more successful friend, a society artist. But Bertha Cross loves Warburton, and accepts him as he is. Shopkeeping does not lead to disgrace, but to love and a happy ending.

In *New Grub Street* Mr Biffen writes a naturalist novel, *Mr Bailey: Grocer*. Being a grocer stands for a life reduced to its bare necessities. Having defined that life, Biffen kills himself when he realises that in his own life he has no chance of anything better. *Isabel Clarendon* (which was written before *New Grub Street*) took a more positive view of shopkeeping. Having failed with a great lady, the hero marries someone at his own level and takes on a bookshop in a provincial town. As a shopkeeper's son, Gissing could be expected to write novels in which shops play a role. But as a social novel, *Will Warburton* falls below the level of Gissing's earlier work. It is hardly an urgent question whether one may invite one's grocer to tea, taking into account that he was raised as a gentleman. The substance of *Warburton* lies elsewhere, in the way Gissing disposes of the 'guilty secret' theme. Secrets have power only so long as they are secrets, and the consequences of revealing them are unknown. Once Warburton admits how he makes his living, the consequences are mixed, but certainly manageable. In *Born in Exile*, exposure leads inevitably to disgrace and death. In *Warburton* one woman flees the hero as if he were a leper, but another accepts him as her husband-to-be. If Gabrielle had not been sympathetic when Gissing told her of his marital troubles, neither had she abandoned him. Queen Victoria was now dead, and *Will Warburton* showed that Gissing's 'guilty secret' novels had died with her. Secrets are no longer fatal, merely troublesome. *Warburton* becomes a different kind of work: an early 'coming-out' novel, in which the hero embraces a stigmatised identity. 'I'm a grocer,' Warburton says, 'and probably shall be a grocer all my life.' This may be bathetic, but it is also a claim for acceptance and dignity. Gissing was not planning to become a grocer himself, but, unlike Ryecroft, he was going to remain a literary tradesman for as long as he could put pen to paper. In *Warburton*, honesty and diligence are rewarded with modest contentment. If it was not one of Gissing's major novels, it was still an embrace of the reality principle, between two escapist works – *Ryecroft* and *Veranilda*.

It took Pinker nearly four months to sell *Will Warburton*, mainly because Gissing had complicated publishing plans. He wanted *Warburton* to appear in both serial and book form, and he wanted *Veranilda* to be published first because he considered it a much stronger and more commercial book. When the dust settled, Pinker had done well for his client. He got £100 from the Northern Newspaper Syndicate to serialise *Warburton*, and £300 from Constable for book publication. This was an advance against good royalties: 20 per cent on the first 2,500 copies, 25 per cent after that. Constable were making money with *Ryecroft*, which encouraged them to make good offers for both *Warburton* and *Veranilda*. In the spring of 1903 Gissing's commercial prospects were higher than they had ever been, just as his health and his ability to write were on the point of final collapse. But he still had not solved the mystery of how to get a steady income from his books. 'I never count on money from a publisher,' he told his sister Ellen, 'when once he has a book in his hands.'[44] Gissing could write *New Grub Street*, but could not beat the economic system that determined writers' incomes.

After sending off the manuscript of *Warburton* in mid-March 1903, Gissing went through another of his barren periods. Most of the time his sciatica and shortness of breath left him in too much discomfort to be able to work at all. He had enjoyed a five-day visit from Morley Roberts in

February, the one friend he had remained close to since the days of his own guilty secret, twenty-five years past. There were new friends at St Jean de Luz too, but Gissing's life was narrowing down to the single question of how long he could hope to survive. He went for a week in April to the spa at Cambo, twenty kilometres away. Hot springs might help his sciatica, but could not cure what lay deeper. It was time to try another move, to escape the summer heat on the coast and find that mythical place of healing.

In October of 1902 Gissing and Gabrielle had made a scouting expedition to St Jean Pied-de-Port, where there was a chalet for rent at nearby Ispoure. Despite the romantic name, they were at first disappointed by the town itself. It was surrounded by mountains, but not really a mountain town. The 'Port' in its name was the Pass of Roncesvalles, a romantic spot for Gissing that gave him a reason to live in the town at its foot. In all battles there is a losing side; Roncesvalles was about losing totally, but doing so in style. The death of Roland at Roncesvalles was the only kind of war-making that Gissing could allow himself to like. St Jean Pied-de-Port was also the gathering point for pilgrims making their way to Santiago de Compostela, on the west coast of Spain. Perhaps it helped Gissing's morale to connect his situation with that of the great doomed warrior, and of the hopeful pilgrims of the past thousand years. There was a practical reason for moving to St Jean Pied-de-Port also: Dr Lasserre of Bayonne insisted that its summer climate would suit Gissing. It does not seem to have occurred to any of these doctors that a stable home might be better for an invalid than trailing around from one resort to the next.

In June Gissing and Gabrielle wound up their lease at Ciboure and set up house again at the Chalet Elgue. It was true to type in being a large, plain nineteenth-century house, situated right on the main road about a mile from St Jean Pied-de-Port. It had pretty meadows behind the house, an old church nearby, and a fine view of the mountains. St Jean itself was one of the most attractive places Gissing had lived, with its narrow medieval streets and the river Nive running through, filled with plump trout. For a while he believed that the mountain air was repairing the damage caused by the sea air at Ciboure, and his sciatica became less painful, though insomnia still plagued him. Most important, he had enough energy to launch his new novel. In the last few weeks at Ciboure he had started to plan the book, and he changed the title from 'The Vanquished Roman' to *Veranilda*. At Ispoure Gissing set himself a modest quota of a thousand words a day, with a view to finishing *Veranilda* by the end of the year. He was able to work both in the morning and after tea, more than he had been able to manage at Ciboure when writing *Will Warburton*.

Gissing was a few steps away from open country at Ispoure, which was a relief from his enclosed life on the village square at Ciboure. Each day, he told Meredith, he could walk 'in lanes very like those of southern England, except for the great chestnut trees by which they are shadowed – the little spleenwort on the stone wall, the foxgloves and bracken, with meadowsweet and loosestrife by the river side, all remind me of home'.[45] In the euphoria of his improved health, he and Gabrielle set off in mid-August on an excursion to Roncesvalles and on into Spain. It was a gruelling journey by horse-drawn cart, over mountain roads and sometimes in great heat. Both of them showed that they were sturdy travellers; those less sturdy – Maman and their little dog Bije – were left behind at Ispoure. Gissing was better at travelling than at staying home, and he faced greasy food and horrible toilets with the same boldness he had shown in Calabria six years before.

On their first day, Gissing and Gabrielle passed Roncesvalles and spent the night below the pass at Burguete. They enjoyed the magnificent mountain scenery, though Gissing insisted that the Apennines were more magnificent yet. The next day they got up at four so as to go to Pamplona for lunch and return to Burguete that same night – on exhausting journey for anyone as sick as Gissing was. From Burguete they went up to stay at Roncesvalles, at a primitive little posada. In the monastery, they saw Roland's mace, and a vial containing milk from the Virgin Mary. Women were not allowed in the library but Gissing revelled in its old volumes, 'which made him wish he could live for a year free from personal work and troubles, shut up in this library. Envied the monks for that.'[46] Even after they were back at Ispoure, Gissing dreamed of living as a monk in an ancient library at Monte Cassino or the Vatican; an ambition impossible to realise, but which could be indulged vicariously in *Veranilda*. Gabrielle did not seem to be bothered by her husband's fantasies of living in some book-lined hermit's cell. Troubles were things that came from outside the marriage, she thought, not from within it. The biggest problem in Gissing's third marriage came from Maman, and if he could have had Gabrielle to himself he might have been truly happy in his last years. At least he had escaped the fate of John Shortridge, whose appalling troubles had continued since Gissing had stayed with him at Massa Lubrense in 1888–9. If Shortridge was to be believed, Edith Gissing was a choirgirl compared to his Italian wife.

Having seen Roncesvalles and the inns of Spain – which he liked because they seemed unchanged from the time of *Don Quixote* – Gissing saw nothing in front of him except to finish *Veranilda*, in five hours of work a day. 'Regularity is everything,' he told Algernon, his irregular brother.[47] By the end of September the novel was half done. Chained to his desk, Gissing sent Gabrielle off on her own for a week, to look at towns further to the west where they might spend the summer of 1904. He wanted to get closer to the Mediterranean, though he also thought of Geneva as a good place to write. Another possibility was Amélie les Bains, a spa town just inland from Perpignan. They had no solid evidence that one place would be better than another for Gissing's ailments, but if nowhere was chosen, that didn't rule out that somewhere might exist. They just had to keep looking for it.

Veranilda was hard going, but Gissing still hoped to follow it up with another historical novel, this time about Pythagoras in the sixth century BC. There was also the planned tribute to Gabrielle, as a sequel to *Henry Ryecroft* (and a corrective to it). Perhaps because he sensed that his literary career was ending, Gissing kept up his correspondence with writers he admired. He sent Morley Roberts a glowing letter about *Rachel Marr*, a novel that was also a popular success, and he never failed to send Wells a careful reading of his books as they came out. Hardy, the man of Wessex, asked Gissing how he could keep writing when separated from his roots:

> I am such a stay-at-home – or have been of late years – that I can hardly understand how you induce your ideas to become portable, e.g., to write of Italy when in France. If I go to a new place – particularly abroad – my imagination is its slave; which has been an inconvenience when in the past I have wished to continue at a foreign lodging a novel begun in England.[48]

The real answer to Hardy was that, in the long run, Gissing's imagination was *not* portable. He needed to get back to England, and hoped to do so in the coming summer. If it were not for Gabrielle and Maman, he might have joined the constellation of writers living near each other in Kent and Sussex: Wells, James, Conrad and Ford Madox Ford. The best he could do was to keep in touch with Hardy, and with Meredith and Conrad too. Conrad had wanted to come and visit the Basque country, but was too much embroiled in the struggle to write *Nostromo* – 'floundering in deep water', as he put it.[49]

The deep water was about to pull Gissing down. It began when Gabrielle fell ill with flu and laryngitis, in mid-October. Gissing became very anxious about her, as she was slow to improve. They were starting to feel trapped at Ispoure. Gissing felt he needed to stay there until *Veranilda* was finished, but the house was not well heated and might make them all ill as the weather closed in. They had renewed the lease until June 1904, and there was nowhere in France where the weather was certain to be better. Gissing took Gabrielle into Bayonne on 3 November to see Dr Lasserre, but refused to see the doctor for himself. Then Maman fell ill with flu and heart spasms; on 22 November (Gissing's forty-sixth birthday) they had to bring Dr Lasserre from Bayonne. Maman wanted Gissing to hold her hand and reassure her; she asked him if he was afraid of death and he said, 'No, not at all, *Je ne la crains pas du tout.*'[50] In the midst of these struggles came a letter from H. G. Wells saying that he wanted to put Gissing up for membership of the National Liberal Club and the Savile. 'Your fame in England grows steadily,' Wells reported, 'and you are the most respectable and respected of novelists next to Hardy Meredith and James. You should come and savour it.'[51] Gissing would have been happy to do so, but his immediate reality was sickness, cold, and a flooded cellar at Ispoure.

As Gabrielle and Maman suffered, Gissing himself felt better than he had for some time. He was still making steady progress on *Veranilda*, and expected to complete it in January. At the end of November Pinker told him that the *Daily Mail* wanted a story; Gissing begrudged taking any time at all from *Veranilda*, but it was quick money. He wrote a story in two days, 28 and 29 November, and it came out in the *Mail* on 9 December. 'Topham's Chance' tells of a poor drudge of a tutor who gets himself a comfortable job by impersonation and forging letters. It was another story of a man with a guilty secret who confesses, but then escapes punishment. Gissing went back to *Veranilda* for five days, during which a stranger wrote asking him for information about his life. 'No account of my life has ever appeared in print,' Gissing replied. 'I am of opinion that that kind of thing may well wait till after a writer's death – if even then it is really called for.'[52] That was the last letter Gissing wrote, and the next day, when he worked on *Veranilda*, was the last that he wrote anything at all.

Living in a cold and wet house, with two women who had been sick for a month and a half, made it almost inevitable that Gissing would catch some infection himself. It began on 4 December, with vague stomach trouble and headache. Four days later he went to bed, feeling feverish. Raboul, the local doctor, came and said that Gissing just had his usual congestion from emphysema. It was five more days before Gabrielle became so alarmed that she brought Dr Lasserre again from Bayonne, fifty kilometres away. He listened to Gissing's chest, and pronounced that he had pneumonia in both lungs. Pneumonia can be either viral or bacterial, though in 1903 there was no way of distinguishing them. In any case, either your native resistance pulled you through, or you died. Gissing was already weakened by his emphysema and his other systemic ailments; at forty-six, he was physically already an old man. His doctors came every day, and his nursing was adequate by the standards of the time. Little more could have been done for him, though H. G. Wells would muddy the waters with his tales of Gissing's last days.

For Gabrielle, Gissing's last illness was simply a lesson in how to accept the inevitable:

> But always so kind, so patient, so sweet to everybody, so thankful for the slightest service given to him! Never one word of impatience; from the first to the last day of his illness, so long and painful, always equal to himself, and the same gentleness to all, and tenderness to me. A great lesson of how to bear sufferings and pains, moral and physical, – and, too, how to die—[53]

No doubt Gabrielle was sweetening her memories somewhat. Gissing had a high fever and was full of restlessness, anxiety and fear. He struggled with his illness, knowing that so many things were left unfulfilled. There were five chapters of *Veranilda* left to write (he had done thirty), and his imagination was still at work on the novel. If he could not go back to England, he could at least see his English friends, Morley Roberts and H. G. Wells. They might still take him somewhere that would make him feel better, if not all the way to that mythical cottage by the Exe. Then there was the agony of trying to provide for Walter and Alfred. Wells had plenty of money, and might be willing to do something for them.

Three weeks after Gissing had been taken ill, Gabrielle sent Wells a telegram: 'George dying entreat you to come in greatest haste.'[54] It was Christmas Eve, Wells had two small children, and he was sick with a cold. He sent a telegram to Morley Roberts, asking if he could go instead; getting no reply, Wells packed a bag and set off on the next boat from Folkestone to Calais. By the time he arrived at St Jean Pied-de-Port, late on Christmas day, Gissing's heart was failing and there was no hope of recovery. He had been hallucinating for some days, seeing figures from the ancient world and moving towards a glorious light:

> 'It is the light of the supernatural world,' he said. 'Oh, my girlie, how I grieve you cannot see it also! It is unspeakably beautiful. And those voices singing in Eternity! I see how foolish I was to doubt the existence of the supernatural world; now it is revealed to me; I see it! And I also see what a large place it takes in our every day life, though we are not aware of it.'

'Curious indeed,' Gabrielle commented, 'considering G's anti-mystical leanings, his unqualified agnosticism, his lack of sympathy for any form of metaphysics.'[55] The local Anglican chaplain set off a furore after Gissing's death by claiming that he had returned to the Church, chanting the hymn 'Te Deum Laudamus' in his last hours. Wells's view was more pragmatic: Gissing's visions demonstrated that his mind was disintegrating, not that the hand of God had reached down to the sickroom:

> Only once did the old Gissing reappear for a moment, when abruptly he entreated me to take him back to England. For the rest of the time this gaunt, dishevelled, unshaven, flushed, bright-eyed being who sat up in bed and gestured weakly with his lead hand, was exalted.
>
> 'What are these magnificent beings!' he would say. 'Who are these magnificent beings advancing upon us?' Or again, 'What is all this splendour? What does it portend?' He babbled in Latin; he chanted fragments of Gregorian music. All the accumulation of material that he had made for *Veranilda* and more also, was hurrying faster and brighter across the mirrors of his brain before the lights went out for ever.[56]

By the time Wells wrote his *Autobiography*, in the early 1930s, he had read Morley Roberts's *The Private Life of Henry Maitland* and accepted its claim that Gissing had syphilis. Wells speaks of Gissing's good looks when he first met him, at the end of 1897, 'his appearance betraying little then of the poison that had crept into his blood to distress, depress and undermine his vitality and at last to destroy him'.[57] In retrospect, Wells might savour the irony of Gissing's love of low women bringing him to his doom, or that his religious mania on his deathbed was the work of spirochetes. But from Gabrielle's account of Wells's behaviour at Ispoure, there is no sign that he thought he was dealing with a case of syphilis. Wells saw Gissing's immediate symptoms of pneumonia and inflammation of the heart; being Wells, he took it for granted that Gabrielle and the French doctors were doing things wrong, and set about doing things differently. He thought that Gissing needed a professional nurse; this was fair enough, except that Gabrielle had already scoured the region as far as Bayonne and St Jean de Luz in search of one. There was an epidemic of flu and pneumonia, and every nurse was engaged. Wells also brought up his old obsession: that Gissing's real problem was malnutrition, and he would get better if he was stuffed with food and drink. Since Gissing had been in the Basque country he had not complained of being starved. Food was cheaper than in Paris, and he was less worried about money once Edith was committed to the asylum in January 1902. If he looked emaciated when Wells arrived it was mainly because he had been deathly ill for three weeks.

In his autobiography Wells says nothing about feeding Gissing, and only takes credit for finding him a nurse.[58] Gabrielle's memoir records that

Gissing's doctors prescribed continuous feeding of small amounts of liquid food (including champagne!). Dr Malpas, an English doctor from Biarritz, agreed with this regime, which was standard practice at the time. It was followed strictly, Gabrielle says, 'even if the patient was hungry, illusively hungry as people who are seriously ill are apt to be, and as G. was'.[59] If Gissing had been given only spoonfuls of broth and the like for three weeks, he may well have been truly hungry (not illusively, whatever that might be). Wells sent Gabrielle off to rest on 26 December, and set to work; Gabrielle was too anxious to sleep, and came back an hour later:

> Alas! The moment I open the door I stand horror-stricken at the sight of the empty bottles, basins, glasses, etc, containing the fluids prescribed to feed the patient in doses of a spoonful every 30 minutes. Mr Wells triumphantly announces that he has made him swallow *all that* during the fateful hour: coffee, tea, highly concentrated beef tea, champagne, milk, somatose, etc!! I reply: 'You have killed him, Mr Wells.' He rubs his hands gleefully, protesting that the patient has refused nothing and that 'substantial nour- ishment in plenty' is all that is needed to cure him. Thereupon he returns to his hotel.[60]

After Wells's treatment, Gissing's fever shot up overnight and he became delirious. When the doctor came in the morning, he said, '[Wells] has poisoned him.' Wells came back to say goodbye, and tell the English nurse to get in a good supply of beefsteaks; this made her think that Wells was either mad, or a drug addict! As Wells left, Gissing began a terrible death-agony: 'fits of suffocation, wild agitation, rattle in the throat, ceaseless delirium'. In the morning of the next day Dr Raboul decided that there was no hope of recovery, and Gissing should be given an overdose of morphia. He came out of his delirium and said: 'It is useless, doctor, to continue – the struggle'![61] At one o'clock in the afternoon, on Monday 28 December, Gissing's struggle came to an end.

Although he was sick himself, Morley Roberts had also set out for Ispoure. After a long and difficult journey he arrived on the morning of 29 December, only to hear that Gissing was already dead. Roberts took over the arrangements for his friend's burial. Gabrielle and Maman were dis-traught, and after quarrelling with their landlady had moved into a hotel in St Jean Pied-de-Port. Gabrielle had taken a deep dislike to the town, and did not want her husband buried there. It was Roberts who took Gissing's body down to the English church at St Jean de Luz, where it rested in front of the altar overnight. Even if Gissing was not a believer, an Anglican church was a little piece of England on foreign soil. The Reverend Cooper was eager to reclaim Gissing for the Church – far too eager, in Roberts's view. Cooper intoned the Anglican rite of burial over Gissing, and chose Psalm 39 for his farewell: 'Surely every man walketh in a vain show: surely they are disquieted in vain: he heapeth up riches, and knoweth not who shall gather them.' That was not a bad summary of the message of Gissing's books. France had nothing like a country churchyard for him to rest in, but he was buried at the highest point of the cemetery of St Jean de Luz. From it there is a magnificent open view across to the mountains of Spain. Gissing had not wanted to die in exile, but at least he took his rest far from the Victorian confinements that had haunted him – the shop, the parlour, the asylum, the workhouse, the prison.

Afterword

Soon after Gissing was buried, Gabrielle and Maman came down to stay at the Pension Larréa in St Jean de Luz. Gissing had spent a month there in the spring of 1902, after leaving Arcachon. Gabrielle had no share in Gissing's estate, because even after he met her he made no changes to the will he had made at Naples in November 1897. She had agreed to this, since she had her £100 a year from her father's estate and would have more when Maman died.[1] Gissing left only £959; for three million or so published words that meant about twelve words for each penny of profit. The commercial success of *The Private Papers of Henry Ryecroft* had come too late, though it secured his great hope for his sons, a public-school education. Edith got one third of the estate in trust; that would make no difference at all to her life in the asylum.

In April 1904 Gabrielle came to England and spent twelve days at Wakefield with Gissing's mother and sisters. They welcomed her kindly and sympathetically, she told Bertz, and told her that religion consoled them for George's untimely death: 'The worst calamities of earthly life only touch them very lightly, because they refer everything to the future world where all the apparent injustices and cruelties of this life will be explained and amply compensated.'[2] Gissing's mother and sisters were sure that he was waiting for them in heaven. He had often said that Christian faith helped those – women especially – who could not face the truth about the futility and misery of human existence.

Gabrielle went to visit Walter at Gresham's School, Holt. She saw little resemblance to his father, and signs of bad heredity from his mother. That was the end of her contact with him. She never saw Alfred, lodged at his farm in Cornwall. Clara Collet put Gabrielle up for a while in London, where she joined in the quarrel over a condescending preface written by H. G. Wells for the posthumous publication of *Veranilda*.[3] By the autumn of 1904 Gabrielle was living in Provence, plagued by bad nerves and thoughts of suicide. Clara Collet remained a staunch friend, and even paid

Gabrielle's rent for years to come. The Fleurys were not poor, though they must have spent much of their income on medical expenses. As Jane Miller observed, Gabrielle was the kind of person who spoke of her 'doctors' in the plural.[4]

Gabrielle made no attempt to manage Gissing's literary heritage. Her life would be passed in the world of bourgeois invalidism, 'taking the cure' at some spa when not at her Paris apartment. Invalid or not it would be a long life, fifty-one years more after Gissing's death. Maman succumbed finally in 1910, at the age of seventy-one; after that, Gabrielle found no other companion. Jane Miller went to see her in Paris in the 1940s, and was told in advance that Gabrielle must be addressed as 'Madame Gissing'.

It was Clara Collet who stepped forward to guard the interests of Gissing's sons and keep his books in print. Algernon quarrelled with Collet about her dealings with publishers, but was not too proud to ask her for the loan of £50 (she sent £20). The money that Gissing left would only have yielded about £40 a year; Edmund Gosse and others arranged Civil List pensions of £37 each for Walter and Alfred. With the royalties from Ryecroft, and Collet's income held in reserve, the boys were in no danger of ending up in the place that haunted their father's nightmares, the Marylebone workhouse. Both went to Gresham's School, acquiring the public-school stamp that Gissing firmly believed necessary for happiness and success. They probably never saw their mother again after she went to the asylum. Collet paid Edith's fees of 25/- a week, until she died at Salisbury in 1917 of 'organic brain disease'.

Walter Gissing trained as an architect and by 1914 was working as a church restorer (the same profession as Thomas Hardy). At Gresham's he had been in the cadet corps, like almost all public-school boys, and when war broke out he joined the Queen's Westminster Rifles.[5] Like his father, Walter disliked military discipline, which may be why he remained a private. In theory, Territorial units could refuse overseas service; but Walter's regiment signed up for France and he went with them. Their first action was at the Battle of the Somme, where they were assigned to attack at Gommecourt, on the extreme left of the British line. The role of the forces in this sector was to make the Germans think that this was the spearhead of the attack, so when they went over the top on 1 July 1916 the Germans had known for weeks that they were coming. The London Division was only a pawn in Haig's game. It was probably Walter's first day of action and within a few hours he was dead, along with hundreds of his comrades in the regiment. His body was never recovered, and his only memorial is with the seventy-two thousand names of the missing on the Somme Memorial at Thiepval.

Alfred Gissing became an officer and had the good fortune to be sent to India. After the war he lived for a while with his aunts in Wakefield (Mrs Gissing had died in 1913). Margaret and Ellen kept up their little school and never married. Alfred taught, wrote a biography of Holman Hunt, and ended up running a small hotel in Switzerland. The Gissing line has continued in his descendants.

The Private Papers of Henry Ryecroft made Gissing into a popular author, at the price of creating a false idea of what his life had been like. *Ryecroft* left out the martyrdom of the bedroom. Morley Roberts opened that door with *The Private Life of Henry Maitland* in 1912, asking how there could be such a split between the life Gissing had led, and the life he had wanted for himself. Virginia Woolf's review of *Ryecroft* in 1907 had already grasped the fundamental tension between Gissing's life and work.[6] If Ryecroft had enjoyed his private income from the beginning, he would have been a flabby and insignificant person. His cosy existence in Devon may be justified as a reward for his dire struggles in Grub Street, but in itself it has little value. In 1907 Woolf had a shrewder sense of the value of literary struggle than when she came to write *A Room of One's Own*, with its callow assumption that one needs £500 a year to have a good prose style. Gissing also directed Woolf's attention to the specific world of the lower middle class. Septimus Smith, in *Mrs Dalloway*, is a beleaguered Gissing character driven into madness by the war. Charles Tansley, in *To the Lighthouse*, is there to show that scholarship boys will always be square pegs to the round hole of middle-class self-assurance. At least Tansley, unlike Gissing, stays out of jail and gets his fellowship.

Gissing, like Forster's Leonard Bast, remained an awkward figure on the fringes of the middle-class social conscience. 'The works of Gissing,' Woolf wrote, 'will live longer than many of their more celebrated contemporaries. For though the angle was sharp and the vision narrow, Gissing beheld with his own eyes the perpetual struggles and sufferings of human beings.'[7] Nevertheless, Gissing's literary standing declined in the period between the wars. Writers on the left, with the exception of Orwell, did not find Gissing helpful to their cause. His concern for the sufferings of the poor was all very well, but his elitism and pessimism ruled him out as any kind of proletarian writer. Christopher Caudwell, in his essay on H. G. Wells, castigated the lower middle class as one 'whose whole existence is based on a lie'.[8] 'Marxist criticism of the time defined writers like Gissing by their origins. But if Gissing was a typical *petit bourgeois*, he was also one who had starved and gone to prison; that made him far from typical in his deepest beliefs.

Orwell's essay on Gissing in 1945 was a crucial step for Gissing's revival, but it was not until the 1960s that he started to receive the respect and attention that have continued until the present. Scholarly interest in him revived with Jacob Korg's 1963 biography and the start, at about the same time, of Pierre Coustillas's monumental contributions to Gissing studies. John Speirs, at Harvester Press, laid the foundations by bringing almost all of Gissing's work back into print. The culmination of Gissing scholarship has come with publication of the *Collected Letters* in 1990–9 and of Coustillas's great *Bibliography* in 2005. The justification for this scholarly revival was a major critical reconsideration of Gissing's novels. This began with critics on the left, such as Raymond Williams, Adrian Poole, John Goode and Frederic Jameson. It was criticism against the grain in that, as John Goode remarks, 'Reading Gissing is not a comfortable experience.'[9] Much of that discomfort came from the dismissive attitude towards the working class that Gissing had settled into by the middle of his career. Yet if Gissing set these critics' teeth on edge, he also examined the injuries of class with a stern clarity beyond any of his novelistic peers. More recently, academic interest in Gissing has moved towards his documentary value. Among British novelists of his time, he reveals most about the everyday lives of the urban poor and lower middle class. What Gissing may lack in literary inventiveness, he makes up in his appreciation of the exterior circumstances that constrain individual lives. Where other novelists take it as given that individuals seek their own fates, Gissing shows that, most of the time, their fates are made for them.

This tension between personal will and the force of circumstances has informed my biography of Gissing. He was a typical scholarship boy of his generation who might normally have climbed as far as the high table of an Oxbridge college. But he would not have climbed further, nor would he have wanted to. What seemed to be the greatest misfortunes of his life – his two disastrous marriages – were also what made him an exceptional man, and an artist. Yet he never saw the cure for his sorrows in giving them an aesthetic form, as writers like Joyce, Lawrence or Thomas Mann aspired to do. Rather than resolve his miseries, Gissing sought to generalise them. He came at the end of belief in the consolations of religion, but before the consolations of psychotherapy. In contemporary terms, he suffered from a personality disorder rather than a neurosis. He did not blame himself for his chronic unhappiness; he blamed the malignancy of the external world.

John Goode argues that 'Gissing was Gissing precisely because he was not Dickens'.[10] This was because he chose not to be. One such choice was his removal of Lionel Tarrant's dream from *In the Year of Jubilee*. If the reader knew about the dream, there would be an excuse for Tarrant's coldly egotistical manner. It would be a way of compensating for being unloved as a child. Gissing believed that men should hide their wounds, not least because a prison term and marriage to a prostitute were not the kind of wounds that it was safe to show. More important, he directed his analysis to what was outside the individual, rather than what was going on inside. He did care about the thinking and suffering person, but mainly from the perspective of what he or she was up against. Circumstances were the real enemy, not the enemy within.

Nonetheless, Gissing always insisted on the differences between himself and the French naturalists, especially Zola. He was not particularly impressed by the social machinery of great cities – how people in the mass cooperated to provide for their needs. Wherever there was a crowd, Gissing took care to keep well away from it. The only crowds that inspired him were those who lay silently in cemeteries. The doctrines on which Naturalism was founded – Marxism, Zolaism, Darwinism – were alike in their indifference to particular individuals. For Gissing, it was only the exceptional individual who really counted. Yet the late Victorian 'death of God' had made that individual into an absurd figure. Whether we are ruled by natural selection, or by the laws of the market, we are fools to think we are personally important. But where can we look to find comfort? For Gissing this was the modern dilemma, one that afflicted people of all conditions. At the end, he could find little consolation in power, status or religious faith. The love of power led only to war; religion was simply a delusion; and his guilty secret denied Gissing any assured place in society. The best defence against the pain of life was a mundane one: to have enough money – the bag of gold that Gissing could never quite lay his hands on. With money one could enjoy Henry Ryecroft's solution: retirement to the country, modest comfort, solitary contemplation. Yet few people could qualify for such a refuge; and it had no answer for the fearsome reality of Victorian London. Gissing came to believe that nothing much could be done about that. Yet if one could not change London, one could at least bear witness to it. That was Gissing's calling as a writer: to walk the streets, to see and hear the people, to record it all in sorrow and in pity.

Notes

Abbreviations

Bibliography   Coustillas, Pierre. *George Gissing: The Definitive Bibliography*. High Wycombe: Rivendale Press, 2005

CH   Coustillas, P., and C. Partridge, eds. *Gissing: The Critical Heritage*. London: Routledge & Kegan Paul, 1972

Diary   *London and the Life of Literature in Late Victorian England: The Diary of George Gissing, Novelist*, ed. P. Coustillas. Hassocks: Harvester Press, 1978

GN   *Gissing Newsletter* (from 1991, *Gissing Journal*)

Letters   *The Collected Letters of George Gissing*, ed. Paul F. Mattheisen. Arthur C. Young, Pierre Coustillas. Nine volumes, Athens, Ohio: Ohio UP, 1990–7.

Introduction

1 In the middle of writing *Nineteen Eighty-Four*, Orwell had to be treated for TB at Hairmyres Hospital, near Glasgow. While there he wrote his major essay on Gissing.

2 'Not Enough Money: a Sketch of George Gissing' in *The Complete Works of George Orwell* (London: Secker & Warburg, 1986–98), xv, 45–7.

3 Edmund Wilson, *The Thirties: From Notebooks and Diaries of the Period* (NY: Farrar, Straus & Giroux, 1980), 652.

Chapter 1

1 *Diary*, 338.

2 *Miscellaneous Poems*, by T. W. G. (Framlingham: W. D. Freeman, 1851), was printed by a bookseller in a nearby town, and dedicated to Miss Whittington. The others, also published by Freeman, were *Metrical Compositions*, by T. W. G. (1853) and *Margaret, and Other Poems*, by an East Anglian (1855).

3 Thomas may have been inspired by Tennyson's early poem: 'O sweet pale Margaret,/ O rare pale Margaret,/ Come down, come down, and hear me speak: / Tie up the ringlets on your cheek . . .'

4 *The Ferns and Fern Allies of Wakefield and its Neighbourhood* (Wakefield: R. Micklethwaite, 1862) and *Materials for a Flora of Wakefield and its Neighbourhood* (Huddersfield: Geo. Tindal, 1867).

5 *Workers in the Dawn*, lxxxv–lxxxvi.

6 'Reminiscences of my Father', MS notebook, Yale.

7 Brook, 17. Thomas took out mortgages for more than 90 per cent of the price, his good credit reflecting his status in the town. One cannot be precise in converting mid-nineteenth-century prices into modern equivalents, but he paid something in the region of £750,000 to £1 million in today's money.

8 *Letters* II, 170; 14 Oct. 1893.

9 Ellen Gissing, in *Letters of George Gissing to Members of his Family*, ed. Algernon & Ellen Gissing, 404.

10 The cause of death was listed as 'congestion of the lungs', a vague diagnosis that suggests pneumonia, with an underlying weakness of the lungs. Brook, 10.

11 *Workers in the Dawn*, lxxxvii (cancelled passage). Brook, 10.

12 For Wood's background see *GN* IX: 2 (April 1973).

13 Quoted in Coustillas, *Alderley Edge*, 6.

14 Ibid., 10.

15 The religious tests for entry to Oxford and Cambridge were abolished in 1871.

16 *Born in Exile*, 1.

17 *Letters* I, 18; 13 Jul. 1873. *Born in Exile*, 13.

18 Ward was only thirty-five when Gissing arrived; he became Vice-Chancellor of Victoria University, the successor to Owens College, and later Master of Peterhouse, Cambridge.

19 *Letters* IX, 250; 1 Sep. 1875.

20 *Letters* I, 38; late 1875.

21 Roberts, *Maitland*, 15–16. Roberts used the pseudonym 'Henry Maitland' to avoid giving offence to Gissing's relatives and his widow, Gabrielle Fleury. They were offended anyway.

22 Ibid., 23. In his biography, Roberts was recalling events of nearly forty years ago, and he has been criticised for minor inaccuracies and for his patronising attitude towards Gissing. Nonetheless, there are no major conflicts between Roberts's narrative and independent documentary evidence, and I accept him as a generally reliable source. Some doubt has to remain, necessarily, when Roberts is a sole source for Gissing's actions or feelings (as in this quoted passage).

23 *Born in Exile*, 39.

24 The first version of 'Jenny' dates from 1847–8, though it was not published until 1870.

25 It was the former home of the great crusader for Free Trade, Richard Cobden.

26 *Sins of the Fathers*, 1.

27 In the 1881 census Gissing and his wife, then living at 55 Wornington Road in

London, were mistakenly enumerated as 'Gilling'. This record provides Nell's place of birth, which corresponds to the 'little market-town in the south of England' of the story. Gissing told Frederic Harrison that Nell was 'a farm girl': *Letters* IX, 227.

28 Roberts, *Maitland*, 24.

29 *Letters* I, 40–1; 29 Feb. 1876.

30 *Letters* I, 40; 29 Feb. 1876.

31 Black to Gissing, *Letters* I, 43; 26 Mar. 1876. The note to this letter in *Letters* proposes a diagnosis of balanitis, but this is considered unlikely by my informant at the STD Clinic, Center for Disease Control, Vancouver, British Columbia.

32 Estimate by the syphilologist Alfred Fournier, cited in Hayden, xv.

33 *A Victim of Circumstances*, 65–6.

34 *Born in Exile*, 36.

35 Marnham, 277.

36 Roberts, *Maitland*, 26.

37 5/2d: five shillings and two pence, 62 old pence or about 26p in today's money. But this shows the arbitrariness of price comparisons across time: 26p is now a trivial sum, but 5/2d was about one-sixth of the average weekly wage in 1875. Median weekly pay in the UK in 2006 was £447.

38 John Halperin says that Greenwood bailed Gissing out, but this is contradicted by the minutes of the Disciplinary Council of Owens College, reproduced in Coustillas, 'Gissing à Manchester', 260. Halperin, 19.

39 Bellevue was demolished in the 1890s, but its layout resembled the existing Strangeways Prison in Manchester (designed by Alfred Waterhouse, the architect of Owens College).

40 *The Unclassed*, 243.

41 *Demos*, 415.

42 *Charles Dickens: A Critical Study*, 17.

43 Anon, 365.

44 For details see *GN* VI: 2 (April 1970).

45 These poems are in a manuscript notebook, 'Verses by G. R. Gissing', in the Yale University Library.

46 *Workers in the Dawn* II, 429.

47 *Letters* I, 57; 28 Jan. 1877.

48 *Free Press*, 9 Mar. 1877.

49 *Sins of the Fathers*, 11.

50 Roberts, *Maitland*, 38–9.

51 *Workers in the Dawn* II, 430.

52 This is assuming that Whelpdale's narrative, in chapter 28 of *New Grub Street*, mirrors Gissing's own experience in Troy.

Chapter 2

1 *In the Year of Jubilee*, 283, 279.

2 *Letters* I, 167; 28 Apr. 1879.

3 *Dickens's Dictionary of London* (1879).

4 *George Gissing: Essays and Fiction*, ed. Coustillas, 180–1.

5 Ibid., 182: 'beasts at Ephesus', 1 Cor. 15: 32.

6 *The Private Papers of Henry Ryecroft*, 39. Gissing owned such a set, so the story in *Ryecroft* is probably true to life.

7 Ibid., 27.

8 By lying about his age, since readers were supposed to be twenty-one. Captain Mercier, the Treasurer of St John's Hospital, was his referee.

9 *Letters* I, 97; 12 Jul. 1878.

10 *The Unclassed* II, 18. When Gissing revised *The Unclassed* for its second edition in 1895 he cut this passage.

11 Ibid. II, 249. Cut in 1895.

12 Ibid. II, 139. Cut in 1895.

13 *Letters* I, 98; 24 Jul. 1878.

14 *Letters* I, 124; 21 Nov. 1878.

15 *Letters* I, 129; 4 Dec. 1878.

16 *The Unclassed* II, 280. Cut in 1895.

17 *Letters* III, 160. Gissing read the novel in French; he went to a dramatisation of *Crime and Punishment* in Paris in 1888, and reread the novel in 1894. *Diary*, 46, 327.

18 Gissing's friend Eduard Bertz had been a student at Tübingen and Gissing drew on his experiences in writing this chapter, which was a late addition to the novel.

19 *Workers in the Dawn* I, 214, 215.

20 Ibid., 216.

21 *Letters* I, 146; 26 Jan. 1879.

22 *The Unclassed*, 39–40. The original advertisement has not been found, and it is possible that it was Gissing who placed it, rather than Bertz – for example, so that he could practise his German.

23 Ibid., 39.

24 In 1897 Gissing wrote to Bertz: 'Do you remember speaking to me about the man long before he became popularly known?' *Letters* VI, 242; 23 Feb. 1897.

25 Edward Street is now Varndell Street.

26 *Letters* I, 215; 3 Nov. 1879.

27 *Letters* I, 235; 25 Jan. 1880.

28 *Letters* I, 236; 25 Jan. 1880.

29 Ibid.

30 *Letters* I, 234; 24 Jan. 1880.

31 *Letters* I, 281; 8 Jun. 1880.

32 In *George Gissing: Essays and Fiction*, ed. Coustillas.

33 Some cuts are visible in the MS at the Humanities Center, University of Texas;

others were made by discarding about twenty of the original 728 pages. For a detailed account see Pierre Coustillas's edition of *Workers in the Dawn*.

34 *Letters* I, 262; 23 Apr. 1880.

35 *Letters* I, 265; 2 May 1880.

36 *Letters* I, 282; 8 Jun. 1880.

37 *CH*, eds, 51–2.

38 *Letters* I, 252; 20 Mar. 1880.

39 *Letters* I, 295; 23 Jul. 1880.

40 Gissing returned to the idea in 1891 with a novel called 'The Coming Man', eventually published as *Denzil Quarrier*.

41 *Letters* I, 289; 9 Jul. 1880.

42 *Letters* I, 291–2; 22 Jul. 1880.

43 *Letters* I, 292; 22 Jul. 1880.

44 *Letters* I, 293; 23 Jul. 1880.

45 *Letters* V, 12; 16 Feb. 1892.

46 *Letters* I, 265; 2 May 1880.

47 Comte assumed that in marriage, as in society as a whole, the man should rule; but Gissing could not make Nell submit. 'Biological analysis presents the female sex, in the human species especially, as constitutionally in a state of perpetual infancy.... Sociology will prove that the equality of the sexes, of which so much is said, is incompatible with all social existence.' *Positive Philosophy* (NY: Calvin Blanchard, 1855), 504–5.

48 See James, *Unsettled Accounts*.

49 *Workers in the Dawn* I, 3.

50 This was the title of a short story Gissing wrote in 1891.

51 *Workers in the Dawn* I, 8.

Chapter 3

1 *CH*, 56.

2 *Notes on Social Democracy*, 13–14.

3 *Letters* I, 298; 10 Sep. 1880.

4 *Letters* I, 301; 3 Oct. 1880.

5 *Letters* II, 11; 30 Jan. 1881.

6 *Letters* II, 20; 26 Feb. 1881.

7 *Letters* II, 27; 9 Apr. 1881.

8 *Letters* II, 33; 4 May 1881.

9 Cited in Hobsbawm, 285.

10 *Letters* II, 34–5; 15 May 1881.

11 *Letters* II, 54; 29 Jul. 1881.

12 *Letters* II, 56; 8 Aug. 1881.

13 The Scrapbook is at the Lilly Library, Indiana University. An edition by Bouwe Postmus and Pierre Coustillas is in preparation.

14 Scrapbook, folder 6.

15 *Letters* II, 65; 23 Nov. 1881.

16 The footnote on Ridsdale in *Letters* II, 70, misses the connection.

17 *Letters* II, 69; 16 Jan. 1882.

18 Thomas, *Eclectic Practice*.

19 *Letters* II, 69–70; 16 Jan. 1882.

20 *Letters* II, 71; 19 Jan. 1882.

21 *Letters* II, 74; 8 Mar. 1882.

22 *Letters* II, 76; 14 Mar. 1882.

23 *Letters* II, 84–5; 18 May 1882.

24 *Letters* II, 87; 29 May 1882. Gissing developed these ideas in the chapter '*Io Saturnalia*' of *The Nether World*.

25 *Letters* II, 88; 29 May 1882.

26 *Letters* II, 90; 17 Jun. 1882.

27 *Letters* II, 106; 2 Nov. 1882.

28 Noel Ainslie, 'Some Recollections of George Gissing', *GN* III: 4 (Oct. 1967), 2. Gissing said that his despair occurred in 'an old house with a little balcony', which fits Oakley Crescent.

29 *Letters* II, 99; 20 Sep. 1882.

30 Gissing later wrote a sonnet about the statue of Carlyle by the Thames, printed in *Letters* II, 133.

31 'The Hope of Pessimism', in *George Gissing: Essays and Fiction*, ed. Coustillas, 82.

32 Ibid., 90.

33 Ibid., 95.

34 *Letters* II, 116; 14 Feb. 1883.

35 Comte, 453.

36 By the contract, Bentley did not have to pay Gissing until the book was actually published. He had forgotten that the original offer was for fifty guineas; he soon realised his mistake and sent the extra £2.10.

37 *Letters* II, 134; 12 May 1883.

38 *Letters* II, 146; 18 Jul. 1883.

39 *Letters* II, 155; 2 Sep. 1883.

40 *Letters* II, 157; 8 Sep. 1883.

41 *Letters* II, 162–3; 24 Sep. 1883.

42 Ibid., 163.

43 *Letters* II, 167; 10 Oct. 1883.

44 *Letters* II, 167–8; 10 Oct. 1883. The poem appeared in *Temple Bar*, Nov. 1883.

45 *Letters* II, 189; 4 Jan. 1884.

46 *Letters* II, 203; 16 Mar. 1884.

47 The manuscript of *The Unclassed* has not survived.

48 *Letters* II, 197; 14 Feb. 1884.

49 *Letters* II, 353.

50 Nicholas Joukovsky, 'According to Mrs Bennet: A Document Sheds a New and

Kinder Light on George Meredith's First Wife', *TLS* (8 Oct. 2004), 13–15.

51 Meredith's constant gastric pains may also have been a symptom of syphilis.

52 *Letters* II, 200; 4 Mar. 1884.

53 *Letters* II, 235; 4 Jul. 1884.

54 *GN* XI: 3 (Jul. 1975).

55 The street, which was near Marylebone station, no longer exists.

56 *Letters* II, 228; 23 Jun. 1884.

57 *Letters* II, 232; 25 Jun. 1884.

58 *Letters* II, 231; 24 Jun. 1884.

59 *The Unclassed* III, 9. Cf. Flaubert, in a letter to Louise Colet: 'It is perhaps a depraved taste, but I love prostitution. . . . My heart begins to pound every time I see one of those flashily dressed women walking under the lamplight in the rain. . . . The idea of prostitution is a meeting point of so many elements – lust, bitterness, complete absence of human contact, muscular frenzy, the clink of gold – that to peer into it deeply makes one reel. One learns so many things in a brothel, and feels such sadness, and dreams so longingly of love!' Quoted in Steegmuller, 284. Gissing probably did not know of this specific passage in 1884, though the topic was often touched on in nineteenth-century French literature.

60 *CH*, 68.

61 *CH*, 68, 70.

62 Since three-deckers were bought overwhelmingly by libraries, for the book to succeed it needed repeat orders beyond the first printing. If a thousand copies had sold, Gissing would have made a total of £180 for the novel. After Chapman & Hall's one-volume remainder edition, Gissing regained his copyright in *The Unclassed*, though it was not reprinted (in revised form) until 1895.

63 *Letters* II, 244; 17 Aug. 1884.

Chapter 4

1 *Letters* II, 245; 25 Aug. 1884.

2 James Gaussen, 'George Gissing and My Boyhood Contact With Him', *GN* XII: 4 (Oct. 1976).

3 *Born in Exile*, 126.

4 It is possible that she confided in Gissing about her origins, and he then adapted what he heard to the character of Ada Warren in *Isabel Clarendon*. After Isabel's husband dies, a foundling girl of seven is brought to her house, the illegitimate child of Mr Clarendon by an unknown working-class woman. Perhaps Mrs Gaussen was simply adopted by the Apcars because both her parents had died; but if so, why should Gissing introduce a more melodramatic adoption plot into *Isabel Clarendon*?

5 *Letters* II, 248; 1 Sep. 1884.

6 In Rutland Street, which no longer exists.

7 *Letters* II, 259; 26 Sep. 1884.

8 *Letters* II, 261; 12 Oct. 1884.

9 *Letters* II, 234; 29 Jun. 1884.

10 *Letters* II, 266; 9 Nov. 1884.

11 *Letters* II, 272; 24 Nov. 1884. The flat cost £40 a year, plus about £6 for a woman to come in daily and clean.

12 *Letters* II, 278; 23 Dec. 1884.

13 Roberts, *The Private Life of Henry Maitland*, 136–7.

14 Coustillas, Introduction to *Isabel Clarendon*, xxi. Roberts had no direct knowledge of the affair, since he was working in a sawmill in British Columbia at the time. His account, if credible, was based on what Gissing told him later.

15 Halperin, 65.

16 *Letters* II, 310; 16 Jun. 1885.

17 *In the Year of Jubilee*, 153.

18 The real-life David Gaussen appears in *Isabel Clarendon* under the guise of Colonel Stratton, a thick-headed and inarticulate neighbour. Stratton has four sons being raised to be soldiers (like the Gaussen boys), 'red-cheeked and hammer-fisted'. A granddaughter recalled that he 'later in life reformed and devoted himself to good works'; she doesn't say what he reformed from. *Letters* II, 250.

19 In *The Odd Women*, Mr Bevis backs out after Monica Widdowson has agreed to leave her husband; Gissing presents him as a feeble, contemptible figure.

20 *Isabel Clarendon* II, 182–3, 106.

21 Ibid. 217; see also II, 48.

22 This would be consistent with the story 'A Lodger in Maze Pond', where the protagonist says that he can make love with servant girls, but not with 'the women one meets in the big houses'.

23 Quoted in V. S. Pritchett, 'A Novelist Born Too Soon', *The Listener*, 28 Nov. 1946.

24 *Isabel Clarendon* II, 222–3.

25 James Gaussen, *GN* XII: 4, 5.

26 *Letters* II, 295; 14 Mar. 1885. The doctor refused to charge a fee, perhaps because Mrs Gaussen secretly paid him.

27 *Letters* II, 286; 31 Jan. 1885. Gissing had finished tutoring the Harrison boys, now that they were going on to public school.

28 *Letters* II, 320; 19 Jul. 1885.

29 *Letters* II, 311; 18 Jun. 1885.

30 *Letters* II, 319; 19 Jul. 1885.

31 *Letters* II, 341; 24 Aug. 1885.

32 *Letters* II, 325–6; 5 Aug. 1885.

33 *Letters* II, 328; 9 Aug. 1885. When he read over the novel, Gissing was 'delighted to find how good it is; there are pieces of writing, which, for the mere English, can stand by anything in recent fiction' (ibid., 330).

34 *Letters* II, 336; 18 Aug. 1885.

35 *Letters* II, 336–7; 18 Aug. 1885.

36 Gissing first called the novel 'Clara Wace' and then 'Emily Hood', before arriving at his final title.

37 *Letters* II, 332; 12 Aug. 1885.

38 *Letters* II, 360.

39 *Letters* II, 365; to Algernon Gissing, 9 Nov. 1885.

Chapter 5

1 *Letters* II, 375; 24 Dec. 1885.

2 *Letters* III, 89; 8 Mar. 1887.

3 See *Letters* II, 113. Gissing particularly liked the neo-Chaucerian style of Morris's *The Earthly Paradise*.

4 *Letters* II, 197; 14 Feb. 1884.

5 *Letters* II, 227; 21 Jun. 1884. Ingersoll, an American who campaigned for agnosticism, called himself 'Minister in America of the Gospel of Freethought'.

6 Quoted in MacCarthy, 466.

7 Quoted in MacCarthy, 467.

8 *Letters* II, 349.

9 *Letters* II, 333; 13 Aug. 1885.

10 *Letters* II, 370; 24 Nov. 1885.

11 *Demos*, 56. In his letter of 24 November, Gissing said he was one-third of the way through the first volume of *Demos*; this passage appears in chapter 6, so it would have been written four or five days after the Kelmscott House meeting, which took place on 22 November.

12 MacCarthy, 136–8.

13 *Demos*, 27.

14 Ibid., 149, 381.

15 Ibid., 383–4.

16 Around 1885 Morris was earning about £1,800 from his business, £120 from his writings, and an unknown amount from his inherited wealth and savings. However, he did contribute up to £500 a year to the movement. (MacCarthy, 457–8, 581.) Ironically, May fell in love with a lower-middle-class socialist in 1886 and married him, against her parents' misgivings. The marriage ended in divorce.

17 *Demos*, 384–5.

18 Ibid., 61.

19 *Letters* III, 10; 6 Mar. 1886.

20 *Demos*, 221. Twenty years later, James Joyce read *Demos* in Rome and took little pleasure in it; but when he wrote 'The Dead' soon after, his vision of the cemetery of the West at Oughterard had echoes of Gissing's Manor Park in the 'dread East'.

21 *Letters* III, 6; 15 Feb. 1886.

22 *Letters* III, 9; 24 Feb. 1886.

23 Morris said of the Trafalgar Square riots: 'I do not agree with you that Monday's

affair will hurt the movement. . . . any opposition to law and order in the streets is of use to us, *if the price of it is not too high* . . . an English mob is always brutal at any rate until it rises to heroism' (MacCarthy, 534).

24 This is Gissing's exaggeration of the split between Morris and H. M. Hyndman within the Social Democratic Federation.

25 *Demos*, 450.

26 Ibid., 453.

27 Ibid., 282.

28 Examples of the former are Kingcote in *Isabel Clarendon*, Reardon in *New Grub Street* and Peak in *Born in Exile;* of the latter, Julian Casti in *The Unclassed*. Mutimer, in *Demos*, fails with two women, one of each type.

29 An exception is Quarrier's betrayal by his friend Eustace Glazzard in *Denzil Quarrier*; though, as discussed below, this is really a form of self-betrayal.

30 *Letters* III, 14; 14 Mar. 1886.

31 *Demos*, 102. Adela's neighbour, Hubert Eldon, has been living in Paris, where he had a Jewish mistress and fought a duel. These misdeeds do not prevent Adela falling in love with him.

32 Zola, *Thérèse Raquin*, tr. Tancock, 109–10.

33 *Letters* III, 19; 22 Mar. 1886.

34 *Letters* III, 20; 27 Mar. 1886.

35 See Adler, 86–7.

36 *The Unclassed*, 22.

37 Korg, 151–2; Halperin, 135–6.

38 *CH*, 80–1.

39 *CH*, 85.

40 *Letters* III, 9; 26 Feb. 1886.

41 Moore, 20.

42 There were also translations into French and German, in 1888 and 1892.

43 *Letters* III, 39; 13 Jun. 1886.

44 *CH*, 96.

45 *CH*, 98.

Chapter 6

1 Gissing cannot have known that the original for 'Thyrza' was a boy whom Byron loved when he was a student at Cambridge.

2 *Numbers* 27: 1–11. See also Song of Solomon 6: 4.

3 *Letters* III, 39; 21 May 1886.

4 *Letters* III, 43; 1 Jul. 1886.

5 *Letters* III, 138–9; 24 Jul. 1887.

6 For Gissing's judgement of Zola, see 'The Place of Realism in Fiction', in Jacob and Cynthia Korg, eds, *George Gissing on Fiction*.

7 Hardy had already read *Demos* when he met Gissing, who then sent him copies

of *The Unclassed* and *Isabel Clarendon*, and received *The Mayor of Casterbridge* in return.

8   *Letters* III, 42; 30 Jun. 1886.

9   *Letters* III, 47; 31 Jul. 1886. He had told Margaret earlier that his hero would be 'a middle-class man who is driven into revolt by the character of our age, the persistent lying and swindling found on every hand, and who makes an attempt to carry on a business in a thoroughly straightforward way, – of course with disastrous results' (*Letters* III, 33; 15 Apr. 1886). This does not fit with the final version of *Thyrza*, but may have been the focus of the manuscript abandoned in July.

10 Booth, 289.

11 *Demos* I, 65.

12 *Letters* III, 48; 31 Jul. 1886.

13 *Letters* III, 61; 14 Oct. 1886.

14 *Letters* III, 59–60; 27 Sep., 1 Oct. 1886.

15 *Letters* III, 59; 27 Sep. 1886.

16 *Letters* III, 64; 28 Oct. 1886.

17 *Letters* III, 94; 22 Mar. 1887.

18 *Letters* III, 89; 8 Mar. 1887.

19 Roberts, *Henry Maitland*, 66.

20 Ibid., 49.

21 Payn also accepted an article by Roberts for *The Cornhill*, 'Concerning Sheep'.

22 Quoted in Gissing's letter to Algernon, *Letters* III, 70; 16 Dec. 1886.

23 However, they were sitting on the manuscript of *A Life's Morning* and it would be another year before it started to appear.

24 *Letters* III, 72; 28 Dec. 1886.

25 *Thyrza*, 377.

26 *Letters* III, 73; 28 Dec. 1886.

27 *Letters* III, 76–7; 16 Jan. 1887.

28 *Thyrza*, 444.

29 *Thyrza* was also reprinted in a cheap format in 1895, so all these editions together must have had a substantial sale.

30 *Letters* III, 80; 31 Jan. 1887.

31 *Letters* III, 81, 84; 3, 4 Feb. 1887.

32 *Letters* III, 83; 4 Feb. 1887.

33 *Letters* III, 85; 5 Feb. 1887.

34 *Letters* III, 86; 3 Mar. 1887.

35 *Letters* III, 90; 8 Mar. 1887. To Ellen Gissing.

36 *Letters* III, 104; 17 Apr. 1887.

37 *Letters* III, 107; 24 Apr. 1887.

38 *Letters* III, 102; 12 Apr. 1887. Twenty-one pages, in the format of the first edition of *Thyrza*, was about 4,000 words.

39 12 May 1887; *CH*, 105.

40 *CH*, 104.

41 *CH*, 110. Stead was notorious as the author of *The Maiden Tribute of Modern Babylon* (1885), an exposé of child prostitution that led to his imprisonment. He died on the *Titanic*.

42 *CH*, 105.

43 *Letters* III, 104–5, to Eduard Bertz; 17 Apr. 1887. Gissing must have been thinking of Casaubon the Renaissance scholar and theologian, not the Casaubon of *Middlemarch*.

44 *Letters* III, 112; 14 May 1887.

45 *Letters* III, 96; 22 Mar. 1887. Mrs Wood: Mrs Henry Wood.

46 *Letters* III, 134, 135; 8, 10 Jul. 1887.

47 *Letters* III, 108, 110; 6, 7 May 1887.

48 *Letters* III, 130–1; 4 Jul. 1887.

49 *Letters* III, 106; 24 Apr. 1887.

50 *Letters* III, 125; 21 Jun. 1887. Gissing presumably did not mean 'farmer's daughter' literally; Victoria's father, Edward Augustus, Duke of Kent, was a soldier who died in the year of her birth.

51 *Letters* III, 129; 1 Jul. 1887.

52 Harte's poem 'Miss Blanche Says' included the lines: 'You lean from your window, and watch life's column/ Trampling and struggling through dust and dew.' Gissing had bought a volume of Harte's poems in 1879.

53 *Letters* III, 139; 25 Jul. 1887.

54 *Letters* III, 156; 16 Oct. 1887.

55 *Letters* III, 162; 13 Nov. 1887.

56 *Letters* III, 146–7; 1 Sep. 1887.

57 Despite Gissing's enthusiasm, Mrs Woods did not succeed as a novelist.

58 *Letters* III, 171; 20 Dec. 1887.

59 Ibid.

60 *Letters* III, 179; 31 Jan. 1888.

61 The diary has been edited by Pierre Coustillas under the title *London and the Life of Literature in Late Victorian England: The Diary of George Gissing, Novelist*. The original survives in three closely written copybooks, now at the Berg Collection in the New York Public Library. The cover of the first book records the dates of composition of *Isabel Clarendon* (July–Sep. 1885), A *Life's Morning* (Sep.–Nov. 1885), and *Demos* (Dec.–Mar. 1885–6). Gissing's affair with Mrs Gaussen, if it happened, would have occurred around the beginning of 1885; that might have been a reason for him to destroy the pages covering 1885–7.

62 *Diary*, 540. This suggests that the surviving volume I was intact in 1902; Mrs Gaussen was still alive when Gissing died at the end of 1903, and either he or Gabrielle may have wished to spare her any possible embarrassment. Alternatively, the earlier entries may have contained material about Nell that was too painful to be preserved.

63 *Diary*, 295; 24 Jan. 1893.

Chapter 7

1 *Diary*, 21; 7 Feb. 1888.

2 Roberts, *Henry Maitland*, 59–61. 'Burning marl' is the fiery ground over which Satan walks in hell: *Paradise Lost* I, 296. The evidence of the *Diary* overrides Roberts's claim that he was with Gissing at Eastbourne when the news of Nell's death arrived; but I see no reason to doubt Roberts's account of the psychological impact on Gissing.

3 Roberts, *Henry Maitland*, 62.

4 *Diary*, 22–3; 1 Mar. 1888.

5 Jameson, 189.

6 *Diary*, 23; 2 Mar. 1888.

7 *Letters* III, 188; 3 Mar. 1888.

8 Ibid.

9 Ibid.

10 *Letters* III, 189; 14 Mar. 1888.

11 *Letters* III, 190; 14 Mar. 1888.

12 Ibid.

13 *Letters* III, 191; 14 Mar. 1888.

14 Ibid.

15 *Diary*, 28; 8 May 1888.

16 *Letters* III, 206–7; 27 Apr. 1888.

17 *Letters* III, 209; 9 May 1888.

18 *Diary*, 32; 17 Jun. 1888.

19 *Diary*, 35; 8 Jul. 1888.

20 *The Nether World*, 312.

21 Ibid., 248.

22 Ibid., 232.

23 Ibid., 233.

24 *Letters* IV, 286.

25 Scrapbook, Lilly Library, Indiana University; entry for 12 June 1888.

26 *Letters* IV, 288; 26 Apr. 1891.

27 *Diary*, 40.

28 *Letters* III, 236; 30 Aug. 1888.

29 *Letters* III, 245–6; 24 Sep. 1888.

30 *Letters* III, 247; 24 Sep. 1888.

31 *Letters* III, 251; 30 Sep. 1888.

32 *Diary*, 43; 28 Sep. 1888.

33 *Diary*, 46; 3 Oct. 1888.

34 *Diary*, 45; 2 Oct. 1888.

35 By this time *Demos* had done quite well, with four thousand copies printed in cheap editions; except that Gissing received no payment for these sales. Smith, Elder also recouped £15 of their payment for *The Nether World* by selling the US rights to Harper, who did not publish until 1899.

36 *Diary*, 51; 14 Oct. 1888.

37 *Diary*, 54; 19 Oct. 1888.

38 *Diary*, 58; 26 Oct. 1888.

39 The fare in second class was 70 francs (just under £3), including berth and meals. The Paris–Marseille train was 58 francs.

40 *Letters* III, 279; 28 Oct. 1888.

41 Goethe, *Italian Journey*, tr. W. H. Auden; quoted in Santore, 5.

42 A British journalist writing in 1884; quoted in Snowden, 19.

43 *Letters* III, 295; 9 Nov. 1888.

44 *Diary*, 71.

45 *Diary*, 73–4; 19 Nov. 1888.

46 *Diary*, 82; 20 Nov. 1888.

47 *Letters* II, 324; 27 Jul. 1885.

48 *Letters* III, 322; 17 Dec. 1888.

49 *Letters* III, 332–3; 31 Dec. 1888. '7. K': Gissing's London flat.

50 *Diary*, 98; 14 Dec. 1888.

51 *Letters* IV, 3; 2 Jan. 1889.

52 *Diary*, 114.

53 *Letters* IV, 20; 20 Jan. 1889.

54 *Letters* IV, 24; 21 Jan. 1889.

55 *Letters* IV, 26; 21 Jan. 1889.

56 *Letters* IV, 26; 21 Jan. 1889.

57 *Diary*, 131; 7 Feb. 1889. I assume this was what Gissing meant by references to 'his old ailment'.

58 *Letters* IV, 42; 13 Feb. 1889.

59 *Diary*, 148; 18 Apr. 1889.

Chapter 8

1 *Letters* IV, 51; 11 Mar. 1889.

2 *Letters* IV, 50; 11 Mar. 1889.

3 *Diary*, 144; *Letters* IV, 53; 22 Mar. 1889.

4 *Diary*, 150; 2 May 1889.

5 *Letters* IV, 66; 6 May 1889.

6 *Diary*, 145, 146; 29 Mar., 3 Apr. 1889.

7 *CH*, 137.

8 *CH*, 142.

9 *CH*, 146.

10 The novel was *Both of This Parish*, published in 1890.

11 *Letters* II, 61; 18 Sep. 1881.

12 *Letters* IV, 73; 2 Jun. 1889.

13 *The Emancipated*, 197. 'Elgar' is Miriam's maiden name.

14 Ibid., 199.

15 *The Emancipated*, 203.

16 Edith Sichel, 'Two Philanthropic Novelists: Mr Walter Besant and Mr George Gissing', *Murray's Magazine* III (April 1888), 506–18.

17 *Letters* III, 197, 199; 3, 8 Apr. 1888.

18 *Letters* IV, 75; 8 Jun. 1889.

19 *Letters* IV, 76; 8 Jun. 1889.

20 *Letters* IV, 80; 30 Jun. 1889. 'The Season' was the London social season, revolving around Ascot, Henley and the like, and ending in July.

21 *Diary*, 154; 17, 18 Jun. 1889.

22 *Diary*, 159; 13 Aug. 1889.

23 Published by Lippincott and Harper's respectively. Gissing was also included in a biographical dictionary of authors published by Lippincott.

24 It was published by Victor Ottman in 1892.

25 The article, 'Christmas on the Capitol', appeared in the *Bolton Evening News*, 28 Dec. 1889.

26 *Letters* IV, 107; 5 Sep. 1889.

27 *Diary*, 161; 25 Aug. 1889.

28 *Letters* IV, 107; 5 Sep. 1889.

29 *Letters* IV, 111; 11 Sep. 1889.

30 Scrapbook, Folder 5. MS Lilly Library, Indiana University.

31 The French translation appeared in 1890 and the German one in 1892.

32 *Diary*, 167; 27 Sep. 1889.

33 *Letters* IV, 115; 29 Sep. 1889.

34 Woolf, *Letters* I, 426; 13 Jun. 1910. Woolf wrote a review of Sichel's *Catherine de Medici* in 1905, but it was not published.

35 *Letters* IV, 116; 29 Sep. 1889.

36 *Letters* IV, 121; 11 Oct. 1889. Gissing's scrapbook in the Lilly Library contains notes on this research.

37 *The Emancipated*, 391.

38 *Letters* IV, 117; 29 Sep. 1889.

39 *Letters* IV, 131; 21 Oct. 1889.

40 *Diary*, 170; 9 Nov. 1889.

41 *Diary*, 171, 181, 195; 12, 27 Nov., 27 Dec. 1889.

42 Sichel compiled a tribute volume for Coleridge after her death, and Ritchie performed a similar service for Sichel. (Coleridge; Sichel)

43 Triangles include Miriam Baske, Cecily Doran, Ross Mallard (*The Emancipated*); Widdowson, Everard Barfoot, Monica Madden (*The Odd Women*). Two years later, when writing *Denzil Quarrier*, Gissing may have been more sensitive to lesbianism. In that novel there is an intellectual feminist widow, Mrs Wade, who has some qualities similar to Edith Sichel's. Mrs Wade describes herself as 'hommasse' (i.e. masculine), and is a passionate friend of the heroine Lilian.

44 *Letters* IV, 119; 30 Sep. 1889.

45 *Letters* IV, 127; 20 Oct. 1889.

46 *Diary*, 174; *Letters* IV, 145; 18 Nov. 1889.

47 *Letters* IV, 163 14 Dec. 1889.

48 *Letters* IV, 159; 6 Dec. 1889.

49 *Letters* IV, 160; 6 Dec. 1889.

50 *Letters* IV, 183; 8 Jan. 1890.

51 *Letters* IV, 183; 8 Jan. 1890.

52 *Letters* IV, 188; 22 Jan. 1890.

53 *Letters* IV, 194, 196; 22, 26 Feb. 1890.

54 *Letters* IV, 214, 190; 13 Apr., 22 Jan. 1890.

55 *Diary*, 212; 1 Apr. 1890.

56 *Letters* IV, 208; 1 Apr. 1890.

57 *Letters* IV, 212; 3 Apr. 1890.

58 *Letters* IV, 209; 1 Apr. 1890.

59 *CH*, 160, 163.

60 *CH*, 162.

Chapter 9

1 *Diary*, 219; 20 Jun. 1890.

2 *Diary*, 222; 1 Aug. 1890.

3 *Letters* IV, 231; 9 Aug. 1890.

4 To Ellen Gissing; *Letters* IV, 231; 12 Aug. 1890.

5 The words are spoken by Shergold, a character whose romantic history resembles Gissing's, in 'A Lodger in Maze Pond'. *The House of Cobwebs*, 257.

6 *Letters* IV, 234; 28 Aug. 1890.

7 *Letters* IV, 235; 6 Sep. 1890.

8 *Letters* IV, 232; 15 Aug. 1890.

9 *Diary*, 226; 16 Sep. 1890.

10 Roberts, *Henry Maitland*, 144.

11 Kift, 137–8.

12 *Letters* VI, 236; 17 Feb. 1897.

13 *The Unclassed*, 115.

14 *Letters* IV, 254; 11 Jan. 1891.

15 *Letters* IV, 240–1; 7 Oct. 1890.

16 *Commonplace Book*, 23. The entry dates from the summer of 1889, when Gissing was living with his mother and sisters.

17 Roberts, *Henry Maitland*, 145.

18 Ibid., 146–8.

19 *Commonplace Book*, 35.

20 *Letters* IV, 263; 23 Jan. 1891.

21 Nancy Lord of *In the Year of Jubilee* allows herself to be seduced by Lionel Tarrant, but they are married three days later.

22 Roberts, *Henry Maitland*, 154.

23 *Diary*, 227; 6 Oct. 1890. Gissing wrote to Ellen that day, saying that he might get

married at the end of December; he had gone to Richmond with Edith the day before, a Sunday.

24 *Diary*, 231; 5 Dec. 1890.

25 Roberts, *Henry Maitland*, 155. In the story Shergold comes back from the Continent and goes through with the marriage, but dies soon after.

26 That is, *Demos*, *A Life's Morning* and *The Nether World*; by 1890 Smith, Elder had published nine cheaper editions of these novels in various formats.

27 *Diary*, 233; 19 Dec. 1890.

28 Another reason may have been that the Underwoods were Catholic: Gissing had gone to a Catholic church with Edith one Sunday evening.

29 *Diary*, 235; 9 Jan. 1891.

30 *Letters* IV, 260, 263; 20, 23 Jan. 1891.

31 *Diary*, 237; 17 Jan. 1891.

32 *Letters* IV, 277–8; 7 Mar. 1891.

33 Quoted in *Letters* IV, 287; written in the early 1930s.

34 *Letters* IV, 285; 21 Apr. 1891.

35 *Letters* IV, 320; 7 Sep. 1891.

36 'Mental states of the mother affect the character of the child during its embryonic life. . . . Therefore indulgence of the mother at this period is sure to implant in the child's nature abnormal sexual desires.' Parker, 140.

37 *CH*, 182.

38 *CH*, 183.

39 *CH*, 177–8.

40 *CH*, 169.

41 *Diary*, 247; 27 May 1891.

42 *Letters* IV, 302; 21 Jun. 1891.

43 *Letters* IV, 303; 26 Jun. 1891.

44 The international copyright agreement of 1891 held out the possibility of British authors getting higher payments for US editions of their works. However, *Born in Exile* was not published in the US until after Gissing's death.

45 *Diary*, 253; 7–9 Aug. 1891. Cheaper editions at 2/6d and 2/- were issued in 1892.

46 *Diary*, 253; 15 Aug. 1891.

47 1 St Leonard's Terrace was destroyed by a bomb in the Second World War.

48 *Letters* IV, 317, 320; 27 Aug., 7 Sep. 1891.

49 *Diary*, 259; 20 Oct. 1891.

50 *Diary*, 260; 6 Nov. 1891.

51 The Colonial edition was published by George Bell, the Continental by Heinemann, and the US by Macmillan. The US edition sold for $1.00.

52 'A Casual Acquaintance' may have resurfaced in revised form as chapter V of *The Odd Women*, which had the same title. It describes the developing relationship between Monica Madden and Mr Widdowson after they have met on a park bench. 'The Fate of Humphrey Snell', published in 1895, also uses the phrase to describe Snell's meeting with a servant girl who has just been dismissed.

53 *A Victim of Circumstances*, 26.

54 *Denzil Quarrier*, 110–11.

55 *Denzil Quarrier*, 161.

56 Glazzard also has had an affair with an upper-class woman not unlike Mrs Gaussen: 'He held the dainty little note, and mused over it. At one time the sight of this handwriting had quickened his pulses with a delicious hope; now it stimulated his gloomy reflections' (*Denzil Quarrier*, 200).

57 *Denzil Quarrier*, 154; *Letters* V, 22; 17 Mar. 1892.

58 *Letters* V, 18; 14 Mar. 1892.

59 *Denzil Quarrier*, 111.

Chapter 10

1 *Diary*, 262; 26 Nov. 1891.

2 *Diary*, 263; 9–10 Dec. 1891.

3 *Letters* V, 118; 25 Apr. 1896.

4 *Diary*, 265; 25 Dec. 1891.

5 *Diary*, 268; 23 Jan. 1892.

6 Gissing used the phrase to suggest that both he and his hero were born outside the social class to which they naturally belonged. He may also have been referring to two figures of exile: Ovid, one of his favourite poets, and Pope Gregory VII, who said on his deathbed: 'I have loved justice and hated iniquity: therefore I die in exile.'

7 *Letters* V, 31; 24 Apr. 1892.

8 *Letters* V, 35; 11 May 1892.

9 *Human Odds and Ends*, 302. For syphilis to be transmitted to a newborn, the mother would have to be infected too.

10 *Diary*, 273; 14 Mar. 1892.

11 *Letters* V, 18; 14 Mar. 1892.

12 *CH*, 189; 13 Feb. 1892.

13 *CH*, 194.

14 *CH*, 200.

15 *CH*, 204.

16 *Letters* V, 36; 20 May 1892.

17 *Born in Exile*, 160.

18 Ibid., 177.

19 *Diary*, 286; 4 Oct. 1892.

20 *Letters* V, 58; 14 Oct. 1892.

21 Orwell, *Collected Essays* IV, 416.

22 *The Odd Women*, 273, 274.

23 *Letters* V, 54; 17 Sep. 1892.

24 *Letters* V, 56; 6 Oct. 1892; *Letters* IX, 26; 16 Nov. 1902.

25 *Letters* V, 64; 3 Nov. 1892.

26 *Diary*, 287; 30 Oct. 1892.

27 *Letters* V, 92; 28 Feb. 1893.

28 *Letters* V, 83; 30 Dec. 1892.

29 *Letters* V, 87; 29 Jan. 1893.

30 *Diary*, 291; 9 Dec. 1893.

31 *Diary*, 293; 31 Dec. 1892.

32 *Diary*, 295; 24 Jan. 1893.

33 *Diary*, 296; 29 Jan. 1893.

34 *Letters* IV, 285; 21 Apr. 1891.

35 *Letters* IV, 287.

36 *Letters* V, 74; 26 Nov. 1892.

37 *Letters* V, 98–9; 20 Mar. 1893. Gissing's comments were appended to Gosse's *Questions at Issue* (London: Heinemann, 1893).

38 *CH*, 219.

39 *CH*, 217.

40 *CH*, 220.

41 *Letters* V, 113; 2 Jun. 1893.

42 *Odd Women*, 287.

43 *Letters* V, 104, 105; 11, 16 Apr. 1893.

44 *Diary*, 302; 20 Apr. 1893; Roberts, *Henry Maitland*, 185.

45 Nothing more was heard of this story.

Chapter 11

1 In September he moved to a better room that Edith found for him at 32 Crawford Road, Camberwell.

2 *Letters* V, 116; 13 Jan. 1893.

3 *Letters* V, 159; 11 Nov. 1893.

4 *Letters* V, 18; 14 Mar. 1892. Ethical Culture resembled Unitarianism; it tried to replace institutional religion with a progressive idealism that would unite believers rather than divide them.

5 *Letters* V, 134, 155; 27 Aug., 26 Oct. 1893.

6 See, for example, Edith's addition to Gissing's letter to Walter, 10 Jul. 1897; MS at Yale University Library.

7 *Letters* V, 144; 17 Sep. 1893.

8 Munden also appears in the story 'An Inspiration' and as a journalist friend of Lionel Tarrant in *In the Year of Jubilee*.

9 *The House of Cobwebs*, 263.

10 *Diary*, 314; 2 Sep. 1893.

11 *Diary*, 316; 22 Sep. 1893.

12 The stories were: 'The Day of Silence', 'A Capitalist', 'A Lodger in Maze Pond', 'Under an Umbrella,' and 'His Brother's Keeper'.

13 However, payment for stories was usually delayed until publication, which might be a year or more after the story was written; Gissing's novels up to this point

were mostly paid for in full as soon as the manuscript was submitted and accepted.

14 *Letters* V, 149; 29 Sep. 1893.

15 Gissing told Colles he liked the story, though earlier he had said: 'I strongly suspect that the man Barrie is monstrously and unaccountably over-rated' (*Letters* V, 26; 9 Apr. 1892).

16 *Letters* V, 148; 29 Sep. 1893.

17 *Letters* V, 149; 29 Sep. 1893.

18 *Diary*, 309; 10 Jul. 1893.

19 Somerset Maugham's first novel, *Liza of Lambeth*, was not published until 1897.

20 The stories were: 'The Pessimist of Plato Road'; 'The Poet's Portmanteau'; 'A Midsummer Madness'; 'The Honeymoon'; 'Comrades in Arms'; 'In Honour Bound'. All appeared in the *English Illustrated Magazine* in 1894 and 1895.

21 *Letters* V, 172; 2 Jan. 1894.

22 *Letters* V, 172; 2 Jan. 1894.

23 *Letters* V, 175; 19 Jan. 1894.

24 For the book version Gissing would receive about £80.

25 *Letters* V, 182; 4 Feb. 1894.

26 *Diary*, 328; 23 Jan. 1894.

27 *Letters* V, 183; 10 Feb. 1894.

28 *Letters* V, 179; 30 Jan. 1894.

29 'Hugger-mugger marriage is a defilement and a curse': *In the Year of Jubilee*, 342.

30 *Letters* V, 210; 17 Jun. 1894.

31 *Letters* V, 214; 7 Jul. 1894.

32 *Eve's Ransom* appeared in thirteen instalments, and had twenty-seven chapters in book form. *The Odd Women*, more than three times as long, had thirty-one chapters.

33 *Eve's Ransom*, 84.

34 Ibid., 84, 102.

35 *Letters* V, 214; 7 Jul. 1894.

36 *Diary*, 343; 9 Aug. 1894.

37 *Diary*, 345; 28 Aug. 1894.

38 *Diary*, 374; 29 May 1895.

39 *The Private Papers of Henry Ryecroft*, x.

40 In 1900 Gissing published his thoughts on vegetarianism: 'More than once I have tried to do without meat, for a month or two together; the result, each time, has been such a serious loss of vital force, and such irritation of the temper, that I found it impossible to persevere. I cannot do mental work on a vegetable diet, however good and varied. Neither can I eat *much* flesh. A moderate mixed diet is indispensable to my health and spirits.' He thought that some people, and all children, would benefit from vegetarianism. *Letters* VIII, 82; Aug.–Sep. 1900.

41 *Letters* V, 251, 254; 20, 23 Nov. 1894.

42 One exception is Gissing's sketch of Theresa, a servant at Agbrigg around 1888: 'Is between 13 and 14, but looks 10. Been starved all her life; originally came begging to the door, being sent by her family. ... Story of how her father went

into the pit to work when he was seven years old. . . . She sings all about the house, all day. . . . Her peculiar laugh, just like the breaking into a sob. – Her round, cherubic face, with little tip-tilted nose and bright eyes and bud of a mouth' (Scrapbook, Lilly Library, Indiana University).

43 *Diary*, 350; 10 Oct. 1894.

44 *In the Year of Jubilee*, 204.

45 *Diary*, 358; 31 Dec. 1894.

46 *CH*, 231–2.

47 *CH*, 235.

48 *Letters* V, 296; 10 Feb. 1895.

49 *In the Year of Jubilee*, 388–9.

50 We should be cautioned by Gissing's comment on a review: 'I strongly object to the writer's crediting *me* with all the sentiments put into the mouth of Lionel Tarrant' (*Letters* V, 290–1; 31 Jan. 1895). Still, this implies that Gissing agreed with *some* of them.

Chapter 12

1 *Diary*, 357; 19 Dec. 1894.

2 *Letters* V, 284; 17 Jan. 1895.

3 *Diary*, 364; 21 Feb. 1895.

4 *Diary*, 367; 31 Mar. 1895.

5 *Letters* V, 316; 8 Apr. 1895.

6 The serial ended on 30 March 1895.

7 *CH*, 248.

8 *CH*, 257–8.

9 He wrote *Hygeia*, a vision of the sanitary city of the future, and a biography of the great epidemiologist John Snow.

10 *Letters* V, 339; 27 May 1895.

11 Allen's *The Typewriter Girl* (1894) was another topical and superficial novel.

12 *Diary*, 375; 6 Jun. 1895.

13 *Letters* V, 351; 23 Jun. 1895.

14 *Diary*, 379; 13 Jul. 1895.

15 *Diary*, 382; 30 Jul. 1895.

16 *Diary*, 383; 30 Jul. 1895.

17 *Diary*, 385; 3 Sep. 1895.

18 *Letters* VI, 21; 3 Sep. 1895.

19 *Letters* VI, 23; 6 Sep. 1895.

20 *Diary*, 387–8; 15 Sep. 1895. *Letters* VI, 30; 22 Sep. 1895.

21 *Letters* VI, 30; 22 Sep. 1895.

22 *Diary*, 388; 16 Sep. 1895.

23 He received an advance of fifty guineas for the new edition of *The Unclassed*.

24 *Letters* VI, 34–5; 3 Oct. 1895.

25 *Letters* VI, 35; 3 Oct. 1895.

26 *Letters* VI, 35–6; 3 Oct. 1895.

27 *A Victim of Circumstances*, 216.

28 *CH*, 267–8.

29 *CH*, 268.

30 *Letters* VI, 76; 6 Jan. 1896.

31 *Letters* VI, 49, 76; 8 Nov. 1895, 6 Jan. 1896.

32 *Letters* VIII, 275; 21 Nov. 1901.

33 *Letters* VI, 74; 30 Dec. 1895.

34 *Letters* VI, 45; 3 Nov. 1895.

35 Roberts, *A Question of Instinct*, 25.

36 *Letters* VI, 93; 31 Jan. 1896.

37 *Letters* VI, 93; 31 Jan. 1896.

38 The stories were 'Joseph', 'Spellbound', 'One Way of Happiness' and 'The Hapless Boaster'. 'One of the Luckless' was not published.

39 *CH*, 261.

40 *Letters* VI, 112; 22 Mar. 1896.

41 *Letters* VI, 117; 23 Apr. 1896.

42 *Diary*, 407; 10 Apr. 1896.

43 *Letters* VI, 115; 22 Apr. 1896; *Letters* VI, 118; 25 Apr. 1896.

44 *Letters* VI, 117; 23 Apr. 1896.

45 *Letters* VI, 118; 25 Apr. 1896.

46 *Letters* VI, 129; 24 May 1896.

47 *Letters* VI, 151–2; 3 Jul., 11 Sep. 1896.

48 *Diary*, 413; 20 Jan. 1896.

49 Gabrielle Fleury's recollections of Gissing; *Letters* IX, 279.

50 Zangwill, letter to Montagu Eder, 2 Sep. 1896; quoted in *Letters* VI, 150.

51 *CH*, 274. To judge by the current second-hand market, *Jubilee* must have sold very well in the US – perhaps in part because it was carefully expurgated by Appleton, its publishers. One of the passages cut was the description of Nancy Lord lying naked in bed, which had provoked an indignant letter to Gissing from an English woman who signed herself 'A mother of girls'. *Letters* IX, 289.

52 *CH*, 274.

Chapter 13

1 *Letters* VI, 155; 20 Jul. 1896.

2 *Diary*, 418; 9 Aug. 1896.

3 *Letters* VI, 156–7; 31 Jul. 1896.

4 *The Whirlpool*, 31.

5 *Letters* VI, 190; 31 Oct. 1896.

6 *Letters* VI, 201; 29 Nov. 1896.

7 *Letters* VI, 200; 27 Nov. 1896.

8 The cuts are enumerated in Coustillas's *Bibliography*, 211–14.

9 *Diary*, 430; 25 Dec. 1896.

10 *Letters* VI, 233; 13 Feb. 1897.

11 *Diary*, 430; 27 Dec. 1896.

12 *Diary*, 427; 20 Nov. 1896.

13 *Letters* VI, 197; 25 Nov. 1896.

14 *Letters* VI, 198; 25 Nov. 1896.

15 *Letters* VI, 200; 27 Nov. 1896.

16 Wells usually called his second wife 'Jane', referred to her as 'Amy' in correspondence with Gissing, and after she died published a tribute, *The Book of Catherine Wells*.

17 Webb, 241.

18 Quoted in Smith, 199. The letter was disingenuous in that Wells had shown passion to several other women, and probably was trying to excuse his diminishing interest in Amy Catherine.

19 *Letters* VI, 219; 19 Jan. 1897.

20 *Letters* VI, 247; 2 Mar. 1897.

21 *Letters* VI, 236; 17 Feb. 1897.

22 *Letters* VI, 241; 21 Feb. 1897.

23 *Letters* VI, 244; 27 Feb. 1897.

24 *Letters* VI, 249; 11 Mar. 1897.

25 *Letters* II, 93; 12 Jul. 1882.

26 *Letters* VI, 273; 18 Apr. 1897.

27 *Letters* VI, 249; 11 Mar. 1897.

28 *Letters* VI, 257; 26 Mar. 1897.

29 Including *The Whirlpool*, Bell's Library now had seven of Gissing's novels in print. But his income from these substantial sales was very small, because Bell bought their copies in sheets for 10d or so each, and bound them themselves. Gissing was entitled to 'half-profits' on these sales, which meant that Lawrence & Bullen deducted from each 10d their costs for printing and advertising, then split the remainder with Gissing. For *The Odd Women*, 1,500 copies were sold to Heinemann at 10d for a colonial edition, and Gissing's share was £8.3 – equivalent to a royalty of just over a penny per copy.

30 However, by November 1899 Gissing was complaining that he was only earning about £10 a year from Lawrence & Bullen, because they failed to advertise his books (soon they would fail altogether).

31 *CH*, 291–2.

32 *CH*, 291.

33 *CH*, 294.

34 *CH*, 276.

35 *CH*, 277.

36 *CH*, 303.

37 *CH*, 304.

38 *The Whirlpool*, 415–16.

39 *CH*, 304.

40 *Letters* VI, 412; 11 Dec. 1899.

41 *Diary*, 435.

42 *Letters* VI, 283; 11 May 1897.

43 *Letters* VI, 290; 21 May 1897.

44 That is, some loss of capacity in one lung because it had to compensate for the lung previously damaged by tuberculosis.

45 *Letters* VI, 300; 13 Jun. 1897.

46 *Diary*, 437; 26 Jun. 1897.

47 *Diary*, 437; 22 Jun. 1897. When Victoria died, Gissing explained to his son Walter that she could have been worse: 'Kings and Queens have not so much power now as they used to have in the old days, but they can still do a great deal of harm if they are foolish or wicked. Queen Victoria always acted for the good of her country, and it is because the English people know she did so, that they grieve for her death. I am very much afraid that her life was shortened by the miserable war in South Africa, which she seems never to have approved.' (*Letters* VIII, 132; 23 Jan. 1901.)

48 *Human Odds and Ends* disappointed Gissing by failing to find a publisher in the US.

49 *Diary*, 436; 7 Jun. 1897.

50 *Letters* VI, 312; 17 Jul. 1897.

51 *Diary*, 441; 11 Aug. 1897.

52 *Diary*, 442–3; 25 Aug. 1897.

53 *Diary*, 442; 18 Aug. 1897.

Chapter 14

1 *Letters* VI, 330; 28 Aug. 1897.

2 *Diary*, 444; 6 Sep. 1897.

3 *Diary*, 445; 10 Sep. 1897.

4 *Diary*, 445; 17 Sep. 1897.

5 *Letters* VI, 355; 3 Oct. 1897.

6 *Diary*, 449; 14 Oct. 1897.

7 *Letters* VI, 352; 28 Sep. 1897.

8 Algernon was given control of Gissing's papers and literary estate, but any money coming from future publications would go to Edith and the children.

9 *Charles Dickens: A Critical Study*, 219.

10 *Letters* VI, 357; 3 Oct. 1897.

11 *Letters* VI, 359; 12 Oct. 1897.

12 *Letters* VI, 365; 25 Oct. 1897.

13 The US edition, by Dodd, Mead, appeared in 1898.

14 *Letters* VI, 381; 13 Nov. 1897.

15 *By the Ionian Sea: Notes of a Ramble in Southern Italy*, 5.

16 Karl Baedeker, *Italy: Handbook for Travellers. Southern Italy and Sicily* (Leipsic: Baedeker, 1900), 176.
17 *Letters* VI, 386; 22 Nov. 1897.
18 *By the Ionian Sea*, 24.
19 Ibid., 26–7.
20 Ross received the Nobel Prize for his discovery.
21 *By the Ionian Sea*, 65–6.
22 *Diary*, 470; 10 Dec. 1897.
23 *By the Ionian Sea*, 126–7.
24 Ibid., 131.
25 *Diary*, 471; 11 Dec. 1897.
26 Gissing might have ended *By the Ionian Sea* with a chapter on Monte Cassino, and it is not clear why he chose not to do so. He was deeply impressed by the monastery, and wrote about it in a 'Summer' section of 'An Author at Grass', the first version of *The Private Papers of Henry Ryecroft*. This section, in the manuscript at the Lilly Library, was suppressed before publication.
27 *The Whirlpool*, 202.
28 *Letters* VII, 22; 26 Dec. 1897.
29 *Letters* VII, 18; 20 Dec. 1897.
30 *Letters* VII, 52; 1 Feb. 1898.
31 Dunne, 117.
32 Ibid., 48.
33 Ibid., 51.
34 Ibid., 57.
35 *Letters* VII, 57–8; 10 Feb. 1898.
36 Dunne, 117; *Letters* VII, 29; 3 Jan. 1898.
37 *Letters* VII, 32; 6 Jan. 1898.
38 Wells, *Experiment in Autobiography*, 575.
39 Quoted in Gettmann, ed., 77.
40 Ibid., 71; 1 Jan. 1898.
41 Hornung, letter to F. Whyte; quoted in *Letters* VII, 82. 'Oscar' was Hornung's son.
42 *Diary*, 487; 24 Mar. 1898.
43 Williams, unpublished autobiography, quoted in Caine, 39.
44 Caine, 106, 104–5.
45 Ibid., 105.
46 Ibid., 221.
47 *Diary*, 490; 15 Apr. 1898.

Chapter 15

1 *Letters* VII, 94; 22 May 1898.
2 *Letters* VII, 102; 20 Jun. 1898.
3 *Stories and Sketches*, 240.

4 *A Victim of Circumstances*, 97–8.

5 *Stories and Sketches*, 241.

6 *Letters* VII, 107; 24 Jun. 1898.

7 *Letters* VII, 29; 3 Jan. 1898.

8 Gissing's letters are missing between 10 February 1898 and 22 July 1899.

9 Wells, *Experiment in Autobiography* II, 568.

10 *Letters* VII, 181; 9 Sep. 1898.

11 Wells, *Experiment in Autobiography* II, 576.

12 *Letters* IX, 157; 6 Nov. 1903.

13 *Letters* VII, 200; Sep. 1898.

14 However, only Gissing's side of the correspondence has survived.

15 *Letters* VII, 130–1; 5 Aug. 1898.

16 *The Crown of Life*, 2, 23.

17 *Letters* VII, 190; 15 Sep. 1898.

18 *Letters* VII, 134; 6 Aug. 1898.

19 *The Crown of Life*, 103.

20 *Letters* VII, 125; 30 Jul. 1898.

21 Brewster made the change on his own initiative, but Gissing accepted it.

22 *Diary*, 501; 7 Sep. 1898.

23 In *The Crown of Life*, Dr Derwent is very conscious of having married into an old upper-class family: 'Now and then, a friend who heard him speak of his wife's family smiled with the thought that he only just escaped being something of a snob. Which merely signified that a man of science attached value to descent. Dr Derwent knew the properties of such blood as ran in his wife's veins, and it rejoiced him to mark the characteristics which Irene inherited from her mother' (83).

24 *Letters* VIII, 201; 24 Jun. 1901.

25 *Letters* VII, 150; Aug. 1898.

26 *Letters* VII, 156; 20 Aug. 1898.

27 *Letters* VII, 195; 22 Sep. 1898.

28 *Letters* VII, 170; 30 Aug. 1898.

29 Gettmann, ed., 228. Wells believed that Gissing's mother was there at the same time as Gabrielle, which was not the case.

30 *Letters* VII, 247; 18 Dec. 1898.

31 *Diary*, 503; 15 Oct. 1898.

32 *Letters* VII, 215; 1 Nov. 1898.

33 *Letters* VII, 295, 299; 15, 20 Feb. 1899.

34 *Letters* VII, 259; 2 Jan. 1899.

35 *Letters* VII, 255; 27 Dec. 1898.

36 *Letters* VII, 259; 2 Jan. 1899.

37 *Letters* VII, 261; 2 Jan. 1899.

38 Edith even accused him of being 'a disciple of Wilde'! There is no evidence at all for this accusation.

39 *Letters* VII, 276; 29 Jan. 1899.

40 *Letters* VII, 267; 15 Jan. 1899.
41 Quoted in *Letters* VII, 273.
42 *Letters* VII, 277; 29 Jan. 1899.
43 *Letters* VIII, 180; 10 Jun. 1901.
44 *Letters* VII, 300; 25 Feb. 1899.
45 *Letters* VII, 302; 28 Feb. 1899.
46 *Letters* VII, 333; 1 Apr. 1899.
47 *Letters* VII, 322; 25 Mar. 1899.
48 *Letters* VII, 328; 29 Mar. 1899.
49 *Letters* VII, 328; 29 Mar. 1899.
50 *Letters* VII, 339; 11 Apr. 1899.
51 A picturesque occasion if, as some have argued, Sickert was Jack the Ripper. This seems unlikely, even though he did take a gruesome relish in painting London's underworld. See Patricia Cornwell, *Portrait of a Killer*. Gissing himself has been suggested as the Ripper, though he was in Italy at the time of three of the murders. Whittington-Egan, *Casebook on Jack the Ripper*.

Chapter 16

1 *Diary*, 513; 7 May 1899.
2 *Diary*, 513; 11 May 1899.
3 *The Immortal Dickens*, 104. The reference is to Rosa Bud in *Edwin Drood*.
4 *Letters* VII, 349; 11 May 1899.
5 *Letters* VIII, 180; 10 Jun. 1901.
6 £21 from *Truth* in New York and £13.13 from *The Cornhill*. This was probably the first time that Gissing got more for a piece of writing in the US than in England.
7 *Diary*, 517; 13 Aug. 1899.
8 *Letters* VII, 367; 11 Aug. 1899.
9 *Letters* VII, 361; 22 Jul. 1899.
10 *Diary*, 517; 16 Aug. 1899.
11 *The Times*, 9 Oct. 1899.
12 Gissing called his piece 'Tyrtaeus', after the poet who wrote warlike songs for the Spartans.
13 Conrad, however, argued that the Boer War was an idealistic and disinterested enterprise by Britain and its allies.
14 *The Crown of Life*, 164.
15 Ibid., 286.
16 Sacher-Masoch's letters to Bertz are at the Beinecke Library, Yale.
17 'Mon grand regret est de n'avoir pas eu moi-même d'enfant, comme je l'aurais dû il y a 4 ans – peut être l'avez vous su.' Gabrielle/Bertz, May 1904. Unpublished, Yale.
18 *The Crown of Life*, 289.

19. Ibid., 289, 291, 268.

20 Gissing's views were close to those of Norman Angell, author of *The Grand Illusion* (1910), who was working in Paris as a journalist in 1899. There is no evidence that they met, however.

21 *CH*, 353.

22 *CH*, 358.

23 *CH*, 361–2.

24 *CH*, 364.

25 *Letters* VIII, 207–8; 26 Jun. 1901.

26 *Letters* VIII, 199; 24 Jun. 1901.

27 'An Author at Grass', MS Lilly Library, Indiana University, 35.

28 The story was published in *The Sphere*, 17 February 1900. Gissing received £20, more than he had got for the furniture.

29 Gissing had done forty-five manuscript pages, about ninety thousand words.

30 *Letters* VII, 412; 11 Dec. 1899.

31 *Letters* VII, 412; 11 Dec. 1899.

32 *Letters* VIII, 4, 11; 21 Jan., 10 Feb. 1900.

33 *Letters* VIII, 11; 10 Feb. 1900.

34 *Letters* VII, 419; 29 Dec. 1899.

35 *Letters* VIII, 11; 10 Feb. 1900.

36 *Letters* VIII, 17; 25 Feb. 1900.

37 Quoted and translated in *Letters* VIII, 43.

38 *Letters* VIII, 57; 7 Jun. 1900.

39 *Letters* VIII, 73; 5 Aug. 1900.

40 *Our Friend the Charlatan*, 262–3.

41 *Letters* VIII, 54; 31 May 1900.

42 *Our Friend the Charlatan*, 37.

43 Ibid., 285.

44 Ibid., 222, 402.

45 Huxley, 13.

46 *Our Friend the Charlatan*, 403.

47 Ibid., 405.

48 Ibid., 381–2.

Chapter 17

1 Paul-Emile Morhardt notes that when Langhans cells are present the lesions cannot be distinguished: *Les Maladies Vénériennes* (Paris: Octave Doin, 1906), 26. J. E. R. McDonagh gives a differential description of each, but Gissing does not say enough about his lesion to indicate which it was: *Venereal Diseases: Their Clinical Aspect and Treatment* (London: Heinemann, 1920), 31.

2 She received 300 francs (£12) for the book publication of her translation of *New Grub Street* in 1902, *La Rue des Meurt-de-Faim*.

3　In the first draft, Gissing placed Ryecroft's cottage in the Mendip Hills near Wells, Somerset.

4　*Letters* IX, 61; 15 Feb. 1903.

5　*Diary*, 533; 23 Oct. 1900.

6　This judgement is supported by the high proportion of ex-library copies of Gissing's books on today's second-hand market.

7　*Letters* VIII, 120; 26 Dec. 1900.

8　*Letters* VIII, 125; 3 Jan. 1901.

9　*Letters* VIII, 116; 17 Dec. 1900.

10　*Diary*, 534.

11　Holt reduced their offer to £100 when Gissing insisted that the book should be published in the spring rather than the autumn.

12　*Letters* VIII, 139; 17 Feb. 1901.

13　*Letters* VIII, 151–2; 7 Apr. 1901.

14　Wells, *Experiment* II, 577.

15　*Letters* VIII, 122, 147; 27 Dec. 1900, 17 Mar. 1901.

16　The pioneer of this treatment was the chemist R. W. Bunsen. Arsenic was sometimes used for tubercular lesions too, however.

17　*Letters* VIII, 159; 26 Apr. 1901.

18　*Letters* VIII, 161–2; 2 May 1901.

19　Wells, *Correspondence*, ed. David Smith, 379.

20　*Letters* VIII, 177; 7 Jun. 1901.

21　*Letters* VIII, 179; 10 Jun. 1901. Gabrielle's erratic English is left uncorrected throughout.

22　*Letters* VIII, 181; 10 Jun. 1901.

23　*Letters* VIII, 185; 11 Jun. 1901.

24　*Letters* VIII, 189; 13 Jan. 1901.

25　*Letters* VIII, 187; 11 Jun. 1901.

26　Quoted in Halperin, 7.

27　*Letters* VIII, 193; 20 Jun. 1901. Gissing's letter, to which this was a reply, has not survived.

28　The sanatorium still stands, but has been converted into flats. The Canadian painter Emily Carr wrote a memoir, *Pause*, about her stay there in 1903.

29　*Letters* VIII, 205; 25 Jun. 1901.

30　*The House of Cobwebs*, 135–6.

31　*Letters* VIII, 214; 3 Jul. 1901.

32　*CH*, 377.

33　*CH*, 384.

34　*Letters* VIII, 215; 3 Jul. 1901.

35　*Letters* VIII, 222; 12 Jul. 1901.

36　*Letters* VIII, 24; 12 Jul. 1901.

37　*Letters* VIII, 226; 17 Jul. 1901.

38　*Letters* VIII, 230–1; 30 Jul. 1901.

39　*Letters* VIII, 232, 234; 2, 6 Aug. 1901.

Chapter 18

1 Twenty-five years later, Ellen Gissing wrote a memoir that contains what is probably a confabulated memory:

> The last glimpse of my brother comes to me vividly. It was the day on which we saw him off to London from the Wakefield station, in August 1901, at the end of his last visit to England. He had improved in health and was going back to France quite hopefully, trusting to carry out some of his plans for work. I remember that, as we walked up and down in the station, our talk was cut short by a porter who hurried him into a relief train for Kings Cross, in which he said there would be more comfortable travel. So the wave of the hand, and cheery smile for his boy Walter and for ourselves, who were standing on the platform, proved to be our last farewell. (*The Letters of George Gissing to Members of his Family*, 406.)

The problem with this touching scene is that Ellen was on holiday in Switzerland in August 1901. Gissing's farewell to Wakefield was in April 1900, and he did not take the train to King's Cross, but to Lincoln. It is barely possible that he did not leave Nayland on the 10th of August (as he said he would in a letter to Hick of 8 August), but on the 9th in order to pay a visit to Wakefield that he concealed from Gabrielle. Such a visit would have allowed him to discuss with Margaret what he had told her in his letter of 30 July, that he was living with Gabrielle. If so, Ellen's account of the parting was derived from Margaret. The last time that Gissing left Wakefield by a London train was on 28 January 1899.

2 *Letters* VIII, 237; 21 Aug. 1901.

3 *Diary*, 540; 7 Apr. 1902.

4 *Letters* IX, 58; 11 Feb. 1903.

5 *Letters* VIII, 264; 20 Oct. 1901.

6 *Letters* VIII, 285; 8 Dec. 1901.

7 *Letters* VIII, 282; 7 Dec. 1901.

8 *Letters* VIII, 302; 28 Dec. 1901.

9 *Letters* VIII, 289–90; 14 Dec. 1901.

10 Gabrielle Fleury, 'Recollections of Gissing', in *Letters* IX, 276.

11 *Diary*, 541; 8 Apr. 1902.

12 The stories were 'Christopherson' and 'Miss Rodney's Leisure'.

13 Coustillas, ed., *Gissing's Writings on Dickens*, 21–5.

14 *Letters* VIII, 329; 31 Jan. 1902.

15 *Letters* VIII, 345; 24 Feb. 1902.

16 *Letters* IX, 91; 3 Jun. 1903.

17 *Letters* VIII, 377; 25 Apr. 1902.

18 *Diary*, 545; 21 May 1902.

19 *Letters* VIII, 411; 6 Jul. 1902. Charles Lamb was offered a pension at age fifty; he immediately accepted and walked out of his office, never to return.

20 *Letters* VIII, 423; 10 Aug. 1902.

21 *Letters* IX, 4–5, 5 Oct. 1902.

22 *Letters* IX, 70; 3 Mar. 1903.

23 *Letters* IX, 13; 26 Oct. 1902.

24 *Letters* IX, 14.

25 *Letters* IX, 29; 30 Nov. 1902.

26 Gissing did not specify the story; in December 1902 he said he had not read 'Youth', so the likely remaining candidates would be 'The Lagoon' in *The Cornhill* (January 1897), or 'Karain' in *Blackwood's* (November 1897).

27 *Letters* IX, 31; 30 Nov. 1902.

28 *Letters* IX, 39; 25 Dec. 1902.

29 Joseph Conrad, *Youth: A Narrative and Two Other Stories*, 205.

30 *Letters* IX, 36; 21 Dec. 1902.

31 *Letters* IX, 39; 24 Dec. 1902.

32 *Letters* IX, 38; 24 Dec. 1902.

33 *Letters* IX, 85; 13 May 1903.

34 *The Private Papers of Henry Ryecroft*, ix.

35 Before commission the earning would have been £83. In standard contracts at this time, thirteen copies sold counted as twelve; for *Ryecroft*, 1,080 sales would earn £60 before commission. Gissing told Henry Hick that his royalty was a shilling a copy; it was actually twelve shillings for ten copies, but he probably factored in the commission and the 'thirteen for twelve' rule. *Letters* IX, 91; 3 Jan. 1903.

36 *The Private Papers of Henry Ryecroft*, 56.

37 *CH*, 419.

38 *Letters* IX, 281.

39 *Letters* IX, 96; 16 Jun. 1903.

40 *Letters* IX, 66; 23 Feb. 1903.

41 *The Private Papers of Henry Ryecroft*, 'Winter', VIII; 'Summer', XIV.

42 *Letters* IX, 303.

43 *Will Warburton: A Romance of Real Life*, 187, 316, 317.

44 *Letters* IX, 72; 21 Mar. 1903. In April he received a royalty cheque for the eight titles published by Lawrence & Bullen; it was for £12.15.

45 *Letters* IX, 106; 2 Aug. 1903.

46 Gabrielle's *Recollections*; *Letters* IX, 300.

47 *Letters* IX, 125; 12 Sep. 1903.

48 *Letters* IX, 136; 9 Oct. 1903.

49 Conrad/Gissing, *Letters* IX, 167; 1 Dec. 1903.

50 'I don't fear it at all'; *Letters* IX, 305.

51 *Letters* IX, 161; 23 Nov. 1903.

52 *Letters* IX, 168; 3 Dec. 1903.

53 *Letters* IX, 306.

54 *Letters* IX, 171; 24 Dec. 1903.

55 *Letters* IX, 307.

56 Wells, *Experiment in Autobiography* II, 580.

57 Ibid., 567–8.

58 The nurse was an Englishwoman, Mrs Bayman, who came the day before Gissing died.

59 *Letters* IX, 308.

60 *Letters* IX, 308–9. Somatose was a patent food for invalids.

61 *Letters* IX, 309.

Afterword

1 Eduard Bertz; 2 Apr. [1904], Yale.

2 GF/EB; May 1904, Yale.

3 Wells's preface was replaced by some discreet reminiscences by Frederic Harrison.

4 McDonald, 193; Miller, 143.

5 The 16th Regiment of the London Division, part of the Territorial Army.

6 Woolf, *Essays* I, 131–4.

7 Woolf, *Essays* III, 374.

8 Caudwell, 76.

9 Goode, 201.

10 Goode, 15.

Bibliography

Adler, Laure. *La Vie Quotidienne dans les Maisons Closes 1830–1930*. Paris: Hachette, 1990

Ainslie, Noel. 'Some Recollections of George Gissing', *Gissing Newsletter* III: 4 (Oct. 1967)

Anon, *Five Years' Penal Servitude by One Who Has Endured It*. London: Richard Bentley, 1877

Booth, Charles. *Life and Labour of the People in London, First Series: Poverty* vol. I. London: Macmillan, 1902

Brook, Clifford. *George Gissing and Wakefield*. Wakefield: Gissing Trust, 1992

Caine, Barbara. *Destined to Be Wives: The Sisters of Beatrice Webb*. Oxford: Clarendon Press, 1986

Carr, Emily. *Pause: a Sketch Book*. Toronto: Clarke, Irwin, 1953

Connelly, Mark. *Orwell and Gissing*. New York: Peter Lang, 1977

Caudwell, Christopher. *Studies in a Dying Culture*. New York: Monthly Review Press, 1971

Coleridge, Mary. *Gathered Leaves from the Prose of Mary E. Coleridge*. London: Constable, 1910

Comte, Auguste. *Positive Philosophy*, tr. Harriet Martineau. New York: Calvin Blanchard, 1855

Conrad, Joseph. *Youth: A Narrative and Two Other Stories*. Edinburgh: Blackwood, 1902

Cornwell, Patricia. *Portrait of a Killer: Jack the Ripper Case Closed*. New York: Berkeley, 2003

Coustillas, Pierre. 'George Gissing à Manchester', *Etudes Anglaises* XVI: 3, (1963) 261–5.

——. *George Gissing at Alderley Edge*. London: Enitharmon, 1969

——. *George Gissing: The Definitive Bibliography*. High Wycombe: Rivendale Press, 2005

——. & C. Partridge, eds. *Gissing: The Critical Heritage*. London: Routledge & Kegan Paul, 1972

Dunne, Brian. *With Gissing in Italy: The Memoirs of Brian Ború Dunne*. Athens: Ohio UP, 1999

Gaussen, James. 'George Gissing and My Boyhood Contact With Him', *Gissing Newsletter* XII: 4 (Oct. 1976)

Gettmann, Royal, ed. *George Gissing and H. G. Wells*. Urbana: University of Illinois Press, 1961

Gissing, George. *Born in Exile*. London: J. M. Dent, 1993

——. *By the Ionian Sea: Notes of a Ramble in Southern Italy*, ed. P. Coustillas. Northampton, MA: Interlink, 2004

——. *Charles Dickens: A Critical Study*. London: Gresham, 1902

——. *The Collected Letters of George Gissing*, ed. Paul Mattheisen, Arthur Young, Pierre Coustillas. Nine volumes, Athens, Ohio: Ohio UP, 1990–7

——. *Commonplace Book*. New York: New York Public Library, 1962

——. *Demos*. Brighton: Harvester, 1972

——. *Denzil Quarrier*. London: Lawrence & Bullen, 1892; repr. AMS Press, 1969

——. *Eve's Ransom*. New York: Dover, 1980

——. *George Gissing: Essays and Fiction*, ed. P. Coustillas. Baltimore: Johns Hopkins UP, 1970

——. *George Gissing on Fiction*, ed. Jacob and Cynthia Korg. London: Enitharmon, 1978

——. *Gissing's Writings on Dickens*, ed. Pierre Coustillas. London: Enitharmon, 1969

——. *Human Odds and Ends*. London: Lawrence & Bullen, 1898

——. *In the Year of Jubilee*. London: Dent, 1994

——. *Isabel Clarendon*. Hassocks: Harvester Press, 1969

——. *Letters of George Gissing to Members of his Family*, ed. Algernon & Ellen Gissing. London: Constable, 1926

——. *London and the Life of Literature in Late Victorian England: The Diary of George Gissing, Novelist*, ed. P. Coustillas. Hassocks: Harvester Press, 1978

——. *Notes on Social Democracy*. London: Enitharmon, 1968

——. *Our Friend the Charlatan*. Hassocks: Harvester Press, 1976

——. *Sins of the Fathers*. Chicago: Pascal Covici, 1924

——. *Stories and Sketches*. London: Michael Joseph, 1938

——. *The Crown of Life*. London: Methuen, 1899

——. *The Emancipated*. Hassocks: Harvester Press, 1977

——. *The House of Cobwebs*. London: Constable, 1906

——. *The Immortal Dickens*. London: Cecil Palmer, 1925

——. *The Nether World*. Oxford: Oxford UP, 1992

——. *The Odd Women*. Peterborough, Ont.: Broadview, 1998

——. *The Private Papers of Henry Ryecroft*. Brighton: Harvester, 1982

——. MS Scrapbook. Lilly Library, Bloomington, Indiana

——. *The Unclassed*. London: Chapman & Hall, 1884; 2nd ed., Lawrence & Bullen, 1895

——. *The Whirlpool*. London: J. M. Dent, 1997

——. *Thyrza*. Brighton: Harvester, 1974

——. 'Verses by G. R. Gissing'. MS notebook. Yale University Library

———. *A Victim of Circumstances*. Boston: Houghton Miflin, 1927

———. *Will Warburton: A Romance of Real Life*. London: Constable, 1915

———. *Workers in the Dawn*. Brighton: Harvester, 1985

Goode, John. *George Gissing: Ideology and Fiction*. New York: Barnes & Noble, 1979

Halperin, John. *Gissing: A Life in Books*. Oxford: Oxford UP, 1987

Hayden, Deborah. *Pox: Genius, Madness, and the Mysteries of Syphilis*. New York: Basic Books, 2004

Hobsbawm, Eric. *Labouring Men*. London: Weidenfeld & Nicolson, 1968

Huxley, T. H. *Evolution and Ethics*. New York: Greenwood, 1968

James, Simon. *Unsettled Accounts: Money and Narrative in the Novels of George Gissing*. London: Anthem Press, 2003

Jameson, Fredric. *The Political Unconscious: Narrative as a Socially Symbolic Act*. Ithaca: Cornell UP, 1981

Kift, Dagmar. *The Victorian Music Hall: Culture, Class and Conflict*. Cambridge: Cambridge UP, 1996

Korg, Jacob. *George Gissing: A Critical Biography*. Seattle: University of Washington Press, 1963

MacCarthy, Fiona. *William Morris: A Life for our Time*. London: Faber & Faber, 1994

McCracken, Scott. *Masculinities, Modernist Fiction and the Urban Public Sphere*. Manchester: Manchester University Press, 2007

McDonagh, J. E. R. *Venereal Diseases: Their Clinical Aspect and Treatment*. London: Heinemann, 1920

McDonald, Deborah. *Clara Collet*. London: Woburn Press, 2004

Marnham, Patrick. *The Man Who Wasn't Maigret*. New York: Farrar, Straus, Giroux, 1993

Miller, Jane. *Relations*. London: Jonathan Cape, 2003

Moore, George. *Literature at Nurse or Circulating Morals*. London: Vizetelly, 1885

Morhardt, Paul-Emile. *Les Maladies Vénériennes*. Paris: Octave Doin, 1906

Orwell, George. 'George Gissing' in *The Collected Essays, Journalism and Letters*. London: Secker & Warburg, 1968. IV, 428–36

———. 'Not Enough Money: a Sketch of George Gissing' in *The Complete Works of George Orwell*. London: Secker & Warburg, 1986–98. XV, 45–7

Parker, Thomas. *Dr Parker's New Marriage Guide*. New York: J. S. Ogilvie, 1916; 1st ed. 1895

Roberts, Morley. *A Question of Instinct*. London: H. Henry, 1895

———. *The Private Life of Henry Maitland*. London: Eveleigh Nash, 1912

Santore, John. *Modern Naples: A Documentary History 1799–1999*. New York: Italica Press, 2001

Sichel, E. *Edith Sichel: Letters, Verses and Other Writings*. Privately printed, 1918

Smith, David C. *H. G. Wells: Desperately Mortal*. New Haven: Yale UP, 1986

Snowden, Frank. *Naples in the Time of Cholera, 1884–1911*. Cambridge: Cambridge UP, 1995

Steegmuller, Francis. *Flaubert and Madame Bovary*. NY: Vintage, 1957

Thomas, Rolla. *The Eclectic Practice of Medicine*. Cincinnati: Scudder, 1907

Trotter, David. *Cooking with Mud: The Idea of Mess in Nineteenth-Century Art and Fiction*. Oxford: Oxford University Press, 2000

Webb, Beatrice. *The Diary of Beatrice Webb* II. London: Virago, 1983

Wells, H. G. *Experiment in Autobiography*. London: Gollancz, 1934

——. *The Correspondence of H. G. Wells*. ed. David Smith. London: Pickering & Chatto, 1998

Whittington-Egan, Richard. A *Casebook on Jack the Ripper*. London: Wiley, 1975

Wilson, Edmund. *The Thirties: From Notebooks and Diaries of the Period*. New York: Farrar, Straus and Giroux, 1980

Woolf, Virginia. *The Essays of Virginia Woolf* I, III. London: Hogarth, 1986, 1988

——. *The Flight of the Mind: Letters* I; London: Hogarth Press, 1975

Zola, Emile. *Thérèse Raquin*, tr. Leonard Tancock. Harmondsworth: Penguin, 1962

Acknowledgements

Anyone who writes on Gissing knows that their first debt is to Pierre Coustillas of the University of Lille, who for more than forty years has been the pre-eminent scholar and interpreter of Gissing's work. Apart from his personal kindness and hospitality (and that of Hélène Coustillas), five of Pierre's contributions have been indispensable to me: his edition of Gissing's diary, his co-editing of the *Critical Heritage* and the *Collected Letters*, his editing of the *Gissing Journal*, and most recently his monumental *Bibliography*. I must also mention his collaborators on the *Collected Letters*, the late Paul F. Mattheisen and Arthur C. Young. I have benefited from their work in almost every page of my biography, and the *Letters* is one of the most impressive editorial projects in recent years. Peter Morton's Gissing website also has been a constant help.

The major collections of Gissing's books and manuscripts are in the US, and for my research there I am indebted to the staff at the Berg Collection, New York Public Library; the Beinecke Library, Yale; and the Lilly Library in Bloomington, Indiana. In England I am grateful to the Wakefield Public Library, Yorkshire, and to the John Rylands Library and Manchester Public Library. Kathy Willeard of the H. M. Prison Service found the records of Gissing's commitment to Bellevue Prison, Manchester; Ray Jack gave me a tour of Strangeways Prison, which was designed by Alfred Waterhouse (also the architect of Owens College).

The Gissing conferences in Amsterdam in 1999 and at the University of London in 2003 provided much background and critical insight. There and elsewhere I have benefited from discussions with Scott McCracken, Bouwe Postmus, Simon James, Arlene Young, Michael Collie, John Speirs, and Jacob Korg. Stephen Ogden at Simon Fraser University combines enthusiasm for Gissing with intimate knowledge of his Yorkshire origins. As always, I am indebted to my agents, Georges Borchardt in New York and Bruce Hunter in London. I must thank Simon Fraser University for research grants, and Clare Hall, Cambridge, for a visiting fellowship in 1999.

For Gissing, writing was a grim and lonely task, made grimmer by one of the most disastrous family lives of any English writer. At times this misery threatened to become contagious. Without naming them all, I would like to record my gratitude to the family and friends who brought this book, long in the making, to a happy ending for its author, if not his subject.

Vancouver, British Columbia
September 2007

Index

Abbot, Evelyn, 63
Aberdeen, 66
Academy, The, 72, 320
Acropolis, 170
Acton, 157
Agbrigg, 44, 56, 156, 160, 162, 163, 173
Airolo, 317
Alaric, 278
Aldeburgh, 235, 239
Alderley Edge, 9, 232–3 *see also* Lindow
    Grove School
Alexander II, Tsar, 55
Allen, Grant, 235–6, 245
    The Woman Who Did, 235
Alnwick, 117, 123
Alps, 314, 315–17, 329, 353, 366
Amalfi, 150
Amélie les Bains, 371
America
    fund to send GG to, 19
    GG in, 20–5
    GG has no wish to return to, 26, 82
    Bertz goes to, 54, 87
    Roberts in, 23–4, 87 and GG's work, 108,
        163, 196, 220, 232, 234, 251, 264, 276,
        286, 309, 364 brief references, 27, 354
Anderson, Reverend Charles, 259
Anglicanism, 4 *see also* Church of
    England/Anglican Church
Anti-Aggression League, 330
Apcar family, 75
Apennines, 370
Arcachon, 352–5, 357, 360
Aristophanes, 170
Art, Georges, 296
Arts and Crafts movement, 91
Ash, Connie, 175–6

Aston, 202
Athenaeum, 45
Athens, 169, 170
Atlantic Monthly, 21
Austin, L.F., 228, 235
Author, The, 226, 297
Authors' Club, 214, 226
Authors' Syndicate, 216
Autun, 335–6, 341, 342, 345, 347, 350, 351,
    352

Back Lane School, Wakefield, 5
Baedeker, 277
Bainton, Reverend George, 145
Balliol College, Oxford, 63, 144, 204
Balzac, Honoré de, 112, 228, 315
Barker, Arthur, 72
Barnard, Fred, 231
Barnes, Martha McCullough, 21, 22, 232
Barrie, J.M., 216, 250, 259
    Sentimental Tommy, 250
Basel, 274
Baseley, Catherine *see* Gissing (*née*
    Baseley), Catherine
Bashkirtseff, Marie, 175
Battersea, 58
Baudelaire, Charles, 105
Bayonne, 372, 3 74
Beachy Head, 221, 350
Beardsley, Aubrey, 242
Beaumont, Dr, 255, 256
Bedford, Elizabeth, 2
Bedford, Margaret *see* Gissing (*née*
    Bedford), Margaret
Bedford, Mary, 130
Bedford, Tom, 130
Bedford, William, 2

Bedford Head pub, Covent Garden, 183

Beerbohm, Max, 270

Beesly, Edward, 51

Belleville, Paris, 104, 105

Bellevue Prison, Manchester, 17–19

Bellini, 154

Belloc, Hilaire, 94

Bell's Indian and Colonial Library, 264

Benedict, St, 282, 330

Bennett, Arnold, 163, 320–1

    A Man From the North, 320

Bentley, George, 60, 63–4, 67–8, 75, 87, 88,
    125–6, 127, 128, 166, 169, 181

Bentley's, 60, 63–4, 67, 68, 163, 164

Berkhamsted, 224

Berlin, 290, 291

Bernhardt, Sarah, 105.

Bertz, Eduard

    newspaper advertisement placed by,
        37–8

    friendship with G G, 38, 53, 118

    Nell jealous of, 54

    joins Utopian colony in America, 54, 87

    returns to England and joins Salvation
        Army and Blue Ribbon Army, 65

    and G G's visit to Italy, 150, 152

    becomes secretary of German Society of
        Authors, 163

    publishes article on G G in Germany, 163

    and Whitman, 164–5

    not told about G G's marriage, 183

    G G advises about his literary career,
        216–17

    G G visits, 290–1

    told about G G's relationship with
        Gabrielle, 305

    receives photograph of G G and
        Gabrielle, 316

    receives letter from Wanda von Sacher-
        Masoch, 319

    receives letter from Gabrielle, 319, 377

    G G's comments to: on Edith, his wife,
        180; on Edith Sichel, 168; on Fellows
        of Oxford and Cambridge, 144; on
        feminism, 207; on Gabrielle, 305, 313;
        on Hardy, 239; on his lack of marriage
        prospects, 176; on his writing, 216,
        219, 268, 336–7, 338; on Shortridge's
        wife, 171

brief references, 50, 52, 82, 160, 169, 208

Besant, Mrs, 142

Besant, Walter, 185–6, 216, 219, 226

Birmingham, 201, 202, 203, 216

Bismarck, Otto von, 50

Black, A. & C., 194

Black, John George, 14–15, 17, 59, 246

Blackie, 256

Blackwood, William, 203, 204

Blackwood's, 190, 202–3, 204, 362

Blazy, Dr Jean, 361

Blue Ribbon Army, 65

Board of Trade, 211

Boer War, 317, 325–6, 329, 330, 333

Booth, Charles, 54, 114, 211, 213

    Life and Labour of the People in London,
        211

Borchardt, Dr Louis, 26, 27

Boston, 20, 21, 25

Boughton, Mrs, 292, 304

Boulogne-Billancourt, 358–9

Bovet, Ernest, 317

Bovet, Madame, 317

Bowes, Arthur, 9

Boxer Rebellion, 329

Box Hill, 237, 238, 250, 259, 327–8

Bradley, George, 132

Brampford Speke, 194, 195, 198, 210

Brewster, S.N.P., 301

Brighton, 115, 305

Brindisi, 170

British Columbia, 82

British Museum, 27, 30, 36, 37, 84, 167, 172,
    201, 205, 214, 220, 263

Brixton

    Tate donates library to, 203

    GG based in, 210–21

    Edith in, 356

Brontë, Charlotte, 125, 127, 145

Broughton, Rhoda, 125, 134

Broughton Hall, 74, 82

Brown, Ford Madox, 95

Brownings, the, 150, 153, 304

Buchanan, Robert, 325

Buckley, Abel, 10

Budapest, 194

Budleigh Salterton

    GG visits with Edith, 187

    GG stays in, 260–9, 342

Bullen, Arthur H., 189, 190, 196, 199, 208, 219, 220, 225, 231, 255, 270, 324
Bunn family, 237–8
Burford Bridge Hotel, 237
Burger, Adele, 194
Burguete, 370
Burne-Jones, Edward, 95, 289
Burnham-on-Sea, 188, 208
Bury, Yetta Blaze de, 297
Busento, River, 278
Butler Clarke, H., 360
Byron, Lord, 3, 6, 127, 136, 150
    'Elegy to Thyrza', 111

Caine, Hall, 134
Calabria (*Magna Graecia*), 274, 276–81, 326
Calais, 274, 373
Calcutta, 75
Camberwell, 217–18
Cambo, 357, 358, 369
Camden Town, 177, 179, 201, 210
Canadian Pacific Railway, 82
Cape Matapan, 170
Capri, 290, 357
Carlyle, Jane, 365–6
Carlyle, Thomas, 57, 61, 365–6
    Latter-day Pamphlets, 57
Cassell's, 237
Cassiodorus, 263, 280–1, 282, 330
Castle Bolton, 271
Catanzaro, 280
Catherine of Siena, St, 274
Caudwell, Christopher, 379
Cervantes: *Don Quixote*, 360
Chalet Elgue, 369
Chalet Feuillebois, 350
Chamonix, 315
Chapman, Frederic, 68, 69, 70, 81, 87
Chapman and Hall, 68–9, 80, 85, 87, 109, 326, 331, 339, 352
Charity Organisation Review, 211
Chasnays, Château de, 338
Chatto & Windus, 40, 41, 68, 189
Chauffard, Dr Anatole, 340–1, 352, 353, 359
Chelsea, 59, 60, 117, 158, 292, 295
Chesterton, G.K., 94
Chicago, 22, 23, 24
Chicago Tribune, 22, 23, 195–6
Chiddingfold, 166–7

China, 329
Christianity, 35, 62, 65, 197
Church of England/Anglican Church, 34, 37, 40, 264 *see also* Anglicanism
Ciboure, GG based in 357–69
Civil List, 328, 359, 378
Clarence Hotel, Exeter, 190
Clerkenwell, 113, 129, 140, 142
Clevedon, 187–8, 189, 221, 223, 224
Clodd, Edward, 234–5, 237, 239, 327, 328, 359, 362
Col de Balme, 315
Coleridge, Mary, 169
Colles, William
    and GG's short stories, 216, 225, 276
    and GG's novels, 166, 219–20, 231, 233, 255, 259, 270, 273, 286, 287
    and GG's study of Dickens, 276, 280
    dropped as GG's agent, 306–7
    brief reference, 236
Collet, Clara
    background and career, 211
    publishes article on 'George Gissing's Novels', 211
    lectures on GG, 212
    friendship with GG, 211, 212, 214
    and Edith Gissing, 212–13, 233, 240–1, 261–2, 263, 378
    and GG's treatment of Edith, 240–1, 261–2
    and GG's children, 213, 240, 254, 261, 275, 378
    GG informs about his move to new accommodation, 218
    GG introduces American friends to, 246
    perceives GG's obsessiveness, 260
    GG writes from Rome to, 285–6
    hopes for more intimate relationship with GG, 294–
    and relationship between GG and Gabrielle, 308, 316, 322, 343, 345, 353
    supports Gabrielle, 377–8
    GG's comments to: on Edith, 177, 240, 241, 263, 274–5; on his children, 246, 249; on his health, 255; on his restlessness, 341; on his writing, xiv, 218, 221, 339 brief references, 84, 220, 226, 236, 248, 283, 347, 349, 363
Collins, Wilkie, 40

Colwyn Bay, 9, 248
Comte, Auguste, xiii, 36, 37, 43, 44, 46, 47, 56, 61, 62, 63
   Positive Philosophy, 63
Congreve, Richard, 45
Conrad, Joseph, 362–3, 371
   'The End of the Tether', 362, 363
   'Heart of Darkness', 363
   Nostromo, 371
   Typhoon, 363
   Youth, 363
Constable, 364, 368
Cooper, Reverend, 375–6
Corelli, Marie, 125
Cornforth, Fanny, 95
Cornhill Magazine, 87, 118, 326
Cornoy, Dr, 335
Cornwall, 194, 357, 377
Cornwall Residences, 76, 77, 78, 89, 117, 123, 141, 144, 146, 157, 159, 172, 175, 179, 181, 182, 215, 256
Cosenza, 276, 278
Cosmopolis, 287
Cotrone, 279, 280, 285
Cotswolds, 74, 82, 130, 140, 159, 202, 273
Court Journal, The, 158
Courtney, W.L., 352, 364
Coustillas, Pierre, 76, 380
Crabbe, George, 145
Crane, Mrs Stephen, 307
Crawshay, Walter, 338
Cromwell family, 327
Cumbria, 5
Cunninghame Grahame, R.B., 142
Curtis, Miss, 134, 140, 157

Daily Chronicle, 196, 225, 274
Daily Mail, 217, 305, 372
Daily Telegraph, 364
Dalston, 52
Dante, 158
   Divine Comedy, 93
Dartmoor, 269
Darwin, Charles, 34, 35, 79
   The Origin of Species, 4, 35, 168
Darwinism, 34, 183, 185, 197, 235, 253, 330, 381 *see also* Social Darwinism
Daudet, Alphonse, 103

Froment Jeune et Risler Aîné, 140–1
Davos, 353
Davray, Henri, 328
Declaration of Independence (USA), 21
Defoe, Daniel, 239
Derby, the, 224
Deutsche Presse, 163
Dickens, Charles
   Orwell's comment on, ix
   childhood stint in blacking factory, xiii, 19, 30
   attachment to Ellen Ternan, xiii, 355
   does not make research notes, 56
   visits Paris Morgue, 103
   GG's study of, 256, 274, 275, 276, 280, 284
   GG's opinion of work of, 262–3
   GG's prefaces for novels on, 294, 303, 309, 313, 315, 316, 326
   GG abridges Forster's biography of, 352, 353, 355, 358
   GG writes article for *Literature* on, 353
   GG reviews Kitton's biography of, 355–6   brief references, xii, 81, 90, 109, 113, 154, 211, 239
   Works:
   Little Dorrit, 262, 263
   Nicholas Nickleby, 313
Dieppe, 145, 312, 313
Dispatch, 145
Dobbs, George, 290
Dodd, Mead, 280
Dorchester, 3, 201, 237, 238
Dorking
   GG based in, 292–311
   Gabrielle visits GG in, 298, 304
   Edith finds GG in, 301–2
   GG's mother visits, 303
   brief references, 224, 247, 248, 324, 338
Dorney House, Weybridge, 236
Dostoevsky, Fyodor, xii, 109, 191
   Crime and Punishment, 35
Dover, 274
Doyle, Arthur Conan, 288–9
Dreyfus, Captain Alfred, 308, 321
Dudley, 202
Duino, 351
Dunne, Brian Ború, 276, 284–5, 288
Durance, 148

Eastbourne, 115–16, 121, 134–5, 140, 191, 221, 232, 350
East End, 93, 211
Echo, 257
Eder, Montagu, 251
Education Acts, 203
Eiffel Tower, 146, 173
Eleusis, 170
Eliot, George, 30, 47, 57, 98, 109, 125, 185, 239, 308
   Middlemarch, 47
Elliot and Fry, 341, 342
Engels, Friedrich, xii
English Illustrated Magazine, 1, 208, 213, 214
English Positivist committee, 46
Epsom
   GG finds house to rent in, 224
   GG based in, 224–59, 269–70
   GG's domestic life in, 226–7, 233, 240
   Hick visits GG in, 234
   Clara Collet visits, 240
   Edith is persuaded to remain in, 261
   GG decides not to renew Worple Road lease, 272, 273
Epsom Downs, 224
Ethical Society, 212
Eustache, Mme, 338
Eustache, Robert, 338
Evening News, 72
Exeter
   GG decides to move to, 181
   GG based in, 182–209

Fabian Society, 202
Falmouth, 357
Farrar, F.W., 158–9
Festal, Dr, 357
Fin Haut, 315
First World War, 130, 378–9
Fisher Unwin, 231, 233
Fitzgerald, Caroline, 289
Flaubert, Gustave, 65
Fleury, Mme Anna ('Maman')
   agrees to Gabrielle's sham marriage to GG, 305
   meets GG and witnesses ceremony between GG and Gabrielle, 313
   rules Fleury household, 314, 343
   health problems, 314, 322, 372

   and relationship between GG and Gabrielle, 314, 319, 322, 370
   and food, 323, 324, 340, 343
   goes to St Honoré les Bains, 329
   visits relations, 338
   in Autun, 345, 350
   goes to St Jean de Luz, 359
   and death of GG, 375
   stays in St Jean de Luz, 377
   death, 378
   brief references, 317, 321, 336, 339, 356, 357
Fleury, Gabrielle Edith
   asks permission to translate *New Grub Street*, 295–6
   visit to Worcester Park, 296, 297
   GG's first impressions of, 296, 297
   described by Wells, 296
   background, 296–7
   engagement to Sully-Prudhomme, 297
   translation work, 298, 335
   spends day with GG in Dorking, 298
   GG falls in love with, 298–300
   and GG's relationship with Rosalind Williams, 300, 301
   and Edith's visit to Dorking, 302
   and GG's inability to divorce Edith, 302–3
   GG describes his relationship to his mother to, 303
   spends a week in Dorking with GG, 304
   and plans for living with GG, 304–5, 305–6, 308, 310–11
   mother accepts relationship between GG and, 305
   and GG's health problems, 309, 322, 328, 339–40, 341, 352
   ceremony between GG and, 313
   honeymoon period, 313–14
   returns to Paris, 314
   relationship with her mother, 314
   married life in Paris, 314–15, 321, 322–4, 326
   holiday in the Alps, 315, 316, 317
   as intellectual and emotional companion for GG, 316
   sexual relationship with GG, 319
   and GG's restlessness, 322

Fleury, Gabrielle Edith—*contd*
  attitude to GG's family situation in
    Wakefield, 322–3, 348
  unable to visit GG's family in Wakefield,
    327
  in St Honoré les Bains, 329
  visits relations, 338, 352
  returns to Paris, 338
  persuades GG to see Dr Chauffard,
    340–1
  rents house at Autun, 341
  visits England with GG, 342
  and GG's decision to remain in England,
    343
  letter to Amy Catherine Wells, 343, 348
  and GG's ideas about self-assertion, 344,
    348
  in Autun, 345, 350
  does not visit GG at Nayland, 345
  GG writes to, 347–8
  keeps GG away from Wakefield, 348–9
  GG tells his family about, 349
  GG returns to, 350
  at Arcachon, 353 spends winter in Paris,
    353, 355
  and GG's plans to go to south of France,
    357, 358
  in St Jean de Luz district, 359, 360
  and GG's plans for sequel to *Henry
    Ryecroft*, 365, 371
  not allowed to read typescript of *Will
    Warburton*, 366
  moves with GG to chalet at Ispoure, 369
  excursion to Roncesvalles and Spain, 370
  looks at possible places to stay, 371
  illness, 371, 372
  and GG's final illness, 372, 373, 374–5
  after GG's death, 377–8
  brief references, 137, 176, 212, 334, 336,
    346, 356, 362, 368
Fleury, René, 314, 315, 338
Florence, 151, 152–4, 155, 274
Folkestone, 373
Ford, Ford Madox, 371
Forster, John: biography of Dickens,
    abridged by GG, 352, 353, 355, 358
Fortnightly Review, 50, 326, 351, 352, 359,
    362, 364
Fourchambault, 338, 352, 353

France
  Comte's aims in, 36
  Turgenev in exile in, 70
  GG visits, 103–6, 145–8, 173
  Demos published in, 139
  and plans of GG and Gabrielle, 304, 305,
    310
  femme d'artiste concept in, 310
  GG based in, 313–15, 321–7, 328–42,
    350–75
  GG's death and burial in, 375–6
  Walter in action in, 378
  brief references, 161, 164, 298
Frascati's, 256
Frederic, Harold, 234, 307, 308
  The Damnation of Theron Ware, 307
  Maggie, A Girl of the Streets, 307
Frederic, Mrs Harold, 307
Frederick, Crown Prince, 129–30
Freud, Sigmund, 358

Garibaldi, Giuseppe, 281
Garrison, William Lloyd, 20–1
Gaussen, Charles, 325–6
Gaussen, David, 74–5
Gaussen, Elizabeth
  background, 75
  GG meets, 75
  and *Isabel Clarendon*, 75, 78–9, 80, 81,
    82–3, 109, 110
  and GG's lodgings, 75
  GG's relationship with, 76–80, 82, 84, 86,
    157–8
  and Ellen Gissing, 80, 81, 160
  GG's difficulties with social life of, 81
  and *Demos*, 107
  brief references, 90, 167, 199, 212
Gaussen, Ellen, 74, 75
Gaussen, James, 74, 75, 76, 80
Geneva, 371
Gentz, Jean-Baptiste, 360
German Society of Authors, 163
Germany, 38, 87, 107, 130, 156, 164, 171–2,
    207, 290–1
Gibbon, Edward: *Decline and Fall of the
    Roman Empire*, 10, 29
Gislebertus, 336
Gissing, Alfred Charles (GG's son)
  birth, 246

infancy and childhood, 252, 260, 261, 271, 272, 273, 292, 301, 302, 305, 323, 327, 356–7, 377

GG tries to ensure financial security for, 255

GG anxious about, 274

guardianship, 275

Civil List pension for, 378

educated at Gresham's School, 378

adult life, 379

brief references, 193, 247, 249, 259, 269, 336, 373

Gissing, Algernon (GG's brother)

birth, 3

sent to boarding school, 7

gives money to GG, 31

hopes to succeed in London matriculation exam, 33

GG preaches Comteanism to, 37

stays with William, 43

and death of William, 43

moves to Agbrigg, 44

works in Wakefield, 44

and GG's newspaper project, 53, 64

conservative views, 55

comes to London to study, 56, 59

passes law exams, 59

opens law office, 64

letters to newspapers, 65, 68

and Bentley's failure to publish, 68

failure of law practice, 68

writing career, 68, 89, 117, 122, 125, 132, 140, 145, 156, 159, 172, 203, 242, 337

dislikes *The Unclassed*, 70

drain on GG's nervous energy, 82

lives with GG in London, 89

fails Civil Service exam, 89

engaged to Catherine Baseley, 115, 123

moves to Northumberland, 116–17

unable to settle to an occupation, 117

GG concerned about, 122–3, 130

financial help given to, 123, 202, 223, 232, 242, 254, 292, 309, 311, 378

moves to the Cotswolds, 130

marries Catherine, 130–1

GG visits, 132, 145, 202, 223, 273, 322

at Agbrigg, 156

birth of daughter, 156

goes north for a short time, 159–60

visits GG and Edith, 219

joint guardian of GG's children, 240, 275

breakdowns, 254, 309

goes to Richmond, Yorkshire, 254

thinks of studying for Church of England ministry, 264

GG plans to seek refuge with, 285

and GG's attempts to avoid contact with Edith, 292

family conference about, 322

and Clara Collet, 378

GG's comments to: on dangers of changing one's occupation, 84–5; on Edith, 261; on events in Russia, 55; on Florence, 152; on the Harrisons, 119; on his depression, 80; on his domestic situation with Nell, 54, 56, 58, 60, 66; on his financial situation, 38; on his intention to travel, 169, 173; on his lack of social life, 83; on his need for reading room, 203; on his plans to move to France, 305; on his refusal of social invitations, 157, 210; on his visits to working-class events, 51; on his writing, 39, 41, 44–5, 53, 63, 87, 120, 123, 128, 137–8, 208; on Italy, 275; on mixing with the upper classes, 74, 75; on Paris Morgue, 104; on Thomas Hardy, 201; on Walter, 248, 252; on William Morris, 92 brief references, 32, 40, 73, 76, 185, 247, 270, 336, 371

Works:

A Dinner of Herbs, 89, 122, 125, 126

Joy Cometh in the Morning, 132, 140, 156

The Sport of Stars, 242

A Vagabond in Arts, 337

A Village Hampden, 172

Gissing (*née* Baseley), Catherine (GG's sister-in-law), 84, 115, 123, 130–1, 132, 137, 145, 156, 159, 195, 273

Gissing (*née* Underwood), Edith (GG's second wife)

GG begins relationship with, 177–80

as spur for GG's writing, 180–1

pressurised by GG, 182

marries GG, 183

early married life, 183–4, 187

becomes pregnant, 184

Gissing (*née* Underwood), Edith (GG's second wife)—*contd*
holidays, 187–8, 194, 201, 208, 221, 232, 237, 271
birth of Walter, 193
treatment of Walter, 193, 204, 227, 233, 247, 248, 262, 282
depressed and aggressive, 193–4
health problems, 194–5
problems in care of Walter, 195
in London with her sister, 202
returns to Exeter, 203
and Morley Roberts, 208, 214
marriage problems, 208, 227–8, 240–1, 249, 256, 258, 259, 260, 261–2, 263, 269, 271–2
and the move to London, 208, 210
and Clara Collet, 212–13, 233, 240–1, 261–2, 263, 378
and Algernon, 219
in London and Dorking while GG house-hunts, 224
quarrels with servants, 226
avoids social contact, 233
becomes pregnant again, 233
birth of Afred, 246
goes to Dorking after house fire, 247
returns home, 248
and GG's decision to place Walter with his sisters, 248–9, 254
letters to Walter, 249–50, 254
and GG's health problems, 256, 309
and GG's decision to go to Italy, 273
stays with Miss Orme, 273
and GG's will, 274–5
and guardianship of children, 275
Miss Orme reports to GG about behaviour of, 282, 287
mental health problems, 282–3, 287–8, 356
refuses to divorce GG, 290
tries to find GG on his return to England, 292
attacks landlord and his wife, 301
GG makes payments to, 301
finds GG in Dorking, 301–2
GG unable to divorce, 302, 305
diagnosed as insane and sent to asylum, 356

and GG's estate, 377
death, 378
brief references, 95, 106, 198, 209, 239, 245, 266, 310, 312, 323, 336, 343, 357
Gissing, Ellen (GG's sister)
birth, 3
moves to Agbrigg, 44
GG tries to launch in London, 80–1, 86
and Mrs Gaussen, 80, 81, 160
becomes a governess, 116
stays with GG after Nell's death, 138
and Daudet's novel, 140–1
and her suitor, 156–7
beliefs and mentality, 160, 161
and *The Emancipated*, 172–3
visits France, 173
thinks GG is deluded about Edith, 178
and *Denzil Quarrier*, 191, 195
remains single, 200, 379
starts a school with her sister, 247
and Walter, 248, 249, 327, 340
offers financial help to Algernon, 309
dislikes Edith, 310
and GG's relationship with Gabrielle Fleury, 310, 316
GG's comments to: on Algernon, 130, 132, 311; on Clara Collet's lecture, 212; on Edith Sichel's household, 167; on her personal life, 139, 156; on her response to Daudet's book, 141; on his health, 352; on his life in Exeter, 184, 203; on his prospects, 175; on his relationship with Edith, 178; on his success, 169; on his visit to the Continent, 145, 148; on his writing, 98, 111, 114, 119–20, 126, 127–8, 129, 172–3, 218; on Keats, 151; on London, 56–7; on Mrs Gaussen, 75, 77, 82–3; on publishers, 368; on time-wasting, 11
brief references, 90, 102, 349
Gissing, Enid (GG's niece), 156
Gissing, George
and George Orwell, ix–x
family background, 1–4
birth, 4
childhood, 3–5
death of his father, 6
at Lindow Grove School, 7–8

as student at Owens College, 8–13, 16

begins affair with Nell, 13, 14, 15, 16–17

friendship with John George Black, 14, 59, 246

arrested for stealing, 17

in prison, 17–19

expelled from Owens College, 19

fund established to assist, 19

in America, 20–5

reunited with Nell, 26–7

first year in London, 26–31

first attempts to write novels, 30, 34

financial situation, x-xiv, 31, 32–3, 38–9, 44, 52, 53, 54, 61, 90–1, 123, 189, 218, 228, 233, 242, 273, 292–3, 309, 311, 337, 339

relationship with Nell, 31, 32

development of ideas, 34–7, 61–3, 64–5

beginning of friendship with Eduard Bertz, 38

marries Nell, 39–40

married life with Nell, 40, 47, 52, 53–4, 55, 56, 57–8

death of his brother William, 43–4

first contact with Frederic Harrison, 45–7

career helped by Harrison, 50

writes articles on Social Democracy, 50–1

writes for *Vyestnik Evropy*, 51, 55

teaching work, 52, 61, 70, 75, 130, 144

becomes more militant Positivist, 52–3

'Scrapbook', 56, 100

separates from Nell, 58–9

lives with Nell again, 60

final separation from Nell, 60–1

informed about Nell's charge against three men, 66

hopes to divorce Nell, 66

encourages Algernon to write, 68

friendship with George Meredith, 69, 238

on holiday at Ullswater with the Harrsions, 73

introduced to the Gaussen family, 74–5

relationship with Mrs Gaussen, 75, 76–80

attempts to launch his sister Ellen, 80–1

exhaustion, and disillusionment with upper class society, 81

end of relationship with Mrs Gaussen, 82–3, 86

disciplined approach to writing, 85

Algernon lives with, 89

and political and social questions, 90–103, 106–7

and William Morris, 91–3, 94, 95

and problems in relation to women, 84, 101–3, 176–7

spends two weeks in Paris, 103–6

and Thomas Hardy, 111–13, 201, 238–9, 244–5

explores Lambeth, 114, 115

visits Brighton, 115

visits to Eastbourne, 115–16, 121–2, 134–5, 140, 221, 232

wishes his mother and sisters to move south, 116

enjoys company of Morley Roberts, 117–18

negative response to invitations, 119, 126, 157, 162, 175, 210

at George Smith's dinner party, 127

and Queen Victoria's Golden Jubilee, 128

pessimistic about the future, 129–30

refuses to attend wedding of Algernon and Catherine, 131

spends evening at house of George Bradley, 132

and Oscar Wilde, 132, 235

visits to Algernon and Catherine, 132, 145, 202, 223, 273

diary, 133

and Miss Curtis, 134, 140

and death of Nell, 135–8

Ellen stays with, 138

loneliness, 138–9, 141–2

shocks Ellen with gift of novel by Daudet, 140–1

visits Oxford, 144

holiday in Seascale, 144–5

visits Wakefield, 145

on the Continent, 145–55

returns to England and visits his family, 156–7

returns to London, 157

visits the Jolly family, 157

restricted social life, 157–8

Gissing, George—*contd*
  works on his novel in Agbrigg, 160–1,
    162, 163
  and Edith Sichel, 161–2, 166–7, 168–9,
    175
  holiday in the Channel Islands, 163–5
  correspondence with Bertz about
    Whitman, 164–5
  visits Marylebone workhouse, 165–6
  attitude to the women's movement,
    167–8, 206, 207
  visits Greece, 169–70
  visits Italy again, 170–1
  returns to England, 171–2
  returns to London, 172
  visits Paris with his sisters, 173
  spends the summer with his family,
    173–4, 175–6
  and Connie Ash, 175–6
  returns to London, 177
  begins relationship with Edith, 177–81
  decides to move to Exeter, 181
  attitude towards Edith, 182
  marries Edith, 183
  early married life with Edith, 183–4, 187,
    193–4
  social isolation in Exeter, 183, 201
  and Edith's pregnancy, 184
  holiday in Clevedon, 187–8
  finds new lodgings in Exeter, 188–9
  encouraged by Bullen, 189, 190
  birth of Walter, 193
  boards Walter out, 194
  holiday in Cornwall, 194
  difficult domestic life in Exeter, 193–4,
    195, 198, 203, 204
  crisis in writing, 198–9
  holiday in Weymouth, 201–2
  stays in Birmingham, 202–3
  returns to Exeter, 203
  decides he needs to move away from
    Exeter, 203, 207–8
  rents a room for writing, 204
  visited by Walter Grahame, 204–5
  and Edmund Gosse, 205
  holidays in Paignton and Burnham-
    on-Sea, 208
  leaves Exeter, 208–9
  moves back to London, 210

  reclusive, 210–11
  begins friendship with Clara Collet,
    211–13, 214
  and guardianship of his children, 213,
    240, 275
  concentrates on short-story writing,
    213–15, 216, 218, 225, 236, 247–8, 293
  engages Colles as agent, 216
  Algernon visits for a month, 219
  in Hastings, 220–1
  in Clevedon, 221, 223
  looks for new lodgings, 224
  moves to Epsom, 224–5
  leads more sociable life, 225–6, 234–6,
    237, 238, 239, 250, 259
  difficult domestic situation continues,
    226–8, 233, 240–1, 245–6, 247, 248–9,
    256, 259
  corresponds with Martha Barnes, 232
  visits Father Osborne Jay, 232
  visits Wakefield, Manchester and
    Alderley Edge, 232–3
  and Edith's second pregnancy, 233
  holiday at Gorleston and Yarmouth,
    237–8
  birth of Alfred, 246
  reflects on his boyhood, 246–7
  leaves Walter with his sisters, 248–9
  writes to Walter, 249
  and Israel Zangwill, 250–1
  holiday at Mablethorpe, 252, 253
  comments about Walter, 252, 253
  visits Frederic Harrison, 254
  health problems, 255–6, 260, 263, 269
  begins friendship with H.G. Wells,
    256–7
  walks out on Edith, 259–60
  consultations with Philip Pye-Smith,
    260, 269
  goes to stay in Budleigh Salterton, 260
  discusses his marital problems, 261–2
  reading, 262–3
  and Algernon's plans, 264
  visited by the Wellses, 268–9
  agrees to return to Edith in Epsom,
    269–70
  and Queen Victoria's Diamond Jubilee,
    270
  holiday in Yorkshire Dales, 270–2

domestic strife continues, 271–2

decides to go to Italy, leaving Edith and Alfred in lodgings, 272, 273

makes farewell visits to his family, 273–4

in Italy, 274–90

health problems inn Italy, 279–80, 285

and Edith's problems, 282–3, 287–8

and Rosalind Williams, 289–90, 295, 300–1

visits Bertz in Germany, 290–1

returns to England and finds house in Dorking, 292

agrees to write prefaces for Dickens novels, 294

receives proposition from Grant Richards, 294

unwilling to enter relationship with Clara Collet, 294–5

receives letter from Gabrielle, 295–6

start of romantic attachment to Gabrielle, 296, 297–300

more problems with Edith, 301

discovered in Dorking by Edith, 301–2

unable to divorce Edith and marry Gabrielle, 302–3, 305

mother visits, 303

Gabrielle spends a week in Dorking with, 304

plans for new life with Gabrielle, 304–6, 308, 310–11, 312

drops Colles as agent, 306–7

and scandal over Harold Frederic's mistress, 307–8

further health problems, 309–10, 328, 335, 339–40, 340–1, 342–3, 345–6, 352, 361, 363

visits family before his departure, 311

leaves for France, 312

ceremony with Gabrielle, 313

honeymoon, 313–14

domestic life in Paris, 314–15, 326, 340

and Parisian intellectual circles, 315, 321

holiday in the Alps, 315–17

gloomy about world events, 317, 329–30

relationship with Gabrielle, 319, 322–4, 344, 345, 348, 353

visits England, 327–8

goes to St Honoré les Bains, 329

sees physician in St Honoré, 335

visits Autun, 335–6

visits Gabrielle's relations, 338

returns to Paris, 338

receives letter about Walter, 340

consults doctor in Paris, 340–1, 352, 359

spends period in England, 342–9, 350

visits Henry James, 344–5

in sanatorium, 345–6

agrees not to visit Wakefield, 348–9

tells his family about Gabrielle, 349

returns to France, 350

goes to Autun, 350

agrees to abridge Forster's biography of Dickens, 352

in Arcachon, 352–5

hears about Edith's mental condition, 356–7

makes arrangements for Alfred, 357

finds house near St Jean de Luz, 357–8

and change of flat in Paris, 358–9

stays in St Jean de Luz area, 359–69

and Joseph Conrad, 362–3, 371

moves to Ispoure, 369, 370

excursion to Roncesvalles and Spain, 370

and Gabrielle's illness, 371–2

and Maman's illness, 372

final illness, 372–5

death, 375

burial, 375–6

scholarly interest in, 380

Works:

'All For Love', 42

'Among the Prophets' (unpublished), 326, 331

'The Artist's Child', 30

'At a Week's Notice', 188

Born in Exile, xiii, 2, 4, 9, 10, 12, 16, 61, 74, 86, 90, 129, 184, 187, 188, 189, 194, 196–8, 206, 208, 216, 264, 331, 367, 368

By the Ionian Sea, 276–7, 315, 316, 326, 331, 339, 346, 347

'A Capitalist', 215

'A Casual Acquaintance', 190

Charles Dickens: A Critical Study, 256, 274, 275, 276, 280, 284

'Christopherson', 354

'Clement Dorricott' (unpublished), 122, 123–4, 125, 126, 127–8, 129

Gissing, George—*contd*

The Crown of Life, 299, 300, 303–4, 305,
306, 307, 308–9, 316, 317–20, 325, 334,
337, 339

'A Daughter of the Lodge', 328

'The Day of Silence', 215

Demos, 18–19, 63, 75, 76, 87, 89, 90, 91,
92, 93, 94–5, 95–101, 102, 103, 106–8,
109, 111, 114–15, 118, 120, 122, 124,
128, 129, 138, 139, 158, 161, 163, 164,
166, 250

Denzil Quarrier ('The Radical
Candidate'), 6, 189, 190–2, 193,
195–6, 199, 220, 324

'A Despot on Tour', 276

'Dickens in Memory', 353

'Dust and Dew' / 'The Insurgents'
(unfinished), 122, 129, 130, 132, 134,
139

'The Elixir', 293

The Emancipated ('The Puritan'), 6, 68,
152, 160–1, 162, 163, 166, 167, 169,
172, 173, 174, 180, 181, 234

Eve's Ransom, 202, 219, 221–3, 225, 231,
233–4, 236, 255, 295–6

'A Farewell', 20

'The Fate of Humphrey Snell', 15–16,
285

'Fleet-footed Hester', 214

'The Foolish Virgin', 242–3

'A Graven Image' (unfinished), 68, 70

'Great Men in Little Worlds', 236

'The Head-Mistress' (unfinished), 167,
168, 172, 177, 199

'Hilda Wolff' (unfinished), 177

'The Honeymoon', 1

'The Hope of Pessimism' (unpublished),
xiii, 61–3

'The House of Cobwebs', 327

'How a Misfortune Made a Philosopher',
208

Human Odds and Ends, 270, 280

'Humplebee', 316

In the Year of Jubilee ('Miss Lord of
Camberwell'), 26, 77–8, 91, 206,
217–18, 219, 220–1, 223, 224, 227,
228–30, 231, 232, 234, 236, 246, 251,
255, 260, 344, 381

'The Iron Gods' / 'Gods of Iron'

(unfinished), 201, 202, 203, 204, 208,
221, 222

Isabel Clarendon, 75, 77, 78–9, 80, 81–2,
82–3, 84, 85, 86, 87, 88, 90, 109, 110,
141, 158, 230, 337, 367

'The Last Half-Crown', 28

A Life's Morning, 81, 85–6, 87, 88, 99, 102,
109, 118, 128, 150, 158, 163, 164

'A Lodger in Maze Pond', 106, 180, 215

'Lou and Liz', 208, 213, 214

'The Minstrel of the Byways', 204

'Miss Rodney's Leisure', 346

'Mrs Grundy's Enemies' (unpublished),
58, 60, 61, 63–4, 67, 68, 75, 85, 87, 88,
122, 125

The Nether World, ix, 63, 91, 121, 139–40,
141, 142–4, 145, 146, 147, 153, 154,
157, 158–9, 162, 163, 164, 169, 182, 183,
208, 211, 232, 250

New Grub Street ('A Man of Letters'), 22,
28, 30, 51, 84, 85, 90, 102, 121, 128,
133, 154, 165, 172, 175, 180–2, 183,
184–6, 188, 194, 197, 198, 203, 205,
206, 210, 216, 222, 228, 229, 250, 256,
259, 265, 295, 296, 297, 298, 310, 316,
321, 331, 336, 344, 359, 367, 368

'Nobodies at Home' sketches, 231

The Odd Women, xi, 2, 7, 77, 84, 102, 131,
141, 145, 154, 157, 168, 169, 199–201,
204, 205–6, 207, 208, 210, 212, 216, 217,
221, 228, 229, 235, 236, 241, 247, 254,
321, 335

Our Friend the Charlatan ('The Coming
Man'), 317, 324, 325, 330, 331–4, 335,
337, 339, 346–7

The Paying Guest, 237, 238, 243, 244, 251

'The Peace Bringer', 293, 298

'Phoebe', 67

'The Pig and Whistle', 327, 328–9

'Polly Brill' (unfinished), 259

The Private Papers of Henry Ryecroft ('An
Author at Grass'), 8, 29, 102, 122, 224,
280, 330, 333, 334, 335, 336–7, 347,
351–2, 359, 362, 364–5, 366, 368, 371,
377, 378, 379

Ravenna, 10

'The Riding-Whip', 58, 351

'The Ring Finger', 287

'R.I.P', 23

'Sandray the Sophist' (unpublished), 122, 127, 128
'The Scrupulous Father', 315
'Simple Simon', 225
'The Sins of the Fathers', 13–14, 22–3, 24
Sleeping Fires, 231, 233, 243, 251
'Snapshall's Youngest', 324
'Song' ('O maiden, simple, pale and sweet'), 66–7
'A Son of the Age' (unfinished), 45
'A Son of the Soil', 195
'The Spendthrift' (unfinished), 232
'Storm-Birds' (unfinished), 175
Thyrza, 43, 63, 106, 108, 111, 113–15, 118–21, 122, 123, 124, 125, 126, 127, 128, 129, 130, 140, 146, 157, 158, 161, 175, 181, 182, 183, 250
'Topham's Chance', 372
'To Sleep', 19
The Town Traveller, 166, 231, 264, 270, 273, 280, 286–7, 292, 309, 339
'The Two Gardens', 20
The Unclassed ('The Burden of Life'), xiii, 18, 31–2, 34–5, 38, 43, 46, 63, 64, 67–8, 68–9, 70–3, 81, 85, 87, 88, 90, 99, 101, 104–5, 108, 140, 165, 178, 234, 237, 240, 339
'Under an Umbrella', 214
Veranilda ('The Vanquished Roman'), 339, 340, 365, 368, 369, 370–1, 372, 373, 374, 377
'A Victim of Circumstances', 190, 202–3
'Victor Yule' (unfinished), 177
The Whirlpool ('Benedict's Household'), 228, 248, 249, 251, 252, 254, 255, 256, 264, 265, 266–8, 283, 344, 347
Will Warburton, 6, 357, 359, 360, 366–8, 369
Workers in the Dawn ('Far, Far Away'), 3, 6, 20, 22, 24, 35, 36, 39, 40, 41, 42–3, 44–5, 45–6, 47, 48–9, 50, 51, 56, 72, 88, 90, 91, 108, 137, 158, 337
Gissing, Jane (GG's grandmother), 1
Gissing (*née* Bedford), Margaret (GG's mother)
family background, 2
marries Thomas, 2
married life, 2–3
death of husband, 6
financial situation, 6–7, 33
moves house and sends boys to boarding school, 7
unwilling to receive Nell at Wakefield, 40
and death of her son William, 43
moves to Agbrigg, 44
and possibility of living in the south, 116
GG spends holiday in Seascale with, 145
in the Cotswolds with Algernon, 202
visits GG, 208, 303
as mother, 247
GG's relationship with, 303
Gabrielle visits after GG's death, 377
death, 379
Gissing, Margaret (GG's sister)
birth, 3
moves to Agbrigg, 44
visits London, 54
views men as egotistical, 64
remains single, 156, 200, 379
beliefs and mentality of Ellen and, 160, 161
holidays with GG, 163, 164, 173
warns GG about Connie Ash, 175
visits GG, 201, 268
dislikes Edith, 201, 310
starts a school with her sister, 247
and Walter, 248, 249, 268, 311, 327, 340
and GG's relationship with Gabrielle Fleury, 310, 316, 349
visits Algernon, 311
GG's comments to, 64, 109, 113, 151–2
brief references, 12, 65, 111, 253, 272
Gissing (*née* Harrison), Nell (Marianne Helen) (GG's first wife)
and 'The Sins of the Fathers', 13–14
GG meets, 13
prostitution, 13, 14, 15
alcoholism, 14, 32, 114
GG decides to save, 14
and John George Black, 14–15
and 'The Fate of Humphrey Snell', 15–16
relationship with GG develops, 16–17
and GG's financial situation, x, 16, 17, 44, 52, 53, 54, 61, 90
GG steals because of relationship with, 17

Gissing (*née* Harrison), Nell (Marianne
　　Helen) (GG's first wife)—*contd*
　GG sent away from, 19
　GG corresponds with, 20, 24
　reunited with GG in London, 26–7
　lives with GG, 31, 32, 33, 38–9
　and *The Unclassed*, 31, 32
　health problems, 32, 39, 52, 53–4, 57,
　　58–9, 60
　spends four weeks at Wilmslow, 39
　marries GG, 39–40
　married life, 40, 47, 52, 53–4, 55, 56, 57–8
　lives apart from GG, 58–9
　returns to live with GG, 60
　final separation from GG, 60–1
　charges three men of rape, 65–6
　GG tries to find evidence to divorce, 66
　GG tells Frederic Harrison about, 71,
　　79
　Mrs Gaussen unaware of, 79–80
　impact on GG's life and aspirations, xiii,
　　90, 102
　and GG's views on marriage, 131
　death, 135
　GG sorts out possessions of, 135–7
　GG arranges funeral of, 137
　GG feels impelled to write after death of,
　　137–8
　burial, 138
　and *The Nether World*, 142, 143, 144, 159
　brief references, xv, xvi, 22, 95, 157, 177,
　　298, 300, 312
Gissing, Robert Foulsham (GG's
　　grandfather), 1, 33
Gissing, Thomas Waller (GG's father),
　　1–5, 6, 7, 33, 34, 246–7
　'Margaret', 2, 12, 136
　Margaret and Other Poems, 137
Gissing, Walter Leonard (GG's son)
　birth, 193
　appearance, 193, 195
　Edith's treatment of, 193, 204, 227, 233,
　　247, 248, 262, 282
　early years, 194, 195, 198, 201–2, 203,
　　204, 208, 210, 212, 220, 221, 224, 225,
　　232, 237, 238, 246–7
　guardianship, 213, 275
　GG tries to ensure financial security for,
　　233, 255

　placed in care of GG's sisters, 248–9
　letters from GG, 249, 316, 326
　letters from Edith, 249–50, 254
　on holiday in Mablethorpe, 252, 253
　GG's reflections on, 252–3
　visited by Clara Collet, 254
　holiday in Budleigh Salterton, 268
　and his parents' row in Castle Bolton,
　　271–2
　GG anxious about, 274, 323
　stays with Hick, 303
　remains with his aunts on GG's move to
　　France, 310
　at Willersey, 311
　and GG's thoughts about military
　　service, 326
　causes problems to his aunts, 327
　sent away from his aunts, 340
　Gabrielle visits, 377
　Civil List pension for, 378
　educated at Gresham's School, 378
　military service and death, 378–9
　brief references, 269, 273, 292, 301, 302,
　　322, 336, 343, 347, 357, 373
Gissing, William (GG's brother), 3, 26,
　　33–4, 37, 39, 40, 41, 43, 44, 171, 220,
　　232
Gladstone, William Ewart, 140, 159
Glastonbury, 188, 208, 336
Goethe, J.W. von: *Italienische Reise*, 147,
　　148–9
Gommecourt, 378
Goode, John, 380, 381
Gorleston, 237
Gosse, Edmund, 205, 237, 378
Grahame, Walter, 70, 111, 123, 130, 144,
　　183, 204–5
Grand Union Canal, 40
Grasmere, 2
Gray, Thomas, 122
Greece, 168, 169–70, 366
Greene, Charles, 224
Greene, Graham, 224
Greenwood, J.G., 17
Gresham's School, 377, 378
Guardian, 106–7, 196
Guernsey, 164, 172
Guildford, 366
Guy's Hospital, 260

Hachette, 139
Hackney, 27
Halesworth, 1
Halperin, John, 76–7, 106, 179, 181
Harbottle, 159–60
Hardy, Thomas
    impressed by *The Unclassed*, 73
    friendship with GG, 111–13, 238
    GG's opinion of writing of, 112, 185, 201,
        239, 244, 245
    GG makes comments on his writing to,
        112, 113, 129
    GG refuses invitation from, 162
    marriage, 162, 239
    invites GG to visit, 237
    GG visits, 3, 238–9
    GG's criticism of, 238–9
    praises GG's article in *Review of the
        Week*, 317
    comments on GG's ability to write
        abroad, 371
    brief references, 117, 226, 342, 363, 372
    Works:
    Jude the Obscure, 112, 113, 244, 245
    The Mayor of Casterbridge, 112
    Tess of the d'Urbervilles, 201
Hardy, Mrs, 239
Harper, 108
Harper's Weekly, 265
Harrison, Austin, 52, 254
Harrison, Bernard, 52, 119, 130, 254
Harrison, Frederic
    and Comte and Positivism, xiii, 36, 45–6,
        51
    and GG's writing, 45–7, 48, 50, 63, 68,
        70, 71, 87
    becomes GG's patron, xiii, 50
    employs GG to teach his sons, 52, 130
    GG receives income from, 54
    and GG's decision not to publish essay
        refuting Comte, xvii, 61
    advises GG to seek divorce, 66
    GG on holiday with family of, 73
    puts GG in touch with Gaussen, 74
    knows about aspects of GG's private life,
        79
    and GG's attitude to the upper classes,
        81
    invites GG to dinner, 119
    GG stays with, 254
    brief references, 90, 106, 251
Harrison, Mrs Frederic, 71, 184
Harrison, Henry, 330
Harrison, Reverend Joseph, 5
Harrison, Nell *see* Gissing (*née* Harrison),
        Nell
Harte, Bret, 129
Hartley, Alfred, 158
Harvester Press, 380
Harvey's Academy for Boys, Halesworth,
        1
Haslemere, 254
Hastings, 55, 56, 220, 221
Hauteville, 164
Heine, Heinrich, 21, 315
Heinemann, 337
Hemingway, Ernest, 5
Hertfordshire, 224
Herwegh, Mme Emma, 315
Hick, Henry, 5, 234, 239, 260, 274, 292, 303,
        339, 342, 343, 357, 361
Hick, Matthew, 19
Holmwood, 295, 300
Holt, 339
Horace, 281
Hornung, E.W., 288, 289
Hotel Concordia, Cotrone, 279
Hôtel Cujas, Paris, 103, 145
Hôtel de Londres, Paris, 145–6
Hôtel de Paris, Rouen, 313
Hôtel des Terrasses, St-Pierre-en-Port, 313
Hotel Leonetti, Cosenza, 278
Hudson, W.H., 158, 170, 211, 214, 328, 359
Hughes, Arthur, 52
Hughes, Thomas, 54
Hugo, Victor, 164
    Les Misérables, 164
    Ninety-Three, 164
    The Toilers of the Sea, 164
Hunt, Holman, 95, 379
Hurst and Blackett, 132, 140, 159, 242
Huxley, T.H., 234, 332
Hyndman, H.M., 92

Ilkley, 340
Illustrated London News, 213, 214, 218, 219,
        221, 231, 233, 236, 351
India, 75, 379

International Copyright Agreement, 286
Irish Home Rule, 51, 55
Islington, 40, 52, 113
Ispoure, G G's last months in, 369–70,
    371–5
Italy, 103, 147, 159, 160, 316, 357
    GG's visits to, 148–55, 170–1, 274–90
    see also names of places
Izoulet, Jean: *La Cité Moderne*, 331

Jack the Ripper, 146, 148
James, Henry, 109, 265–6, 344–5, 351,
    353–4, 363, 371, 372
    The Ambassadors, 344
    The Bostonians, 246
    Guy Donville, 294
    'The Real Thing', 214
Jameson, Frederic, 136, 380
Jay, Father Osborne, 232
    The Social Problem, 232
Jerome, Jerome K., 231
    Three Men in a Boat, 231
Jolly, Mrs, 157
Joyce, James, 239, 380
    Dubliners, 294
Judaism, 162

Keats, John, 151
Kegan Paul, 41, 42
Kelley, Mary, 146
Kelmscott, 75
Kelmscott House, 94, 100, 101
Kennington, 58, 208, 210, 356
Kew, 179
Kingdom of the Two Sicilies, 149
Kingston, 212
Kipling, Rudyard, 21, 268, 278, 317, 325
    'The Absent-Minded Beggar', 325
    Barrack-Room Ballads, 267–8
    Stalky and Co, 325
Kitton, Frederick, 355
Koch, Robert, 171
Korg, Jacob, 106, 380
Kurz, Frau, 152

Lambart, Mr, 286
Lambart, Mrs, 284
Lambeth, 111, 114, 115
Lambeth Cemetery, 138

Lambeth Workhouse Infirmary, 356
Lamb House, 345
Landor, W.S., 145, 153
Landseer, Sir Edwin, 136
Lane, John, 242
Lang, Andrew, 186
Lasserre, Dr, 369, 372
Lawrence, D.H., 16, 239, 380
    The Rainbow, 213
Lawrence, H.W., 208, 225, 226, 261
Lawrence, Lady, 238
Lawrence and Bullen, 189, 226, 231, 233,
    240, 264, 270, 273, 292, 324, 337
League of Nations, 317
Le Breton, Fanny, 139, 148, 163
Leicester, 213
Lenormant, François: *La Grande Grèce*, 278
Lewes, 134, 312
Lewes, George Henry, 36, 308
Liberalism, 107
Liberal Party, 4
Lincoln, 327
Lindow Grove School, Alderley Edge, 7–8,
    9, 10, 248
Literature, 341, 347, 353
Liverpool, 20, 24, 26
London
    GG lives in, 26–103, 106–44, 156,
        157–60, 165–8, 172, 177–82, 209,
        210–20, 221
    and G G's writing, xiii, 26, 28, 29, 48–9,
        63, 98, 112, 114, 115, 124, 129, 143,
        154, 215, 217–18, 252, 254, 263, 267,
        326, 366, 381
    poverty in, 54
    Algernon in, 56, 59, 89
    GG's comments on life in, 56–7, 59, 87
    Bertz returns to, 65
    Ellen visits, 80–1
    William Morris's contacts with the
        masses in, 93
    political meetings in, 94
    riots in, 99
    GG wants his mother and sisters to live
        near, 116
    Morley Roberts returns to, 117
    Plitt returns to, 155
    GG dislikes the 'Season' in, 162
    GG visits Edith Sichel's flat in, 168

GG marries Edith Underwood in, 183
Edith sees a doctor in, 195
Edith's visit to her sister in, 201
GG's decision to return to, 208
GG joins in social scene of, 225–6, 231
GG consults lung specialist in, 260
GG fears having to stay away from, 263
brief references, 1, 269, 284, 295, 310, 327, 377
see also names of districts in London
London Correspondence College, 258
London Division, 378
London Figaro, 122
London University, 11, 19, 226
Louis Napoleon, 164
Louvre, 147
Lugano, 317
Lushington, Kitty (later Kitty Maxse), 52, 67, 254
Lushington, Margaret, 67
Lushington, Mrs, 52
Lushington, Vernon, 51, 52
Lyon, 148
Lyon, Kate, 307–8

Mablethorpe, 252, 253
Macmillan, 220
Macmillan's Magazine, 190
Magna Graecia see Calabria
Malpas, Dr, 375
Manchester
GG as student in, 8–13, 16
GG begins affair with Nell in, 13, 14, 15, 16
GG arrested for stealing in, 17
GG in prison in, 17–19
GG visits, 232, 233
brief references, 26, 45
Manchester Examiner, 50
Manchester Guardian, 229, 234, 266
Mann, Thomas, 380
Manor Park Cemetery, 98, 99, 106
Marlow, 250
Marseille, 148, 169–70, 296
Martial, 12
Martineau, Harriet, 36
Marx, Karl, 36–7
    Capital, 50
    Communist Manifesto, 50

Marxism, 37, 381
Marylebone Female Protection Society, 26–7
Marylebone Workhouse, 165–6, 171, 378
Mason, Mrs, 271
Massachusetts, 24
Massa Lubrense, 151, 155, 170–1, 370
Massingham, H.W., 225
Maugham, Somerset: *Liza of Lambeth*, 326–7
Maupassant, Guy de, 214
Max Gate, Dorchester, 238
Maxse (*née* Lushington), Kitty *see* Lushington, Kitty
Maxse, Leopold, 254
Mechanics Institution, Wakefield, 4
Menai Bridge, 9
Mercier, St Vincent, 27–8
Meredith, George
    as reader at Chapman and Hall, 68–9, 81
    GG's friendship with, 69
    social origins, 69–70, 239
    marriage, 69–70, 162
    advice to GG on subject matter, 87, 88
    Omar Khayyam Club dinner in honour of, 237
    GG visits at Box Hill, 238, 250, 327–8
    GG writes from Ispoure to, 370
    brief references, 72, 109, 117, 259, 363, 371, 372
    Work: *Modern Love*, 69
Meredith (*née* Nicholls), Mary Ellen, 69–70
Messina, 276
Metaponto, 279
Methuen, 231, 286, 292, 294, 303, 309, 324, 325, 326
Michaelis, Kate, 251
Milan, 274
Mill, John Stuart, 36, 206, 303
Miller, Jane, 378
Milner, Miss, 5
Minehead, 188
Monahan, Bridget, 18
Montaigne: 'Of Cruelty', 182–3
Mont Blanc massif, 315
Monte Cassino, 281–2, 370
Montmartre cemetery, Paris, 173

Moore, George, 107
  The Celibates, 234
  Esther Waters, 234
Morgue, Paris, 103–4, 105
Morley, John, 50, 51
Morris, Jane, 75, 95
Morris, May, 94
Morris, William, 91–2, 93, 94, 95, 96, 99,
    107, 120
  The Earthly Paradise, 93
  'The Pilgrims of Hope', 92
Morrison, Arthur: *A Child of the Jago*, 255,
    326
Morvan hills, 329
Mother's Act (1886), 275
Mount Taygetos, 170
Mudie's, 60, 72, 107, 223, 224
Murger, Henri: *Scènes de la Vie de Bohème*,
    29, 103, 179
Musset, Alfred de, 296, 304
Musset, Madame Lardin de, 296, 304, 315
My Secret Life, xii

Naples, 145, 148–50, 151, 170, 171, 241, 276,
    277, 290
Narodniks, 55
National Hospital for Diseases of the Heart
    and Paralysis, 57, 58–9
National Liberal Club, 225–6, 372
National Review, 254
Naturalism, 381
Nayland, GG's stay in, 345–7, 350
Nefyn, 248
Nevers, 338
New England Hospital for Women and
    Children, 246
Newhaven, 145, 312
Newnham College, Cambridge, 346
New Romney, 260, 303
New York, 24, 220, 280, 339
New York Times, 234
New York Tribune, 320
Niagara Falls, 22
Nicholas II, Tsar, 308–9
Nicholls, Mary Ellen (later Mary Ellen
    Meredith), 69–70
Nietzsche, Friedrich Wilhelm, 38, 62
  The Birth of Tragedy, 62
Nineteenth Century, The, 140

Norman, Henry, 274
Normandy, 311, 312, 313, 314
Northallerton, 271
Northern Newspaper Syndicate, 368
North London Collegiate School for Girls,
    211
Northumberland, 5, 116, 123, 160

Omar Khayyam Club, 237, 250, 256, 288
Orient, 171
Orme, Eliza
  GG meets, 226
  and GG's marital problems, 261, 262,
    263, 269, 270
  GG writes about his decision to, 272
  Edith and Alfred live with, 273
  Edith moves out of home of, 292
  sends news of Edith to GG, 282, 287,
    301, 356
  brief references, 212, 357
Orwell, George, ix–x, 102, 166, 199, 267, 380
  Down and Out in Paris and London, ix
  Nineteen Eighty-Four, ix, x
Ovid, 12
  Amores, 164
Owens, John, 9
Owens College, Manchester
  GG as student at, x, xi, 8–13, 16, 19
  GG expelled from, 19
  fund established for GG, 19
  brief references, 20, 191, 250, 256
Oxford, 144 *see also* Balliol College, Oxford
Oxford Junior Local Examination, 8
Oxford Music Hall, London, 177

Paddington, 27
Paestum, 150, 154, 290
Paignton, 208
Palazzo Swift, Venice, 154
Palermo, 281
Pall Mall Gazette, 50, 205, 206, 267, 365
Pamplona, 370
Pancras Registry Office, 183
Paola, 276
Paris
  syphilis in, 15
  Comte in, 36
  Turgenev in, 51
  GG visits, 103–6, 145–8, 173

lecture on G G's work in, 297
GG's life with Gabrielle and Maman in,
    314–15, 321–2, 323–4, 326, 338–9, 340
GG consults doctor in, 340–1, 352
Gabrielle returns from Arcachon to, 353
Gabrielle and Maman change flat in, 357,
    358–9
brief references, 112, 299, 313, 320, 327,
    328, 337, 342, 378
Passy, 314
Patras, 170
Payn, James, 87, 99–100, 101, 107, 118–19,
    120, 125, 188, 189
Peacock, T.L., 69
Pease, Edward, 92
Pension Larrea, Ciboure, 357, 377
Pent Farm, Postling, 362
Penzance, 194
Père Lachaise cemetery, Paris, 146, 173
Perpignan, 371
Petit Journal, Le, 146
Petremant, Robert, 24
Phillips, Mrs, 194
Pinker, James B.
    becomes G G's agent, 306
    and G G's novels, 306, 308, 309, 324, 326,
        331, 337, 351, 352, 364, 368
    and G G's short stories, 315, 372
    brief references, 327, 338, 342, 343, 355
Piraeus, 170
Plato: Republic, 101
Plitt, Ernst, 145, 146–7, 148, 151, 155
Plutarch, 254
Poe, Edgar Allan, 23
Pompeii, 151
Poole, Adrian, 380
Portland Maine, 24
Positivism, 36, 46, 50, 51, 52–3, 55, 57, 61,
    63
Postling, 362
Potsdam, 290
Potter, Richard, 289
Pre-Raphaelites, xvi, 95
Previtali's Hotel, Piccadilly, 259, 260
Procter, Anne, 127
Protestant Cemetery, Rome, 151
Provence, 377
Pye-Smith, Philip, 260, 269, 342
Pythagoras, 279, 371

Queen's Westminster Rifles, 378

Raboul, Dr, 372, 375
Rahardt, Paul, 52
Rahardt, Maria, 27
Raphael, 136, 137
Reform Bill (1832), 4
Regent Canal, 42
Regent's Park, 55, 218
Reggio, 280, 281
Remington, 42, 43, 45, 51, 54, 60
Renaissance, 152, 154
Review of the Week, 317
Richards, Grant, 294, 308, 309
Richardson, Sir Benjamin Ward, 235
Richardson, Samuel, 239
Richmond, Surrey, 178, 179, 211, 212
    Park, 59
Richmond, Yorkshire, 254
Rickards, Miss, 340
Ridsdale, Dr, 57
Rilke, Rainer Maria, 351
Ritchie, Anne, 167
Ritchie, Emily Marion, 167, 168, 169
Robbins, Amy Catherine see Wells (née
    Robbins), Amy Catherine
Roberts, Morley
    friendship with G G, 11, 118
    on G G's student days, 11, 14, 17
    on G G's time in Chicago, 23
    and G G's relationship with Mrs
        Gaussen, 76, 77, 78
    in America and Canada, 23–4, 82, 87
    returns to London, 117
    on G G's flat, 117
    on G G's cooking, 117–18
    writes about his travels in North
        America, 118
    visits G G in Eastbourne, 134
    and Nell's death, 135
    in Cornwall, 141
    GG meets friends of, 158
    and G G's relationship with Edith, 177,
        178, 180
    on G G's relationship with women,
        179
    recommends G G to Bullen, 189
    on Edith, 208
    visits G G in Devon, 208

Roberts, Morley—*contd*
  encourages GG to write more short
    stories, 208, 213, 214
  GG gives money to, 232
  hears about GG's plans to live with
    Gabrielle, 304–5
  comments on *The Crown of Life*, 320
  writes survey article on GG, 347
  visits GG in France, 368–9
  arrives at Ispoure, 375
  arranges GG's funeral, 375–6
  GG's comments to: on his life in France,
    361; on his writing, 360; on Wilde, 235
  brief references, 38, 121, 165, 169, 203,
    211, 326, 360, 373
  Works:
  The Private Life of Henry Maitland, 177,
    374, 379
  A Question of Instinct, 245–6
  Rachel Marr, 371
  The Western Avernus, 24, 118
Rockett, Mr and Mrs, 188
Rome
  GG in, 151–2, 276, 282, 284, 285–6,
    288–9, 290
  Plitt in, 155
  sack of, 278
  brief references, 150, 155, 169, 275, 278,
    316, 366
Roncesvalles, Pass of, 366, 369, 370
Rose, J.H. (Holland), 256
Rosherville Gardens, 208
Ross, Robert, 235
Ross, Ronald, 279
Rossetti, Dante Gabriel, 75, 95
  The House of Life, 95
  'Jenny', 12–13, 95
Rothenstein, William, 270, 312
Rouen, 313
Royal Literary Fund, 235
Rugby, Tennessee, 54, 65
Ruskin, John, 61, 63, 68, 145
  The Stones of Venice, 154
Russia, 51, 55, 70
Rye, 344, 351

Sacher-Masoch, Leopold von, 296
Sacher-Masoch, Madame Wanda von, 296,
  304, 319

Saglio, Alfred, 338
Saglio, Mlle, 352
St Honoré les Bains
  Gabrielle takes lease on house in, 329
  GG spends summer based in, 329–38, 351
  GG's enjoyment of, 329
  GG visits physician in, 335
St Ives, 194
St James's church, Hampstead Road, 39, 40
St Jean de Luz
  GG finds house near, 357–8
  GG based near, 359–69
  GG visits doctor in, 361
  GG buried in, 375–6
  brief references, 374 377
St Jean Pied-de-Port, 369, 373, 375
St John's Hospital for Diseases of the Skin,
  27–8
St Just, 194
St Neot's, 327
St Peter's, Rome, 152
St Peter Port, 164
St Petersburg, 51
St-Pierre-en-Port, 313, 314
St Ruth, Sergeant, 8
Saintsbury, George, 50
Salamis, 170
Salisbury, 378
Salisbury, Lord, 325
Salvation Army, 65, 237–8
Sampson, Low, 41, 210
Samoëns, 315
Sandgate, 328, 340, 342, 362
Santiago de Compostela, 369
Sark, 164, 165, 172
Saturday Review, 109, 174, 186, 205, 251
Savile Club, 328, 372
Schopenhauer, Artur, 35, 36, 62, 63
Schreiner, Olive, 168
  The Story of an African Farm, 168
Scott, Sir Walter, 113, 228
Sculco, Riccardo, 279
Seaford, 58
Seascale, 144–5
Shailer, Emma, 130
Shakespeare, William, 9, 151
Shaw, Bernard: *Pygmalion*, 241
Shelley, Percy Bysshe, 127, 150, 151
Shoreditch, 232

Shorter, Clement, 208, 213, 214, 215, 218, 219, 221, 225, 228, 235, 236, 237, 239

Shortridge, Carmela, 171

Shortridge, Ellen, 157

Shortridge, Herbert, 171

Shortridge, Jack, 171

Shortridge, John, 151, 155, 157, 170–1, 370

Shrewsbury, 13

Sichel, Edith, 161–3, 166–7, 168–9, 175, 177,180, 199, 207, 212

Sicily, 278, 281

Sickert, Ellen, 312

Sickert, Walter, 312

Siddal, Lizzie, 95

Siena, GG's stay in, 274–6, 284

Similis, 359

Sistine Chapel, 151

Sketch, The, 213, 215, 228, 236, 239, 270

Smallbrook Cottage, Willersey, 130

Smith, Alfred, 357

Smith, Elder
    rejection of *Workers in the Dawn*, 41
    rejection of 'Mrs Grundy's Enemies', 60
    acceptance of *A Life's Morning*, 87, 99
    acceptance of *Demos*, 99
    advertising campaign for *Demos*, 106
    cheaper editions of *Demos* issued, 108
    acceptance of *Thyrza*, 118–19
    cheaper editions of *Thyrza* issued, 120–1, 183
    poor treatment of GG, 121, 189
    advertising campaign for *Thyrza*, 124
    'Clement Dorricott' not sent to, 127–8
    GG sends *The Nether World* to, 144
    acceptance of *The Nether World*, 146
    GG dissatisfied with, 163–4
    purchase of copyright for *Thyrza*, 121, 181, 182
    acceptance of *New Grub Street*, 181–2
    cheaper editions of *New Grub Street* issued, 185
    GG sends *Born in Exile* to, 188
    Born in Exile manuscript retrieved from, 188
    GG's break with, 189
    request a novel from GG, 231
    continue to advertise GG's novels, 231–2
    give permission for translation of *New Grub Street*, 298
    no reason to sell GG's titles to Methuen, 324–5
    do not wish to increase their investment in GG, 327
    brief references, 126, 166, 180, 265, 296, 337

Smith, George, 107, 126, 127, 157

Snowdon, 9

Social Darwinism, 165, 330, 331

Social Democracy, 50

Social Democratic Federation, 92, 99

Socialism, 96, 99, 106, 107

Society of Authors, 216, 337

Socrates, 182–3

Somersby, 253

Somme, Battle of the, 378–9

Somme Memorial, Thiepval, 379

South Africa, 69, 70, 325

Southampton, 123

South Downs, 116, 121–2, 134

South Place Ethical Society, 212

Southport, 16

Southwold, 1

Spain, 360, 369, 370

Spectator, The, 50, 106

Speirs, John, 380

Spencer, Herbert, 36, 62, 330
    Facts and Comments, 330

Sprague, Julia, 246

Squillace, 280

Stannard, Ann, 27

Stannard, William, 27, 33, 37

Stead, William, 124

Steinitz, Clara, 163

Stephen, Lesley, 52

Stephen, Virginia *see* Woolf (*née* Stephen), Virginia

Stephen family, 52, 254

Stevenson, R.L., 21, 24
    An Amateur Emigrant, 24

Stewart, Charles, 210

Stockwell, 210

Stokes, Frederick, 264, 286

Strait of Messina, 281

Strand Magazine, 276

Strauss, David, 35
    Leben Jesu, 34, 35

Sturmer, Herbert, 283, 284

Sue, Eugène: *Mystères de Paris*, 103

Sully-Prudhomme, René, 297
Summers, William, 9–10, 86
Sutherland, Duke of, 58
Swinburne, Algernon, 317
Swindon, 202
Swinton-Hunter, Robert, 284
Switzerland, 315–17, 379

Taranto, 277, 278–9
Tate, Henry, 203
Tauchnitz, 107
Taylor, Harriet, 303
Tazières, Château de, 338, 352
Temple Bar, 67, 125–6
Tennyson, Alfred, Lord, 136, 185, 201, 205, 253, 304
  'In Memoriam', 165
  'The May Queen', 179
Ternan, Ellen, xvii, 355
Thackeray, W.M., 30, 81, 113, 211, 262
Theatre Français, Paris, 105
Theberton, 1
Thesiger, Wilfred, 279
Thiepval, 379
Thomson, J.J., 9
Ticino, 317
Tillotson's newspaper syndicate, 163
Times, The, 106, 183, 196, 232, 317, 346–7
Times Literary Supplement, 355
Tinckam, C.W., 210
Tinsley's Magazine, 30
Tintoretto, 154
Tit-Bits, 217
Today, 231
Tolstoy, Leo, 342
Trafalgar Square, 94, 99, 100, 101
Travers, Rosalind, 236
Treverva, 357
Tribune, ix
Trient, holiday in, 315–17, 366
Trollope, Anthony, 30, 108–9, 125, 211
  The Way We Live Now, 267
Trollope, Fanny, 150
Troy, 24
Tufnell Park, 327
Tulse Hill, 273
Turgenev, I.S., 51, 70, 344
  Fathers and Sons, 70

Uffizi, Florence, 153
Ullswater, 73
Underwood, Edith *see* Gissing (*née* Underwood), Edith
Underwood, Herbert, 259
University Hospital, London, 57
University of London, 11, 19, 226

Vatican, 370
Venice, 151, 154–5, 156, 289
Vesuvius, 148, 150
Veules, 314
Victoria, Queen, 368
  Golden Jubilee, 128
  Diamond Jubilee, 270
Villa des Roses, St Honoré les Bains, 329
Villa Souvenir, Archachon, 353, 355
Virgil, 6, 149
Visigoths, 278
Vyestnik Evropy, 51, 54, 55, 60

Wahltuch, Dr, 17
Wakefield
  GG's family background and childhood in, 2–7
  GG visits but is unable to live in, 26
  GG does not visit at Christmas, 40
  response to *Workers in the Dawn* in, 44
  GG thinks of starting a newspaper in, 53, 64
  Algernon writes letters to newspapers in, 65, 68
  GG's mother and sisters remain in, 116, 173
  GG's visits to, 145, 156, 157, 160, 173–4, 175–6, 232, 233, 327
  GG's sisters start a school in, 247
  GG takes Walter to, 248
  Walter remains in, 248
  GG says goodbye to Walter in, 273–4
  Gabrielle's attitude towards, 322–3, 340, 348
  GG wishes to visit, 347
  GG agrees not to visit, 348–9
  Gabrielle visits, 377
  Alfred lives for a time in, 379
  brief references, 27, 45, 81, 84, 85, 151, 177, 195, 252, 269, 271, 303, 316, 324
Wales, 9, 248

Walker, Dr Jane, 345
Waller, Emily, 1, 6–7, 33
Wallis, Henry, 69
Walsall, 202
Waltham Free Press, 21–2
Waltham High School, 21–2, 232
Ward, Adolphus, 10
Ward, Alice, 297, 335
Ward, Mrs Humphrey, 189
Waskett, the Misses, 58, 60
Wassermann test, 361
Waterhouse, John, 10
Watt, A.P., 188, 189, 194, 215–16
Watts-Dunton, Theodore, 237
Way, Hal, 342
Webb (*née* Potter), Beatrice, 98, 258, 289, 290
Webb, Sidney, 98, 289
Webster, Wentworth, 360
Wedd, Nathaniel, 346
Wells, 208, 336
Wells (*née* Robbins), Amy Catherine
    GG meets, 257
    Wells's marriage to, 258
    visits GG in Budleigh Salterton, 268
    walks on Dartmoor with her husband, 269
    in Italy with her husband, 288, 290
    GG stays at home of, 296, 342
    Gabrielle's letters to, 314, 343, 348
    visits GG in Paris with her husband, 340
    expecting first child, 344
    GG's letter to, 345
Wells, Frank, 328
Wells, H.G.
    and GG's relationship with Mrs Gaussen, 79
    and GG's poverty, 105
    and GG's writing, 221–2, 243–4, 248, 251, 267–8
    meets GG, 256
    invites GG to his house, 256–7
    GG visits, 256, 259
    compared with GG, 256, 340
    first marriage, 257–8
    second marriage, 258–9
    financial success, 258, 328
    dines with GG and Hicks, 260
    visits GG in Budleigh Salterton, 268–9
    and GG's second marriage, 287
    in Italy, 288, 289, 290
    and GG's cycling, 296
    and Gabrielle, 296, 301, 302, 304, 323
    sees Rosalind Williams as suitable partner for GG, 301
    stays with Hick, 303
    and publishers and agents, 306–7
    GG refuses offer of money from, 311
    builds house at Sandgate, 328
    views about GG's domestic life in France, 340
    GG compares himself with, 340
    GG spends time at home of, 342
    visits Henry James, 344
    writes to GG about his growing recognition, 372
    and GG's last illness, 373, 374, 375
    writes preface for *Veranilda*, 377
    GG's comments to: on Chalet Feuillebois, 350; on Edith, 287; on God, 244–5; on Naples, 276; on Rosalind Williams, 300
    brief references, xii, 163, 245, 309, 345, 347, 360, 371, 379
    Works:
        Autobiography, 374
        The Time Machine, 258
        The War of the Worlds, 328
        When the Sleeper Wakes, 288
Wells, Isobel, 257–8
Wensleydale, 271
Westminster Gazette, 259
Westminster Hospital, 60
Wessex, 112
Weybridge, 236
Weymouth, 201
Whale, George, 235
White, Rachel, 346, 353
Whitechapel, 146
Whitehall Review, 124, 186
White Hart, Lewes, 312
Whitman, Walt, 38, 164–5, 342
Whittington, Sophia, 1, 2, 6, 33
Who's Who, 275–6
Wilde, Oscar, 18, 132, 165, 235, 284, 308
    'A Ballad of Reading Gaol', 284
Wilhelm II, Kaiser, 130

Willersey, 130, 223, 254, 273, 292, 311, 312, 322
Williams, Dyson, 290
Williams, Raymond, 380
Williams (*née* Potter), Rosalind, 212, 289–90, 292, 295, 300–1
Williams, Trevor, 33
Williamson, Charles and Alice, 355
Williamson, George, 366
Wilmslow, 33, 39, 43, 232
Wilson, Edmund, xii
Wood, James, 7–8, 9, 248
Wood, Mrs, 125
Woods, Margaret: *A Village Tragedy*, 132
Wooler, 122
Woolf (*née* Stephen), Virginia, 52, 167, 254, 379
  Mrs Dalloway, 52, 379
  A Room of One's Own, 379

To the Lighthouse, 379
Worcester, 2
Worcester Park, 257, 296, 297, 342
Wordsworth, William, 2, 6, 64, 73

Xerxes, Emperor, 170

Yarmouth, 238, 241
Yellow Book, The, 242
Yorkshire Dales, 270–1

Zakrzewska, Dr Marie, 246
Zangwill, Israel, 250–1
  Children of the Ghetto, 250
Zola, Émile, 46, 47, 103, 104, 109, 112, 159, 219, 321, 381
  L'Argent, 214
  L'Assommoir, 104
  Thérèse Raquin, 103–4